test cricket grounds

john woods

Acknowledgements

I have many people to acknowledge for their help and friendship over the last 16 months. Randall Northam, my publisher, gave me the opportunity to write this book – I cannot thank him enough. My family have provided constant support especially Audrey, my mother, who read tirelessly through every word, correcting the occasional grammatical error! I am grateful to Mark Clinch for his support, the use of his computer and for retrieving mysteriously disappearing files; and to Killian Cregan for his encouragement throughout.

Many friends, old and new, welcomed me into their homes. Thanks to the Licciardo clan (Melbourne) who always entertain me at Christmas, to Wayne Howard and Georgina Cohen who opened their doors to me during the Boxing Day Test, Don Neely and his wife Paddi Anne in Wellington, Duane Wilson and his parents in Auckland, Frank Thayer and his family in Johannesburg, the Springer family and Bronie and Brett in Cape Town, Kamille and Winston at the Bay Hotel in Cape Town, Basil and Lindy Rowlands in Harare and Francis McGovern and his family in Bulawayo.

To all I travelled and partied with especially those on the West Indies tour: Danny Byrne, Justin Peacock, Kip Barr, Perth Ian, Cameron Russo, Ali Perkins, Garry Taylor, Nifty Fowler, Luke Donnelly, Damien Coleman, Matthew Colbert, Jamie Zell, Rob Pennington and Karen, Dillo, Jonno and Kath, the mob from Waving the Flag, including Luke Gillian, Darren Moulds, Tim Crowley, Big Matty, Darren Glover and Dean Marshall – thank you all, it was brilliant.

Thanks to Sonny Shaw and Tim Dryden with whom I shared the Indian experience and to the English fans in Bangladesh and Sri Lanka who know how to party especially Ken Watkins, Bury Phil, Lindsay, Big Harvey, Rob Grace, Will, Chris Phillips, Newport Mark, Graham, Cheap Steve, Andy Newton, David Birch, Will Davies, Mark Villa, Anna Woodhouse, Sarah Jane and Paul, Andrew Miller, and Andy Clarke of the Corridor of Uncertainty fame, and to all the other great people I had the pleasure to meet during a remarkable year, thank you!

Researching this book would not have possible without some incredible websites including Test Cricket Tens (http://tc.has.it) and Cricinfo (www.cricinfo.com). Thanks also to Anna Woodhouse and Peter Garrod for their photographs.

Published by SportsBooks Ltd

Copyright: John Woods, August 2004 ©

SportsBooks Limited
PO Box 422
Cheltenham
GL50 2YN
United Kingdom
Tel: 08700 713 965
Fax: 08700 750 888
e-mail   randall@sportsbooks.ltd.uk
Website   www.sportsbooks.ltd.uk

Photographs by John Woods except where stated.

ISBN 1899807 20 9

Printed by Compass Press.

The fellowship of cricket: John Woods (left) with Kip Barr and Justin Peaock on their travels through the Caribbean

It started, as all good ideas do, in a bar. At around 2 a.m. I was talking to friends at the Elsternwick Cricket Club in Melbourne about the places where I'd watched the game when one of them suggested I should write a guidebook to the world's Test grounds. This is it.

It took a year and a day to fit in all the grounds and in the time I was trekking around them their number went from 56 to 58 because the Australians decided to play Tests against Bangladesh in Cairns and Darwin. I'd already watched cricket in the West Indies, South Africa, Australia and England but now I had to research how I could get to all the grounds used in the last six years by the ten Test playing nations. Obviously I wouldn't be able to watch Test cricket at every ground, indeed at a couple of them I didn't watch any cricket at all due to the refusal of South Africa to play at Peshawar and because Kanpur and Nagpur grounds in India were not awarded international cricket in 2003. And the ground in Dehli was a building site. But I managed to catch 16 Tests and 48 one-dayers. What a trip it was – 175,000km and 72 flights.

It started with England against Sri Lanka, in the one-day triangular series, at the Gabba in Brisbane, sadly only a quarter full, before going on to the Boxing Day Test at the MCG. I love this match – the only one I've missed in 14 years was because I was elsewhere researching this book – and as I'm Irish, which I ought to make clear right away, I have no particular allegiance to any of the Test playing countries. Yes, Ireland has an international cricket team and, yes, I play the game... but our only real claim to cricketing fame is scuttling out the 1969 West Indians – Basil Butcher, Clive Lloyd and even Clyde Walcott (OK he was the team's manager at the time, not in his prime) – for just 25 runs. As someone wrote, the pitch was wet and the hospitality was wetter. So I tend to side with the home team when I watch cricket and this was easy in that Boxing Day Test as Justin Langer (250) and Matthew Hayden (102) laid the foundations for a five wicket win against England.

From Melbourne I had to fly to New Zealand; otherwise I wouldn't have fitted in the land of the long white cloud. First was Christchurch, then Wellington, Auckland and finally Hamilton – all low scoring one-dayers against India. New Zealand was quiet. I did meet Don Neely, the former chairman of the New Zealand selectors, in Wellington. He's the author of 'Men in White', the massive history of New Zealand cricket. He

introduction

kindly gave me dinner in his house, even digging up potatoes from his back garden to go with it. The most excitement was a bungy jump I made in Queenstown but even that didn't match one I'd done in South Africa a year before – 216 metres high it was, the biggest in the world.

Back then across the Tasman Sea to Australia and one-dayers in Adelaide, Hobart and Sydney before flying to Perth. The Sydney match was the first final of the triangular series against England and the lights had hardly come on before Australia had taken only 12.2 overs to knock off the required 118. The match was over at 7.20p.m... still didn't get back to the hotel before 5a.m. though. I awoke at 9a.m. for my noon flight, so decided on a couple more hours sleep. Woke up again and it was still 9a.m. The clock was broken and the actual time was 2.30p.m. I missed the flight; not even Qantas will wait that long. When I finally got to the WACA in Perth the match was between Western Australia and New South Wales or rather the Western Warriors v New South Wales Blues. Good standard though. NSW played Slater, Katich, Clarke and both Waughs with Slater scoring 204. The 'Warriors' had Langer and Hussey and lost by five wickets.

Then it was off to South Africa for the World Cup. I was based in Centurion where I saw three matches including Australia and India before going north to Zimbabwe and taking in India v Zimbabwe in Harare and Australia v Zimbabwe in Bulawayo. Harare was scary, loads of security, long queues for bread and petrol and generally a hostile atmosphere. At the airport the British were charged £55 for a visa whereas, when I mentioned I was Irish, I was moved to the top of the queue and didn't have to pay anything. At the match there were a lot of spectators wearing black armbands in sympathy with the stand made by Grant Flower and Henry Olonga against their country's regime. I bumped into New Zealander Sonny Shaw in Harare and we travelled up to Victoria Falls because he knew a Kiwi girl who wanted to bungy jump off the Falls. It used to be a thriving tourist area but the place was deserted on our visit. The jump was great, though. I was persuaded to have a go and it was nothing like I'd experienced before. In South Africa and New Zealand they are very safety conscious. Not at Victoria Falls. "Never had a man as big as you before," the attendant grinned as I made my way onto the bridge. As I'm 18 stone I was a little put out and startled when he suddenly shouted "stop, stop" as I was about to take off. "No man," he said. "There's a train coming and we can't have a train and Big John on the bridge at the same time." He was winding me up as his great big grin showed.

Bulawayo was totally different to Harare. There were still queues but it was possible to walk around safely whereas in Harare it was not. In Bulawayo I met a fellow Irishman who, hearing my accent, started talking and ended putting me up and entertaining me to dinner in the Cattleman's restaurant he owned.

Back to Johannesburg and a train ride to Potchefstroom to watch Australia beat Namibia. After a late night a local policeman drove me 145km back to Joburg. When I suggested he might still be over the limit and was more drunk than I was, he said it didn't matter because of his job! I then travelled to Capetown for Sri Lanka v West Indies and bumped into Jack McDonnell, ex-President of my former club, Leinster CC. I was in the Bay Hotel watching the cricket on TV when he came in and asked what was the score. "Hello Jack," I said. Was he surprised! I hadn't seen him for 20 years. We were not to meet again, as I heard the sad news of his death later in the year.

People were incredibly friendly in South Africa. At Centurion watching India thrash Sri Lanka, I met Frank Thayer, a businessman who stopped me to ask for a light for his cigar. He put me up in his house, got his PA to arrange air tickets to Port Elizabeth and secured tickets for me to both semi-finals and the final. I don't know how I'm going to repay him and his family when they come to London but fortunately my brother-in-law and sister do own a Michelin starred restaurant.

While watching Zimbabwe lose to Kenya in Bloemfontein I met up with Sonny Shaw again and we ended up in the ground's Long Room being really well entertained by Allan Donald and Andy Moles, the ex-Warwickshire opening batsman, now coaching the Kenyan national side. After the game it was off to the pub where we met Joel Stransky, the rugby World Cup winning outside half...

Donald and Stransky, two South African sporting icons in one day. Sonny was interviewed on the radio the next morning... I wasn't because I hadn't got home by that time.

A drive down to Port Elizabeth for Australia v New Zealand and one of the best guesthouses I've ever stayed in – St. George's. When I was talking to the landlady she mentioned there were other Irishmen staying there. And so I bumped into Ian Lewis, a former President of the Irish Cricket Union, and some friends. I hadn't seen them for 20 years either. Durban was memorable for watching the Natal Sharks at rugby the night before the semi-final. The South Africans go mental for their Friday night rugby. For the final at the Wanderers, Frank Thayer had arranged tickets for the hill in front of the dressing room. The only downside was that someone nicked my bag with my camera in it. I'd like to say a big "thank you" to them!

I spent a week holidaying in Capetown before flying to London for five days and then to the West Indies for the Australian tour.

The first Test was in Guyana which is virtually lawless. There were about 60 Australian supporters including Justin Peacock and Kip Barr who became very good travelling companions. I also met up with Danny Byrne, from the UK, whom I continued to meet during the year around the cricket world. Danny scores each match and his aim is to score a Test at each ground. He has done more than 30 at present. It was great fun at the cricket, the locals smoking huge amounts of ganja and having a big party in the tented area after the match, but we were warned to leave before it got dark. There are four or five pubs worth going to in Guyana and while they are all within 400 yards of each other it was advisable to get a cab when travelling between them. One unfortunate thing that remains in my mind from Georgetown is the disgusting state of the toilets at the ground. We either sneaked into the press section or used the match referee's toilet. There was a great party at the teams' hotel. There was Brett Lee on the guitar, Brian Lara, Darren Lehmann... half the people were in the swimming pool at 3 a.m. along with a lot of the hotel's furniture.

It was off to Trinidad for the second Test the next morning and another experience I won't forget. We were delayed on the tarmac, the pilot explaining that those on the left-hand side of the plane could see the reason; an ancient military plane had crashed on the runway. Trinidad was another all-day, all-night party. Great guesthouses, all day in the Trini Posse stand for $35 USD a day... all the booze you could drink, dancing girls, free tee-shirts. Reminded me of Lord's! The party continued in the 'Cricket Wicket' bar opposite the ground, with dancing in the streets. I needed a few days off after that, chilling out in Tobago with Kip and some other friends. Kip is an Aussie with a fine Rastafarian hairstyle, if you can believe. Outside a KFC restaurant some local Rastas drove by and shouted something to us. "Is that a fraternal greeting" I asked Kip. "No they are just wondering if that's vegetarian chicken," he replied. Rastas are vegetarian, it seems. You learn things when you travel around the world watching cricket.

Barbados for the third Test was again a big party although the island is very expensive. Next was Antigua for the last test. Here we pestered Arlene Richardson, Richie's wife, so much that she let us stay in staff accommodation in Lashings, the inn and bar she runs on the beach and the greatest place to stay on the island. If you are lucky you get to hear Dread & the Baldhead, the band in which Curtly Ambrose plays bass and Richie is on guitar. When we were there the beach was used for cricket each night with Brett Lee bowling to Michael Clarke and others. The Australians don't shy away from their fans like the more reserved English team does.

Then there was Jamaica for the first one-dayer. Don't stay out late and definitely don't walk around Kingston after dark. I had to miss the second match in Kingston to get to St. Lucia for the third one-dayer. I flew to Antigua and met my connecting flight the following day which contained everybody I'd been partying with in Jamaica. They had diverted the flight to go to St. Lucia! St. Lucia was delightful, a new ground and a different type of fan, boisterous and French patois speaking. Then to Grenada for the sixth and seventh one-dayers where there were very few Aussies, before flying back to London for the English side of this adventure.

First to the Oval for a Twenty 20 day/night match. Then to Chester-le-Street for the same. I'm not a huge fan of English county cricket but this innovation makes it more exciting. I watched the Headingley Test, a Lord's one-dayer, Lancashire and Middlesex at Old Trafford and then a glorious day at Trent Bridge when England beat South Africa. Finally it was Warwickshire against Leicestershire at Edgbaston.

Then it was back to Australia to check out Darwin and Cairns before the subcontinental leg of this world tour. I was dreading Pakistan. I'd been wound up by all my mates – dry country, no beer – and totally freaked by the BBC and CNN. I shouldn't have been... Pakistan was fabulous. I flew into Karachi where I had an eight hour wait before going to Multan for a one-dayer between Pakistan and Bangladesh. Pakistan Airways were brilliant. The return ticket from London cost me £490 but they threw in six internal flights for just £15 and put me up in a hotel room all day, free of charge; fed and watered me as well. There was I thinking that men with big beards wanted nothing to do with western culture when I walked out of Karachi airport and saw the biggest McDonald's I'd ever seen.

Got into Multan at 8.30p.m. without a hotel booked. It was total chaos. Every taxi driver was touting for business and I eventually ended up paying £9 a night. It seems there are no lanes on Multan's roads. Cars, auto-rickshaws, trucks, buses, bicycles, cows, hens, sheep, goats... all using both sides of the road. And the dust is amazing. Everybody stared at me but were really friendly. Getting a ticket for the match was a mystery. I didn't realise then that they were sold in banks. When I got to the ground it was heaving. But the police took one look at me and started knocking people out of my way with their sticks and let me in. It was in Multan that I met the Pakistani ICC representative who I'd like to thank for all his help in Pakistan. I didn't realise who he was until I got to Bangladesh. The spectators in Multan were so hospitable towards me. The stand was packed but the older spectators made a young lad get up to give me his seat. When I went for a walk outside at lunchtime I was again the subject of great interest. I was soon surrounded by a crowd ten deep. One person would try his English: "Your name, your country?" and soon they were all saying it, even the ones who didn't know any English. As soon as the leader went away they all vanished. There must have been 30,000 inside the ground and more outside. There was always the chance of getting over the fence any time a policeman turned his back.

In Faisalabad I asked in several hotels what there was to do and they all answered with one word – "nothing". The trick here was to stay in a cheaper hotel and go to one of the big ones where for £2 you could stay all day and use the swimming pool and gym. Mind you, it cost £1 for a bottle of water rather than the 4p elsewhere. The secret with water is to check the seal on the bottle. The locals were very friendly once again, but there really is nothing to do and very little English spoken. Eating might have been a problem but if you act like a chicken and say "jalfrezi" you can get by and the food was great, much better than on the Indian leg of my trip.

Lahore was fascinating, both the new city, built about 200 years ago, and the old which is more than two thousand years old. It's as safe as houses as well but it was lucky I'd taken cash because banking is difficult and travellers' cheques are rarely accepted. The Gadaffi stadium is so-called because the Libyan leader paid for it. PR I suppose. There's a mixture of very rich and very poor in Lahore. I stayed in the Amer hotel for £10 a night and went swimming in one of the big ones where I met Michael Palin who was making a TV programme about his trek through the Himalayas.

Rawalpindi is a little more western but getting tickets is again a nightmare if you don't go to the bank. Also the ground is 10km from the centre, which means an hour's drive through the traffic.

Peshawar was interesting. There was no cricket as South Africa had pulled out, so I took some photos and arranged a trip to the Khyber Pass. I seemed to be the only person there without a gun. Some had AK47s, others just muskets, but everyone appeared to be armed. I don't usually like organised tours but I was pleased I'd gone with this one. Going back into town from the ground in a rickshaw I passed through bazaars like I had never seen before, selling every type of food and spice. Next was a dusty field with cock-fighting going on, then a dog market where I quickly realised they were selling fighting dogs.

Karachi wasn't like the rest of Pakistan. There was unbelievable poverty, just like India and very heavy security. The South African tour had just been called off so security was tighter than Shane Warne's waistband circa 1998... or mine for that matter. You can take your camera into the ground but not take any photos I was told. Security was that tight!

I had 12 days at home in Battersea before going to India. First to Ahmedabad in Gujarat for the first Test with New Zealand. Gujarat is dry, just like Pakistan... so no beer unless you know the system. I met up again with Sonny Shaw from New Zealand. He's known as the Kiwi's biggest supporter who travels the world following his team and waves two New Zealand flags all day when he watches cricket! He knew the system, which is to register as an alcoholic. He got his allowance of 20 beers on the second day. You don't have to get them yourself. A member of the hotel staff will go – his reward is usually a bottle of Scotch!

The pollution was incredibly bad in Ahmedabad. I went out for a look around by rickshaw to get the feel of the stadium and ended up getting a lift back by the chief of police in his jeep. We had two crashes in 15 minutes... first into a motorbike, second into a truck. Next day we got a lift in a police van and the third day in a council truck. Sonny didn't give me even one of his beers but I wasn't unhappy because he got sick.

He was better by the time it came to go to Chandigarh which is a modern city. We travelled with another Kiwi, Tim Dryden, and stayed in a really nice hotel for £5 a night. I'd broken my trip to Chandigarh by visiting Delhi to see the Feroz Shah Kolta stadium. It was a builder's yard and will not be used again for Test cricket until 2005. After the Chandigarh match it was off to Chennai... 35 hours in a train in the two-tier carriages. Better than first-class because you've got air-conditioning and two bunks each side of the carriage. Sonny had been given tickets by New Zealand spinner Daniel Vettori but unfortunately the match was rained off after 25 overs. Still it meant I met Indian coach, John Wright, another Kiwi, in the bar.

I took a 13-hour train ride to Nagpur while Sonny went to Faribad. There was no match but I needed to visit the ground. I even visited a ground I did not need to, Gwailor for Australia v India during Devali, the great Indian festival, when the crowd set fire to everything, even the advertising hoardings. I watched a match between two police teams in Kanpur before a detour to Delhi to check that the building site I'd been to was the correct ground. Because of its condition I really feared that I had gone to the wrong place. I need not have worried.

Mumbai was next for Australia v India in the one-day series. Afterwards Sonny went to Pune while I went to Kolkata (that's Calcutta for anyone over 35) for a flight to Dhaka in Bangladesh and then Chittagong. Here I caught up with the Bangladesh/England series and the demonstration put on by the English supporters who were annoyed at being ripped off. They staged a sit-down outside the ground because they were expected to pay £30 a day while everybody else paid less than £1 each. They compromised on a fiver and I met up with friends of Danny Byrne, who I'd last seen in Trinidad. We celebrated our meeting in the cha bars until 4a.m. I joined them again in Dhaka where we had a roast dinner in the Bagha Club. I needed to leave halfway through the next match to catch a flight back to Kolkata. A three hour delay meant I watched the match I'd just left on TV at the airport! A one-and-a-half hour taxi ride from Kolkata airport to the train station meant I missed my train to Bangalore by 17 minutes and had to return to the airport and fly down. Sonny was in Bangalore, knackered after a 36 hour train trip, whereas I was refreshed, if impoverished, after the flight! We had to con our way into the ground with out-of-date press passes but were worried about being trampled to death because it was so crowded. Three days later I was in Hyderbad for India v New Zealand (that isn't a Test ground) and to watch Australia beat New Zealand in the Rugby World Cup. Sonny and I stayed up until 2.30a.m. to make sure we watched the match, but 3.30, then 4.30, then 5 o'clock came before the match started. We both saw the first try but slept through the rest of the game.

Next was the one-day final between India and Australia in Kolkata, Eden Gardens was heaving... 110,000 fans, but I managed to get a ticket on the black market. It was one of the most wonderful sporting experiences of my life even though the crowd thought we were Australian and spat at us, threw things at us, bags of water (at least I hope it was water!), apples, anything they could get their hands on when Australia won. Tim turned up again and he and Sonny went off to watch New Zealand in Pakistan while I went to Chennai for a flight to Colombo.

When I arrived in Sri Lanka it was raining, so I went to the Cricket Club Cafe and met up with English supporters, Kinky Ken from Merthyr, Bury Phil and the Mad Monk from Manchester. Also in Colombo were Mad Dog Mark from Newport who has not missed an overseas Test involving England in ten years and Cheap Steve, leader of the Jungle Army. They propound the notion of 'Free Cricket' so if they can get away without paying they will. Good on them! The first two one-dayers were rained off so we went off to Galle for the first Test and a few days at Unawatuna, one of the world's most wonderful beaches. Danny Byrne arrived with some friends and we all went to Kandy in the hill country for the second Test, leaning out of the window of the train to get natural air-conditioning and see the incredible view. Staying in the official observation car would have been too stuffy. Kandy has only two pubs. We got to know them quite well. The 'Free Cricket' supporters watched the Kandy match from a hill outside the ground. If there is a choice between a 50p train ride and a 40p bus ride they will take the bus. Not because they cannot afford 50p but for the principle.

Back to Colombo for a match between the Barmy Army and a local side and then four days of my final Test at the SSC. I also visited the Premadasa and Saravanamuttu grounds while in Colombo. Then off to Dubai to visit Sharjah for photographs because Test matches are occasionally played there.

So I started in a quarter-full Gabba at Brisbane and ended up in an empty Sharjah in Dubai. The trip from Australia to Dubai via New Zealand, South Africa, Zimbabwe, the West Indies, England, Australia again, Pakistan, India, Bangladesh and Sri Lanka had taken a year and a day, giving me an experience I will never forget.

John Woods

NB: All the statistics are up to date to the end of June 2004

Contents

the grounds

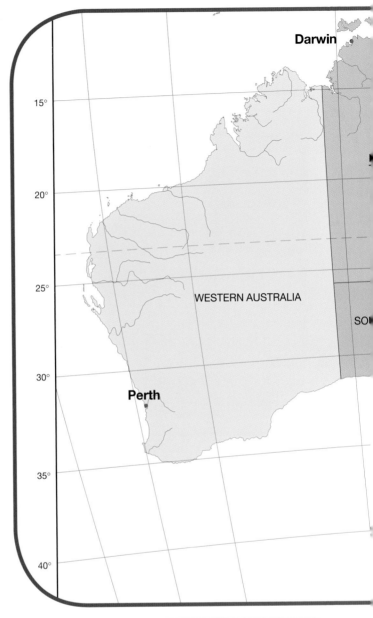

Darwin

15°

20°

25°

WESTERN AUSTRALIA

SO

30°

Perth

35°

40°

The Melbourne Cricket Ground became the first ground to host a Test when it staged the inaugural match between Australia and England on 15th March 1877 when the home side won by 45 runs. It also staged the next three Tests before the Sydney Cricket Ground became the second Test venue when it hosted the second match of the 1882 series in February. The Adelaide Oval was the third ground in Australia used for Test cricket when England visited two years later.

The Exhibition Ground in Brisbane became the fourth Australian Test venue, for the first match of the 1928/29 Test series against England. The ground was only used for one more Test, against the West Indies in December 1931. Woolloongabba, known as the Gabba, had hosted a Test against South Africa the month before and was chosen to be Brisbane's Test ground because of its larger capacity. The Exhibition Ground is the only Australian ground which has staged Test cricket and is not currently used.

The WACA, in Perth, was the next Test venue when it hosted the second

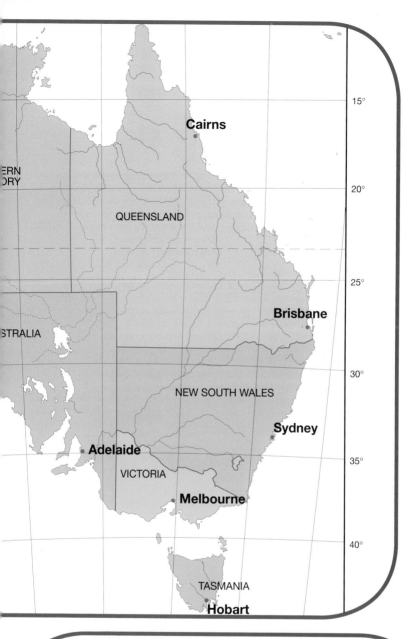

match of the 1970/71 series in December 1970. Bellerive Oval in Hobart, Tasmania became the seventh when Sri Lanka visited in 1989 and the Marrara in Darwin was the next ground to be used for Test cricket when it hosted Bangladesh on 18th July 2003. The Bundaberg Rum Stadium in Cairns became the ninth and newest Test venue in Australia a week later.

Airlines

Australia's national airline is Qantas. All Test match cities have their own airports. International visitors can take advantage of Qantas' Boomerang Pass which permits travel throughout Australia and selected destinations in New Zealand at a reduced rate. Domestic flights in Australia are expensive and the pass is certainly good value. It must be purchased prior to arrival in Australia. Details www.qantas.com.au

Qantas   13 13 13

Distance between Cities (in kms)

	Adelaide	Brisbane	Cairns	Darwin	Melbourne	Perth	Sydney
Adelaide		2055	3384	3051	732	2716	1415
Brisbane	2055		1699	3429	1671	4289	982
Cairns	3384	1699		2885	3055	6050	2685
Darwin	3051	3429	2885		3789	4049	4301
Melbourne	732	1671	3055	3789		3456	873
Perth	2716	4363	6050	4049	3456		3972
Sydney	1415	982	2685	4301	873	3972	

Buses

Australia has two excellent interstate coach companies, providing reliable and luxurious services throughout the country. Most services are air-conditioned, show videos and have toilet facilities. Both companies offer a variety of passes, including unlimited travel, for between seven and 90 days, preset route passes and the very popular kilometre pass which allows visitors to choose their own itinerary and travel from 2,000 to 20,000 kilometres.

Greyhound Pioneer   13 20 30   www.greyhound.com.au
McCafferty's   13 14 99   www.mccaffertys.com.au

Trains

Due to the distance between each of the Test match cities most visitors choose to fly between destinations however RailAustralia does offer an alternative. Services between Melbourne, Sydney and Adelaide run overnight and offer sleeping cars and catering facilities. The Indian Pacific runs from Sydney to Perth via Adelaide. The three day journey across the Nullabor Plain is quite an experience. There are a number of services between Brisbane and Cairns including the luxurious Great South Pacific Express.

RailAustralia have a number of passes offering unlimited travel around their network. The Austrailpass is an unlimited travel pass for up to 30 days. The Austrail Flexi-pass is an alternative valid for 8, 15, 22 and 29 days within a six month period. Both passes have limitations which can prove frustrating. Visitors should examine the terms and conditions carefully before purchase. Both passes must be bought prior to arrival in Australia and are valid for 12 months from date of purchase.

Car hire

Avis, Budget, Hertz and Thrifty have desks at airports in each of the cities which host Test cricket. An International Driving Licence is required and all drivers must be over 21.

Taxis

Metered taxis are available at airports, outside hotels and at ranks throughout Australia.

Emergency Numbers

Police, Fire, Ambulance   000

Embassies/Consulates

British High Commission
Commonwealth Avenue, Yarralumla, Canberra
Tel: 02 6270 6666
Fax: 02 6273 3236
bhc.canberra@mail.uk.emb.gov.au

New Zealand High Commission
Commonwealth Avenue, Canberra
ACT 2600
Tel: 02 6270 4211
Fax: 02 6273 3194
nzhcca@austarmetro.com.au

South Africa Embassy
Corner of Rhodes Place and State Circle, Yarralumla, Canberra
Tel: 02 6273 2424
Fax: 02 6273 3543
info@rsa.emb.gov.au

High Commission for the People's Republic of Bangladesh
35 Endeavour Street, Red Hill, ACT 2603
Tel: 02 6295 3328
Fax: 02 6295 5331

High Commission of India
3 Moonah Place
Yarralumla
Canberra
ACT 2600
Tel: 026 273 3999
Fax: 026 273 1308
hcoffice@bigpond.com

Visas

All visitors to Australia must carry a valid passport and all but New Zealand passport holders must have a visa. Australia issue Electronic Travel Authority visas free to tourist visitors. They are valid for 12 months from date of issue and allow a maximum stay of 3 months per visit. ETA visas are issued through Australian Embassies, travel or visa agents.

Customs

Visitors over the age of 18 may take the following goods into Australia without incurring customs duty – 250 cigarettes, 1.125 litre of alcohol

Time Difference

Australia has three different time zones
Western Australia – GMT + 8 hours
South Australia, Northern Territory – GMT + 10 ½ hours
Victoria, New South Wales, Queensland and Tasmania – GMT + 11 hours.

Electricity

220/240 volts AC at 50 cycles per second. Most hotels have adaptors.

Departure Tax

Departure Tax is included in the price of airline ticket.

Banks

Opening times at most banks are Monday to Thursday 09.30-16.00 and Friday 09.30-17.00. Most banks have foreign exchange facilities and accept travellers' cheques in major currencies. Commission is charged for this service. ATM facilities are widespread. All major credit cards are accepted.
Currency is the Australian Dollar (A$). Notes are issued in denominations of A$100, 50, 20, 10 and 5 and coins in denominations of A$2, 1 and 50, 20, 10 and 5 cents.

Telecoms

International Direct Dialling is available throughout Australia. Public payphones are widespread and accept coins and phone cards (A$5, 10, 20) which are available in newsagents. Australia's dialling code is 61. The outgoing international code is 0011.

Post

Official opening times for post offices throughout Australia are Monday-Friday 09.00-17.00. General Post Offices in major cities open on Saturday from 09.00-12.00.

Tourist Offices

All major cities have Tourist Information Centres. Most airports also have tourist information desks, other have information boards which have brochures on accommodation, attractions etc.
Australian Tourist Commission
80 William St.
Woolloomooloo
Sydney
Tel: 02 9360 1111
Fax: 02 9331 6469

adelaide

the oval

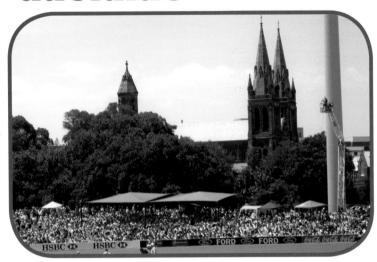

Opened in 1873, the Adelaide Oval is the home of the South Australia Cricket Association. One of the world's most picturesque grounds, it lies in the north of the city on the banks of the river Torrens with St. Peter's Cathedral standing proudly behind the historic scoreboard and the Mount Lofty Ranges as a backdrop.

The Oval held its first Test on 12th December 1884 when Australia entertained England. The home side batted first and made 243 with Percy McDonnell scoring 124 and Billy Bates taking 5/31 for England. England replied with 369, Billy Barnes scoring 134 and George Palmer taking 5/81. McDonnell scored 83 in Australia's second innings score of 191 with Bobby Peel taking 5/51. England, chasing 67, won by 8 wickets.

Many remarkable Tests have played at the ground. With the series level at one all, the third Test of the 1933 'Bodyline' series against England attracted a total crowd of 172,361, including a record 50,962 on the third day. England batted first, making 341 with Maurice Leyland top scoring with 83. Tim Wall took 5/72 for Australia. In reply the home team scored 222, Bill Ponsford making 85. England made 412 in their second innings leaving Australia a massive target of 532 for victory. Harold Larwood and Gubby Allen each took four Australia wickets as the home team crumbled to 193 all out to give England a 338 run victory. England went on to win the series 4-1, provoking a political storm.

In January 1993, the West Indies visited the Adelaide Oval for the fourth Test of the 1992/93 series. One-nil down with two to play, the West Indies were in danger of losing their first series in 13 years. Batting first, they made 252, Merv Hughes taking 5/64. Curtly Ambrose kept the Australian reply down to 213 with figures of 6/74. Then the West Indies collapsed to 146 all out with Richie Richardson scoring 72 and Tim May returning figures of 6.5 overs, 3 maidens, 5 wickets for 9 runs. Needing 186 to win Australia, under severe pressure from Ambrose, Bishop, Benjamin and Walsh, slumped to 108/8 and 144/9 before Tim May and Craig McDermott took them to within two runs of victory. McDermott was controversially given out, caught behind by Junior Murray off the bowling of Courtney Walsh, which gave West Indies victory by one run. They went on to win the series 2-1 and retain the Frank Worrell Trophy.

Sir Donald Bradman recorded the Oval's highest individual score with 299no against South Africa in 1932. The highest aggregate is held by Alan Border with 1415 runs at an average of 58.76 including four centuries and a highest score of 205. The highest team score was 674 by Australia against India in 1948. The lowest team score was 82 by Australia against West Indies in 1951.

On a ground that has always been known for favouring batsmen the best match figures are 14/199 by Clarrie Grimmett versus South Africa in 1932. Lance Gibbs of the West Indies took the only Test hat-trick at Adelaide in 1961. Unlike other Test grounds in Australia, the Adelaide Oval has not sacrificed tradition for commercialism. One long structure runs down the west side of the ground. The George Giffin (members), the Sir Edwin Smith and the Mostyn Evan stands provide a wonderful reminder of the history of the Oval and are protected on Adelaide's Heritage list. These stands are covered and spectators are sheltered from the harsh sun. The seats in front of these stands down by the fence are not covered and spectators should protect themselves. To the right of the west stands at the south end of the ground is The Sir Donald Bradman stand which was added in 1980, its architecture respecting the traditional stands while being given a modern interior. Most seats in the Bradman stand are under cover.

To the right of this stand at fine leg is the Southern Mound which is a wonderful place from which to watch. It has a small covered area which is always the first part of the ground to fill up each day. The Eastern Stand is totally uncovered and can get extremely hot. The Northern Mound, where the Georgian Scoreboard is situated, is the liveliest part of the ground with all-day drinking and chanting and a lot of banter. The area to the west of the sightscreen at the Northern end is a 'Dry and Family Area'.

There are numerous bars around the ground, the two largest being under the scoreboard at the northern end and beside the Southern Mound at the end of the Sir Donald Bradman Stand. There is also a bar inside here with a wonderful viewing area. The western stands also have bars. Burgers, hot dogs and other fast food are on offer. In addition to the bars in the ground a lot of spectators made the three-minute pilgrimage to the Cathedral Hotel for a cool beer at lunchtime.

Facilities and access for people with disabilities are good, with viewing areas in different parts of the ground. Tickets for the Test can be purchased from Venue*Tix Tel : 08 8225 8888 Fax : 08 8232 8363 or "http://www.venuetix.com.au" www.venuetix.com.au Tickets are also available on the door on match days, doors open at 08.00. The cost of tickets ranges from A$24 for general admission to A$72 for the best stand seats. Tickets for all five days cost between A$72-A$141.

The Oval is only a ten-minute walk from the city centre and the majority of spectators walk. A bus does run from both South and North Terrace. Parking is available in the public car parks in the Southern and Northern Stadium.

The Adelaide Oval Cricket Museum on the ground floor of the Bradman Stand is a trip down memory lane, a wonderful journey of the Oval's cricketing history from Bradman's bats and scorebooks, to Joel Garner's one-day uniform to the little bird that did not survive a run-in with a ball during a match in the fifties.

Adelaide is the capital of South Australia and, with a population of one million, Australia's fourth largest city. It is situated on the south coast between the Gulf St. Vincent to the west and the Mount Lofty Ranges to the east. Named after the wife of King William IV, it is a quiet city nestling at the foot of the Adelaide Hills with the Torrens River meandering its way through to the Southern Ocean. It has wide, tree-lined streets with elegant Victorian and Edwardian buildings which can be attributed to Colonel William Light who spent two years designing the grid pattern layout of the city's square mile in 1832 ten miles inland from its port. The square mile is surrounded by parklands, botanical and zoological gardens.

The Dutch sighted the South Australia coast in 1627. In 1792 the French landed, followed in 1800 by the British under Lieutenant James Grant. However it was not until 1836 that the first settlers arrived after a short stay on Kangaroo Island. This was a private venture by free settlers from the south of England. Adelaide never received any convicts, South Australia being the only state not to.

Adelaide has a great reputation for art and culture. The South Australian Museum in North Terrace has the largest collection of Aboriginal artefacts in the world. The Art Gallery of South Australia has one of the finest collections in the country. The museum and gallery are housed in some of Adelaide's beautiful buildings with stunning architecture. Others include the Adelaide Railway Station, Parliament House and The Institute, the home of the Bradman Collection. The Adelaide Festival Centre is home to four theatres including the Festival Theatre and the Playhouse.

The Royal Botanical Gardens are beautiful and home to the bicentennial conservatory, the largest single span conservatory in the southern hemisphere. Adelaide Zoo is another major attraction with some 1,400 mammals, birds, reptiles and fish. Adelaide has a Mediterranean climate with warm summers and cool winters. Lightweight cottons and linens are recommended all year around. The climate is pleasant for walking the city and for alfresco dining. The city has an almost European feel with sidewalk cafés, churches, galleries and antique shops. Many of the Adelaide restaurants certainly have a German touch but particularly in the Barossa Valley.

Crayfish and crabs are on offer in many of the excellent seafood restaurants.

Hilton Adelaide

233 Victoria Square
Tel: 08 8217 2000
Fax: 08 8217 2001

Hyatt Regency Hotel

North Terrace
Tel: 08 8231 1234
Fax: 08 8231 1120

Stamford Plaza Adelaide

150 North Terrace
Tel: 08 8461 1111
Fax: 08 8231 7572
sales@spa.stamford.com.au
www.stamford.com.au
City centre opposite casino, this is a top class hotel with restaurants, bars and a fantastic roof-top pool. 5 minute walk to Oval.

Radisson Playford Hotel

120 North Terrace
Tel: 08 8213 8888
Fax: 08 8213 8833
www.radisson.com/adelaideau
Five star hotel in the centre. 182 rooms with restaurants, bars.

The O'Connell Inn

197-199 O'Connell Street, North Adelaide
Tel: 08 8239 0766
Fax: 08 8239 0560
Near Oval. Excellent rooms, café restaurant. A very good choice if you would rather stay out of the centre.

Festival City Hotel Motel

140 North Terrace
Tel: 08 8212 7877
Fax: 08 8211 8137
festival@ecite.net.au
A 45-room hotel in the centre; inexpensive tariff. All rooms are en suite and have fridge and cable TV. Opposite the casino and only five minutes from the Oval.

City Central Motel

23 Hindley St.
Tel: 08 8231 4049
Fax: 08 8231 4804
Another small hotel in the centre of town. Air-conditioned with fridge and TV. Inexpensive.

Barossa Valley

Australia's most popular wine region. Wine-making has taken place here since 1842. An hour's drive north of Adelaide, through tiny villages, wildlife sanctuaries and orchards, provides the opportunity to stop at cafés, hotels and wineries to sample the famous product, great food and wonderful scenery of the region. The Barossa has quite a German heritage which can be seen in the buildings of the 50 or so wineries in the area.

Sir Donald Bradman Museum

The most wonderful collection of the memorabilia, film footage, audiotape, photographs, bats, balls and press billboards of the greatest cricketer who ever played the game. For the cricket lover this is a dream come true. Hours can be spent perusing this fine collection, listening to the early tapes from Bradman's tours of England. The museum is housed in The Institute on the corner of North Terrace and Kintore Avenue Tel: 08 8207 7595 www.bradman.sa.com.au

Tram journey to Genelg

One of the best excursions in Adelaide. A tram runs the 16km from the city centre to Genelg. The first settlers landed here in 1836 and it has grown into a very pleasant seaside town with a beautiful sandy beach, a long pier where kids are always fishing or jumping off and sidewalk cafés to sit back and watch the world go by. There are beach volleyball courts and other sport activities down by the water.

Kangaroo Island

The third biggest island in Australia and a nature lovers' paradise with more than 30 per cent being National Park. An opportunity to see much flora and fauna that is extinct on mainland Australia. The island has some excellent beaches, a good golf course and some wonderful restaurants and bars. Flights to the island are available from Adelaide airport and there is also a ferry service.

Adelaide Gaol

An historic site which gives an insight into the plight of prisoners in Australia's younger years. Tours visit the prisoners' cells, the exercise yards, the hanging tower and the graveyard. 18 Gaol Road, Adelaide 08 8231 4062 Open Monday to Friday 11.00-16.00, Saturday closed, Sunday 11.00-15.00

Her Majesty's Theatre

58 Grote St.
Tel: 08 8236 0555
Fax: 08 8236 0566

Adelaide Festival Centre

King William Road
Tel: 08 8216 8600
Fax: 08 8212-7849
Four theatres under the one roof.

South Australia Museum

North Terrace
Tel: 08 8207 7500
Home to the largest collection of Aboriginal culture in the world. Other highlights include the Egyptian Room and an exhibition of Douglas Mawson, Adelaide's most famous explorer.

Migration and Settlement Museum

82 Kintore Avenue
Tel: 08 8207 7580
Traces migration history of people from many lands back to Adelaide early settlers. It is housed in the beautifully restored building of a former asylum.

Art Gallery of South Australia

North Terrace
Tel: 08 8207 7000
The gallery features contemporary and heritage art displays. Open 10.00-17.00 daily.

Adelaide Airport is located 6km west of the city. A taxi ride will take 15 minutes and cost A$25. A Skylink Airport Bus runs between the airport and the city every 20 minutes at a cost of $6. There are ATM machines in the arrivals area and a bureau de change. There is no tourist information desk but there are information boards in the arrivals area with details of accommodation, tourist attractions and tours. There are cafés, newsagents and other shops in the departure hall. Car hire is available from Avis (08 8234 4558), Budget (08 8234 4111), Hertz (08 8234 4566) and Thrifty (1300 367 227).

Airlines

Qantas	13 12 23
Virgin Blue	13 67 89
Air New Zealand	13 24 76
British Airways	08 238 2138
Singapore Airlines	13 12 23

Buses

There is an extensive local bus service. Enquiries 08 8210 1000.
Two free buses, the City Loop and Bee Line, visit most of the attractions.
The Interstate Central bus station is in Franklin Street.

Trains

Suburban Trains leave from Adelaide Station on North Terrace. Enquiries 08 8210 1000

Interstate Trains arrive and depart from Adelaide Rail Passenger Terminal, Keswick Enquiries 13 21 47. It should be noted that this terminal is a fair way out of town and is not served well by bus connections or taxis.

Taxis

Adelaide Independents	13 22 11
Suburban Taxis	13 10 08
Diamond Cabs	13 24 48
Yellow Cabs	13 22 27

Trams

Glenelg Tram Service runs between Victoria Square and Mosley Square in Glenelg.

Car Hire

Avis
136 North Terrace
Tel: 08 8410 5727
Fax: 08 8410 4001

Budget
274 North Terrace
Tel: 08 8223 1440
Fax: 08 8224 0025

Hertz
233 Morphett St.
Tel: 08 8231 2856
Fax: 08 8212 4050

Thrifty
296 Hindley St.
Tel: 08 8211 8788
Fax: 08 8211 8193

Stanley's Great Aussie Fish Café

76 Gouger St.
Tel: 08 8410 0909
One of the city's busiest seafood restaurants, sporty bar with beer garden. Lunch Sunday to Friday. Dinner 7 days a week.

Pasta Palace

100 Hindley St.
Tel: 08 8231 9500
Excellent Italian food. Lunch Monday to Friday. Dinner 7 days a week.

La Guillotine

125 Gouger St.
Tel: 08 8212 2536
French cuisine in rustic atmosphere. Courtyard dining an option. Fine wine list. Open for dinner Tuesday-Saturday.

Café Tapas

147-149 Hindley St.
Tel: 08 8211 74446
Wine, cocktails and tapas in a relaxed atmosphere. Lunch Monday-Saturday, Dinner Wednesday-Saturday.

Red Rock Noodle Bar

187 Rundle St.
Tel: 08 8223 6855
Noodle and rice dishes. Extensive menu at inexpensive prices. Open for lunch and dinner seven nights a week.

Kublai Khan

3 St. Ann's Place, Parkside
Tel: 08 8272 8688
A Mongolian barbeque. Choose your own food and watch chef cook it. Fantastic food, great value, something different. Lunch Tuesday-Friday. Dinner 7 days a week.

Jasmin Indian

31 Hindmarsh Square
Tel: 08 8223 7837
Best curry in town. Excellent Indian food. Dinner Tuesday-Saturday.

There are plenty of pubs to go partying in Adelaide. The main area is Hindley and the surrounding streets. Listed below are just some of the more lively ones.

Cathedral Hotel

45 Kermode Street, North Adelaide
Tel: 08 8267 2197
The perfect pub to go to at lunchtime or after the match. Very lively.

PJ O'Briens

14 East Terrace
Irish pub on East Terrace. Very busy with live music. Open very late.

Adelaide Casino

North Terrace

Austral Hotel

205 Rundle St.
Busy city centre pub with loud music and a young, trendy crowd.

The London Tavern

Terrace Level, Myer Centre
175 North Terrace
Tel: 08 8231 5464
English pub serving good English ales and good food.

Brecknock Hotel

401 King William St
Nice pub at the south end of the city. Good pub food and nice atmosphere.

Royal Admiral Hotel

125 Hindley St.
Tel: 08 8231 5929
Lively pub. Good crowd.

Fox and Hounds

Stamford Hotel, 150 North Terrace
Upmarket pub in the Stamford Hotel. Very busy after the cricket.

Talbot Hotel

104 Gouger St.
Tel: 08 8231 9780
Another haunt frequented by cricket supporters after a day at the Oval.

Post Office

General Post Office
Corner of King William and Franklin
Streets
Tel: 08 8216 2222

Tourist Information

South Australia Travel Centre
18 King William St.
1300 655 276
Monday-Friday 08.30-17.00, Saturday-
Sunday 09.00-14.00

Rundle Mall Information Centre
Tel: 08 8203 7611
Monday-Thursday 10.00-17.00, Friday

10.00-09.00, Saturday 10.00-15.00,
Sunday 11.00-16.00

Royal Adelaide Hospital

North Terrace
Tel: 08 8222 4000

Emergency Dentist   08 8272 8111

Midnight Chemist (07.00-midnight)
Corner West and North Terrace
Tel: 08 823 316 333

Emergency Dentist   08 8272 8111

stats

Win/Loss Record

Country	Played	Won	Drawn	Lost	Tie
Australia	62	30	16	16	-
West Indies	12	5	3	4	-
South Africa	7	2	2	3	-
Pakistan	4	-	3	1	-
England	28	8	5	15	-
India	8	1	2	5	-
New Zealand	2	-	1	1	-
Sri Lanka	1	-	-	1	-

Highest Individual Aggregates (all Australia)

Player	Mat	Inn	NO	Runs	Ave	HS	50	100
Allan Border	16	29	5	1415	58.96	205	9	4
Steve Waugh	15	26	2	1056	44.00	170	4	3
Don Bradman	7	11	2	970	107.78	299*	3	3
David Boon	12	23	3	920	46.00	135	2	4
Mark Waugh	12	23	2	837	39.86	138	6	2
Ricky Ponting	8	15	0	814	54.27	242	2	3
Mark Taylor	11	21	1	811	40.55	169*	5	2
Bob Simpson	6	11	0	805	73.18	225	5	3
Clem Hill	6	11	0	714	64.91	160	6	1
Kim Hughes	7	13	0	676	52.00	213	3	2

Top Wicket Takers (all Australia)

Player	Mat	Bll	Md	Runs	Wkt	Ave	BB	FWI	S/R	RPO
Dennis Lillee	9	2479	63	1206	45	26.80	6/171	4	55.09	2.92
Craig McDermott	8	2325	98	1162	42	27.67	5/76	3	55.36	3.00
Shane Warne	10	2908	134	1188	41	28.98	5/113	1	70.93	2.45
Glenn McGrath	7	1773	87	708	35	20.23	4/41	0	50.66	2.40
Clarrie Grimmett	4	2097	96	769	34	22.62	7/83	4	61.68	2.20
Richie Benaud	6	2134	54	890	27	32.96	5/91	2	79.04	2.50
Ashley Mallett	6	1673	55	656	25	26.24	8/59	1	66.92	2.35
Bill Johnston	4	1531	46	500	25	20.00	6/62	2	61.24	1.96
Merv Hughes	7	1563	56	843	24	35.13	5/64	2	65.13	3.24
Jeff Thomson	6	864	18	504	24	21.00	4/68	0	36.00	3.50

Highest Individual Scores (Australia unless stated)

299*	Don Bradman	v South Africa 1931-32
242	Ricky Ponting	v India 2003-04
233	Raul Dravid (Ind)	2003-04
225	Bob Simpson	v England 1965-66
216	Dean Jones	v West Indies 1988-89
214*	Victor Trumper	v South Africa 1910-11
213	Kim Hughes	v India 1980-81
212	Don Bradman	v England 1936-37
206	Arthur Morris	v England 1950-51
205	Allan Border	v Nz 1987-88

Best Individual Bowling (Australia unless stated)

27-10-43-8	Albert Trott	v England 1894-95
23.6-6-59-8	Ashley Mallett	v Pakistan 1972-73
38-6-106-8	Kapil Dev (Ind)	1985-86
40-7-112-8	Geoff Lawson	v West Indies 1984-85
64.5-21-126-8	Jack White (Eng)	1928-29
16.5-4-38-7	Ray Lindwall	v India 1947-48
49.2-17-83-7	Clarrie Grimmett	v South Africa 1931-32
48-19-87-7	Clarrie Grimmett	v West Indies 1930-31
41-11-87-7	Shaun Pollock (SA)	1997-98
30-6-89-7	Mike Whitney	v West Indies 1988-89

Highest Partnerships

Wkt	Runs	Batsmen	Match
1st	244	Bob Simpson & Bill Lawry (Australia)	1965-1966 v England
2nd	275	Colin Mcdonald & Lindsay Hassett (Australia)	1952-1953 v South Africa
3rd	341	Eddie Barlow & Graeme Pollock (South Africa)	1963-1964
4th	214	Dean Jones & Allan Border (Australia)	1988-1989 v West Indies
5th	303	Raul Dravid & v VVS Laxman (India)	2003-2004
6th	191	Imran Khan & Wasim Akram (Pakistan)	1989-1990
7th	168	Rod Marsh & Kerry O'keefe (Australia)	1973-1974 v New Zealand
8th	243	Roger Hartigan & Clem Hill (Australia)	1907-1908 v England
9th	122	David Holford & Jackie Hendriks (West Indies)	1968-1969
10th	94	Sunil Gavaskar & Shivial Yadav (India)	1985-1986

Results at the Adelaide Oval

Date	Countries	Result
12/12/1884	v England	lost by 8 wickets
24/03/1892	v England	lost by an innings and 230 runs
11/01/1895	v England	won by 382 runs
14/01/1898	v England	won by an innings and 13 runs
17/01/1902	v England	won by 4 wickets
15/01/1904	v England	won by 216 runs
10/01/1908	v England	won by 245 runs
07/01/1911	v South Africa	lost by 38 runs
12/01/1912	v England	lost by 7 wickets
14/01/1921	v England	won by 119 runs
16/01/1925	v England	won by 11 runs
01/02/1929	v England	lost by 12 runs
12/12/1930	v West Indies	won by 10 wickets
29/01/1932	v South Africa	won by 10 wickets
13/01/1933	v England	lost by 338 runs
29/01/1937	v England	won by 148 runs
31/01/1947	v England	draw
23/01/1948	v India	won by an innings and 16 runs
02/02/1951	v England	won by 274 runs
22/12/1951	v West Indies	lost by 6 wickets
24/01/1953	v South Africa	draw
28/01/1955	v England	lost by 5 wickets
30/01/1959	v England	won by 10 wickets
27/01/1961	v West Indies	draw
25/01/1963	v England	draw
24/01/1964	v South Africa	lost by 10 wickets
28/01/1966	v England	won by an innings and 9 runs
23/12/1967	v India	won by 146 runs
24/01/1969	v West Indies	draw
29/01/1971	v England	draw
22/12/1972	v Pakistan	won by an innings and 114 runs
26/01/1974	v New Zealand	won by an innings and 57 runs
25/01/1975	v England	won by 163 runs
23/01/1976	v West Indies	won by 190 runs
24/12/1976	v Pakistan	draw
28/01/1978	v India	won by 47 runs
27/01/1979	v England	lost by 205 runs
26/01/1980	v West Indies	lost by 408 runs
23/01/1981	v India	draw
30/01/1982	v West Indies	lost by 5 wickets
10/12/1982	v England	won by 8 wickets

09/12/1983	v Pakistan	draw
07/12/1984	v West Indies	lost by 191 runs
13/12/1985	v India	draw
12/12/1986	v England	draw
11/12/1987	v New Zealand	draw
03/02/1989	v West Indies	draw
19/01/1990	v Pakistan	draw
25/01/1991	v England	draw
25/01/1992	v India	won by 38 runs
23/01/1993	v West Indies	lost by 1 run
28/01/1994	v South Africa	won by 191 runs
26/01/1995	v England	lost by 106 runs
25/01/1996	v Sri Lanka	won by 148 runs
25/01/1997	v West Indies	won by an innings and 183 runs
30/01/1998	v South Africa	draw
11/12/1998	v England	won by 205 runs
10/12/1999	v India	won by 285 runs
15/12/2000	v West Indies	won by 5 wickets
14/12/2001	v South Africa	won by 246 runs
21/11/2002	v England	won by an innings and 51 runs
12/12/2003	v India	lost by 4 wickets

Climate

	ave temp	rain cm
January	22	17
February	22	19
March	19	22
April	16	36
May	14	56
June	12	54
July	11	66
August	12	55
September	13	43
October	16	37
November	18	24
December	20	20

brisbane

the gabba

The Brisbane Cricket Ground at Woolloongabba, better known as the Gabba, is home to the Queensland Cricket Association. It is situated on Vulture Street to the east of the city.

Brisbane's first two tests were played at the Exhibition Ground for capacity reasons in the late 1920s. The first Test at the Gabba was in 1931, when Australia comfortably beat South Africa by an innings and 163 runs, Don Bradman scoring 226 and Bertie Ironmonger taking match figures of 9/86 as the visitors were dismissed for 170 and 117. One of the most historic Test matches ever played took place at the Gabba when Australia tied with the West Indies in the first match of 1960/61 series. The West Indies batted first, reaching 453, with Garfield Sobers scoring 132 and Alan Davidson taking 5/135. Australia replied with 505, Norm O'Neill scoring 181 and Bobby Simpson 92. Wes Hall took 4/141. In their second innings West Indies scored 284, Frank Worrell top-scoring with 65 and Davidson capturing another six wickets for 87 runs. Chasing 233 to win, Davidson made 80 before being one of three run outs as Australia lost their last four wickets for six runs to end up with the scores equal, the first ever tied Test and a feat which has only occurred on one other occasion, when India and Australia tied in Chennai in 1986.

Bradman's 226 remains the highest score. There have been two other double centuries; Keith Stackpole's 207 in 1970 against England and Greg Chappell's 201 against Pakistan in 1981. The highest team score was 645 by Australia in 1946 when they beat England by an innings and 332 runs. The lowest team score of 58 has been recorded twice, by Australia in their second innings against England in 1936 and India in their first innings in 1947. The highest chase at the Gabba is 236/7 by Australia against the West Indies in 1951.

In 1985/86 Richard Hadlee took 9/52 in the first innings in New Zealand's innings and 41 run victory. His match figures of 15/123 are the fifth best bowling return in Test cricket. In 1994/95 Shane Warne took 8/71 in England's second innings to secure a 184 run win. Warne shares the most wickets taken at the Gabba with Glenn McGrath. In 1988 Courtney Walsh of the West Indies became the only bowler to take a hat-trick at the Gabba.

The Brisbane Cricket Ground was redeveloped for the 2000 Olympics when football was played there. It meant saying goodbye to the beloved hill and the old stands at the southern end of the ground but in their place Brisbane has a state of the art, modern cricket stadium. With the exception of the Brisbane Lions Social Club, the whole ground is surrounded by grandstands. At the Vulture Street end of the ground the Northern Stand houses the players' dressing room and provides some of the best seats in the ground, particularly behind the bowler's arm. The Western and Southern Stands are also excellent vantage points with no viewing restrictions. The Eastern Stand is not used at Test matches. Most of the seats in these stands are covered.

The General Admission seats sweep around the boundary in front of the West, South and East stands. The majority of these seats are in the open for a large part of the day and spectators need to protect themselves from the hot Queensland sun. The Gordon Chalk stand in front of the social club is at fine leg and is a wonderful place from which to watch, with a great party atmosphere. Again, there is no protection from the sun.

Facilities and access for the disabled are excellent with seats in the northern and southern stands. Enquires regarding wheelchair seats should be directed to Customer Services on 1300 136 122. Tickets for the tests can be purchased at Ticketmaster7, Tel: +61 1300 13 61 22 Fax: +61 7 3331 9050 or www.ticketmaster7.com . Tickets prices range from A$29 – A$45 per day to A$80-A$128 for a five day ticket. Tickets can be collected from the office at Gate 3. Gates open at 08.30 on Test match days and play commences at 10.00.

There are plenty of well-organised bars around the ground with little queuing. It should be noted that there are many areas in the ground where alcohol cannot be consumed. The ground is also non-smoking. Food outlets are again well organised and serve the usual hot dogs, burgers, chips and soft drinks.

The Brisbane Cricket Ground is a half-hour walk from the centre of the city through Southbank and up Vulture or Stanley Streets. Buses and trains run from the city to the ground. All pre-purchased match tickets include public transport to and from the Gabba. Transport enquires 13 12 30. Car Parking is available in Brisbane Lions Car Park on Stanley Street but not around the ground. The local Council have restricted parking around the ground to 15 minutes.

Brisbane International Airport is 16km from the city centre, the domestic airport is 18km. A taxi ride takes 20 minutes and costs A$25. Taxis are available directly outside both terminals. The Brisbane Airport Transfer runs from both terminals and costs A$11. Tel: 07 3236 1000 Fax: 07 3236 3870. The Airtrain runs every 15 minutes and take 20 to get into the city. Single A$9. Times : Airport to City 05.35-08.32, City to Airport 05.01-07.58 each day.

There is a Visitor Information Centre in the Arrivals Hall on level 2. There are restaurants, coffee shops, bars, fast food outlets and shops, including a duty free shop in the terminal. Mobile telephone rental is available in Arrivals Hall. Car rental is available from Avis (07 3860 4200), Budget (07 3860 4744), Hertz (07 3860 4522) and Thrifty (1300 367 227).

Airlines
Qantas Domestic 13 13 13

Qantas International 13 12 11
Virgin Blue 13 67 89

Buses
Local services include City Circle, City Bus and City Express.
Coachtrans Airport Commuter Service 07 3236 1000
Greyhound 13 20 30

Trains
Regular air-conditioned trains link the city, suburbs and beyond. Enquiries Roma Street Transit Centre Tel: 13 12 30
Interstate and Long Distance 13 2232

Ferries
City Cats are fast catamaran ferries with regular stops along the river. Services run every ten to 15 minutes.

Taxis
Yellow Cabs 13 19 24

Car Hire
Avis
275 Wickham St. ➡

Brisbane is the capital of Queensland, Australia's sunshine state. It is situated on the north east coast on the River Brisbane.

With a population of 1.6 million, it is the country's fastest growing city. It was named after Sir Thomas Brisbane, the Governor of New South Wales, who sent John Oxley to survey potential penal settlement sites north of Sydney in 1823. It hosted the Commonwealth Games in 1982, the World Expo in 1988 and the Goodwill Games in 2001. It also staged some of the the 2000 Olympics. Aborigines have inhabited the area for 40,000 years. In 1606 the Dutch explorer Willem Jansz explored Northern Queensland. He was followed by another Dutchman in 1623, Jan Carstens, who did not venture as far south as Brisbane's location today. On 16th May 1770 Captain James Cook founded and named Moreton Bay. In 1824 a penal settlement was established at Redcliffe Point in Moreton Bay, however within a year, the settlement moved to Brisbane's current location. This closed in 1837 and in 1842 free settlers arrived and inhabited Moreton Bay, Brisbane and the surrounding area. In 1859 Brisbane was declared the capital of Queensland.

Tourism is a huge part of the Queensland economy. Brisbane is the gateway to many coastal resorts and huge attractions such as the Gold Coast and the Great Barrier Reef.

A modern city with some very tall skyscrapers, Brisbane has still been able to maintain some of its colonial roots with fine heritage buildings such as City Hall which was built in 1829, Newstead House (1846), Parliament House, a magnificent sandstone building built in 1868 and the Old Custom House. The Government Treasury is another heritage building which now houses the Treasury Casino.

The Brisbane River runs through the city and is used to transport commuters. It also affords the most wonderful views of the city and the City Cat Ferry provides the opportunity to see not only the centre, but also the beautiful leafy tree-lined suburbs and parklands that surround it. Brisbane is fortunate to have wonderful Botanical Gardens in the heart of the city by the river. It is hard to believe that the entrance to the Gardens is less than three-minute walk from Adelaide Mall, the city centre. The Gardens of Roma Street and Alma Park Zoo are also stunning.

In addition to the Great Barrier Reef and the Gold Coast, there are a multitude of other tourist attractions in Queensland. The islands of Fraser, Bribie and North and South Stradbroke off the south east coast have some of the best beaches in Australia.

Brisbane has a subtropical climate with high daytime temperatures between October and March, with an average of 26 degrees. Sea breezes temper the humidity at this time of year. The rest of the year is warm with an average of 20 degrees.

The city is quiet during the week but comes alive at the weekends when its many good pubs and clubs thrive. The hippest area in town is Fortitude Valley with an abundance of pubs, clubs and restaurants. Many of the pubs stay open late into the night.

➡ Fortitude Valley
Tel: 07 3252 7111
Fax: 07 3854 1057

Budget
105 Mary St.
Tel: 07 3220 0699
Fax: 07 3220 0955

Hertz
55 Charlotte St.
Tel: 07 3221 6166
Fax: 07 3221 5263

Thrifty
49 Barry Parade
Fortitude Valley
Tel: 07 300 367 227
Fax: 07 3006 3299

Southbank Parklands

Situated on 16 hectares of land along the banks of the Brisbane River opposite the city centre, it is the product of the £67 million investment for World Expo 88. It has a wonderful man-made beach and lagoon, a popular venue with locals and tourists alike, a rainforest area and an entertainment area. Also home to the Queensland Cultural Centre. There are at least a dozen cafés in the park serving everything from seafood to Chinese and Indian. A wonderful place to spend an afternoon or early evening.

North Stradbroke Island

Less than 50km south-east of Brisbane and ideal for visitors looking for a laid-back break. Very popular with the locals, the island has some fine wilderness areas and beaches with huge sand dunes. Every type of accommodation is available from camping and backpackers to luxury resorts. The island also has art galleries and museums.

Noosa

Has to be seen to be believed. The beach is magnificent, the National Park stunning, with shady walks, peaceful coves and some very long beaches and the restaurants are second to none. An hour-and-a-half drive from Brisbane, Noosa cannot be missed. It has style. A bye-law preventing any building more than two storeys high has preserved the beachfront. The main street, Hastings Street, buzzes with clothes, book and souvenir shops and some excellent restaurants and cafés.

Brisbane River Cruise

A wonderful way to get to know Brisbane is to jump on one of the ferries that journey up and down the river. From the water the city stands proud with its sky-scrapers towering over the heritage buildings along the riverside. You travel from the University of Queensland, via the Casino, Southbank, Eagle Street Pier and the Botanical Gardens to the other end of Brisbane and the beautiful parks that surround the city. Hop on and off wherever you want and take the opportunity to enjoy the riverside cafés and the markets. The City Cat runs from 06.00-10.30 seven days a weeks.

The Gold Coast

An hour outside Brisbane, this has everything one expects from a seaside holiday resort from adrenalin-stirring activities such as bungy jumping and cable skiing to wildlife sanctuaries and museums. Dreamworld, Sea World and Warner Bros. Movie World and Wet'n'Wild Waterworld are theme parks to visit. Golf, diving, sailing and 4-wheel driving add to the fun. All types of accommodation are available at affordable prices.

Queensland Cultural Centre Museum

South Bank
Tel: 07 3846 1918
Museum of Natural History, Science and Human achievement. Wonderful dinosau garden and whale exhibition. Open seven days.

Queensland Maritime Museum

South Bank Parklands
Tel: 07 3844 5361
Many fascinating nautical relics including World War II frigate and 1925 steam tug

Queensland Performing Arts Centre

Southbank
Tel: 07 3840 7444
Fax: 07 3844 1839

Royal on the Park

Corner Alice and Albert St.
Tel: 07 3221 3411
Fax: 07 3229 9817
res@royalonthepark.com.au
Beside the botanical gardens in the
CBD and shopping district. 153
rooms. Wood panelling, leather
couches and brass lamps. Bar,
Restaurant, spa, gym and the largest
swimming pool in Brisbane.

Conrad Treasury Brisbane

130 William St.
Tel: 07 3303 8888
Fax: 07 3306 8880
hotelres@conrad.co.au
www.conrad.co.au
Right in the centre. 130 beautiful
rooms with excellent restaurant and
bars. Casino one of the city's top
attractions. No swimming pool.

Novotel Brisbane

200 Creak St.
Tel: 07 3309 3309
Fax: 07 3309 3308
res@novotelbrisbane.com
Really friendly hotel in the centre. 295
rooms with cable TV, good restaurant,
gym and swimming pool.

Rydges South Bank

9 Glenelg Stree
Southbank
Tel: 07 3255 0822
Fax: 07 3255 0899
reservations.southbank@rydges.com
Very large. 10 minutes walk to city
but closer to the Gabba. 305

rooms, cable TV, spas
but no swimming pool.

Explorers' inn

Corner George and Turbet Streets
Tel: 07 3211 3488
Fax: 07 3211 3499
stay@explorers.com.au
Budget accommodation in the centre.
58 comfortable rooms with TV.

Hotel George William

317 – 325 George St.
Tel: 07 3308 0700
Fax: 07 3308 0733
hgw@ymca.org,au
Excellent central budget accommo-
dation. Great gym and fine rooms.
Highly recommended.

Brisbane City Backpackers'

380 Upper Roma St.
Tel: 07 3211 3221
Fax: 07 3236 0474
Good backpackers' in centre. 53
rooms with swimming pool.

Palace Backpackers'

Corner Edward and Ann Streets
Tel: 07 3211 2433
Fax: 07 3211 2466
Brisbane@pbp.co.au
Probably one of the best city backpackers' in Australia. 117 rooms,
singles, doubles, twin and dormitories. Roof top terrace and basement
bar. Without doubt the liveliest bar
in town.

Queensland's major cultural venue for performing arts incorporating the
Lyric Theatre. Tickets and enquiries from Qtix on 13 62 46

Queensland Cultural Centre Art Gallery

Southbank
Tel: 07 3840 7303
A collection of rare Australian, Aboriginal, European and Asian art.

Brisbane City Gallery

City Hall
King George Square
Brisbane's best gallery for local, national and international visual arts, craft and
design.
Tel: 07 3403 8888

California Café
The Valley
The only way to start the day with the Truckies Breakfast. Excellent value

River Canteen
South Bank Boardwalk
South Bank
Tel: 07 3846 1880
Fax: 07 3846 1839
info@rivercanteen.com.au
Beautiful food in a warm atmosphere in South Bank. Wonderful views of city

F.I.X. Food Wine Bar
Post Office Hotel
Corner Edward and Margaret St.
Tel: 07 3210 6016
Brisbane's busiest eating and meeting place. Great food in relaxed surroundings.

Pier Nine
Eagle Street Pier
Eagle St.
Tel: 07 3229 2194
Mediterranean/Australian, seafood restaurant on the pier. Wonderful views through floor to ceiling glass windows. Excellent wine list. Highly recommended. Reservations necessary.

Vino's Cellar Bar and Café
Eagle Street Pier
Eagle St.
Tel: 07 3221 0811
Excellent Mediterranean food in a relaxed atmosphere.

Circa
Adelaide St.
Tel: 07 3882 4722
Without doubt one of the best restaurants in the city with fantastic food and a fine wine list.

Friday's Bar, Restaurant and Club
Riverside Centre

123 Eagle St.
Tel: 07 3832 2121
Steak and seafood on an Aussie menu in one of the finest bars in town. Has served the city's best vegetarian food for 15 years.

The Zoo
711 Ann St.
The Valley
Tel: 07 3854 1381

Adrenalin Sports Bar
127 Charlotte St.
Tel: 07 3229 1515

Aces Bar
Ground Floor
Treasury Casino
Corner Queen and George St.
Tel: 07 3306 8888

Elephant and Wheelbarrow
230 Wickham St.
The Valley
Tel: 07 325 4136

Gilhooleys
Corner Elizabeth and Creek St.
Tel: 07 3221 8566

Down Under Bar and Grill
308 Edward St.
Palace Backpackers
Tel: 07 3211 9277

Fihellys Arms Hotel
270 Ann St.
Tel: 07 32 35 1887

Irish Murphys
175 George St.
Tel: 07 3221 4377
Self explanatory!

The Rat and Parrott
Corner Ann and Constance St.
The Valley
Tel: 07 3252 9833

Post Office

Australia Post
261 Queen St.
Tel: 07 3405 1434
Open 07.00 – 19.00 daily.

Tourist Information

There is an information kiosk in Queen Street Mall which provides all the necessary information about Queensland. Telephone enquiries to Tourism Queensland on 07 3535 3535 and Visitor Information on 07 3409 9555.

Hospitals

North
  Royal Brisbane Hospital
    Herston Road
Herston
Tel: 07 3252 8111

South
Princess Alexandra Hospital
Ipswich Road
Woolloongabba
Tel: 07 3240 2111

Travellers' Medical Service 07 3211 3611

Dentist

11/138 Albert St.
Tel: 07 3221 0677

Emergency Numbers

Police	07 3364 6464
Fire	07 3247 5539
Ambulance	07 3364 1246

Climate

	ave temp	rain cm			
January	25	106	July	15	57
February	25	154	August	16	46
March	24	137	September	18	45
April	22	88	October	21	78
May	18	68	November	23	97
June	16	60	December	24	101

Win/Loss Record

	Played	Won	Drawn	Lost	Tie
Australia	46	26	11	8	1
Sri Lanka	1	-	1	-	-
West Indies	10	3	2	4	1
England	17	4	4	9	-
New Zealand	6	1	1	4	-
South Africa	3	-	1	2	-
Pakistan	4	-	1	3	-
India	5	-	1	4	-

Highest Individual Aggregates (all Australian)

Player	Mat	Inn	NO	Runs	Ave	HS	50	100
Greg Chappell	7	11	2	1006	111.78	201	4	5
Steve Waugh	17	26	4	915	41.59	147*	5	3
Mark Taylor	10	18	2	912	57.00	164	6	2
Alan Border	15	22	1	779	37.10	152*	2	3
David Boon	12	20	0	750	37.50	143	4	2
Don Bradman	5	7	0	736	105.14	226	1	3
Bill Lawry	6	11	1	710	71.00	166	4	2
Mark Waugh	11	16	1	689	45.93	140	4	2
Ian Healy	11	17	4	689	53.00	161*	1	2
Michael Slater	6	9	1	675	84.38	176	1	3

Top Wicket Takers (Australian unless stated)

Player	Mat	Bll	Md	Runs	Wkt	Ave	BB	S/R
Glenn Mcgrath	10	2577	128	1131	51	22.18	6/17	50.53
Shane Warne	8	2643	139	1071	51	21.00	8/71	51.82
Craig Mcdermott	8	1887	69	905	40	22.63	6/53	47.18
Dennis Lillee	6	1175	35	625	31	20.16	6/53	37.90
Jeff Thomson	6	1396	30	697	29	24.03	6/46	48.14
Merv Hughes	6	1285	53	608	28	21.71	4/50	45.89
Geoff Lawson	6	1240	47	545	28	19.46	6/47	44.29
Richie Benaud	5	1895	64	603	23	26.22	6/115	82.39
Richard Hadlee (NZ)	3	807	29	343	21	16.33	9/52	38.43
Ray Lindwall	6	1111	30	358	21	17.05	5/60	52.90

Highest Individual Scores (Australian unless stated)

226	Don Bradman	v South Africa 1931-32
207	Keith Stackpole	v England 1970-71
201	Greg Chappell	v Pakistan 1981-82
197	Matthew Hayden	v England 2002-03
188	Martin Crowe (NZ)	1985-86
187	Don Bradman	v England 1946-47
185	Don Bradman	v India 1947-48
181	Norm O'neill	v West Indies 1960-61
176	Michael Slater	v England 1994-95
169	Brian Booth	v South Africa 1963-64

Best Individual Bowling (Australian unless stated)

23.4-4-52-9	Richard Hadlee (NZ)	1985-86
50.2-22-71-8	Shane Warne	v England 1994-95
16.1-9-23-7	Shane Warne	v Pakistan 1995-96
22-4-60-7	Keith Miller	v England 1946-47
20-12-17-6	Glenn Mcgrath	v West Indies 2000-01
17-6-29-6	Ernie Toshack	v India 1947-48
20.6-5-41-6	Bill Voce (Eng)	1936-37
17.5-3-46-6	Jeff Thomson	v England 1974-75
18.3-4-47-6	Geoff Lawson	v England 1982-83
22-7-47-6	Terry Alderman	v England 1990-91

Highest Partnerships

Wkt	Runs	Batsmen	Match
1st	269	Michael Slater & Greg Blewett (Australia)	1999-2000 v Pakistan
2nd	272	Matthew Hayden & Ricky Ponting (Australia)	2002-2003 v England
3rd	276	Don Bradman & Lindsay Hassett (Australia)	1946-1947 v England
4th	198	Laurence Rowe & Alvin Kallicharran (West Indies)	1975-1976
5th	187	Bill Lawry & Doug Walters (Australia)	1965-1966 v England
6th	197	Allan Border & Greg Matthews (Australia)	1985-1986 v New Zealand
7th	144	Aravina de Silva & Ravi Ratnayeke (Sri Lanka)	1989-1990
8th	135	Adam Gilchrist & Brett Lee (Australia)	2001-2002 v New Zealand
9th	92	Eddie Paynter & Hedley Verity (England)	1932-1933
10th	86	Shane Warne & Scott Muller (Australia)	1999-2000 v Pakistan

Results at the Gabba

Date	Countries	Result
27/11/1931	v South Africa	won by an innings & 163 runs
10/02/1933	v England	lost by 6 wickets
04/12/1936	v England	lost by 322 runs
29/11/1946	v England	won by an innings & 332 runs
28/11/1947	v India	won by an innings & 226 runs
01/12/1950	v England	won by 70 runs
09/11/1951	v West Indies	won by 3 wickets
05/12/1952	v South Africa	won by 96 runs
26/11/1954	v England	won by an innings & 154 runs
05/12/1958	v England	won by 8 wickets
09/12/1960	v West Indies	tied
30/11/1962	v England	draw
06/12/1963	v South Africa	draw
10/12/1965	v England	draw
19/01/1968	v India	won by 39 runs
06/12/1968	v West Indies	lost by 125 runs
27/11/1970	v England	draw
29/11/1974	v England	won by 166 runs
28/11/1975	v West Indies	won by 8 wickets
02/12/1977	v India	won by 16 runs
01/12/1978	v England	lost by 7 wickets
01/12/1979	v West Indies	draw
28/11/1980	v New Zealand	won by 10 wickets
27/11/1981	v Pakistan	won by 10 wickets
26/11/1982	v England	won by 7 wickets
25/11/1983	v Pakistan	draw
23/11/1984	v West Indies	lost by 8 wickets
08/11/1985	v New Zealand	lost by an innings & 41 runs
14/11/1986	v England	lost by 7 wickets
04/12/1987	v New Zealand	won by 9 wickets
18/11/1988	v West Indies	lost by 9 wickets
08/12/1989	v Sri Lanka	draw
23/11/1990	v England	won by 10 wickets
29/11/1991	v India	won by 10 wickets
27/11/1992	v West Indies	draw
03/12/1993	v New Zealand	won by an innings & 96 runs
25/11/1994	v England	won by 184 runs
09/11/1995	v Pakistan	won by an innings & 126 runs
22/11/1996	v West Indies	won by 123 runs
07/11/1997	v New Zealand	won by 186 runs
20/11/1998	v England	draw
05/11/1999	v Pakistan	won by 10 wickets
23/11/2000	v West Indies	won by an innings & 126 runs
08/11/2001	v New Zealand	draw
07/11/2002	v England	won by 384 runs
04/12/2003	v India	draw

cairns

bundaberg rum stadium

The stadium lies to the south west of the city and, with its wonderful hilly back drop, is one of the most scenic of Test grounds.

It became the ninth Australian Test ground on 25 July 2003 when Bangladesh were entertained in the second Test of a two-match series

Bangladesh, one down in the series, began well with a first innings score of 295, Hannan Sarker top-scoring with 76. Stuart MacGill continued his good work from the first Test, taking 5/77. In reply Australia scored a massive 556/4, Darren Lehmann (177), Steve Waugh (156) and Martin Love (100) each scoring centuries. Steve Waugh shared a fourth wicket partnership of 250 with Lehmann and an unbeaten fifth wicket partnership of 174 with Love. Needing 261 to force the hosts to bat again, Bangladesh could only manage 163 and so lost by an innings and 98 runs. Sarker made another half-century but MacGill was again the destroyer, taking another five wickets (5/56). Formerly known as the Cazaly's Australian Rules Football Park, the Bundaberg Rum Stadium has a capacity of 12,000. On the south west side of the ground is the 3,000 seat grandstand which was formerly the Western Stand at the Gabba in Brisbane. It was moved to Cairns in 1995 when the redevelopment of the Brisbane ground began. The remainder of the ground is surrounded by grassy banks which are ideal for spectating. The Test was very well attended by locals, delighted that an international match had been awarded to their city. The mild winter climate in June/July is an ideal time for cricket when the other Australian Test cities are experiencing more severe winter conditions. The stadium will entertain Sri Lanka in 2004 and Cricket Australia is committed to using the ground regularly.

The ground lies 5km from the centre of Cairns on the corner of Mulgrave Street and Tills Street. Buses run from the city each morning of the Test while a taxi should cost no more than $12. However, catching a taxi after the day's play can be difficult with large numbers queueing. If driving from the city you should go up Florence Street until it joins with Mulgrave Road. There is only limited parking near the ground and the bus or taxi are probably better options.

Tickets can be purchased from the ticket office on the day of the game and cost $35 for reserved seating and $25 general admission. Tickets can also be bought from Ticketmaster7 on www.ticketmaster.com.au. The facilities in the ground are excellent with good food stalls and efficiently run bars without long queues. The toilets around the ground are all well looked after. There are a number of first-aid points around the ground.

All in all the Bundaberg Rum Stadium did a wonderful job in hosting their first international.

Cairns lies on Trinity Bay on the north east coast of Queensland about 1,800km to the north of Brisbane. It is said to be the capital of the Tropical Far North and is a modern cosmopolitan city. Named after the state's first Irish born Governor Sir William Wellington Cairns, the population is 124,000.

The area was first inhabited by the Aborigines and the Torres Strait Islanders and was known as Gimuy. Although the Dutch charted the coastline in the late 1600s, Captain James Cook was the first European to land in the area in June 1770. Cook landed because of the difficulty with navigating his ship, the Endeavour, through the Great Barrier Reef. The sheltered bay attracted him and he named it Trinity Bay as he arrived on Trinity Sunday. Cook claimed the land for Britain and spent some time there repairing his ship before leaving. Due to the treacherous reefs, the dense vegetation and the harsh climate, it was nearly one hundred years before the first Europeans settled in the area which was a sand ridge fringed by mangrove swamps. The discovery of gold north of Cairns in 1872 brought many prospectors to the area. The settlement grew steadily, becoming a town in 1876 and a city in 1923 when the population reached 10,000. The development of the tin mines and timber industry in the Atherton Tablelands also had a great deal to do with the growth of Cairns. A railway line was built between the city and the Tablelands and Cairns handled the distribution of its products.

In addition to the tin and timber industries, sugar cane is an important industry and vast amounts of the land around Cairns are dedicated to cane. In the hinterland dairy farming, fruit and vegetables and tobacco are also important industries. The export of these products makes Cairn a busy port. Tourism is the city's major industry with the number of visitors growing steadily every year since the early 1980s. The Great Barrier Reef is by far the main attraction followed by the rainforest which surrounds the city.

Cairns itself is a charming place built in a grid pattern and it is easy to walk around the wide streets viewing the incredible old buildings. The Boland Centre built in 1912, Earl Court (1926) and the Central Hotel (1909) in Spence St, and the School of Arts (1907) and Hides Corner (1930) in Lake Street are just some examples of the colonial architecture that can be found in the city. Abbott Street is the most historic area with the Regional Gallery (1936), the Old Court House (1919) and the Cairns Post Building (1908). Cairns also has some lovely parks including the wonderful Esplanade with the newly built swimming lagoon in Fogarty Park Drive which adds so much to the city. There is no beach in the city itself so the new lagoon is really well used. The Marlin Marina is worth a stroll.

Deep sea fishing and big game trips leave from the marina. The Skyrail Rainforest Cableway and the train journey to Kuranda are the major attractions. Daytrips to Cape Tribulation and Cooktown are also popular.

Great Barrier Reef

Cairns' biggest tourist attraction. Every morning cruises leave the Marlin Marina to take divers, snorkellers and sightseers. The journey takes about 90 minutes and the snorkelling is excellent with good coral and plenty of fish to see. The visibility for diving is good and a lot of tourists take the opportunity to do an introductory dive.

Flecker Botanic Gardens

4km to the north of Cairns. Collections of both native and exotic tropical plants. Daily guided walks are conducted to the Orchid House, the Aboriginal Plant Section, the Fernery and Palms, Bamboo and Tropical fruits. The gardens are open 07.30-17.30 Monday to Friday and 08.30-17.30 on Saturday and Sunday. Guided walks are available on weekdays at 13.00. Admission is free.

White Water Rafting

Some of the world's best white water rafting. Cairns' original rafting company, Raging Thunder Adventures (07 40 30 7990), run a 12-hour trip which includes five hours rafting and a barbeque lunch. Everyone receives a photo and video of the day's action. Rafting can be quite strenuous and you are guaranteed an early night after an eventful day.

Atherton Tablelands

An hour's drive west of Cairns through lush rainforest covered mountains. The Tablelands have some natural wonders such the Curtain and Cathedral fig trees and The Twin Kauri Pines. There are some incredible waterfalls cascading down the mountain. The area offers the opportunity to swim, canoe, sail or fish in the beautiful lakes and to see some of the local wildlife including kangaroos, platypus and many species of birds. Can be reached by taking the Rex and Kennedy highways from Cairns.

Port Douglas

A sleepy town with some of the best restaurants in Australia. Less than an hour's drive from Cairns, it has wonderful beaches. It also has great markets, boutiques and shops. The Bally Hooley Railway runs trips to the nearby rainforest. Just outside the town it is possible to catch the cable-driven ferry on the Daintree River.

The Shipwreck Museum

Pier Market Place
Tel: 07 4031 0102
madive@smartchat.net.au
Very interesting maritime museum.

The Cairns Museum

City Place
Tel: 07 4051 5582
www.carinsmuseum.org.au
Looks into the city's history, aboriginal culture, and the mining industry.

The Australian Sugar Industry Museum

Bruce Highway
Mourilyan
Tel: 07 4063 2656
www.sugarmuseum.org.au
An unusual museum exploring the history of sugar cane in the state.

Cairns Regional Gallery

Corner of Abbott and Shields Streets
Offers changing exhibitions by local, Australian and international artists.
Open 10.00-17.00 Monday to Saturday
13.00-17.00 Sunday

Cairns International Airport is 6km from the centre. A taxi should cost no more than $14. Australia Coach Services provides a service to all the major hotels for $7.00. The International Airport has currency exchanges in baggage reclaim and the Arrivals Hall which also has an ATM. There is a tourist information desk, also shops, food counters and a newsagent. A post box is located beside tourist information. Car hire is available from Avis (07 4035 9100), Hertz (07 4035 9299), Budget (07 4035 9500) and Thrifty (07 4035 9033).

Cairns Domestic Terminal is a five minute covered walk. Australia Coaches run a service between the terminals for $2. The domestic terminal also has ATMs, currency exchange, tourist information, shops and cafés.

Airlines

Qantas	13 13 13
Virgin Blue	13 67 89
Air New Zealand	13 24 76
Singapore Airlines	13 10 11

Buses

The local terminal is beside City Place on Lake St. The Intercity Transit Centre is down by Trinity Wharf on Wharf St.
McCafferty's   13 20 30

If you want to watch the winter Tests in Cairns and Darwin there is a wonderful four-day overland trip between the two organised by Desert Venturer (1800 079 119 – www.desertventurer.com. au) which travels through Townsville, Mount Isa and Renner Springs for approximately $400.

Trains

Cairns Railway Station in on Bunda St.
All Railway Enquiries 13 22 32

Taxis

Cairns Black and White Taxis
13 10 08

Car Hire

Avis
135 Lake St.
Tel: 07 4051 5911
Fax: 07 4052 1487

Countrywide 13 63 33
reservations@avis.com.au

Budget
153 Lake St.
Tel: 07 4051 9222
Fax: 07 4052 1158
Country 13 27 27
www.budget.com.au

Hertz
147 Lake St.
Tel: 07 4051 6399
Fax: 07 4051 8005

Thrifty
Corner Sheridan and Aplin Streets
Tel: 07 4051 8099
Fax: 07 4051 8949

Countrywide 13 61 39

Motor Cycle Rentals

Easy Rider Motor Cylces
134 Sheridan St.
Tel: 07 4051 4229
Fax: 07 4041 4251
sales@easyridemotorcyclehire.com.au
www.easyridermotorcyclehire.com.au

Post Office

Cairns Main Post Office
13 Grafton St.
Tel: 07 4031 4303

Tourist Information

Cairns Tourist information Centre
Corner The Esplanade and Shields St.
Tel: 07 4031 1751
Fax: 07 4051 9682

Tourism Tropical North Queensland
Visitor information Centre
51 The Esplanade

Tel: 07 4051 3588
Fax: 07 4051 0127
Open Monday-Sunday 08.30-17.30.

Hospital

Cairns Base Hospital
Lake St/Kerwin St.
Tel: 07 4050 6333

24hr Doctor   07 4041 1699

Cairns Police Headquarters

5 Sheridan St.
Cairns.
Tel: 07 4030 7000

Hog's Breath Café
64 Spence St.
07 4031 771
Part of the famous Australian chain serving prime rib, chicken, burgers, tex mex. Great atmosphere. Well worth a visit

Kanis on the Esplanade
59 The Esplanade
Tel: 07 4051 1550
Out-and-out seafood restaurant serving fresh local produce. Indoor and verandah dining. Open 7 days a week from 17.30.

Yanni's Greek Taverna
Corner Aplin and Grafton Streets
Tel: 07 4041 1500
City centre restaurant with excellent food and an atmosphere to match. Belly dancers at weekends. Open for dinner 7 nights a week until late. Lunch Monday-Friday.

Dundee's Seafood, Steaks and Pasta
29 Spence St.
Tel: 07 4051 0399
Australian cuisine including seafood, beef, crocodile at very reasonable cost.

Catina Bar and Restaurant
96 Lake St.
Tel: 07 4041 2412
Great Mexican restaurant serving traditional gourmet cuisine with cactus garden. Great bar open from 17.30 til late.

Raw Prawn Seafood
103 The Esplanade
Tel: 07 40315400
Excellent seafood restaurant with great ocean views.

Roma Roulette
48 Aplin St.
Tel: 07 4051 1076
Well established BYO Italian restaurant with excellent steaks and seafood. Open Wednesday to Sunday from 18.00.

Tandoori Oven
62B Shields St.
Tel: 07 4031 0043

Finest curry house in Cairns serving North Indian cuisine in great atmosphere.

Barnacle Bill's Seafood Inn
65 The Esplanade
Tel: 07 4051 2241
Great seafood restaurant, indoor and outdoor tables. Crocodile and kangaroo on menu.

Verdi's Restaurant
Corner Sheridan and Shields Streets
Tel: 07 4052 1010
Award winning seafood, steak, pasta and wood fired pizzas served in a good fun atmosphere.

Food Court in the Night Markets
The Esplanade
A variety of different food counters to suit everybody's taste. Open each night from 17.00-23.00. Very good food

Shenannigans
Corner Spence and Sheridan Sts
Tel: 07 4051 2490
Liveliest bar in town, great atmosphere, always busy with big screen constantly showing sport.

Cock and Bull
Corner Grove and Digger Streets
Tel: 07 4031 1160
Lively British pub with excellent food.

Chapel Bar Restaurant
91 The Esplanade
Tel: 07 4041 4222
Upstairs bar with good music open until late. Great food.

Serpent Hostel Bar
341 Lake St.
Tel: 07 4040 7777
Lively young bar, always busy with good prices.

Rydges Plaza

Corner Grafton and Spence St.
Tel: 07 4041 1022
Excellent hotel in the heart of city
with 98 en suite rooms. Restaurant,
bar, swimming pool and fitness centre.

Raddisson Plaza on the Pier

Pierpoint Road
Tel: 07 4031 1411
Ideally positioned on the Marlin
Marina this is one of Cairns' finest.
219 splendid en suite rooms with
balconies. The Rainforest lobby and
Great Barrief Reef aquarium are very
impressive. Swimming pool, gym and
sauna.

Holiday Inn Cairns

Corner The Esplanade and Florence St.
Tel: 07 40506070
Fax: 07 40313770
232 en suite rooms with fine ocean
and mountain views. Restaurant,
swimming pool, gym. Fabulous
atrium.

Rainbow Inn

179 Sheridan St.
Tel: 07 4051 1022
5 minutes from the city centre with
excellent restaurant and bar. All
rooms en suite, with cable TV and
kitchenette.

The Great Northern Hotel

69 Abbot St.
Tel: 07 4051 5966
Good, comfortable en suite, recently
renovated rooms with cable TV. Bar
with very friendly and helpful service.

Comfort Inn Tropical

2026 Digger St.
Tel: 07 4051 0123
One and two bedroom apartments
with cable TV, kitchenette and balcony.

Best Western Flying Horseshoe Hotel

281-289 Sheridan St.
Tel: 07 4051 3022

Family run hotel with
air-conditioned en suite rooms,
balcony and kitchenette.

Compass Motor Inn

232 Mulgrave Road
Tel: 07 4051 5466
Good budget accommodation with
clean, air-conditioned rooms with TV.

Club Crocodile Hides Hotel

87 Lake St.
Tel: 07 4051 1266
Good budget accommodation in
colonial style hotel in centre . Air-
conditioning, TV and internet.

Shenannigans Motel

Corner Spence and Sheridan Sts
Tel: 07 4051 2490
Fax: 07 4051 2288
shenannigans3@bigpond.com
www.shenannigans.com.au
Very good budget accommodation in
the centre. Fine bar downstairs. Good
food. Reservations advisable.

Global Palace

City Place
Corner Lake and Shields Sts
Tel: 07 4031 7921
Fax: 07 4031 3231
www.globalpalace.com.au
Right in the centre. Well established
backpackers' with air-conditioned
twin, double rooms and 3, 4 and 5 bed
dormitories. Rooftop swimming pool,
pool tables and big screen TV.

Pete's Backpackers' Resort

242 Grafton St.
Tel: 07 4031 6472
Fax: 07 4031 4872
www.petescairns.com.au
Not far from the centre. Good pool,
great atmosphere. Big Screen TV,
internet, airport pickups.

stats

Win/Loss Record

Country	Played	Won	Drawn	Lost
Australia	1	1	-	- -
Bangladesh	1	-	-	1 -

Highest Individual Aggregates

Player	Mat	Inn	NO	Runs	Ave	HS	50	100
Darren Lehmann (Aus)	1	1	0	177	177.00	177	0	1
Steve Waugh (Aus)	1	1	1	156	-	156*	0	1
Hannan Sarkar (Bangla)	1	2	0	131	65.50	76	2	0
Martin Love (Aus)	1	1	1	100	-	100*	0	1
Habibul Bashar (Bangla)	1	2	0	71	35.50	46	0	0

Top Wicket Takers

Player	Mat	Bll	Md	Runs	Wkt	Ave	BB	S/R
Stuart MacGill (Aus)	1	264	12	133	10	13.30	5/56	26.40
Jason Gillespie (Aus)	1	226	10	95	7	13.57	4/38	32.29
Sanwar Hossain (Bangla)	1	180	2	128	2	64.00	2/128	90.00
Brett Lee (Aus)	1	174	3	133	2	66.50	1/45	87.00
Mashrafe Mortaza (Bangla)	1	150	7	60	1	60.00	1/60	150.00

Highest Individual Scores

177	Darren Lehmann (Aus)	2003
156*	Steve Waugh (Aus)	2003
100*	Martin Love (Aus)	2003
76	Hannan Sarkar (Bangla)	2003
59	Ricky Ponting (Aus)	2003

Best Individual Bowling

20-3-56-5	Stuart MacGill (Aus)	2003
24-9-77-5	Stuart MacGill (Aus)	2003
12.4-3-38-4	Jason Gillespie (Aus)	2003
25-7-57-3	Jason Gillespie (Aus)	2003
30-2-128-2	Sanwar Hossain (Bangla)	2003

Highest Partnerships

Wkt	Runs	Batsmen	Match
1st	47	Hannan Sarkar & Javed Omar (Bangla)	2003-2004 v Aus
2nd	108	Hannan Sarkar & Habibul Bashar (Bangla)	2003-2004 v Aus
3rd	27	Ricky Ponting & Darren Lehmann (Aus)	2003-2004 v Bangla
4th	250	Darren Lehmann & Steve Waugh (Aus)	2003-2004 v Bangla
5th	174*	Steve Waugh & Martin Love (Aus)	2003-2004 v Bangla
6th	60	Sanwar Hossain & Khaled Mashud (Bangla)	2003-2004 v Aus
7th	20	Khaled Mashud & Khaled Mahmud (Bangla)	2003-2004 v Aus
8th	51	Khaled Mashud & Tapash Baisya (Bangla)	2003-2004 v Aus
9th	14	Tapash Baisya & Mushrafe Mortaza (Bangla)	2003-2004 v Aus
10th	7	Mashrafe Mortaza & Anwar Hossain Monir (Bangla)	2003-2004 v Aus

Results at Bundaberg Rum Stadium

Date	Countries	Result
25/07/2003	v Bangladesh	won by an Innings and 98 runs

Climate

	ave temp	rain cm
January	28	405
February	27	435
March	27	420
April	26	197
May	24	100
June	22	45
July	21	30
August	22	26
September	23	35
October	26	39
November	27	89
December	28	171

marrara

The home of the Northern Territory Cricket Association, Marrara is a small ground surrounded by trees just 15km from Darwin on the north side of the city beyond the airport. It became Australia's eighth Test venue on 18th July 2003 when Australia played Bangladesh for the first time. Unfortunately it was one-sided with the hosts winning by an innings and 132 runs. Bangladesh scored 97 in their first innings, Glenn McGrath and Brett Lee taking three wickets each. In reply Australia hit 407/7dec, Darren Lehmann (110) and Steve Waugh (100 not out). Mashrafe Mortaza was the only Bangladeshi bowler of note taking 3/74. The visitors scored 178 in their second innings as Stuart MacGill took 5/65 to end the match within three days.

Because of its climate, Darwin is an ideal location to play Test cricket in the June/July period when the other Test grounds in Australia are rested for the winter. Cricket Australia plan to use both grounds regularly in the future. Marrara is also used for Australian Rules Football and uses a 'drop in' wicket.

The capacity is 15,000 with a grandstand on the west side. The north end is a grass bank and a 'dry' area. The east side is partially covered with temporary shade and houses the scoreboard. The south end is also partially covered. The grandstand has excellent facilities with a wide range of food and drink available. The east side has food and drink stalls which can become very busy and are prone to long queues. Only low and mid-strength alcohol is served in public areas. The toilet facilities are good with blocks on each level of the grandstand, in front of the scoreboard and at both ends. First-Aid points are located underneath the grandstand, on level two at the south end of that stand and beneath the scoreboard.

Tickets cost $25 for general admission and $35 for reserved seating and are available from the Bonson and Scoreboard gates. Prepaid tickets can be also be collected from these gates. There is no direct bus to the ground from the city centre, but there are buses from Casuarina Bus Interchange between 7.30 and 10.00 each morning of the match. Buses do run to Darwin, Palmerston and Casuarina after play. If driving from Darwin one should take the Stuart Highway, turn left onto Bagot Road before taking a right onto McMillan Road. Car parking is available at the south end of the ground in the Darwin Gun Club and at the north end in the South Darwin Sports Club for a fee of $2. Taxis are also available outside the ground.

Disabled access is through the north end of the ground and there are excellent disabled viewing areas in the Grandstand. Smoking is prohibited apart from designated areas. No alcohol, glass or cans may be brought into the ground. Collapsible seats and stools are permitted.

Darwin is the capital of the Northern Territory and is situated on a peninsula on Clarence Strait. Formerly known as Palmerston, after the British Prime Minister of the time, and Port Darwin, the city was named after the British scientist Charles Darwin by John Lort Stokes, of the HMS Beagle, upon landing in the area in 1839. Darwin had spent five years as botanist on the ship circumnavigating the globe in the early 1830s. The city has a remarkably varied history of gold rushes, cyclones and World War II bombings. Despite its harsh climate Darwin has always attracted the adventurous, from prospectors, pearl fishermen, cattlemen and crocodile hunters of times past to the entrepreneurs of today. The population is 90,000.

When gold was discovered in the area, many migrants from Europe and Asia were attracted to the area. The city reverted to the name Darwin in 1911 when South Australia handed over control to the Commonwealth. Two events above all others dominate the history of Darwin – the World War II bombings and the advent of Cyclone Tracey on Christmas Day 1974. The cyclone killed 64 people, injured thousands more and wiped out most of the city. Darwin was rebuilt in line with strict construction standards and building codes specially devised for cyclone-prone cities. It was planned in a modern grid pattern unrecognisable from its original layout.

The city and surrounds have a lot to offer. It is quiet, clean, friendly and pleasant to stroll around. The old buildings which survived the cyclone, Government House at the south end of the Esplanade and Fannie Bay Gaol, both built in 1883, and the Old Admiralty House, 1920, are reminders of old Darwin. Parliament House, the Supreme Court in State Square and the Civic Centre with its 'Tree of Knowledge' Banyan tree are worth visiting. Bicentennial Park on the Esplanade overlooking the harbour is a lovely place to relax.

Darwin is compact and most of the attractions are within walking distance of the centre, but there is an air-conditioned tour bus called The Tour Tub that runs all day from Smith Street Mall. One-hour and half-day cruises of Darwin harbour are also available. Darwin has a wealth of art and cultural activities with its own Symphony Orchestra that tours the Territory playing in some fine but unusual places. In addition to the attractions in the city, the Territory has some places that should not be missed when visiting Darwin. Kakadu National Park, 200km to the east of Darwin, Litchfield National Park, Edith Falls and Katherine Gorge all have to be seen to be believed.

what to see

Kakadu National Park

200km south of Darwin, this is without doubt one of the most exciting and amazing places to visit in the world. Rich in natural beauty and culture, Kakadu has so much for the visitor including spotting crocodiles while cruising on the East Alligator River, exploring Ubirr Rock with wonderful panoramic views of the area, studying the Aboriginal Art at Nourlangie Rock and Nanguluwur, walking through the Manngarre rainforest and visiting Jim Jim and Twin Falls in a 4X4. Visitors can organise their own trip or use one of the many tour companies which include Kakadu Parklink (08 8979 2411) and Kakadu Gorge and Waterfall Tours (08 8979 0111 – www.kakadu-touring.com.au)

Litchfield National Park

Closer than Kakadu to Darwin, around 130km from the city, the park has some fantastic waterfalls where swimming is a must. Wangi, Tolmer and Florence are the best and Buley Rock Holes must also be visited. The park is a wildlife sanctuary providing wonderful opportunities to view animals and birds in their environment. Reptiles of many varieties abound. Picnic areas with barbeques are available. Again, visitors can make their own way to Litchfield in less than two hours by car or avail of one of the many tours such as those run by Nature Territory Tours (08 8981 6473) or Goanna Eco Tours (08 8927 2781).

Darwin Botanical Gardens

Just to the north of the city centre, the gardens provide a wonderful escape from the city bustle. The 42 hectares include rainforest, mangroves and beautiful flower gardens with rose and orchids. There are 400 different types of palm. There are three self-guide walks through different environments. Entrance is free. Open from 07.30-17.00 Monday to Friday and 08.30-17.00 on Saturday and Sunday.

Mindil Beach Markets

On Gilruth Ave, the markets are a mixture of art, craft and food stalls with free entertainment thrown in as well. Held every Thursday evening and Sunday afternoon from April to November. Darwin's most popular market venue and offers local produce along with food from all over Asia. Open Thursdays from 17.00-22.00 and Sundays from 16.00-22.00.

Darwin Harbour Cruise

A number of companies operate cruises around the harbour to view sights such as the Stokes Hill Wharf, Doctors Gully, the Navy Bas, Cullen Bay, East Point and, of course, the city skyline. Cruise can be as short as an hour or take a leisurely half-day or evening. The Spirit of Darwin (08 8981 3711) and Australian Harbour Cruise (08 8941 4000) both leave from Cullen Bay Marina.

Post Office

Darwin General Post Office
48 Cavenagh St.
13 13 18
Open 08.30-17.00 Monday-Saturday

Tourist Information

Tourism Top End Visitor Information Centre, Beagle House
Corner of Knuckley and Mitchell Streets
Tel: 08 8936 2499

Fax: 08 8981 0653
info@tourismtopend.com.au

Hospital

Royal Darwin Hospital
Rocklands Drive, Tiwi
Tel: 08 8922 8888
Located on the northern side As you approach the suburb of Casuarina blue signs indicate the direction to the hospital. The Darwin Private Hospital (08 8920 6011) is on the same site.

where to eat & drink

Tim's Surf and Turf
Corner of Smith Street and Packard Place
One of Darwin's best bargains. Small restaurant serving local seafood, crocodile and huge steaks.

Christo's
28 Mitchell St.
Tel: 08 8941 1444
Excellent Greek restaurant specialising in seafood. Fantastic.

Pee Wee's Beachfront Café
Alec Fong Lim Drive
East Point Reserve
Fannie Bay
Tel: 08 8981 6868
Great seafood restaurant with fine views of the harbour. Award winning restaurant not to be missed. 10 minutes from city centre.

The Magic Wok
Darwin GPO Centre
48 Cavenagh St.
Tel: 08 8981 3332
Lovely, small restaurant serving local food including crocodile, kangaroo, buffalo and seafood. Highly recommended.

Hog's Breath Café
85 Mitchell St.
Tel: 08 8941 3333
Part of the famous Australian chain serving prime rib, chicken, burgers, tex mex. Good honest food in great atmosphere with lively bar.

Crustaceans on the Wharf
Stokes Hill Wharf
Tel: 08 8981 8658
Excellent seafood restaurant with fabulous ocean and city views.

Hanuman
28 Mitchell St.
Tel: 08 8941 3500
One of Darwin's finest restaurants serving Thai dishes based on local seafood. Excellent.

Some of the top hotels have some fine restaurants. The MGM Grand has E'voo (á la carte), Sunset (buffets) and Dragon Court (Asian) Restaurants and the Saville Park suites has the excellent Colonnade Café Restaurant.

Shenannigans Irish Pub
69 Mitchell St.
Tel: 08 8981 2100
Irish pub in the heart of Darwin's nightlife. Busy with great atmosphere, live music, friendly staff and good food.

Victoria Hotel
Smith Street Mall
Tel: 08 8981 4011
The most famous pub in Darwin. Always busy with loud music and good food.

Top End Hotel
Corner of Mitchell and Day Streets
Tel: 08 8981 6511
Very popular venue with live music at the weekends. Great atmosphere.

Rorkes' Drift Bar/Café
46 Mitchell St.
Tel: 08 8941 7171
One of the liveliest pubs in Darwin with excellent food and a wonderful beer garden.

Climate

	ave temp	rain cm			
January	28	406	July	25	0
February	28	349	August	27	11
March	28	311	September	28	19
April	29	21	October	28	79
May	28	0	November	28	154
June	26	0	December	29	230

MGM Grand Darwin Hotel Casino

Gilruth Ave
Tel: 08 8943 8888
Fax: 08 8943 8999
reservations@mgmgrand.com.au
www.mgmgrand.com.au
One of Darwin's best hotels. Just outside the city. All rooms have private balconies. Business centre, casino, 3 restaurants, bars, gym, swimming pool and tennis courts.

Crowne Plaza Darwin

32 Mitchell St.
Tel: 08 8982 0000
Fax: 08 8981 1765
crowneplazadarwin@6c.com
City centre, five star hotel with deluxe rooms, some with ocean views. Restaurant, bar, swimming pool, gym. Excellent accommodation.

Novotel

100 The Esplanade
Tel: 08 8941 0755
Fax: 08 8981 9025
www.noveteldarwin.com
Excellent hotel with 138 en suite rooms with cable TV, internet services overlooking Bicentennial Park and the harbour. Friendly atmosphere with bar in atrium. Terraced restaurant, swimming pool and spa.

Saville Park Suites

88 The Esplanade
Tel: 08 8943 4333
Fax: 08 8943 4388
Freecall 1300 881 686
Darwin.info@shg.com.au
204 air-conditioned rooms, one, 2 and 3 bedroom apartments. Cable TV, minibar, fully licensed restaurant and bar, swimming pool, spa and beauty salon.

Darwin Central Hotel

21 Knuckey St.
Tel: 08 8944 9000
Fax: 08 8944 9100
resereavations@darwincentral.com.au
www.darwincentral.com.au
Locally owned and managed friendly hotel with fine rooms, restaurant and cocktail bar. Swimming pool.

Top End Hotel

Corner Mitchell and Daly Streets
Tel: 08 8981 6511
Freecall 1800 626 151
Reasonably priced hotel in quiet grounds. Air-conditioned rooms with TV, in-house movies. Outdoor Bar and Grill, Sportsman Bar, restaurant. Salt water swimming pool in beautiful surrounds.

Steeles at Larrakeyah

4 Zealandia Crescent
Larrakeyah
Tel: 08 8941 3636
rustynt@octa4.net.au
www.steeles-at-larrakeyah.com.au
Fabulous guesthouse within a ten-minute walk of the centre. All rooms air-conditioned, saltwater pool. Mid-range price-wise but one of the best places to stay in Darwin.

Plantation House

102 East Point Road
Tel: 08 8981 8850
Fax: 08 8981 1650
www.plantationhouse.com.au
plantationhousedarwin@hotmail.com
Amazing guesthouse outside the city. Wonderful en suite rooms, brilliant breakfasts, swimming pool, tennis court and fine gardens. A haven by the sea.

Chillis Backpackers'

69a Mitchell St.
Tel: 08 8941 9722
Fax: 08 8941 9835
info@chillis.com.au
www.chillis.com.au
One of the best backpackers, offering twins, doubles and 4, 6 and 8 bed dormitories. Air-conditioning. Spa, sundeck and TV room. Internet.

Globetrotters Lodge

97 Mitchell St.
Tel: 08 8981 5385
Fax: 08 8981 9096
globe@octa4.net.au
www.globetrotters.com.au
Backpackers' with air-conditioned dormitories, twins, and doubles. Swimming pool, TV, pool tables, kitchen.

Darwin International YHA

69 Mitchell St.
Tel: 08 8981 3995
Fax: 08 8981 6674
darwinyha@yhant.org.au
www.yha.com.au
Without doubt one of the finest YHA anywhere! Superb accommodation in clean rooms. Beautiful swimming pool, sundeck, large kitchen, pool table, friendly and helpful staff. One of the best bargains in Darwin.

Darwin International Airport is 13km to the north of the city. A taxi takes around 20 minutes and should cost no more than $22. An airport/city shuttle bus (1800 358 945) runs every half hour, 24 hours a day and costs $9.50. It is a modern airport with an ATM machine, a bureau de change, an excellent tourist information office and a small café is the arrivals hall. In the international departures there are duty free shops with gifts, jewellery, clothing and souvenirs. Car hire is available from Avis (08 89450662), Budget (132727 or 08 8941 0300) Hertz (08 8945 0999) or Thrifty (08 8981 8555).

Airlines

Qantas	131313
Virgin Blue	13 6789
Royal Brunei	13 12 23

Buses

Darwin has an extensive local bus service which runs throughout the city and up to the northern suburbs. McCaffertys runs the interstate buses from 67 – 69 Mitchell St, Tel 08 8941 0911.

If your intention is to watch the winter tests in Darwin and Cairns it should be noted that as well as flying there is a four day overland trip between the two cities organised by Desert Venturer (1800 079 119 – www.desertventurer.com.au) which travels through Renner Springs, Mount Isa and Townsville for approximately $400.

Taxis

Darwin Radio Taxi 131 008
City Radio Taxis 8981 3777

Car Hire

Avis
BP Service Station
89 Smith St.
Tel: 08 8981 9922
Fax: 08 8981 3155
Countrywide 13 63 33
reservations@avis.com.au

Budget
Corner Daly and Doctors Gully Road
Tel: 08 8981 9800
Fax: 08 8981 0750
Countrywide 13 27 27
www.budget.com.au

Hertz
Corner Smith and Davy St.
Tel: 08 8941 0944
Fax: 08 8941 0895
Countrywide 13 30 39

Thrifty
64 Stuart Highway
Stuart Park
Tel: 08 892 4000
Fax: 08 8981 5247
Countrywide 13 61 39

Fannie Bay Gaol Museum

Corner East Point Road and Ross Smith Ave.
A museum of incarceration giving an insight into the horrors of being a prisoner in the past. Built in 1883 the gaol was notoriously tough even by Australian standards.

The Museum and Art Gallery of the Northern Territory

Conacher St.
Fannie Bay
Tel: 08 8999 8201

Traces the history and culture of the Territory. Wonderful Aboriginal art and craft collections. Open Monday to Friday 09.00-17.00 Saturday-Sunday 10.00-17.00. No entrance fee.

Win/Loss Record

Country	Played	Won	Drawn	Lost
Aus	1	1	-	-
Bangla	1	-	-	1

Highest Individual Aggregates

Player	Ct	Mat	Inn	NO	Runs	Ave.
Darren Lehmann (Aus)	1	1	0	110	110.00	110
Steve Waugh (Aus)	1	1	1	100	-	100*
Justin Langer (Aus)	1	1	0	71	71.00	71
Habibul Bashar (Bangla)	1	2	0	70	35.00	54
Adam Gilchrist (Aus)	1	1	0	43	43.00	43

Top Wicket Takers

Player	Ct	Mat	Bll	Md	Runs	Wkt	Ave	BB
Stuart MacGill (Aus)	1	157	5	86	7	12.29	5/65	22.43
Glenn McGrath (Aus)	1	138	6	45	4	11.25	3/20	34.50
Jason Gillespie (Aus)	1	144	4	75	4	18.75	2/27	36.00
Brett Lee (Aus)	1	122	7	57	4	14.25	3/23	30.50
Mashrafe Mortaza (Bangla)	1	138	7	74	3	24.67	3/74	46.00

Highest Individual Scores

110	Darren Lehmann (Aus) 2003
100*	Steve Waugh (Aus) 2003
71	Justin Langer (Aus) 2003
54	Habibul Bashar (Bangla) 2003
43	Adam Gilchrist (Aus) 2003

Best Individual Bowling Performances

13.1-1-65-5	Stuart MacGill (Aus) 2003
13-6-20-3	Glenn McGrath (Aus) 2003
8.2-2-23-3	Brett Lee (Aus) 2003
23-7-74-3	Mashrafe Mortaza (Bangla) 2003
13-4-21-2	Stuart MacGill (Aus) 2003

Highest Partnerships

Wkt	Runs	Batsmen	Match
1st	13	Justin Langer & Martyn Hayden (Aus)	2003-2004 v Bangla
2nd	81	Hannan Sarkar & Habibul Bashar (Bangla)	2003-2004 v Aus
3rd	141	Justin Langer & Darren Lehmann (Aus)	2003-2004 v Bangla
4th	59	Darren Lehmann & Steve Waugh (Aus)	2003-2004 v Bangla
5th	1	Alok Kapali & Mohammed Ashraful (Bangla)	2003-2004 v Aus
		Steve Waugh & Martin Love (Aus)	2003-2004 v Bangla
6th	69	Steve Waugh & Adam Gilchrist (Aus)	2003-2004 v Bangla
7th	64	Steve Waugh & Brett Lee (Aus)	2003-2004 v Bangla
8th	30*	Steve Waugh & Jason Gillespie (Aus)	2003-2004 v Bangla
9th	19	Mushrafe Bin Mortaza & Al Sahariar Rokon (Bangla)	2003-2004 v Aus
10th	7	Al Sahariar Rokon & Manjural Islam (Bangla)	2003-2004 v Aus

Results at the Marrara Cricket Ground

Date	Countries	Result
18/07/2003	v Bangladesh	won by an Innings and 132 runs

hobart

bellerive oval

When the Bellerive Oval was awarded a Test match on 16 December 1989 it became Australia's seventh Test ground and the only one in Tasmania. It is situated near the Derwent River to the south of the city of Hobart and has a wonderful backdrop of the surrounding hills. Home to the Clarence Cricket Club since the turn of the century, the ground has undergone an £8million refurbishment, completed in January 2003. The first Test played here was against Sri Lanka with the home side winning by 173 runs. Having scored a modest first innings total of 224, Rumesh Ratnayake taking 6/66, Australia restricted Sri Lanka to 216 before amassing 513/5 dec. in their second innings, Mark Taylor (108), Dean Jones (118) and Steve Waugh (134) all scoring centuries. Set 506 to win, Sri Lanka scored 348 with Merv Hughes taking 5/88. In Bellerive's short history the 1999 Test against Pakistan certainly rates as the most exciting. Pakistan batted first, scoring 222 with Mohammed Wasim contributing 91. Australia replied with 246, Michael Slater scoring 97 and Saqluin Mushtaq taking 6/46. Inzaman-ul-Haq with 118 led Pakistan to 392 in their second innings. Shane Warne took 5/110. In reply Australia slumped to126/5 before Adam Gilchrist joined Justin Langer at the wicket. A partnership of 238 brought Australia to within four runs of victory, Gilchrist scoring 149no and Langer 127. Australia won by four wickets with a total of 369/6.

The highest team score is 558/8 by Australia against New Zealand in a rain-affected draw in 2001. The lowest score is 161 by New Zealand in 1993. Shane Warne's 6/31 and match figures of 9/67 against New Zealand is the best bowling performance at the Oval. Warne has taken five wickets in an innings three times.

The refurbishment has totally transformed the Oval. The new Members' pavilion with additional seating and food and beverage facilities and the new Southern Stand with a capacity of 5,500 and its own Media Centre were the two main changes. In addition, modern entrance gates with more turnstiles were fitted, new changing rooms were added, a video replay screen was installed and a perimeter fence around the boundary was erected. A fine cricket museum was opened in the Members' pavilion. This museum, which has a very unusual and modern design, traces the history of cricket in Tasmania, Australia and the world.

The Players' and Members' pavilion spans the northern end of the ground and the upgraded facilities provide an excellent position for spectators. The view from the pavilion is still spectacular with the hills behind the scoreboard, but the new Southern Stand has obscured part of the river view. To the left of the pavilion is the small North East Stand. Sweeping around the eastern side of the ground is the very popular Hill. The scoreboard and video replay screen are located at the back of the Hill. The new Southern Stand towering above the pitch provides an ideal vantage point. There are bars and food outlets underneath the Stands and around the ground. They are well organised and queuing is not excessive.

The Members' Pavilion and the Southern Stand have facilities and viewing areas for wheelchair users. Tickets can be purchased from Ticketmaster7 Tel : 13 61 00 Overseas Tel : +61 3 9256 8800 or www.ticketmaster7.com. Ticket prices range from A$26 – A$36 per day. Gates open two hours before play.

Bellerive Oval is on the opposite side of the river to Hobart, which provides an opportunity for match-goers to catch the ferry from the city. Bellerive Wharf is a five minute walk from the ground. It is certainly one of the most attractive ways of travelling to a Test cricket ground. Metrobus Services also run between the city and the ground. The closest parking is in South Street Car Park off Alexandra Street. A Shuttle service runs from the car park to the ground. A taxi ride from the city to the Oval costs approximately A$22.

Hobart is the capital of Tasmania, Australia's smallest state and named after Robert Hobart, 4th Earl of Buckinghamshire and British Colonial Secretary from 1801-1804. Australia's second oldest city, it has a population of 195,000. The city is in the south east of the island at the base of Mount Wellington which towers over it. The suburbs of Hobart line the Derwent River and the centre is based around the impressive Constitution and Victoria Docks.

Dutch Explorer Abel Janszoon Tasman sighted the western coast of the island in 1642 and named it Van Diemans Land. In 1803 the British arrived to survey the area. The natural harbour was identified as an important strategic point for the British Navy. The first settlement was set up in Risdon Cove, the scene of infamous battles with the indigenous people, but was moved to Sullivan's Cove where Hobart now is. A year later, in February 1804, the first convict ship arrived with 226 men, 15 women and 21 children on board. Hobart became a major penal location for the 'Convict System' and in 1840, when transportation to the mainland ceased, the city became the headquarters of the system.

Hobart has preserved much of its colonial architecture. The Tasmanian Museum and Art Gallery, the Maritime Museum, the Theatre Royal and the Commissiariat Bond Store are all housed in buildings erected between 1808 and 1837. Wherever you look there are mid-19th century terraced houses. Battery Point has some fine examples of buildings of the convict era.

Housed in an 1830's warehouse in the heart of the city, Salamanca Market is a bustling area with galleries, studios, shops, restaurants and cafés. Mount Wellington to the west of the city is a popular destination for tourists with its great views of the city and surrounds. Cruises along the Derwent river are also popular.

Royal Tasmanian Botanical Gardens

More than 5,000 native and exotic plant species are in this lovely setting. Guided walks can be arranged and include visits to the Sub-Antarctic Plant House and the Discovery Centre. St. David's Gardens and the Waterworks Reserve Gardens are also worth visiting.

Port Arthur

One of Australia's most historic sites, with a range of buildings and ruins of those built by convicts more than 150 years ago when the site was a penal colony. Port Arthur was infamous for its harsh treatment of convicts and was one of the last to end the convict system. Historic Ghost tours, beautifully landscaped gardens and cruises are among the attractions. Visitor Information 03 6251 2371

Cadbury Chocolate Factory

Book this tour as limited numbers are allowed. Upon completion of the tour it is possible to buy chocolate at very reasonable prices. Tour 03 6249 0333.

Female Factory Historic Site

Located quite near the Cascade Brewery and the women's prison from 1828 until 1877. Guide Tours are available of what is regarded as Australia's most significant historical site for women. Tour 03 6223 1559

Cascade Brewery Tours

Cascade has been brewed in Hobart since 1824. The brewery has wonderful gardens and a museum. Of course one of the highlights is tasting the many Cascade products. The two-hour tour is strenuous with some climbing involved. Shoes must be worn.

Theatre Royal

29 Campbell St.
Tel: 03 6233 2299
Fax 03 6233 2129

Federation Concert Hall

Hotel Grand Chancellor
1 Davey St.
Tel: 03 6235 4535

The State Library

91 Murray St. (Corner of Bathurst St)
Tel: 03 6233 7484
The state's history and fine arts are displayed in the Heritage Collection.

Maritime Museum of Tasmania

Corner Argyle & Davey Streets
Tel: 03 6234 1427
Museum depicting Tasmania's shipping history including paintings, photographs and whaling implements.

Tasmanian Museum and Art Gallery

40 MacQuarie St.
Tel: 03 6211 4177
Gallery displaying Australian, British and European art and the work of local artists.

Hobart International Airport is 15km outside the city of Hobart. A taxi to the city costs approximately A$28 and takes 20 minutes. An Airporter Shuttle leaves from outside the terminal every 30 minutes at a cost of A$9. Hobart is a small airport. There is no manned information desk in the terminal however there are stands with leaflets for accommodation, tours etc. There is a small information office in the car park. There is an ATM machine in the terminal, also a café and newsagent. Car rental is available from Avis (03 6248 5424), budget (03 6248 5333), Hertz (03 6237 1155) and Thrifty (03 6248 5678).

Airlines
Qantas   13 13 13
Virgin Blue   13 67 89

Buses
Metro Hotline (City Area) 13 22 01
Tassie Link (Outlying Areas) 1300 300 520

Taxis
City Cabs 13 10 08
Taxi Combined 13 22 27

Car Hire
Avis
125 Bathurst St.
Tel: 03 6234 4222
Fax: 03 6234 4190

Budget
96 Harrington St.
Tel: 03 6234 5222
Fax: 03 6231 0252

Hertz
122 Harrington St.
Tel: 03 6237 1111
Fax: 03 6234 1935

Thrifty
11-17 Argyle St.
Tel: 03 6234 1341
Fax: 03 6231 2475

Post Office
General Post Office
Bus Mall

Tourist Information
Tasmanian Travel And Information Centre
Corner Davey And Elizabeth Streets
Tel: 03 6230 8233

Hospital
Royal Hobart Hospital
Corner Liverpool And Campbell St.
Tel: 03 6222 8308

Emergency Dentist 03 6248 1546

Emergency Doctor 03 6222 8423

Climate

	ave temp	rain cm
January	16	48
February	17	40
March	16	47
April	13	52
May	11	49
June	9	55
July	9	55
August	9	54
September	11	53
October	12	65
November	14	54
December	15	51

Hog's Breath Café

2 MacQuarie St.
Tel: 03 6236 9955
Part of a well-known Australian chain. Excellent value and good fun. Lively bar.

Ball and Chain Grill

87 Salamanca Place
Tel: 03 6223 2655
Charcoal grill steak house. Beef, game, poultry and seafood all on the menu. Good value.

Noobar

37A Elizabeth St.
Tel: 03 6234 6669
Noodles. Excellent food, reasonably priced. Trendy setting in the centre.

Drunken Admiral

17 Hunter St.
Tel: 03 6234 1903
Seafood on the waterfront. Old warehouse with a wonderful atmosphere. Very busy.

Fish Frenzy

Elizabeth St. Pier
Tel: 03 6231 2134
Something quick, relaxed and fresh. Fish and chips on the pier. Could do a lot worse.

Mures

Victoria Dock
Tel: 03 6231 2121
Sit on the upper deck and enjoy seafood of the highest standard, fresh from the ocean. Situated on Hobart's fishing docks.

Athena on the Pier

Elizabeth St. Pier
Tel: 03 6224 2200
Greek restaurant with a contemporary twist. Good dining. Reservations advised.

Mr Wooby's

Wooby's Lane
Salamanca Place
Tel: 03 6234 3466
Local restaurant serving local produce and seafood. Excellent food and service.

Point Revolving Restaurant

Wrest Point
410 Sandy Bay Road
Tel: 03 6221 1701

Tasmania's only revolving restaurant. Modern cuisine with 360-degree views of Hobart. Slightly outside city centre.

The Elbow Room

9-11 Murray St.
Tel: 03 6224 4254
A basement restaurant serving local seafood and game. An absolute gem.

Custom House Hotel

1 Murray St.
Tel: 03 6234 6645
1846 waterfront hotel, fine seafood restaurant. Quite a rowdy bar with live entertainment

Bridie O'Reilly's

124 Davey St.
Tel: 03 6224 9494
Irish pub, good food. Good atmosphere with 20 beers on tap.

Republic Bar and Café

299 Elizabeth St.
Tel: 03 6234 6954
Live Blues and Jazz five nights a week. Excellent food in relaxed surroundings.

Irish Murphys

21 Salamnca Place
Tel: 03 6223 1119
Lively Irish pub with a great atmosphere. Great food with live entertainment. Outside seating.

Wrest Point Casino

410 Sandy Bay
Sandy Bay
Tel: 03 6225 0112
Probably one of the best night spots in Hobart. Restaurant, bars and casino.

New Sydney Hotel

87 Bathurst St.
Tel: 03 6234 4516
Lively Irish pub with entertainment every night and great food.

There are many other pubs and clubs in Hobart including the Salmanca Inn and the Shamrock. In Battery Point the Prince of Wales Hotel and the Shipwright Arms are well worth a visit.

Hotel Grand Chancellor

1 Davey St.
Tel: 03 6235 4535
Fax: 03 6223 8175
eservations@hgchobart.com.au
ww.grandhotelsinternational.com
ocated on the waterfront with a
eautiful view of the Derwent river
nd Mount Wellington, this is one of
Hobart's top hotels. 234 high quality
ooms. Restaurant, bar, lobby shops,
ym and swimming pool.

akford on the Pier

lizabeth St. Pier
el: 03 6220 6600
ax: 03 6224 1277
ww.the-ascott.com
ll-suite hotel on Hobart Harbour. Fine
r-conditioned rooms with cable TV.
afé, restaurant, bar.

Wrest Point Hotel and Casino

10 Sandy Bay
andy Bay
el: 03 6225 0112
ax: 03 6225 3909
Hobart's casino. Little way out of
own. Modern hotel with all the com-
orts. Gym, pool, spa, sauna, tennis.
estaurants and bars.

he Old Woolstore Hotel

Macquarie St.
el: 03 6235 5355
ax: 03 6234 9954
ws@southcom.com.au
entrally located, reasonably priced
ith excellent rooms with kitchen and
eparate living/dining area, video and
ereo. All rooms en suite.

uest Waterfront

Brooke St.
el: 03 6224 8630
ax: 03 6224 8633
uestwaterfront@questapartments.com.au
ocated in Sullivan's Cove in the centre
f Hobart. Offers a range of studio and
ne-bedroom apartments. All with
itchenettes.

adleys Hotel

4 Murray St.
el: 03 6223 4355
ax: 03 6224 0303
es.hadleys@dohertyhotels.com.au
1 heritage guestrooms in this 1834
hotel. Centre of town, all rooms have
mini-bar, TV and coffee making.

Alexandra On Battery

3 Sonning Crescent
Sandy Bay
Tel: 03 6225 2574
Fax: 03 6225 3522
bdienaar@trump.net.au
Comfortable B&B, 10 minutes drive to
the city. Sweeping views of the city and
the Derwent River.

Battery Point Guest House

7 McGregor St.
Battery Point
Tel: 03 6224 2111
Fax: 03 6224 3648
maritime1@iprimus.com.au
Closest B&B to the city centre. All
rooms have en suite facilities with TV
and tea and coffee making.

Clydesdale

292 Sandy Bay Road
Sandy Bay
Tel: 03 6223 7289
Fax: 03 6223 2465
Lovely guesthouse with a warm, homely
atmosphere. All rooms have television,
fridges tea and coffee facilities. 5 minute
walk from casino.

Barton Cottage

72 Hampden Road
Battery Point
Tel: 03 6224 1606
Fax: 03 6224 1282
5 minutes walking distance from the
centre. 6 en suite rooms with TV
and tea and coffee making facilities.
Generous, full cooked breakfast.

New Sydney Hotel

87 Bathurst St.
Tel: 03 6234 4516
Excellent backpackers' at incredibly
cheap rates. Great pub.

Central City Backpackers'

138 Collins St.
Tel: 03 6224 2404
Fax: 03 6224 2316
centralbackpackers@mbox.com.au
www.centralbackpackers.com.au
Kitchen, bar and pool table. Great
atmosphere.

Narrara Backpackers'

88 Goulburn St.
Tel: 03 6231 3191
nigelruddock@hotmail.com
Kitchen, off-street parking, friendly
atmosphere.

where to stay

Win/Loss Record

Country	Played	Won	Drawn	Lost	Tie
Australia	6	4	2	-	-
New Zealand	3	-	2	1	-
Sri Lanka	1	-	-	1	-
Pakistan	2	-	-	2	-

Highest Individual Aggregates (Australia unless stated)

Player	Mat	Inn	NO	Runs	Ave	HS	50	100
Mark Taylor	4	7	1	405	67.50	123	1	2
Michael Slater	3	5	0	365	73.00	168	2	1
Justin Langer	2	3	0	309	103.00	127	1	2
Mark Waugh	5	8	0	309	38.63	111	2	1
Steve Waugh	6	10	3	272	38.86	134*	0	1
Greg Blewett	3	6	0	230	38.33	99	2	0
Inzamam-ul-Haq (Pak)	2	4	0	197	49.25	118	0	1
Adam Gilchrist	2	3	1	194	97.00	149*	0	1
David Boon	3	5	0	181	36.20	106	0	1
Allan Border	2	3	0	169	56.33	85	2	0

Top Wicket Takers (Australia unless stated)

Player	Mat	Bll	Md	Runs	Wkt	Ave	BB	S/R
Shane Warne	5	1074	44	461	24	19.21	6/31	44.75
Glenn McGrath	3	693	39	274	13	21.08	5/61	53.31
Paul Reiffel	3	449	21	195	11	17.73	4/38	40.82
Mushtaq Ahmed (Pak)	1	408	13	198	9	22.00	5/115	45.33
Saqlain Mushtaq (Pak)	1	413	17	176	8	22.00	6/46	51.63
Wasim Akram (Pak)	2	496	19	233	8	29.13	3/42	62.00
RJ Ratnayake (SL)	1	328	7	189	8	23.63	6/66	41.00
Merv Hughes	1	320	14	156	8	19.50	5/88	40.00
Daniel Vettori (NZ)	2	372	7	231	7	33.00	5/138	53.14
Tim May	1	339	23	110	7	15.71	5/65	48.43

Highest Individual Scores (Australia unless stated)

168	Michael Slater	v New Zealand	1993-94
157*	Ricky Ponting	v New Zealand	2001-02
149*	Adam Gilchrist	v Pakistan	1999-00
134*	Steve Waugh	v Sri Lanka	1989-90
133	Matt Horne (NZ)		1997-98
127	Justin Langer	v Pakistan	1999-00
123	Mark Taylor	v Pakistan	1995-96
123	Justin Langer	v New Zealand	2001-02
118*	Dean Jones	v Sri Lanka	1989-90
118	Inzamam-ul-haq (Pak)		1999-00

Best Individual Bowling Performances (Australia unless stated)

19.5-9-31-6	Shane Warne	v NZ 1993-94
24-8-46-6	Saqlain Mushtaq (Pak)	1999-00
19.4-2-66-6	Rumesh Ratnayake (SL)	1989-90
24.3-7-61-5	Glenn McGrath	v Pakistan 1995-96
31.3-10-65-5	Tim May	v NZ 1993-94
31.4-8-88-5	Merv Hughes	v Sri Lanka 1989-90
28-6-88-5	Shane Warne	v NZ 1997-98
45.5-11-110-5	Shane Warne	v Pakistan 1999-00
30-5-115-5	Mushtaq Ahmed (Pak)	1995-96
36-5-138-5	Daniel Vettori (NZ)	2001-02

Highest Partnerships

1st	223	Justin Langer & Matthew Hayden (Aus)	2001-2002 v NZ
2nd	235	Michael Slater & David Boon (Aus)	1993-1994 v NZ
3rd	70	Amir Sohail & Inzamam-Ul-Haq (Pakistan)	1995-1996
4th	163	Mark Taylor & Allan Border (Aus)	1989-1990 v Sri Lanka
5th	97	S P Fleming & C D McMillan (New Zealand)	2001-2002
6th	260*	Dean Jones & Steve Waugh (Aus)	1989-1990 v Sri Lanka
7th	145	Ricky Ponting & Shane Warne (Aus)	2001-2002 v NZ
8th	77	Ricky Ponting & Brett Lee (Aus)	2001-2002 v NZ
9th	47	Mark Waugh & Michael Kasprowicz (Aus)	1997-1998 v NZ
10th	34	Wasim Akram & Shoaib Akhtar (Pakistan)	1999-2000

Results at Bellerive Oval

Date	countries	result
16/12/1989	v Sri Lanka	won by 173 runs
26/11/1993	v New Zealand	won by an innings and 222 runs
17/11/1995	v Pakistan	won by 155 runs
27/11/1997	v New Zealand	match drawn
18/11/1999	v Pakistan	won by 4 wickets
22/11/2001	v New Zealand	match drawn

melbourne

mcg

The Melbourne Cricket Ground has the distinction of hosting the first ever Test match in 1877. In fact it staged the first three Test matches. The Melbourne Cricket Club moved to the ground in 1853 and entertained interstate and English touring sides until 15 March 1877 when the fourth English touring side led by James Lillywhite contested the first Test match against Australia. Australia batted first, scoring 245 with Charles Bannerman completing the first ever Test century with 165 before retiring hurt with a split thumb. England replied with 196, Henry Jupp scoring 63 while William Midwinter took 5/78. Australia were dismissed for 104 in their second innings, Alfred Shaw taking 5/33 which left England 154 to win. However Thomas Kendall took 7/55 to restrict England to 108 and Australia won the inaugural Test by 45 runs.

There have been 95 tests played at the MCG but none have been tighter than the matches of 1908 and 1951. In 1908, chasing 282, Syd Barnes and Arthur Fielder had a tenth wicket partnership of 39 to bring England home by one wicket. In 1951 Australia, with a target of 260, also relied on a tenth wicket partnership, this time of 38 between Doug Ring and Bill Jones to defeat the West Indies by one wicket.

In 1937 a record aggregate crowd of 350,534 saw the Australians, two down in the five match series, beat England by 365 runs. Jack Fingleton (136) and Don Bradman (270) shared a sixth wicket partnership of 346, a record that still stands. Australia went on to win the series 3-2. The largest daily Test attendance at MCG was 90,800 in 1961 when Australia defeated the West Indies.

The Centenary Test in 1977 was one of the MCG's great occasions. Australia scored a disappointing 138 before Dennis Lillie ripped through the English side with 6/26 dismissing them for 95. In Australia's second innings Rod Marsh hit 110 to lead Australia to 419/9 declared. Set a formidable total of 463 to win, England's Derek Randall hit a wonderful 174. But it was not enough and England were dismissed for 417 leaving victory to Australia by 45 runs, the same result as the inaugural Test match. Lillie ended with match figures of 11/165.

The highest individual score at the MCG is 307 by Bob Cowper for Australia against England in 1965. However this was Bradman's ground. His aggregate of 1,671 at an average of 128.54 included nine centuries and a highest score of 270. The highest team total is 604 by Australia versus England in 1937 and the lowest 36 by South Africa in 1932 – the fifth lowest Test score of all time. The highest run chase is 332/7 by England in 1928.

The best match bowling performance came in 1904 when Wilfred Rhodes returned figures of 15/124 for England in their 185 run victory. Lillie took five wickets in an innings seven times with a best of 7/83 against the West Indies in 1981. Five of the 31 Test hat-tricks have happened at the MCG, Fredrick Spofforth in 1879, the first in Test cricket, Billy Bates for England in 1883, Hugh Trumble twice in 1902 and 1904 for Australia against England and, more than 90 years later, Shane Warne against England in 1994.

The MCG is in the middle of a huge redevelopment plan to replace the Ponsford Stand, the Members' Pavilion and The Olympic Stand with a new ultra modern stand. Work should be completed by the end of 2005. At present the members sit in a pavilion steeped in history. It is a remarkable building with some of the finest cricket memorabilia. However, it was decided time had caught up with it. To the left of the Members' Pavilion is the Olympic Stand, huge and uncovered. The Great Southern Stand sweeps around the boundary covering almost half the ground. It is a magnificent edifice with four levels and offers a fantastic view. The seats at the top of the fourth tier are very high and a long way from the pitch. The General Admission areas are on the ground floor of this stand. The next area is where the Ponsford stand used to be. It was many people's favourite but, unfortunately, its time had come.

Facilities and access for the disabled are good. Any enquires should be directed to Customer Services on 1300 136 122. There are wheelchair bays in the Great Southern Stand in sections N and P with ramp access at Gate 7. Wheelchair access for the Olympic Stand is at Gate 3. Tickets can be purchased for Ticketmaster7 Tel : +61 1300 13 61 22 Fax : 03 9256 8840 or www.ticketmaster7.com Ticket prices ranges from A$34 – A$68 per day. A five day general pass costs A$90. Gates open at 09.00.

The MCG is a very pleasant 15-minute walk from the centre of Melbourne. Trains run to Jolimont and Richmond stations which are both very near the ground. Trams Nos. 48 and 75 from Flinders Street in the city run along Wellington Parade which is beside the ground. Parking is available inYarra Park, but is very limited on the streets around the ground.

Behind the Members' Pavilion is the Australian Gallery of Sport and Olympic Museum which documents the history of Australian sport. It also holds extensive collections of artefacts and photographs from the 1956 Olympics. Tours of the MCG include the Gallery of Sport, the Long Room, the MCG Cricket Museum and Library, the Cricket Hall of Fame and the Australia Rules Exhibition.

arrival

Tullamarine International Airport is 20km north of Melbourne. A taxi rank is directly outside the Arrivals Hall, A taxi from the airport to the city takes 25 minutes and costs A$35. A 24-hour bus service, the Skybus, runs every 30 minutes to Spencer Street in the city at a cost of A$14 one way. Tel:03 93353066. A Travellers' Information Desk is located on the ground floor of International Arrivals. There are ATM machines and Bureaux de Change throughout the international and domestic terminals. There is a wide range of shops including duty free shopping, and restaurants in each terminal. Car hire is available from Avis (03 9338 1800), Budget (03 9241 6336), Hertz (03 9338 4044) and Thrifty (1300 367227).

the city

Melbourne is the capital of Victoria, Australia's smallest mainland state. It has a population of 3.2 million and is one of the biggest cities in the world, spreading over 6000 square km. The city was named after the British Prime Minister, Lord Melbourne. It is situated in the southeast corner of Australia on Port Phillip Bay at the mouth of the River Yarra. The city is easy to get around due to the symmetrical pattern of wide leafy treelined streets in a rectangular grid bounded by Latrobe, Spencer, Flinders and Spring Streets.

Aborigines occupied the land for over 40,000 years. In 1834 John Batman and John Fawkner established a settlement called Bearbrass. In 1837 the name was changed to its present day title. Melbourne prospered in the 1850s when gold was discovered in Bendigo and Ballarat. Melbourne was the seat of the Federal Government from 1901-1927. Since the Second World War Melbourne has been transformed by the arrival of immigrants from all over the world. It has become a wonderfully multicultural city.

Melbourne has managed to fit in the old with the new. Skyscrapers are commonplace in the centre of the city, however there is still some wonderful 19th century architecture to appreciate. The Royal Exhibition Buildings, Flinders Street Station, Parliament Buildings and the Old Melbourne Gaol are all reminders of times gone by. The splendid Victoria Market, an institution for Melbournians, is another example. Trams have been running in Melbourne for more than one hundred years and still provide an incredibly efficient service today.

Melbourne is Australia's cultural capital with many museums, galleries and theatres. The Melbourne Museum, the Immigration Museum and the National Gallery of Victoria are all fine examples of the city's culture. The city has many parks including the Royal Botanical Gardens and the Zoological Gardens. In the last decade the city has changed remarkably. The Crown Casino was built in the Southgate Centre, an aquarium opened, shopping centres appeared all over the city, the docklands was redeveloped and the new Colonial Stadium built.

There is a lot more to Melbourne than the centre. The suburbs are cosmopolitan and stylish. Carlton, Fitzroy, Williamstown, Richmond and St. Kilda all have their own identities. Carlton is Melbourne's little Italy, Richmond's Victoria Street has scores of Vietnamese restaurants and St. Kilda is Melbourne's playground. A trip down to St. Kilda to the Sunday markets and the sidewalk cafés on Acland Street will confirm this.

transport

Airlines

Qantas	13 13 13
Virgin Blue	13 67 89
Air New Zealand	13 24 76
Singapore	13 10 11

Buses/Trams

Melbourne has an excellent tram and bus network running throughout the city. Trams run from 05.30 in the morning until midnight. A free tram circles in the city with stops on Spring, Flinders, Spencer, La Trobe and Victoria Streets. Enquires 13 16 38

Skybus run a service between Spencer Street Station and Tullamarine Airport. 03 9335 3066 Interstate Buses and country services are run by Greyhound Pioneer Australia from the corner of Swanston and Franklin Streets.

Trains

Suburban	The Met	13 16 38
Country	Vic Rail	03 9563 4788
Interstate	V/Line	13 61 96

Taxis

Yellow Cabs	13 19 24
Embassy Cabs	13 17 55
Silver Top Cabs	13 10 08

Hilton on the Park

192 Wellington Parade
Tel: 03 9419 2000
Fax: 03 9419 2001
info_Melbourne@hilton.com
www.hilton.com
The perfect place to stay. 2 minutes walk to the ground. Well appointed rooms, restaurants, bars and an outdoor swimming pool.

The Windsor

103-115 Spring St.
Tel: 03 9633 6000
Fax: 03 9633 6001
info@the windsor.com.au
www.the windsor.com.au
Melbourne's finest. Oozes elegance and grandeur. Beautifully decorated rooms with marble bathrooms. Restaurant and cricket memorabilia bar. 5 minutes from MCG.

Grand Hyatt

123 Collins St.
Tel: 03 9657 1234
Fax: 03 9650 3491
In centre. 547 rooms and 48 suites with 2 restaurants, 2 bars, nightclub, tennis court, swimming pool and health club.

Novotel St. Kilda

16 The Esplanade
Tel: 03 9536 6191
Fax: 03 9525 5678
reservations@novotel-stkilda.com.au
Overlooking St. Kilda esplanade and Port Phillip Bay. 209 rooms, restaurant, café, bar, swimming pool.

Batman's Hill Hotel

66-70 Spencer St.
Tel: 03 9614 6344
Fax: 03 9614 1189
res@batmanshill.com.au
www.batmanshill.com.au
Affordable, central hotel with the casino, aquarium and the MCG within walking distance. Compact rooms with shower only. Small, but comfortable with all mod cons.

Annie's Bed and Breakfast

93 Park St, St. Kilda
Tel: 03 8500 3755
Fax: 03 9534 8705
annies_stkilda.bigpond.com
B&B in a renovated Edwardian cottage. 3 rooms with en suite facilities. Splendid breakfast.

Clifton Hill Bed and Breakfast

49 Heidelberg Road, Clifton Hill
Tel: 03 9482 3837
Fax: 03 9481 0722
csnedden@alphalink.com.au
Historical building where one can relax. Spacious rooms.

King

122 Nicholson St, Fitzroy
Tel: 03 9417 1113
Fax: 03 9417 1116
www.kingaccomm.com.au
B&B. 15 minute walk from the MCG. The 1867 listed building has spacious rooms with marble bathrooms. Good breakfast.

Victoria Hall Accommodation

380 Russell St.
Tel: 03 9662 3888
Fax: 03 9639 0101
reception@victoriahall.com.au
www.victoriahall.com.au
In the heart of Melbourne. Singles, twin and triples are available at very affordable prices. Shared bathrooms, kitchen, and laundry. Excellent value.

Hotel Claremont

189 Toorak Road, South Yarra
Tel: 03 9826 8000
Fax: 03 9827 8652
info@hotelclaremont.com
www.hotelclaremont.com
B&B in 1886 building with 77 rooms catering for budget travellers. Situated in the beautiful suburb of South Yarra, within walking distance of the MCG.

The Ritz Backpackers'

169 Fitzroy St, St. Kilda Beach
1800 670 364
Tel: 03 9593 9166
ritz@backpackerscentre.com
www.backpackerscentre.com
Liveliest suburb in town. Single, doubles and dormitories.

All Nations Backpackers' Hotel and Bar

2 Spencer St.
Fax: 03 9620 1022
Tel: 03 9620 1033
www.allnations.co.au
One of the most comfortable hostels in centre. Great bar, with cable TV.

Victoria Market

A city institution. For more than a century the market has supplied the people of Melbourne. It has more than a thousand stalls throughout its vast warehouses. Arts, crafts, fruit, vegetables, meat, fish and much more are on offer to 100,000 shoppers who visit the market each week. Restaurants and cafés serve every type of food imaginable from top cuisine to take away food. The market is surrounded by some very trendy bars and weekends are hectic. A very popular place to visit. www.qvm.co.au

Melbourne Zoo

Certainly worth a visit. Set in the beautifully laid out gardens, it has some 350 species. Highlights include gorillas raising their young, the African/Asian rainforest, the Aussie Bush area with koalas, kangaroos and wombats, the World of Bugs and Butterflies and the underwater seal viewing. On the edge of the city on Elliott Ave in Parkville. Tram No. 55 runs from William Street in the city to the entrance. There are a number of cafés, restaurants, kiosks and souvenir shops. Open 09.00-17.00 daily. Enquiries 03 9285 9300. www.zoo.org.au

The Great Ocean Road

400km of spectacular coastal road south west of Melbourne leading to Adelaide. World renowned for its beautiful scenery. The most famous landmark is The Twelve Apostles, huge sandstone pillars that rise up from the ocean. Other rocks formations such as London Bridge, The Blowhole and The Grotto line the coast. It is believed that some 700 ships have been wrecked along the coast. Bells Beach, just outside Torquay, one of the most famous surfing beaches in the world, and Erskine Falls at Lorne are other highlights. The National Park of Otway, inland from the coast, has some incredible waterfalls and the park in Port Campbell has remarkable limestone cliffs. Visit the resort towns of Lorne and Apollo Bay and the historic towns of Queenscliff and Port Fairy. www.tgor.org

Ballarat

The centre of Victoria's goldrush is the 1850s. Nowadays a beautiful town with grand old buildings. There are many art galleries, theatres and museums to visit and the most glorious parks and gardens to enjoy. Plenty of fine restaurants. Only 110km from Melbourne on the Western Freeway.

Mornington Peninsula

Within easy driving distance of the city, this is the coastal strip on the eastern side of Port Phillip Bay and offers everything from farmland to ocean views. A variety of attractions include 150 wineries, notably the Dromana Estate, Arthur's Seat chairlift, antique markets, art and crafts shops, and, of course, bay beaches for safe swimming, diving and snorkelling. The ocean beaches on the other side of the Peninsula are renowned for their surfing conditions. The restaurants in the area offer wonderful food and wine.

Car Hire

Avis
20-24 Franklin St.
Tel: 03 9663 6366
Fax: 03 9663 2551

Budget
398 Elizabeth St.
Tel: 03 9203 4844
Fax: 03 9639 3930

Hertz
97 Franklin St.
Tel: 03 9663 6244
Fax: 03 9663 4205

Thrifty
390 Elizabeth St.
1300 367 227
Fax: 03 8661 6022

Licciardo's
Mt Eliza Way
Tel: 03 787 0317
Fabulous Italian. Bookings advised.

Chinta Blues
6 Acland St, St. Kilda
Tel: 03 9534 9233
Malaysian style coffee house in one of city's trendiest streets. Simple décor, wonderful food.

Donovan's
40 Jacka Boulevard, St. Kilda
Tel: 03 9534 8221
One of the best restaurants on the beach. Fine Italian food.

Est, Est, Est
440 Clarendon St, South Melbourne
Tel: 03 9682 5688
Modern Australian food in top restaurant. Bookings essential.

Vlado's
61 Bridge Road, Richmond
Tel: 03 9428 5833
A must for meat eaters. Just around the corner from the MCG. One of the remarkable restaurants anywhere. Focused on meat with liver, sausage and beef. No vegetables and very little salad. Do not eat for about two days beforehand because it is the feast of a lifetime. Bookings essential.

Flower Drum
17 Market Lane
Tel: 03 9662 3655
Melbourne's finest Chinese, serving Cantonese cuisine. Bookings essential.

Dog's Bar
54 Acland St.
St. Kilda
Tel: 03 9525 3599
Italian restaurant. Fabulous food with fine wine. Wonderful décor.

Café di Stasio
31 Fitzroy St, St. Kilda
Tel: 03 9525 3999
An institution. Lively, stylish Italian with terrific atmosphere. Booking essential.

Stokehouse
30 Jacka Boulevard, St. Kilda
Tel: 03 9525 5555
Excellent café/restaurant on the beach with fantastic views, great food and professional service. Trendy place.

The Curry Club
394-396 Bridge Road, Richmond
Tel: 03 9428 6f458
Popular restaurant with traditional and contemporary North Indian cuisine. Fun atmosphere. Open for lunch Tuesday-Saturday, Dinner nightly.

LemonGrass
176 Lygon St, Carlton
Tel: 03 9662 2244
Lovely Royal Thai cuisine in elegant surroundings. Excellent value.

Syd's Café and Bar
132 Wellington, East Melbourne
Tel: 03 9419 1951
Casual, stylish café opposite MCG. Perfect for lunch.

The Colonial Tramcar Restaurant
Tel: 03 9696 4000
A different way of dining while touring the centre. Fine cuisine. Departs from Claredon Street nightly.

Post office
General Post Office
Corner of Bourke and Elizabeth St.
Open 09.00-17.00 Monday-Friday
09.00-13.00 Saturday

Tourist Information
Victoria Tourist Information Centre
Melbourne Town Hall
Corner Little Collins and Swanston St.
Tel: 03 9658 9955
Open 09.00-18.00 Monday-Friday
09.00-17.00 Saturday-Sunday

City of Melbourne Information Booth
Bourke St. Mall

Hospital
The Alfred Hospital
Commercial Road
Prahan
Tel: 03 9276 2000

St. Vincent's Hospital
Victory Parade
Fitzroy
Tel: 03 9288 2211

The Esplanade Hotel

11 Upper Esplanade
St. Kilda
Tel: 03 9534 0211
Great bar, a live band and chaos.
Fabulous. Established spot for live
rock, punk and grunge music.

The Elms Family Hotel

Spring St.
A very friendly, lively pub not too
far from the MCG. Popular after the
cricket each day.

The Dog's Bar

54 Acland St.
St. Kilda
Tel: 03 9525 3599
Ultra cool bar with live music.

Hilton on the Park

192 Wellington Parade
Tel: 03 9419 2000
A great bar to visit after the cricket.
Great atmosphere.

P J O'Briens

Southgate Complex
Tel: 03 9686 5011
Very busy Irish pub with music and
dancing. Great atmosphere, great fun.

The Pint on Punt

Punt Road
St. Kilda
Tel: 03 9510 3310

Very lively pub with backpackers' upstairs. Live bands, open late.

The Continental

132 Grevill
St, Prahan
Tel: 03 9510 2788
Excellent bar and restaurant that
attracts big name performers.

Dan O'Connell Hotel

225 Canning St
Carlton
Tel: 03 9347 1502
Yet another Irish pub with fantastic
atmosphere. Very popular pub, open
late most nights.

The Sherlock Holmes

415 Collins St.
Tel: 03 9629 1146
English pub in the middle of
Melbourne. Fine ales and good food.

There is a seemingly never-ending list
of pubs and clubs in Melbourne. Try
the Cricketers' Arms and The Royal Oak
outside the ground, the Prince of Wales
and the Ritz in St. Kilda and the Prince
Alfred Hotel in Grattan St. in Carlton.
Nightclubs include the Mercury Lounge
and Heat in the Crown Casino and
Metro at the top of Bourke Street.

The Victorian Arts Centre
129 Ferrars St.
Southbank
Tel: 03 9242 1000
Three theatres – State, Playbox and the George Fairfax Studio – plus the Concert Hall.

Regent Theatre
191 Collin St.
Tel: 03 9299 9500

Princess Theatre
165 Spring St.
Tel: 03 9299 9800

Melbourne Museum
Carlton Gardens
Carlton
Includes an Aboriginal Centre, Children's Museum, Mind and Body Museum, Australian Gallery and Forest Gallery.

Immigration Museum
Corner of William and Flinders St.
Tel: 03 9927 2700
Located in original Customs House. Has a 17 metre ship to re-enact, through voice and image, the lives of thousands of immigrants. Open 10.00-17.00 daily

Scienceworks Museum
2 Booker St.
Spotswood
Tel: 03 9392 4800
Hands-on exhibits and demonstrations.

Australian Racing Museum
Gate 22
Caulfield Racecourse
Station St.
Tel: 03 9257 7279
A fascinating look at Australia's racing history.

Comedy Theatre
The Victoria Arts Centre
129 Ferrars St.
Southbank
Tel: 03 9242 1000

National Gallery of Victoria
Federation Square
Corner Flinders and Russell Streets.
Tel: 03 9298 0203
www.ngv.vic.gov.au
The world's finest collection of Australian art. More than 20 galleries on three floors. The gallery has been open for nearly 150 years. The permanent collections range from Egyptian to contemporary art.

Climate

	ave temp	rain cm			
January	20	48	July	10	49
February	20	48	August	11	51
March	18	52	September	12	60
April	16	59	October	14	68
May	13	58	November	16	60
June	11	50	December	18	59

Win/Loss Record

Country	Played	Won	drawn	lost	Tie
Australia	96	53	15	28	-
England	52	19	7	26	-
Pakistan	7	2	2	3	-
New Zealand	3	-	2	1	-
South Africa	10	2	2	6	-
India	9	2	1	6	-
West Indies	14	3	1	10	-
Sri Lanka	1	-	-	1	-

Highest Individual Aggregates (Australia unless stated)

Player	Mat	Inn	NO	Runs	Ave	HS	50	100
Don Bradman	11	17	4	1671	128.54	270	3	9
Steve Waugh	17	30	6	1284	53.50	131*	6	3
Allan Border	20	36	3	1272	38.55	163	5	4
Greg Chappell	17	31	4	1257	46.56	121	9	4
Jack Hobbs (Eng)	10	18	1	1178	69.29	178	4	5
Bill Lawry	8	13	0	1023	78.69	205	5	4
Ian Chappell	12	19	2	948	55.76	165	5	3
Neil Harvey	12	23	2	947	45.10	205	3	3
Warwick Armstrong	11	20	5	918	61.20	133*	3	3
Doug Walters	11	19	2	846	49.76	115	6	2

Top Wicket Takers (Australia unless stated)

Player	Mat	Bll	Md	Runs	Wkt	Ave	BB	S/R
Dennis Lillee	14	3833	105	1798	82	21.93	7/83	46.74
Hugh Trumble	7	1708	71	646	46	14.04	7/28	37.13
Garth McKenzie	7	2370	35	1019	45	22.64	8/71	52.67
Craig McDermott	10	2345	84	1201	41	29.29	5/42	57.20
Monty Noble	8	1324	55	521	39	13.36	7/17	33.95
Shane Warne	8	2305	99	894	37	24.16	7/52	62.30
Bruce Reid	4	1144	53	475	35	13.57	7/51	32.69
Bill Johnston	8	2247	48	852	35	24.34	6/152	64.20
Sydney Barnes (Eng)	5	1723	83	632	35	18.06	7/121	49.23
Alan Davidson	5	1646	32	643	34	18.91	6/53	48.41

Highest Individual Scores (Australia unless stated)

307	Bob Cowper	v England 1965-66
270	Don Bradman	v England 1936-37
268	Graham Yallop	v Pakistan 1983-84
257	Ricky Ponting	v India 2003-04
250	Justin Langer	v England 2002-03
208	Viv Richards (I)	1984-85
205	Neil Harvey	v South Africa 1952-53
205	Bill Lawry	v West Indies 1968-69
204	Aubrey Faulkner (SA)	1910-11
200	Wally Hammond (Eng)	1928-29

Best Individual Bowling Performances (Australia unless stated)

35.4-7-86-9	Sarfraz Nawaz (Pak)	1978-79
47-8-121-9	Arthur Mailey	v England 1920-21
15-0-68-8	Wilfred Rhodes (Eng)	1903-04
28-5-71-8	Graham McKenzie	v West Indies 1968-69
29.1-6-81-8	Len Braund (Eng)	1903-04
42.2-7-143-8	Max Walker	v England 1974-75
7.4-2-17-7	Monty Noble	v England 1901-02
20-7-23-7	Bert Ironmonger	v West Indies 1930-31
12.3-1-27-7	Frank Tyson (Eng)	1954-55
26.2-14-28-7	Billy Bates (Eng)	1882-83

Highest Partnerships

Wkt	Runs	Batsmen	Match
1st	323	Jack Hobbs & Wilfred Rhodes (England)	1911-1912
2nd	298	Bill Lawry & Ian Chappell (Australia)	1968-1969 v. West Indies
3rd	249	Don Bradman & Stan McCabe (Australia)	1936-1937 v. England
4th	192	Mike Denness & Keith Fletcher (England)	1974-1975
5th	223*	Don Bradman & Arthur Morris (Australia)	1947-1948 v. India
6th	346	Don Bradman & Jack Fingleton (Australia)	1936-1937 v. England
7th	185	Graham Yallop & Greg Matthews (Australia)	1983-1984 v. Pakistan
8th	173	Nip Pellew & Jack Gregory (Australia)	1920-1921 v. England
9th	100	Albert Hartkopf & Bert Oldfield (Australia)	1924-1925 v. England
10th	120	Reggie Duff & Warwick Armstrong (Australia)	1901-1902 v. England

Results at The MCG

Date	Countries	Result
15/03/1877	v England	won by 45 Runs
31/03/1877	v England	lost by 4 Wickets
02/01/1879	v England	won by 10 Wickets
31/12/1881	v England	drawn
10/03/1882	v England	drawn
30/12/1882	v England	won by 9 Wickets
19/01/1883	v England	lost by an Innings and 27 Runs
01/01/1885	v England	lost by 10 Wickets
21/03/1885	v England	lost by an Innings and 98 Runs
01/01/1892	v England	won by 54 Runs
29/12/1894	v England	lost by 94 Runs
01/03/1895	v England	lost by 6 Wickets
01/01/1898	v England	won by an Innings and 55 Runs
29/01/1898	v England	won by 8 Wickets
01/01/1902	v England	won by 229 Runs
28/02/1902	v England	won by 32 Runs
01/01/1904	v England	lost by 185 Runs
05/03/1904	v England	won by 218 Runs
01/01/1908	v England	lost by 1 Wicket
07/02/1908	v England	won by 308 Runs
31/12/1910	v South Africa	won by 89 Runs
17/02/1911	v South Africa	won by 530 Runs
30/12/1911	v England	lost by 8 Wickets
09/02/1912	v England	lost by an Innings and 225 Runs
31/12/1920	v England	won by an Innings and 91 Runs
11/02/1921	v England	won by 8 Wickets
01/01/1925	v England	won by 81 Runs
13/02/1925	v England	lost by an Innings and 29 Runs
29/12/1928	v England	lost by 3 Wickets
08/03/1929	v England	won by 5 Wickets
13/02/1931	v West Indies	won by an Innings and 122 Runs
31/12/1931	v South Africa	won by 169 Runs
12/02/1932	v South Africa	won by an Innings and 72 Runs
30/12/1932	v England	won by 111 Runs
01/01/1937	v England	won by 365 Runs
26/02/1937	v England	won by an Innings and 200 Runs
01/01/1947	v England	drawn
01/01/1948	v India	won by 233 Runs
06/02/1948	v India	won by an Innings and 177 Runs
22/12/1950	v England	won by 28 Runs
23/02/1951	v England	lost by 8 Wickets
31/12/1951	v West Indies	won by 1 Wicket
24/12/1952	v South Africa	lost by 82 Runs
06/02/1953	v South Africa	lost by 6 Wickets
31/12/1954	v England	lost by 128 Runs
31/12/1958	v England	won by 8 Wickets
13/02/1959	v England	won by 9 Wickets
30/12/1960	v West Indies	won by 7 Wickets

10/02/1961	v West Indies	won by 2 Wickets
29/12/1962	v England	lost by 7 Wickets
01/01/1964	v South Africa	won by 8 Wickets
04/12/1964	v Pakistan	drawn
30/12/1965	v England	drawn
11/02/1966	v England	drawn
30/12/1967	v India	won by an Innings and 4 Runs
26/12/1968	v West Indies	won by an Innings and 30 Runs
31/12/1970	v England	Match Abandoned
21/01/1971	v England	drawn
29/12/1972	v Pakistan	won by 92 Runs
29/12/1973	v New Zealand	won by an Innings and 25 Runs
26/12/1974	v England	drawn
08/02/1975	v England	lost by an Innings and 4 Runs
26/12/1975	v West Indies	won by 8 Wickets
31/01/1976	v West Indies	won by 165 Runs
01/01/1977	v Pakistan	won by 348 Runs
12/03/1977	v England	won by 45 Runs
30/12/1977	v India	India Won by 222 Runs
29/12/1978	v England	won by 103 Runs
10/03/1979	v Pakistan	lost by 71 Runs
29/12/1979	v West Indies	lost by 10 Wickets
01/02/1980	v England	won by 8 Wickets
26/12/1980	v New Zealand	drawn
07/02/1981	v India	lost by 59 Runs
11/12/1981	v Pakistan	lost by an Innings and 82 Runs
26/12/1981	v West Indies	won by 58 Runs
26/12/1982	v England	lost by 3 Runs
26/12/1983	v Pakistan	drawn
22/12/1984	v West Indies	drawn
26/12/1985	v India	drawn
26/12/1986	v England	lost by an Innings and 14 Runs
26/12/1987	v New Zealand	drawn
24/12/1988	v West Indies	lost by 285 Runs
12/01/1990	v Pakistan	won by 92 Runs
26/12/1990	v England	won by 8 Wickets
26/12/1991	v India	won by 8 Wickets
26/12/1992	v West Indies	won by 139 Runs
26/12/1993	v South Africa	drawn
24/12/1994	v England	won by 295 Runs
26/12/1995	v Sri Lanka	won by 10 Wickets
26/12/1996	v West Indies	lost by 6 Wickets
26/12/1997	v South Africa	drawn
26/12/1998	v England	lost by 12 Runs
26/12/1999	v India	won by 180 Runs
26/12/2000	v West Indies	won by 352 Runs
26/12/2001	v South Africa	won by 9 Wickets
26/12/2002	v England	won by 5 Wickets
26/12/2003	v India	won by 9 Wickets

The WACA is home to the Western Australia Cricket Association and is one of the fastest tracks in the world. Reclaimed from swampland in 1893, the ground lies beside the Swan River in East Perth. Incredibly, no Test was played here until England's tour of 1970/71. England batted first and scored 397, Brian Luckhurst contributing 131. Australia replied with 440, Ian Redpath hitting 171 and Greg Chappell 108 on his Test debut. John Edrich top-scored with 115 in England's second innings total of 287. Set 245 to win, Australia could only reach 100/3 by the close.

The closest match was in 1977 when Australia scored 342/8 to beat India by two wickets, the highest chase at the WACA. However the last match in the 2001 series between Australia and New Zealand matched the excitement. Following draws in Brisbane and Hobart, four New Zealand batsmen – Lou Vincent (104), Stephen Fleming (105), Nathan Astle (156no) and Adam Parore (110) – scored centuries in the first innings total of 534/9 dec. In reply Australia scored 351 with Shane Warne dismissed on 99. New Zealand's second innings of 256 set the Australians a target of 439. Australia reached 381/7 by close of play with Gilchrist on 83no. The series was drawn.

The highest individual score at the WACA is 380 by Matthew Hayden against Zimbabwe in 2003. It broke the world record of 375 by Brian Lara which had stood since 1994, Lara regained the record in 2004 by scoring 400no against England in Antigua. One of the greatest innings seen at the ground was Doug Walters' 100 between tea and close in the nine-wicket victory over England in 1974. Walters brought up his century with a six off the last ball of the day. The highest team score is 617/5 by Australia when Slater scored his 219, the lowest is 62 by Pakistan in 1981.

The best bowling performance is Merv Hughes' 8/87 against the West Indies in 1988. Craig McDermott also took eight wickets, for 97, against England two years later. Hughes' figures of 13/217 are the best match return. Hughes has also taken most wickets, 39, closely followed by Glenn McGrath and McDermott, each with 38. Hughes' 1988 performance included a hat-trick, which he took across two innings. The only other hat trick was taken by McGrath against the West Indies in 2000.

The WACA has had a face-lift over the last couple of years. Rather than getting rid of the hills like other Test grounds, the authorities have replaced seats with grass and it has transformed the ground. It feels more comfortable and with the new layout it is possible to walk around most of the ground.

The refurbished Lillie Marsh Stand, the WACA members stand, is at the southern end of the ground. There are grass areas with scoreboard and video replay screens on both sides of the pitch.

The northern end of the ground has the Inverarity and Prindiville Stands which are excellent vantage points. The WACA is a wonderful ground and although temperatures soar in the summer, the mid-afternoon breeze nicknamed 'The Fremantle Doctor' cools players and spectators alike.

There are well-run bars throughout the ground and queues do not get excessively long. Food outlets serve the usual hot dogs, burgers and chips. Facilities and access for the disabled can be arranged by contacting the WACA 9265 7222. Entrances for wheelchairs are at Gates 3 and 6. Tickets can be purchased from Ticketmaster7 on +61 1300 13 61 22 or www.ticketmaster7.com. Ticket prices range from A$28 – A$50 per day and A$75 – A$140 per Test match. Tickets can be collected by Gate 6. Gates open at 09.00.

The WACA is a 25-minute walk from the middle of town, a very pleasant stroll down Hay Street. Central Area Transport buses drop and collect from Queen's Gardens and the Metro buses drop and collect at Hale Street, both points very near the ground. Enquiries Transperth 13 62 13. Driving to the ground is not advised as parking has become increasingly difficult in the last few years. A taxi ride from the centre should cost no more A$12.

Perth is the capital of Western Australia, the country's largest state. It is the most isolated city in the world, flanking the Indian Ocean on the south west coast at the foot of Mount Eliza and on the banks of the Swan River. It is Australia's fourth largest city with a population of 1.38 million and was named in memory of Sir George Murray, Secretary of State for the Colonies and the Member of Parliament for Perth in Scotland. The Dutch explorer Dirk Hartog first sighted the west coast of Australia in 1616. Eighty years later Willem de Vlamingh landed in Perth, naming the river the Swaene after the black swans he encountered there, but described the area as an arid, barren and wild land and departed. In 1801 a Frenchman, Francois Heiresses charted the area but also rejected settling. In 1829 the British under Captain Sir James Stirling landed and set up the Swan River Settlement.

Although it is a modern city with many skyscrapers and new buildings it has retained a number of heritage buildings such as the Old Court House and Law Museum, the Supreme Court, Government House in St. George Terrace, Her Majesty's Theatre in Hay St, the 1865 Western Australian Museum and the Perth Town Hall. The Perth Culture Centre is a modern building housing the Western Australian Art Gallery and The State Library.

Rottnest Island is one of Perth's big tourist attractions. A beautiful island with no cars and plenty for the visitor to do. Fremantle is 19km outside Perth and has many historical buildings, large markets, restaurants and cafés. The Pinnacles and Wave Rock in the heartlands are mysterious rock formations, and the south eastern part of the state is also worth a visit with wineries in Yallingup and Margaret River, the towering Karri forests and the towns of Bunbury and Albany.

There is a Mediterranean climate with hot summers from November to March with an average temperature of 26 degrees. Winter is cooler but still very pleasant. Perth's weather and brilliant blue skies allow visitors to take advantage of the superb white sandy beaches at Scarborough and Cottesloe to name but two. The people of Perth enjoy an outdoor lifestyle and spend much off their time on the beach. Popular activities include swimming, surfing, sailing diving and fishing.

Fremantle

Port town 19km south west of Perth and a cosmopolitan and stylish place with historic buildings, museums, huge markets and the fantastic Round House Gaol built in 1830. The sidewalk cafés, restaurants with courtyards and bars with beer gardens are always busy with visitors enjoying Western Australia's superb climate.

Perth Zoo

Located in South Perth, only minutes away from the city with shaded walkways and grassy banks, this is a wonderful place to spend an afternoon. Ferries from Barrack Street Jetty in the city run every half hour. The Zoo has a huge array of animals, reptiles and birds. Open 09.00-17.00 daily and remains open until 21.00 throughout January.

King's Park

Western Australia's most visited tourist attraction. Located on Mount Eliza no more than five minutes away from the city centre. Within the 400 hectares are the wonderfully presented Botanical Gardens. Viewing platforms on Fraser Avenue provide a bird's eye view of the city. Memorials remember those who lost their lives in the World Wars. A tram runs through the park providing an opportunity to see the whole area.

Rottnest Island

This trip is a must when in Perth. Although most visitors are day-trippers who catch the ferry from Barrack Street or Fremantle and spend the day cycling or bussing around the island, stopping to swim and snorkel in the Indian Ocean, an overnight stay is recommended if at all possible. One of most fascinating things about Rottnest is the small marsupial whose appearance gave the island its name. The Quokka is a small marsupial which looks like a cross between a kangaroo and a rat. There are thousands of them throughout the island. There is a hotel and resort, with excellent restaurant, on the island.

The Swan Bells

Perth's newest tourist attraction, It is said to be one of the largest musical instruments in the world, housing the 12 bells of the church of St. Martin in the Fields in London. The bells, which date back to the 1300's, are said to have rung to celebrate victory over the Spanish Armada, the homecoming of Captain Cook and the victory at El Alamein in 1942. They also rang in the New Year in Trafalgar Square for 275 years. They were presented to the University of Western Australia and the people of Perth on the occasion of the bi-centenary in 1988.

Perth International Airport is 16km from the centre of the city. A taxi costs from A$28 to $32 and takes approximately 20 minutes. Feature Tours Coach Service run into the city costs A$13 one way, A$18 return. The local bus service costs A$2.90. There is an information board in the arrival area with accommodation, tourist attractions and other information on the city. There are ATM machines and bureaux de change in both arrival and departure halls. There are cafés, restaurant, bars and shops in the terminal. Mobile phone rental in available. Car hire is available from Avis (08 9477 1302), Budget (08 9277 9277), Hertz (08 9479 4788) and Thrifty (08 9464 7333).

Airlines

Qantas	13 13 13
Virgin	13 67 89
Skywest Airlines	1300 660 088
Rotto Air Taxi	1800 500 006
Emirates	1300 303 777
South African	08 9216 2200
British Airways	08 9425 7711
Air New Zealand	13 24 76
Singapore Airlines	13 10 11

Buses

The city and suburbs of Perth have an excellent bus network. Perth Bus Station is situated on Mounts Bay Road. All tickets are valid for two hours and can also be used on trains and ferries. Local buses run daily between 06.00-11.30. The CBD is a Free Transit Zone. Cat buses circle the city every ten minutes. Enquiries 13 22 13.

Interstate and Long Distance
Greyhound Pioneer Australia 13 20 30

Trains

Transperth run trains between Wellington Street, Perth and Fremantle and other suburban destinations. Enquiries 13 62 13
Westrail run interstate services across the Nullarbor Plain from East Perth Terminal, West Parade 13 10 53

Ferries

Perth Water Transport run regular ferry services run between Barrack Street Jetty across the Swan to South Perth. Ferry services to Fremantle and Rottnest Island also leave Barrack Street Jetty.

Taxis

Black and White	13 10 08
Swan Taxis	13 13 30
Coastal Cabs	13 22 27
Yellow Cabs	13 19 24

Car Hire

Avis
46 Hill St.
Tel: 08 9325 7677
Fax: 08 9325 9021

Budget
960 Hay St.
Tel: 08 9480 3111
Fax: 08 9480 3188

Hertz
39 Milligan St.
Tel: 08 9321 7777
Fax: 08 9321 7770

Thrifty
198 Adelaide Terrace
Tel: 08 9464 7444
Fax: 08 9464 7499

arrival & transport

44 King St.
44 King St.
Tel: 08 9321 4476
Modern Australian cuisine. Fine food with fast friendly service.

Frasers
Fraser Ave.
Kings Park
Tel: 08 9481 7100
Seafood the speciality. Australian cuisine with the most wonderful Devonshire Teas. Great views of Perth and the Swan River. Outdoor dining most of the year. Open 07.30 until late daily.

Coco's
Southshore Centre
The Esplanade
South Perth
Tel: 08 9474 3030
Award winning restaurant. Australian, French, Japanese cuisine, specialising in seafood. Overlooks the Swan River, has outstanding food and stunning views. Bookings essential. 09.00 until late daily.

C Restaurant
Level 33
44 St. George's Terrace
Tel: 08 9220 8333
Fax: 08 9325 1533
pat@crestaurant.co.au
A large revolving restaurant at St. Martin's Tower providing spectacular views . Award winning Australian cuisine. Bookings essential.

Kallis Fish Market Café
Fishing Boat Harbour
46 Mews Road
Fremantle
Tel: 08 9335 7755
Fax: 08 9430 4695
seafood@kailis.com
Founded in 1928, this family-run restaurant offers fresh quality seafood. On the waterfront.

Shun Fung
Barrack Square Jetty
Tel: 08 9221 1868
One of the finest Chinese restaurants in Perth. Down by the river, Specialises in seafood.

The Thai House
63 Aberdeen St.
Northbridge
Tel: 08 9328 6074
Delicious food in a relaxed atmosphere.

Anarkali Indian Restaurant
171 James St.
Northbridge
Tel: 08 9228 4464
Excellent curries.

The Bog
361 Newcastle St.
Northbridge
Tel: 08 9228 0900
Busy Irish pub with live music seven days a week. Open late every night.

The Deen
84 Aberdeen St.
Northbridge
Tel: 08 9227 9361
Huge pub. Large bar at front of house with dance floor on one side and live music on the other. Open until 01.00 most nights.

The Brass Monkey Pub and Brassiere
209 William St.
Northbridge
Tel: 08 9227 9596
Very popular with visiting cricket fans.

The Astoria
37 Bay View Terrace
Claremont
Tel: 08 9384 1372
One of the best pubs in Perth. Lively pub, trendy crowd.

The Sail and Anchor
64 South Terrace
Fremantle
Tel: 08 9335 8433
A brewery in a pub! This is an institution. A heritage listed building, the pub serves good food and excellent beer. The first floor décor is stunning.

Paddy Hananns
Burswood International Resort and Casino
Great Eastern Highway
Tel: 08 9362 7777
Yet another Irish pub. One of many in the Burswood Resort. Great atmosphere and excellent pub food.

Margeaux's Nightclub
Parmeila Hilton Hotel
Mill St.
Tel: 08 9322 3622
One of Perth's finest nightclubs, but expensive.

Burswood International Resort and Casino

Great Eastern Highway
Burswood
Tel: 08 9362 7777
Fax: 08 9362 8866
reserve@burswood.com.au
www.burswood.com.au
Perth's finest. 414 rooms and 20 suites, golf course, tennis courts, gym, pool, sauna, 6 restaurants, 7 bars and a casino. Stunning panoramic views.

Rydges

Corner of Hay and King Streets
Tel: 08 9263 1800
Fax: 08 9263 1801
ridges_perth@rydges.com
www.rydges.com/perth
245 rooms with cable TV, minibar. Very trendy bar and street- side restaurant. Complimentary access to pool and gym next door.

The Holiday Inn

788 Hay St.
Tel: 08 9261 7200
Fax: 08 9261 7277
bookings@holidayinnperth.co.au
Well-appointed rooms with cable TV, minibar and safe. Restaurant and bar on the first floor and a beautiful swimming pool in the basement.

Duxton Hotel

St. George's Terrace
Tel: 08 9261 8000
Fax: 08 9261 8020
duxton@global.net.au
www.duxtonhotels.com.sg
Fine hotel. 306 rooms featuring cable TV, personal bar and generous bathrooms. Brasserie is one of WA's finest. Good Bar and superb swimming pool and gym.

Acacia Hotel

5 Robinson Ave.
Northbridge
Tel: 08 9328 0000
Fax: 08 9328 0100
bookings@acaciahotel.com.au
www.acaciahotel.com.au
Surprisingly affordable prices considering area. 94 rooms with cable TV and minibar. Restaurant, bar and gym.

Hotel Ibis

334 Murray St.
Tel: 08 9322 2844
Fax: 08 9321 6314
gm@htlibis.com.au

Excellent, affordable place to stay in the centre. 192 air-conditioned rooms with cable TV. Bistro and bar.

Sunmoon Resort

200 West Coast Highway
Scarborough
Tel: 08 9245 8000
Fax: 08 9245 8055
www.sunmoon.com.au
An alternative to staying in the centre. 2 minutes from the beach in Scarborough and a beautiful place to stay in relaxed surroundings. with good rooms, café, excellent swimming pool

Cottesloe Beach Chalets

6 John St.
Cottesloe
Tel: 08 9383 5000
Fax: 08 9385 4196
davies@git.com.au
Affordable beachfront accommodation. Self-contained chalets sleep 5 comfortably at a reasonable price. Lovely swimming pool with BBQ facilities.

City Beach Bed and Breakfast

11 Helston Ave.
City Beach
Tel: 08 9385 8824
city.beach.bedand.b@bigpond.com
Lovely. Situated between Scarborough and Cottesloe beaches. Self-contained kitchen, spacious living area.

Pension of Perth

3 Throssell St.
Tel: 08 9228 9049
Fax: 08 9228 9290
stay@pensionperth.com.au
www.pensionperth.com.au
Sumptuous surroundings. 7 wonderfully furnished en suite rooms. Great breakfast which can be eaten out by the pool.

Underground Backpackers'

268 Newcastle St.
Northbridge
Tel: 08 9228 3755
Fax: 08 9228 3744
Fine backpackers' with swimming pool close to the city centre. Singles, twins, doubles and dormitories.

Billabong Backpackers' Resort

381 Brauford St.
Tel: 08 9328 7720
Fax: 08 9328 7721
info@billabongresort.com.au

where to stay

Western Australian Museum

Perth Cultural Centre
James St.
Tel: 08 9427 2700
Western Australia's largest museum of the history and culture of the state's people. Also a bird, butterfly and marine gallery. Open 9.30-17.00

Western Australian Cricket Association Museum

Gate 2
Nelson Crescent
East Perth
Tel: 08 9265 7318

Museum of Performing Arts

Her Majesty's Theatre
825 Hay St.
Tel: 08 9265 0900
The museum traces Western Australian's entertainment history from settlement to present.

Western Australia Maritime Museum

Victoria Quay
Fremantle
Tel: 08 9431 8444
A wonderful look at Western Australian's maritime past.

Her Majesty's Theatre

825 Hay St.
Tel: 08 9265 0900
Home to the West Australian Ballet Company and the West Opera Company. Also hosts productions to Shakespeare to local productions.

Playhouse Theatre

Pier St.
Tel: 08 9235 3344

Perth Concert Hall

St. George's Terrace
Tel: 08 9231 9900
Fax: 08 9325 1283

Art Gallery of Western Australia

Perth Cultural Centre
James St.
Tel: 08 9492 6600
Western Australia's principal art gallery with Aboriginal art and visiting exhibitions. Open 10.00-7.00 daily.

Post Office

General Post Office
Forrest Place
Tel : 13 13 18

Tourist Information

Western Australian Visitor Centre
Corner of Wellington Street and Forrest Place
Tel : 1300 361 351
Fax : 08 9481 0190
www.wa.net

Hospital

Royal Perth Hospital
Victoria Square
Tel: 08 9224 2244

City Centre Medical Centre
Tel: 08 9221 4747

Health Direct
1800 022 222

Climate

	ave temp	rain cm			
January	24	9	July	13	164
February	25	12	August	13	118
March	23	14	September	14	65
April	19	43	October	16	45
May	16	111	November	20	26
June	14	167	December	22	18

Win/Loss Record

Country	Played	Won	Drawn	Lost	Tie
West Indies	6	5	-	1	-
Australia	31	18	6	7	-
New Zealand	6	1	3	2	-
England	10	1	3	6	-
Zimbabwe	1	-	-	1	-
Sri Lanka	2	-	-	2	-
Pakistan	4	-	-	4	-
India	2	-	-	2	-

Highest Aggregates (all Australian)

Player	Mat	Inn	NO	Runs	Ave	HS	50	100
Alan Border	16	26	3	931	40.48	125	6	2
David Boon	11	19	2	846	49.76	200	6	2
Steve Waugh	15	21	2	843	44.37	99*	8	0
Mark Waugh	11	16	1	766	51.07	119	4	2
Matthew Hayden	5	7	0	583	83.29	380	2	1
Michael Slater	6	9	0	567	63.00	219	1	2
Greg Chappell	8	13	1	497	41.42	117	1	2
Mark Taylor	9	15	1	490	35.00	142*	4	1
Dean Jones	5	7	1	488	81.33	150*	2	2
Ricky Ponting	8	9	0	487	54.11	197	2	1

Top Wicket Takers (Australian unless stated)

Player	Mat	Bll	Md	Runs	Wkt	Ave	BB	S/R
Merv Hughes	6	1618	63	752	39	19.28	8/87	41.49
Glenn McGrath	9	2256	104	977	38	25.71	4/49	59.37
Craig McDermott	8	1781	67	847	38	22.29	8/97	46.87
Dennis Lillee	7	1856	77	817	30	27.23	5/18	61.87
Rodney Hogg	5	1240	37	502	25	20.08	5/57	49.60
Brett Lee	4	1002	31	588	24	24.50	5/61	41.75
Jason Gillespie	5	985	36	486	24	20.25	5/88	41.04
Curtley Ambrose (WI)	3	639	28	310	24	12.92	7/25	26.63
Shane Warne	9	1983	69	980	23	42.61	4/83	86.22
Jeff Thomson	5	1097	25	571	21	27.19	5/93	52.24

Highest Individual Scores (Australian unless stated)

380	Matthew Hayden	v Zimbabwe 2003-04
219	Michael Slater	v Sri Lanka 1995-96
200	David Boon	v New Zealand 1989-90
197	Ricky Ponting	v Pakistan 1999-00
176	Bob Simpson	v India 1977-78
171	Ian Redpath	v England 1970-71
169	Roy Fredericks (WI)	1975-76
162	Chris Broad (Eng)	1986-87
159	Wayne Phillips	v Pakistan 1983-84
156	Ian Chappell	v West Indies 1975-76

Best Individual Bowling Performances (Australian unless stated)

37-9-87-8	Merv Hughes	v West Indies 1988-89
24.4-2-97-8	Craig McDermott	v England 1990-91
18-9-25-7	Curtley Ambrose (WI)	1992-93
12.1-3-27-7	Mike Whitney	v India 1991-92
14-3-54-7	Andy Roberts (WI)	1975-76
9.2-3-21-6	Michael Holding (WI)	1984-85
17.2-4-34-6	Greg Dymock	v England 1979-80
15-4-38-6	Craig Mcdermott	v England 1994-95
16-4-40-6	Ian Bishop (WI)	1992-93
35-9-78-6	Ian Botham (Eng)	1979-80

Highest Partnerships

Wkt	Runs	Batsmen	Match
1st	228	Mark Taylor & Michael Slater	1995-1996 v. Sri Lanka
2nd	259	Wayne Phillips & Graham Yallop	1983-1984 v. Pakistan
3rd	208	Robert Samuels & Brian Lara (WI)	1996-1997

4th	207	Matthew Hayden & Steve Waugh	2003-2004 v. Zimbabwe
5th	327	Justin Langer & Ricky Ponting	1999-2000 v. Pakistan
6th	233	Matthew Hayden & Alan Gilchrist	2003-2004 v. Zimbabwe
7th	149	Larry Gomes & Jeff Dujon (WI)	1984-1985
8th	253	Nathan Astle & Adam Parore (NZ)	2001-2002
9th	81	Sachin Tendulkar & Kiran More (Ind)	1991-1992
10th	74	Heath Streak & Ray Price (Zim)	2003-2004

Results at The Waca

Date	Countries	Result
11/12/1970	v England	drawn
13/12/1974	v England	won by 9 wickets
12/12/1975	v West Indies	lost by an innings and 87 runs
16/12/1977	v India	won by 2 Wickets
15/12/1978	v England	lost by 166 runs
24/03/1979	v Pakistan	won by 7 Wickets
14/12/1979	v England	won by 138 runs
12/12/1980	v New Zealand	won by 8 Wickets
13/11/1981	v Pakistan	won by 286 runs
12/11/1982	v England	drawn
11/11/1983	v Pakistan	won by an innings and 9 runs
09/11/1984	v West Indies	lost by an innings and 112 runs
30/11/1985	v New Zealand	lost by 6 wickets
28/11/1986	v England	drawn
12/02/1988	v Sri Lanka	won by an innings and 108 runs
02/12/1988	v West Indies	lost by 169 runs
24/11/1989	v New Zealand	drawn
01/02/1991	v England	won by 9 Wickets
01/02/1992	v India	won by 300 runs
30/01/1993	v West Indies	lost by an innings and 25 runs
12/11/1993	v New Zealand	drawn
03/02/1995	v England	won by 329 runs
08/12/1995	v Sri Lanka	won by an innings and 36 runs
01/02/1997	v West Indies	lost by 10 Wickets
20/11/1997	v New Zealand	won by an innings and 70 runs
28/11/1998	v England	won by 7 Wickets
26/11/1999	v Pakistan	won by an innings and 20 runs
01/12/2000	v West Indies	won by an innings and 27 runs
30/11/2001	v New Zealand	drawn
29/11/2002	v England	won by an innings and 48 runs
09/10/2003	v Zimbabwe	won by an innings and 175 runs

sydney

SCG

The Sydney Cricket Ground, home to New South Wales Cricket Association, is in Moore Park, 4km to the south of the city centre. Opened in 1810, the first recorded match was in 1854. The first Test played at the SCG was against England in February 1882, the sixth match in Test history, when Australia won by five wickets. Not surprisingly Sydney has seen many great matches from George Lohmann's 8/35 in 1887 (still the best at the ground) when England won by 71 runs to Shane Warne's match haul of 11/109 when Australia beat South Africa by an innings and 21 runs.

Lohmann liked Sydney. In 1888 he had match figures of 9/52 as England won by 126 runs. His first innings 5/17 came when Australia managed just 42, still their lowest Test score. Left arm spinner Robert Peel took 5/18 at the other end. In that match Charlie Turner took 12/87 – still the best match figures at the SCG – but finished on the losing side. In 1892 Australia beat England by 72 runs but Lohmann still took 8/58.

The best run chase came in 1898 when Australia scored 276/4 thanks to Joe Darling's 160. In Australia's first innings Tom Richardson had collected 8/94 but to no avail.

The closest match at the SCG was in 1994 when South Africa won by five runs despite Warne taking 10/147. One of the biggest thrashings came in 1969 when Australia beat the West Indies by 382 runs. The home side made 619 thanks to Bill Lawry (151) and Doug Walters (242) before bowling out West Indies for 279. But instead of enforcing the follow-on Australia batted again to reach 394-8 dec. Walters hit 103 and Ian Redpath 132, The Windies faced a mammoth task of scoring 735 to win. Typically they went down with all guns blazing. Garry Sobers hit 113 and Seymour Nurse 137 as they reached 352 scored in only 64.2 overs at 5.47 an over. Australia also scored 659 against England in 1946 when Sid Barnes and Don Bradman eached notched 234.

England got a measure of revenge in 1971 when John Snow's 7-40 after a Geoff Boycott second innings' 142 gave them victory by 299 runs. Astonishingly Bill Lawry (60) and Keith Stackpole (30) scored all but 26 of Australia's second innings 126 as Snow ripped through them.

The highest team score, though, is India's 705 (Sachin Tendulkar 241, VVS Laxman 178 – 353 for the fifth wicket) in the draw of 2004.

There have been two hat-tricks at the SCG, both by English bowlers – Johnny Briggs in 1892 and Darren Gough in 1998.

The ground has a capacity of 43,562. The Members' Pavilion, built in 1886, is one of the most beautiful in Test cricket. The Pavilion and the 1896 Ladies' Pavilion have stood the test of time as the ground has developed around them. To the left of the pavilions are the Noble and Bradman stands, both fine places to watch cricket. The Bradman Stand has private suites on its top tier.

Moving around the ground, the uncovered Messenger Stand is positioned beside the O'Reilly which stretches down the mid wicket boundary to Yabba's Hill. Unfortunately, Yabba's Hill, formerly a world famous grass hill at the Randwick end of the ground, is now covered with concrete seats. The atmosphere is still wonderful at this end of the ground, but many cricket lovers still miss the Hill. A giant electronic scoreboard and video replay screen are situated at the back of the hill, as is the small, uncovered, Doug Walters Stand which provides a wonderful view of the ground. Moving around, the much bigger Churchill and the Brewongle Stands have corporate and private suites.

The general admission area is the concourse which circles the whole ground. These seats are close to the playing area and great fun although they can get very hot. Food and beverages outlets are located throughout. Unfortunately the queues get very long and spectators can miss quite a bit of cricket while waiting for refreshments. Facilities and access for persons with disabilities are good. Wheelchair access can be arranged by contacting the Sports Department on 02 926 4000 and designated disabled parking is available in Moore Park parking area. Tickets can be purchased from Ticketek on Tel : 02 9266 4800or www.ticketek.com.au. The cost of the tickets range from A$40-A$70 and can be collected from the Box Office located underneath the Brewongle on Driver Ave.

The SCG is a half-an-hour walk from Circular Quay and many spectators walk there. Buses run from Central Station and Circular Quay and special shuttles are rostered on Test match days. Public Transport Information Line 13 15 00. Parking is available in Moore Park, A$10 and Fox Studios, A$22. There is a taxi rank on Errol Flynn Boulevard at Fox Studios. Sydney Cricket Ground has a fine museum with a lot of memorabilia and a spectravision show featuring players from the past. There are numerous pubs and restaurants in the area to visit after the game. The nearest pub is the Captain Cook where the talk is cricket, cricket, and cricket.

the city

Sydney is the capital of New South Wales with a population of four million. Regarded as Australia's premier city, it has become one of the world's most dynamic. It is situated on the east coast of Australia on the south shore of Sydney Harbour. The Sydney Opera House, the Sydney Harbour Bridge and the city skyline all contribute to make the harbour one of the most remarkable locations in the world. in 2000 Sydney hosted the Olympics which were a resounding success and helped to raise the city's profile throughout the world.

Aborigines inhabited the area around the harbour for 40,000 years. In 1770 Captain James Cook, the English explorer, sighted the harbour on his epic journey down the east coast. In 1788 the First Fleet arrived in Botany Bay under the command of Captain Arthur Phillips and set up Britain's first penal settlement. The area was named after Viscount Sydney, the British Home Secretary at the time.

No trip to Sydney is complete without taking a ferry trip to Manley or Taronga Zoo as the journey provides an ideal opportunity to get that perfect photograph of the city's wonderful skyline. Harbour cruises are also very popular.

The Royal Botanic Gardens are down by the harbour. Mrs. MacQuarie's seat in the gardens is considered to be the best place for photographing the Opera House and the Bridge together. Groves of palms trees, lakes and plants fill the gardens. Olympic Park has become a huge attraction since the Games and tours around the series of wonderful stadia at the venue at Homebush are very popular.

The Sydney Opera House

Since opening in 1973 the Opera House has become Australia's home for performing arts as well as an international architectural icon. It is home to the Symphony Orchestra, Opera Australia, Sydney Theatre Company and the Australia Ballet. Guided tours cost A\$16 and take approximately one hour. 02 9250 7777.

Sydney Harbour Bridge Climb

The climb is a three-hour experience no-one will never forget. After a full safety briefing, climb the bridge to savour the 360 degrees view of Sydney Harbour and take incredible photographs of the city and harbour. Enquiries 02 9252 0077.

Sydney Aquarium

Situated on Aquarium Pier in Darling Harbour. Since opening in 1988 it has become one of Sydney's leading tourist attractions. It is a unique display of Australian aquatic life. Walk through transparent tunnels to view all the multicoloured reef fish, sharks, eels, turtles and coral. There is a seal sanctuary and a touch pool outdoors. The aquarium is open daily 09.30-10.00. (02 9262 2300 www.sa.com.au).

Ferry ride to Taronga Park Zoo and Manley

One of the best ways to see the harbour is to catch a ferry from Circular Quay to either Taronga Zoo on Sydney's North Shore (open 0900-1700 daily 02 9969 2777) or to Manley which has one of the best beaches in the area along with some excellent cafés and restaurants. The ferry ride is magnificent and provides the opportunity to photograph Sydney's skyline as you leave Circular Quay.

Sydney Tower, Centre Point

Following a lift ride to the top, one is treated to superb 360 degree views of the city and harbour from the observation desk. There are two revolving restaurants. Open daily 09.30-10.30. 02 9223 0933 www.centrepoint.com.au

Sydney Airport is 8km from the centre of Sydney. It is without doubt one of the most customer-friendly airports in the world. Refurbished for the 2000 Olympics, it is the ultimate airport. A taxi ride into the city costs A\$25. The ranks are located directly outside International Arrivals. A hotel shuttle bus, The Sydney Airporter, runs from the airport to Darling Harbour, Kings Cross and the city at a cost of A\$9. Trains run from the airport to the city every ten minutes. The journey takes 15 minutes and costs A\$8.
There is an Information Desk in the Arrival Hall and an Airport Help Desk in the Departure Hall and help phones located throughout the airport. There are bookshops, many restaurants, fashion shops, pharmacies, Post Offices, and a medical centre.
There are ATM machines in all terminals and foreign exchange bureaux throughout the airport. Mobile Rental service is available in Arrivals Hall.
Car Rental is available from Avis (02 8374 2870), Budget (13 28 48), Hertz (02 9669 2444) and Thrifty (02 9582 1701).

Sydney has numerous accommodation options from top class five star hotels to bed and breakfasts and backpackers. Listed below is a small selection of the that available.

ANA Hotel
176 Cumberland St.
Tel: 02 9250 6000
Fax: 02 9250 6250
www.anahotelsyd,com
Towering over Sydney Harbour, the ANA is the largest and probably best hotel in Sydney. It certainly has the most wonderful views of the harbour. Great bar on the 36th Floor. 524 rooms, 3 restaurants, three bars, cable TV, pool, gym, sauna.

Menzies Hotel
14 Carrington St.
In the centre. Overlooks Wynard Park and is just a short walk from Circular Quay. 446 rooms, restaurant, bars, cable TV, swimming pool with sauna.

Sydney Marriott Hotel
36 College St.
Tel: 02 9361 8400
Fax: 02 9361 8599
Near the centre. Excellent rooms with cable TV, minibar. Swimming pool.

Novotel Sydney
100 Murray St.
Pyrmont
Tel: 02 9934 0000
Fax: 02 9934 0099
www.accordhotels.com.au
h1181@accord-hotels.com
Great hotel in Darling Harbour. Fine rooms with cable TV. Restaurant, bar, gym and swimming pool

Harbour Rocks Hotel
34-52 Harrington St.
The Rocks
Tel: 02 9251 8944
Fax: 02 9251 8900
Located in the historic Rocks area, the Harbour Rocks is in the hub of Sydney. 55 rooms with cable TV, restaurant and bar.

Sullivans
21 Oxford St.
Tel: 02 9361 0211
Fax: 02 9360 3735
www.sullivans.com.au
Small family hotel, 15 minutes walk to the city, 5 minutes walk to the cricket ground. 62 rooms, restaurant, café and swimming pool.

Ravesi's on Bondi Beach
Corner Campbell Parade and Hall St.
Bondi
Tel: 02 9365 4427
Fax: 02 9365 1481
www.ravesis.co.au
Small boutique hotel with some wonderful ocean front rooms with fabulous views. 16 rooms and bar.

Surfside Backpackers'
186 Arden St.
Coogee
Tel: 02 9315 7888
Fax: 02 9315 7892
Excellent backpackers' by the beach. Great atmosphere, clean, safe with cooking facilities.

Climate

	ave temp	rain cm			
January	23	104	July	12	100
February	23	117	August	14	81
March	21	135	September	15	69
April	18	129	October	18	79
May	16	121	November	20	82
June	13	131	December	25	17

The Tea Room
Level 3, North End
Queen Victoria Building
55 George St.
Tel: 029269 0774
Traditional lunch and afternoon tea in
the most stylish setting. Beautiful décor
with an amazing ceiling. Bookings
essential.

Harry's Fish Café
The Spit Bridge
Mosman
Tel: 02 9968 3049
Famous for seafood.

e Mela Ristorante
00 George St.
The Rocks
Tel: 02 9251 9323
Lively Italian restaurant. Sit outside in
atmospheric courtyard.

The Waterfront Restaurant
Campbells cove
7 Circular Quay West
Tel: 02 9247 3466
Excellent seafood in fantastic location
by harbour. Reservations essential.

Chinta Ria
Roof Terrace
Cockle Bay Wharf
Darling Harbour
Tel: 02 9264 3211
Top quality Malaysian restaurant with
good prices. No reservation policy

ensures a table early in the evening. Very busy. Loud music.

Doyle's on the Beach
11 Marine Parade
Watson's Bay
Tel: 02 9337 2007
One of Sydney's most famous restaurants, with a reputation for serving the
best fish in town. Wonderful views of
the harbour and certainly the place to
be seen. Bookings essential

Pavilion on the Park
1 Arts Gallery Road
Tel: 02 9232 1322
Fine restaurant on the edge of the
Botanic Gardens. Seafood, lamb and
the finest vegetarian menu in Sydney.
Bookings essential.

Rockpool
107 George St.
The Rocks
Tel: 02 9252 1888
One of the best restaurants in Sydney.
Fabulous food, excellent service,
fine wine. Another place to be seen.
Bookings essential.

Sailor's Thai
106 George St.
The Rocks
Tel: 02 9251 2466
Thai restaurant is the Old Sailor's
Home in the rocks. Delicious food.
Bookings essential.

General Post Office
Pitt St.
Sydney
Open 08.15-17.30 Monday-Friday
10.00-14.00 Saturday
Australia Post Enquiries 13 13 18

Tourist Information
Sydney Visitor Centre
The Rocks
106 George St.
Tel: 02 9240 8786

Sydney Visitor Centre
Darling Harbour
3 Wheat Road
Tel: 02 9281 0788

Airport Tourist Information
Tel: 02 9667 6065
There are information kiosks at the
Town Hall, Circular Quay and Martin
Place.

Hospital
Sydney Hospital
MacQuarie St.
Tel: 02 9382 1111

St. Vincent's Hospital
Victoria St.
Darlinghurst
Tel: 02 9339 1111

Dental Emergency Information Service
Tel: 02 9369 7050

Jackson's on George

George St.
Circular Quay
Lively pub with dancing and pool tables.
Late night opening. Great fun.

The Mercantile

25 George St.
The Rocks
Tel: 02 9247 3570
Irish pub under the shadow of the
Harbour Bridge. Very lively pub with
live bands. Open late seven days a week.

The Orient Hotel

89 George St.
The Rocks
One of the liveliest pubs in Sydney.
Huge pub with bands. Late opening.

The Pontoon Bar

Cockle Bay Wharf
Darling Harbour

Tel: 02 9267 7099
Groovy pub. Very popular.

Bourbon and Beefsteak Bar

24 Darlinghurst Road
Kings Cross
Tel: 02 9358 1144
Open 24 hours a day. Dining, drinki
dancing and gambling. Lively pub.

Q Bar

Level 2
44 Oxford St.
Darlinghurst
Pool Hall bar and dance floor .

Home

101 Cockle Bay Wharf
Darling Harbour
Tel: 02 9266 0600
Very popular dance club in Darling
Harbour.

Sydney Opera House

Bennelong Point
Tel: 02 9250 7250
Home to all performing arts including
the Australia Ballet and Sydney Dance
Company.

Her Majesty's Theatre

107 Quay St.
Haymarket
Tel: 02 9212 3411
The thespian centre of Sydney, hosting a
wide range of world productions.

The Art Gallery of New South Wales

Art Gallery Road
The Domain
Tel: 02 9225 1744
www.artgallerynsw.gov.au
One of the world's best art/sculpture col-
lections including Australian, Asian and
European Art. Open 1000-1700 daily.

Australian Museum

6 College St.
Tel: 02 9320 6000
www.amonline.net.au
Established in 1827, this is a discovery
of Australian natural environment and
indigenous cultures. A large section covers the anthropology of the Aboriginal
people. Open 09.30-17.00 daily.

Power House Museum

500 Harris St.
Ultino
Darling Harbour
Tel: 02 9217 0111
www.phm.gov.au
Some of the oldest steam engines in
world, displays of aircraft, satellites a
musical instruments. Every aspect of
human creativity.

National Maritime Museum

2 Murray St.
Tel: 02 9298 3777
www. Anmm.gov.au
Situated in Darling Harbour with
indoor and outdoor attractions inclu
ing tall ships and a fleet of historic ve
sels.

Hyde Park Barracks Museum

Queens Square
MacQuarie St.
Tel: 02 9223 8922
hht.nsw.gov.au
Australia's most comprehensive displ
of convict life. Built in 1819 to house
prisoners, the barracks is now a wond
ful museum giving an insight into th
way they lived. Open 09.30-17.00 dai

Airlines

Qantas	13 13 13
Virgin Blue	13 67 89
Air New Zealand	13 24 76
British Airways	02 9258 3300
Singapore	13 10 11

Buses

Sydney Explorer and Bondi Express are the two main tourist shuttle buses with running commentary.
Main bus terminals are Circular Quay, Wynard and Town Hall.
Enquiries   13 15 00
Interstate buses operate from Central Station on Eddy Ave.
Greyhound Pioneer 13 20 30
McCafferty's   13 14 99

Trains

City Rail trains run an extensive service throughout Sydney and the suburbs. Airport link is the quickest mode of transport to the airport.
Enquiries   13 15 00.
Central Station is the terminal for long distance and interstate trains.
Enquiries   13 22 32.

Ferries

Ferries operate from Circular Quay to a many destinations including Manley, Darling Harbour, Taronga Zoo and Watson Bay.
Enquiries   13 15 00.

Taxis

There are taxi ranks at railway stations, hotels and other location throughout the centre of Sydney. They can also be hailed in the street.
RSL Cabs   02 9581 1111
Combined Cabs   02 8332 8888
ASC Cabs   13 25 22
Water taxi operates from Circular Quay to other wharves.
Harbour Taxi Boats 02 9555 1155
Taxis Afloat   02 9955 3222

Car Hire

Avis
200 William St.
Kings Cross
Tel: 02 9357 2000
Fax: 02 9335 1930

Budget
93 William St.
Kings Cross
Tel: 02 8255 9600
Fax: 02 9332 1260

Hertz
Corner William & Riley St.
Kings Cross 2011
Tel: 02 9360 6621
Fax: 02 9360 5145

Thrifty
75 William St.
Kings Cross
Tel: 1300 367 227
Fax: 02 8374 6188

transport

Win/Loss Record

Country	Played	Won	Drawn	Lost	Tie
Australia	91	47	17	27	-
Pakistan	5	2	1	2	-
England	52	21	7	24	-
India	8	1	4	3	-
New Zealand	2	-	1	1	-
South Africa	9	1	2	6	-
West Indies	14	2	2	10	-
Zimbabwe	1	-	-	1	-

Highest Individual Aggregates (Australia unless stated)

Player	Mat	Inn	NO	Runs	Ave	HS	50	100
Allan Border	17	29	8	1177	56.05	89	11	0
Greg Chappell	12	22	4	1150	63.89	204	3	4
David Boon	11	21	3	1127	62.61	184*	4	4
Steve Waugh	17	25	1	1084	45.17	103	7	3
Doug Walters	11	19	2	900	52.94	242	3	3
Clem Hill	12	22	0	824	37.45	191	4	1
Victor Trumper	10	19	2	809	47.59	185*	2	3
Wally Hammond (Eng)	5	7	2	808	161.60	251	1	4
Don Bradman	8	12	0	703	58.58	234	3	2
Syd Gregory	10	19	2	690	40.59	201	1	1

Top Wicket Takers (Australia unless stated)

Player	Mat	Bll	Md	Runs	Wkt	Ave	BB	S/R
Shane Warne	10	3120	143	1291	49	26.35	7/56	63.67
Charlie Turner	6	2106	209	602	45	13.38	7/43	46.80
Dennis Lillee	8	2191	61	1036	43	24.09	4/40	50.95
Ray Lindwall	8	1968	41	726	42	17.29	7/63	46.86
Richie Benaud	10	3136	95	1022	36	28.39	5/83	87.11
George Lohmann (Eng)	4	1219	114	331	35	9.46	8/35	34.83
Glenn McGrath	8	1777	73	796	34	23.41	5/48	52.26
George Giffen	7	1427	82	593	33	17.97	7/117	43.24
Stuart MacGill	5	1870	65	910	32	28.44	7/50	58.44
Frederick Spofforth	5	1194	122	482	32	15.06	7/44	37.31

Highest Individual Scores (Australia unless stated)

287	Tip Foster (Eng)		1903-04
277	Brian Lara (WI)		1992-93
251	Wally Hammond (Eng)		1928-29
242	Doug Walters	v West Indies	1968-69
241*	Sachin Tendulkar Ind)		2003-04
234	Sid Barnes	v England	1946-47
234	Don Bradman (Aus)	v England	1946-47
231*	Wally Hammond (Eng)		1936-37
223	Justin Langer	v India	1999-00
206	Ravi Shastri (Ind)		1991-92

Best Individual Bowling Performances (Australia unless stated)

27.1-12-35-8	George Lohmann (Eng)	1886-87
43.2-18-58-8	George Lohmann (Eng)	1891-92
36.1-7-94-8	Tom Richardson (Eng)	1897-98
46.5-7-141-8	Anil Kumble Ind)	2003-04
34.2-20-40-7	Dick Barlow (Eng)	1882-83
17.5-5-40-7	John Snow (Eng)	1970-71
38-23-43-7	Charlie Turner	v England 1887-88
41.1-23-44-7	Frederick Spofforth	v England 1882-83
26-10-46-7	Allan Border	v West Indies 1988-89
20.1-4-50-7	Stuart MacGill	v England 1998-99

Highest Partnerships

Wkt	Runs	Batsmen	Match
1st	234	Geoff Boycott & Bob Barber (Eng)	1965-1966 v Australia
2nd	224	Warren Bardsley & Clem Hill (Aus)	1910-1911 v South Africa
		Sunil Gavaskar & Mohinder Amarnath (Ind)	1985-1986 v Australia
3rd	293	Richie Richardson & Brian Lara (WI)	1992-1993 v Australia
4th	353	VVS Laxman & Sachin Tendulkar (Ind)	2003-2004 v Australia
5th	405	Sid Barnes & Don Bradman (Aus)	1946-1947 v England
6th	187	Warwick Armstrong & Charles Kelleway (Aus)	1920-1921 v England

7th	160	Richie Benaud & Garth McKenzie (Aus)	1963-1964 v South Africa
th	154	George Bonnor & Sammy Jones (Aus)	1884-1885 v England
h	154	Syd Gregory & Jack Blackham (Aus)	1894-1895 v England
)th	130	Tip Foster & Wilfred Rhodes (Eng)	1903-1904 v Australia

esults at Sydney Cricket Ground

ate	Countries	Result
7/02/1882	v England	won by 5 wickets
3/03/1882	v England	won by 6 wickets
6/01/1883	v England	lost by 69 runs
7/02/1883	v England	won by 4 wickets
)/02/1885	v England	won by 6 runs
6/03/1885	v England	won by 8 wickets
8/01/1887	v England	lost by 13 runs
5/02/1887	v England	lost by 71 runs
)/02/1888	v England	lost by 126 runs
)/01/1892	v England	won by 72 runs
4/12/1894	v England	lost by 10 runs
/02/1895	v England	won by an innings and 147 runs
3/12/1897	v England	lost by 9 wickets
5/02/1898	v England	won by 6 wickets
3/12/1901	v England	lost by an innings and 124 runs
4/02/1902	v England	won by 7 wickets
1/12/1903	v England	lost by 5 wickets
6/02/1904	v England	lost by 157 runs
3/12/1907	v England	won by 2 wickets
1/02/1908	v England	won by 49 runs
9/12/1910	v South Africa	won by an innings and 114 runs
3/03/1911	v South Africa	won by 7 wickets
5/12/1911	v England	won by 146 runs
3/02/1912	v England	lost by 70 runs
7/12/1920	v England	won by 377 runs
5/02/1921	v England	won by 9 wickets
)/12/1924	v England	won by 193 runs
7/02/1925	v England	won by 307 runs
4/12/1928	v England	lost by 8 wickets
/01/1931	v West Indies	won by an innings and 172 runs
7/02/1931	v West Indies	lost by 30 runs
3/12/1931	v South Africa	won by an innings and 155 runs
2/12/1932	v England	lost by 10 wickets
5/03/1933	v England	lost by 8 wickets
8/12/1936	v England	lost by an innings and 22 runs
6/12/1946	v England	won by an innings and 33 runs
4/02/1947	v England	won by 5 wickets
2/12/1947	v India	drawn
5/01/1951	v England	won by an innings and 13 runs
9/11/1951	v West Indies	won by 7 wickets
5/01/1952	v West Indies	won by 202 runs
9/01/1953	v South Africa	won by an innings and 38 runs
7/12/1954	v England	lost by 38 runs
5/02/1955	v England	drawn
)/01/1959	v England	drawn
8/01/1961	v West Indies	lost by 222 runs
/01/1963	v England	won by 8 wickets
5/02/1963	v England	drawn
)/01/1964	v South Africa	drawn
7/02/1964	v South Africa	drawn
7/01/1966	v England	lost by an innings and 93 runs
5/01/1968	v India	won by 144 runs
4/01/1969	v West Indies	won by 10 wickets
4/02/1969	v West Indies	won by 382 runs
1/01/1971	v England	lost by 299 runs
2/02/1971	v England	lost by 62 runs
5/01/1973	v Pakistan	won by 52 runs
5/01/1974	v New Zealand	drawn
4/01/1975	v England	won by 171 runs
3/01/1976	v West Indies	won by 7 wickets
4/01/1977	v Pakistan	lost by 8 wickets
7/01/1978	v India	India won by an innings and 2 runs
06/01/1979	v England	lost by 93 runs

10/02/1979	v England	lost by 9 wickets
04/01/1980	v England	won by 6 wickets
02/01/1981	v India	won by an innings and 4 runs
02/01/1982	v West Indies	drawn
02/01/1983	v England	drawn
02/01/1984	v Pakistan	won by 10 wickets
30/12/1984	v West Indies	won by an innings and 55 runs
22/11/1985	v New Zealand	won by 4 wickets
02/01/1986	v India	drawn
10/01/1987	v England	won by 55 runs
29/01/1988	v England	drawn
26/01/1989	v West Indies	won by 7 wickets
03/02/1990	v Pakistan	drawn
04/01/1991	v England	drawn
02/01/1992	v India	drawn
02/01/1993	v West Indies	drawn
02/01/1994	v South Africa	lost by 5 runs
01/01/1995	v England	drawn
30/11/1995	v Pakistan	lost by 74 runs
29/11/1996	v West Indies	won by 124 runs
02/01/1998	v South Africa	won by an innings and 21 runs
02/01/1999	v England	won by 98 runs
02/01/2000	v India	won by an innings and 141 runs
02/01/2001	v West Indies	won by 6 wickets
02/01/2002	v South Africa	won by 10 wickets
02/01/2003	v England	lost by 225 runs
17/10/2003	v Zimbabwe	won by 9 wickets
02/01/2004	v India	drawn

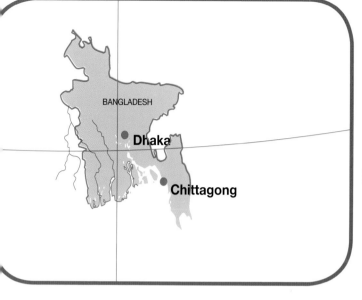

The Bangabandhu Stadium in Dhaka hosted Pakistan's first ever home Test on New Year's Day 1955 when the city was the capital of East Pakistan. It staged seven Tests between 1955 and 1969 but when in 1970 Bangladesh won its independence Test cricket ceased to be played there until 1999 when Pakistan and Sri Lanka used it as a neutral ground because of trouble in Pakistan. And when Bangladesh became a Test nation in 2000 its inaugural match against India was played at the Bangabandhu. India won by nine wickets. The only other ground to be used in Bangladesh is the M. A. Aziz Stadium in Chittagong. It staged its first match against Zimbabwe on 15th November 2001. The visitors won by eight wickets.

Distance between cities (in km)
The distance between Dhaka and Chittagong is 260 kms.

Airlines
Bangladesh's national airline is Biman Bangladesh Airlines. Both Dhaka and Chittagong have international airports. Biman and GMG Airlines both fly in between the two cities. GMG are slightly more expensive but a lot more comfortable.

GMG Airlines	881 3246
Biman Bangladesh Airlines	891 7400

Buses
There is a bus service between Dhaka and Chittagong however it is slow, over-crowded and not recommended.

Trains
Train run between Dhaka and Chittagong three times each day. The 260km journey takes between five and eight hours depending on the service chosen. Train travel in Bangladesh is extremely inexpensive.

Car Hire
The Bangladesh Parjatan Corporation which is the national tourist board can arrange car hire if required. An International Driving Licence is required and all drivers must be over 21 years of age. Most visitors to Bangladesh chose to hire a driver as well as a car as it is inexpensive and also as driving can be quite hazardous for visitors who have no local knowledge.

Taxis

Taxis are available outside the airport in both Dhaka and Chittagong and outside most major hotels. Your hotel or restaurant host will happily order a taxi for you. Auto and cycle rickshaws are the most popular forms of transport in Bangladesh. They are very cheap and are a good way to see and feel the cities. One drawback is the proximity to the pollution which is very heavy especially in Dhaka.

Emergency Numbers

Police Emergency   999
Fire Brigade Emergency   199

Embassies/Consulates

British High Commission
United Nations Road
Baridhara
Tel: 02 882 2705
Fax: 02 988 2819
ppabhc@citecho.net

Australian High Commission
184 Gulshan Ave.
Gulshan, Dhaka   Tel: 02 881 3101
Fax: 02 881 1125

Embassy of Pakistan
House-NE (C) 2
Road 71
Gulshan, Dhaka

Visas

All visitors must hold a passport valid for at least three months after departure. Visas and return tickets are also required by everyone. A single entry visa varies in price depending which country's passport one holds, British passport holders pay £40. Applicants must fill in application form, have three passport photos and a letter from ones employer. Please allow three days for the embassy to deal with applications personally delivered to the embassy, at least seven working days for postal applications. The visa is valid for three months from the date of issue.

Customs

Visitors over the age of 18 may take the following goods into Bangladesh without incurring customs duty: 200 cigarettes or 50 cigars, 2 litres of alcohol, 250ml of perfume.

Time Difference

Bangladesh is six hours ahead of GMT.

Electricity

220/240 volts AC at 50 cycles per second. Some hotels have adaptors.

Tipping

Tipping is common in Bangladesh in restaurants, hotels and rickshaws. A small gratuity will suffice.

Departure Tax

There is a departure tax of Tk300 on all passengers leaving Bangladesh.

Banks

Opening times for banks in Dhaka and Chittagong are generally 09.00-15.00 Saturday to Wednesday and 09.00-13.00 on Thursdays. They do not open on Fridays. The international banks have foreign exchange counters and some accept travellers' cheques. American Express are the most widely accepted. ATM facilities are available. Major credit cards are accepted in larger hotels in both Dhaka and Chittagong. Bangladesh uses the Taka (Tk). Notes are issued in denominations of Tk 500, 100, 50, 20, 10, 5 , 2 and 1 and coins in denominations of Tk5, 2, 1 and 50, 25, 10, and 5 paisa.

Telecoms

International Direct Dialling is available in most hotels in Dhaka and Chittagong. Public payphones do not have IDD. Bangladesh's dialling code is 880. The outgoing international code is 0011.

Post

Both Dhaka and Chittagong have General Post Offices. Dhaka GPO opening hours are 09.30-20.00 daily except Fridays. Chittagong GPO is open from 08.00-20.00. Airmail can take a week or more to Britain.

Tourist Offices

Both Dhaka and Chittagong have tourist information offices. The head office is in Dhaka.

Bangladesh Parjatan Corporation
National Tourism Organisation
233 Airport Road
Tejgaon
Tel: 02 811 7855
Fax: 02 811 7235
bpcho@bangla.net
www.parjatan.org

chittagong

chittagong stadium

Chittagong Stadium, formerly known as the M. A. Aziz Stadium, is Bangladesh's second Test ground.

The first Test match played there was the second and final one of the 2001 series with Zimbabwe, when after winning the toss, Bangladesh invited the opposition to bat and were forced to endure centuries by three of the visitors, Andy Flower, 114no, Craig Wishart, 114, and Trevor Gripper, 112, before Zimbabwe declared at 542/7. Habibul Basher scored 108 in the home side's first innings total of 251. Forced to follow-on, Bangladesh batted well reaching 201/2, before slumping to 301 all out. Zimbabwe lost two wickets chasing the required 11 runs to win by eight wickets.

Pakistan beat Bangladesh by an innings and 169 runs in 2002. and later the same year, the West Indies visited the 27,000 capacity stadium for the second and final Test of the series and won by seven wickets.

The ground hosted the first match in the 2003 series against South Africa, again losing by a large margin. The home side scored 173, as Habibul Basher hit 60 and Paul Adams took 5/37. The visitors replied with 470/2 before declaring. Jacques Rudolph, 222no, and Boeta Dippenaar, 177no, shared an unbeaten partnership of 429 for the third wicket. Trailing by 297 runs, Bangladesh could only manage 237, Basher again top scoring with 60 and Adams taking another five wickets, this time for 49.

The stadium's next Test was the second match of the 2003 series with England. England had already won the first Test in Dhaka and completed a 2-0 series win with a convincing 329 run victory in Chittagong. Nasser Hussain was England's batting star with 76 and 95, while Richard Johnson finished with match figures 9/93.

The stadium is 2km from the city centre The pavilion is a small, comfortable building which includes the players' dressing rooms, the members' enclosure and the international enclosure where visiting supporters are expected to sit. Unfortunately, this part of the ground is very expensive and totally out of line with the prices of the other enclosures in the ground. The reasonably priced stand to the left of the pavilion is a fine place from which to watch cricket and has a terrific atmosphere. The stand to the right of the pavilion is reserved for corporate entertainment. The rest of the ground is terracing which is partially under cover and can get very crowded, although the people are very friendly and excited to meet visiting supporters. The toilet facilities around the ground are generally well tended.

Tickets are available through branches of the Prime Bank and the State Janata Bank which are located throughout Chittagong. Prices are minimal for all parts of the ground with the exception of the International enclosure. All bags are searched at the entrance and glass bottles are not allowed in the ground. The Stadium is within walking distance of CDA Avenue where some of the popular hotels are located. Auto and cycle rickshaws costing around Tk 20 are available from Station Road and the city centre.

the city

Chittagong is Bangladesh's second largest city and lies on the Karnaphuli River, 20km from its mouth in the Bay of Bengal in the south east of the country. It is the capital of the south eastern administrative division and has a population of 2.4 million. An attractive city surrounded by green hills, forests and beaches, a seventh century Chinese poet described the city as "a sleeping beauty emerging from mists and water."

It is an ancient city that has experienced repeated conquests by Arakanese, Arab, Mughal, Portuguese and British in turn. Originally part of an ancient Hindu kingdom, the city was conquered by the Arakanese in the ninth century before becoming part of the Mughal Empire in the 13th century. The Arakanese retook the city in the 16th century, but the Portuguese soon seized control and developed it as a trading and commercial centre, naming it Porto Grande. The Mughals temporarily wrested it back before the British took control in 1760 and established it as a headquarters of the British East India Company. In the early 19th century, Burma's claim of the city as a dependency led to the Burmese war in 1824. The city remained British until 1947 when it became part of East Pakistan. It became part of the new country of Bangladesh in 1971.

The old city has some fine Portuguese colonial buildings and many mosques, including the Qadam Mubarek Mosque and the Shahi Jama-e-Masjid which sits on top of a hill in the centre. The city also has some notable Hindu temples, Buddhist ruins and a number of shrines. The Ethnological Museum in the new city is another interesting attraction and traces the history of the local tribes. A good vantage point to view the city is to the northwest where the British settled and today is the main commercial area. Other places of interest of include the Portuguese Arsenal, the port Area and the Zia Museum. There are excellent beaches close to Chittagong, such as Patenga and Fouzdarhat. There are three main seasons; the pre-monsoon season in April and May when the temperature rises to over 30 degrees with plenty of sun, the rainy season from June to October which is wet, warm and muggy and the dry season from November to March which coincides with the cricket season and is sunny and cooler than the rest of the year. Light tropical clothing is recommended all year round.

Lake Foy

A man-made lake in the hills of Chittagong. Created by a railway engineer named Foy in 1942 it is a favourite spot for picnicking and relaxation. The lake is within 10km of the centre of the city and can be reached by taxi or train to the Pahartali railway station. It has restaurants, barbecues and snack bars and is a beautiful place to watch the sun set over the city.

Cox's Bazaar

The top tourist resort in Bangladesh and situated on the Bay of Bengal. Named after Lieutenant Cox who established a colony for Moghuls in British territory during the Burmese war. It has miles of sandy beaches and steep cliffs. It is renowned for excellent seafood and is a popular destination for supporters between Test matches in Bangladesh.

The Tomb of Sultan Bayazid Bostami

6km to the north of Chittagong in the suburb of Nasirabad. A large tank at the base of the Tomb contains hundreds of tortoises said to be descendants of evil spirits who incurred the wrath of a great saint who visited Nasirabad more than 1,000 years ago.

The War Cemetery

The World War II Cemetery is a well-preserved burial ground for more than 750 members of the Allied forces who gave their lives on the Indo-Burmese Front. Located on a picturesque hill in the south west corner of the Chittagong Medical College Hospital. A solemn, tranquil and thought-provoking place.

Sitakunda

40km from Chittagong, it is the site of the Chandranath Hindu Temple, one of the oldest temples on the subcontinent, as well as many other beautiful temples of a variety of faiths. Sitakunda is a very popular place with both Hindu and Buddhists pilgrims. The Buddhist Temple said to have a footprint of Lord Buddha and considered sacred by Buddhists and Hindus. To the north of the town is a hot water spring which is also worth a visit.

Chittagong M.A. Hannan International Airport is modern and 20km from the centre. Taxis are available outside the terminal and should cost no more than Tk 200 for the 30 minute journey. There are no buses or coaches from the airport to the city. There are a number of small cafés within the well run terminal. There are no car hire facilities.

Hotel Agrabad
Agrabad Commercial Area
Tel: 031 713 311
Fax: 031 710 572
aliotel@spnetctg.com
The best and most expensive in Chittagong. Luxurious rooms, cable TV. Two restaurants, bar and swimming pool.

Hotel Meridian
1367 CDA Ave.
Tel: 031 654 000
Fax: 031 650 154
meridian@spctnet.com
A fine hotel in the centre. Good rooms, cable TV. Restaurant, coffee shop and bar.

Hotel Harbour View
721 CDA Ave.
Nasirabad
Tel: 031 617 868
Fax: 031 610 607
hview@spctnet.com
www.harbourviewbd.com
One of the best. Luxurious air conditioned rooms with satellite TV and mini bar. Business centre, restaurant and bar.

Hotel Silmoon
134 CDA Ave
Dampara
Tel: 031 628 302
A new hotel less than 10 minutes walk from the stadium. It has luxurious en suite rooms with cable TV, 2 great restaurants and a business centre. Excellent value and good service.

Hotel Golden Inn
336 Station Road
Fax: 031 611 004
A good budget hotel with clean rooms and restaurant.

Dream Hotel
91 Station Road
Tel: 031 619 401

Clean budget hotel in the city centre. Good rooms at very good prices.

Hotel Mishtka
95 Station Road
Another city centre budget hotel. Good rooms and restaurant.

Restaurants
All the major hotels have their own restaurants and are popular with cricket fans. Other restaurants include

Meredian Tondoor
Nasirabad
Excellent restaurant serving Bangladeshi, Chinese and Indian food.

Silver Spoon
Sattar Chamber
99 Agrabad Commercial Area
Popular restaurant serving Bangladeshi Indian, Indonesian and Chinese food.

Bonanza Restaurant
1692 CDA Ave.
Tel: 031 652 564
Another restaurant popular with cricket fans. Serves Bangladeshi, Thai, Korean and Indian food.

Tai Wah
Nur Ahmed Road
Good Korean restaurant in the centre of town.

Chungking Restaurant
Sheikh Mujibur Rahman Road
Excellent Chinese restaurant.

Nightlife
Some of the better hotels have bars and the Chittagong Club opposite the Stadium is very popular with visiting fans, however it is worth noting that the club has a strict dress code. The Sharjan, a small hotel near Station Road, has an excellent little bar that also serves good food.

Airlines

Biman Airways
CDA Ave.
Tel: 031 650 7671

GMG Airlines
Hotel Agrabad
Agrabad Commercial Area
Tel: 031 503 147

Buses

Chittagong bus station is in
Bardarhat, 4km to the north of the
city. Buses run from the station to
Cox's Bazaar, a popular resort with
fans in between Tests.

Trains

Chittagong train station is in the centre of the city. Trains run to Dhaka
three times a day and the journey
takes six to seven hours. Tickets cost
Tk 300 first class, Tk 150 second
class. Enquiries 031 720 121.
Trains also run from Chittagong to
Cox's Bazaar.

Taxis

AB Enterprise
1248 Dhaniala Para
Dhaka Trank Road
Tel: 031 723 145

Cheora Automobiles
601 Sk. Mujib Road
Tel: 031 724 853

Car Hire

Agrabad Tours   031 724 062
Alam Enterprise   031 714 566
Bangladesh Enterprise 031 670 512

Post Office

General Post Office
Suhrawardi Road
Open 08.00-20.00 daily except
Fridays.

Tourist Information

Chittagong Tourist Information
Centre
Motel Shaikat
Station Road
Tel: 031 209 845

Hospital

Chittagong General Hospital
Anderkillah
Tel: 031 220 404

Chattagram Metropolitan Hospital
O.R. Nizam Road
Tel: 031 651 242

Emergency Numbers

Ambulance   725 056
Fire   716 326
Police   630 691

Climate

	ave temp	rain cm
January	20	7
February	23	15
March	25	54
April	27	116
May	26	247
June	28	604
July	28	719
August	28	553
September	28	284
October	27	242
November	25	58
December	21	10

Win/Loss Record

Country	Played	won	drawn	Lost	Tie
Zimbabwe	1	1	-	-	-
Pakistan	1	1	-	-	-
West Indies	1	1	-	-	-
South Africa	1	1	-	-	-
England	1	1	-	-	-
Bangladesh	5	-	-	5	-

Highest Individual Aggregates

Player	Mat	Inn	NO	Runs	Ave	HS	50	100
Habibul Bashar (Ban)	5	10	0	414	41.40	108	4	1
Javed Omar (Ban)	4	8	0	224	28.00	80	2	0
Jacques Rudolph (SA)	1	1	1	222	-	222*	0	1
Yousuf Youhana (Pak)	1	1	1	204	-	204*	0	1
Boeta Dippenaar (SA)	1	1	1	177	-	177*	0	1

Top Wicket Takers

Player	Mat	Bll	Md	Runs	Wkt	Ave	BB	S/R
Paul Adams (SA)	1	187	8	106	10	10.60	5/37	18.70
Richard Johnson (Eng)	1	199	7	93	9	10.33	5/49	22.11
Mashrafe Mortaza (Ban)	3	514	19	302	9	33.56	4/60	57.11
Grant Flower (Zim)	1	325	21	104	8	13.00	4/41	40.63
Tapash Baisya (Ban)	2	321	10	187	7	26.71	4/72	45.86

Highest Individual Scores

222*	Jacques Rudolph (SA)	2003
204*	Yousuf Youhana (Pak)	2001-02
177*	Boeta Dippenaar SA)	2003
119	Younis Khan (Pak)	2001-02
114*	Andy Flower (Zim)	2001-02

Best Individual Bowling Performances

16.4-3-35-5	Saqlain Mushtaq (Pak)	2001-02
12.3-3-37-5	Paul Adams (SA)	2003
21-6-49-5	Richard Johnson (Eng)	2003-04
18.4-5-69-5	Paul Adams SA)	2003
8.5-0-36-4	Waqar Younis (Pak)	2001-02

Highest Partnerships

Wicket	Runs	Batsmen	Match
1st	126	Marcus Trescothick & Michael Vaughan (Eng)	2003-2004
2nd	131	Javed Omar & Habibul Bashar (Ban)	2002-2003 v South Africa
3rd	429*	Jacques Rudolph & Boeta Dippenaar (SA)	2002-2003
4th	70	Younis Khan & Yousuf Youhana (Pak)	2001-2002
5th	116	Nasser Hussain & Rikki Clarke (Eng)	2003-2004
6th	123	Craig Wishart & Dougie Marillier (Zim)	2001-2002
7th	73	Alok Kapali & Enamul Haque (Ban)	2002-2003 v West Indies
8th	99	Yousuf Youhana & Saqlain Mushtaq (Pak)	2001-2002
9th	36	Khaled Mashud & Manjural Islam (Ban)	2002-2003 v West Indies
10th	34	Khaled Mashud & Mohammed Sharif (Ban)	2001-2002 v Zimbabwe

Results at Chittagong Stadium

Date	Countries	Result
15/11/2001	v Zimbabwe	lost by 8 wickets
16/01/2002	v Pakistan	lost by an innings and 169 runs
16/12/2002	v West Indies	lost by 7 wickets
24/04/2003	v South Africa	lost by an innings and 60 runs
29/10/2003	v England	lost by 329 runs

bangabandhu

photo by Peter Garod

Right in the heart of Dhaka, this is an unusual cricket ground with shops and offices around its exterior beneath the massive stands. The stadium has a remarkable history, having hosted Pakistan's first Test match in 1955 and Bangladesh's first in 45 years later. Seven of Pakistan's home Tests were held at the ground until Bangladesh gained its independence in 1971. Originally the venue was named Dacca Stadium and then the National Stadium, before its present name in honour of Bangabandhu Sheikh Mujibur Rahman, the Father of the Nation.

The stadium's inaugural Test was the first of a five match series between Pakistan and India whch ended 0-0 after five draws. The next Test, against New Zealand, was also a draw.

The ground also hosted the first Test of the 1959 Test series between Pakistan and Australia. Put into bat by their opponents, the home side scored 200, Hanif Mohammad top scoring with 66 as Alan Davidson, 4/24 and Richie Benaud, 4/69 took the wickets. The visitors replied with 225, Neil Harvey scoring 96 and Wally Grout, 66no. Fazal Mahmood took 5/71 for Pakistan. The home side could only manage 134 in their second innings as Ken Mackay, 6/42 and Benaud, 4/42 ran through their line up. Set 110 to win, Australia reached their target with eight wickets to spare. Pakistan's last three home matches at the stadium ended in draws, a high scoring affair against England in 1962 and two tame draws in 1969 against England and New Zealand.

In 1999, due to trouble in Pakistan, the stadium hosted an Asian Championship Test between Pakistan and Sri Lanka. Pakistan won the game by an innings and 175 runs, as Ijaz Ahmed, 211 and Inzamam-ul-Haq, 200, scored double centuries in a one-sided affair.

Bangladesh's inaugural Test against India was played at the stadium in 2000 and although the home side reached a creditable 400 with Aminul Islam becoming the first Bangladeshi player to score a Test century, hiting 145, India went on to win. They scored 429 in their first innings and then skittled out Bangladesh for

91.India reached their target for the loss of only one wicket.

The first Test of a two match series against Zimbabwe in 2001 resulted in a draw. Unfortunately, Bangladesh were on the receiving end of some big defeats at the ground after this. Pakistan beat them by an innings and 178 runs in 2002, the West Indies, by an innings and 310 runs also in 2002, when Jermaine Lawson ripped the Bangladesh side apart, reducing them from 80/3 to 87 all out in a spell of 6.5 overs, 4 maidens, 6 wickets for 3 runs, and by South Africa in 2003 by an innings and 18 runs. The home side put up a better performance against England in the first Test of a series in 2003. Having won the toss, Bangladesh made 203, Khaled Mashud contributing 51 and Steve Harmison taking 5/35 for England. The visitors made 295 in their first innings, Marcus Trescothick hitting 113 and Graham Thorpe, 64. Trailing by 92 runs, Bangladesh made 255 in their second innings, Hannan Sarkar and Habibul Bashar both scoring half centuries as Harmison, 4/44 and Matthew Hoggard, 4/48 took the wickets. It was not enough and England reached their target of 164 with seven wickets to spare thanks to a fine 81no by Michael Vaughan.

The stadium has a capacity of 55,000 and is located in the centre of Dhaka. Its three-tier pavilion is a modern building which houses the players' changing rooms, the members' enclosure and corporate hospitality suites. The rest of the stadium has two-tier enclosures with the top tier partially covered. Most visiting supporters sit in the International enclosure directly opposite the pavilion. A large fence encircles the playing area. Food is available underneath the stands and vendors move through the crowd selling various foods and soft drinks. The toilet facilities are sparse, but generally acceptable.

Tickets are available through branches of the Prime Bank and the State Janata Bank which are located throughout Dhaka. Prices range from Tk 20 for the cheapest seat to T 2000 for a five-day pass in the International enclosure. Security is tight and all bags are searched upon entering the ground. Glass bottles are not allowed in the stadium. The ground is within walking distance of many of the central hotels. Auto-rickshaws and taxis are always available for those supporters staying in Gulshan and other suburbs of the city. Plenty of time should be allowed for even the shortest journeys by road, as the traffic in the centre of Dhaka is horrendous.

the city

Dhaka, formerly Dacca, is the capital of Bangladesh and is situated on the Dahaleswari River in the Ganges Brahmaputra Delta in the centre of the country. It is surrounded by rivers, the Tongi Kahl to the north, the Buriganga to the south, the Shitalakhya to the east and the Turag to the west. Historically known as the "city of mosques and muslin", it is a huge vibrant place with a blend of old and new. But it suffers from air pollution and chronic traffic congestion. The old section is a maze of bazaars and alleyways whereas the new section, Ramna, is modern and well laid-out, housing the business area, government offices and educational institutions.. The name originated from the Dhakesshwari Temple, built by Raja Ballal Sen in the 9th century in the ancient town of Bengalla. The Romanised spelling was changed from Dacca to Dhaka in 1982.

Dhaka was part of the Buddhist Kingdom of Kamrup during the 7th and 8th centuries until it was taken over by the Sena Kings of Vikrampur at the end of the 8th century. It remained in their control until the Turks captured it in 1298. The Pathans and the rulers of Sonargaon invaded before the city became the Mughal capital of Bengal Province in 1608 under Islam Khan, the first Mughal Viceroy of Bengal. The city grew in importance during the Mughal reign and became one of the biggest trading centres in South East Asia. It suffered a setback when the capital was moved to Murshidabad in 1704, however the trading centre continued to thrive with the arrival of the Portuguese, British, French and Dutch until the East India Company took control of the city in 1764. Hard times followed with not only famines and floods to contend with but also the growth of the neighbouring port of Calcutta, which, as the capital of British India, was preferred by the British.

The city began to thrive again when power was transferred from the East India Company to the Crown in 1858. In 1911 the city became capital of East Bengal and remained so until the Partition of British India in 1947 when it became the capital of the Pakistan Capital Province of East Bengal and later in 1956 capital of East Pakistan. After the war of independence in 1971 Dhaka became the capital of the new republic, Bangladesh. The leader of the uprising, Sheikh Mujibur Rahman became the first head of state. He was later assassinated and the country has suffered from political instability with states of emergencies, assassinations and military coups.

Dhaka has a strong Muslim influence with more than 750 mosques. The Shaat Gombuj on the banks of the Buriganga River is known for its wonderful domes and the Tara Masjid on Islampur Road for its extravagant mosaics. The Hussain Dalan mosque is also worth visiting.

Zia International Airport is a modern airport 20km to the north of Dhaka. Taxis are available outside the arrivals hall. Unfortunately, the city's traffic is so heavy the journey can take up to two hours to the centre and should cost approximately Tk 400. Parjatan, the national tourist authority, runs coaches to and from the city every hour from 08.00-22.00. Local buses also run to the city but can become ridiculously overcrowded. Auto rickshaws are not allowed to pick up at the airport. Facilities at the airport include restaurants, banks and a post office. The domestic terminal for flights to Chittagong is within walking distance.

arrival

photo by Peter Garod

Lalbagh Fort

Built in 1678 AD by Prince Mohammad Azam, son of Aurangazeb, the Mughal emperor, the fort lies on the banks of the Buriganga River. It was used in the unsuccessful first war of independence against the British in 1857. Outstanding monuments in the fort include the three-domed mosque, the tomb of Pari Bibi, daughter of Nawab Shaista Khan and the Audience Hall.

The Central Shahid Minar

A monument which has become a place of pilgrimage for all Bangladeshi people. It was built in honour of the martyrs who died for the Language Movement on 21 February 1952. The Movement was part of the nationalist struggle of the people of Bangladesh and demanded that Bangla become the first language of their state.

National Memorial

Situated 35km from the city centre in the suburb of Savar, it was designed by Moinul Hossein and is dedicated to the memory of those who lost their lives during the 1971 war of liberation.

Suhrawardy Uddyan

A wonderful garden in the city centre. Formerly known as the Race Course, it is where Bangabandhu Sheikh Mujibur Rahman, the Father of the Nation, called for the independence for Bangladesh in March 1971. It was also the scene of the surrender of the occupying forces in December the same year.

Ahsan Manzil Museum

Set in magnificent gardens and originally the home of the Nawab of Dhaka. This beautiful pink palace situated on the banks of the river Buriganga has over 20 galleries exhibiting portraits, furniture and other historical items.

Climate

	ave temp	rain cm
January	20	6
February	22	13
March	26	37
April	28	109
May	29	166
June	28	614
July	28	818
August	28	550
September	28	244
October	26	200
November	24	22
December	21	16

Dhaka Sheraton Hotel

1 Minto Road
Tel: 02 861 1191
Fax: 02 831 2915
One of Dhaka's finest. Situated 3km from the centre of the city, it has 233 superb rooms with cable TV, mini bar and kitchenette. Three restaurants, a number of cafés and a bar.

The Pan Pacific Sonargaon

107 Kazi Nazrul Islam Ave.
Tel: 02 811 1005
Fax: 02 813 324
Central. Five star, with 279 well appointed rooms, 25 beautiful suites and excellent facilities including a health and leisure club. Number of restaurants, lounges and bars.

Hotel Lake Castle

House No. 1A Road 68A
Gulshan 2
Tel: 02 881 2812
Fax: 02 881 4137
htllake@agni.com
Tasteful with excellent rooms 25 minutes drive from the stadium, the hotel is close to the Australian High Commission and the American Club.

Hotel de Crystal Garden

House No. 28, Road No. 63
Gulshan
Tel: 02 882 3147
Fax: 02 882 7076
degarden@citechco.net
Fine hotel with luxurious rooms. Excellent restaurant and good health and leisure facilities.

The White House Hotel

155 Shantinagar Road
Tel: 02 813 4601
Fax: 02 813 7720
Middle of the range. Good rooms with cable TV. Business centre and a restaurant.

Hotel Pacific

120B Motijheel Commercial Area
Tel: 02 956 7583
Fax: 02 956 5162
wafaltd@citechco.net

Excellent budget hotel within walking distance of the Bangabandhu National Stadium. Very comfortable en suite rooms and a fine restaurant. Highly recommended.

Hotel Ramna

45 Bangabandhu Ave.
Tel: 02 956 2279
Good standard budget accommodation at very low prices close to the stadium. Restaurant, bar.

Hotel Midway International

30 Inner Circular Road
Tel: 02 831 5360
Fax: 02 831 6935
Budget hotel within a mile of the stadium.

Restaurants

Most of the top hotels have very good restaurants offering local and international cuisine. Others include

Nightingale Restaurant

35 inner Circular Road
Excellent Chinese restaurant in the centre.

Saffron

Kemal Ataturk Ave.
Gulshan
Leading Indian restaurant.

Hotel Ramna

45 Bangabandhu Ave.
Tel: 02 956 2279
Good restaurant on the seventh floor serving local cuisine.

Café Baghdad

20 Topkhana Road
Small café serving kebabs at very reasonable prices.

Nightlife

Most of the larger hotels have their own bars and are most popular with cricket supporters. The Bagha Club (British) and the Australian Club, both in Gulshan are also very popular.

transport

Airlines

Biman Bangladesh Airlines
Balaka Bhaban
Kurmitola
Tel: 02 891 7400
Fax: 02 891 3005
dmsbiman@bdbiman.com

British Airways
First Floor
Star Centre
Block SE© Road 138
Gulshan 1
Tel: 02 881 5111
Fax: 02 881 5346

Emirates
116 Gulshan Ave.
Tel: 02 956 3825
988 4900
shaheda.muid@emirates.com

Indian Airlines
Sena Kalyan Bhaban
195 Motijheel
Tel: 02 955 5915
Fax: 02 956 9027
ialdhaka@connectbd.com

GMG Airlines
ABC House
8 Kernal Ataturk Ave.
Banani
Tel: 02 881 3246
Fax: 02 882 6115
gmgair@gmggroup.com
GMG Airlines is a domestic airline that flies between Dhaka and
Chittagong. Although slightly more
expense than Biman, the service and
comfort provided make it a pleasant
alternative.

Buses

Buses in Dhaka are always overcrowded and are not recommended. Traffic
congestion is a huge problem and the
buses take an eternity to reach their
destination.

Trains

Kamalapur railway station in
Motijheel is Dhaka's main train sta-
tion. Trains run between Dhaka and
Chittagong three times a day and
take between six and seven hours.
Enquiries 02 831 5857.

Taxis

As buses are so overcrowded, taxis and
auto rickshaws are the best forms of
transport in Dhaka. The traffic is very
bad and ample time should be given
for even the shortest of journeys.

Anudip Autos Ltd	912 5138
Cab Express	934 8401
Capital Cab Company	935 2847
Cosmo Cabs	812 7191
Kool Cabs	813 0485
Navana Taxi Cabs	955 2212
Orion Taxi Cabs	934 7277

Car Hire

Bangaldesh Parjatan Corporation
233 Airport Road
Tejgaon
Tel: 02 914 0790
812 6501
bpcho@bnagla.net

Dhaka Tours Rent-A-Car Association
Shahbag
Tel: 02 966 3134
Fax: 02 861 1313

Hertz International
House 6 Road 9
Banani
Tel: 02 988 4311
Fax: 02 988 1290
hertz@bangla.net

Harney's Rent-A-Car
Tower Hamlet
16 Kernal Ataturk Ave.
Banani
Tel: 02 881 3021
Fax: 02 881 0399
hbe@bdcom.com

Post Office

General Post Office
Abdul Gani Road
Tel: 02 955 5533
Open 09.30-20.00 daily except Fridays.

Tourist Information

National Tourism Organisation
233 Airport Road
Tejgaon
Tel: 02 811 7855
Fax: 02 811 7235
bpcho@bangla.net
www.parjatan.org

Hospital

Dhaka General Hospital
Swamibagh
Tel: 02 235 351

Dhaka National Hospital
Dhanmondi
Tel: 02 812 2588

Emergency Numbers

Dhaka Metropolitan Police
Emergency   999
Control Room   861 6552

Win/Loss Record

Country	Played	won	drawn	Lost	Tie
South Africa	1	1	-	-	-
Australia	1	1	-	-	-
India	2	1	1	-	-
England	3	1	2	-	-
Pakistan	9	3	5	1	-
Zimbabwe	1	-	1	-	-
New Zealand	2	-	2	-	-
West Indies	2	1	-	1	-
Bangladesh	6	-	1	5	-
Sri Lanka	1	-	-	1	-

Highest Individual Aggregates (Bangladesh unless stated)

Player	Mat	Inn	NO	Runs	Ave	HS	50	100
Hanif Mohammad (Pak)	5	9	0	474	52.67	111	1	3
Habibul Bashar	6	12	0	372	31.00	71	4	0
Inzamam-ul-Haq (Pak)	2	2	1	243	243.00	200*	0	1
Aminul Islam	4	8	1	222	31.71	145	0	1
Saeed Ahmed (Pak)	4	8	0	214	26.75	69	1	0
Ijaz Ahmed (Pak)	1	1	0	211	211.00	211	0	1
Javed Burki (Pak)	2	4	1	179	59.67	140	0	1
Mark Burgess (NZ)	1	2	1	178	178.00	119*	1	1
Geoff Pullar (Eng)	1	2	1	173	173.00	165	0	1
Asif Iqbal (Pak)	2	4	0	168	42.00	92	1	0

Top Wicket Takers (Bangladesh unless stated)

Player	Mat	Bll	Md	Runs	Wkt	Ave	BB	S/R
Fazal Mahmood (Pak)	4	1053	74	321	22	14.59	6/34	47.86
Mohammad Rafique	3	835	28	338	14	24.14	6/77	59.64
Khan Mohammad (Pak)	2	511	42	101	14	7.21	6/21	36.50
Intikhab Alam (Pak)	3	838	46	325	11	29.55	5/91	76.18
Mahmood Hussain (Pak)	2	383	10	157	11	14.27	6/67	34.82
Pervez Sajjad (Pak)	2	732	41	202	10	20.20	4/60	73.20
Steve Harmison (Eng)	1	281	17	79	9	8.78	5/35	31.22
Danish Kaneria (Pak)	1	232	9	113	9	12.56	7/77	25.78
Mashrafe Mortaza	3	516	19	246	9	27.33	4/106	57.33
Enamul Haque	3	772	35	311	8	38.88	4/136	96.50

Highest Individual Scores (Bangladesh unless stated)

211	Ijaz Ahmed (Pak)	v Sri Lanka 1998-99
200*	Inzamam-ul-Haq (Pak)	v Sri Lanka 1998-99
165	Geoff Pullar (Eng)	v Pakistan 1961-62
145	Aminul Islam	v India 2000-01
140	Javed Burki (Pak)	v England 1961-62

134	Abdul Razzaq (Pak)	v Bangladesh 2001-02
119*	Mark Burgess (NZ)	v Pakistan 1969-70
119	Ramnaresh Sarwan (WI)	v Bangladesh 2002-03
114*	Basil D'Oliveira (Eng)	v Pakistan 1968-69
113	Marcus Trescothick (Eng)	v Bangladesh 2003-04

Best Individual Bowling Performances (Bangladesh unless stated)

19.4-4-77-7	Danish Kaneria (Pak)	2001-02
6.5-4-3-6	Jermaine Lawson (WI)	2002-03
16.2-6-21-6	Khan Mohammad (Pak)	v New Zealand 1955-56
18.3-9-34-6	Fazal Mahmood (Pak)	v West Indies 1958-59
45-27-42-6	Ken Mackay (Aus)	v Pakistan 1959-60
16.2-2-55-6	Waqar Younis (Pak)	2001-02
27-10-66-6	Fazal Mahmood (Pak)	v West Indies 1958-59
27-6-67-6	Mahmood Hussain (Pak)	v India 1954-55
37.2-7-77-6	Mohammad Rafique	v South Africa 2003
44.3-9-132-6	Naimur Rahman	v India 2000-01

Highest Partnerships

Wkt	Runs	Batsmen	Match
1st	198	Geoff Pullar & Bob Barber (Eng)	1961-1962 v Pakistan
2nd	147	Geoff Pullar & Ken Barrington (Eng)	1961-1962 v Pakistan
3rd	366	Ijaz Ahmed & Inzamam-Ul-Haq (Pak)	1998-1999 v Sri Lanka
4th	176	Ramnaresh Sarwan & Marlon Samuels (WI)	2002-2003 v Bangladesh
5th	107	Jacques Rudolph & Mark Boucher (SA)	2002-2003 v Bangladesh
6th	175	Abdul Razzaq & Rashid Latif (Pak)	2001-2002 v Bangladesh
7th	121	Sourav Ganguly & Sunil Joshi (Ind)	1998-1999 v Sri Lanka
		Sourav Ganguly & Sunil Joshi (Ind)	2000-2001 v Bangladesh
8th	108	Heath Streak & Travis Friend (Zim)	2001-2002 v Bangladesh
9th	96	Mark Burgess & Bob Cunis (NZ)	1969-1970 v Pakistan
10th	73	Hashan Tillakaratne & Sajeewa de Silva (SL)	1998-1999 v Pakistan

Results at Bangabandhu Stadium

Date	Countries	Result
01/01/1955	Pakistan v India	drawn
07/11/1955	Pakistan v New Zealand	drawn
06/03/1959	Pakistan v West Indies	won by 41 runs
13/11/1959	Pakistan v Australia	lost by 8 wickets
19/01/1962	Pakistan v England	drawn
28/02/1969	Pakistan v England	drawn
08/11/1969	Pakistan v New Zealand	drawn
12/03/1999	Sri Lanka v Pakistan	Pakistan won by an innings and 175 runs
10/11/2000	Bangladesh v India	lost by 9 wickets
08/11/2001	Bangladesh v Zimbabwe	drawn
09/01/2002	Bangladesh v Pakistan	lost by an innings and 178 runs
08/12/2002	Bangladesh v West Indies	lost by an innings and 310 runs
01/05/2003	Bangladesh v South Africa	lost by an innings and 18 runs
21/10/2003	Bangladesh v England	lost by 7 wickets

SCOTLAND

Chester-le-Street

Leeds
(Headingley)

Manchester
(Old Trafford)

Nottingham
(Trent Bridge)

Birmingham
(Edgbaston)

ENGLAND

WALES

London
(Lord's, The Oval)

The Oval in London was the first ground in England to host a Test, staging England v Australia, the fourth ever Test match on 6 September 1880. Only the MCG in Melbourne has a longer Test history. England won the one-off match by five wickets. Manchester's Old Trafford was the second English Test venue, holding the first match of the three-match series between the two countries in 1884. The match ended in a draw. Lord's hosted the second Test of the series with England winning by an innings and five runs.

Trent Bridge in Nottingham became the fourth Test venue in England when five years later on 1 June England played Australia in the first Test of a five match series. Headingley Cricket Ground in Leeds was next, staging the third Test of the series four weeks later. The Edgbaston Cricket Ground in Birmingham was the next ground to be used for Test cricket, in May 1902 when it hosted the first match of the Ashes series. Bramall Lane, Sheffield, was used for the third match of this series in July but was the ground's only Test. It was more than one hundred years before England used another ground, The Riverside hosting the second Test of the series against Zimbabwe in June 2003.

Distance Between Cities (in km)

	Birmingham	C-le-Street	Leeds	London	Manchester	Nottingham
Birmingham		316	193	192	142	86
Chester-le-Street	316		129	436	206	236
Leeds	193	129		318	70	116
London	192	436	318		326	209
Manchester	142	206	70	326		112
Nottingham	86	236	116	209	112	

Airlines

The United Kingdom's national airline is British Airways. London, Birmingham, Manchester, Leeds and Nottingham all have airports and Chester-le-Street is less than 32km from Newcastle airport. Enquiries 0870 850 4850 or www.ba.com

British Airways	0845 773 3377
British Midland	0870 607 0555
Ryanair	ryanair.com
Easyjet	easyjet.com

Buses

National Express operates nationwide coach services. Daily services run between all Test cities. Travelling by coach is certainly cheaper than flying or travelling by train. Enquiries 08705 80 80 80 or www.nationalexpress.com

Trains

A consortium of service providers operates services to and from all of the Test venues. Travelling by train is expensive and visitors should try and pre-book tickets at least 14 days in advance to take advantage of reduced fares. A BritRail pass is available to non-British residents. The pass must be purchased in the country of origin. Enquiries 08457 48 49 50. InterRail passes, the European rail pass are valid in the UK.

Car Hire

Car hire is available from Avis, Budget, Hertz and Thrifty at most airports and cities in the UK.

Taxis

Taxis are available throughout each of the cities, outside airports, hotels and at taxi ranks.

Banks

Opening times at most banks are Monday to Thursday 09.00-15.30 and Friday 09.00-14.30. Most banks have foreign exchange facilities and accept travellers cheques in major currencies. Commission is charged for this service. ATM facilities are wide-spread. All major credit cards are accepted.

The UK uses the Sterling Pound (£). Notes are issued in denominations £50, 20, 10 and 5 and coins in denominations of £2, 1 and 50, 20, 10 and 5 pence.

Telecoms

International Direct Dialling is available throughout the UK. Public pay-phones are widespread and accept coins and phone cards which are available in newsagents. The UK's dialling code is 44. The outgoing international code is 00.

Post

Post office opening times throughout the UK are 09.00-17.30 Monday to Friday and 09.00-12.30 on Saturday. The main post offices in each city have extended hours.

Tourist Offices

All major cities and airports have Tourist Information Centres.
Britain and London Visitor Centre
1 Regent Street
Piccadilly Circus
London SW1Y 4XT
Tel: 0870 608 2000
Open Monday 09.30-18.30, Tuesday -Friday 09.00-18.30, Saturday and Sunday 10.00-16.00

Emergency Numbers

Police   999
Ambulance   999
Fire   999

Embassies/Consulates

Australian High Commission
Australia House
The Strand
London
WC2B 4LA
Tel: 0207 379 4334
Fax: 0207 240 5333
www.australia.org.uk

High Commission for the People's
Republic of Bangladesh
28 Queen's Gate
London
SW7 5JA
Tel: 0207 584 0081
Fax: 0207 581 7477
www.bangladeshhighcommission.org.uk

Office of the High Commissioner for
India
India House
Aldwych
London
WC2B 4NA
Tel: 0207 836 8484
Fax: 0207 836 4331
www.hcilondon.net

New Zealand High Commission
New Zealand House
80 Haymarket
London
SW1Y 4TQ
  0207 930 8422
  0207 839 4580
nzembassy@newzealandhc.org.uk

High Commission for the Islamic
Republic of Pakistan
34- 36 Lowndes Square
London
SW1X 9JN
Tel: 0207 664 9200
Fax: 0207 664 9224
www.pakmission-uk.gov.uk

South African High Commission
South Africa House
Trafalgar Square
London
WC2N 5DP
Tel: 0207 451 7299
Fax: 0207 451 7283

High Commission of Sri Lanka
13 Hyde Park Gardens
London
W2 2LU
Tel: 0207 262 1841
Fax: 0207 262 7970
www.slhe.globalnet.co.uk

High Commission for the Republic of
Zimbabwe
Zimbabwe House
429 The Strand
London
WC2R 0JR
Tel: 0207 836 7755
Fax: 0207 379 1167
zimlondon@callnetuk.com

Visas

With the exception of nationals of EU countries all visitors to Britain must carry a valid passport. Tourist visas are required and should be applied for at the consular section of the British High Commission in the country of origin. Applicants must complete application form and have two passport photographs. The fee varies from country to country. Applications take upto five working days.

Customs

Visitors over the age of 18 may take the following goods into Britain without incurring customs duty.
200 cigarettes or 50 cigars
1 litre of alcohol
50g of perfume

Time Difference

The UK is on Greenwich Mean Time.

Electricity

240 volts AC at 50 cycles per second. Most hotels have adaptors.

Departure Tax

There is none

birmingham

edgbaston

Edgbaston, which became the fifth Test venue in England in 1902 when it hosted the first Test of a series against Australia, is the home of Warwickshire County Cricket Club and is situated in the south of Birmingham.
In that initial rain-affected Test the home side won the toss and, scoring 376/9 before declaring. Johnny Tyldesley led the way with 138, and England were also helped by a fine unbroken 10th wicket partnership of 81 between Bill Lockwood, 52no, and Wilfred Rhodes, 38no. Australia managed only 36 in reply, their lowest ever Test score, as Rhodes took 7/17 and George Hirst, 3/15.

Forced to follow-on, Australia reached 46/2 before time ran out and the match ended in a draw.

The first Test of the 1924 series against South Africa saw an even lower first innings total. Having lost the toss, England were put in but scored 438 before dismissing the visitors for 30 in only 12.3 overs, South Africa's lowest ever Test score. Arthur Gilligan, 6/7 and Maurice Tate, 4/12 did the damage. Tate became only the fifth bowler to take a wicket with his first ball in Test cricket when he dismissed Fred Susskind – a feat only seven more bowlers have managed. Forced to follow-on, South Africa performed much better. But, despite 120 from Bob Catterall, they were dismissed for 390 to lose by an innings and 18 runs. Gilligan, 5/83 and Tate, 4/103 were again the wicket takers.

After a draw against South Africa in 1929 Edgbaston had to wait until 1957 before hosting another Test but what a match. England managed only 186 as Sonny Ramadhin took 7/49 for the West Indies. In reply the West Indies, inspired by Collie Smith, 161, and Clyde Walcott, 90, scored 474 to leave England trailing by 288 runs. The home side got right back into the game with a massive 583/4 dec., thanks to 285no by Peter May and 154 by Colin Cowdrey. Set a target of 295 in 60 overs, the West Indies struggled against the bowling of Jim Laker and Tony Lock and crawled to 72/7 at the close to draw the game. Laker ended the innings with the remarkable figures of 24 overs, 20 maidens, two wickets for 13 runs and Lock 27 overs, 19 maidens, three wickets for 31 runs.

England had a superb victory over India in Edgbaston in 1974 in third and final Test. India scrambled to a modest 165 with Mike Hendrick taking 4/28. The home side, with David Lloyd hitting an unbeaten 214 on debut, reached an impressive 459/2 dec. There were other fine contributions from Mike Denness, 100 and Dennis Amiss, 79. Trailing by 294, India could only manage 216 as England won by an innings and 78 runs to clinch the series..

A year later the Australians beat England by an innings and 85 runs in the first Test of the Ashes series, a game noted for a pair for Graham Gooch on his Test debut. Dennis Lillee and Max Walker took five each in the first innings, Lillee getting Gooch, while Jeff Thomson grabbed five in the second innings, including Gooch. It was England captain Mike Denness's last Test.

The fourth Test in the 1981 Ashes series was eagerly awaited after England's sensational win in the third Test at Headingley to level the series. England made a disappointing 189, as Terry Alderman took 5/42. In reply Australia scored 258, a lead of 69. John Emburey took four wickets for England to keep them in the match. He also top scored in England's second innings with 37no and enabled them to reach 219 after they had collapsed to 115/6. Ray Bright was the pick of the Australian bowlers with 5/68. Set a modest target of 151, Australia reached 105/4 before Ian Botham, the hero of the third Test, took five wickets for one run to reduce them to 121 and hand England victory by 29 runs. Botham's second innings figures read 14-9-11-5. No batsman reached 50 in the match. England had turned a 1-0 deficit into a 2-1 lead which they extended to 3-1 at Old Trafford to win the series.

The fifth Test of the 1985 Ashes series was another excellent match. With the series level at 1-1, England won the toss and invited Australia to bat. They scored 335, Kepler Wessels top scoring with 83 and Richard Ellison taking 6/77. The home side's reply was a superb 595/5 dec. David Gower hit a masterful 215, while Tim Robinson, 148, and Mike Gatting, 100, also hit centuries. Trailing by 260, Australia could muster only 142 to lose by an innings and 118 runs. Ellison took 4/27 and Ian Botham, 3/52.

The third Test of the six match series against the West Indies in 1995 was staged at Edgbaston. The series was level at one match apiece. England scored a paltry 147 as Courtney Walsh and Ian Bishop took three wickets each The visitors replied with 300, Sherwin Campbell hitting 79 and Richie Richardson, 69. Facing a deficit of 153, England collapsed to 89 all out in their second innings to lose by an innings and 64 runs. Walsh, 5/45 and Bishop, 4/29 were the match winners for the West Indies.

The first Test of the 1997 Ashes series started with a thrilling morning's cricket. Australia were reduced to 54/8 as Andy Caddick, 5/50 and Darren Gough, 3/43 ripped their batting order apart. Shane Warne hit a brisk 47 to push the Australians first innings total to 118. England replied with 478/9dec., 360 ahead. Nasser Hussain top scored with 207 and Graham Thorpe, 138, also scored a century. Mark Taylor, 129 and Greg Blewett, 125 helped Australia to 477. Set a target of 118, England, despite losing Mark Butcher for 14, coasted home with nine wickets to spare as Michael Atherton finished up on 57no and Alec Stewart on 40no.

The highest team score is 633/5 declared by England against India in 1979, the lowest the 30 by South Africa. The highest run chase is 211/3 by England against New Zealand in 1999.

The ground is on the corner of Pershore Road and Edgbaston Road in the suburb of Edgbaston to the south of Birmingham city centre. It is a well designed stadium surrounding by tall trees. The pavilion, at the southern end, is a modest building with limited seating. To the left of the pavilion are the Leslie Deakin Stand, a two tier structure, its top uncovered, its lower tier partially covered and the William Ansell Stand, both part of the members' area. On the west side of the ground are the open Priory and Raglan Stands with the Aylesford Executive boxes on the highest level.

The R. E. S. Wyatt stand is at the north end of the ground as is one of the most famous scoreboards in Test cricket. Also at the north end is the Press Box Stand. The Stanley Barnes and the Eric Holles Stand are on the east side of the ground. The R. V. Ryder Stand in the south east corner is also part of the members' area.

The Dollery Restaurant and Bar in the pavilion are exclusively for members and their guests. There are food villages at both ends of the ground with stalls and bars all around the ground. The R. E. S. Wyatt Stand has quite a pleasant non-members bar. There are two designated wheelchair viewing areas in the front of the R. V. Ryder Stand and the Stanley Barnes Stand. Lift access is available to the restaurant and bar in the pavilion. First-Aid is available in the Old Cricket School and behind the Stanley Barnes Stand.

Tickets can be purchased by post or in person from the Ticket Office at Warwickshire County Cricket Club, County Ground, Edgbaston, Birmingham B5 7QU which is open from 09.30-16.30 Monday to Friday and 10.00-13.00 Saturday. The ticket office telephone number is 0121 446 5506 and facsimile 0121 440 7516. Tickets can also be ordered online on tickets@thebears.co.uk Ticket are also available on the ECB Ticketline 08705 338 833.

Official car parks within a ten minute walk of the ground are clearly signposted on all approach roads. Birmingham New Street train station is less than two miles away and taxis should cost around £5. Buses no's 45 and 47 run from the centre of Birmingham to Edgbaston.

Birmingham International Airport is 12km to the south east of the city. Taxis are available outside the Arrival Hall and a journey should take about 20 minutes and cost no more than £16. The main terminal is linked to Birmingham International Station which is a 10 minute journey from Birmingham New Street with Intercity (08457 48 49 50). An Airbus service every 30 minutes between 05.00-21.00 links the airport with the city (0870 606 2608) and local bus no. 900 runs in between the city and airport every 20 minutes.

Facilities at the airport include banks, ATM's, bureaux de change, restaurants, cafés, bars, medical centre, view gallery. Car hire is available from Avis (0121 782 6183), Budget (0800 181 181), Europcar (0121 782 6507) and Hertz (0121 782 5158).

Birmingham is England's second largest city with a population of 1.1 million. Situated in the West Midlands it is considered to be the geographical centre of the country.

It has a manufacturing background and is a main industrial hub, but today it has also become an important financial and business centre. Its location has helped it become the conference and exhibition capital of the United Kingdom.. Birmingham has some fine tourist attractions. The city's Museum and Art Gallery in Chamberlain Square and the Museum of Science and Industry are both absorbing places to visit. The city has some magnificent religious buildings, including St. Philip's Cathedral and the 13th century St. Martin's Church, one of its oldest churches.

The city also has some splendid parks including Cannon Hill Park and King's Heath Park and, believe it or not, more canals than Venice.

Birmingham's climate is typically English, like the rest of England's is temperate with warm wet summers and cold winters. Temperatures average between 10 and 20 degrees during the summer months. Unfortunately the city does get its fair share of rain even during the summer.

Edgbaston, the suburb after which the cricket ground is named, has plenty of hotels and guesthouses to accommodate visiting cricket supporters but does not have many bars or restaurants. However the centre of Birmingham some two miles away has excellent restaurants especially at the recently developed Brindley Place at the Water's Edge that has continental style restaurants and bars and along the Balti Mile, which has scores of Pakistani and Kashmiri restaurants. Broad Street and Bennett's Hill have some fine pubs and bars for night-time entertainment.

Royal Shakespeare Company

One of Britain's national theatre companies and based in Shakespeare's birthplace of Stratford-upon-Avon. The RSC perform throughout the year with both matinee and evening performances in its three theatres. Many of the buildings frequented by Shakespeare are open to visitors. For enquiries contact 01789 403 404 or info@rsc.org.uk

Birmingham Botanical Gardens

Designed by J C Loudon in 1832 and situated close to the centre. A place to relax, walk and enjoy 15 acres of parkland. See the Historic Gardens with Roman, Tudor and Medieval designs, the Herb Garden with culinary and medicinal herbs, the British Wetlands Habitat, the Rhododendron Walk and the National Bonsai Collection. There is a tea room serving light lunches and afternoon teas, a gift shop and an art gallery. The Gardens are on Westbourne Road near Edgbaston and Bus no's 10, 21, 22, 23, 29 and 103 stop near the entrance. Open 09.00-dusk each day. For enquiries contact 0121 454 1860 or www.birminghambotanicalgardens.org.uk

Birmingham Cathedral

Built in 1725 by Thomas Archer with four famous pre-Raphaelite stained-glass windows by Sir Edward Burne-Jones. Open all year round 08.00-18.00 Monday to Friday and 09.00-16.00 on weekends. For enquiries contact 0121 262 1840 or enquiries@birminghamcathedral.com

Cadbury World

Devoted to chocolate. It traces the history of it, and of the Cadbury family. Near Bournville railway station which is connected to Birmingham New Street. For all enquiries contact 0121 451 4159 or cadbury-world@csplc.com

The National Sea Life Centre

An excellent display of underwater life in a one million litre tank. It is located in Brindley Place in the heart of Birmingham and is home to sharks, giant turtles and tropical reef fish. Open 10.00-17.00 seven days a week. quiries 0121 633 4700 or www.sealifeeurope.com

Copthorne Hotel
Paradise Circus
B3 3HJ
Tel: 0121 200 2727
One of Birmingham's best. 212 well
appointed en suite rooms with cable
TV. Restaurant and bar.

Jurys Inn
245 Broad Street
B1 2HO
Tel: 0121 626 0626
Fax: 0121 698 7840
jurysinn_Birmingham@jurydoyle.com
Central with 415 en suite rooms with
cable TV. Restaurant and bar.

City Inn
1 Brunswick Square
Brindley Place
B1 2HW
Tel: 0121 643 1003
Fax: 0121 643 1005
Birmingham.resvations@cityinn.com
Very popular central hotel. 238 en suite
rooms with cable TV.

Woodlands Hotel
379 Hagley Road
B17 8DL
Tel: 0121 420 2341
Fax: 0121 429 3935
hotel@woodlands2000@freeserve.co.uk
Very popular with cricket fans. 20 en
suite rooms, restaurant and bar.

Westbourne Lodge Hotel
27 Fountain Road
B17 8NJ
Tel: 0121 429 1003
Fax: 0121 429 7436
info@westbournelodge.co.uk
Very comfortable small hotel near the
ground.

Hagley Court Hotel
229 Hagley Road
Edgbaston
B16 9RP
Tel: 0121 454 6514
Fax: 0121 456 2722
reception@hagleycourt.com
26 well appointed rooms. Near the
ground. Restaurant and bar.

Thistle Hotel
Hagley Road
B16 9RY
Tel: 0121 455 9777
Fax: 0121 454 9432
Part of the nationwide chain, offering
151 comfortable rooms, all en suite
with cable TV. Restaurant and bar.

Beechwood Hotel
201 Bristol Road
B5 7UB
Tel: 0121 440 2133
Fax: 0121 446 4549
Affordable hotel close to the ground.
Excellent restaurant and bar.

Smithys Hotel
415 Hagley Road
B17 8BL
Tel: 0121 420 1123
sales@smithysbirmingham.co.uk
Close to ground. 34 rooms, some en
suite with cable TV. Restaurant and bar.

Comfort Inn, Norfolk Hotel
257 Hagley Road
B16 9NA
Tel: 0121 454 8071
Fax: 0121 455 6149
Very close to ground. 166 en suite
rooms with cable TV, some very rea-
sonably priced.

The Quality Hotel
166 Hagley Road
B16 9NZ
Tel: 0121 4546621
Fax: 0121 456293
Near the ground and popular with
cricket fans. It has 213 en suite rooms,
some very reasonably priced.

Prince Hotel
4 Stanmore Road
B16 9TA
Tel: 0121 429 2598
Fax: 0121 429 2061
princehotelb16@yahoo.co.uk
Affordable rooms, some en suite, near
ground.

Cook House Hotel
425 Hagley Road
Edgbaston
Birmingham B17 8BL
Tel: 0121 429 1916
Cheap accommodation with shared
bathrooms.

Paris

109 Wharfside Street
The Mailbox
B1 1RF
Tel: 0121 632 1488
Top of the range restaurant in the city centre. Excellent French food and superb service.

Bank Restaurant & Bar Four

Brindley Place
B1 2JF
Tel: 0121 633 4466.
One of Birmingham's finest. Fine food and service.

Ipanema Latin American Restaurant and Bar Nine

Brindley Place
B1 2HJ
Tel: 0121 643 5577
Latin/Caribbean in centre. Excellent food in great atmosphere.

Lasan Restaurant

3 Dakota Buildings
James Street
St. Paul's Square
B3 1 SD
Tel: 0121 212 3664
Excellent Indian restaurant. Highly recommended.

Cielo Italian

6 Oozells's Square
Brindley Place
B1 2JB
Tel: 0121 632 6882
New, offering good Mediterranean cuisine.

Shogun Teppanyaki

The Water's Edge
Brindley Place
B1 2HL
Tel: 0121 643 1856
Busy Japanese restaurant serving good food in nice surroundings.

Café Soya

Unit 106 The Arcadian Centre
70 Hurst Street
B5 4TD
Tel: 0121 683 8350
Very popular Chinese restaurant serving good food at very reasonable prices.

Los Canarios

105 Albert Street
B5 5JY
Tel: 0121 233 3759
Small, family run Spanish restaurant with a friendly atmosphere. Good food at good prices.

Bushwackers

Exchange Building
Edmund Street
B3 2HZ
Tel: 0121 236 4994
Australian restaurant in the middle of Birmingham! Inexpensive food in fun surroundings.

Hard Rock Café

263 Broad Street
B1 2HF
Tel: 0121 665 6562
Part of the international chain serving hamburgers, steaks etc.

The Jamhouse

3 St. Paul's Square
B3 1QU
Tel: 0121 200 3030
Very popular dining venue with restaurants on each of its three floors. International cuisine.

The Mongolian Bar

24 Ludgate Hill
B3 1DX
Tel: 0800 294 2055
Cheap restaurant where you choose your and watch the chef cook it on a barbeque. Good value.

Mokhams of Digbeth

140 Digbeth High Street
B5 6DR
Tel: 0121 643 7375
When in Birmingham you must have a Balti and this is the restaurant to have it in. Excellent food in a great atmosphere.
Balti (meaning bucket) dishes originated in Birmingham and for the truly authentic experience a trip to the triangle of Balsall Heath, Moseley and Sparkbrook takes you to the birthplace of the cuisine

The Windsor

33 Cannon Street
B2 5EE
Tel: 0121 633 3013
Friendly city centre pub serving excellent food. Open late at weekends.

Bennetts

8 Bennetts Hill
B2 5RS
Tel: 0121 643 9293
Excellent old pub in the centre with satellite TV for sporting events.

Briar Rose

25 Bennetts Hill
B2 5RS
Tel: 0121 634 8100
Part of the Wetherspoon chain serving good food in a relaxed atmosphere.

Factotum and Firkin

23 Bennetts Hill
B2 5 QP
Tel: 0121 631 3548
Another popular city centre pub serving good food in a relaxed atmosphere.

Sputnik Bar

Temple Street
B2 5BN
Tel: 0121 643 0426
Lively young bar with music and good food.

McClusky's

63 Smallbrook
Queensway
B5 4HX
Tel: 0121 616 3939
Excellent bar in the centre, offering live music, good food and a late licence.

Edward's

36 Broad Street
B1 2DY
Tel: 0121 643 0444
Lively city centre pub serving good food during the day and offering a great atmosphere at night. Beer garden for summer days.

The Prince of Wales

84 Cambridge Street
B1 2NP
Tel: 0121 643 9460

Famous for its real ale and home cooked food. 150 years old and very popular with locals and visitors alike.

Brasshouse on Broad Street

44 Broad Street
B1 2HP
Tel: 0121 633 3383
Another lively city centre pub with beer garden, satellite TV, good food and live music. Very popular with relaxed atmosphere.

Walkabout Inn

266A Broad Street
B1 2DS
Tel: 0121 632 5712
Australian bar. Entertainment every night Great bar to catch up with sporting events on the large TV screens.

Flapper and Firkin

Cambrian Wharf
Kingston Row
B1 2NU
Tel: 0121 236 2421
Young people's pub in the centre with regular live music, beer garden, pool table and good food.

Casa

The Waters Edge
Brindley Place
B1 2HL
Tel: 0121 633 3049
Trendy bar with beer garden overlooking the canals and serving excellent food.

Bar 2 Sixty

260 Broad Street
B1 2HF
Tel: 0121 633 4260
Very trendy bar with restaurant and beer garden.

O'Neills

Broad Street
B1 2HG
Popular Irish bar with a great atmosphere offering live music, satellite TV and good food.

Birmingham Museum and Art Gallery

Chamberlain Square
B3 3DH
Tel: 0121 303 2834
Fax: 0121 303 1394
www.bmag.org.uk
Wonderful collection of pre-Raphaelite art and exhibitions outlining the city's past, industries and people. Open Monday-Saturday 10.00-7.00

Symphony Hall

Broad Street
B1 2EA
Tel: 0870 730 0196
Ecs.boxoffice@necgroup.co.uk
Purpose built home to the prestigious City of Birmingham orchestra. Also stages pop and jazz concerts.

Airlines

British Airways	0845 773 3377
British Midland	0870 607 0555
Ryanair	ryanair.com
Easyjet	easyjet.com
Qantas	0870 572 6827
Singapore	0870 608 8886
South African Airways	0870 747 1111

Buses

Birmingham bus station is in Digbeth Street. National Express Enquiries 0990 808080.

Trains

The city is served by three main train stations, Birmingham New Street, Birmingham Snow Hill and Birmingham International. Trains run from these stations to all parts of the country.

Rail Enquiries   08457 484950

Taxis

TOA Taxi's	0121 427 8888
BB's Taxi's	0121 693 3333

Car Hire

Avis	0121 622 5666
Budget	0121 643 0493
Europcar	0121 622 5311
Hertz	0121 643 5387

Post Office

Edgbaston Post Office
13-15 Islington Row
Middleway
Birmingham Post Office
1 Pinfold Street
B2 4AA

Tourist Information

Birmingham Tourist Office
2 City Arcade
Birmingham B2 4TX
Tel: 0121 643 2514
Fax: 0121 616 1038

Hospital

City Hospital
Dudley Road
Tel: 0121 554 3801

Queen Elizabeth Hospital
Queen Elizabeth Medical Centre
Birmingham
Tel: 0121 472 1311

Emergency Numbers

Police HQ   0121 626 5000

Climate

	ave temp	rain cm		ave temp	rain cm
January	4	9	July	11	0
February	3	7	August	12	0
March	5	2	September	9	6
April	6	6	October	8	4
May	8	5	November	6	2
June	10	6	December	6	6

Win/Loss Record

Country	Played	won	drawn	Lost	Tie
West Indies	7	4	2	1	-
England	39	19	13	7	-
Australia	11	3	4	4	-
South Africa	5	-	3	2	-
Pakistan	6	-	3	3	-
India	5	-	1	4	-
Sri Lanka	1	-	-	1	-
New Zealand	4	-	-	4	-

Highest Individual Aggregates (England unless stated)

Player	Mat	Inn	NO	Runs	Ave	HS	50	100
David Gower	9	14	1	767	59.00	215	3	2
Colin Cowdrey	8	13	0	737	56.69	159	3	3
Michael Atherton	9	18	2	664	41.50	103	6	1
Alex Stewart	11	18	1	566	33.29	190	1	1
Nasser Hussain	9	16	2	537	38.36	207	0	2
Graham Gooch	10	16	0	525	32.81	154	1	1
Mike Gatting	5	9	2	523	74.71	183*	0	3
Graham Thorpe	7	12	2	506	50.60	138	1	2
Ted Dexter	5	9	1	483	60.38	180	4	1
Geoff Boycott	6	10	2	418	52.25	155	1	1

Top Wicket Takers (England unless stated)

Player	Mat	Bll	Md	Runs	Wkt	Ave	BB	S/R
Fred Trueman	7	1709	55	798	39	20.46	7/44	43.82
Ian Botham	9	2128	74	1087	29	37.48	5/11	73.38
Andy Caddick	5	1145	36	597	22	27.14	5/32	52.05
Chris Old	5	1108	43	508	22	23.09	7/50	50.36
Ray Illingworth	6	1478	88	505	22	22.95	4/92	67.18
Courtney Walsh (WI)	3	601	32	220	19	11.58	5/36	31.63
Chris Lewis	4	994	36	515	17	30.29	6/111	58.47
Imran Khan (Pak)	3	818	33	381	17	22.41	7/52	48.12
Brian Statham	4	1020	38	461	17	27.12	4/54	60.00
Bob Willis	5	1024	34	525	16	32.81	3/69	64.00

Highest Individual Scores (England unless stated)

285*	Peter May	v West Indies 1957
277	Graeme Smith (SA)	2003
274	Zaheer Abbas (Pak)	1971
215	David Gower	v Australia 1985
214*	David Lloyd	v India 1974
207	Nasser Hussain	v Australia 1997
200*	David Gower	v India 1979
190	Alex Stewart	v Pakistan 1992
183*	Mike Gatting	v India 1986
180	Ted Dexter	v Australia 1961

Best Individual Bowling Performances (England unless stated)

11-3-17-7	Wilfred Rhodes	v Australia 1902
14.3-2-44-7	Fred Trueman	v West Indies 1963
31-16-49-7	Sonny Ramadhin (WI)	1957
22.4-6-50-7	Chris Old	v Pakistan 1978
25.3-11-52-7	Imran Khan (Pak)	1982
6.3-4-7-6	Arthur Gilligan	v South Africa 1924
23-6-44-6	Charlie Blythe	v Australia 1909

24-4-58-6	Chetan Sharma (Ind)		1986
27.3-10-58-6	Eddie Hemmings	v New Zealand	1990
22.5-3-71-6	Paul Reiffel (Aus)		1993

Highest Partnerships

Wkt	Runs	Batsmen	Match
1st	338	Graeme Smith & Herschelle Gibbs (SA)	2003
2nd	331	Tim Robinson & David Gower	1985 v Australia
3rd	227	Alex Stewart & Robin Smith	1992 v Pakistan
4th	411	Peter May & Colin Cowdrey	1957 v West Indies
5th	153	Mark Waugh & Steve Waugh (Aus)	1993
6th	190	Collie Smith & Frank Worrell (WI)	1957
7th	159	Alan Knott & Peter Lever	1971 v Pakistan
8th	104	Jonty Rhodes & Lance Klusener (SA)	1998
9th	150	Eldine Baptiste & Michael Holding (WI)	1984
10th	103	Alex Stewart & Andy Caddick	2001 v Australia

Results at Edgbaston

Date	Countries	Result
29/05/1902	Australia	drawn
27/05/1909	Australia	won by 10 wickets
14/06/1924	South Africa	won by an innings and 18 runs
15/06/1929	South Africa	drawn
30/05/1957	West Indies	drawn
05/06/1958	New Zealand	won by 205 runs
09/06/1960	South Africa	won by 100 runs
08/06/1961	Australia	drawn
31/05/1962	Pakistan	won by an innings and 24 runs
04/07/1963	West Indies	won by 217 runs
27/05/1965	New Zealand	won by 9 wickets
13/07/1967	India	won by 132 runs
11/07/1968	Australia	drawn
03/06/1971	Pakistan	drawn
09/08/1973	West Indies	drawn
04/07/1974	India	won by an innings and 78 runs
10/07/1975	Australia	lost by an innings and 85 runs
01/06/1978	Pakistan	won by an innings and 57 runs
12/07/1979	India	won by an innings and 83 runs
30/05/1981	Australia	won by 29 runs
29/07/1982	Pakistan	won by 113 runs
14/06/1984	West Indies	lost by an innings and 180 runs
15/08/1985	Australia	won by an innings and 118 runs
03/07/1986	India	drawn
23/07/1987	Pakistan	drawn
06/07/1989	Australia	drawn
05/07/1990	New Zealand	won by 114 runs
25/07/1991	West Indies	lost by 7 wickets
04/06/1992	Pakistan	drawn
05/08/1993	Australia	lost by 8 wickets
06/07/1995	West Indies	lost by an innings and 64 runs
06/06/1996	India	won by 8 wickets
05/06/1997	Australia	won by 9 wickets
04/06/1998	South Africa	drawn
01/07/1999	New Zealand	won by 7 wickets
15/06/2000	West Indies	lost by an innings and 93 runs
05/07/2001	Australia	lost by an innings and 118 runs
30/05/2002	Sri Lanka	won by an innings and 111 runs
24/07/2003	South Africa	drawn

chester-le-street

riverside stadium

The home of Durham County Cricket Club, the Riverside is a purpose built stadium completed in 1995. With a capacity of 15,000 allowances have been made for expansion. It became the eighth ground in England, and the first newcomer in more than 100 years, to host Test cricket on 5 June 2003 when England took on Zimbabwe in the second match of the series. Unfortunately it turned out to be a one sided affair.

England limped to 156/5 before Andrew McGrath, 81 and Alec Stewart, 68 shared a partnership of 149 to guide them to 416. Zimbabwe struggled from the start, collapsing to 48/8 before Tatenda Taibu put up some resistance with 31 as his team fell to a paltry 94. Richard Johnson took 6/33 in 12 overs for England. Seven of the Zimbabwean batsmen were out lbw, five of them to Johnson. Forced to follow-on the visitors fared better in their second innings, Travis Friend scored 65 not out and Dion Ebrahim, 55. However it was not enough and they were dismissed for 253, as England won by an innings and 69 runs in less than three days. Jimmy Anderson and Steve Harmison had identical figures of 4/55.

The stadium is a mile outside the town of Chester-le-Street. The Don Robson pavilion is on the west side of the ground along with the Members' Balcony and the County Stand. The north and south ends of the ground have terraces and the east side of the ground has temporary stands which all provide good vantage points. The scoreboard is on the east side of the ground.

The Riverside Stadium has some of the most up-to-date disabled facilities in the UK. Wheelchair access is available at Gate 1 in Ropey Lane. There are 31 wheelchair bays in the West Stand and there are a variety of ramps and lifts providing access to all parts of the pavilion. All doors have been designed with wheelchairs in mind. Other facilities include match day commentary for the visually impaired by volunteers. There are six disabled toilets in the Don Robson Pavilion, three on the east side of the ground and two on the west.

Tickets can be purchased by post or in person from the Durham County Cricket Club Ticket Office at the County Ground, Riverside, Chester-le-Street,

Co. Durham DH3 3QR which is open from 09.00-17.00 Monday to Friday and 09.00-15.00 Saturday. They can also by purchased by telephone 0191 387 5151, facsimile 0191 388 9210 or online on www.crickettickets.net or wwwdurhamccc.co.uk. Tickets are also available on the ECB Ticketline 08705 338 833. Tickets are priced between £25 and £32.50 for adults and £10 for under 16's. The pavilion has an excellent restaurant, Austin's Bistro and Bar, and there are food outlets around the ground. There are two bars in the public area. There is also a club shop and cricket museum in the main pavilion. The First-Aid centre is located in the main enclosure. The Riverside Stadium is within walking distance of Chester-le-Street railway station and 6km away from Durham railway station. A taxi from Durham to the ground should cost around £8. Newcastle is 20km away and a taxi will cost around £15. There is ample parking directly outside the ground.

A small town in County Durham in the north east of England. There are a few small guesthouses in Chester-le-Street, however most visitors elect to stay either in Durham or Newcastle.

Durham is dominated by its Norman Cathedral and Castle which stand on the banks of the River Wear. Other places of interest in the city are the Durham Heritage Centre and Museum which details the history of the city and its people, the Durham University Botanic Garden on Hollingside Lane and the Durham Art Gallery. The Beamish Museum is an open air museum that gives visitors a glimpse of life in the area in the 19th century and Cook Hall is a splendid mansion set in magnificent gardens within walking distance of the city centre. The city is compact with narrow streets, perfect for strolling around.

The city of Newcastle is also worth visiting. The Tyne Bridge, one of the city's top landmarks and built in 1928, was the largest single span bridge in the world until the Sydney Harbour Bridge, designed with the Tyne Bridge in mind, was built five years later. Castle Garth is where the city gets its name. It was built in wood in the 11th century by the son of William the Conqueror and rebuilt in stone by Henry II in the 12th century. Places of interest include the Discovery Museum in Blandford House and St. Nicholas Cathedral.

Durham is an administrative centre and an outlet of the surrounding agricultural area whereas Newcastle's history is steeped in shipbuilding and heavy industry. Chester-le-Street is an agricultural area.

Transport from both cities to the Riverside Stadium or Chester-le-Street is available. The choice of restaurants and pubs in Chester-le-Street is also limited and most cricket visitors tend to eat and drink in either of the neighbouring cities. Durham's most popular restaurants and pubs are mostly in Claypath in the centre of the city. Newcastle's most popular venues are along the Quayside and in Bigg and Groat Markets.

Newcastle International Airport is 9km to the north west of the city. Taxis are available outside the terminal and the approximate journey time to the centre is 15 to 20 minutes. The Tyneside Metro Rapid Transit system runs from Newcastle Central Station to the airport and takes 23 minutes at a cost of £2. (0870 08 2608). Busways run coaches between the city centre and the airport every 30 minutes. Local bus No's 76, 76A, 77, 77A, 78, 78E, 79 and 79A run from Newcastle City Centre to the airport between the hours of 06.00-23.00. The journey should take 5 minutes.

Facilities at the airport include a bank, ATMs, a bureau de change, restaurants, bars, coffee shops and newsagents. There is a tourist information desk on the ground floor. Car hire is available from Avis (0191 214 0116), Europcar (0191 286 5070) and Hertz (0191 286 6748).

Durham Castle

Built by the Normans in 1072 and the seat of the Prince Bishops, the King's representatives in this border area until 1830. They ran the area independently of the rest of England with their own tax system, currency and army. Together with the Cathedral, it is now a World Heritage site and is home to part of Durham University. One of the most impressive English castles in England it sits on a hill overlooking the city. Open 10.00-12.30 and 14.00-16.30 during university holidays. Enquiries 0191 334 3800

Durham Cathedral

A wonderful example of Norman architecture it dates from 1093. The Cathedral is a shrine to St. Cuthbert whose coffin and cross are on display. The Cathedral and the Castle dominate the city skyline. Visitors can tour the Tower, the Monks' dormitory and the Treasury Museum which has an exhibition of artefacts from the cathedral's 900 years history, including some relics belonging to St. Cuthbert. Open from 07.30-16.15 each day. Enquiries 0191 386 4266.

Durham University Botanic Garden

Open all year around. The gardens are pleasant and relaxing with outdoor collections from New Zealand, Chile, North America and the Orient. Other highlights are the Monkey Puzzle tree, the Woodland Garden and the Alpine Garden. The glasshouse is well worth a visit with tropical plants, a cactus house and a conservatory with tropical butterflies. There is also some fine artwork around the garden. Open 10.00-17.00. Enquiries 0191 374 7971

Angel of the North

A remarkable sculpture on the Durham Road outside Gateshead. It is the largest in Britain and was created by Anthony Gormley in 1998. It stands 65 feet high and has a wingspan of 177 feet. It can be seen from all over the county. For more details contact 0191 477 3478.

Hadrian's Wall

One of the most famous monuments in the Roman Empire, it was built by order of Emperor Adrian in 122 AD and took six years to complete. The wall stretches from Wallsend on Tyne in the east to Bowness on Solway in the west. It was built to separate the Romans from the Barbarians, not, as is often thought, the Scots who arrived later. It has some terrific forts and museums. There are many walks along the wall through the beautiful countryside of the north east. The wall was designated a World Heritage Site in 1987. Bus AD122 runs from Newcastle to the wall each day. Enquiries 01434 322 002.

Photo: durhamccc.co.uk

Chester-le-Street

Waldridge Fell Guesthouse
Old Waldridge Village
DH2 3RY
Tel: 0191 389 1908
bbchesterlestreet@btinternet.com
Converted from a 19th century
Methodist Chapel. Family run, with 6
lovely en suite rooms with TV.

Low Urpeth Farmhouse
Ouston
DH2 1BD
Tel: 0191 410 2901
Fax: 0191 410 0088
stay@lowurpeth.co.uk
Excellent B&B with 3 en suite rooms
with TV in the countryside. Self cater-
ing accommodation also available.

The Cookson
Cookson Terrace
DH2 2AN
Tel: 0191 389 2044
Another B&B. 5 rooms with TV and tea
and coffee facilities. Licensed bar.

Lilac Cottage
Wheatley Well Lane
Plawsworth
DH2 3LD
Tel: 0191 371 2969
Small B&B with 3 nice rooms, each
with TV and tea and coffee making
facilities.

Durham

Ramside Hall Classic Hotel
Carville
DH1 1TD
Tel: 0208 722 6904
Fax: 0191 386 0399
enquiries@classicbritishhotels.com
Magnificent four star hotel built in
1820 and set in 220 acres. 80 en suite
rooms with all modern amenities.
Excellent a` la carte restaurant, bar.
Own golf course, gym and sauna.

Kings Lodge Hotel
Flass Vale
DH1 4BG
Tel: 0191 370 9977
Fax: 0191 370 9988
reservations@kingslodge.info
21 en suite rooms with cable TV, restaurant and champagne bar. Restaurant
one of the best in Durham.

Farnley Tower Hotel
The Avenue
DH1 4DX
Tel: 0191 375 0011
Fax: 0191 383 9694
12 well appointed en suite rooms, each
with cable TV. Restaurant and bar.

The Georgian Town House
10 Crossgate
DH1 4PS
Tel: 0191 386 8070
Fax: 0191 386 8070
Grade II listed building in the centre-
with 7 beautiful rooms.

Three Horse Shoes
Running Waters
Sherburn House
DH1 2SR
Tel: 0191 372 0286
Fax: 0191 372 3386
Lovely country inn. 6 en suite rooms
with TV. 3 miles from Durham. Serves
excellent food.

Green Grove
99 Gilesgate
DH1 1JA
Tel: 0191 384 4361
B&b with 7 rooms, all en suite.

Newcastle

Copthorne Hotel
The Close
Quayside
NE1 3RT
Tel: 0191 222 0333
Fax: 0191 230 1111
sales.newcastle@mill-cop.com
On quayside with 156 en suite rooms,
many with fine views of the city.
Modern with a good restaurant and bar

Royal Station Hotel
Neville Street
Tel: 0191 232 0781
Fax: 0191 222 0786
info@royalstationhotel.com
Victorian building in the centre with 133
well appointed rooms, an excellent restaurant and bar. It also has a health centre
with swimming pool, jacuzzi and gym.

Rosebery Hotel
2 Rosebery Crescent
NE2 1ET
Tel: 0191 281 3363
Lovely guest house 5 minutes from the
centre. 16 rooms with TV, some
en suite. Country atmosphere.

Chester-le-Street

Da Vinci's
Black Horse Yard
Front Street
Tel: 0191 389 1919
Small Italian restaurant. Good value.

Riverside
Bridge End
Tel: 0191 389 3101
Chinese restaurant that serves an excellent lunch during the cricket.

Memories of India
3 Pelaw Bank
Tel: 0191 388 7777
The best Indian restaurant in town.

Durham

Emilio's Restaurant
96 Elvet Bridge
Tel: 0191 384 0096
Probably the most popular restaurant in the city, serving excellent Italian food in an enchanting atmosphere. Great service.

El Molino's
St. Nicholas Cottage
Durham Markets
Tel: 0191 383 9444
Popular Mexican restaurant.

The New Dragon
72 Claypath
Tel: 0191 384 8683
Good Chinese restaurant.

Pizzeria Venezia
4 Framwelgate Bridge
Tel: 0191 384 6777

Shaheen's at the Old Post Office
48 North Bailey
Tel: 0191 386 0960
Probably the best Indian restaurant in Durham. Good value.

Newcastle

Treasures of the Orient
26 Stowell Street
Tel: 0191 230 4008
Smashing little restaurant. Great menu and very reasonably priced.

Heartbreak Soup
77 Quayside
Tel: 0191 222 1701
On the waterside and one of the most popular restaurants in town. Mainly Mexican with South American dishes. Good value.

Simply Greek
6 Bigg Market
Tel: 0191 232 0750
Really popular. Great food, great atmosphere, great fun.

Rupali
6 Bigg Market
Tel: 0191 232 8629
Fabulous Indian restaurant in the heart the city. If you can manage a plate of the hottest curry, it's free.

The Godfather
3 Market Street
Tel: 0191 232 6171
Small but excellent restaurant in the centre of Newcastle. Great value.

Post Office
Durham Post Office
33 Silver Street
Durham DH1 3RE

Pelton Post Office
Ernest Street
Chester Le Street
DH2 1DU

Tourist Information
Durham City Tourist Information Centre
Millennium Place
DH1 1WA
Tel: 0191 384 3720
touristinfo@durhamcity.gov.uk

Hospital
University Hospital of North Durham
North Road DH1 5TW
Tel: 0191 333 2333

Shotley Bridge General Hospital
Shotley Bridge
Consett
Co Durham DH8 0NB
01207 583583

Emergency numbers
Durham Constabulary Police HQ
Aykley Heads
DH1 5TT
Tel: 0191 3864929

Chester-le-Street

Chesters Wine Bar
87 Front Street
Tel: 0191 388 4657
Handy for a drink after the cricket.

Durham

The Fighting Cocks
South Street
Tel: 0191 386 4822
Great little pub located at the intersection of two ancient routes. Food is excellent and the atmosphere very friendly.

The Jug
Claypath
Tel: 0191 384 8354
Lovely pub on the main street. Good beer, fine food. Evening entertainment.

The Garden House
North Road
Tel: 0191 384 3460
Characterful old pub with character just outside the centre. Excellent food and friendly service. Also has rooms to let.

Newcastle

Lord Chancellors
31 Groat Market
Tel: 0191 261 0924
Excellent pub in centre . Very lively.

Ram Jam Inn
11 Bigg Market
Very popular pub in the centre. Young crowd, loud music, great fun.

The Bridge Hotel
Castle Square
Tel: 0191 232 6400
Wide range of real ales. Varied music and good food. Great view from beer garden.

Cooperage
32 The Close
Quayside
Tel: 0191 232 8286
Real ale pub. Very popular place overlooking the River Tyne. Good music.

The Crown Posada
The Side
Close to Tyne Bridge tower. On CAMRA's inventory of historic pubs, the interia is outstanding.

The Duke
High Bridge
Tel: 0191 2618852
Wide range of real ale and large screen that regularly shows sporting events.

Airlines

British Airways	0845 773 3377
British Midland	0870 607 0555
Ryanair	ryanair.com
Easyjet	easyjet.com
Qantas	0870 572 6827
Singapore	0870 608 8886
South African Airways	0870 747 1111

Buses

National Express (0990 80 80 80) runs daily services between Durham and the other Test venues. The journey from London to Durham takes about eight hours compared to three hours by train. The bus station is on North Road in the city centre.

Trains

Durham train station is located in the centre of the city off Millburngate Bridge Roundabout. There are 15 high speed trains to and from the station each day. A taxi from Durham station to the Riverside will cost £8. Chester-le-Street station is quieter with fewer trains, but it is within walking distance of the ground. Newcastle Central is in the centre of the city and is 12 miles from the ground. A taxi should cost about £15. All train enquiries 08457 48 49 50.

Taxis

Access Taxis	0191 383 2043
Chester Town Taxis	0191 387 1077
Chester-le-Street Taxi Co.	0191 388 2728
City Taxis (Durham)	0191 384 0433

Car Hire

Avis
7 George Street
Newcastle upon Tyne
NE4 7JP
Tel: 0191 232 5283

Budget
223 Westgate Road
Newcastle upon Tyne
NE4 6AD
Tel: 0191 261 8282
Fax: 0191 230 5056

culture

The Anker's House Museum
St. Mary and St. Cuthbert's Church
Chester-le-Street
Small museum which details the life
of the Anchorites, a reclusive order of
monks who lived in isolation in the
14th and 15th centuries.

The Durham Art Gallery
Aykley Heads
Durham DH1 5TU
Tel: 0191 384 2214
Changing programme of exhibitions by
artists and craftsmen. Open 10.00-17.00
daily.

Beamish Museum
Chester-le-Street
DH9 0RG
Tel: 0191 370 4000
Tel: 0191 370 4001
 Internationally famous open air
 museum

The Baltic
South Shoe Road
Gateshead
NE8 3BA
Tel: 0191 478 1810
Opened in 2003, renowned centre for
contemporary art.

The Laing Gallery
 New Bridge Street,
Newcastle upon Tyne
NE1 8AG
Tel: 0191 232 7734
Renowned art gallery, recently celebrat-
ed 100th anniversary.

Theatre Royal
100 Grey St.
Tel: 0870 905 5060
Newcastle upon Tyne
NE1 6BR
Second home to Royal Shakespeare
Company but not in cricket season.

Climate

	ave temp	rain cm			
January	3	58	July	15	49
February	3	37	August	14	61
March	5	48	September	12	50
April	7	41	October	9	55
May	10	50	November	5	50
June	13	51	December	4	56

Photo: Paul McGregor

Win/Loss Record

Country	Played	won	drawn	Lost	Tie
England	1	1	-	-	-
Zimbabwe	1	-	-	1	-

Highest Individual Aggregates (England unless stated)

Player	Mat	Inn	NO	Runs	Ave	HS	50	100
Anthony McGrath	1	1	0	81	81.00	81	1	0
Alex Stewart	1	1	0	68	68.00	68	1	0
Travis Friend (Zim)	1	2	1	65	65.00	65*	1	0
Dion Ebrahim (Zim)	1	2	0	61	30.50	55	1	0
Ashley Giles	1	1	0	50	50.00	50	1	0

Top Wicket Takers (England unless stated)

Player	Mat	Bll	Md	Runs	Wkt	Ave	BB	S/R
James Anderson	1	198	10	85	6	14.17	4/55	33.00
Steve Harmison	1	185	7	77	6	12.83	4/55	30.83
Richard Johnson	1	204	11	100	6	16.67	6/33	34.00
Heath Streak (Zim)	1	205	11	64	4	16.00	4/64	51.25
Douglas Hondo (Zim)	1	132	1	98	3	32.67	3/98	44.00

Highest Individual Scores (England unless stated)

81	Anthony McGrath	v Zimbabwe 2003
68	Alex Stewart	v Zimbabwe 2003
65*	Travis Friend (Zim)	2003
55	Dion Ebrahim (Zim)	2003
50	Ashley Giles	v Zimbabwe 2003

Best Individual Bowling Performances (England unless stated)

12-4-33-6	Richard Johnson	v Zimbabwe 2003
21.4-4-55-4	Steve Harmison	v Zimbabwe 2003
23-8-55-4	James Anderson	v Zimbabwe 2003
34.1-11-64-4	Heath Streak (Zim)	2003
22-1-98-3	Douglas Hondo (Zim)	2003

Highest Partnerships

Wkt	Runs	Batsmen	Match
1st	49	Marcus Trescothick & Michael Vaughan (Eng)	2003 v Zimbabwe
2nd	60	Marcus Trescothick & Mark Butcher (Eng)	2003 v Zimbabwe
		Dion Ebrahim & Stuart Carlisle (Zim)	2003
3rd	37	Mark Butcher & Nasser Hussain (Eng)	2003 v Zimbabwe
		Dion Ebrahim & Grant Flower (Zim)	2003
4th	11	Grant Flower & Tatenda Taibu (Zim)	2003 v Zimbabwe
5th	18	Tatenda Taibu & Sean Ervine (Zim)	2003
6th	149	Alex Stewart & Anthony McGrath (Eng)	2003 v Zimbabwe
7th	19	Anthony McGrath & Ashley Giles (Eng)	2003 v Zimbabwe
8th	32	Ashley Giles & Richard Johnson (Eng)	2003 v Zimbabwe
9th	34	Ashley Giles & Steve Harmison (Eng)	2003 v Zimbabwe
10th	26	Ashley Giles & James Anderson (Eng)	2003 v Zimbabwe

Results at The Riverside Stadium

Date	Countries	Result
05/06/2003	England v Zimbabwe	won by an innings and 69 runs

leeds

headingley

The home of Yorkshire County Cricket Club, Headingley is named after the suburb to the west of Leeds city centre in which is lies.

The first match played at the ground was the drawn third Test in the 1899 series between England and Australia.

England's fortunes varied at Headingley in the early years. They had a terrific record against South Africa with victories in 1907, 1912, 1924, 1929 and 1947 along with two draws in 1935 and 1951 until, eventually, South Africa beat them in 1955. However, their record against Australia was dismal. Losses in 1909, 1921, 1938 and 1948 were accompanied by six draws. No wins at all. The dismal run ended in the third Test of the 1956 series. England, 1-0 down after losing the second Test at Lords, were well served by spinners Jim Laker and Tony Lock who took 18 wickets between them to help England to an innings and 42 runs victory. .

This victory was the start of an incredible run at Headingley. England won four of their next five matches – against the West Indies, New Zealand, India and Pakistan – by an innings. Then came victory over Australia by eight wickets in 1961 and Pakistan by an innings and 117 runs in 1962 before they lost to the West Indies by 221 runs in 1963. They won again in 1971 when the match against Pakistan was the series decider. Geoff Boycott made 112 in that match but it was the fourth Test of the Ashes series in 1977 for which one of Yorkshire's favourite sons will always be remembered. Opening the batting at the start of the match Boycott became the first batsman to score his 100th first class century in a Test match in front of his home crowd. He went on to score 191 to give England victory by an innings and 85 runs.

The third Test of the 1981 series against Australia was one of the greatest of all time. England were 1-0 down after the first two matches and Ian Botham had been replaced as captain by Mike Brearley after bagging a pair at Lord's in the second Test. Australia scored 401/9 before declaring and England could only manage 174 in reply. Botham, who took six wickets, was the only batsman to make an impression with 50. Forced to follow-on, England found themselves 135/7 and on the verge of defeat. Botham had other ideas! He made 149no in one of the best knocks of all time.

He took England's score to 356, a lead of 129. Remarkably, the

Australians struggled from the start, unable to handle the inspired bowling of Bob Willis who took eight wickets to dismiss the visitors for 111 to give England victory by 18 runs.

England won the next Headingley Ashes Test by five wickets but were thrashed in 1989, 1993 and 1997. They also beat Australia in 2001, but it was the fourth Test and Australia were already 3-0 ahead However, Mark Butcher's amazing knock of 173 was one of the great Ashes innings.

The highest team score is 653/4dec. by Australia in 1993, the lowest, the West Indies' 61 in 2000. The highest run chase is 404/3 by Australia in 1948. At the time this chase was the highest in Test cricket and still remains the third best of all time.

Two bowlers have taken hat-tricks at the ground. Jack Hearne became the fifth player and fourth Englishman to take a hat-trick in 1899 against Australia. Peter Loader repeated the feat against the West Indies in 1957 to become the 11th player and seventh Englishman to perform the feat.

Headingley Cricket Ground is situated on St. Michael's Lane, two miles from Leeds city centre and has a capacity of 16,500. The Headingley Pavilion is situated in the south east corner of the ground and is reserved exclusively for members and their guests. It has a number of suites, including the Premier Suite on the fourth floor with its own balcony and area, the Taverners' Suite on the second floor and the Legends' Suite on the first floor. The balconies on the upper two tiers are partially covered, however the enclosure at ground level is open to the elements.

To the left of the pavilion at the south end of the ground is the main grandstand, an old structure whose upper level is totally covered and lower level uncovered. The West Stand runs along the whole west side of the ground and has no cover. This is the liveliest part of the ground and generally has a very good atmosphere. The scoreboard, a replay screen and the Dickie Bird Clock are situated at the back of this open stand. The North Stand at the Kirkstall Lane End of the ground provides an excellent view of the pitch, its top tier and lower tier are both uncovered. The middle tier is reserved for corporate entertainment. The Winter Shed, also at the north end of the ground, has executive boxes while the North Enclosure is general admission seating on temporary stands with no cover. The East Stand is a three tier structure, its upper two levels reserved for corporate entertainment. Its lower level is uncovered.

There are numerous food stalls and bars around the ground. The toilet facilities are adequate. Wheelchair access to the ground can be made through all gates and viewing areas are available in the West and Wintershed Stands and the Northern Enclosure. There are St. John Ambulance posts around the ground. The club shop is located behind the pavilion between gate B and C. There is no museum at the ground.

Tickets can be purchased by post or in person from the Ticket Office which is open from 10-17.00 Monday to Friday and is located at Yorkshire Country Cricket Club, Headingley Cricket Ground, Leeds LS6 3 BU or telephone on 0113 278 7394, facsimile 0113 278 4099 online on www.yorkshireccc.org.uk Ticket are also available on the ECB Ticketline 08705 990 833. The ticket collection point is at Gate C.

There is no parking near Headingley Cricket Ground. A park and ride scheme is in operation during Test matches with free bus services from Beckett Park at the University campus to the ground. Leeds City train station is just over two miles away and taxis are available. The journey should take 15 minutes and cost around £5. Bus No's 73, 74. 75, 76 and 77 run from the city centre to Headingley. (Leeds Buses 0113 245 7676).

Leeds/Bradford International Airport is 12km to the north of the city. Taxis are available outside the Arrivals Hall and cost £12 to the centre of Leeds. An Airlink coach service runs between the airport and Leeds city centre at a cost £1.60. Facilities at the airport include an executive lounge, ATM's, bureau de change, cafés, sandwich bars, pubs and newsagents.

arrival

Leeds is situated on the River Aire in West Yorkshire in North England. It has a population of 740,000. The city is compact and easy to walk around.

Leeds has a background in the wool trade, but has developed into a financial and banking centre and is the commercial capital of Yorkshire.

Leeds was mentioned in the Venerable Bede's Ecclesiatical History in about 730 as being Loidis, a country estate. It was also in the Domesday Book of 1086, although by then it was called Ledes but it became a town in the 13th century, now called Leedes.

It was the site of fierce battles in the 17th civil war in England and devastated by the plague a few years later. By then it was famous for producing woollen cloth and when this industry declined it turned to tailoring and then, late in the 20th century, to information technology.

The Industrial Revolution saw the population increase from around 30,000 at the end of the 18th century to more than 150,000 by 1840. It became a city in 1893.

Armley Mills

A former textile mill built in 1805 it was once the largest woollen mill in the world. It ceased trading in 1969 and has since become Leeds Industrial Museum with many exhibits relating to the city's industrial era. Some exhibits date back to the 18th and 19th centuries. The Museum is situated on Canal Road, Armley, two miles to the west of the city centre. Enquiries 0113 263 7861.

Royal Armouries

On the banks of the Leeds to Liverpool canal, this is an engrossing collection of arms with over 7,500 exhibits on display. It is divided into five galleries, War, The Orient, Tournament, Self Defence and Hunting. Exhibits are from far and wide and include Henry VIII's tournament armour and armour from the Mughal empire. Demonstrations of jousting and falconry in the Tiltyard are ongoing during the day. Situated a mile south east of the city centre.

Kirstall Abbey

A medieval Cistercian monastery on the banks of the River Aire. Built in 1182 it is one of the country's best preserved abbeys. It was closed in 1539 under the orders of King Henry VIII. Over the years, it has been stripped of its roof and stained glass windows but the church, the tower, the transepts and the cloisters remain standing. Kirkstall Abbey is situated near Headingley and can be reached by bus no's 33, 732, 733 and 736 from Central Bus Station.

Leeds Town Hall

The symbol of the city, the Town Hall was built in 1858 by Cuthbert Brodrick with millstone grit and local sandstone. Opened by Queen Victoria it was originally named after her. The tower and bell were added later. Over the years it has been used as courtrooms, council headquarters and mayor's chambers. Today it is Leeds' main concert venue. Enquiries 0113 247 7989.

The Henry Moore Institute

Established to increase public interest and appreciation of art and sculpture., the Institute has a magnificent sculpture collection and also shows temporary exhibitions of various styles of the art in its four galleries. Based in Victorian warehouses which were refurbished in 1993 and are situated on the Headrow in the centre of Leeds. Enquiries 0113 234 3158

The Queen's Hotel

City Square
LS1 1PL
Tel: 0113 243 1323
Fax: 0113 242 5154
One of Leeds' finest. 190 well appointed rooms with cable TV. Excellent restaurant and bar.

Radisson SAS Hotel

No. 1 The Light
LS1 8TL
Tel: 0113 236 6000
Fax: 0113 236 6100
sales.leeds@radissonSAS.com
147 luxurious rooms all with cable TV. restaurants, coffee shop and bar. The hotel is connected to the Light Centre which has a health club.

Ramada Jarvis

Otley Road
LS16 8AG
Tel: 0113 269 9000
Fax: 0113 281 7260
Comfortable hotel with 118 en suite rooms all with cable TV. Juliana's restaurant and bar are well worth a visit. Swimming pool and gym

Crowne Plaza

Wellington St.
LS1 4DL
Tel: 0113 244 2200
Fax: 0113 244 0460
sales.cpleeds@ichotelsgroup.com
142 en suite rooms, restaurant and cocktail lounge. It also has a business centre and health club with swimming pool and gym.

Ascot Grange Hotel

28 Otley Road
Headingley
LS16 5JX
Tel: 0113 293 4444
Fax: 0113 293 5555
ascotgrangehotel@hotmail.com
Newly refurbished, family-run hotel close to the ground. 22 en suite rooms with cable TV. Licensed restaurant and bar.

The Golden Lion

Lower Briggate
LS1 4AE
Tel: 0113 243 6454
One of the city's oldest hotels. 89 well decorated rooms with cable TV. Restaurant and bar.

Abbey Guest House

44 Vesper Road
Kirkstall
LS5 3NX
Tel: 0113 278 5580
Fax: 0113 278 7780
abbeyleeds@aol.com
Within walking distance of ground. Its 6 rooms are individually decorated with private bathroom, radio and TV.

Cardigan Hotel

36 Cardigan Road
Headingley
LS6 3AG
Tel: 0113 278 4301
Fax: 0113 230 7792
Close to ground. 10 en suite rooms with TV. Bar.

Aintree Hotel

38 Cardigan Road
Headingley
LS6 3AG
Tel: 0113 275 8290
Very convenient for cricket fans. Overlooking the ground, the hotel has en suite rooms with TV, restaurant and licensed bar.

The Manor Hotel

30 Cardigan Road
Headingley
LS6 3AG
Tel: 0113 275 7991
Fax: 0113 275 7991
Another overlooking the ground. Good affordable accommodation with friendly service.

St. Michaels Tower Hotel

5 St. Michaels Villas
Caridgan Road
LS6 3AF
Tel: 0113 275 5557
Fax: 0113 230 7491
23 rooms with TV, some en suite with cable TV. Licensed bar. Close to ground.

Broomhurst Hotel

12 Chapel Lane
Headingley
LS6 3BW
Tel: 0113 278 6836
Fax: 0113 230 7099
broomhursthotel@yahoo.co.uk
Another near the ground. 18 en suite rooms with TV. Restaurant and licensed bar.

Flying Pizza

60 Street Lane
Tel: 0113 266 6501
Best pizzeria in Leeds with extensive Italian menu. Very popular.

La Cantina 44 Ristorante

1A Austhorpe Road
Cross Gates
Tel: 0113 368 0066
Italian and Mediterranean restaurant to the east of the city centre.

Café Vianna

2 St. Anne's Road
Headingley
Tel: 0113 278 3678
Excellent Portuguese restaurant near ground. Indoor and outdoor dining.

La Tasca

4 Russell St.
Tel: 0113 244 2205
Lovely Spanish restaurant and bar in the centre. Very popular, bookings essential.

Pietro

70 Otley Road
Tel: 0113 274 4262
Great little Italian restaurant near ground. Excellent service.

Calls Grill

36 The Calls
Tel: 0113 245 3870
In a converted warehouse overlooking the river.

Brasserie Forty 4

44 The Calls
Tel: 0113 234 3232
Renowned as one of Leeds' best restaurants serving continental food.

Pool Court

42 The Calls
Tel: 0113 244 4242
One of the city's best restaurants. Serves traditional and modern British dishes.

The Italian Job

9 Bridge End
Tel: 0113 242 0185
Excellent Italian restaurant, very popular.

The Chemic Tavern

9 Johnson St.
Headingley LS6 2NG

Great pub to pop into after the cricket. Friendly atmosphere and good food.

The Feast and Firkin

Party pub in the centre. Very popular with the young.

The Observatory

40 Barr Lane
LS1 5DA
Popular city centre pub.

The Whip

Duncan St.
Turks Head Yard
Ls1 6NB
Traditional pub with a dart board and friendly atmosphere.

Whitelocks

Turks Head Yard
LS1 6HB
Old English style pub with fine ales and excellent home-cooked food.

All Bar One

27 East Parade
LS1 5BN
Part of excellent national chain.

The Elbow Room

64 Call Lane
LS1 6DT
Trendy bar in the centre with pool table, music and a great atmosphere.

The Slug and Lettuce

159 The Headrow
LS1 5RG
Part of national chain.

The Dry Dock

Woodhouse Lane
LS2 3AX
Probably Leeds' most unusual pub. Housed in an old boat on a traffic island. Great atmosphere.

Duck and Drake

43 Kirkgate
LS2 7DR
One of the best pubs with a good atmosphere.

Stick or Twist

Marrion Way
LS2 8PD
Traditional pub with a relaxed atmosphere. Good food.

The Grand Theatre and Opera House

46 New Briggate
The centre of Leeds' arts entertainment with musicals, drama, opera and dance productions.

City Art Gallery

The Headrow
LS1 3AA
Tel: 0113 247 8248
Some excellent exhibitions including the Henry Moore sculpture collection. Moore was a graduate of the Leeds School of Art.

Abbey House Museum

Abbey Road
Kirkstall
LS5 3EH
Tel: 0113 230 5492
The streets, shops and workplaces of Victorian Leeds recreated.

Harewood House

LS17 9LQ
Tel: 0113 218 1010.
The family home of the Earl and Countess of Harewood and one of England's great Stately Homes. Designed by John Carr, with the interior created by Robert Adam and furniture made by Thomas Chippendale. Also gardens and Bird Garden with some 600 birds. 11km north of Leeds.

Airlines

British Airways	0845 773 3377
British Midland	0870 607 0555
Ryanair	ryanair.com
easyjet	easyjet.com
Qantas	0870 572 6827
Singapore	0870 608 8886
South African Airways	0870 747 1111

Buses

The bus and coach station is located in New York Street in the centre of the city. Over 100 National Express coaches depart from the station to destinations all over Britain each day. National Express Enquiries 0990 808080.

Trains

City station is the main railway station in Leeds with an hourly Intercity service to London and regular services to the other cricket centres. The station is located in the city centre two miles from the ground.

Taxis

Metro Cars 0113 244 4031
Express Cars 0113 275 5186

Car Hire

Avis
81 Roseville Road
LS8 5DT
Tel: 0113 243 9771

Budget
Unit 8, Hunslet Trading Estate
Servern Way
LS10 1BL
Tel: 0113 272 1177
Fax: 0113 272 1199

Hertz
Unit 2, Emmanuel Trading Estate
Springwell Road
LS12 1AT
Tel: 0870 849 0014
leeds@hertz.com

Post Office

General Post Office
City Square
LS1 2UH

Tourist Information

Gateway Yorkshire
Regional Travel and Tourism Centre
The Arcade
Leeds City Station
LS1 1PL
Tel: 0113 242 5242
Open Monday-Saturday 09.00-17.30
Sunday 10.00-16.00

Hospital

General Infirmary
Great George St.
LS1 3EX
Tel: 0113 243 2799

St. James's University Hospital
Beckett Street,
LS9 7TF.
Tel: 0113) 2433144

Emergency Numbers

West Yorkshire Police   0845 606 0606

Climate

	ave temp	rain cm
January	4	58
February	3	47
March	6	46
April	8	47
May	11	53
June	14	55
July	16	64
August	16	69
September	14	59
October	10	68
November	6	64
December	4	61

stats

Win/Loss Record

Country	Played	won	drawn	Lost	Tie
West Indies	11	6	1	4	-
England	65	28	17	20	-
Australia	23	8	8	7	-
India	6	2	1	3	-
South Africa	11	2	3	6	-
Pakistan	8	1	3	4	-
New Zealand	6	1	1	4	-

Highest Individual Aggregates (England unless stated)

Player	Mat	Inn	NO	Runs	Ave	HS	50	100
Don Bradman (Aus)	4	6	1	963	192.60	334	0	4
Geoff Boycott	10	16	1	897	59.80	246*	0	4
John Edrich	9	17	1	849	53.06	310*	5	1
Graham Gooch	12	22	1	776	36.95	154*	4	2
Alex Stewart	11	19	3	695	43.44	170	4	1
Ian Botham	10	17	1	668	41.75	149*	3	2
Ken Barrington	8	12	1	655	59.55	163	3	1
Mark Butcher	6	12	2	621	62.10	173*	2	2
Nasser Hussain	8	14	1	621	47.77	110	2	2
Peter May	8	11	2	621	69.00	138	2	3

Top Wicket Takers (England unless stated)

Player	Mat	Bll	Md	Runs	Wkt	Ave	BB	S/R
Fred Trueman	9	1764	66	795	44	18.07	6/30	40.09
Bob Willis	8	1513	61	771	40	19.28	8/43	37.83
Ian Botham	10	1647	74	773	33	23.42	6/95	49.91
Darren Gough	6	1228	39	701	31	22.61	6/42	39.61
John Snow	8	2020	73	853	31	27.52	4/77	65.16
Jim Laker	6	1562	103	509	30	16.97	6/55	52.07
Tony Lock	7	1737	112	592	29	20.41	7/51	59.90
Ray Illingworth	7	1867	135	547	26	21.04	6/87	71.81
Derek Underwood	9	1571	112	536	24	22.33	6/45	65.46
Curtly Ambrose (WI)	4	926	39	341	23	14.83	6/52	40.26

Highest Individual Scores (England unless stated)

334	Don Bradman (Aus)	1930
310*	John Edrich	v New Zealand 1965
304	Don Bradman (Aus)	1934
246*	Geoff Boycott	v India 1967
236	Eric Rowan (SA)	1951
200*	Allan Border (Aus)	1993
199	Matthew Elliott (Aus)	1997
193	Sachin Tendulkar (Ind)	2002
191	Geoff Boycott	v Australia 1977
182	Arthur Morris (Aus)	1948

Best Individual Bowling Performances (England unless stated)

15.1-3-43-8	Bob Willis	v Australia 1981
15.5-1-59-8	Charlie Blythe	v South Africa 1907
46.2-15-107-8	Neil Foster	v Pakistan 1987
13.4-1-37-7	Jason Gillespie (Aus)	1997
22.4-9-40-7	Charlie Blythe	v South Africa 1907
19.1-5-40-7	Imran Khan (Pak)	1987
35.2-20-51-7	Tony Lock	v New Zealand 1958
26-9-53-7	Malcolm Marshall (WI)	1984
25.3-6-58-7	Charles Macartney (Aus)	1909
38.2-9-70-7	Frank Worrell (WI)	1957

Highest Partnerships

Wkt	Runs	Batsmen	Match
1st	192	Roy Fredericks & Gordon Greenidge (WI)	1976
2nd	369	John Edrich & Ken Barrington (Eng)	1965 v New Zealand
3rd	229	Don Bradman & Alan Kippax (Aus)	1930
4th	388	Bill Ponsford & Don Bradman (Aus)	1934
5th	332*	Allan Border & Steve Waugh (Aus)	1993
6th	152	Tony Greig & Alan Knott (Eng)	1976 v West Indies
7th	147	Steve Waugh & Merv Hughes (Aus)	1989
8th	150	Gary Kirsten & Monde Zondeki (SA)	2003
9th	108	George Geary & George Macaulay (Eng)	1926 v Australia
10th	103	Tuppy Owen-Smith & Sandy Bell (SA)	1929

Results at Headingley

Date	Countries	Result
29/06/1899	v Australia	drawn
03/07/1905	v Australia	drawn
29/07/1907	v South Africa	won by 53 runs
01/07/1909	v Australia	lost by 126 runs
08/07/1912	v South Africa	won by 174 runs
02/07/1921	v Australia	lost by 219 runs
12/07/1924	v South Africa	won by 9 wickets
10/07/1926	v Australia	drawn
13/07/1929	v South Africa	won by 5 wickets
11/07/1930	v Australia	drawn
20/07/1934	v Australia	drawn
13/07/1935	v South Africa	drawn
22/07/1938	v Australia	lost by 5 wickets
26/07/1947	v South Africa	won by 10 wickets
22/07/1948	v Australia	lost by 7 wickets
11/06/1949	v New Zealand	drawn

26/07/1951	v South Africa	drawn
05/06/1952	v India	won by 7 wickets
23/07/1953	v Australia	drawn
21/07/1955	v South Africa	lost by 224 runs
12/07/1956	v Australia	won by an innings and 42 runs
25/07/1957	v West Indies	won by an innings and 5 runs
03/07/1958	v New Zealand	won by an innings and 71 runs
02/07/1959	v India	won by an innings and 173 runs
06/07/1961	v Australia	won by 8 wickets
05/07/1962	v Pakistan	won by an innings and 117 runs
25/07/1963	v West Indies	lost by 221 runs
02/07/1964	v Australia	lost by 7 wickets
08/07/1965	v New Zealand	won by an innings and 187 runs
04/08/1966	v West Indies	lost by an innings and 55 runs
08/06/1967	v India	won by 6 wickets
25/07/1968	v Australia	drawn
10/07/1969	v West Indies	won by 30 runs
08/07/1971	v Pakistan	won by 25 runs
27/07/1972	v Australia	won by 9 wickets
05/07/1973	v New Zealand	won by an innings and 1 Run
25/07/1974	v Pakistan	drawn
14/08/1975	v Australia	drawn
22/07/1976	v West Indies	lost by 55 runs
11/08/1977	v Australia	won by an innings and 85 runs
29/06/1978	v Pakistan	drawn
16/08/1979	v India	drawn
07/08/1980	v West Indies	drawn
16/07/1981	v Australia	won by 18 runs
26/08/1982	v Pakistan	won by 3 wickets
28/07/1983	v New Zealand	lost by 5 wickets
12/07/1984	v West Indies	lost by 8 wickets
13/06/1985	v Australia	won by 5 wickets
19/06/1986	v India	lost by 279 runs
02/07/1987	v Pakistan	lost by an innings and 18 runs
21/07/1988	v West Indies	lost by 10 wickets
08/06/1989	v Australia	lost by 210 runs
06/06/1991	v West Indies	won by 115 runs
23/07/1992	v Pakistan	won by 6 wickets
22/07/1993	v Australia	lost by an innings and 148 runs
04/08/1994	v South Africa	drawn
08/06/1995	v West Indies	lost by 9 wickets
08/08/1996	v Pakistan	drawn
24/07/1997	v Australia	lost by an innings and 61 runs
06/08/1998	v South Africa	won by 23 runs
17/08/2000	v West Indies	won by an innings and 39 runs
16/08/2001	v Australia	won by 6 wickets
22/08/2002	v India	lost by an innings and 46 runs
21/08/2003	v South Africa	lost by 191 runs
03/06/2004	v New Zealand	won by 9 wickets

london

lord's

Lord's Cricket Ground is the spiritual headquarters of cricket as well as home to the Marylebone Cricket Club and the home ground of Middlesex County Cricket Club. The ground is located in St. John's Wood in north west London. Lord's inaugural Test was the second Test in the 1884 series between England and Australia which England won by an innings and five runs. George Ulyett was England's hero with 7/36.

Following that good start for England, Lord's has seen more than 100 Tests. One of the most memorable was the second Test of the 1930 series against Australia. Leading 1-0 after the first Test, England won the toss and chose to bat with KS Duleepsinhji hitting a wonderful 173 on his debut in a total of 425. Australia replied with a massive 729/6 declared, Don Bradman scoring a masterful 254, ably supported by Bill Woodfull with 155. Facing a deficit of 304, Percy Chapman, 121, top scored for the home side as they made 375, Clarrie Grimmett taking 6/167. The visitors were set a target of 71 for victory and after losing three early wickets for 22 runs, Bill Woodfull and Stan McCabe brought the Aussies home by seven wickets.

Another great battle between the two sides took place in the second Test of the 1961 series. England batted first, having won the toss, and scored a disappointing 206, Raman Subba Row top scoring with 48 as Alan Davidson took 5/42 for Australia. Bill Lawry hit a fine 130 as the visitors made 340 to take a lead of 134. The home side could only manage 202 in their second innings, Ken Barrington alone performing well with 66. Garth McKenzie took 5/37. Set a target of 69, Australia, under pressure from Fred Trueman and Brian Statham, wobbled to 19/4 before Peter Burge steadied the ship with 37 to see them home by five wickets.

The second Test of the 1963 series against the West Indies was another enthralling match. Although Trueman ended with match figures of 11/152, England required 234 for victory on the final day against the awesome bowling combination of Wes Hall and Charlie Griffith. Rain prevented play until midway through the afternoon session and when it eventually began England started well, Barrington, 60, and Brian Close, 70, leading the charge. However, their fortunes changed when Colin Cowdrey's arm was broken by a delivery from Hall. The home side were eight runs short with two wickets left as the last over started. Having scored two off the first three balls Derek Shackleton was run out which meant that Cowdrey had to come back to the wicket with his arm in plaster as David Allen played out the final two balls to earn a draw.

Ten years later the West Indies were in full flow. They made 652/8 declared with Rohan Kanhai hitting 157, Gary Sobers 150no and Bernard Julien 121. England's reply was only 233. Forced to follow-on England were dismissed for 193 to lose by an innings and 226 runs.

England had one of their most emphatic wins at the ground in the second Test of the 1974 series against India. They scored 629 as Denis Amiss hit 188, Mike Denness, 118 and Tony Greig, India, trailing by 32, were forced to follow-on and capitulated to a dismal 42. Chris Old, 5/21, and Geoff Arnold, 4/19, were England's bowling heroes.

Ten years later Gordon Greenidge hit an unbeaten 214 off 232 balls to help the West Indies to an incredible nine wicket victory. The visitors' second innings score of 344/1 is the seventh highest run chase of all time and Greenidge's innings was the seventh fastest double century in Test cricket.

England's victory against India 1990 was a personal triumph for Graham Gooch. India sent in their hosts and could only watch as Gooch made 333 in England's of 653. Allan Lamb, 139, and Robin Smith, 100no, also hit centuries. Mohammed Azharuddin, 121, and Ravi Shastri, 100, batted brilliantly in India's reply but it seemed they would have to follow-on until Kapil Dev, 77no, hit Eddie Hemmings for four successive sixes to avoid the target by one run. It did not matter as Gooch notched another century, 123, and shared a partnership of 204 with Mike Atherton, 72, to enable his side to declare at 272/4, 471 runs ahead. India were dismissed for 224 to give England victory by 247 runs. Gooch's match aggregate of 456 is the highest in Test history.

The second Test of the 1992 series against Pakistan was another fine game. Pakistan won by two wickets although, chasing 138, they were 95 for eight.

The match against the West Indies in 2000 was a remarkable affair. England inserted the visitors, who made 267 after being 162-1. However, Curtly Ambrose, 4/30 and Courtney Walsh, 4/43 ripped through England's first innings and dismissed them for 134 to take a lead of 133. But from being clear favourites the West Indies collapsed to 54 as Andy Caddick took 5/16 and Dominic Cork, 3/13. The drama was not over. Needing 188 to win, Mike Atherton (45) and Michael Vaughan (41) got England off to a good start and at 119/2 they looked comfortable. But Walsh was inspired and reeled back England to 160/8 before Cork (33no) and Darren Gough (4no) saw England home.

The highest team score at the ground is Australia's 1930 729/6 dec. and the lowest the 42 by India in 1974. This is India's lowest total ever and the fifth lowest in Test history. Martin Donnelly of New Zealand is the only batsman to score a double century on debut at Lord's – 206 in the 1949 Test.

Lord's is England's largest ground with a capacity of 30,000. The famous pavilion is exclusively for members and their guests. The Long Room in the pavilion, the most historic hall in cricket, is home to the Ashes trophy. To the left of the pavilion is the Warner Stand, a mostly covered two-tier structure and the new three-tier Grandstand. The upper and lower levels are partially covered and offer splendid views. The middle tier has corporate boxes. At the north east end of the ground, the Nursery End, is the Compton Stand, its upper half uncovered and lower half mostly covered, the NatWest Media Centre and the Edrich Stand, its top uncovered and lower covered. The Mound Stand, the Tavern Stand and the Allen Stand follow-on. The Mound is a three-tier structure with the upper level covered. The middle tier is reserved for corporate entertainment and lower tier is partially covered. The Tavern Stand is similar, although its lower tier is uncovered. The Allen Stand has two partially covered tiers.

There is a food village and a number of bars at the Nursery End and other food outlets and bars around the ground. The club shop is behind the Mound Stand and the museum is behind the pavilion. There are medical centres underneath the Warner Stand and behind the Edrich Stand. Facilities for the disabled are provided. Gate No. 6 in Grove End Road should be used. The Mound Stand has a viewing area by the fence and there are disabled toilets around the ground. The general toilet facilities are excellent and well looked after.

Tickets can be purchased by post or in person from the MCC Ticket Office which is open 09.30-17.30 Monday-Thursday, 09.30-16.30 on Friday and is located at Lord's Cricket Ground, London NW8 8QN or by telephone on 020 7432 1000, fax 0207 616 8700 or online on www.Lord's.org. Tickets are also available on the ECB Ticketline 08705 338 833.

There is no parking in the area and spectators are advised to use public transport to the ground. St. John's Wood underground station is less than a five minute walk. Baker Street and Maida Vale underground stations are also in walking distance. LUL 0845 330 9880 or www.thetube.com Numerous buses run from central London to St. John's Wood including No's 6, 13,16, 46, 82, 98, 113, 139 and 189. London Buses 0207 918 4300.

Win/Loss Record

Country	Played	Won	Drawn	Lost	Tie
Australia	33	14	14	5	-
England	106	40	40	26	-
Pakistan	11	3	5	3	-
West Indies	16	4	6	6	-
South Africa	14	4	3	7	-
New Zealand	14	1	7	6	-
Sri Lanka	4	-	2	2	-
India	14	1	3	10	-
Zimbabwe	2	-	-	2	-

Highest Individual Aggregates (England unless stated)

Player	Mat	Inn	NO	Runs	Ave	HS	50	100
Graham Gooch	21	39	1	2015	53.03	333	5	6
Alex Stewart	20	37	4	1476	44.73	124*	8	3
David Gower	17	30	2	1241	44.32	108	8	2
Geoff Boycott	16	29	3	1189	45.73	128*	6	3
Allan Lamb	13	24	2	959	43.59	139	2	4
Denis Compton	11	17	2	882	58.80	208	5	3
Nasser Hussain	11	18	1	861	50.65	155	5	3
Michael Atherton	15	27	0	852	31.56	99	7	0
Tom Graveney	11	16	1	843	56.20	153	5	2
Ken Barrington	12	18	0	838	46.56	148	7	1

Top Wicket Takers (England unless stated)

Player	Mat	Bll	Md	Runs	Wkt	Ave	BB	S/R
Ian Botham	15	3194	125	1693	69	24.54	8/34	46.29
Fred Trueman	12	3087	113	1394	63	22.13	6/31	49.00
Bob Willis	9	1901	81	882	47	18.77	7/78	40.45
Brian Statham	9	2268	111	786	45	17.47	7/39	50.40
Hedley Verity	7	1923	115	613	42	14.60	8/43	45.79
Darren Gough	8	1548	44	897	39	23.00	5/61	39.69
Derek Underwood	9	1967	140	643	38	16.92	8/51	51.76
John Snow	10	2267	87	1000	38	26.32	5/57	59.66
Dominic Cork	8	1692	64	849	36	23.58	7/43	47.00
Andy Caddick	8	1654	63	802	36	22.28	5/16	45.94

Highest Individual Scores (England unless stated)

333	Graham Gooch	v India 1990
259	Graeme Smith (SA)	2003
254	Don Bradman (Aus)	1930
240	Wally Hammond	v Australia 1938
214*	Gordon Greenidge (WI)	1984
211	Jack Hobbs	v South Africa 1924
208	Denis Compton	v South Africa 1947
206*	Bill Brown (Aus)	v England 1938
206	Martin Donnelly (NZ)	v England 1949
205*	Joe Hardstaff jnr	v India 1946

Best Individual Bowling Performances (England unless stated)

20.5-8-34-8	Ian Botham	v Pakistan 1978

20.3-8-38-8	Glenn McGrath (Aus)		1997
22.3-8-43-8	Hedley Verity	v Australia	1934
34.5-17-51-8	Derek Underwood	v Pakistan	1974
27.2-9-53-8	Bob Massie (Aus)		1972
32.5-7-84-8	Bob Massie (Aus)		1972
27.4-6-103-8	Ian Botham	v West Indies	1984
31-18-32-7	Derek Underwood	v New Zealand	1969
39.1-23-36-7	George Ulyett	v Australia	1884
29-12-39-7	Brian Statham	v South Africa	1955

Highest Partnerships

Wkt	Runs	Batsmen	Match
1st	268	Jack Hobbs & Herbert Sutcliffe (Eng)	1924 v South Africa
2nd	287*	Gordon Greenidge & Larry Gomes (WI)	198
3rd	370	Bill Edrich & Denis Compton (Eng)	1947 v South Africa
4th	248	Len Hutton & Denis Compton (Eng)	1939 v West Indies
5th	216	Allan Border & Greg Ritchie (Aus)	1985
6th	274*	Garry Sobers & David Holford (WI)	1966
7th	174	Colin Cowdrey & Godfrey Evans (Eng)	1957 v West Indies
8th	246	Les Ames & Gubby Allen (Eng)	1931 v New Zealand
9th	130	Steve Waugh & Geoff Lawson (Aus)	1989
10th	83	Ray Illingworth & John Snow (Eng)	1969 v West Indies

Results at Lord's

Date	Countries	Result
21/07/1884	v Australia	won by an innings and 5 runs
19/07/1886	v Australia	won by an innings and 106 runs
16/07/1888	v Australia	lost by 61 runs
21/07/1890	v Australia	won by 7 wickets
17/07/1893	v Australia	drawn
22/06/1896	v Australia	won by 6 wickets
15/06/1899	v Australia	lost by 10 wickets
12/06/1902	v Australia	drawn
15/06/1905	v Australia	drawn
01/07/1907	v South Africa	drawn
14/06/1909	v Australia	lost by 9 wickets
10/06/1912	v South Africa	won by an innings and 62 runs
24/06/1912	v Australia	drawn
15/07/1912	Australia v South Africa	Australia won by 10 wickets
11/06/1921	v Australia	lost by 8 wickets
28/06/1924	v South Africa	won by an innings and 18 runs
26/06/1926	v Australia	drawn
23/06/1928	v West Indies	won by an innings and 58 runs
29/06/1929	v South Africa	drawn
27/06/1930	v Australia	lost by 7 wickets
27/06/1931	v New Zealand	drawn
25/06/1932	v India	won by 158 runs
24/06/1933	v West Indies	won by an innings and 27 runs
22/06/1934	v Australia	won by an innings and 38 runs
29/06/1935	v South Africa	lost by 157 runs
27/06/1936	v India	won by 9 wickets
26/06/1937	v New Zealand	drawn
24/06/1938	v Australia	drawn
24/06/1939	v West Indies	won by 8 wickets
22/06/1946	v India	won by 10 wickets
21/06/1947	v South Africa	won by 10 wickets
24/06/1948	v Australia	lost by 409 runs
25/06/1949	v New Zealand	drawn
24/06/1950	v West Indies	lost by 326 runs
21/06/1951	v South Africa	won by 10 wickets
19/06/1952	v India	won by 8 wickets
25/06/1953	v Australia	drawn
10/06/1954	v Pakistan	drawn
23/06/1955	v South Africa	won by 71 runs
21/06/1956	v Australia	lost by 185 runs
20/06/1957	v West Indies	won by an innings and 36 runs
19/06/1958	v New Zealand	won by an innings and 148

		runs
18/06/1959	v India	won by 8 wickets
23/06/1960	v South Africa	won by an innings and 73 runs
22/06/1961	v Australia	lost by 5 wickets
21/06/1962	v Pakistan	won by 9 wickets
20/06/1963	v West Indies	drawn
18/06/1964	v Australia	drawn
17/06/1965	v New Zealand	won by 7 wickets
22/07/1965	v South Africa	drawn
16/06/1966	v West Indies	drawn
22/06/1967	v India	won by an innings and 124 runs
27/07/1967	v Pakistan	drawn
20/06/1968	v Australia	drawn
26/06/1969	v West Indies	drawn
24/07/1969	v New Zealand	won by 230 runs
17/06/1971	v Pakistan	drawn
22/07/1971	v India	drawn
22/06/1972	v Australia	lost by 8 wickets
21/06/1973	v New Zealand	drawn
23/08/1973	v West Indies	lost by an innings and 226 runs
20/06/1974	v India	won by an innings and 285 runs
08/08/1974	v Pakistan	drawn
31/07/1975	v Australia	drawn
17/06/1976	v West Indies	drawn
16/06/1977	v Australia	drawn
15/06/1978	v Pakistan	won by an innings and 120 runs
24/08/1978	v New Zealand	won by 7 wickets
02/08/1979	v India	drawn
19/06/1980	v West Indies	drawn
28/08/1980	v Australia	drawn
02/07/1981	v Australia	drawn
10/06/1982	v India	won by 7 wickets
12/08/1982	v Pakistan	lost by 10 wickets
11/08/1983	v New Zealand	won by 127 runs
28/06/1984	v West Indies	lost by 9 wickets
23/08/1984	v Sri Lanka	drawn
27/06/1985	v Australia	lost by 4 wickets
05/06/1986	v India	India won by 5 wickets
24/07/1986	v New Zealand	drawn
18/06/1987	v Pakistan	drawn
16/06/1988	v West Indies	lost by 134 runs
25/08/1988	v Sri Lanka	won by 7 wickets
22/06/1989	v Australia	lost by 6 wickets
21/06/1990	v New Zealand	drawn
26/07/1990	v India	won by 247 runs
20/06/1991	v West Indies	drawn
22/08/1991	v Sri Lanka	won by 137 runs
18/06/1992	v Pakistan	lost by 2 wickets
17/06/1993	v Australia	lost by an innings and 62 runs
16/06/1994	v New Zealand	drawn
21/07/1994	v South Africa	lost by 356 runs
22/06/1995	v West Indies	won by 72 runs
20/06/1996	v India	drawn
25/07/1996	v Pakistan	lost by 164 runs
19/06/1997	v Australia	drawn
18/06/1998	v South Africa	lost by 10 wickets
22/07/1999	v New Zealand	lost by 9 wickets
18/05/2000	v Zimbabwe	won by an innings and 209 runs
29/06/2000	v West Indies	won by 2 wickets
17/05/2001	v Pakistan	won by an innings and 9 runs
19/07/2001	v Australia	lost by 8 wickets
16/05/2002	v Sri Lanka	drawn
25/07/2002	v India	won by 170 runs
22/05/2003	v Zimbabwe	won by an innings and 92 runs
31/07/2003	v South Africa	lost by an innings and 92 runs
20/05/2004	v New Zealand	won by 7 wickets

The Brit Oval Cricket Ground is the home of Surrey County Cricket Club.
Formerly known as the Kennington Oval, the Oval, the Foster's Oval and the AMP Oval, the ground is situated in south east London.

The Oval hosted the first Test played in England, against Australia in a one-off in 1880. WG Grace made 152 in England's first innings total of 420 while Australia managed just 149. Forced to follow-on, Australia started badly falling to 14/3 before making a fighting 327, thanks mainly to their captain Billy Murdoch who scored 153no. With only 57 required, England lost five wickets for just 31 runs before Frank Penn steadied the ship to bring his team home by five wickets.

Another one-off Test in 1882 produced a thrilling match and created one of the finest rivalries in world sport. Australia made a paltry 63 in their first innnings as Edmund Peate, 4/31 and Dick Barlow 5/19 ran through them. But England also struggled, reaching just 101 as Fredrick Spofforth took 7/46. Hugh Massie hit 55 in Australia's second innings total of 122 as Peate took 4/40. Set a target of 85, WG Grace scored 32 as England reached 66/4 before collapsing to 77 all out. Spofforth took 7/44. His match figures of 14/90 remained the best return at the Oval until Muttiah Muralitharan took 16/220 for Sri Lanka in 1998. At the end of the week an obituary appeared in the Sporting Times announcing the death of English cricket whose body would be cremated and its ashes taken to Australia. The two countries have played for the Ashes ever since although the urn in which they are held resides at Lord's.

The second Test in 1890 was another close low scoring match. Australia made 92 in their first innings. Harry Trott top scored with 39 as Fred Martin took 6/50 for England. The home side took a slender first innings lead with a score of 100. Australia scored 102 in their second innings as Martin took another six wickets to take his match figures to 12/102. Set a modest target of 95, Maurice Read top scored with 35 as England struggled home with two wickets to spare.

One of the most remarkable Tests took place at the Oval in the 1902 series against Australia. The visitors had already won the series 2-0 entering the fifth and final match. They won the toss and elected to bat making 324. Hugh Trumble top scored with 64no as George Hirst took 5/77 for England. England could only manage 183 in reply, Hirst hitting 43 and Trumble taking 8/65 as Australia took a lead of 141. Bill Lockwood took 5/45 as Australia slumped to 121 all out in their second innings. Set a target of 263, England collapsed to 31/4 and 48/5 as Trumble and Jack Saunders took control. However, Gilbert Jessop, 104, and Stanley Jackson, 49, brought the home side back into it and although they wobbled at 214/8 and 248/9 Hirst, 58no, helped them sneak home by one wicket.

The fifth and final Test of the 1926 series against Australia was the decider after the first four matches all ended in draws. England won by 289 runs after Herbert Sutcliffe hit a masterful 161 and Jack Hobbs made 100. Set a target of 414, Australia collapsed to 125 all out, Wilfred Rhodes 4/44 and Larwood 3/43 doing the damage.

The fifth and final Test of the 1934 series against Australia was also the decider after each side had won one of the earlier matches. Australia made 701 with Bill Ponsford top scoring with 266 and sharing a second wicket stand of 451 with Don Bradman, 244. England replied with 321, Maurice Leyland hitting 110 and Cyril Walters, 64. Australia chose not to enforce the follow-on and made 327 in their second innings, Bradman top scoring with 77 as Bowes took 5/55 and Nobby Clark 5/98. Set 708 to win, England capitulated to 145 all out, Clarrie Grimmet took 5/64.

England got their own back four years later, making 903/7 declared, the highest total in Test cricket at that time and still the second highest of all time. Only Sri Lanka with 952/6 declared against India have scored higher. Len Hutton made a record 364, Maurice Leyland, 187 and Joe Hardstaff jnr, 169no. Australia, having been in the field for more than two days, could only manage 201 in reply. Forced to follow-on without Bradman or Jack Fingleton, who were absent hurt, they were dismissed for 123 to give England victory by an innings and 579 runs.

Bradman's last match in Test cricket took place at the Oval in 1948. England were dismissed for a miserable 52 as Ray Lindwall took 6/20. When Australia replied all eyes were on Bradman who needed just four runs to finish his career with an average of 100. Amazingly he was bowled by Bill Hollies for a duck and had to be content with an average of 99.94, the most remarkable average in Test history. Arthur Morris hit 196 as Australia took control with 389. Trailing by 337 runs, England were dismissed for 188 as Australia won by an innings and 149 runs.

It is not just the games with Australia that have captivated the Oval.

The 1976 Test against the West Indies produced a brilliant 291 from Viv Richards and although Dennis Amiss also got a double century England could not cope with Michael Holding, match figures of 14 for 149, and lost by 231 runs.

The fourth and final Test of the 1979 series against India at the Oval was also magnificent. England set the visitors a target of 438 to win. India got off to a terrific start with an opening partnership of 213 between Sunil Gavaskar, 221 and Chetan Chauhan, 80. However wickets began to tumble and at the close India were a tantalising nine runs short of their target with two wickets remaining, ending up on 429/8. Gavaskar's knock was one of the greatest ever seen at the Oval.

Pakistan scored their highest Test score of 708 in the first innings, thanks to Javed Miandad, 260, Saleem Malik, 102, and Imran Khan, 118, but 150 from Mike Gatting staved off defeat.

The fifth and final Test of the 1991 series against the West Indies was another fabulous match. England, thanks mainly to 109 from Robin Smith, reached 419, The visitors struggled against the bowling of Phil Tufnell, 6/25, in their first innings and could only reach 176. Forced to follow-on, Richie Richardson, 121, and Viv Richards, 60, led the way as the West Indies fought back with 385. Sid Lawrence was England's hero taking 5/106. England, although a little shaky, made the required 146 for the loss of five wickets.

The third and final Test of the 1994 series against South Africa produced some fireworks. South Africa made the mistake of hitting Devon Malcolm on the helmet in England's first innings and the big fast bowler single handedly ripped through their second innings with an amazing 9/57 to dismiss them for 175. Set 204 for victory, England had the momentum and cruised home for the loss of only two wickets.

The one-off Test against Sri Lanka in 1998 was also remarkable. Sri Lanka sent their hosts in to bat only to watch them score 445 as John Crawley hit 156no and Graham Hick, 107. Mutiah Muralitharan took 7/155. Sri Lanka's reply was an astonishing 591 as Sanath Jayasuriya hit 213 and Aravinda De Silva, 152. Trailing by 146 runs, England were dismissed for 181 as Muralitharan took 9/65 in an amazing performance. The only English batsman not to fall to him was Alec Stewart who was run out. Sri Lanka's openers scored the required 37 runs to win by 10 wickets. Muralitharan ended the match with figures of 16/220, the fifth best bowling return in Test history.

Ian Botham hit the fourth fastest double century in Test history against India in 1982. He also hit the sixth fastest 50 in Test history off 32 balls against New Zealand in 1986. This innings included 24 off one over from Derek Stirling. Len Hutton became the only batsman ever to be dismissed for obstructing the field against South Africa in 1951.

The Oval is the oldest ground in England and has a capacity of 18,500. It is located in Kennington in south east London. The glorious pavilion towers above the playing area and provides a tremendous view from each of its four levels. Seats in the top tier are probably the most sought after in the ground. Also at the southern end of the ground to the right of the pavilion are the Laker and Lock Stands, both with two floors of corporate boxes above an uncovered balcony enclosure and a partially covered ground level enclosure. The Bedser Stand is a modern stand with four levels to the left of the pavilion. The top two levels are exclusively for corporate entertainment, while the second level houses the players' dressing rooms. There are a number of large uncovered enclosures in front of the dressing rooms providing excellent vantage points. The new scoreboard is situated in the Bedser Stand. The Ken Barrington Sports Centre is housed underneath the Bedser Stand. The Surridge Enclosure runs along the west side of the ground and is totally uncovered. The replay screen is situated at the northern end of the enclosure. At the northern end of the ground, known as the Vauxhall End, the Gover, Fender and Jardine Stands are partially covered. The Jardine Stand incorporates the Vauxhall Chalet Complex and Restaurant. However, a £22 million redevelopment of this end to improve seating and hospitality facilities should be completed in 2005. The Vauxhall End will be covered by a lightweight roof and the improvements will provide an additional 4,000 seats, raising the capacity of the ground to 23,000. The Peter May Enclosure runs down the east side of the ground and is a very popular area. The old scoreboard still operates behind this enclosure.

There are food villages and bars at both ends of the Oval. The club shop selling memorabilia and other cricket products is behind the pavilion. There are first-aid points underneath the Bedser Stand at the southern end of the ground and behind the Peter May Enclosure on the east side. Facilities for the disabled are provided. There are wheelchair viewing areas in a number of the stands. Wheelchair access is through the Hobbs Gate. There are disabled toilets around the ground. The general toilet facilities in the ground are excellent and well serviced.

Tickets can be purchased by post or in person from the Ticket Office at Surrey County Cricket Club, The Brit Oval, Kennington, London SE11 5SS which is open from 09.30-12.30 and from 1.30-16.00 Monday to Friday. Their telephone number is 020 7582 7764 and facsimile 0207 735 7769. Tickets can also be ordered online on www.surreycricket.com Tickets are also available on the ECB Ticketline 08705 338 833.

There is no parking in the surrounding area and spectators are advised to use public transport to the ground. The Oval underground station on the Northern Line is a minute's walk from the ground. LUL 0845 330 9880 or www.thetube.com Vauxhall Network Rail Station is less than a ten minute walk from the ground. (Enquiries 08457 48 49 50). Numerous buses run between the Oval and central London including No's 3, 36, 36A, 36B, 59, 95, 109, 133, 155, 156, 157, and 158.

Win/Loss Record

Country	Played	Won	Drawn	Lost	Tie
Sri Lanka	1	1	-	-	-
England	86	34	34	18	-
Pakistan	7	3	2	2	-
West Indies	15	6	3	6	-
India	9	1	6	2	-
Australia	33	6	12	15	-
New Zealand	9	1	4	4	-
South Africa	12	-	7	5	-

Highest Individual Aggregates (England unless stated)

Player	Mat	Inn	NO	Runs	Ave	HS	50	100
Len Hutton	12	19	2	1521	89.47	364	5	4
Graham Gooch	12	22	1	1097	52.24	196	9	1
Wally Hammond	12	17	4	930	71.54	217	3	4
Herbert Sutcliffe	7	11	1	916	91.60	161	3	5
David Gower	11	20	1	905	47.63	157	1	4
Michael Atherton	12	24	0	859	35.79	108	7	1
Denis Compton	13	22	4	798	44.33	113	5	1
Geoff Boycott	8	15	1	747	53.36	137	2	3
Colin Cowdrey	11	18	2	717	44.81	182	3	2
Alan Knott	12	20	2	673	37.39	92	7	0

Top Wicket Takers (England unless stated)

Player	Mat	Bll	Md	Runs	Wkt	Ave	BB	S/R
Ian Botham	11	2615	90	1379	52	26.52	6/125	50.29
Derek Underwood	10	3401	199	1251	45	27.80	7/50	75.58
Jim Laker	8	1833	114	638	40	15.95	6/55	45.83
Tony Lock	8	1793	126	538	34	15.82	6/20	52.74
Bob Willis	9	1709	55	928	33	28.12	5/42	51.79
Brian Statham	9	1942	80	761	31	24.55	5/40	62.65
Fred Trueman	8	1244	42	543	30	18.10	5/48	41.47
Devon Malcolm	6	1227	37	724	27	26.81	9/57	45.44
Michael Holding (WI)	3	820	31	393	27	14.56	8/92	30.37
Dennis Lillee (Aus)	3	1136	54	475	27	17.59	7/89	42.07

Highest Individual Scores (England unless stated)

364	Len Hutton	v Australia 1938
291	Viv Richards (WI)	1976
266	Bill Ponsford (Aus)	1934
260	Javed Miandad (Pak)	1987
244	Don Bradman (Aus)	1934
240	Zaheer Abbas (Pak)	1974
232	Don Bradman (Aus)	1930
221	Sunil Gavaskar (Ind)	1979
219	Marcus Trescothick	v South Africa 2003
217	Wally Hammond	v India 1936

Best Individual Bowling Performances (England unless stated)

16.3-2-57-9	Devon Malcolm	v South Africa 1994
54.2-27-65-9	Muttiah Muralitharan (SL)	1998
16.4-4-29-8	Sydney Barnes	v South Africa 1912

31-13-65-8	Hugh Trumble (Aus)	1902
33-9-92-8	Michael Holding (WI)	1976
21.4-8-25-7	Gerry Hazlitt (Aus)	1912
30.2-17-36-7	George Lohmann	v Australia 1886
15.5-5-36-7	Michael Kasprowicz (Aus)	1997
28-15-44-7	Frederick Spofforth (Aus)	1882
36.3-18-46-7	Frederick Spofforth (Aus)	1882

Highest Partnerships

Wkt	Runs	Batsmen	Match
1st	290	Geoff Pullar & Colin Cowdrey	1960 v South Africa
2nd	451	Bill Ponsford & Don Bradman (Aus)	1934
3rd	268	Marcus Trescothick & Graham Thorpe	2003 v South Africa
4th	266	Wally Hammond & Stan Worthington)	1936 v India
5th	191	Javed Miandad & Imran Khan (Pak)	1987
6th	215	Len Hutton & Joe Hardstaff (Jnr)	1938 v Australia
7th	142	Jack Sharp & Kenneth Hutchings	1909 v Australia
8th	217	Tom Graveney & John Murray	1966 v West Indies
9th	190	Asif Iqbal & Intikhab Alam (Pak)	1967
10th	128	Ken Higgs & John Snow	1966 v West Indies

Results at The Oval

Date	Countries	Result
06/09/1880	v Australia	won by 5 wickets
28/08/1882	v Australia	lost by 7 runs
11/08/1884	v Australia	drawn
12/08/1886	v Australia	won by an innings and 217 runs
13/08/1888	v Australia	won by an innings and 137 runs
11/08/1890	v Australia	won by 2 wickets
14/08/1893	v Australia	won by an innings and 43 runs
10/08/1896	v Australia	won by 66 runs
14/08/1899	v Australia	drawn
11/08/1902	v Australia	won by 1 Wicket
14/08/1905	v Australia	drawn
19/08/1907	v South Africa	drawn
09/08/1909	v Australia	drawn
12/08/1912	v South Africa	won by 10 wickets
19/08/1912	v Australia	won by 244 runs
13/08/1921	v Australia	drawn
16/08/1924	v South Africa	drawn
14/08/1926	v Australia	won by 289 runs
11/08/1928	v West Indies	won by an innings and 71 runs
17/08/1929	v South Africa	drawn
16/08/1930	v Australia	lost by an innings and 39 runs
29/07/1931	v New Zealand	won by an innings and 26 runs
12/08/1933	v West Indies	won by an innings and 17 runs
18/08/1934	v Australia	lost by 562 runs
17/08/1935	v South Africa	drawn
15/08/1936	v India	won by 9 wickets
14/08/1937	v New Zealand	drawn
20/08/1938	v Australia	won by an innings and 579 runs
19/08/1939	v West Indies	drawn
17/08/1946	v India	drawn
16/08/1947	v South Africa	drawn
14/08/1948	v Australia	lost by an innings and 149 runs
13/08/1949	v New Zealand	drawn
12/08/1950	v West Indies	lost by an innings and 56 runs
16/08/1951	v South Africa	won by 4 wickets
14/08/1952	v India	drawn
15/08/1953	v Australia	won by 8 wickets
12/08/1954	v Pakistan	lost by 24 runs
13/08/1955	v South Africa	won by 92 runs
23/08/1956	v Australia	drawn
22/08/1957	v West Indies	won by an innings and 237 runs
21/08/1958	v New Zealand	drawn
20/08/1959	v India	won by an innings and 27 runs
18/08/1960	v South Africa	drawn
17/08/1961	v Australia	drawn
16/08/1962	v Pakistan	won by 10 wickets
22/08/1963	v West Indies	lost by 8 wickets
13/08/1964	v Australia	drawn

26/08/1965	v South Africa	drawn
18/08/1966	v West Indies	won by an innings and 34 runs
24/08/1967	v Pakistan	won by 8 wickets
22/08/1968	v Australia	won by 226 runs
21/08/1969	v New Zealand	won by 8 wickets
19/08/1971	v India	lost by 4 wickets
10/08/1972	v Australia	lost by 5 wickets
26/07/1973	v West Indies	lost by 158 runs
22/08/1974	v Pakistan	drawn
28/08/1975	v Australia	drawn
12/08/1976	v West Indies	lost by 231 runs
25/08/1977	v Australia	drawn
27/07/1978	v New Zealand	won by 7 wickets
30/08/1979	v India	drawn
24/07/1980	v West Indies	drawn
27/08/1981	v Australia	drawn
08/07/1982	v India	drawn
14/07/1983	v New Zealand	won by 189 runs
09/08/1984	v West Indies	lost by 172 runs
29/08/1985	v Australia	won by an innings and 94 runs
21/08/1986	v New Zealand	drawn
06/08/1987	v Pakistan	drawn
04/08/1988	v West Indies	lost by 8 wickets
24/08/1989	v Australia	drawn
23/08/1990	v India	drawn
08/08/1991	v West Indies	won by 5 wickets
06/08/1992	v Pakistan	lost by 10 wickets
19/08/1993	v Australia	won by 161 runs
18/08/1994	v South Africa	won by 8 wickets
24/08/1995	v West Indies	drawn
22/08/1996	v Pakistan	lost by 9 wickets
21/08/1997	v Australia	won by 19 runs
27/08/1998	v Sri Lanka	lost by 10 wickets
19/08/1999	v New Zealand	lost by 83 runs
31/08/2000	v West Indies	won by 158 runs
23/08/2001	v Australia	lost by an innings and 25 runs
05/09/2002	v India	drawn
04/09/2003	v South Africa	won by 9 wickets

London, one of the world's great, most cosmopolitan cities, is the capital of the United Kingdom with a population of 7.2 million. It straddles the River Thames in the south east of England.

Tourism is a major industry with 25 million visitors each year. The City of London, known as the Square Mile, is the one of the leading financial centres of the world.

London has an almost inexhaustible list of places for the tourist to visit. The five most popular in 2001, the last available figures were the National Gallery, British Museum, London Eye, Tate Modern and the Tower of London.

Then, of course, there is Buckingham Palace, the home of the Royal Family, the Houses of Parliament, St. Paul's Cathedral and Trafalgar Square which is home to Nelson's Column as well the National Gallery. There is a wealth of other museums, theatres, concert halls and art galleries in the city. As well as the British Museum in Russell Street there is the Victoria and Albert Museum in Cromwell Road.

On the south side of the river is the renovated Shakespeare's Globe Theatre which was destroyed by fire during a performance of Hamlet in 1613. It is an open-air theatre and a must see when visiting London.

Other venues include squares such as Piccadilly Circus, Leicester Square and Covent Garden. An excellent way to see the city is from an open-top bus which tours many of the sights London has to offer. The London Eye affords an excellent bird's eye view over the city. The 450 foot observation wheel was erected to celebrate the Millenium and has become one of the major tourist attractions in London. On a clear day you can see for 25 miles in any direction. London is also an excellent place for shopping especially on Oxford Street, Regent Street and Knightsbridge.

The city has many splendid parks. Regents Park is just around the corner from Lord's and houses London Zoo. Hyde Park, Green Park and St. James Park are other areas of recreation in central London. Kew Gardens in Richmond in Surrey is less than 30 minutes journey by tube and is a glorious park and a world-renowned botanical centre.

There is a wide variety of accommodation available in London although it is more expensive than the rest of the country. It has hotels in every price range, however budge accommodation is rather hard to find. St. John's Wood and the surrounding area has a plethora of accommodation for visitors planning to attend a Test at Lord's. There are also some fine hotels in south east London for visitors to the Oval.

London has some of the best restaurants, pubs and bars in the world. Soho, Fitzrovia and Holborn, all in central London, offer every type of restaurant imaginable. It also has fine pubs and bars that cater for all visitors. Covent Garden, Leicester Square and Piccadilly are just some of the nightlife locations. The area around Lord's has some good restaurants and a couple of good pubs whereas the Oval is more pub than restaurant orientated.

Buckingham Palace

One of the British Royal Family's homes since 1837. The Changing of the Guard is a wonderful spectacle taking place each day at 11.00 which always attracts a huge audience. The Palace has been open to public during the summer months since 1993. Queues for this can be long. Enquiries 0207 930 4832. The nearest tube stations are St. James Park and Victoria.

The London Eye

The 450-foot observation wheel was erected by British Airways to celebrate the new millennium. On the south bank of the Thames between Westminster and Waterloo bridges. A 30-minute ride on the wheel allows panoramic views of London. Considering its popularity, queuing time is minimal and a trip should not be missed. Enquiries 0870 0500 0600. The nearest tube station is Waterloo.

The Tower of London

Another famous attraction on the Thames which should not be missed. Built by William the Conqueror in the 11th century, the Tower has a fascinating history of murders, incarcerations and beheadings. It is also home to the Crown Jewels. Beefeaters, the guardians of the Tower, lead tours. Enquiries 0207 709 0765. The nearest tube is Tower Hill. Visitors should also visit Tower Bridge, one of the most famous bridges in the world.

St. Paul's Cathedral

Christopher Wren built St. Paul's Cathedral between 1674 and 1710. It provides an insight into England's religious history and was the venue for the wedding of Princess Charles and Lady Diana Spencer in 1981. Highlights of the cathedral are the Whispering Gallery, the Crypt and the Dome which provides an amazing view across London once one has climbed the 500 steps to the top! The nearest tube station is St. Paul's on the Central Line.

The Houses of Parliament

Neo-Gothic buildings on the River Thames incorporating the Houses of Commons and Lords. Big Ben, the four-faced clock, is the most recognisable feature of the buildings. The Strangers' Gallery gives an opportunity to see Parliament in session. Guided tours are available. Enquiries 0207 219 4272. Visitors should also visit Westminster Abbey, the burial place of many royal personages, which is on the other side of Parliament Square.

London has hundreds of hotels. This is a selection in the centre and nearer the two grounds

Central

Radisson Edwardian Mayfair
Stratton St.
W1J 8LL
Tel: 0207 629 7777
Fax: 0207 629 1459
resmyf@radisson.com
One of London's best. 289 superb rooms, with satellite TV and modem. Several restaurants and bars.

Charlotte Street Hotel
15 Charlotte St.
W1T 1RJ
Tel: 0207 806 2000
Fax: 0207 806 2002
charlotte@firmdale.com
Luxury boutique hotel. 52 rooms with cable TV, VCR. CD player, modem points and fabulous bathrooms. Excellent restaurant, private screening room and gym.

Convent Garden Hotel
10 Monmouth St.
WC2H 9HB
Tel: 0207 806 1000
Fax: 0207 806 1100
covent@firmdale.com
Boutique hotel in the middle of theatre and surrounded by dozens of theatres, restaurants and bars. 58 spacious rooms with all modern amenities. Its restaurant Brassiere Max is a very popular spot.

Radisson Edwardian Grafton Hotel
130 Tottenham Court Road
W1T 5AY
Tel: 0207 666 5444
Fax: 0207 387 7394
resgraf@radisson.com
Comfortable. 224 splendidly designed rooms. All modern amenities.

Lord's

Ramada Plaza Regents Park
18 Lodge Road
NW8 7JT
Tel: 0207 722 7722
Fax: 0207 483 2408
Excellent, directly opposite Lord's. 374 well-appointed rooms, all en suite with cable TV. Several restaurants and a number of very popular bars.

The New Inn
2 Allitsen Road
NW8 6LA
Perfect location to stay, within walking distance of Lord's. Five comfortable rooms, restaurant and bar.

Regent's Park Hotel
156 Gloucester Place
NW1 6DT
Tel: 0207 258 1911
Fax: 0207 258 0288
Attractive family run hotel within walking distance of Lord's. All 23 en suite rooms have cable TV, modem point and trouser press. Excellent garden restaurant.

The Americana Hotel
172 Gloucester Place
NW1 6DS
Tel: 0207 723 1452
Fax: 0207 723 4641
Pleasant Georgian style hotel with 29 en suite rooms with walking distance of Lord's. Cable TV. TV lounge and bar.

Wyndham Hotel
30 Wyndham St.
W1H 1DD
Tel: 0207 723 7204
Fax: 0207 724 2893
wyndhamhotel@talk21.com
Family run Georgian hotel. 10 comfortable rooms, all with TV.

Craven Gardens Hotel
16 Leinster Terrace
W2 3ES
Tel: 0207 262 3167
Fax: 0207 262 2083
Privately run, suitable for budget travellers. 43 rooms, mostly en suite and convenient for Lord's, Hyde Park, Oxford Street. Rooms have TV and tea and coffee making facilities.

The Oval

City Inn Westminster
30 John Islip St.
SW1P 4QP
Tel: 0207 630 5447
Stunning, with 460 rooms overlooking Thames. Rooms have flat screen TV with satellite channels, DVD and CD players and internet access. Restaurant and cocktail bar. Within walking distance of The Oval

Comfort Inn
87 South Lambeth Road
SW8 1RN
Tel: 0207 735 9494
Fax: 0207 735 1001
stay@comfortinnyx.co.uk
Convenient for The Oval. 94 en suite rooms, gym and business centre. Breakfast only.

The Mad Hatter
3 Stamford St.
SE1 9NY
Tel: 0207 401 9222
Fax: 0207 401 7111
madhatter@fullers.co.uk
Lovely hotel. Ideally located for The Oval. 30 large comfortable en suite roo with cable TV. Restaurant and bar.

Carlton Hotel
90 Belgrave Road
SW1V 2BJ
Tel: 0207 976 6634
Fax: 0207 821 8020
info@cityhotelcarlton.co.uk
Budget hotel near Victoria. 19 rooms, mostly en suite with cable TV and tea a coffee making facilities. Breakfast only.

culture

London has many commercial theatres and there are a number of half-price ticket kiosks which offer the opportunity of purchasing tickets on the day of the performance. The theatre centre is Shaftesbury Avenue in the west end, which is also home to the Royal Opera House and English National Opera.

South Bank Complex
Includes National Theatre and National Film Theatre.
SE1 8XT
Tel: 0207928 3232
Culture alongside the Thames, despite its concrete exterior. Nearest tube is Waterloo

Shakespeare's Globe Theatre
21 New Globe Walk
SE1 9DT
Tel: 0207 401 9919
The Globe Theatre, where many of Shakespeare's plays were originally performed, was rebuilt in the late 1990's. It had burnt down in the 17th century. Today the plays are recreated in this outdoor theatre. Tours are held daily. Nearest tube is London Bridge.

The British Museum
Great Russell St.
WC1B 3DG
Tel: 0207 636 1555
Highlights include the Great Court, the Egyptian mummies, the Assyrian treasures and a 2000-year-old corpse recovered from a bog in Cheshire.
A tour is probably the best way to see the museum. Nearest tube is Russell Square.

The Victoria & Albert Museum
Cromwell Road
SW7 2RL
Tel: 0207 938 8500
An absolute treasure trove with over four million artefacts on display. Tour are available. Nearest tube station is South Kensington.

The National Gallery
Trafalgar Square
WC2 5DN
Tel: 0207 747 2885
More than 2000 pieces on display. Covers all eras and also has visiting exhibits from all over the world. Tours available. Nearest tube station is Charing Cross.

The Tate Modern
25 Sumner St.
SE1 9TG
Tel: 0207 887 8000
Housed in the huge Bankside Power Station. Galleries trace the history of international modern art with works from Bacon, Dali, Matisse and Picasso Tours are available. There is an excellent seventh floor restaurant overlooking the Thames and the city. Nearest tube station is London Bridge. Sister gallery in on the other side of the river at Millbank.

London has many high class restaurants and pubs. Here is a selection.

Pied-a-Terre
34 Charlotte St.
W1T 2NH
Tel: 0207 636 1178
Fax: 0207 916 1171
One of London's finest. Ideal for dining after visiting either ground. Food and wine is superb and service is impeccable.

Rules
35 Maiden Lane
Covent Garden
Tel: 0207 836 5314
Opened in 1798, this is London's oldest restaurant and offers superb food including game and fish pies and traditional deserts. Stylishly decorated and is well worth a visit.

The Rock & Sole Plaice
7 Endell St.
Covent Garden
Tel: 0207 836 3785
One of the London's oldest fish and chips shops and is popular with tourists and Londoners alike. It has a small restaurant but also does takeaways.

Philpott's Mezzaluna
424 Finchley Road
NW2 2HY
Tel: 0207 794 0455
www.philpotts-mezzaluna.com
Excellent restaurant serving Italian food, very convenient for Lord's.

A Tavola
St. Johns Wood High St.
NW8 7NG
Tel: 0207 586 4776
Small Italian restaurant near Lord's. Ideal for a lunchtime snack or dinner.

Harry Morgans
1 St. John's Wood High St.
NW8 7NH
Tel: 0207 722 1869
Excellent restaurant within walking distance of Lord's. Fine food, friendly staff and good atmosphere.

Royal China
8 Queen's Grove
NW8 6ER
Tel: 0207 586 4280
Very popular Chinese within walking distance of Lord's. Suitable for lunch and dinner. Excellent food and service.

The Lavender
24 Clapham Road
SW9 0JG
Tel: 0207 793 0770
Very popular restaurant near The Oval, with varied menu offering everything from risottos and vegetarian dishes to bangers and mash. Relaxed atmosphere.

The Lamb and Flag
33 Rose St.
WC2E 9EB
Tel: 0207 497 9504
Popular Covent Garden pub. An absolute must for cricket fans. Wonderful atmosphere.

Cross Keys
31 Endell St.
WC2H 9BA
Tel: 0207 836 5185
Popular pub serving good beer and food.

Lord's Tavern
St. John's Wood Road
NW8 8QN
Alongside the Grace Gates at Lord's and has a terrific atmosphere during Test matches. It also serves good food.

The Anchor
34 Park St.
SE1 9EF
Tel: 0207 407 1577
Thameside pub with a superb view. Very popular pub with locals and tourists alike and convenient for The Oval.

Kings Arms
25 Roupell St.
Kings Arms
SE1 8TB
Quaint little pub quite near Waterloo Station. Great atmosphere. Convenient for The Oval.

The Far Side
144 Stockwell Road
SW9 9TQ
Excellent beer and food in friendly surroundings. Close to The Oval.

The Hanover
326 Kennington Park Road
SE11 4PP
Very popular lunchtime pub for The Oval. Gets pretty crowded and the majority end up drinking on the pavement.

transport

Airlines

British Airways	0845 773 3377
British Midland	0870 607 0555
Ryanair	ryanair.com
Easyjet	easyjet.com
Qantas	0870 572 6827
Singapore	0870 608 8886
South African Airways	0870 747 1111

Buses

Victoria Coach Station on Buckingham Palace Road is London's main coach station. National Express coaches depart from here to all over the United Kingdom. The station has snack bars and a travel shop. Enquiries 0207 730 3466

Trains

Kings Cross (to Leeds and Durham), Euston (to Birmingham and Manchester), St. Pancreas (to Nottingham) for other Test venues.

Taxis

The three most reliable Black Cab firms in London are:

Dial a Cab	0207 253 5000
Radio Cabs	0207 272 0272
Computer Cabs	0207 286 0286

Car Hire

Avis
88 Eversholt St.
London
NW1 1BP
Tel: 0870 010 7967

Hertz
35 Edgware Road
W2 2JE
Tel: 0870 846 0011
march@hertz.com

Budget Rent a Car
66 York Way
N1 9AG
Tel: 01344 484 100

Thrifty Car Hire
Chelsea Cloisters Garage
Sloane Avenue
SW3 3DL
Tel: 0207 262 2223

arrival

London is served by four airports:

Heathrow, London's largest, is located 25 km to the west. It has four terminals with taxis available. A journey to central London should take 35 minutes and cost about £38. There are two underground stations, one at Terminals 1, 2 and 3 and the other at Terminal 4. The journey takes about 60 minutes to the centre and costs £3.70. The Heathrow Express (0845 600 1515) to Paddington every 15 minutes and takes 23 minutes. The cheapest fare is £13. Airbuses are every 30 minutes to central London taking just under two hours. Jetlink run a service between Heathrow and Gatwick airport every 30 minutes which takes just over an hour.

All terminals have banks, ATM's, restaurants, bars, cafés, left luggage facilities, hotel reservations desks and a variety of shops. There are post offices in Terminal 2 and Terminal 4 and post boxes in all terminals. There is a business centre in Terminal 2. Car hire is available from Avis, Budget, Hertz and Thrifty.

Gatwick, London's second largest, is 43km to the south. There are two terminals, North and South, and there are taxi ranks outside both. A taxi journey should take one hour and cost approximately £50. There is a main line train station at the airport which has a number of services to central London. The Gatwick Express (08705 301 530) runs a service every 15 minutes to Victoria Station and London Bridge Station in the centre of London. The journey takes 30 minutes and costs £15. There are slower trains which cost considerably less. (08457 48 49 50). Coaches run between the airport and Victoria Coach Station every hour taking one hour 30 minutes.

Facilities at both terminals include banks, ATM's, bureaux de change, restaurants, bar, coffee shops, left luggage and medical centres. There is a business centre in the South Terminal. Car hire is available from Avis, Budget, Hertz and Thrifty.

London City Airport, the city's closest airport, is situated 10km to the east of the centre. It is small but very convenient. There is a taxi rank outside the arrival hall. A journey will take between 30 to 45 minutes and cost approximately £25 to £30 to the centre.

Facilities include a bank, ATM's, bureaux de change, business centre, restaurant, bar and newsagent. A coach runs between the airport and Canary Wharf DLR expand station and Liverpool Street underground and mainline station. Car hire is available from Avis, Budget, Hertz and Thrifty.

Stansted is London's fourth airport and is located 50km to the north east. Taxis are available outside the airport and a journey takes 90 minutes and costs approximately £70. Trains run between the airport and Liverpool Street Station in central London every 15 minutes and the journey takes 40 minutes. (08457 48 49 50). Coaches run between the airport and Victoria Coach Station every 30 minutes and take approximately 90 minutes. Facilities include ATM's, restaurants, coffee shops, bars, medical centre and a variety of shops. Car hire is available from Avis, Budget, Hertz and Thrifty.

It should be noted that the traffic in London is very heavy and taxi journeys to and from all the airports can vary in length of time and price depending on the time of day.

Post Office

Trafalgar Square Post Office
24 William IV St.
WC2N 4DL
Tel: 0207 930 9580
Open 08.00-20.00 Monday to Saturday

Tourist Information

Britain and London Visitor Centre
1 Regent St.
Piccadilly Circus
W1Y 4XT
Tel: 0870 608 2000
Open Monday 09.30-18.30, Tuesday-
Friday 09.00-18.30, Saturday and
    Sunday 10.00-16.00

Visitor Centre
Arrivals Hall
Waterloo International Terminal
SE1 7LT

Hospital

St. Thomas' Hospital
Lambeth Palace Road
SE1 7EH
Tel: 0207 188 7188

St. Mary's Hospital
Praed St.
W2 1NY
Tel: 0207 886 6666

manchester

old trafford

Old Trafford is the home of Lancashire County Cricket Club and is situated in the south west of Manchester. It was the second ground to stage a Test in England.

The first Test to be played here was the first of the three match series in 1884 against Australia. Despite England sliding to 95 in their first innings, rain affected the match and it ended in a draw.

England and Australia played a number of close matches at Old Trafford in the la nineteenth century, England won by four wickets in 1886 and Australia by three wickets in 1896. However, neither was as exciting as the fourth Test of the 1902 Ashes series. Australia were 1-0 up after a win in the one and only Bramall Lane Test. They elected to bat and with Victor Trumper hitting 103 before lunch (he lasted one run afterwards) scored 299. Bill Lockwood took 6/48. Stanley Jackson 128 in England's first innings total of 262. But the visitors managed only 86 in the second innings as Lockwood took 5/28 and Wilfred Rhodes 3/26. Set 124 to win, England reached 107/5 before collapsing to 120 all out to lose by three runs.

Old Trafford hosted a Test match between Australia and South Africa during a triangular series in 1912. Australia won by an innings and 88 runs and Australian Jimmy Matthews took hat-tricks in both innings, a feat that has never been equalled in Test cricket. Remarkably, those were his only wickets in the match!

The fourth Test of the Ashes series in 1956 is the one for which Old Trafford is be remembered. It has gone down in history as the first time a bowler took ten wick in an innings. England scored 459, David Sheppard, 113, and Peter Richardson, 104, contributing most. Australia started well in their reply, reaching 48/0 before Jim Laker came on and took 9/37 to dismiss the visitors for 84. Forced to follow-Australia had no answer to Laker, who went one better taking all ten wickets for runs in 51.2 overs. The feat has been equalled only once in Test history when Ani Kumble took all ten wickets against Pakistan in Delhi in 1999. Laker's match figu of 19/90 are by far the best ever return in Test cricket. Surprisingly Laker took on eight wickets in four other Tests at Old Trafford.

Australia gained a measure of revenge five years later. Despite Brian Statham taki 5/53 on his home ground to reduce Australia to 190, and England scoring 367 in their first innings, Australia won by 54 runs.

The Australians scored 432 in their second innings, thanks mainly to Bill Lawry' 102, Norm O'Neill's 67 and a last wicket partnership of 98 between Alan

Davidson, 77no and Garth McKenzie, 32. England reached 150/1 in reply before Richie Benaud took 6/70. England crumbled to 201 to lose by 54 runs.

The third Test against the West Indies in 1976 was one of the most one-sided matches at Old Trafford. The visitors elected to bat and scored 211, Gordon Greenidge top scoring with 134. England could only make a paltry 71 in reply as Michael Holding, 5/17 and Andy Roberts, 3/22 ripped through them. The West Indies piled on the pressure in their second innings, Viv Richards hitting 135 and Greenidge 101 in their team's total of 411/5 dec. Trailing by 551 runs, England were dismissed for 126 as Roberts took 6/37 giving the Windies victory by 425.

The first Test of the 1993 Ashes series will be remembered for one ball, Shane Warne's first in Test cricket in England. Having put Australia in and seen them score 289, England were 80/1 when Warne bowled a leg break a foot outside Mike Gatting's leg stump that spun through the defensive shot to take the top of his off stump. Warne took 4/86 in England's 210. Australia then scored 432/5 before declaring 511 runs ahead. England batted well but could only make 332 to lose by 179 runs. Graham Gooch scored 133 before he became only the fifth batsman to be dismissed for handling the ball. Warne took 4/86.

The highest team score is 658/8 declared by Australia in 1964, the lowest, 58 by India in 1952. The highest run chase is 145/7 by South Africa in 1955. Sachin Tendulkar became the second youngest Test centurion, now the third youngest, when he scored 119no in 1990 at the age of 17 years and 107 days. Another Indian, Sandeep Patil hit 24 off a Bob Willis over in 1982.

In 1995 Dominic Cork joined Jimmy Matthews as the only other hat-trick taker at the ground. He became the 21st bowler and eighth Englishman to achieve the feat when he dismissed Richie Richardson, Junior Murray and Carl Hooper in England's win over the West Indies. Bill Bradley of Australia became the second player to take a wicket with his first ball when he had Frank Laver caught in the 1899 Test. Tom Richardson took 10/156 against Australia on debut in 1893 becoming only the second bowler and first Englishman to do so. Alf Valentine took 11/204 to become the eighth player and second West Indian to achieve the feat in 1950.

Old Trafford lies to the south west of Manchester and has a capacity of 19,500. The pavilion on the north side of the ground is a beautiful building with plenty of seating for members at ground level. There are also two balconies in the pavilion. The Eddie Paynter Stand, uncovered with excellent vantage points, is on the left of the pavilion. Behind it is the Old Trafford Lodge, the ground's hotel. The Red Rose Press Gallery is on the east side of the ground and provides a fine view from behind the bowler's arm. In the south east corner is the A. N. Hornby Stand, another uncovered stand. The Washbrook and Statham Stands are opposite the pavilion on the south side of the ground and are partially covered. The Executive Boxes, the Ladies' Stand and the scoreboard are all on the west side of the ground.

There is a food village between the Executive Boxes and the Washbrook and Statham stands. There are other food outlets and bars around the ground. The club shop, museum and library are under the Eddie Paynter Stand and are well worth a visit. There are wheelchair viewing areas outside the pavilion and in front of the Washbrook and Stratham stands. There are two medical points, one behind the Washbrook Stands and the other at the side of the Eddie Paynter Stand.

Tickets are available by post or in person Ticket Office, Lancashire County Cricket Club, Old Trafford, Manchester M16 0PX which is open 09.00-17.00 Monday to Friday or by telephone 0161 282 4040, facsimile 0161 873 8363 or online www.lcc.co.uk. Tickets are also available on the ECB Ticketline 08705 338 833.

The Old Trafford Metro Link Tram Station is right outside the ground and takes 10 minutes to and from Piccadilly in the centre of town. Buses No's 114, 115, 120 252, 253, 254, 255, 256, 257, 263 and 264 run from the city centre to the Chester Road near the ground. Local Bus and Rail Enquiries 0161 228 7811.

Manchester was founded when future Roman Emperor Agricola built a fort just north of the site of present day city 2000 years ago,. But it was not until the 18th century that the small town became the birthplace of the Industrial Revolution and world renowned. The city and many small towns and villages surrounding it saw a massive growth of textile factories and became the prime region for this industry until its decline in the 1950s, when cheaper foreign imports sounded the death knell for the region's pre-eminence.

Manchester is in the north west of England. It has a population of 430,000 although it is the centre of a conurbation with a population of nearly seven million.

It has now developed into an important commercial and banking centre. It is also major industrial centre for engineering, chemicals and clothing products.

In 1996 an IRA bomb ripped out much of the city centre but is had been rebuilt now and is expanding rapidly, moving north into what was once a manufacturing area.

New buildings such as the MEN arena, which stages pop concerts and boxing shows, have been built and areas with restaurants and bars are spreading throughout the city. Manchester has always been proud of its multicultural heritage and this is evident throughout the city.

Granada Studios

One of Manchester's premier tourist attractions and where the popular TV soap Coronation Street is made. Daily tours to see the set and witness how the show is created are available. Bookings are essential. Enquiries 0161 832 4999.

Manchester United Football Club

A visit to the "Theatre of Dreams", Old Trafford, home of one of the world's greatest football clubs is a great experience for any sports fan. It provides an opportunity to see the stadium, the trophy room and the legends' corridor dedicated to players such as Bobby Charlton, George Best, Denis Law and Eric Cantona. Other exhibitions include photographs and newspapers relating to the 1958 Munich Disaster, the Treble Exhibition which celebrates the successful 199 season and the Manchester United Roll of Honour which lists every player for the club since 1886. The museum is open from 9.30-17.00 daily. Enquiries 0870 442 1994 or tours@manutd.co.uk

Manchester Town Hall

A neo-Gothic building built in 1874 by Alfred Waterhouse. In the centre of the city overlooking Albert Square it is home to Manchester City Council. Tours are available and provide the chance to see the many murals depicting the history of the city. There are also sculptures, paintings and carvings on display. Manchester Town Hall also has a tourist information centre. Enquiries regarding tours 0161 234 5000

The Lowry

The new centre of culture in Manchester although it is located on the redeveloped Salford Quays. It has a number of art galleries, including one totally dedicated to the works of the painter L. S. Lowry, Salford's most famous son, two theatres, shops and restaurants. Less than 10 minutes walk from the centre of Manchester. Open 09.30-23.30. Enquiries 0161 876 2000.

Manchester Cathedral

Dates back to medieval times. Located in Victoria Street in the centre of the city it has some magnificent medieval carvings, stained glass windows and fine art. Services are held daily and the choir is well worth hearing.
Enquiries 0161 833 2220

Crown Plaza-The Midland

Peter St.
M60 2DS
Tel: 0161 236 3333
Fax: 0161 932 4100
sales.cpmanchester@ichotelsgroup.com
One of oldest and finest hotels in city.
Always busy. 300 beautifully decorated
rooms, three excellent restaurants, two
bars, health club with swimming pool,
gym.

Piccadilly Hotel

Piccadilly Plaza
M60 1QR
Tel: 0161 236 8414
Excellent rooms with cable TV.
Restaurants and bars. Coffee shop and
a good health centre.

Thistle Hotel Manchester

3-5 Portland St.
M1 6DP
Tel: 0161 228 3400
Fax: 0161 228 6347
Manchester@thistle.co.uk
In the centre. 205 en suite rooms with
cable TV. Restaurant, bar, leisure centre
with small swimming pool, gym, sauna

Jurys Inn

56 Great Bridgewater St.
M1 5LE
Tel: 0161 953 8888
Fax: 0161 953 9090
info@jurysdoyle.com
City centre. 265 en suite rooms, cable
TV. Good informal restaurant and bar.
10 minute tram ride to Old Trafford.

Trafford Hall Hotel

Talbot Road
M16 0PE
Tel: 0161 848 7791
Fax: 0161 848 0219
info@traffordhallhotel.com
Fine old Victorian building located close
to ground. 35 en suite rooms with TV.
Excellent restaurant.

Chesters Hotel

730 Chester Road
M32 0RS
Tel: 0161 877 5375
Fax: 0161 877 5431
info@chestershotel.co.uk
The perfect place for cricket fans during the Test. Within walking distance
of the ground, rooms are air conditioned with cable TV and private
bathroom. Fine restaurant and bar.

Britannia Hotel

35 Portland St.
M1 3LA
Tel: 0161 228 2288
Fax: 0161 236 9154
res704@britanniahotels.com
363 room hotel in a prime location in the
centre. The 1858 building is listed and
has excellent rooms with cable TV. Very
popular restaurant and trendy bars.

Golden Tulip

Waters Reach
M17 1WS 50 quid
Tel: 0161 873 8899
Walking distance of the ground. 50 en
suite rooms, satellite TV and minibar.
Restaurant and bar.

Cornelius Hotel

175 Manchester Road
M16 0ED
Tel: 0161 862 9565
Very reasonably priced Edwardian
hotel providing comfortable accommodation near the ground. All 20
rooms are air conditioned with cable
TV and in-house movies. Excellent café
and bar.

Hotel Campanile

55 Ordsall Lane
M5 4RS
Tel: 0161 833 1845
Popular mid-range hotel close to Old
Trafford. 104 recently refurbished en
suite rooms with cable TV. Bistro restaurant and bar.
Peppers Hostel

17 Great Stone Road

0161 848 9770
Small privately run, provides cheap
accommodation next to Old Trafford.
TV lounge, internet, laundry.

Manchester Youth Hostel

Potato Wharf
Tel: 0161 839 9960
Fax: 0161 835 2054
Centre of city and ideal for budget
cricket fan. 2, 4 and 6 bed dormitories.
TV lounge, games room with pool
table, and kitchen. Less than a 10 minute tram ride from Old Trafford.

Le Petit Blanc

55 King St.
M2 4LQ
Tel: 0161 832 1000
Fax: 0161 832 1001
French food with a hint of Asia.

The River Room

50 Dearmans Place
M3 5LH
Tel: 0161 827 4000
One of the city's best restaurants. In
Lowry hotel.

The Market Restaurant

104 High St.
M4 1HQ
Tel: 0161 834 3743
Small restaurant. Prides itself on using
fresh seasonal ingredients.

Choice Restaurant

Castle Quay
M15 4PR
Tel: 0161 833 3400
Modern British restaurant. Excellent
food, fine wine and live piano music.

The Drawing Room Restaurant

254 Moston Lane
M40 9WF
Tel: 0161 203 4967
Worldly and exciting menu.

Old Wellington Inn

4 Cathedral Gates
M3 1SW
Tel: 0161 830 1440
Built in 1552, one of the city's oldest
buildings. Very good restaurant serving
English food with a modern twist.

That Café

1031 Stockport Road
M19 2BO
Tel: 0161 432 4672
Renowned award winning restaurant
serving modern British food.

Cocotoo

57 Whitworth St.
M1 5WW
Tel: 0161 237 5458
Italian restaurant with a fabulous menu
and an atmosphere to match.

Pizza Express

Old Colony House
6A South King St.
M2 6DQ
Tel: 0161 834 0145
Part of national chain. Top pizzas.

Red Café

Manchester United Football Club
M16 0RA
Tel: 0161 868 8303
The Manchester United experience.

Stock4

Norfolk St.
M2 1DW
Tel: 0161 839 6644
Excellent Italian in the heart of city.
Fine food and service in a marvellous
setting.

Mr Thomas' Chop House

52 Cross St.
Tel: 0161 832 2245
Traditional English pub food at
extremely good prices in fascinating
surroundings.

Little Yang Sing

17 George St.
Cantonese restaurant renowned for
excellent food good value.

Darbar

65 Wilmslow Road
Tel: 0161 224 4392
One of the best curry houses in city.
Great food at cheap prices.

Britons Protection Pub

50 Great Bridgewater St.
M1 5LE
Tel: 0161 236 5895
Edwardian hostelry with an excellent
beer garden.

The Bulls Head

84 London Road
M1 2PN
Tel: 0161 236 1724
Friendly, central. Excellent beer and food.

O'Shea's

80 Princess St.
M1 6NF
Tel: 0161 236 3906
Irish bar with nightly live music.
Excellent pub food and service.

Springbok Bar

The Circus
Oxford St.
M1 4BH
Tel 0161 237 5051
Busy with a great atmosphere.

Waxy O'Connor's

Corporation St.
M4 2BS
Tel: 0870 220 0823
Huge Irish bar with a fabulous décor.
Good beer, great food; always busy.

The Circus Tavern

86 Portland St.
Tel: 0161 236 5818
Tiny, 19th century pub with a great atmosphere.

The Manchester Museum

The University of Manchester
Oxford St.
M13 9PL
Tel: 0161 275 2634
Fax: 0161 275 2676
15 galleries including those for
Egyptology, Zoology and Science for
Life . Also has fine fossil collection.
Opening Monday-Saturday 10.00-17.00
Sunday 11.00-16.00

Imperial War Museum

Trafford Wharf Road
M17 1TZ
Tel: 0870 220 3435

Recently opened with engrossing
exhibitions describing the impact of
war on Britain throughout the centuries. On the Manchester Canal near Old
Trafford. Open 10.00-18.00 daily.

Manchester Art Gallery

Mosley St.
M2 3JL
Tel: 0161 235 8888
Recently renovated, with fine collection
of local and international art including pieces by Henry Moore, Turner,
Gainsborough and Bacon. Opening
10.00-17.00 daily except Mondays.

Manchester International Airport is 18km to the south west of the
city. There are taxi ranks outside all three terminals and a journey should
take 25 minutes, costing around £15. (Advance bookings 0161 499 9000). Buses
No's 43A and 105 take about an hour to Piccadilly bus station. The railway station is adjacent to Terminal 1 and trains run to and from Piccadilly station in
the centre every ten minutes from 06.00-23.15 and hourly during the night. The
journey takes 30 minutes.
Facilities include restaurants, cafés, bars, business centre, duty free shops, banking
services, bureaux de change, ATM's, post office and medical centre in Terminal 3,
post office in Terminal 1. Car hire is available from Avis (0161 934 2300), Budget
(0161 437 0151), Europcar (0161 436 2200) and Hertz (0161 499 3320).

Post Office

Manchester Post Office
26 Spring Gardens
M2 1BB
Newton Street Post Office
3 Newton St.
M1 1NS

Tourist Information

Manchester Visitor Information Centre
Town Hall Extension
St. Peter's Square
M60 2LA
Tel: 0161 234 3157

Monday-Saturday 10.00-17.30
and Sundays 10.30-16.30

Hospital

Manchester Royal Infirmary
Oxford Road
M13 9WL
Tel: 0161 276 1234
Fax: 0161 273 6211

Emergency Numbers

Great Manchester Police Enquiries
Tel: 0161 872 5050

transport

Airlines

British Airways	0845 773 3377
British Midland	0870 607 0555
Ryanair	ryanair.com
Easyjet	easyjet.com
Qantas	0870 572 6827
Singapore	0870 608 8886
South African Airways	0870 747 1111

Buses

Manchester Central coach station is in Chorlton Street. National Express Enquiries (08705 80 80 80)

Trains

Piccadilly station is the city's main station and is in the centre of the city. Direct services to other major cities including London, Birmingham, Leeds and Nottingham. Enquiries contact 08457 48 49 50 or www.nationalrail.co.uk

Taxis

Manchester Cars 0161 236 3555

Radio Cars	0161 236 8033
Taxifone	0161 236 2322
Yellow Cars	0161 228 3355

Car Hire

Avis Rent-A-Car
1 Ducie St.
M1 2GH
Tel: 0161 236 6716
Monday-Friday 08.00-18.00 Saturday 08.00-13.00

Thrifty
Anderton House
Warwick Road
M16 0QQ
Tel: 0161 877 7374
Fax: 0161 877 3099

Budget
Unit 1B Ringway Trading Estate
Shadowmoss Road
M22 6LX
Tel: 0161 499 7861
Fax: 0161 499 7874

Climate

	ave temp	rain cm
January	3	71
February	4	59
March	6	58
April	8	52
May	12	62
June	14	71
July	16	87
August	16	93
September	13	82
October	10	93
November	6	85
December	4	87

stats

Win/Loss Record

Country	Played	Won	Drawn	Lost	Tie
Pakistan	4	1	3	-	-
England	67	20	33	14	-
West Indies	13	5	4	4	-
Australia	28	8	13	7	-
New Zealand	6	-	4	2	-
South Africa	9	1	4	4	-
India	8	-	5	3	-
Sri Lanka	1	-	-	1	-

Highest Individual Aggregates (England unless stated)

Player	Mat	Inn	NO	Runs	Ave	HS	50	100
Denis Compton	8	13	3	818	81.80	158	4	3
Michael Atherton	10	18	0	729	40.50	131	3	2
Alex Stewart	9	14	2	704	58.67	164	1	3

Len Hutton	9	15	1	701	50.07	104	4	2
Ken Barrington	6	11	0	642	58.36	256	3	1
Graham Gooch	9	15	0	568	37.87	133	3	2
Ted Dexter	6	10	0	544	54.40	174	3	1
Wally Hammond	10	14	1	543	41.77	167	3	1
Gordon Greenidge (WI)	4	5	0	503	100.60	223	0	3
John Edrich	8	15	2	491	37.77	100*	2	1

Top Wicket Takers (English unless stated)

Player	Mat	Bll	Md	Runs	Wkt	Ave	BB	S/R
Alec Bedser	7	1816	88	686	51	13.45	7/52	35.61
Jim Laker	5	1038	54	325	27	12.04	10/53	38.44
Lance Gibbs (WI)	3	1228	76	359	23	15.61	6/98	53.39
Tom Richardson	2	892	59	400	23	17.39	7/168	38.78
Tich Freeman	2	740	48	264	22	12.00	7/71	33.64
Darren Gough	5	1322	34	715	21	34.05	4/47	62.95
Fred Trueman	6	1192	39	532	21	25.33	8/31	56.76
Hugh Trumble (Aus)	4	1091	69	449	21	21.38	6/53	51.95
Bob Willis	5	893	23	550	19	28.95	4/63	47.00
John Snow	3	813	22	406	19	21.37	4/41	42.79

Highest Individual Scores (English unless stated)

311	Bob Simpson (Aus)	1964
256	Ken Barrington	v Australia 1964
223	Gordon Greenidge (WI)	1984
210	Gary Kirsten (SA)	1998
205	Aamer Sohail (Pak)	1992
191	Bill Edrich	v South Africa 1947
182	Conrad Hunte (WI)	1963
179	Mohammad Azharuddin (Ind)	1990
174	Ted Dexter	v Australia 1964
169*	George Headley (WI)	1933

Best Individual Bowling Performances (English unless stated)

51.2-23-53-10	Jim Laker	v Australia 1956
16.4-4-37-9	Jim Laker	v Australia 1956
18.2-7-31-8	Frank Laver (Aus)	1909
8.4-2-31-8	Fred Trueman	v India 1952
50-14-104-8	Alf Valentine (WI)	1950
36-3-141-8	Craig McDermott (Aus)	1985
15.4-5-22-7	Malcolm Marshall (WI)	1988
26.2-17-31-7	Bobby Peel	v Australia 1888
24-11-35-7	Tony Lock	v New Zealand 1958
52-34-44-7	Dick Barlow	v Australia 1886

Highest Partnerships

Wkt	Runs	Batsmen	Match
1st	225	Graham Gooch & Michael Atherton (Eng)	1990 v India
2nd	238	Gary Kirsten & Jacques Kallis (SA)	1998
3rd	267	Graham Thorpe & Michael Vaughan (Eng)	2001 v Pakistan
4th	189	Sanjay Manjrekar & Mohammad Azharuddin (Ind)	1990
5th	219	Bob Simpson & Brian Booth (Aus)	1964
6th	180*	Steve Waugh & Ian Healy (Aus)	1993
7th	160*	Sachin Tendulkar & Manoj Prabhakar (Ind)	1990
8th	168	Ray Illingworth & Peter Lever (Eng)	1971 v India
9th	104	Rod Marsh & John Gleeson (Aus)	1972
10th	98	Alan Davidson & Garth McKenzie (Aus)	1961

Results at Old Trafford

Date	Countries	Result
11/07/1884	v Australia	drawn
05/07/1886	v Australia	won by 4 wickets
30/08/1888	v Australia	won by an innings and 21 runs
25/08/1890	v Australia	abandoned
24/08/1893	v Australia	drawn

16/07/1896	v Australia	lost by 3 wickets
17/07/1899	v Australia	drawn
24/07/1902	v Australia	lost by 3 runs
24/07/1905	v Australia	won by an innings and 80 runs
26/07/1909	v Australia	drawn
27/05/1912	Australia v South Africa	Australia won by an innings and 88 runs
29/07/1912	v Australia	drawn
23/07/1921	v Australia	drawn
26/07/1924	v South Africa	drawn
24/07/1926	v Australia	drawn
21/07/1928	v West Indies	won by an innings and 30 runs
27/07/1929	v South Africa	won by an innings and 32 runs
25/07/1930	v Australia	drawn
15/08/1931	v New Zealand	drawn
22/07/1933	v West Indies	drawn
06/07/1934	v Australia	drawn
27/07/1935	v South Africa	drawn
25/07/1936	v India	drawn
24/07/1937	v New Zealand	won by 130 runs
08/07/1938	v Australia	abandoned
22/07/1939	v West Indies	drawn
20/07/1946	v India	drawn
05/07/1947	v South Africa	won by 7 wickets
08/07/1948	v Australia	drawn
23/07/1949	v New Zealand	drawn
08/06/1950	v West Indies	won by 202 runs
05/07/1951	v South Africa	won by 9 wickets
17/07/1952	v India	won by an innings and 207 runs
09/07/1953	v Australia	drawn
22/07/1954	v Pakistan	drawn
07/07/1955	v South Africa	lost by 3 wickets
26/07/1956	v Australia	won by an innings and 170 runs
24/07/1958	v New Zealand	won by an innings and 13 runs
23/07/1959	v India	won by 171 runs
21/07/1960	v South Africa	drawn
27/07/1961	v Australia	lost by 54 runs
06/06/1963	v West Indies	lost by 10 wickets
23/07/1964	v Australia	drawn
02/06/1966	v West Indies	lost by an innings and 40 runs
06/06/1968	v Australia	lost by 159 runs
12/06/1969	v West Indies	won by 10 wickets
05/08/1971	v India	drawn
08/06/1972	v Australia	won by 89 runs
06/06/1974	v India	won by 113 runs
08/07/1976	v West Indies	lost by 425 runs
07/07/1977	v Australia	won by 9 wickets
10/07/1980	v West Indies	drawn
13/08/1981	v Australia	won by 103 runs
24/06/1982	v India	drawn
26/07/1984	v West Indies	lost by an innings and 64 runs
01/08/1985	v Australia	drawn
04/06/1987	v Pakistan	drawn
30/06/1988	v West Indies	lost by an innings and 156 runs
27/07/1989	v Australia	lost by 9 wickets
09/08/1990	v India	drawn
02/07/1992	v Pakistan	drawn
03/06/1993	v Australia	lost by 179 runs
30/06/1994	v New Zealand	drawn
27/07/1995	v West Indies	won by 6 wickets
03/07/1997	v Australia	lost by 268 runs
02/07/1998	v South Africa	drawn
05/08/1999	v New Zealand	drawn
03/08/2000	v West Indies	drawn
31/05/2001	v Pakistan	lost by 108 runs
13/06/2002	v Sri Lanka	won by 10 wickets

The home of Nottinghamshire County Cricket Club, Trent Bridge has the reputation for the best atmosphere at Test cricket in England. The first Test played here was the first of the 1899 series which ended in a draw.

The legendary Jack Hobbs top scored in each of the innings of the first Test of the 1930 Ashes series, hitting 78 and 74, although Clarrie Grimmett had match figures of 10/201. Facing a total of 428 to win Don Bradman led from the front but his 131 was not enough and England came home by 95.

The corresponding Test in 1938 saw a high scoring draw. England notched 658/8 dec. Eddie Paynter was 216no on debut and Charlie Barnett (126), Denis Compton (102), and Len Hutton (100) each scored centuries. Australia replied with 411, Stan McCabe scoring a wonderful 232, his double century coming in 223 minutes, the third fastest in Test history. Forced to follow-on, Australia made 427/6 declared Don Bradman hit an unbeaten 144 and Bill Brown, 133, for the match to end in a draw.

Bradman clearly liked Trent Bridge. Back for the first Test of the 1948 series Australia reduced England to 165, Jim Laker top scoring with 63 as Bill Johnston took 5/36. Bradman led the way with 138 and Lindsay Hassett hit 137 as Australia reached 509. England scored 441 to make Australia bat again after Compton made a fine 184 and Hutton 74. Needing 98 to win, Sid Barnes hit 64no to see Australia home by eight wickets.

The West Indies were in this sort of form during the third Test of the 1950 series. The West Indies replied to England's 223 with 558, Frank Worrell hitting a masterful 261 and Everton Weekes, 129. Alec Bedser took 5/127 for the home side. Trailing by 335 runs, England scored 436 as Cyril Washbrook hit 102. Sonny Ramadhin took 5/135 for the visitors. Requiring just 102 to win, Jeffrey Stollmeyer, 52no, and Allan Rae, 46no, led their team home by 10 wickets.

There were runs galore in the first Test of the 1951 series against South Africa as well. Dudley Nourse made 208 in the visitor's 483/9 dec. England replied with 419/9 dec., Reg Simpson, 137, and Compton, 112, contributing centuries. The visitors collapsed in their second innings to 121 as Alec Bedser took 6/37 to leave England with a target of 186. But Athol Rowan, 5/68 and Tufty Mann, 4/24 dismissed the home side for 114 to win the Test for South Africa by 71 runs.

New Zealand strove manfully to chase 479 in the first Test of the 1973 series but fell short by 38. After being routed for 97 in their first innings, Bev Congdon hit 176 and Vic Pollard 116 as they reached 440.

South Africa were leading the series 1-0 when the fourth Test of the 1998 series began in Nottingham. Having been put in, the visitors made 374, with captain Hansie Cronje leading the way with 126. England replied with 336, Allan Donald taking 5/109. South Africa managed only 208 in the second innings with Angus Fraser taking 5/62. England reached their target of 247 easily even though it required the highest chase in Trent Bridge Test history. They lost only two wickets as Michael Atherton ended up on 98no and Alec Stewart, 45no.

The third Test of the 2003 series between the two was far more tense. England led by Nasser Hussain, 116, and Mark Butcher, 106, made 445, while South Africa replied with 362 thanks mainly to Neil McKenzie, 90 and Shaun Pollock, 62. James Anderson took 5/102 for the home side. Pollock ruined England's second innings with 6/39 as the home side were dismissed for 118. Requiring 202 to win, South Africa never settled and James Kirtley, on his debut, took 6/34 as they fell to 131 all out, frightening England with a ninth wicket partnership of 45 before losing by 70 runs.

It must have been well worth the money during lunch and tea when Compton was batting against Pakistan in 1954. Compton, whose 278, is the highest Test innings at the ground, struck 173 between the intervals, the most runs ever scored in a session.

The highest team score is Australia's 1938, the lowest, 88 by South Africa in 1960. The highest run chase is 247/2 by England against South Africa in 1998.

Alec Bedser's 14/99 is the best return at the ground. Ken Farnes took 10/179 on his debut against Australia in 1934 and Richard Illingworth became the 11th bowler to take a wicket with his first ball in Test cricket when he bowled Phil Simmons of the West Indies in 1991.

Trent Bridge is in the suburb of West Bridgford, 5km to the south of Nottingham centre, and has a capacity of 15,300. It is a glorious ground. The Members' Pavilion built in 1886 is a multi-tiered building exclusive to members and their guests. The West Wing Upper and Lower and the Parr Upper and Lower Stands are to the left of the pavilion. The lower sections of both these stands are totally covered. The Parr is an alcohol free zone. The partially covered William Clarke Stand is also on the west side. The replay screen is behind this stand.

The Radcliffe Road Stand is one of the greatest stands in Test cricket, stretching the length of the north end of the ground. Its top two tiers are uncovered and provide a wonderful view. Below these tiers are the corporate boxes and at ground level, more public seating. The modern, partially covered, Fox Road Stand is on the east side of the ground. The Larwood and Voce Stand and the Hound Road Upper and Lower Stands are in the south east corner of the ground. The lower part of the Hound Road Stand is partially covered. It should be noted that some seats in the Ratcliffe Road and the Larwood and Voce Stands have a restricted view of the scoreboard and replay screen.

There are food outlets and bars at each corner of the ground. The Trent Bridge Inn in the north west corner is a very popular haunt during breaks in play. There is a club shop and a museum behind the pavilion. Wheelchair access is through any gate and there are viewing areas in the Fox Stand, the Upper and Lower Hound Road Stand, the Radcliffe Road middle and upper tiers and in the lower West Wing. There are disabled toilets in all areas. There are three first-aid points around the ground.

Tickets can be bought by post or in person from the Ticket Office which is open from 09.30-16.30 Monday to Friday, 09.30-13.00 on Saturday and is located at Nottingham County Cricket Club, Trent Bridge, Nottingham NG2 6AG or by telephone on 0870 168 8888, fax 0115 982 2753 or online on www.nottsccc.co.uk

Tickets are also available on the ECB Ticketline 08705 338 833.

There is little parking in the surrounding area and spectators are advised to use public transport. Nottingham train station is situated two miles away and taxis are available. The fare should be around £5. Bus no.'s 1, 1X, 2, 4, 6, 7, 7X, 8, 9, 10 all run from the centre of Nottingham to the ground.

Nottingham lies on the River Trent in the heart of the East Midlands and has a population of 270,000. It is located to the south east of the popular Peak District.

The city is known throughout the world as the home of Robin Hood who legend has it lived in nearby Sherwood Forest, now a 450-acre country park. There are some fine trails through the ancient forest which are perfect for walking. A guided tour of the World of Robin Hood is a fun afternoon.

Tourism is an important industry for Nottingham with increasing numbers of visitors each year. The city has a history in the coal, textile and lace industries.

Nottingham Castle Museum and Art Gallery

Built in 1067 and set in beautiful grounds overlooking the city. The museum traces the history of the castle. while the excellent art gallery shows traditional and modern works of art. Tours of the castle are available. Open 10.00-17.00 daily. Enquiries 0115 915 3700.

The Birthplace of D. H. Lawrence

The author of 'Lady Chatterley's Lover' and other novels was born in Victoria Street in Eastwood close to Nottingham in 1885. The house is now a museum dedicated to his works and his life. Many of his novels, plays, short stories and travel stories are exhibited. Enquiries 0177 376 3312

Nottingham Caves

A number of 700 year-old caves run under the city. They are man-made, carved from the sandstone in medieval times. Over the years they have have served in diverse ways as a medieval tannery, and an air-raid shelter in World War II. The entrance is through the Broadmarsh Centre in Drury Walk and visitors can explore these remarkable caves and discover their history between 10.30-16.30 each day. Audio tours are available. Enquiries 0115 952 0555.

Newstead Abbey

Beautiful historic house built in the 12th century by monks and the former home of the poet Lord Bryon. Today it is one of Nottingham's biggest tourist attractions with ghost and theme tours available daily. Situated 10 miles north of the city it is open every day. Enquiries 0162 379 3557.

Galleries of Justice

Absorbing museum tracing crime through the centuries. Actors playing criminals, policemen and judges help to relive the 300 years sufferings of the 17th century prison accompanied by sounds, sights and smells. The Galleries are on High Pavement in the centre. Open 10.00-17.00, Tuesday to Sunday. Ghost tours are held in the evenings. Enquiries 0115 952 0555.

East Midlands Airport is 16km outside Nottingham. Taxis are available outside Arrivals. The journey into the centre should take 20 minutes and cost £17. Buses run from the airport to the Victoria Centre in Nottingham from 06.00-22.00. Facilities at the airport include ATM's, bureau de change, a food hall, bars, pharmacy and newsagents. There is a information desk in the main terminal building. There are a number of car hire desks in the Arrivals Hall.

Lace Market Hotel

29 High Pavement
NG1 1HE
Tel: 0115 852 3232
Fax: 0115 852 3223
reservations@lacemarkethotel.co.uk
Small hotel in the centre with 42 elegant rooms with all mod cons.

Park Plaza

41 Maid Marian Way
NG1 6GD
Tel: 0115 947 7200
Fax: 0115 947 7300
info@parkplazahotels.co.uk
Luxurious city centre hotel. 178 comfortable rooms, restaurant and bar.

Nottingham Royal Moat House

Wollaton St.
NG1 5RH
Tel: 0115 936 9988
Fax: 0115 947 5667
rmnry@queensmoat.co.uk
Modern with 200 en suite rooms, restaurants, bar, swimming pool and gym.

Comfort Hotel

George St.
NG1 3BP
Tel: 0115 947 5641
Fax: 0115 948 3292
enquiries@comfort-hotels-nottingham.com
Reasonably priced hotel in the centre. 70 rooms with cable TV, restaurant and bar.

Nottingham Moat House

Mansfield Road
NG5 2BT
Tel: 0115 935 9988
Fax: 0115 924 5227
revnhm@queensmoat.co.uk
On the outskirts. 172 comfortable rooms with cable TV. Restaurant, bar, swimming pool and gym.

Rutland Square Hotel

St. James' St.
Tel: 0115 941 1114
Fax: 0115 941 0014
rutland.square@forestdale.com
87 pleasant rooms. Opposite Castle.

Greenwood Lodge Guesthouse

Third Avenue
Sherwood Rise
NG7 6JH
Tel: 0115 962 1206
coolspratt@aol.com
Award winning guest house close to the centre with 6 bedrooms and excellent food.

Acorn Hotel

4 Radcliffe Road
West Bridgford
NG2 5RH
Tel: 0115 981 1297
Fax: 0115 981 7654
reservations@acorn-hotel.co.uk
Family run hotel within walking distance of ground. 12 rooms. Very popular with cricket fans.

The Gallery

8 Radcliffe Road
West Bridgford
NG2 5FN
Tel: 0115 981 3651
Very pleasant guest house near ground with 16 clean rooms.

The Grantham Hotel

24 Radcliffe Road
West Bridgford
NG2 5FW
Tel: 0115 981 1373
Fax: 0115 981 8567
granthamhotel@netlineuk.net
Small, comfortable family run hotel with 22 rooms near ground.

Milford Hotel

Pavilion Road
West Bridgford
NG2 5FG
Tel: 0115 981 1464
Fax: 0115 982 2204
Family hotel with 15 clean rooms close to ground.

Mange Caribbiene

10 Alfreton Road
Canning Circus
Tel: 0115 978 1930
Excellent restaurant offering traditional
Caribbean food in relaxed atmosphere.

Aquarium

16-22 Goosegate
Hockley
Tel: 0115 950 0111
Fish restaurant with growing reputation.

The Belfry

The Bell
8 Angel Row
Tel: 0115 947 5241
Excellent restaurant serving traditional
English food.

Le Pub Francais

9 Warser Gate
The Lace Market
Tel: 0115 912 6969
Small eatery serving good food.

Eviva Taverna

Barkergate
Tel: 0115 958 0243
Greek restaurant serving good value
food in a great atmosphere.

4550 Miles from Delhi

41 Mount St.
Tel: 0115 947 5111
Best curries in Nottingham.

Tequila Mexican Restaurant

101 Derby Road
Tel: 0115 950 8189
Good value.

Hard Rock Café

King St.
Tel: 0115 947 4201
Part of the worldwide chain.

Brass Monkey

11 High Pavement
Tel: 0115 840 4101
Small but popular cocktail bar with DJ
music, a good atmosphere and good
food. Strict dress code.

Canalhouse

48-52 Canal St.
Tel: 0115 955 5011
Pub and restaurant in a converted warehouse by the waterway. Very popular
with young crowd.

Libertys

Upper Parliament St.
Tel: 0115 988 1491
American theme bar . Very popular
with live music every night.

Scruffys

Stone St.
The Lace Market
Tel: 0115 947 0471
Popular bar and restaurant in the centre
serving excellent food. It has a great
atmosphere and plays good music.

The Pitcher and Piano

The Lace Market
Tel: 0115 958 6081
Converted church which has a great
atmosphere and is very popular with
locals.

The Slug and Fiddle

Upper Parliament St.
Tel: 0115 924 1779
Another popular pub city centre pub
with live music and a great atmosphere.

Post Office

Nottingham Post Office
Queen St.
NG1 2BN
Tel: 0345 740740

Radcliffe Road Post Office
5 Radcliffe Road
West Bridgford
NG2 5FF
Tel: 0115 981 6951

Tourist Information

Nottingham Tourist Information Centre
1-4 Smithy Row, NG1 2BS
Tel: 0115 915 5330
Fax: 0115 915 5323
tourist.information@nottinghamcity.
gov.uk

Hospital

Nottingham City Hospital
Hucknall Road, NG5 1PB
Tel: 0115 969 1169

Airlines

British Airways	0845 773 3377
British Midland	0870 607 0555
Ryanair	ryanair.com
Easyjet	easyjet.com
Qantas	0870 572 6827
Singapore	0870 608 8886
South African Airways	0870 747 1111

Buses

Broad Marsh bus station is the city's main station and is situated less than five minutes walk from Nottingham railway station. National Express (0990 80 80 80).

Trains

Nottingham railway station is located in the centre. Midland Mainline run services to and from London St. Pancras. Central Trains run services to Birmingham. Enquiries 08457 48 49 50.

Taxis

A to Z	0115 854 7474
County Cars	0115 942 5425
Granada Cars	0115 977 1111

Car Hire

Avis Rent-A-Car
Arndale Centre
Maid Marion Way
NG1 3AE
Tel: 0115 950 1872
Open Monday to Friday 08.00-18.00
Saturday 08.00-13.00.

Nottingham Playhouse

Wellington Circus
NG1 5AF
Tel: 0115 941 9419
One of Nottingham's main theatres presenting local and visiting drama and music groups.

Angel Row Gallery

3 Angel Row
Central Library Building
NG1 6HP
Tel: 0115 915 2869
angelrow.info@nottinghamcity.gov.uk
Leading contemporary art and craft gallery. Open Monday to Saturday 10.00-17.00.

The Museum of Nottingham Lace

3-5 High Pavement
NG1 1HF
Tel: 0115 9484221
Fax: 0115 9483102

Describes a very important part of Nottingham's history. Daily 10:00-17:00 Last admission 16:00.

The Brewhouse Yard Museum

The Museum of Nottingham Life
Castle Boulevard,
NG7 1FB
Tel: 0115 915 3600
A small museum housed in 18th century cottages, also provides an insight into the city's past. Open all year except Xmas Day, Boxing Day and New Year's Day

Climate

	ave temp	rain cm			
January	3	71	July	16	87
February	4	59	August	16	93
March	6	58	September	13	82
April	8	52	October	10	93
May	12	62	November	6	85
June	14	71	December	4	87

Win/Loss Record

Country	Played	won	drawn	Lost	Tie
West Indies	8	4	4	-	-
Australia	20	7	10	3	-
Zimbabwe	1	-	1	-	-
England	50	15	21	14	-
South Africa	9	2	3	4	-
India	3	-	2	1	-
New Zealand	8	1	2	5	-
Pakistan	3	-	1	2	-

Highest Individual Aggregates (England unless stated)

Player	Mat	Inn	NO	Runs	Ave	HS	50	100
Michael Atherton	11	19	1	1083	60.17	160	3	5
Denis Compton	7	10	0	955	95.50	278	1	5
Graham Gooch	10	17	0	936	55.06	210	4	3
Tom Graveney	8	11	2	735	81.67	258	1	3
Geoff Boycott	10	17	2	663	44.20	131	4	2
David Gower	8	15	1	628	44.86	166	3	1
Colin Cowdrey	8	14	1	594	45.69	105	4	1
Viv Richards(WI)	4	6	0	567	94.50	232	4	1
Graham Thorpe	5	9	3	544	90.67	114*	3	2
Don Bradman (Aus)	4	8	1	526	75.14	144*	1	3

Best Individual Bowling Performances (England unless stated)

Player	Mat	Bll	Md	Runs	Wkt	Ave	BB	S/R
Alec Bedser	6	2289	111	829	41	20.22	7/44	55.83
Fred Trueman	5	1299	52	528	32	16.50	5/27	40.59
Brian Statham	6	1608	78	640	28	22.86	5/31	57.43
John Snow	6	1806	66	912	26	35.08	5/92	69.46
Ian Botham	7	1541	60	709	25	28.36	6/34	61.64
Richard Hadlee (NZ)	5	1459	59	649	24	27.04	6/80	60.79
Shane Warne (Aus)	3	1032	59	381	21	18.14	6/33	49.14
Bob Willis	5	1081	41	481	21	22.90	5/65	51.48
Phil DeFreitas	4	832	33	407	20	20.35	5/53	41.60
Angus Fraser	4	1047	56	417	18	23.17	5/60	58.17

Highest Individual Scores (England unless stated)

278	Denis Compton	v Pakistan	1954
261	Frank Worrell (WI)		1950
258	Tom Graveney	v West Indies	1957
232	Stan McCabe (Aus)		1938
232	Viv Richards (WI)		1976
219	Mark Taylor (Aus)		1989
216*	Eddie Paynter	v Australia	1938
210	Graham Gooch	v New Zealand	1994
209*	Basil Butcher (WI)		1966
208	Dudley Nourse (SA)		1951

Best Individual Bowling Performances (England unless stated)

32.4-2-107-8	Bernard Bosanquet	v Australia	1905
17.2-7-44-7	Alec Bedser	v Australia	1953
41.4-24-54-7	Bill O'Reilly (Aus)		1934
38.3-16-55-7	Alec Bedser	v Australia	1953
31.3-14-64-7	Frank Laver (Aus)		1905
21.3-7-28-6	Frank Tyson	v South Africa	1955
18-5-33-6	Shane Warne (Aus)		2001
21-9-34-6	Ian Botham	v New Zealand	1978
16.2-7-34-6	James Kirtley	v South Africa	2003
23.5-9-35-6	Morris Nichols	v South Africa	1935

Highest Partnerships

Wkt	Runs	Batsmen	Match
1st	329	Geoff Marsh & Mark Taylor (Aus)	1989
2nd	266	Peter Richardson & Tom Graveney (Eng)	1957 v West Indies
3rd	319	Alan Melville & Dudley Nourse (SA)	1947
4th	283	Frank Worrell & Everton Weekes (WI)	1950

stats

5th	237	Denis Compton & Norman Yardley (Eng)	1947 v South Africa
6th	215	Geoff Boycott & Alan Knott (Eng)	1977 v Australia
7th	154	Collie Smith & John Goddard (WI)	1957
8th	107	Lindsay Hassett & Ray Lindwall (Aus)	1948
9th	103	Craig White & Matthew Hoggard (Eng)	2002 v India
10th	80	Mike Watkinson & Richard Illingworth (Eng)	1995 v West Indies

Results at Trent Bridge

Date	Countries	Result
01/06/1899	v Australia	drawn
29/05/1905	v Australia	won by 213 runs
05/08/1912	Australia v South Africa	drawn
28/05/1921	v Australia	lost by 10 wickets
12/06/1926	v Australia	drawn
13/06/1930	v Australia	won by 93 runs
08/06/1934	v Australia	lost by 238 runs
15/06/1935	v South Africa	drawn
10/06/1938	v Australia	drawn
07/06/1947	v South Africa	drawn
10/06/1948	v Australia	lost by 8 wickets
20/07/1950	v West Indies	lost by 10 wickets
07/06/1951	v South Africa	lost by 71 runs
11/06/1953	v Australia	drawn
01/07/1954	v Pakistan	won by an innings and 129 runs
09/06/1955	v South Africa	won by an innings and 5 runs
07/06/1956	v Australia	drawn
04/07/1957	v West Indies	drawn
04/06/1959	v India	won by an innings and 59 runs
07/07/1960	v South Africa	won by 8 wickets
26/07/1962	v Pakistan	drawn
04/06/1964	v Australia	drawn
05/08/1965	v South Africa	lost by 94 runs
30/06/1966	v West Indies	lost by 139 runs
10/08/1967	v Pakistan	won by 10 wickets
07/08/1969	v New Zealand	drawn
13/07/1972	v Australia	drawn
07/06/1973	v New Zealand	won by 38 runs
03/06/1976	v West Indies	drawn
28/07/1977	v Australia	won by 7 wickets
10/08/1978	v New Zealand	won by an innings and 119 runs
05/06/1980	v West Indies	lost by 2 wickets
18/06/1981	v Australia	lost by 4 wickets
25/08/1983	v New Zealand	won by 165 runs
11/07/1985	v Australia	drawn
07/08/1986	v New Zealand	New Zealand won by 8 wickets
02/06/1988	v West Indies	drawn
10/08/1989	v Australia	lost by an innings and 180 runs
07/06/1990	v New Zealand	drawn
04/07/1991	v West Indies	lost by 9 wickets
01/07/1993	v Australia	drawn
02/06/1994	v New Zealand	won by an innings and 90 runs
10/08/1995	v West Indies	drawn
04/07/1996	v India	drawn
07/08/1997	v Australia	lost by 264 runs
23/07/1998	v South Africa	won by 8 wickets
01/06/2000	v Zimbabwe	drawn
02/08/2001	v Australia	lost by 7 wickets
08/08/2002	v India	drawn
14/08/2003	v South Africa	won by 70 runs
10/06/2004	v New Zealand	won by 4 wickets

TARIM

ALTUN S

TAN

Chandigarh .

New Delhi

NEPAL

BHUT

Kanpur .

Ahmedabad

BANGLAD

I N D I A

Nagpur .

Kolkata

Mumbai .

Bangalore .

Chennai

SRI LANKA

India's first Test began at the Gymkhana Ground in Mumbai (then Bombay) on December 15 1933 when England were entertained. The visitors won by nine wickets. This was the ground's only Test. Eden Gardens in Kolkata (then Calcutta) was the venue for the second Test of the series which started on 5th January 1934. That match ended in a draw. The third and final Test of that series was played at the M. A. Chidambaram Stadium in Chennai (then Madras). England won by 202 runs. When the West Indies visited in 1948/49 the Feroz Shah Kotla Stadium in Delhi became India's fourth Test venue. The Brabourne Stadium replaced the Gymkhana Ground as Mumbai's Test venue when it hosted the second Test of this series on 9th December. Green Park in Kanpur was the next ground to be granted Test status when England visited in January 1952, winning by eight wickets. The University Ground in Lucknow also became a Test ground in October 1952 when Pakistan paid their first visit to India. This was the only Test played at the ground.

India continued to move Tests around the country and Lal Bahadur Stadium in Hyderabad became the eighth venue during the 1955/56 series against New Zealand. The stadium was only used for three Tests, the last being in December 1988. The Corporation Stadium in Chennai took over from the MA Chidambaram Stadium for nine Tests between January 1956 and February 1965. The Vidarbha Cricket Association Ground in Nagpur was the next ground to be granted Test status in October 1969 when New Zealand were again the visitors. The M. Chinnaswamy Stadium in Bangalore held its first Test in November 1974.

The following year the Wankhede Stadium replaced the Brabourne Stadium in Mumbai. Burlton Park in Jullender became the 13th Test ground in the country when it hosted the second Test of the September 1983 series against Pakistan. The Gujarat Stadium in Ahmedabad held its first Test two months later.

The Barabati Stadium in Cuttack hosted its first Test in January 1987. The ground held just one more Test match, eight years later. The next three grounds to stage Tests were only awarded one Test each. The Sawai Mansingh Stadium in Jaipur became the 16th Test venue in February 1987, the Sector 16 Stadium in Chandigarh followed in 1990 and Test cricket returned to Lucknow in January 1994 when the K. D. Singh Babu Stadium was used. Unfortunately the ground has not held Test cricket since. The most recent venue is the Punjab Cricket Association Ground in Chandigarh. The fabulous, purpose-built stadium hosted the third and final Test of 1994 series against the West Indies. The ground has now become a regular Test match venue.

Airlines

India's national airline is Air India. There are a number of airlines which fly in between the major cities including India Airlines, Sahara Airlines and Jet Airways. Air travel is expensive in India. There are discount fares for Indian residents but not international visitors. For best prices internal flights should be purchased in the country of origin if possible. Indian Airlines do offer a 15 day pass for US$500 and a 21 day pass for US$750 which offers unlimited travel on all domestic routes.

Indian Airlines	033 2211 0730
Sahara Airlines	033 2282 9075
Jet Airways	033 2229 2227

Buses

India has an extensive bus network however bus can be very uncomfortable and overcrowded. Most visitors opt for train travel.

Trains

Inexpensive, comfortable and safe way to travel. Due to the expense of air flights many cricket supporters travel by train from match to match. Indian Railways offer an Indrail pass which entitles travellers to unlimited travel throughout the country. The pass costs US$248 for 30 days in 2-tier AC, air-conditioned accommodation with two-tier bunk beds, and US$200 for 30 days for 3-tier AC. Free reservations can be made upon purchase of the pass which is totally flexible. Journeys can be changed and added to your itinerary. Booking is essential as the trains are always very busy. The standard of services in booking offices and on the trains in second to none. Enquiries www.indiarail.gov.

Distance Between Cities (in kms)

	Ahmedabad	Bangalore	Chandigarh	Chennai	Delhi	Kanpur	Kolkata	Mumbai	Nagpur
Ahmedabad		1495	1153	1826	915	1077	1924	545	970
Bangalore	1495		2298	331	2061	1851	1881	998	1049
Chandigarh	1153	2298		2424	238	646	1646	1637	1249
Chennai	1826	331	2424		2095	1885	1676	1329	1083
Delhi	915	2061	238	2095		408	1461	1407	1012
Kanpur	1077	1851	646	1885	408		1000	1288	802
Kolkata	1924	1881	1646	1676	1461	1000		1987	1124
Mumbai	545	998	1637	1329	1407	1288	1987		863
Nagpur	970	1049	1249	1083	1012	802	1124	863	

...drail passes can be purchased in Britain
...n SD Enterprises on 0208 903 3411 or
...w.indiarail.co.uk

Hire
...lable from most of the major hotels in
...a. An International Driving Licence is
...iired by all foreigners. An alternative is to
...a car and driver as driving in India is very
...cult, especially for visitors with no local
...wledge. Traffic is horrendous in most cities
...cars, cyclists, trucks and animals battling
...supremacy on the roads.

...is
...s and auto-rickshaws are available outside
...orts, hotels, restaurants and on ranks
...oughout the country. Taxis are usually on
...ers but the fare should be agreed with the
...er before commencing an auto-rickshaw
...rney. Hoteliers will advise the correct price
...guideline.

...nks
...king hours in India vary from city to city.
...ally banks are open in the morning and
...ort part of the afternoon. They are also
...n on Saturday morning. Most banks have
...ign exchange facilities and US$ and Ster-
...; traveller cheques are widely accepted.
...ia uses the rupee. Notes are issued in
...ominations of Rs500, 100, 50, 20, 10, 5, 2
...1 and coins in denominations of Rs 5, 2
...1 and 50, 25, 10 and 5 paise.

...ecoms
...rnational Direct Dialling is available in
...st major hotels. Public payphones are
...international. However there are many
...phone and internet shops which offer
...rnational calls at cheap rates. India's dial-
...; code is 91. The outgoing international
...de is 00.

Post
Each city has a General Post Office which is
open Monday to Saturday and in some cases
Sundays. Opening times vary however the larger
post offices should be open from 08.00-18.00.

Tourist Offices
There are offices in most of the cricket playing
cities and at the major airports. The Govern-
ment of India Tourist Office headquarters is in
Connaught Place in Delhi.
Enquiries 011 332 0005.

Emergency Numbers
Police   100
Fire   101
Ambulance   102

Embassies
British High Commission
Shantipath, Chanakyapuri
New Delhi 110 021
Tel: 011 26872161
Fax: 011 26870065

Australian High Commission
Australia Compound
No.1/50 G Shantipath
Chanakyapuri
New Delhi 110–021
Tel: 011 688 8223
Fax: 011 688 5199

New Zealand High Commission
50-N, Nyaya Marg
Chanakyapuri
New Delhi 110-021
Tel: 011 2688 3170
Fax: 011 2688 3165
nzhc@ndf.vsnl.net.in

Visas
All visitors must carry a passport valid for
at least six months and must obtain a visa
before travelling. Multiple entry tourist
visas are issued at Indian embassies for a
fee depending on the passport held.

A British passport holder is charged £30 for the six month visa. Applicants must complete an application form and have two passport photographs. A visa must be used within six months of issue. The visa is usually issued on a same day basis.

Customs

Visitors over the age of 18 may take the following goods into Australia without incurring customs duty.
200 cigarettes or 50 cigars
1 litre of alcohol

Time Difference

India is five-and-a-half hours ahead of GMT GMT + 5

Electricity

220 volts AC at 50 cycles per second. Mos: hotels have adaptors.

Departure Tax

Rs 300 on all visitors leaving India.

ahmedabad

sardar patel stadium

The Sardar Patel Stadium in Ahmedabad is home to the Gujarat Cricket Association. It is a modern stadium, a concrete bowl surrounded by a dustbowl. It became the 14th venue for Test cricket in India in 1983 when India entertained the West Indies. India looked likely to win when Kapil Dev took 9/83 in the second innings, leaving India needing 242. But Michael Holding, 4/30, and Winston Davies, 3/21, ripped out the heart of the innings and India finished 138 runs short on 103. No Indian batsmen got a duck but no less than six of them scored only one run each.

After drawing with Pakistan in 1987, the next match was not until 1994 against Sri Lanka. The visitors batted first being dismissed for 119 with Venkatapathy Raju taking 5/38. In reply India totalled 358 with Mohammed Azharuddin top scoring with 152. In their second innings Raju was again the menace taking 6/87 as Sri Lanka collapsed to 222 all out for India to win by an innings and 17 runs. Two years later in 1996, South Africa were the visitors in a thrilling match. Batting first the home side scored 223 with Alan Donald taking 4/37. South Africa replied with 244, thanks to a knock of 67no from number 9 Fanie De Villiers. Sunil Joshi took 4/34 for the home side. In their second innings a fifty from VVS Laxman was the only decent score of India's total of 190. Set 170 to win South Africa collapsed to 105 all out to lose by 64 runs. Hanse Cronje was left on 48no as six of his team mates did not manage to get off the mark. Javagal Srinath took 6/21.

The highest team score is 583/7dec. by India against New Zealand in 1999 and the lowest is 103 by India in the inaugural Test. Raju's 11/125 against Sri Lanka is the best match return.

The stadium is situated 4km to the west of Ahmedabad, off Relief Road and across Ellisbirdge. The crowd rarely reaches 10,000 for Test matches although the capacity is 50,000. The Pavilion is a fine building at the south end of the ground. The seats in the lower pavilion are the most expensive in the ground and beside the players' area. Above, in the upper pavilion, there are two tiers which is arguably the best place in the ground from which to watch. Most of these seats are undercover. Entrance to this area is through Gate 4. To the left of the pavilion cheaper seats but still undercover are available at Gate 7. At the far end of the ground the North Stand provides a good vantage point to watch the cricket. Moving around to the east side of the ground is the General Admittance Area. This area is totally uncovered and gets incredibly hot as the day progresses. A high fence runs around the whole ground apart from in front of the pavilion.

The crowd is very friendly and very curious. Ahmedabad does not get many tourists and the cricket is about the only time a lot of the crowd will see westerners. They love their cricket and can happily chat about it all day. All around the ground spectators flock to the fence when any of the players comes close. The players are absolutely worshipped. and the crowd are appreciative of good cricket from both teams.

Security is very tight at Ahmedabad. Due to crowd trouble in the past no food, flags, newspapers, water or soft drinks are allowed in the ground. Tickets are constantly checked and bags are constantly searched in what can seem to be an over-the-top manner. Pass-outs are issued when leaving the ground.

Lunchtime can be a wonderful experience at Ahmedabad. It is a chance to go outside and meet the people who are absolutely fascinated by the presence of a westerner. Everybody, including journalists, wants to talk and, of course, the kids all want to sell you sweets, water and cadge any spare tickets. There are food stalls inside the ground behind the pavilion and the stands. They serve Indian food, nuts and cold drinks which unfortunately cannot be brought back to your seats. As Gujarat is 'dry' there is no alcohol. Generally the stalls cater for the locals. The toilet facilities are not the best and are not well looked after. They deteriorate as the game progresses.

Tickets are available from the ticket office at the entrance to the area which one passes 200 metres before reaching the stadium itself. Queues are not long and the service is quick. Tickets can be ordered beforehand from Mr. Vikram Patel, Honorary Secretary, Gujarat Cricket Association, Sardar Patel Stadium, Near Sports Club of Gujarat Ltd, Navrangpura, Ahmedabad 380 014. Tel : 079 644 3787 Fax : 079 640 7978 or from bcci@vsnl.com A rickshaw journey from the city to the ground should not cost any more than 100R, however on the way home everybody offers the visitors lifts in their cars, trucks or jeeps. The local people certainly go out of their way to make your visit to their city as pleasant as possible.

Post Office
General Post Office
Corner of Tilak and Balvantrai Road
Tel: 079 550 3116
Navrangpura H.P.O.079 6442286
Railwaypura P.O.   079 2142961

Hospital
Apollo Hospital
Tel: 079 396 9209
Civil Hospital
Chamanpura Road

Tourist Information
Tourism Corporation of Gujarat Ltd.
H. K. House
Ashram Road
Tel: 079 658 9172

Ahmedabad also known as Ahmadabad, is in the Gujarat State in Western India. The state was formed in 1960 by the Bombay Reorganisation Act with Ahmedabad its capital. This lasted ten years until Gandhinagar took over. Known as the 'Manchester of the East', it is Western India's second largest industrial city with a population of just under four million. Ahmedabad suffered a massive earthquake on India Independence Day in January 2001 which measured 7.9 on the Richter Scale. More than 30,000 people died, 70,000 were injured and more than one million made homeless.

The city was begun in the early 15th century and was named after its founder Sultan Ahmed Shah. However the area dates back to the fourth century when it was part of the Gupta Empire. The area was conquered by the Gurjaras in the 8th century, hence the name. A succession of rulers followed including the Arabs, the Mughals and the Maratha. The British East India Company took control in 1820 and 40 years later Gurajat became a province of British India. Ahmedabad was a major centre during the fight for independence with Mahatma Gandhi directing operations from the Sabarmati Ashram. After independence in 1947 it became part of the state of Bombay until 1960.

It is a huge city divided down the middle by the wide Sabarmati River. It is extremely busy, with chaotic traffic not helped by cattle wandering the streets. Some of these animals are monstrous and regularly cause pile-ups. Without doubt the city is fast and vibrant, especially in the old city's bazaar with its narrow lanes. It is perfectly safe to walk around although the air pollution is incredibly bad and coupled with the humidity makes walking pretty uncomfortable. The Mughal Emperor Jehangir described the city as the 'City of Dust' in the 15th century and unfortunately now in the 21st century that would be a generous description. The climate is hot and humid with temperatures rising to over 40 degrees during the summer. Most visitors use either taxis or auto-rickshaws to move around. There are a number of fascinating sights, mostly religious. The Ahmedabad Municipal Transport Corporation (Tel: 5507739) can arrange tours although using auto-rickshaws is an easy way to see the sights. The Great Mosque, also known as the Jama Masjid, is a must see; another Mosques include the Sidi Saiyad and the Rani Sipri, both constructed in the early 16th century, and the Sidi Bashir Mosque home of the Shaking Minarets. The Hathi Singh and Hatheesing Jain Temples are also wonderfully ornate buildings and visiting them or any of the many temples is a rewarding experience. The Dada Hari Vav, a 15th century stepped well, is a wonderful example of Gujarati architecture. The Gandhi Memorial Museum and Ashram are two of the highlights. There are a number of museums including the Natural History Museum and a couple of art galleries.

There is a varied selection of accommodation with few top class hotels and a large number of mid-range and budget choices. Generally the latter two ranges are clean and comfortable. There are numerous restaurants including those at the top end hotels. The cheaper hotels tend not to have restaurants but do supply room service. Ahmedabad is a dry state with no alcohol available in hotels or restaurants. A permit can be granted for the allocation of a small quantity of alcohol per week however the process is long and tedious.

Sardar Vallabhbhai Patel International Airport is situated 8km to the north east of Ahmedabad. Pre-paid taxis are available in the arrivals hall and should cost no more than R200 and the journey takes approximately 15-20 minutes. Autorickshaws are also available for those with less luggage at a cost of R100. All the major hotels have desks in the tiny Arrival Hall and provide transportation for their guests. Local bus No's 102 and 105 run to and from the airport to Lal Darwaja is the centre of town at a cost of R5. There is very little else at the airport with no sign of any car rental.

Gandhi Ashram

Mahatma Gandhi's headquarters during India's struggle for Independence. Founded in 1915 and situated 7km north of Ahmedabad it is set in a beautiful park alive with birdlife and animals and is the city's major tourist attraction. His spartan living area is preserved and there is a small museum detailing his life. The ashram is open from 08.30-18.30 seven days a week.

Jama Masjid

Built by Ahmad Shah in 1423, it is one of the biggest mosques in India and is a fine example of the exquisite workmanship which is a feature of many mosques. It has over 300 pillars which divide the prayer hall into 15 different squares.

The Shaking Minarets

A pair of minarets, which if one is shaken the other also rocks in sympathy via vibrations through a connecting stone bridge. The reason why remains a mystery. They are situated in the Sidi Bashir Mosque near Ahmedabad railway station. Climbing up the Minarets to feel the shaking is no longer permitted after a tragedy when many people were crushed.

Kankaria Lake

Built by Qutb-ud-Din in 1451 this is a very popular recreational centre. The lake lies in glorious gardens. In the middle is the summer palace known as Nagina Wadi that was visited by Nur Jahn and Jehangir during the Mughal period.

Hatheesing Jain Temple

Kerarisimha Hatheesing Shah, a rich merchant, built this from white marble in 1948 in dedication of Dharmanath. It known as one of the most ornate temples in Ahmedabad with intricate carvings. Situated just outside the Delhi gate.

Airlines

Indian Airlines
Airline House
Lal Barwaja
Tel: 079 902 712

Air India
Airline House
Lal Barwaja
Tel: 079 658 5622

Jet Airways
Madhuvan Complex
Ground Floor
Ellisbridge
Tel: 079 754 3304

British Airways
Tel: 079 656 1703

Emirates
Tel: 079 642 0798

Trains

The General Booking Office is to the left of Ahmedabad Railway Station. The tourist/foreigners counter is No.5 however getting to the front of the queue can be quite difficult. Persistence is required. Trains run to all parts of the country from Ahmedabad including Delhi 19 hours and Mumbai 13 hours.

General Enquiries	131
Reservation Enquiries	135
Arrival / Departures	132

Taxis

Taxi and auto-rickshaws are available throughout the city outside hotels, restaurants, the airport and the cricket stadium. Always agree the price with the driver before commencing your journey.

Holiday Inn Ahmedabad
Khanpur Road, near Nehru Bridge
Tel: 079 2550 5505
Fax: 079 2550 5501
reservations@holidayinnahmedabad.com
Three star hotel. 63 luxury rooms
overlooking the Sabarmati River.
Multi-cusinine restaurant, swimming
pool, health club with Turkish baths.

Hotel Taj Residency Ummed
Airport Cross Road
Tel: 079 2286 4444
Fax: 079 2286 4454
Five star hotel, 2km from centre.
91 excellent rooms, business centre,
health club, restaurants.

Hotel Cama Park Plaza
Khanpur Road
Tel: 079 255 05281
Fax: 079 255 05285
camahotel@vsnl.com
Four star hotel on the banks of the
river. 50 rooms, very good restaurant,
24 hour coffee shop, business centre,
swimming pool, gardens.

Comfort Inn Sunset
Airport Circle
Hansol
Tel: 079 2286 2591
Fax: 079 2286 1627
cisunset@winetoneline.net
Four star hotel 6km from the centre
of the town near airport. 33 luxury
rooms, restaurant serving Indian,
Continental, Italian and Chinese cui-
sine.

Hotel Silver Oak Heritage
Opposite Bhagwat Vidyapeth
Tel: 079 2747 6605
Fax: 079 2748 3540
A two star hotel in the centre of town
with good rooms and restaurant.

Days Inn Chicago
Ellisbridge
Tel: 079 2657 7223
Comfortable budget hotel. Large air-
conditioned en suite rooms. Good
restaurant and friendly staff.

Hotel King Palace
Khanpur
Tel: 079 2550 0280
Fax: 079 2550 0275

Good budget hotel opposite
Cama Hotel. Good clean en suite
rooms with TV. Good restaurant and
room service.

Hotel Capital
Khanpur
Tel: 079 2550 4634
Another good budget hotel with clean
rooms and room service.

Hotel Capri
Relief Road
Tel: 079 2550 6644
Fax: 079 2550 6646
Good budget hotel in the centre of
town.

Vishala
Vasna Tolnaka Ahmedabad
Tel: 079 403357

Timbuktoo Restaurant
Samudra Building
Nagar Road
Tel: 079 408547

Ten Restaurant
Urja House
C G Road
Tel: 079 445070

Tomatoes
Mardia Plaza
CG Road
Tel: 079 441198

RG - The Pizzaria
Mardia Plaza
C G Road
Tel: 079 6566129

Chills Thrills & Frills
3031 Centre Point Panchvati
Tel: 079 467435

Cafe Upper Crust
5 Arohi Complex Vijay
Char Rasta Road
Tel: 079 401554

Sankalp Restaurant
Samir Complex
C G Road
Tel: 079 406707

Mirch Masala
Chandan Complex
C G Road
Tel: 079 403340

The Calico Museum
Opposite Shahibaug under Bridge
Shahibaug
Tel: 079 286 8172
An exhibition of rare textiles dating back to the 17th century which are entwined with the history of the city. It is housed in a wooden Haveli. Open 10.30-12.30 and 14.45-16.45 Monday, Tuesday, Thursday, Friday and Saturday.

Sardar Patel Memorial Museum
Opposite Circuit House
Shahibaug
The Sardar Patel Memorial Museum

houses a rare collection of Jain sculptures and paintings. Open 10.00-17.30. Closed on Mondays.

N. C. Mehta Art Gallery
Sanskar Kendra
Paldo
Tel: 079 78369
Houses a fine collection of miniatures from all over India.

Climate	ave temp	rain cm
January	20	2
February	23	2
March	24	1
April	31	1
May	34	11
June	33	100
July	30	325
August	28	223
September	29	135
October	29	14
November	25	6
December	22	2

Win/Loss Record

Country	Played	won	drawn	Lost	Tie
West Indies	1	1	-	-	-
India	7	2	4	1	-
Pakistan	1	-	1	-	-
New Zealand	2	-	2	-	-
England	1	-	1	-	-
Sri Lanka	1	-	-	1	-
South Africa	1	-	-	1	-

Highest Individual Aggregates (India unless stated)

Player	Mat	Inn	NO	Runs	Ave	HS	50	100
Rahul Dravid	4	8	1	431	61.57	222	1	1
Sachin Tendulkar	5	9	0	431	47.89	217	0	2
Sourav Ganguly	3	6	2	324	81.00	125	1	2
VVS Laxman	3	5	0	245	49.00	75	3	0
Nathan Astle (NZ)	2	3	1	228	114.00	103	2	1
Mohammad Azharuddin	3	4	0	223	55.75	152	0	1
Sunil Gavaskar	2	3	0	154	51.33	90	2	0
Mark Butcher (Eng)	1	2	0	143	71.50	92	2	0
Craig White (Eng)	1	2	0	139	69.50	121	0	1
Craig McMillan (NZ)	1	2	1	137	137.00	83*	2	0

Top Wicket Takers (India unless stated)

Player	Mat	Bll	Md	Runs	Wkt	Ave	BB	S/R
Anil Kumble	5	1969	98	710	28	25.36	7/115	70.32
Kapil Dev	3	651	32	227	14	16.21	9/83	46.50
Harbhajan Singh	3	1179	47	433	12	36.08	5/71	98.25
Javagal Srinath	3	714	34	328	12	27.33	6/21	59.50
Venkatapathy Raju	1	338	16	125	11	11.36	6/87	30.73
Daniel Vettori (NZ)	2	714	14	432	7	61.71	4/200	102.00
Alan Donald (SA)	1	252	17	69	7	9.86	4/37	36.00
Rajesh Chauhan	1	246	22	53	6	8.83	3/8	41.00
Michael Holding (WI)	1	258	10	110	6	18.33	4/30	43.00
Wayne Daniel (WI)	1	108	2	50	6	8.33	5/39	18.00

Highest Individual Performances (India unless stated)

222	Rahul Dravid	v New Zealand 2003-04
217	Sachin Tendulkar	v New Zealand 1999-00
152	Mohammad Azharuddin	v Sri Lanka 1993-94
125	Sourav Ganguly	v New Zealand 1999-00
121	Craig White (Eng)	2001-02
110	Sadagoppan Ramesh	v New Zealand 1999-00
109	Dilip Vengsarkar	v Pakistan 1986-87
105	Ijaz Faqih (Pak)	1986-87
103	Sachin Tendulkar	v England 2001-02
103	Nathan Astle (NZ)	v India 2003-04

Best Individual Bowling Performances (India unless stated)

30.3-6-83-9	Kapil Dev	v West Indies 1983-84
51-13-115-7	Anil Kumble	v England 2001-02
11.5-4-21-6	Javagal Srinath	v South Africa 1996-97
32.3-9-87-6	Venkatapathy Raju	v Sri Lanka 1993-94
23.5-7-38-5	Venkatapathy Raju	v Sri Lanka 1993-94
11.5-0-39-5	Wayne Daniel (WI)	1983-84
43.3-16-67-5	Ashley Giles (Eng)	2001-02
30.2-6-71-5	Harbhajan Singh	v England 2001-02
48-21-82-5	Anil Kumble	v New Zealand 1999-00
17-5-30-4	Michael Holding (WI)	v India 1983-84

Highest Partnerships

Wkt	Runs	Batsmen	Match
1st	131	Matt Horne & Gary Stead (NZ)	1999-2000
2nd	112	Mark Butcher & Nasser Hussain (Eng)	2001-2002
3rd	121*	Craig Spearman & Stephen Fleming (NZ)	1999-2000
4th	281	Sachin Tendulkar & Sourav Ganguly (Ind)	1999-2000 v N Zealand
5th	182	Rahul Dravid & VVS Laxman (Ind)	2003-2004 v N Zealand
6th	59	Mark Ramprakash & Craig White (Eng)	2001-2002
7th	154	Imran Khan & Ijaz Faqih (Pak)	1986-1987

	8th	74	Malcolm Marshall & Michael Holding (WI)	1983-1984
	9th	67	Mohammad Azharuddin & R K Chauhan (Ind) 1993-1994 v Sri Lanka	
			Daniel Vettori & Paul Wiseman (NZ)	2003-2004
	10th	51	Jeff Dujon & Winston Davis (WI)	1983-1984

Results at Sardar Patel Stadium

Date	Countries	Result
12/11/1983	India v West Indies	lost by 138 runs
04/03/1987	India v Pakistan	drawn
08/02/1994	India v Sri Lanka	won by an innings and 17 runs
20/11/1996	India v South Africa	won by 64 runs
29/10/1999	India v New Zealand	drawn
11/12/2001	India v England	drawn
08/10/2003	India v New Zealand	drawn

bangalore

m. chinnaswamy Stadium

The M. Chinnaswamy Stadium in Bangalore is the home of the Karnataka State Cricket Association and named after a former president. The stadium is situated in the heart of the city and is modern, purpose-built and with excellent facilities.

It became the 11th Indian Test venue in 1974 when it hosted the opening match of the series between India and the West Indies.

Having lost the toss, the visitor's batted first making 289 with Alvin Kallicharran hitting 124 and Gordon Greenidge 93. The home side replied with 260, Hrishikesh Kanitkar topscoring with 65. In their second innings the West Indies scored 356/6 dec. with captain Clive Lloyd hitting a glorious 163 and Gordon Greenidge 107. Set a target of 386 and with two players absent, the home side were blasted out for 118 to lose by 267 runs. Andy Roberts (3/24) and Keith Boyce (3/43) were the chief wicket takers.

The next Test was the fourth against England in 1977. England were already 3-0 up in the series but here India turned the tables and won by 140 runs. In reply to India's 253 (Bob Willis 6/53), England could only manage 195, Dennis Amiss scoring 82 of them. Bhagwat Chadnrasekhar took 6/76. In their second innings the home side declared on 259/9 leaving the visitors 318 for victory. England collapsed to 61/6 before Allan Knott hit 81no but not even he could stop Bishan Bedi (6/71) and Chandrasekhar (3/55) dismissing England for 177.

A string of five draws followed; against the West Indies in 1978, Australia and Pakistan in 1979, England in 1981 and Pakistan in 1983. The result was the same in the deciding Test of 1987 series against Pakistan. After draws in Chennai, Kolkata, Jaipur and Ahmedabad there was everything to play for in the decider. After winning the toss, Pakistan managed only 116, Maninder Singh taking 7/27. India replied with 145, Dilip Vengsarkar hitting 50, while Iqbal Qasim (5/48) and Tauseef Ahmed (5/54) took the wickets. Rameez Raja (47) top scored in Pakistan's second innings of 249. Set 221 for victory India fell 17 runs short despite 96 from Sunil Gavaskar, Iqbal (4/73) and Tauseef (4/85) again doing the damage.

Comfortable victories followed against New Zealand by 172 runs in 1988 and, after a five year gap, against Sri Lanka by an innings and 95 runs, and against New Zealand again a year later, this time by eight wickets. In 1998 India had already taken a 2-0 lead in the three match series with Australia when the teams met in Bangalore. India won the toss and batted first making 424 with a glorious 177 from Sachin Tendulkar and 74 from Navjot Sidhu. Australia replied with 400, Mark Waugh hitting 153no and Michael Slater 91. Anil Kumble took 6/98 for India. In their second innings the home side could only manage 169 as Michael Kasprowicz took 5/28. Captain Mark Taylor hit 102no as Australia salvaged some pride with an eight wicket victory.

Bangalore hosted what turned out to be Mohammed Azharuddin's last match for India, an innings and 71 runs defeat by South Africa. The most recent Test to be played at the ground was a rain affected draw with England in 2001 during which Michael Vaughan became only the seventh player in Test history to be given out 'handled the ball'.

The highest team score is 541/6 declared by India against Sri Lanka in 1994, the lowest 116 by Pakistan in 1987. The highest run chase was 195/2 by Australia in 1998. Maninder Singh's match figures of 10/126 are the best return at the ground.

The M. Chinnaswamy Stadium has an official capacity of 35,000 but it feels a lot of bigger. It is on Mahatma Gandhi Road, which has most of the better restaurants and bars in Bangalore, in the centre of the city and the approach to the stadium is entertaining with excitable home supporters giving any visiting fans a loud but friendly welcome. It is modern with a fine pavilion at the south end of the ground. To the left of the pavilion is the three-tier President's Stand which is an excellent vantage point. The rest of the ground is circled by a huge two-tier stand which also provides excellent views and is where the ground's terrific atmosphere is created by a passionate and vocal crowd. The seats in the upper tier provide the best view as there is a fence running around the pitch which restricts some viewing in the lower tier. It is important to get to the ground early if your seat is in the lower tier. The entrance/exits in the lower tier can get very congested during the intervals and can be frightening. The majority of the seats in the ground are undercover. A modern electronic scoreboard is in the north east corner of the ground. Foodstalls under the stands offer Indian food, popcorn, crisps, soft drinks and water. The toilet facilities only offer squat loos and are not well tended.

Tickets should be purchased in the days leading up to the Test as the ticket office can be very busy on the day. They are available from the Karnataka State Cricket Association Tel : 080 286 4487 or 080 286 5010 or on their website www.karnatakacricket.org

Security is tight at the entrances to the ground and each stand with no bottles allowed. Pass-outs are issued for those who wish to leave during the day.

The ground is within walking distance of most of the good hotels. Tuk tuks and taxis are available outside most hotels.

Bangalore lies on the Mysore Plateau in southern India and is the capital of Karnataka State. It is India's fifth largest city, with a population of 6.8 million. Known as the Garden City, Bangalore is like a breath of fresh air with wide, tree-lined streets and beautiful parks. Legend tells us that while out hunting King Veer Ballala of Vijaynagar could not find his way back to his palace. While searching for a way out of the woods he came across a woman who fed him baked beans. He eventually made his way back and named the area Benda Kaluooru which means the place of baked beans. In time the name transformed into Bangalore.

The city was founded by Kempe Gowda, a chieftain of the Vijayanagar empire in 1537. He built a mud fort with eight gates around the city. In 1687 the Mughals captured it and it still has some of their architecture today. They eventually sold it to the Mysore rulers. In 1807 the British took over the city and it grew from a small garrison to a thriving trading centre. Bangalore remained British until independence in 1947 when the Mysore state was included in the Indian Union. Bangalore's growth was increased by the Indian Government's decision to move defence and scientific research centres to the city. It has become India's silicon valley, producing computer software and telecommunication products on a mass scale. Electronics City is a huge industrial park dedicated to these and associated industries. The city has attracted a huge amount of foreign investment and other industries include heavy electrical machinery, aircraft manufacturing, textiles, steel and cement.

It is one the most visited cities in India. There area some fine historical and religious attractions. The old area in the south is home to the Vidhan Soudha, the neo Dravidian style building which house the Secretariat and State and Legislature, and other historical buildings. Other attractions include the 300 acre Cubbon Park which offers an escape in the heart of the city, Lal Bagh the beautiful botanical gardens, Bangalore Palace a granite palace modelled on Windsor Castle, the 18th century Fort and Tipu's Palace and The International Society for Krishna Consciousness one of the many temples in the city. Other temples include Venkataramanasway Temple which was built by theWodevars 300 years ago, the Bull Temple in the south of the city and Gavi Gangadhareswara Temple an unusual cave temple.

Bangalore Airport is 13km from the city centre. There is a prepaid taxi service office in the arrival hall. A taxi ride should take about 15 minutes and cost R230. Auto rickshaws are also available and cost R100 to the city centre. The local bus No's 13 and 333 run from the airport to the city bus stand for R7.50. There is an ATM at the airport along with a café, and tourist information.

Vidhana Soudha

A neo-Dravidian style grey granite building which houses the Secretariat and the State Legislature and other state offices. One of India's finest public buildings, its gleaming white domes, archways and pillars are typical of many palaces in southern India. It is situated by Cubbon Park in the heart of the city.

Lal Bagh

These gardens spread across 240 acres and were design by Hyder Ali and his son Tipu Sultan during the 1760's, the Muslim era. They are within walking distance to the south of the city and are a haven with lakes, flowerbeds and fountains. There is also a wonderful collection of tropical and sub-tropical plants. The glass house which was built in 1840 is a copy of the one at London's Crystal Palace.

Cubbon Park

In the heart of Bangalore, the park was designed in 1864 by the Chief Engineer of the city and has 300 acres of lush parklands with lawns, flower beds, fountains and trees. The park has some Greco colonial buildings including the Public Library, the Government Museum and the High Court. Known as the 'lungs of Bangalore' the park is a great escape from city life. Home to one of India's largest aquariums with a fine collection of exotic fish.

The Fort

Opposite the City Market the fort built initially in 1537 by Kempe Gowda and rebuilt by Hyder Ali in 1760. It is a good example of military architecture in the 18th century. It has a number of temples within its walls with exquisite carvings of Sri Krishna. Only one of the original eight gates survives, the Delhi Gate, which remains in use. Nearby Tipu Sultan's Palace, started by Hyder Ali and completed by his son Tipu. It is well known for its five wonderfully decorated arches. The palace was later used as the British Secretariat. Both the fort and the palace are open to the public from 06.00-18.00 each day.

The Bull Temple

A typical Dravidan style temple built in the 16th century by Kempe Gowda. It is dedicated to Nandi, a bull used as transport by Lord Shiva. The temple is an extraordinary place with musicians strolling around playing their instruments, marriage processions passing by and other festive activities. The gigantic bull statue is more than five metres tall.

Post Office

General Post Office
Raj Bhavan Road
Tel: 080 286 6772
Monday to Saturday 0800-19.00
Sunday 10.30-13.30
There is another post office on
Museum Road (559 7542)

Tourist Information

Government of India Tourist Office
KFC Building
48 Church St.
Tel: 080 257 9517
Open 09.30-18.00 Monday to Friday
09.00-13.00 Saturday

Hospital

St. Martha's Hospital
Kempegowda Road

Bowring and Lady Curson Hospital
Hospital Road

The Leela Palace

23 Kodahalli
Airport Road
Tel: 080 521 2727
Fax: 080 521 1234
admin@theleelablr.com
Set in 7 acres of lush gardens 3km from the centre of town. 254 luxurious rooms with balconies overlooking either the pool or the gardens. Choice of restaurants, bar, swimming pool and health club.

The Taj West End

44 Race Course road
Tel: 080 225 5055
Fax: 080 220 0010
westend.bangalore@tajhotels.com
20 acres of gardens with 129 air-conditioned rooms . Cable TV and mini-bar. 4 restaurants and bars. Swimming pool, health club and floodlit tennis.

Taj Residency

41/3 Mahatma Gandhi Road
Tel: 080 558 4444
Fax: 080 558 4748
residency.bangalore@tajhotels.com
Five star hotel with 163 elegant rooms with cable TV and minibar. 3 restaurants, bar, swimming pool and health and fitness club.

Hotel Grand Ashok

Kumara Krupa High Grounds
Tel: 080 226 9462
Fax: 080 225 0033
htashok@blr.vsnl.net.in
Excellent. 179 rooms with all mod cons. 2 restaurants, coffee shop, bar. Swimming pool, heath centre and tennis.

Le Meridien

28 Sankey Road
Tel: 080 226 2233
Fax: 080 226 7676
leme@vsnl.com
201 tastefully decorated rooms with air-conditioning, cable TV, fax and minibar. Choice of restaurants, bar, swimming pool.

St. Mark's

4/1 St. Mark's Road
Tel: 080 227 9090
Fax: 080 227 5700
stmarks@vsnl.com
Middle of the range hotel with 78 rooms with cable TV. Restaurant, bar, swimming pool and health club.

Comfort Inn Vijay Residency

18 III Main Road
Hotel St.
Gandhinagar
Tel: 080 220 3024
Fax: 080 228 1065
civijay@zeeaccess.com
47 air-conditioned rooms with cable TV. Choice of vegetarian and Chinese restaurants.

Geo Hotel

11 Devanga Hostel Road
Tel: 080 222 1583
Fax: 080 222 1993
hotelgeoblr@rediffmail.com
Small, two star central hotel with excellent reputation. 66 rooms with air-conditioning or fans and cable TV. Very good multi-cuisine restaurants. Good service.

Ramanashree

16 Raja Ram Mohan Roy Road
Tel: 080 222 5152
Fax: 080 223 5250
ramanblr@bgl.vsnl.net.in
Budget hotel. 68 air-conditioned rooms with cable TV. Multi-cuisine restaurant.

Highgates

33 Church St.
Tel: 080 559 7172
Fax: 080 559 7799
highgates@vsnl.net
Government approved hotel with 39 rooms with air-conditioning and cable TV. Two restaurants.

The Chancery

10/6 Lavelle Road
Tel: 080 227 6767
Fax: 080 227 6700
chancery@vsnl.com
Central. 100 clean rooms with good room service.

The Atria

No. 1 Palace Road
Tel: 080 220 5205
Fax: 080 225 6850
Budget hotel with 168 rooms. Cable TV. 3km from centre. Choice of Chinese or Indian restaurants.

Most of the top hotels in Bangalore have fine restaurants. But there are also good restaurants throughout the city. Listed below are just some of them. Mahatma Gandhi Road, Church Street and Brigade Road are three of the most popular areas.

Dahlia
Church St.
Fine Japanese restaurant. Reasonably priced and one of the Bangalore's best eateries.

Taipan
Richmond Road
One of Bangalore's best Chinese restaurants with a little Indian flavour.

Ullas Refreshments
Public Utility Building
MG Road
Small, cheap restaurant serving Indian and Chinese vegetarian dishes.

Coconut Grove
Church St.
Small friendly open air restaurant with excellent Keralan and Goan dishes.

Victoria Hotel
47-48 Residency Road
Good restaurant serving Indian dishes in garden or old fashioned dining hall.

Casa Piccola 131
Residency Road
Western style restaurant, very popular with tourists.

The Only Place
Mota Royal Arcade
MG Road
Continental restaurants serving excellent steaks and good lamb dishes.

Ebony
MG Road
Popular restaurant serving Continental, Mughal and Tandoori dishes.

Sue's Food Place
Indiranagar
Small restaurant serving West Indian food. A real treat.

Mavalli Tiffin Room
Lalbagh
Lovely teahouse in the park.

Indraprastha
Hotel Adore
47 SC Road
Good, cheap Indian restaurant. Highly recommended.

Sukh Sagar
6 SM Road
Excellent south Indian food at very good prices.

Gautam
17 Museum Road
Cheap south Indian vegetarian dishes.

Bangalore has quite a lively nightlife with many bars especially around the Mahatma Gandhi Road. Pub World on Mahatma Gandhi Road has a variety of different themed pubs including a British pub and a German beer hall. The Underground pub on the same road is a good English pub with excellent western music. Nasa on Church Street is the 'in' pub in the city and is laid out like a spaceship with very loud music. Other pubs include

Black Cadillac
50 Residency Road
American theme bar. Good music.

Concorde
Airport Road
The late-night opener. Open after everywhere else closes.

Nightwatchman
Church St.
One of the top pubs/clubs in Bangalore.

180 Proof
St. Marks Road
Up-market pub with good food and music.

Downtown
Residency Road
English pub with snooker tables and loud music.

Pecos
Brigade Road
Small crowded pub with great music.

Ravindra Kalakshetre Theatre
C Road
Tel: 080 222 1271

The Town Hall
C Road
Tel: 080 222 1270

The Government Museum
Kasturba Road
Tel: 080 286 4483
Houses a fine collection of archaeo-logical artefacts. Open 10.00-17.00 Tuesday-Sunday.

Venkatappa Art Gallery
Kasturba Road
Tel: 080 286 4483
This houses the work of the famous Indian artist K. Venkatappa in which he uses both traditional Indian and western techniques. Works of other artists and sculptors are also housed in the gallery. Open 10.00-17.00 Tuesday to Sunday

Airlines
Indian Airlines
Cauvery Bhavan
Kempe Gowda Road
41
Airport   080 522 6233

Jet Airways
Sunrise Chambers
Unit GW 07
2 Ulsoor Road
Tel: 080 555 0858
Airport   080 522 1929

Air Sahara
Church St.
Tel: 080 558 4417
Airport   080 522 0626

Buses
Unlike other cities in India the local bus service in Bangalore is useable and is not too overcrowded. Light blue buses run throughout the city.

Trains
City Central is the main railway sta-tion in Bangalore and is about 2km from the centre of the city. Cantonment station is closer to the centre but few interstate trains stop there.

Railway Enquiries
General	131
Reservations	132
Arrivals/Departures	133

Taxis
Metered taxis are available, along with radio taxis, tourist taxis and auto rick-shaws. The rickshaws are certainly the best and cheapest way to get around the city.
Taxis   080 332 0152 / 080 348 7192

Climate
	ave temp	rain cm
January	21	5
February	23	6
March	26	12
April	28	39
May	27	114
June	25	78
July	24	106
August	24	138
September	24	175
October	231	57
November	22	63
December	21	17

Win/Loss Record

Country	Played	Won	Drawn	Lost	Tie
South Africa	1	1	-	-	-
West Indies	2	1	1	-	-
Australia	2	1	1	-	-
Pakistan	3	1	2	-	-
India	14	4	6	4	-
England	3	-	2	1	-
Sri Lanka	1	-	-	1	-
New Zealand	2	-	-	2	-

Highest Individual Aggregates (India unless stated)

Player	Mat	In	NO	Runs	Ave	HS	50	100
Sunil Gavaskar	8	12	1	600	54.55	172	3	2
Gundappa Viswanath	6	8	2	450	75.00	161*	3	1
Sachin Tendulkar	5	8	1	439	62.71	177	2	1
Mohammad Azharuddin	6	9	0	438	48.67	108	1	2
Dilip Vengsarkar	6	7	0	405	57.86	112	3	1
Navjot Sidhu	3	5	1	376	94.00	116	2	1
Alvin Kallicharran (WI)	2	4	0	245	61.25	124	1	1
Kapil Dev	8	9	2	235	33.57	59	2	0
Javed Miandad (Pak)	3	5	1	229	57.25	99	2	0
Aunshuman Gaekwad	3	5	1	212	53.00	87	2	0

Top Wicket Takers (India unless stated)

Player	Mat	Bll	Md	Runs	Wkt	Ave	BB	S/R
Anil Kumble	5	1420	48	612	29	21.10	6/98	48.97
Kapil Dev	8	1405	43	727	27	26.93	5/68	52.04
Bhagwat Chandrasekhar	3	854	24	478	17	28.12	6/76	50.24
Shivlal Yadav	3	639	20	270	12	22.50	4/49	53.25
Bishan Bedi	2	555	30	231	11	21.00	6/71	50.45
Karson Ghavri	4	666	25	353	11	32.09	5/51	60.55
Javagal Srinath	3	552	26	210	10	21.00	4/73	55.20
Maninder Singh	1	373	16	126	10	12.60	7/27	37.30
Ravi Shastri	3	714	34	234	10	23.40	4/69	71.40
Tauseef Ahmed (Pak)	1	437	19	139	9	15.44	5/54	48.56

Highest Individual Scores (India unless stated)

177	Sachin Tendulkar	v Australia 1997-98
172	Sunil Gavaskar	v England 1981-82
163	Clive Lloyd (WI)	1974-75
161*	Gundappa Viswanath	v Australia 1979-80
153*	Mark Waugh (Aus)	1997-98
126	Mudassar Nazar (Pak)	1979-80
124	Alvin Kallicharran (WI)	1974-75
116	Navjot Sidhu	v New Zealand8-89

| 112 | Dilip Vengsarkar | v Australia 1979-80 |
| 108 | Mohammad Azharuddin | v Sri Lanka 1993-94 |

Best Individual Bowling Performances (India unless stated)

8.2-8-27-7	Maninder Singh	v Pakistan 1986-87
7-2-53-6	Bob Willis (Eng)	1976-77
0-10-59-6	Narendra Hirwani	v New Zealand 1988-89
1.3-4-71-6	Bishan Bedi	v England 1976-77
1.2-7-76-6	Bhagwat Chandrasekhar	v England 1976-77
1.3-8-98-6	Anil Kumble	v Australia 1997-98
8.4-15-143-6	Anil Kumble	v South Africa 1999-00
8-5-28-5	Michael Kasprowicz (Aus)	1997-98
0-15-48-5	Iqbal Qasim (Pak)	1986-87
4-8-51-5	Karson Ghavri	v West Indies 1978-79

Highest Partnerships

Wkt	Runs	Batsmen	Match
st	176*	Aunshuman Gaekwad & Sunil Gavaskar (Ind)	1983-1984 v Pakistan
nd	170	Aunshuman Gaekwad & Dilip Vengsarkar (Ind)	1978-1979 v West Indies
rd	174*	Navjot Sidhu & Dilip Vengsarkar (Ind)	1988-1989 v New Zealand
th	207	Gordon Greenidge & Clive Lloyd (WI)	1974-1975
th	164	Lance Klusener & Jacques Kallis (SA)	1999-2000
th	96	Mohammad Azharuddin & Anil Kumble (Ind)	1999-2000 v South Africa
th	155	Roger Binny & Madan Lal (Ind)	1983-1984 v Pakistan
th	84	Kiran More & Ravi Shastri (Ind)	1988-1989 v New Zealand
th	69	Graham Dilley & Bob Taylor (Eng)	1981-1982
0th	26	Don Anurasiri & Muttiah Muralitharan (SL)	1993-1994

Results at M. Chinnaswamy Stadium

Date	Countries	Result
2/11/1974	West Indies	lost by 267 runs
8/01/1977	England	won by 140 runs
5/12/1978	West Indies	drawn
9/09/1979	Australia	drawn
1/11/1979	Pakistan	drawn
9/12/1981	England	drawn
4/09/1983	Pakistan	drawn
3/03/1987	Pakistan	lost by 16 runs
2/11/1988	New Zealand	won by 172 runs
6/01/1994	Sri Lanka	won by an innings and 95 runs
8/10/1995	New Zealand	won by 8 Wickets
5/03/1998	Australia	lost by 8 Wickets
2/03/2000	South Africa	lost by an innings and 71 runs
9/12/2001	England	drawn

chandigarh

The Punjab Cricket Association ground in Chandigarh is India's youngest Test venue and is one of its best. Situated in the suburb of Mohali, 10km from the centre of the city. It is modern with a wonderful pavilion and up-to-date facilities. It is also one of the best attended grounds in the country. The first match played there was against the West Indies in the third and final test of the 1994 series but it was not an auspicious start, India losing by 243 runs.

Two draws followed, a high scoring match against Sri Lanka in 1997 and quite a remarkable Test against New Zealand in 1999. India were dismissed for 83 after being inserted with Dion Nash taking 6/27. New Zealand scored 215 in their first innings with Javagal Srinath taking 6/45. India turned it around with 505/3 dec, Rahul Dravid, 144, Sachin Tendulkar, 126,no, Sourav Ganguly, 64, Devang Gandhi, 75 and Sadogoppan Ramesh, 73 all contributing heavily. Set a target of 374, New Zealand reached 251/7 as the match ended in a draw.

India finally won when they entertained England in 2001 in the first Test of the three match series. Harbhajan Singh took 5/51 as England reached 238. India amassed 469 in their first innings, Deepak Dasgupta scoring 100, Dravid, 86 and Tendulkar, 88. Trailing by 231 runs from the first innings, England managed only 235 in their second knock as Anil Kumble took 6/81. Requiring five runs to win, it took only two deliveries from Matthew Hoggard to give India the match by ten wickets.

The highest team score is 630/6 by New Zealand in 2003, the lowest India's 83 against New Zealand. The highest run chase is 5/0 by India against England in 2001! The best match return is Srinath's 8/108 in 1999.

Test cricket is not just a game in the Punjab, it is also a huge social occasion. The stadium has a capacity of 50,000 and crowds approaching this number are possible at the weekends. It is amazing to see the crowd visibly grow by thousands just before Tendulkar comes in to bat and diminish again when the master leaves the crease.

The modern pavilion is on the west side of the ground and its upper terrace is one of the few shaded areas. Not surprisingly these are the most expensive seats in the ground and are highly recommended. The terrace is always busy and often gets extremely full.

Many of the young locals treat the game as a chance to catch up with friends and seem to have little interest in the cricket, which can be frustrating for the dedicated cricket fan. The constant movement around the ground results in regular interruptions to the game. This said, the crowd are wonderfully hospitable to visitors and are some of the best hosts in Test cricket.

To the left of the pavilion is the 'VIP' section, an uncovered area with individual seats packed closely together. It is a good place from which to watch, although the heat becomes more intense as the day goes on. The cheaper seats which fill up quickly are on the north side of the ground. One of the scoreboards is behind this uncovered area. The Birla Plus Cement Pavilion provides a fantastic view of the wicket and is totally under cover on the east side of the ground. The south side has the large video replay screen, the scoreboard and uncovered terraces. There are foodstalls behind the VIP and general area stands serving popcorn, soft drinks, water, crisps, ice-cream and Indian dishes.

Behind the pavilion is one of the greatest treats in Test cricket grounds. The Punjab Cricket Association, a wonderful garden with a great bar and excellent food which can enjoyed under parasols. The swimming pool looks tempting but unfortunately it is out of bounds during the Test. The garden is a great place to go at lunch time or at stumps. The service is excellent and the area also has the best toilets in the ground.

Tickets must be obtained from the Gujarat Cricket Association, Sardar, Vallabhbhai Patel Stadium, next to Sports Club of Gujarat Ltd, Navrangpura, Ahmedabad, Telephone 6565391 or 6443787 or from pathfind@satyam.net.in as it is impossible to get them on match days. The queue for tickets needs to be seen to be believed and the crush is certainly not safe. Access through the gates is easy for those who have tickets although security is tight at the each gate, as turbanned policemen search for forbidden items including cigarettes, matches, newspapers and bottles. Cameras are allowed in the ground. Pass-out are issued for those wishing to leave the ground.

The ground is to the north of the city and a taxi from Sectors 17 or 22 takes about 20 minutes along the Himalaya Marg and costs about R200, an auto-rickshaw R80. The roads around the ground are closed during the Tests but taxis can get quite near. At the end of play many rickshaws wait just over the bridge to bring the crowds back into the city.

The Punjab Cricket Association Club are terrific hosts and have a fascinating building opposite the pavilion with the history of cricket on its wall including a tribute to Sir Don Bradman. There is also a fine painting of the last ball of the tied test in Chennai in 1986. The white government cars parked outside the club or ground just add to the feel of India.

It is a very well planned ground and one can see that the organisers have gone that extra yard with nice touches such as pot plants lining the walkways and both team emblems painted on the scoreboards. Just little things, but noticeable.

Chandigarh is situated at the foot of the Shiwalik Hills in Northern India. It is a Union Territory and is capital of both the Punjab and Haryana states. However it does not belong to either state and is under the direct administration of the India Government. The name Chandigarh is derived from the Goddess Chandika Devi, an exceptionally beautiful woman who killed the demon kings Shumbh and Nishumbh. Her temple is on the road between Chandigarh. and Kalka. Known as 'The City Beautiful', it is renowned for its architecture, gardens and splendid surroundings. It was India's first planned city, with tree lined streets, and has a population of just under one million. The earlier capital of the Punjab, Lahore, was ceded to Pakistan in the partition of 1947. The decision to build Chandigarh as the new capital was taken after India independence by Prime Minister Nehru who declared: "Let this be a new town symbolic of the freedom of India. Unfettered by the traditions of the past, an expression of the nation's faith in the future".

Albert Mayer, the American town planner, and Matthew Nowlicki were commissioned to plan and design the city. They proposed a fan shaped outline between the two riverbeds that run on the east and west of the city. They also proposed a sector concept which would divide the city in self-contained sectors each with its own residential, recreational and commercial areas.

the city

Unfortunately, Nowlicki was killed in a plane crash in 1950 and Mayer decided to pull out of the project. The French architect Le Corbusier was brought in as project architect and his plans were finalised early in 1951. Le Corbusier kept most of the original ideas but discarded the fan shaped concept, choosing instead a grid-like mesh of rectangles. He also used unfinished concrete and exposed brickwork on his buildings. Prime Minister Nehru laid the foundation stone in 1952 and President Dr. Rajendra Prasad inaugurated the city in 1953.

Chandigarh is laid out in a grid pattern which divides the city into more than 60 self-contained sectors. It is divided into four main areas. The Capital Complex in the north of the city houses the headquarters of the Punjab and offices of the Union Territories along with the Secretariat, the Assembly and the High Court. There are several monuments along the main piazza of the complex, including the Open Hand, the symbol of the city and The Martyrs Memorial, which remembers those who lost their lives in the Indian Freedom Struggle. Interestingly, there are no monuments dedicated to individuals in the city. Commemoration of people is confined to bronze plaques. Sector 17 is the city centre which houses the city's administrative offices, its banks and main shopping malls. This sector has no residential area. The educational and cultural institutions such as the university, medical school and college of Asian studies are on the west side of town. The east side of the city is the industrial area.

Chandigarh is an easy-going city, easy to get around and very friendly. It is unlike many other Indian cities with wide-open spaces, clean air and clean streets. It has a western feel with a huge choice of shops and restaurants in many of the sectors and less of the markets and bazaars found in the older cities.

where to eat

There is a huge choice of restaurants in Chandigarh serving Indian, Chinese and Continental food.

Indian Restaurants

Bazm
Hotel Shivalikview
Sector 17 C
Tel: 0172 700 001

Chazal
Hotel Shivalikview
Sector 17C
Tel: 0172 700 001

Dastoor
Sector 35
Tel: 0172 608265

Chandigarh City Heart
RestaurantSector 22
Opposite bus station

Continental Restaurants

Hotel Aroma
Sector 22
Tel: 0172 700 046

Khyber
Sector 35
Tel: 0172 607 728

Yangtse
Hotel Shivalikview
Sector 17C
Tel: 0172 700 001

Chinese Restaurants

Chopsticks
Sector 22B
Tel: 0172 774 181

Chopsticks
Sector 7
Tel: 0172 549 863

Shangri-La
Sector 17C

ShangrilaPlus
Sector 35 B
Tel: 0172 608 082

Coffee Shops

La Patisserie Hotel
Mount View
Sector 10

Cream & Crunch
Aroma Complex
Sector 22
Round the Clock Hotel

Mount View
Sector 10-A

Nek Chand's Rock Garden

Without doubt Chandigarh's most popular attraction, the garden was created by a resident of the city in 1958. Using discarded domestic and industrial objects such as glass, plates, metal, stone and paper, Nek Chand created a wonderland with streams, walkways, bridges, sculptures that resemble people and animals. Groups of dancing girls made from motorcycle waste materials, ducks made from stone, flying birds made of broken glass and pappier-mache soldiers are just some of the many treats. The garden is situated in Sector 1 by Sukhna Lake and is open every day from 09.00-13.00 and 14.00-16.00.

The Capital Complex

Situated in Sector 1 under the jagged skyline of the Shivalik Hills it comprises the Secretariat, the largest building in Chandigarh in which more than 4,500 people work. Le Corbusier designed it in such a way that the Secretariat was placed perpendicular to the nearby hills so not to ruin the view. Also included are the Assembly, the most sculptural building in the Complex, and the High Court. The Open Hand Monument, a symbol of harmony and peace, a large metal hand pointed towards the sky, is also there.

Sukhna Lake

An artificial reservoir on the south east of the city. It was created in 1958 to stem the flow of the Suukhna Choe, a seasonal stream flowing from the mountains. Locals and tourists alike come to walk around the lake and to use the boating facilities on offer. There is also an amusement park, a restaurant and shops.

Zakir Hussein Rose Garden

In Sector 16, this is Asia's largest rose garden, spreading over 30 acres with more than 1,500 different types of rose. The best time of the year to visit the garden is in February when the annual competition is held. Unfortunately, many of the roses are not in bloom during the cricket season, but the gardens are still relaxing to walk around.

Guided Tour of the City

A local sightseeing tour is run twice daily by the Tourism Department of Chandigarh Administration and takes in such sights as the Rose Garden, Punjab University, the Capital Complex, the Rock Garden, Sukhna Lake and the Museum and Art Gallery. The tour leaves from Hotel Shivalikview at 09.00 and 14.00 .

Nightlife

There are not many pubs in Chandigarh, but most of the hotels have bars. Two of the most popular bars are in the Sunbeam Hotel and the Piccadilly Hotel. The Mountview Hotel also has a busy bar. Nightclubs include Arizona (0172 700 622) in Sector 9, Cloud 9 (0172 775 133) in Sector 22 and Jail Rock House (0172 714 284) in Sector 17.

The Civil Air Terminal in Chandigarh is a domestic airport situated 10km from the centre of the city. The majority of the flights arriving at the airport are from Delhi. A taxi ride to the centre takes about 15 minutes and should cost R250. An auto-rickshaw should cost R80. There is a prepaid taxi service, a tourist information desk and a number of hotel booking counters in the Arrival Hall. There is a bank and a restaurant in the Departure Hall. There are no car hire services available.

Hotel Regency

Sector 35
Tel: 0172 604 972
Tel: 0172 604 971
Four star hotel in the centre. 25 elegant rooms with air-conditioning and cable TV. Multi-cuisine restaurant, 24 hour coffee shop, bar.

Hotel Mountview

Sector 10
Tel: 0172 740 544
Tel: 0172 742 220
mountview@citcochandigarh.com
One of the best hotels in the city. Some of its 156 luxurious rooms have private balconies, all have cable TV. 2 restaurants, one Chinese, the other Multi-cuisine, 24 hour coffee shop. Business centre, swimming pool and health centre.

Hotel Piccadilly

Himalya Marg
Sector 22B
Tel: 0172 707 521
Tel: 0172 705 692
picadily@ch1.vsnl.net.in
In the centre. 48 air-conditioned rooms with all modern amenities. Restaurants offer Indian, Chinese, Continental and Thai food, bar.

The Majestic Hotel

SCF 77 Phase IX
SAS Nagar
Mohali
Tel: 0172 232 777
Tel: 0172 214 415
themajestic@mail.com
5 minutes from ground. 14 air-conditioned rooms. Good restaurant and bar. One of the best places to stay during the cricket. Early booking is essential.

Hotel Sunbeam

Udyog Path
Sector 22B
Tel: 0172 708 100
Tel: 0172 708 900
sunbeamchd@sancharnet.in
Central. 57 air-conditioned rooms with en suite, cable TV, work area and mini-bar. Multi-cuisine restaurant, cocktail lounge and coffee shop.

Hotel Park Inn

Sector 35C
Tel: 0172 660 111
Tel: 0172 660 110

26 air-conditioned rooms with cable TV. Chinese restaurant.

The Aroma

Himalaya Marg
Sector 22C
Tel: 0172 700 045
Tel: 0172 700 051
Chandigarh's oldest. 30 stylish en suite rooms . Cable TV. 3 restaurants serving Indian, continental, Chinese and Mexican. 24 hour coffee shop, ice-cream parlour and bakery.

Hotel Maya Palace

Sector 35
Tel: 0172 600 547
Tel: 0172 660 555
maya@ehl.vsnl.net.in
26 well furnished rooms with all modern amenities. Multi-cuisine restaurant.

Hotel Shivalikview

Sector 17
Tel: 0172 700 001
Tel: 0172 701 094
citcd@ch1.vsnl.net.in
104 air-conditioned rooms with cable TV. Two restaurants, bar and coffee shop.

Hotel Parkview

Sector 24
Tel: 0172 700 050
Tel: 0172 706 038
parkview@citcochandigarh.com
Good value for budget travellers. 80 rooms, some air-conditioned, some with fans. Restaurant.

Jullendar Hotel

Udyog Path
Sector 22B
Tel: 0172 706 777
Good budget hotel. Clean rooms with TV. Indian restaurant downstairs.

Hotel Satyadeep

Sector 22
Tel: 0172 703 103
Tel: 0172 721 165
Good budget hotel in centre of city. Good vegetarian restaurant.

The following are budget hotels between the centre of Chandigarh and the stadium: KC Residency 0172 615364, GH international 0172 660737, South End 0172 607935

Government Museum and Art Gallery

Sector 10C
Tel: 0172 742 501
Collections of Indian stone sculptures, modern art and Mughal miniature paintings.

Museum of the Evolution of Life

Sector 10C
Tel: 0172 742 501

National Gallery of Portraits

Sector 17C
Tel: 0172 702 565
Opened in 1977, this gallery exhibits portraits of Indian freedom fighters and relives the history of the struggle for independence. Open 09.00-17.00 Weekdays.

Airlines

Indian Airlines
Sector 17
Tel: 0172 704 539

Air India
Sector 17
Tel: 0172 704 014

Jet Airways
Madhya Marg
Sector 14
Tel: 0172 740 550

Buses

Chandigarh Bus Station is in Sector 17. The journey to New Delhi takes five hours.

Trains

Chandigarh Train station is 8km outside the city. There are regular trains to New Delhi including the Shatabadi Express which is the quickest and most comfortable way to travel.

Taxis

There are taxi stands in Sectors 17, 22 (beside Sunbeam Hotel) and 35. Auto rickshaws are the quickest and cheapest way to travel around the city as Chandigarh does not have the traffic congestion seen elsewhere in India. Taxi No's : 0172 703 839/0172 740 544

Car Hire

Tara Brothers
Sector 17 D
Tel: 0172 701 811
Tel: 0172 710 808
tarabrothers@rediffmail.com

Post Office

Chandigarh Main Post Office
Sector 17

Tourist Information

Chandigarh Tourism
Sector 17
Tel: 0172 704614

Punjab Tourism
Sector 22B
Tel: 0172 704570

Hospital

General Hospital
Sector 1
Tel: 0172 780 756

General Hospital
Phase VI
Mohali
Tel: 0172 670 264

Climate

	max	rain cm
January	13	26
February	16	24
March	22	14
April	27	12
May	32	14
June	33	79
July	31	203
August	30	197
September	28	126
October	26	29
November	20	8
December	14	10

Win/Loss Record

Country	Played	won	drawn	Lost	Tie
West Indies	1	1	-	-	-
Sri Lanka	1	-	1	-	-
India	5	1	3	1	-
New Zealand	2	-	2	-	-
England	1	-	-	1	-

Highest Individual Aggregates (India unless stated)

Player	Mat	Inn	NO	Runs	Ave	HS	50	100
Sachin Tendulkar	5	8	1	361	51.57	126*	2	1
Rahul Dravid	4	6	0	283	47.17	144	1	1
Jimmy Adams (WI)	1	2	2	252	-	174*	1	1
Sourav Ganguly	3	4	1	222	74.00	109	1	1
VVS Laxman	2	3	2	199	199.00	104*	1	1
Stephen Fleming (NZ)	2	3	0	146	48.67	73	1	0
Mark Richardson (NZ)	1	1	0	145	145.00	145	0	1
Aravinda de Silva (SL)	1	2	1	143	143.00	110*	0	1
Navjot Sidhu	2	3	0	142	47.33	131	0	1
Craig McMillan (NZ)	2	3	1	140	70.00	100*	0	1

Top Wicket Takers (India unless stated)

Player	Mat	Bll	Md	Runs	Wkt	Ave	BB	S/R
Anil Kumble	5	1570	69	698	21	33.24	6/81	74.76
Javagal Srinath	3	926	27	476	17	28.00	6/45	54.47
Harbhajan Singh	2	549	20	259	9	28.78	5/51	61.00
Kenny Benjamin (WI)	1	315	11	171	8	21.38	5/65	39.38
Daryl Tuffey (NZ)	1	258	9	110	7	15.71	4/80	36.86
Dion Nash (NZ)	1	288	19	106	6	17.67	6/27	48.00
Abey Kuruvilla	1	253	11	117	6	19.50	4/88	42.17
Courtney Walsh (WI)	1	318	11	123	5	24.60	3/34	63.60
Venkatapathy Raju	1	277	5	133	5	26.60	3/73	55.40
Richard Dawson (Eng)	1	258	6	134	4	33.50	4/134	64.50

Highest Individual Scores (India unless stated)

174*	Jimmy Adams (WI)	1994-95
145	Mark Richardson (NZ)	2003-04
144	Rahul Dravid	v New Zealand 1999-00
131	Navjot Sidhu	v Sri Lanka 1997-98
130	Virender Sehwag	v New Zealand 2003-04
126*	Sachin Tendulkar	v New Zealand 1999-00
120	Manoj Prabhakar	v West Indies 1994-95
119	Scott Styris (NZ)	2003-04
110*	Aravinda de Silva (SL)	1997-98
109	Sourav Ganguly	v Sri Lanka 1997-98

Best Individual Bowling Performances (India unless stated)

11-3-27-6	Dion Nash (NZ)	1999-00
22-9-45-6	Javagal Srinath	v New Zealand 1999-00
28.4-6-81-6	Anil Kumble	v England 2001-02
19.3-4-51-5	Harbhajan Singh	v England 2001-02
17-3-65-5	Kenny Benjamin (WI)	1994-95
29-5-80-4	Daryl Tuffey NZ)	2003-04
27-7-88-4	Abey Kuruvilla	v Sri Lanka 1997-98
29-3-90-4	Anil Kumble	v West Indies 1994-95
27.2-4-92-4	Javagal Srinath	v Sri Lanka 1997-98
43-6-134-4	Richard Dawson (Eng)	2001-02

Highest Partnerships

Wkt	Runs	Batsmen	Match
1st	231	Mark Richardson & Lou Vincent (NZ)	2003-2004
2nd	151	Mark Richardson & Scott Styris (NZ)	2003-2004
3rd	229	Rahul Dravid & Sachin Tendulkar (Ind)	1999-2000 v New Zealand
4th	145*	Jimmy Adams & Keith Arthurton (WI)	1994-1995

5th	80	Sourav Ganguly & Sachin Tendulkar (Ind)	2001-2002 v England
6th	103	Aravinda de Silva & Kumar Dharmasena (SL)	1997-1998
7th	99	Jimmy Adams & Anderson Cummins (WI)	1994-1995
8th	38	Jimmy Adams & Courtney Walsh (WI)	1994-1995
9th	89	Sourav Ganguly & Abey Kuruvilla (Ind)	1997-1998 v Sri Lanka
10th	64	Javagal Srinath & Venkatapathy Raju (Ind)	1994-1995 v West Indies

Results at the Punjab Cricket Association Ground

Date	Countries	Result
10/12/1994	India v West Indies	lost by 243 runs
19/11/1997	India v Sri Lanka	drawn
10/10/1999	India v New Zealand	drawn
03/12/2001	India v England	won by 10 wickets
16/10/2003	India v New Zealand	drawn
10/12/1994	India v West Indies	lost by 243 runs
19/11/1997	India v Sri Lanka	drawn
10/10/1999	India v New Zealand	drawn
03/12/2001	India v England	won by 10 wickets
16/10/2003	India v New Zealand	drawn

chennai

m. a. chidambaram

The M A Chidambaram Stadium, formerly known as Chepauk Stadium, is 3km south of the city in a residential area beside the Buckingham Canal. It has a capacity of 55,000 which produces a tremendous atmosphere during big matches. The ground has staged some of the most incredible games ever played including the tied match of 1986 against Australia. It was also the venue for India's first Test win in 1952 after 20 years and 25 matches. Sunil Gavaskar's 30th Test century to pass Sir Don Bradman's record was made at the ground which also hosted the finale of one of the greatest series ever played, again against Australia, in 2001. No Tests were held at the ground between December 1952 and January 1967. During this time nine Tests were played at the Corporation Stadium.

The inaugural Test against England in February 1934 saw defeat for the home side by 202 runs although Amar Singh took 7/86 in England's first innings. The third match at the ground, 18 years later, saw India's first Test victory. Vinoo Mankad took 8 wickets for 55 as England scored 266 while Polly Umrigar, 130no and Pankaj Roy, 111 led India to 457/9 dec. Mankad was again the hero for the home side, taking 4/53 in 30.5 overs and three catches as England were dismissed for 183 to give India victory by an innings and eight runs.

In 1979 India beat the West Indies by three wickets, a close call but nothing compared to what was to come in 1986. In one of the most famous Test matches, Australia batted first and scored 574/7 dec. with Dean Jones (210), David Boon (122) and Alan Border (122) being the chief contributors. India replied with 397, Kapil Dev hitting 119 and Greg Matthews taking 5/103. Border, the Australian captain, made a brave declaration after his team hit 170/5 off 49 overs. The target was 348 off 87 overs and India started well, Gavaskar hitting 90 as his side reached 158/1. From then the game fluctuated; Australia looked on top when they took India's sixth wicket with the score on 291. A 4? run partnership between Ravi Shastri and Chetan Sharma put India back in the drivin? seat until Ray Bright took three wickets to leave the home side requiring four runs from the last over with only one wicket left. Shastri, 48no levelled the scores before Greg Matthews got Maninder Singh lbw on the penultimate ball, to tie the Test. Bright ende? with figures of 5/94 and Matthews, 5/146.

The 1999 season saw another tight match, this time against Pakistan. Anil Kumble too? 6/70 as Pakistan reached a modest 238. India managed just 16 more as Saqlain Mushta? took 5/94. In Pakistan's second innings Shahid Afridi hit a glorious 141 to lead his tear? to 286. Venkatesh Prasad was the pick of the Indian bowlers with 6/33 in only 10.2 overs. Set 271 to win, a wonderful century by Sachin Tendulkar (136) was not enough as India fell 12 runs short. Saqlain was again amongst the wickets with 5/93.

In 2001 India and Australia came to Chennai with the series level 1-1 in a three match series. Australia had won the opening Test easily by 10 wickets in Mumbai, India came back to win the second in Kolkata despite being forced to follow-on, so the final match of the series was set up to be a thriller. It did not disappoint. Batting first, Australia got off to a tremendous start with a double century (203) by Matthew Hayden. They reached 340/3 before collapsing to 391 all out as Harbhajan Singh took 7/133. Steve Waugh became only the sixth player to be given out for handling the ball when on 47 runs. India replied with 501, Tendulkar scoring 126 with support from Shiv Sunder Das, 84 and Rahul Dravid, 81. Trailing by 110, Australia could only manage 264 in the? second innings. Harbhajan was again the tormentor with 8/84. Set 155 to win, India cruised to 76/1 before collapsing to 135/7, only VVS Laxman contributing well with 66 until Sameer Dighe (22no) brought his side home by two wickets at 155/8. India had come back from the dead to take the series.

The highest team innings is 652/7 declared by England in 1985, the lowest, 83 by India? against England in 1977. The highest run chase at the ground is the 155/8 by India in that historic win in 2001.

Narendra Hirwani has the best match figures – 16/136 on debut against the West Indie? in 1988. Hirwani became the first Indian and only the 12th Test player to take ten or more wickets on debut. Harbhajan Singh's figures against Australia in 2001 were 15/21? The Anna Pavilion is at the southern end of the ground as is the pavilion of the Madra? Cricket Club. To the left are the two-tier Met Life India Insurance and the India Overseas Bank Stands which both provide excellent views. A small scoreboard sits above the IOB Bank stand. The single tier Royal Sundaram and United India Insuranc? Stands are at the northern end of the ground. A huge electronic scoreboard, arguably the finest in world cricket, is at this end of the ground. The general enclosure sponsored by Bharat Petroleum, is the single-tier enclosure with the cheapest entrance fee on the east side of the ground. Beside this enclosure is the players' friends and family enclosure. The majority of seats in the ground are covered by the roof which encircles the stadium. Unfortunately the roof is supported by huge concrete pillars which can affect one's view of the pitch giving good reason to arrive at the ground early as attendances of up to 50,000 are common.

The crowd is friendly and appreciative. Some parts, especially the general enclosure, can get very lively with loud music and dancing during the breaks. Huge nets drop down in front of the general enclosure to prevent bottles or other missiles being launched. Fences run along the west and east sides of the ground. Security is tight with metal detectors on each gate, however bottles, flagpoles and cameras are allowed in.

The foodstalls around the ground are good. Well-planned canteens serve tomato soup, coffee, soft drinks, nuts, ice-cream, crisps and Indian food such as samosas and rice. Unfortunately the toilet facilities are disappointing, not looked after well, with only squat loos available.

Tickets should be purchased before the day of the match at the ground or by contacting the Tamil Nadu Cricket Association on www.tnca.org.in as it is absolute chaos queuing for tickets on the day and nigh on impossible to get to the top of the queue. Pass-outs are only issued during intervals.

A rickshaw costs about 40R. The roads around the stadium are closed off and one has to walk the last 500 metres which provides the opportunity so soak up the atmosphere in this cricket-crazy city.

the city

Chennai, formerly Madras, is the capital of the Tamil Nadu State and is situated on the eastern shores of Southern India on the Bay of Bengal, stretching 20km along the Coromandel Coast. It is India's fourth largest city and growing constantly. Known as the Gateway of Southern India it has a population of 5.9 million. Relaxed, with some wonderful architecture, the city is divided into two main areas, Mylapore in the south where the Portuguese first settled and the north which was the centre of British trade in the 19th century

Chennai is the home of the ancient Dravidian civilisation, one of the oldest cultures in the world. For more than 2000 years the east coast of India has been visited by traders and seafarers. The Portuguese were the first Europeans to settle although the city was founded by Francis Day of the East India Company in 1639 when the British leased a beach called Madraspatinam. It was the company's first settlement in India and became one of the country's main trading centres. The British built Fort St. George in 1653 and the surrounding settlement, Georgetown, gradually incorporated the surrounding villages such as Mylapore, Triplicane and Pallavaram to form the city of Madras. It was the capital of the Madras Presidency which comprised most of Southern India until independence in 1947.

Silk production has long been part of the city's life and the textile mills and tanneries provide employment to many. There are two extremes in Chennai, the very rich who live life to the full and the majority who have very little and live in slums in great poverty.

The city has a mixture of Gothic and Dravidian architecture. Some stately buildings include the Indo Saracenic style High Court built in 1892 and The Pantheon Complex which encompasses the city's Museum, National Art Gallery and the Connemara Public Library. Along the Marina the buildings of the University of Madras, Chepauk Palace and the Police Headquarters are also wonderful structures as is Chennai Central Train Station. The War Memorial built in 1932 is also worth visiting.

Marine Beach is one of India's finest, 8km long and perfect for an early morning stroll on its golden sands or a swim or surf in the sea. In the evenings the beach becomes a hive of activity. The Horticultural Gardens are very beautiful and even though it is 85km south of Chennai the Vedanthangal Bird Sanctuary makes a great trip and is a must for bird watchers.

The most popular modes of transport for tourists are taxis or autorickshaws. The traffic is not too bad in the city so taxis do move quite quickly but autorickshaws are definitely the cheapest and fastest way to get around the city. Although open to the pollution and the car fumes it is a great way to get to know the city, its people and, most all, its aroma! They fly around and occasionally the driver will give you a running commentary. It is important that rather than agreeing a price first that one persuades the driver to turn on his meter. He will be reluctant to do so but if you ask him to stop and threaten to get out the meter soon goes on.

There is a wide selection of accommodation in Chennai from glorious five star deluxe hotels which are as good as any in India to middle of the range and budget hotels. These last two categories are cheaper than anywhere else in India with some fantastic bargains at the lower end of the market. For example, an en suite room with fan and cable TV on Kennet Lane in Egmore costs about 400R. Egmore is very central and most budget travellers stay around this area and in Triplicane just to the south. Most of the top hotels are in the centre of Chennai and all are convenient for the stadium. Most hotels in Chennai have their own restaurants or at least a room service menu. Tamil Nadu is known throughout India for its traditional Southern Indian food. One speciality that must be tried is the Masala Dosa, one of the finest foods in India. Most of the top hotels restaurants are inexpensive and the budget travellers tend to use them for breakfasts and dinner. There are also some independent restaurants and cafés serving good Southern Indian food. They are not many bars in Chennai and most cricket fans seem to use their hotel bars to have a drink after the cricket.

Most hotels in Chennai have their own restaurants or at least room service. Some of the five star hotels have very good restaurants including the Hotel Chola Sheraton which has Peshawri, an Indian restaurant, Sagari, a Chinese and Mercara, a coffee shop. The Taj Cormandel has the South Spice restaurant which serves good Indian food and the Golden Dragon, an excellent Chinese. The Ambassador Pallava has The Other Room serving Continental and Indian cuisine and Salt and Pepper, a 24 hour coffee shop.
Other restaurants include

Maris Vegetarian Restaurant
11 Cathedral Road
Tel: 044 2811 0541
Excellent Southern Indian and Tandoori restaurant.

Raj Air-Conditioned Restaurant
Hotel Pandian
9 Kennet Lane
Egmore
Tel: 044 2825 2901
Good Southern Indian food in darkened restaurant.

Jewel in the Crown
Quality Inn Aruna
144 Sterling Road
Tel: 044 2825 9090
Another excellent restaurant serving Indian food.

New Victoria
3 Kennet Lane
Egmore
Tel: 044 2825 3638
Indian food.

Copper Chimney
Cathedral Road
Tel: 044 2827 5770
Well known restaurant serving excellent northern frontier and Tandoori food.

Fort St. George

The first bastion built by the East India Company in 1653. Today it is the home of the Tamil Nadu Legislative Assembly and Council and the offices of the State's Secretariat. The fort has been attacked on numerous occasions including in 1701 by Daud Khan and in1741 by the Marathas. The French admiral, La Bourdonnais took it over in 1746 but it was returned to the British under the treaty of Aix-la-Chapelle in 1749.

Kapaleeswarar Temple

One of the largest and oldest temples in the city and a typical example of Dravidian temple sculpture and architecture, with the walls and pillars intricately carved with scenes of Hindu mythology. The temple is dedicated to Shiva and has inscriptions dating back to the 13th century. A miracle is said to have occurred here when a saint sang a hymn to Lord Kapaleeswarar to resurrect a girl from the dead. The magnificent gopuram is 37 metres high and has the most delicate carvings. .

Kancheepuram

This ancient place is one of the seven sacred cities of Hindu mythology. In the 6th century it was the capital of the Pallava Empire and some of the temples date back to this time. There are numerous temples and in its time this was a major centre of Buddhism, Hinduism and Jainism. Kancheepuram is also famous for its weavers who are said to produce the best woven silk sarees in the world. 7km to the south west of Chennai.

Guindy National Park

Within the city limits which is incredibly rare, this game reserve covers hundreds of acres and is home to a large population of spotted deer, monkeys, reptiles, mangoose and the Indian Civet Cat. The snake park has a wonderful collection of reptiles and Indian snakes. Open from 09.00-18.00 every day.

The High Court

Built in 1892 this is an Indo-Saracenic style building with some fabulous stained glass windows and beautiful domes. It is possible to visit the courtrooms in the law courts by contacting the Registrar. Some of the court rooms have wonderfully carved furniture, stained glass windows and decoratively painted ceilings. The building was designed by Henry Irwin who also designed the National Art Gallery.

Chennai International Airport is 16km to the south west. A taxi journey should take about 25 minutes and should not cost more than 250R. There is a prepaid kiosk is in the arrival hall. A coach service provided by the Tamil Nadu Government meets all flights arrivals and drops at all the top hotels, Egmore and Chennai Central train stations and Air India and Indian Airlines offices. The local No 18A bus runs from the airport to Chennai every 25 minutes.

There are ATM machines in both the international and domestic terminals and also foreign exchange bureaux. There are tourist information booths in both terminals. There is a business centre on the 2nd floor of the domestic terminal and an internet office on the ground floor. There are a number of food counters in both terminals, along with shops, newsagents and a post office. Retiring rooms are available for passengers with long waits for connections. A medical clinic is open around the clock.

The Taj Cormandel
37 Mahatma Gandhi Road
Nungambakkam
Tel: 044 2827 2827
Tel: 044 2825 7104
coromandel.chennai@tajhotels.com
Five star deluxe hotel with 183 luxurious rooms and 22 suites. Centrally
located with 3 restaurants and a fine
bar. Swimming pool, health club,
sauna, jacuzzi and steam room.

Taj Connemara Hotel
Binny Road
Tel: 044 2852 0123
Tel: 044 2825 7361
Another five star hotel in the centre.
141 rooms with all mod cons and 7
suites. Beautiful swimming pool.

Chola Sheraton
10 Cathedral Road
Tel: 044 2828 0101
Tel: 044 2827 8779
Splendid hotel in the centre. 100
elegant rooms. 2 multi-cuisine restaurants, bar, swimming pool, health
club.

New Victoria
3 Kennet Lane
Egmore
Tel: 044 2825 3638
Tel: 044 2825 0070
www.hotelnewvictoria.com
Quiet hotel. 52 air-conditioned en
suite rooms with a good restaurant
and bar.

Quality Inn
144 Sterling Road
Tel: 044 2825 9090
Within a few minutes of the centre.
94 elegant rooms. Multi-cuisine restaurant, coffee shop and bar.

Hotel Savera
69 Dr. Radhakrishnan Road
Tel: 044 2811 4700
Tel: 044 2811 3475
hotsave@md2.vsnl.net.in
Established hotel with a grand
tradition. 125 good en suite
rooms with air-conditioning.
Restaurant and excellent swimming
pool.

Breeze Hotel
850 Poonamallee High Road
Tel: 044 2641 3334
Tel: 044 2641 3301
breeze@vsnl.com
www.breezehotel.com
Centrally located with en suite rooms
with cable TV. Multi-cuisine restaurant with live music.

Hotel Pandian
9 Kennett Lane
Egmore
Tel: 044 2825 2901
Tel: 044 2825 8459
hotelpandian@vsnl.com
www.fhrai.com
Excellent budget hotel near the centre
of the city. 90 good rooms with en
suite and air-conditioning if required.
Cable TV. Restaurant, bar, travel desk
and airport transfers.

Shri Lakshmi Lodge
16 Kennett Lane
Egmore
Tel: 044 2825 4576
Good budget hotel with clean en
suite rooms and fans.

Broadlands
16 Vallabha Agraharam St.
Triplicane High Road
Tel: 044 8545 573
50 clean rooms some with bathrooms
good budget hotel. Friendly service

Tourist Home
21 Gandhi Irwin Road
Egmore
Tel: 044 2825 0079
Good clean budget accommodation
with en suite air-conditioned rooms
with TV near Egmore station.

Airlines

Indian Airlines
City   044 2855 3039
Airport   044 2256 3131

Jet Airways
City   044 2841 4141
Airport   044 2232 8080

Sahara Airlines
City   044 2827 1961
Airport   044 2231 1543

Air India
19 Marshalls Road
Egmore
City   044 2855 4477
Airport   044 2256 7400

British Airways
Raheja Towers
8th Floor Sigma Wing
177 Anna Salai
City   044 2855 4680
Airport   044 2233 2352

Qantas
G-3 Eldorado building
112 Nungambakkam High Road
2827 8680

Emirates
Riaz Garden
1st Floor
12 Kodambakkam High Road
Tel: 044 2822 3700

Buses

Inter-city bus services originate from the Central Bus Station on Broadway. The inter-state services depart from the Express Bus Station on the Esplanade. Enquiries 2534 2835.

Trains

Long distance trains depart from Chennai Central. Trains for the southern cities leave from Egmore station. It is important to check which station your train leaves from. General Enquiries 563 535 and Arrival and Departure 567 575. Internet booking facility www.irctc.co.in
Rail reservations can be made at Central Station 06.30-20.30 daily. Suburban electrical trains run from Beach station to Tambaram and Chennai Central to Gummidipoondi.

Taxis

Call Taxis   044 2538 4455
Rajoo Cabs   044 2499 1680
Metro Cabs   044 2858 7193

Car Hire

Wheels Rent a Car   044 2824 1331
Bala Tourist Service 044 2822 4444

Post Office

Chennai Main Post Office
Rajaji Salai

Kennet Lane Post Office

Anna Salai Post Office

Tourist Information

Indiatourism
154 Anna Salai
2846 0285
2846 0193
indtour@vsnl.com
Opening Monday-Friday 09.15-17.45

Indiatourism
Airport
Tel: 044 2256 0386 open 24 hours.
Tamil Nadu Tourism Development Corporation
4 EVR Salai
Tel: 044 2536 0294

Hospital

Apollo Hospital
21 Greams Road
Tel: 044 2829 1111

Aysha Hospital
91 A Millers Road
Tel: 044 2642 1255

Government Museum

Pantheon Road
Egmore
The Government Museum has been open since 1857 and is without doubt one of the country's finest museums. It houses fine collections concerning geology, archaeology, botany and zoology. Open 08.00-17.00hrs. Closed on Fridays.

Fort Museum

Fort St. George

Very interesting museum detailing the British era in India. Exhibits include weapons, medals, uniforms and other items from the era. Open 09.00-17.00. Closed Fridays.

National Art Gallery

Pantheon Road
Egmore
Houses a fine collection of Asian paintings. Open 08.00-17.00. Closed Friday.

Climate

	max	rain cm
January	25	30
February	26	9
March	28	9
April	30	17
May	32	44
June	32	52
July	31	92
August	30	124
September	29	125
October	28	285
November	26	345
December	25	138

Win/Loss Record

Country	Played	won	drawn	Lost	Tie
India	26	11	8	6	1
Sri Lanka	1	-	1	-	-
Pakistan	4	1	2	1	-
England	7	3	1	3	-
Australia	5	1	1	2	1
West Indies	7	1	2	4	-
New Zealand	2	-	1	1	-

Highest Individual Aggregates (India unless stated)

Player	Mat	Inn	NO	Runs	Ave	HS	50	100
Sunil Gavaskar	12	21	4	1018	59.88	236*	3	3
Gundappa Viswanath	10	17	1	785	49.06	222	3	2
Sachin Tendulkar	6	10	3	714	102.00	165	1	4
Kapil Dev	11	17	4	708	54.46	119	4	2
Mohammad Azharuddin	8	12	0	465	38.75	105	2	1
Mohinder Amarnath	7	13	1	422	35.17	95	5	0
Dilip Vengsarkar	9	13	2	372	33.82	96	4	0
Allan Border (Aus)	2	4	0	345	86.25	162	1	2
Syed Kirmani	9	11	3	341	42.63	75	3	0
Yashpal Sharma	4	6	1	311	62.20	140	1	1

Top Wicket Takers (India unless stated)

Player	Mat	Bll	Md	Runs	Wkt	Ave	BB	S/R
Kapil Dev	11	1863	58	1092	40	27.30	7/56	46.58
Erapalli Prasanna	5	1620	85	672	36	18.67	6/74	45.00
Bishan Bedi	6	1701	108	535	31	17.26	5/48	54.87
Anil Kumble	5	1261	57	554	29	19.10	6/64	43.48
Bhagwat Chandrasekhar	5	1458	58	619	25	24.76	6/90	58.32
Dilip Doshi	4	1512	77	558	23	24.26	6/103	65.74

Harbhajan Singh	2	835	45	352	22	16.00	8/84	37.95
Venkat	4	1149	59	412	18	22.89	4/43	63.83
Narendra Hirwani	1	203	6	136	16	8.50	8/61	12.69
Vinoo Mankad	3	826	31	314	15	20.93	8/55	55.07

Highest Individual Scores (India unless stated)

236*	Sunil Gavaskar	v West Indies 1983-84
222	Gundappa Viswanath	v England 1981-82
210	Dean Jones (Aus)	1986-87
207	Mike Gatting (Eng)	1984-85
203	Matthew Hayden (Aus)	2000-01
201	Graeme Fowler (Eng)	1984-85
166	Sunil Gavaskar	v Pakistan 1979-80
165	Sachin Tendulkar	v England 1992-93
162	Allan Border (Aus)	1979-80
160	Jeffrey Stollmeyer (WI)	1948-49

Best Individual Bowling Performances (India unless stated)

38.5-15-55-8	Vinoo Mankad	v England 1951-52
18.3-3-61-8	Narendra Hirwani	v West Indies 1987-88
15.2-3-75-8	Narendra Hirwani	v West Indies 1987-88
41.5-20-84-8	Harbhajan Singh	v Australia 2000-01
23.5-10-49-7	Hedley Verity (Eng)	1933-34
23.4-7-56-7	Kapil Dev	v Pakistan 1979-80
20.5-5-64-7	Andy Roberts (WI)	1974-75
44.4-13-86-7	Amar Singh	v England 1933-34
38.2-6-133-7	Harbhajan Singh	v Australia 2000-01
41.3-12-143-7	Jim Higgs (Aus)	1979-80

Highest Partnerships

Wkt	Runs	Batsmen	Match
1st	239	Allan Rae & Jeffrey Stollmeyer (WI)	1948-1949
2nd	241	Graeme Fowler & Mike Gatting (Eng)	1984-1985
3rd	316	Gundappa Viswanath & Yashpal Sharma (Ind)	1981-1982 v England
4th	190	Mohinder Amarnath & Moh. Azharuddin (Ind)	1984-1985 v England
5th	169	Rahul Dravid & Sachin Tendulkar (Ind)	2000-2001 v Australia
6th	170	Sunil Gavaskar & Ravi Shastri (Ind)	1983-1984 v West Indies
7th	100	Alvin Kallicharran & Derick Parry (WI)	1978-1979
8th	112	Imran Khan & Wasim Akram (Pak)	1986-1987
9th	143*	Sunil Gavaskar & Syed Kirmani (Ind)	1983-1984 v West Indies
10th	104	Zulfiqar Ahmed & Amir Elahi (Pak)	1952-1953

Results at M. A. Chidambaram Stadium

Date	Countries	Result
10/02/1934	v England	lost by 202 runs
27/01/1949	v West Indies	lost by an innings and 193 runs
06/02/1952	v England	won by an innings and 8 runs
28/11/1952	v Pakistan	drawn
13/01/1967	v West Indies	drawn
24/12/1969	v Australia	lost by 77 runs
12/01/1973	v England	won by 4 wickets
11/01/1975	v West Indies	won by 100 runs
26/11/1976	v New Zealand	won by 216 runs
14/01/1977	v England	lost by 200 runs
12/01/1979	v West Indies	won by 3 wickets
11/09/1979	v Australia	drawn
15/01/1980	v Pakistan	won by 10 wickets
13/01/1982	v England	drawn
17/09/1982	v Sri Lanka	drawn
24/12/1983	v West Indies	drawn
13/01/1985	v England	lost by 9 wickets
18/09/1986	v Australia	tied
03/02/1987	v Pakistan	drawn
11/01/1988	v West Indies	won by 255 runs
11/02/1993	v England	won by an innings and 22 runs
25/10/1995	v New Zealand	drawn
06/03/1998	v Australia	won by 179 runs
28/01/1999	v Pakistan	lost by 12 runs
18/03/2001	v Australia	won by 2 wickets
17/10/2002	v West Indies	won by 8 wickets

feroz shah kotla stadium

The Feroz Shah Kotla Stadium in Delhi is close to India Gate in the centre of the city. It is hoped the reconstruction, begun in 2002, will be finished by 2005.

It became India's fourth Test venue in 1948 in the first match of a five Test series with the West Indies. The visitors scored 631 with four men – Clyde Walcott (152), Everton Weekes (128), Robert Christiani (107) and Gerry Gomez (100) – making centuries. Commandur Rangachari took 5/107 for the Indians. In reply, India could not avoid the follow-on despite scoring 454, Hemu Adhikari top scoring with 114no. In their second innings India collapsed to 162/6 before Adhikari (29no) and Chandu Sarwate (35no) steadied the ship and steered their side safely to a draw, ending on 220/6.

India gained their first win at the ground against Pakistan in 1952. Vinoo Mankad taking 13/131 to help his team to victory by an innings and 70 runs to take a 1-0 lead in the series.

India's first defeat came against Australia in 1959 by an innings. Two years later Mushtaq Mohammad scored 101 against Pakistan to become the youngest Test centurion of the time at the age of 17 years and 78 days. Four years went by until the ground was used again when India defeated New Zealand by seven wickets in 1965.

The next Test played at the ground was the third match in the 1969 series against Australia. The visitors, one up after two matches, scored 296 thanks mainly to Ian Chappell's 138. India managed only 223 as Ashley Mallett took 6/64. But Bishan Bedi (5/37) and Erapalli Prasanna (5/42) ripped through the Australians in their second innings to dismiss them for a meagre 107. Australian captain, Bill Lawry, carried his bat for 49no. Set 181, India won by seven wickets.

A bad run was to follow for India over the next ten years. They lost to England by six wickets in 1972, before losing by an innings and 17 runs to the West Indies in 1974, thanks mainly to an innings of 192no by Viv Richards and a second innings six wicket haul by Lance Gibbs. Another innings defeat occurred in 1976 against England when Dennis Amiss hit 179 and John Lever returned match figures of 10/70 to become the 11th Test cricketer and fifth English bowler to take ten wickets on debut. 1979 saw three draws at the ground against the West Indies, Australia and Pakistan. India could not press home the advantage in the first two matches after forcing the visitors to follow-on. The third draw against Pakistan was a thriller with India, chasing a massive 390 for victory in the fourth innings, only 25 runs short of their target at the close. They still had four wickets remaining and Dilip Vengsarkar was on 146no. Two more draws followed against England in 1981, a game notable for Ian Botham's half century off 6 balls, the fastest in Test cricket, against the West Indies in 1983.

England won the next Test at the ground in 1984 by eight wickets. Tim Robinson was the hero with a first innings score of 160. A draw against Australia followed in 1986 before a remarkable opening Test in the 1987 series against the West Indies when the home side were dismissed for a paltry 75 in the first innings, Patrick Patterson (5/24) and Winston Davis (3/20) inflicting the damage. In reply the visitors collapsed to 49/7 before rallying to 127. Chetan Sharma (5/55) and Kapil Dev (3/41) took the wickets for India. In their second innings Dilip Vengsarkar scored 102 and Courtney Walsh took 5/54 for the visitors as India scored 327 to set the West Indies a daunting target of 276 for victory. However, Viv Richards scored an unbeaten 109 to see his team home with five wickets to spare.

It was more than five years before another Test was played at the ground. In 1993 India beat Zimbabwe by an innings and 13 runs with Vinod Kambli scoring 227 which was the first of five wins on the trot at the Feroz Shah Kotli. In 1996 they defeated Australia by seven wickets; in 1999, Pakistan by 212 runs; in 2000, Zimbabwe by seven wickets and in 2002 Zimbabwe again, this time by four wickets.

The 1999 Test against Pakistan created history. India, 1-0 down in the two match series, batted first and scored 252, Mohammad Azharuddin top scoring with 67 and Saqlain Mushtaq taking 5/94. Pakistan could only manage 172 in reply as Anil Kumble took 4/75. The home side piled on the runs to reach 339 leaving Pakistan an improbable target of 420 for victory. Sadogoppan Ramesh, 96 and Sourav Ganguly, 62no were the main contributors. Saeed Anwar (69) and Shahid Afridi (41) started off well for the visitors with a century opening partnership before Kumble took control. Pakistan went from 101/0 to 128/6 and 207 all out as Kumble ripped through their side to take all ten wickets to become only the second bowler to do so in 123 years of Test cricket. The first was Jim Laker (10/53) 43 years earlier for England against Australia in Old Trafford.

Kumble finished with figures of 26.3 overs, 9 maidens, 74 runs for 10 wickets and match figures of 14/149, the best at the ground. His spell of bowling in which the wickets fell was 17.5-9-37-10. India won the match by 212 runs.

The highest team score at the ground is 644/8 dec. by the West Indies in 1958, the lowest, India's 75 in 1987. The West Indies run-chase in that match is the highest.

Apart from the pavilion which remains standing, the rest of the ground, including the terraces, has been removed to make way for new stands. The proposed capacity is 45,000. Tickets can be purchased from the Delhi District Cricket Association on 011 335 3660 or 011 331 9323. The ground is in the centre of the city. Taxis and auto and cycle rickshaws are available outside most hotels.

The capital of India, Dehli lies in the north on the banks of the river Yamuna, a tributary of the Ganges. It is the country's third largest city with a population of 14 million. One of the world's most elegant capitals, with the ancient and historic buildings of Old Delhi and the modern ones of New Delhi making a pleasing contrast, it evolved from seven historical cities built during the Hindu and Mughal dynasties.

Raja Dhilu is said to have established a settlement on the site as early as 100BC. Coins and jewellery have been found which testify that the area was a trading centre at this time.

As the Mughal dynasty declined, the British took over at the beginning of the 19th century. In 1911 Delhi succeeded Calcutta as capital of the British Administration in India and remained the seat of British rule until India achieved independence in 1947. It continued to be the seat of government in the newly fledged state. As well as being the country's seat of power, Delhi is an important financial, commercial and industrial centre.

There are many places of interest in Delhi, some influenced by Islamic and Hindu culture, others date back to British times. There is Rashtrapati

Bhavan, formerly the Vice Regal Palace and now the Presidential Palace, which is also a magnificent building. No.1 Safdarjung Road is the Indira Gandhi Memorial, the house where she lived and died.

Connaught Place in New Delhi is the centre of the city and is where the airline and tou information offices are based. It is also an upmarket shopping area with many restaurants and cafés. In the past, Chandni Chowk (Silver Street) in Old Delhi was believed t be the most lavish street in the world. Nowadays the style has gone but it remains one of the major commercial areas of the city. Delhi has some fine museums including the National Museum and the Museum of Modern Art. The Lodi Gardens, designed by La Willingdon in the 1930s, are a wonderful retreat from the hustle of the city.

Landmarks outside the city include the Qutab Minar, an 800 year old minaret which stands 15 metres high and is the emblem of Delhi; the royal tomb of Humayan, a fine example of Mughal architecture and Rai Ghat where Mohandas, Indira and Rajiv Gand and Jawaharlal Nehru were cremated.

Delhi's climate is one of extremes. In the summer hot winds and dust storms force the temperature over 40 degrees. The monsoon season from July to September is hot and humid. The cricket season after this is a lot more bearable although the temperature st rises well above 20 degrees each day.

For the sports minded, Delhi has a number of golf courses including the Delhi Golf Cl in the centre of town near India Gate. Tennis, swimming and horse-riding are just som of the other activities available.

Red Fort

Also known as the Lal Qila, it lies on the banks of the river Yamuna. Towering over the city, it is surrounded by a sandstone wall more than 2km long. Shah Jahan, the Mughal ruler, built it in 1648. The two most famous buildings within the fort are Diwan-I-Am, the Hall of Public Audience, where the Emperor listened to the grievances of his subjects and dispensed justice and Diwan-i-Khas, the hall of Private Audiences, where the Emperor held private meetings and met visiting dignitaries.

India Gate

A 42metre high structure built to commemorate the 90,000 Indian soldiers who lost their lives in World War 1. It was designed by Lutyens. The names of the soldiers are engraved on the monument and an eternal flame, the Amar Jawan Jyoti, burns at the foot in commemoration of the unknown soldier. The Gate is situated at the eastern end of Raj Path .

Jama Masjid

The Friday Mosque is the largest in India and can accommodate 25,000 worshippers at one time. Built of red sandstone and white marble by Shah Jahan in 1658, it is opposite the Red Fort and overlooks the Chandni Chowk markets of the old city. There is a marble tank in the middle of the mosque where worshippers wash before praying.

Lotus Temple

The Lotus or Baha'I Temple was built of marble in 1980. It is an elegant structure, shaped like a flowering lotus with white marble petals that rise from nine pools surrounding the temple. All Baha'I temples are dedicated to the worship of God by all races, religions or castes. The temple is a wonderful sight at night when it is lit up.

Agra

The city of the Taj is 203km from Delhi but well worth the trip as it is the home of the Taj Mahal. Built by the Mughal emperor Shah Jahan, it is a monument of sheer beauty situated on the banks of the Yamuna river. Other places of interest include the Fort, Sikandra and Fatehpur Sikri, the deserted city. Same day tours to Agra depart at 07.00 from the Central Reservation Office, 1 Baba Kharak Singh Marg and visit the Taj Mahal, the Fort and Akbar's tomb at SikandraTel (2336 5358).

Taj Mahal

1 Mansingh Road
Tel: 011 302 6162
Fax: 011 301 7299
www.tajhotels.com
The best and probably most expensive. 275 rooms and 12 suites, 2 restaurants, coffee shop, bar, swimming pool and health club.

The Oberoi

Dr Zakir Hussain Road
Tel: 011 436 3030
Fax: 011 436 0484
www.oberoihotels.com
Elegant and quiet. 320 rooms, 5 restaurants, bar, business centre, swimming pool and health club.

Taj Palace

2 Sardar Patel Marg
Tel: 011 611 0202
Fax: 011 301 1252
www.tajhotels.com
388 rooms and 30 suites, 3 restaurants, bar, nightclub, swimming pool and health club. Beautiful.

Imperial Hotel

Jan Path
Tel: 011 334 1234
Fax: 011 334 2255
www.theimperialindia.com
Elegant, with more than 300 spacious rooms. 3 restaurants, 2 bars, swimming pool and health club. Very close to Connaught Place.

Park Hotel

15 Parliament St.
Tel: 011 373 3737
Fax: 011 373 2025
www.theparkhotels.com
Centrally located. 226 rooms and 40 suites, 2 restaurants, bar, swimming pool, health club and dance club.

Ashok

50B Chanakyapuri
Tel: 011 611 0101
Fax: 011 687 3216
www.theashokgroup.com
Huge hotel overlooking Nehru Gardens. 571 elegant rooms and 110 suites, 4 restaurants, 2 bars, coffee shop, business centre, swimming pool, health club and tennis courts.

Claridges

12 Aurangzeb Road
Tel: 011 301 0211
Fax: 011 301 0625
Central with beautifully furnished rooms in Victorian style. 162 rooms and 10 suites some overlooking pool, business centre, 3 restaurants, bar, coffee shop, swimming pool and health club.

Jukaso Inn

50 Sunder Nagar
Tel: 011 469 0754
Fax: 011 469 4402
jukaso@vsnl.com
50 Clean rooms in an up-market guest house in the city centre. Dining area in nice courtyard.

India International

2485 Nalwa St.
Paharganj
Tel: 011 367 7229
hindiandx@vsnl.com
Clean hotel with budget prices. Swimming pool and restaurant.

Maharani Guest House

3 Sunder Nagar
Tel: 011 469 3128
Fax: 011 462 4562
24 clean rooms. Room service meals.

My Hotel

901 Gali Chandi Wali
Paharganj
Tel: 011 361 6215
Budget hotel in backpackers area of town. Clean rooms and good restaurant.

Ajay's Hotel

5084 Main Bazar
Tel: 011 354 3125
Fax: 011 354 0656
Clean rooms in budget hotel in Paharganj. Internet available next door.

YMCA Tourist Hostel

Jai Singh Road
Tel: 011 336 1915
Fax: 011 374 6032
Good, clean budget accommodation. 123 rooms some with showers. Within walking distance of centre.

Bann Thai
The Oberoi
Dr Zakir Hussain Road
Tel: 011 436 3030
Excellent Thai restaurant serving fine, light food in wonderful surroundings overlooking swimming pool

House of Ming
Taj Mahal Hotel
1 Mansigh Road
Tel: 011 302 6162
Fine Chinese restaurant. Excellent value.

La Rochelle
The Oberoi
Dr Zakir Hussain Road
Tel: 011 436 3030
French restaurant where west meets east. One of Delhi's best.

Chor Bizarre
Hotel Broadway
4/15 Asif Ali Road
Tel: 011 327 3821
Serves good north Indian food in the unusual surroundings with a mixture of furniture collected from the city markets.

Coconut Grove
Ashok Yatri Niewa
19 Ashok Road
Southern Indian restaurant serving food from Kerala and Karnthe

The Great Kebab Factory
Radisson Hotel
National Highway 8
Tel: 011 612 9191
Fun place with excellent food in retro décor. Vegetarian and meat kebabs of the finest quality. A real treat.

Kovil
Connaught Place
Tel: 011 371 0585
Southern Indian restaurant in the centre of town. Very popular.

Farsann
30 Saidul Jab
MB Road
Tel: 011 683 8827
Simple restaurant serving Gujurati food at very reasonable prices.

Las Meninas
The Park Hotel
15 Parliament St.
Tel: 011 373 3737
Delhi's only Spanish restaurant. Great.

Sagar
18 Defence Colony Market
Tel: 011 461 7832
Well known cheap restaurant serving delicious Indian food.

Curry on the Roof
35 Greater Kailash
Tel: 011 641 8896
Fine little restaurant serving south Indian dishes, specialising in fish.

Karim Restaurant
168/2 Jha House Basti
Hazrat
Nezamuddin West
Tel: 011 469 8300
Most remarkable. Real Indian food in a huge dining area accommodating hundreds. Just down the road from the Jama Masjid Mosque. More than 990 years old and a great experience.

Most of the pubs and clubs in Delhi are attached to the bigger hotels. Listed below are some favourites.

Club Bar
The Oberoi
Dr Zakir Hussain Road
Nice comfortable bar.

Djinns
Hyatt Regency
Bhikaiji , Cama Place
Trendiest bar in Delhi.

Las Meninas
The Park Hotel
15 Parliament St.
Good wine bar with delicious tapas in the Park Hotel

Someplace Else
The Park
15 Parliament St.
Best nightclub in Delhi. Open late.

Blues
Outer Cirlce
Connaught Place
Popular night spot.

Sports Bar Radisson Hotel
National Highway 8
Good sports bar. On outskirts.

Delhi has two airports in the south west of the city, the Indira Gandhi International Airport (Terminal 2) which handles overseas flights and the Indira Gandhi Domestic Airport (Terminal 1).

The Indira Gandhi International Airport is 23km from the centre of Delhi. Prepaid taxis are available outside the terminal building. A taxi ride should take 30 minutes off peak, 60 minutes during the day and should cost no more than R250. Buses run to the centre and take around 50 minutes. Auto-rickshaws are also available (R150). The tourist information desk is in the baggage reclaim area and a help desk after customs. There are ATM's in the airport and a number of 24 hour Bureaux de Change after customs. The airport has a post office, a pharmacy and a medical unit. There is also a business centre.

The domestic airport is 6km from the international airport. A free air-conditioned bus runs between them every hour during the day and every 30 minutes during the night. The domestic airport also has a prepaid taxi service available and taxis should not cost more than R200. The domestic airport has ATM's, a post office, and a snack bar, however there are no facilities by the departure gates.

Airlines

Jet Airways
13 Community Centre
Yusuf Sarai
Tel: 011 685 3700
Fax: 011 567 5404

Sahara Airlines
7th Floor
14 KG Marg
Tel: 011 332 6851
Fax: 011 567 5234

Air India
124 Connaught Place
Tel: 011 373 1225
Fax: 011 565 2050

British Airways
DLF Plaza Tower
Gurgaon Estate
Barkhamba Road
Tel: 011 332 1286

Qantas
13 Tolstoy Marg
Fax: 011 335 5284

Emirates
18 Barakhamba Road
Tel: 011 331 60 44

Buses

The local bus system is inadequate for the volume of people in the city. Most buses are overcrowded with passengers hanging out of every door. The Inter State Bus Terminus is close to Old Delhi Railway Station in the north of the city.

Trains

There are two major railway stations, Old Delhi Station in the north of the city and New Delhi, close to Connaught Place in the centre of the city. Buses, taxis and rickshaws connect the two stations. Both stations are incredibly busy and visitors should be wary of the numerous unscrupulous touts who wander the platforms and booking halls.
General Enquiries   131 and 3313535
Reservation   011 3348686
Computerised Reservation   1330

Taxis

Metered taxis, radio taxis, tourist taxis and auto rickshaws are plentiful. Rickshaws are certainly the best and cheapest way to get around the city.

Car Hire

Avis
The Oberoi
Dr. Zakir Hussain Marg
Tel: 011 439 5163
Fax: 011 439 5164
promindersingh@avis.co.in

Post Office

General Post Office
Connaught Place

Eastern Court Post Office
Jan Path

Tourist Information

Government of India Tourist Office
88 Janpath
Connaught Place
Tel: 011 332 0005
There are also tourist informa-
tion counters at the airport, the
Interstate Bus Terminus (011
296 2181), Old Delhi Railway Station
(011 251 1083) and New Delhi Railway
Station (011 373 2374).

Hospital

All India Institute of Medical Sciences
Ansari Nagar
Tel: 011 686 4851

Ram Manohar Lohia
Willingdon Crescent
Tel: 011 336 5525

Nehru Museum

Teen Murti Bhavan
Tenn Murti Marg
Tel: 011 301 7635
The Nehru Museum is the former home
of Jawaharlal Nehru, India's first Prime
Minister, and is set in the beautiful
gardens. The museum maps his life and
that of the Independence movement.
Open 09.00-17.00 Tuesday-Sunday.

Gandhi Smriti

5 Tees January Marg
Delhi
Tel: 011 301 2843
The bungalow where Gandhi was
staying when he was assassinated.
Photographs and pictures tell the story
of his life. Open 09.00-17.00.

Climate

	ave temp	rain cm
January	14	22
February	17	20
March	22	15
April	29	10
May	33	15
June	34	68
July	31	200
August	30	200
September	29	122
October	26	18
November	20	3
December	15	10

stats

Win/Loss Record

Country	Played	won	drawn	Lost	Tie
England	7	3	4	-	-
West Indies	6	2	4	-	-
India	27	8	13	6	-
Australia	5	1	2	2	-
Pakistan	4	-	2	2	-
New Zealand	2	-	1	1	-
Zimbabwe	3	-	-	3	-

Highest Individual Aggregates (India unless stated)

Player	Mat	Inn	NO	Runs	Ave	HS	50	100
Dilip Vengsarkar	8	12	2	671	67.10	159	1	4
Sunil Gavaskar	9	14	0	668	47.71	121	2	3
Andy Flower (NZ)	3	6	2	522	130.50	183*	3	2
Chandu Borde	6	9	1	489	61.13	109	3	1
Gundappa Viswanath	8	13	1	480	40.00	131	0	2
Vijay Manjrekar	5	6	2	413	103.25	189*	0	2
Sourav Ganguly	4	8	3	410	82.00	136	3	1
Viv Richards (WI)	3	5	2	399	133.00	192*	1	2
Rahul Dravid	4	7	2	379	75.80	200*	1	1
Nawab of Pataudi	4	6	1	379	75.80	203*	0	2

Top Wicket Takers (India unless stated)

Player S/R	Mat	Bll	Md	Runs	Wkt	Ave	BB	
Anil Kumble	4	1568	81	585	38	15.39	10/74	41.26
Kapil Dev	9	1874	75	849	32	26.53	6/77	58.56
Bhagwat Chandrasekhar	5	1411	80	601	23	26.13	8/79	61.35
Vinoo Mankad	4	1766	114	585	22	26.59	8/52	80.27
Bishan Bedi	4	1578	104	455	19	23.95	5/37	83.05
Venkat	6	1507	89	494	19	26.00	8/72	79.32
Tiny Desai	6	1215	33	633	15	42.20	4/88	81.00
Erapalli Prasanna	2	582	26	300	13	23.08	5/42	44.77
Javagal Srinath	3	631	22	278	12	23.17	5/60	52.58
John Lever (Eng)	2	442	19	174	12	14.50	7/46	36.83

Highest Individual Scores (India unless stated)

230*	Bert Sutcliffe (NZ)	1955-56
227	Vinod Kambli	v Zimbabwe 1992-93
203*	Nawab of Pataudi	v England 1963-64
200*	Rahul Dravid	v Zimbabwe 2000-01
192*	Viv Richards (WI)	1974-75
189*	Vijay Manjrekar	v England 1961-62
183*	Andy Flower (Zim)	2000-01
179	Dennis Amiss (Eng)	1976-77
177	Vijay Manjrekar	1955-56
164*	Vijay Hazare	1951-52

Best Individual Bowling Performances (India unless stated)

26.3-9-74-10	Anil Kumble	v Pakistan 1998-99
47-27-52-8	Vinoo Mankad	v Pakistan 1952-53
21-3-69-8	Sikander Bakht (Pak)	1979-80
51.1-26-72-8	Venkat	v New Zealand 1964-65
41.5-18-79-8	Bhagwat Chandrasekhar	v England 1972-73
23-6-46-7	John Lever (Eng)	1976-77
23.4-7-45-6	Geoff Arnold (Eng)	1972-73
31-5-62-6	Harbhajan Singh	v Zimbabwe 2001-02
32.3-10-64-6	Ashley Mallett (Aus)	1969-70
40.5-17-76-6	Lance Gibbs (WI)	1974-75

Highest Partnerships

Wkt	Runs	Batsmen	Match
1st	159	Conrad Hunte & John Holt (Jr) (WI)	1958-1959
2nd	178	Sunil Gavaskar & Dilip Vengsarkar (Ind)	1983-1984 v West Indies
3rd	222*	Bert Sutcliffe & John Reid (NZ)	1955-1956
4th	267	Clyde Walcott & Gerry Gomez (WI)	1948-1949
5th	136	Javed Burki & Mushtaq Mohammad (Pak)	1960-1961
6th	134	Chandu Borde & Hemu Adhikari (Ind)	1958-1959 v West Indies
7th	118	Everton Weekes & Robert Christiani (WI)	1948-1949
8th	128	Ravi Shastri & Syed Kirmani (Ind)	1981-1982 v England
9th	106	Robert Christiani & Denis Atkinson (WI)	1948-1949
10th	109	Hemu Adhikari & Ghulam Abbas (Pak)	1952-1953

Results at Feroz Shah Kotla

Date	Countries	Result
10/11/1948	v West Indies	drawn
02/11/1951	v England	drawn
16/10/1952	v Pakistan	won by an innings and 70 runs
16/12/1955	v New Zealand	drawn
06/02/1959	v West Indies	drawn
12/12/1959	v Australia	lost by an innings and 127 runs
08/02/1961	v Pakistan	drawn
13/12/1961	v England	drawn
08/02/1964	v England	drawn
19/03/1965	v New Zealand	won by 7 wickets
28/11/1969	v Australia	won by 7 wickets
20/12/1972	v England	lost by 6 wickets
11/12/1974	v West Indies	lost by an innings and 17 runs
17/12/1976	v England	lost by an innings and 25 runs
24/01/1979	v West Indies	drawn
13/10/1979	v Australia	drawn
04/12/1979	v Pakistan	drawn

23/12/1981	v England	drawn
29/10/1983	v West Indies	drawn
12/12/1984	v England	lost by 8 wickets
26/09/1986	v Australia	drawn
25/11/1987	v West Indies	lost by 5 wickets
13/03/1993	v Zimbabwe	won by an innings and 13 runs
10/10/1996	v Australia	won by 7 wickets
04/02/1999	v Pakistan	won by 212 runs
18/11/2000	v Zimbabwe	won by 7 wickets
28/02/2002	v Zimbabwe	won by 4 wickets

kanpur

green park

Green Park in Kanpur is home to the Uttar Pradesh Cricket Association. Situated 2km on the north side of the city it is pleasant and surrounded by trees. Unfortunately the ground has not been used for Test cricket since 1999 and is in a rundown state.

It became the sixth Test ground in India in January 1952 when the home side took on England in the fourth Test of a five match series, Roy Tattersall taking 6/48 as India slumped to 121. In reply England scored 203 with Ghulan Ahmed taking 5/70. The home side could only manage 157 in their second innings, Mark Hilton taking 5/61 and the visitors knocked off the target of 76 for the loss of two wickets.

The next Test at Green Park was six years later against the West Indies. Fergie Gupte took a remarkable 9/102 as the West Indies scored 222, a score matched by the home team, Wes Hall taking 6/50. Gary Sobers was unlucky to be run out on 198 as the Windies totalled 443/7 from their second knock. The West Indies won by 203 runs with Hall taking another five Indian wickets for 76 runs..

India did not have to wait much longer for their first win. The following year saw a visit from Richie Benaud's Australians. India started badly as they were dismissed for 152, Alan Davidson taking 5/31 and Benaud 4/63. Australia reached 149/2 with Colin McDonald and Neil Harvey both hitting fifties, before collapsing to 219 all out as Jasubhai Patel bettered Gupte's performance of the year before by taking 9/69. Spurred on by this comeback, India hit 291 in their second innings although Davidson was devastating again with 7/93 in 57.3 overs to end with match figures of 12/124. Set 225 to win, the Australians were rolled for 105, Patel taking another five wickets for 55 runs and Umrigar 4/27.

After this fine win, Green Park saw a run of seven draws over a 20-year period before a victory over Australia by 153 runs in 1979 when Faoud Bacchus's 250 made him only the ninth batsmen in history to score a double century on debut. In 1983 Gordon Greenidge fell six runs short of a double century as West Indies won by an innings and 83 runs.

After a draw against Sri Lanka in 1986 the ground was not used again for Test cricket until December 1996 when South Africa paid their first visit to India. It was the third and final Test of a thrilling series. With the scores locked at 1-1, Paul Adams took 6/55 to restrict the home side to 237. South Africa were 60 short and up against it when the home side hit 400/7 in their second innings before declaring, Mohammad Azharuddin top scoring with 163no. This was Azharuddin's third century in only his third Test. Set 461 to win, the visitors could only manage 180, their captain Hansie Cronje hitting 50 to no avail, as Javagal Srinath (3/38) and Sunil Joshi (3/66) won the game for India by 280 runs.

In the last Test played at the ground India beat New Zealand by eight wickets in 1999 series. The visitors had no answer to Anil Kumble who ended with match figures of 10/134.

Kapil Dev's 163 against Sri Lanka in 1986 included the seventh fastest 100 of all-time, coming up in 74 balls. Salim Durani hit the second fastest 50 ever on the ground in 29 minutes against England in 1963/64.

The highest team score at the ground is 676/7 by India against Sri Lanka in that 1986 Test. At the time it was India's highest ever total, a record that lasted until January 2004 when they collected 707/5 dec. against Australia at the Sydney Cricket Ground. The lowest team score at Green Park was Australia's in 1959. The highest run chase is India's 83/2 against New Zealand in 1999.

Jasubhai Patel's match figures of 14/124 against Australia in 1959 are the best return on the ground.

Unfortunately, while the Green Park pitch is still up to Test standard, the ground has become run-down with crumbling and unkempt terraces. It would not, though, take much to restore it to its former glory.

It has a capacity of 45,000, although only a fraction of this number come to watch Tests. One-day internationals are slightly busier. The pavilion and grandstand are at the northern end of the ground. The grandstand comprises two enormous stands with a great view of the pitch. There are corporate boxes at the back. The uncovered terraces are to the left of the pavilion. The media centre and a huge uncovered concrete double-decker stand are at the southern end of the ground . There are more uncovered terraces on the west side of the ground. A large fence runs around the entire ground.

Tickets are available on the day of a Test as the capacity far outweighs demand. However they can be purchased in advance by contacting the Uttar Pradesh Cricket Association on 0512 217 200 or 0512 215 755. The ground is only a 15 to 20-minute walk from The Mall where most cricket fans stay while in Kanpur. An auto rickshaw costs R30. The journey is interesting with what seems to be a photographers' market on both sides of the street and, of course, the animals, who, without doubt, rule the roost on the roads!

Kanpur is situated on the southern banks of the River Ganges in Northern India in the Uttar Pradesh State. It is the largest city in the state, sprawling over an area of 300sq. km with a population of two million. It is India's fifth most populous city and its eighth largest in size. The name Kanpur is derived from Kanhiyapur, the town of Lord Krishna. In time Kanhiyapur was abbreviated to Kanhapur and then to Kanpur. The British called the city Cawnpore during their administration.

The city made a significant contribution to the Indian freedom struggle. Unfortunately, it has earned the reputation of being one of the most polluted in the world. This reputation is well deserved due to incessant industrial emissions. Kanpur is not a pleasant place to visit. The roads are traffic-clogged with every type of vehicle, pot-holed and full of rubbish on which the cows, oxen, pigs and dogs dine. The buildings are crumbling with no hope of being repaired and the pathways are lined with beggars and the homeless.

Kanpur's history until the 13th century is unclear, but the history of two neighbouring towns, Bithoor and Jajmau, can be traced back to legendary times. In 1207AD Raja Kanti Deo of Prayag established a village called Kohna on the site where the city is today. Kanpur was first mentioned in 1579 during Sher Shah's regime. In the 18th century it was part of the Oudh kingdom until the British defeated the Nawab Wazir of Awadh in 1765. Kanpur became a district in 1803 and one of the strongest British military garrisons in northern India. In 1857 a revolt led by Nana Saheb Peshwa led to the Indians regaining the city. The Indian Mutiny cost the lives of the entire British Garrison. The women and children were taken prisoner. However, as British relief approached the city they were massacred and thrown into a well at Bibi Ghar. The British retook the city and The Kanpur Memorial Church was built in honour of the fallen. Today, the well, located in the Nana Rao Park, is covered by concrete. The British responded to the atrocities with a reign of terror and retained control of the city until Indian Independence in 1947. Since then Kanpur expanded rapidly as a centre of heavy industry.

Although Lucknow is the capital of the state, Kanpur is the main centre of commercial and industrial activities. The city is known for its cotton and woollen textile industries which have thrived since the 1860s when the first mills were established. Other industries include chemicals, metals, fertilizer, rubber and machinery. The city has two huge power stations. It is also a major defence manufacturer and an important railway junction.

Kanpur is not known for its tourism, but there are a number of places worth visiting. There are a number of fine temples including the Shri Radhakrishna Temple, a blend of ancient and modern architecture, the Dwarka Dhish Temple which is dedicated to the worship of Lord Krishna and the Jain Glass Temple, a highly decorated place of worship. The city has many parks including Nana Rao, Phool Bagh and the Agricultural Gardens. There are also clubs where visitors can swim, play tennis and other sports. These include the Cawnpore Club, the Ganges Club and the Kanpur Union Club.

There are some towns of historical and religious significance in the neighbourhood of Kanpur. Bithoor, the ancient city, Bhitargaon, the site of the only brick temple belonging to the Gupta era and Musanagar, home of the ancient temple of Muktadevi, are of special interest. Kannauj, the 7th century capital of Emperor Harshvardhan's empire on the banks of the Ganges,is not too far. In addition there are some interesting archaeological sites around Kanpur. Temperatures in the cricket season, are cooler than in the summer although the temperature reaches 30 degrees most days. Lightweight tropical clothing is recommended all year round.

The Kanpur Memorial Church

The All Soul's Cathedral was built in 1875 in honour of the British who lost their lives in the Indian Mutiny in 1857. Designed by Walter Granville, it is a Gothic style building made of bright red brick and it contains monuments commemorating the mutiny and other fine sculptures. Near the church is Massacre Ghat on the right bank of the Ganges which was the scene of the massacre. The Ghat has been renamed Nanarao after the Nana Saheb Peshwa who led the revolt against the British.

Jajmau

One of Kanpur's ancient sites. An archaeological dig in the 1950s on the east of the city uncovered antiquities dating back to 600BC. The area, known as Siddhapuri in ancient times, was the kingdom of Yayati, the Pauranic king. Today Jajmau has two beautiful temples, the Siddhnath and Siddha Devi, a 17th century mosque and the 14th century mausoleum of Makhdum Shah Ala-ul-Haq, the Sufi saint.

Kamla Retreat

Kanpur's recreation park. On the west of the city in the Allen Forest, it has a swimming pool with a wave machine, a canal for boating and pathways for walking. There is also a zoo and a museum housing a collection of historical and archaeological artefacts. The Retreat is a great break from the hustle and bustle of Kanpur. Enquiries Tel : 0512 311 478.

Lucknow

Described by Rudyard Kipling as "no city except Bombay, the queen of all, was more beautiful in her garish style than this", Lucknow, the capital of Uttar Pradesh, is 80km to the north east of Kanpur. A city of heritage and tradition it is synonymous with the Nawabi culture. Many of its buildings and historic monuments are crumbling but it is still worth seeing. There are a number of museums and wonderful botanical gardens to visit.

Nawabganj Bird Sanctuary

45km from Kanpur, it attracts rare Siberian migratory birds as well as other fine species. The ideal time to visit the sanctuary is November to February. There is a hotel at the sanctuary.

Chakeri Airport in Kanpur small and handles local flights only. The nearest large airport is Amausi in Lucknow, 80km away. Flights to Delhi, Mumbai, Kolkata, Chennai are available from Lucknow.O.R. Nizam Road Tel: 031 651 242

Post Office

Head Post Office
: Chauraha
e Mall
0512 364 435
en 24 hours

t Office
npur Central Railway Station
0512 266 624

Tourist Information

ah Pradesh Government Tourist
fice
6/51 Birhana Road

Opposite Post Office
Tel: 0512 358 186

Hospital

Mariampur Hospital
Shastri Nagar
Tel: 0512 217 004

Meerpur Hospital
30 Meerpur Cantt
Tel: 0512 318 843

Moti Hospital
Pheel Khana Thana
Birhana Road
Tel: 0512 352 878

where to stay, eat & drink

The Landmark Hotel
10 The Mall
Tel: 0512 317 601
Fax: 0512 315 291
The best in Kanpur with 133 luxurious rooms each with cable TV. Multi-cuisine restaurant, coffee shop, bar, swimming pool, health club.

Meghdoot Hotel
The Mall
Tel: 0512 311 999
Fax: 0512 310 209
100 comfortable rooms with air-conditioning, cable TV, roof top restaurant serving Indian, Mughal, Continental and Chinese food, swimming pool and health club.

The Meera Inn
The Mall
Tel: 0512 319 972
Fax: 0512 319 973
A good budget hotel in the centre of the city. Good clean en suite rooms and cable TV. Good room service food.

Gaurav Hotel
18/54 The Mall
Tel: 0512 368 616
Fax: 0512 369 599
35 en suite rooms with cable TV, restaurant serving Chinese, Indian and Continental cuisine. Situated 1km from centre.

Geet Hotel
18/174 The Mall
Tel: 0512 311 042
Fax: 0512 311 024
Budget hotel with 40 air-conditioned rooms. Good restaurant.

Hotel Ganges
51 Naya Ganj
Tel: 0512 352 853
Fax: 0512 352 965
Budget hotel with 80 en suite rooms, some with air-conditioning. Restaura

Hotel Swagat
80 Feet Road
Tel: 0512 541 923
Fax: 0512 541 900
Recommended budget hotel near to cricket stadium. Restaurant.

Hotel Ashoka
24/16 Birhani Road
Tel: 0512 312 742
Well established budget hotel.

Hotel Mahadev Regency
14/124 The Parade
The Mall
Tel: 0512 319 943
Another budget hotel in the centre.

Most of the hotels in Kanpur have restaurants and bars. Other restauran can be found on The Mall such as the continental Kwality Restaurant and t Chinese Shanghai and Fu Tu. Anothe good Chinese is Chung Fa on Canal Road.

Climate

	ave temp	rain cr
January	15	22
February	17	20
March	21	16
April	28	10
May	32	18
June	33	60
July	31	190
August	30	189
September	29	123
October	27	23
November	20	2
December	14	11

Airlines

Jet Airways
4/1 The Mall   0512 312 787

Indian Airlines
15/54 Civil Lines   0512 311 430

Air India
15/3 M.G. Marg   0512 312 874

Buses

Uttar Pradesh State Road Transport buses connect Kanpur with various centres in the state including Lucknow. Note that buses are very crowded, in fact over-crowded, and safety is a major concern.

Trains

Kanpur Central Train Station in the centre connects with all the major stations in the country including Delhi and Kolkata.

Kanpur Central
Enquiries   0512 212 181
Reservations   67716
Anwar Ganj
Enquiries   0512 245 488

Taxis

Taxis, auto and cycle-rickshaws are the best and freely available on the street-. There is a taxi stand at Kanpur Railway Station and on Canal Road. Most hotels have taxis waiting outside.

Win/Loss Record

Country	Played	won	drawn	Lost	Tie
West Indies	3	2	1	-	-
England	6	1	5	-	-
India	18	4	11	3	-
Sri Lanka	1	-	1	-	-
Pakistan	2	-	2	-	-
New Zealand	2	-	1	1	-
Australia	3	-	1	2	-
South Africa	1	-	-	1	-

Highest Individual Aggregates (all Indian)

Player	Mat	Inn	NO	Runs	Ave	HS	50	100
Gundappa Viswanath	7	12	3	776	86.22	179	4	3
Sunil Gavaskar	9	14	0	629	44.93	176	5	1
Mohammad Azharuddin	3	5	2	543	181.00	199	1	3
Kapil Dev	7	9	0	430	47.78	163	1	2
Dilip Vengsarkar	7	10	1	422	46.89	137	3	1
Polly Umrigar	5	8	1	409	58.43	147*	1	2
Chetan Chauhan	4	7	0	311	44.43	84	4	0
Vijay Manjrekar	5	7	0	268	38.29	96	2	0
Bapu Nadkarni	3	5	2	261	87.00	122*	1	1
Hari Contractor	4	6	0	253	42.17	74	2	0

Top Wicket Takers (India unless stated)

Player	Mat	Bll	Md	Runs	Wkt	Ave	BB	S/R
Kapil Dev	7	1329	39	696	25	27.84	6/63	53.16
Sergie Gupte	3	1141	53	515	19	27.11	9/102	60.05
Anil Kumble	2	664	30	232	15	15.47	6/67	44.27
Jasubhai Patel	1	369	23	124	14	8.86	9/69	26.36
Geoff Dymock (Aus)	1	382	12	166	12	13.83	7/67	31.83
Alan Davidson (Aus)	1	466	30	124	12	10.33	7/93	38.83
Bhagwat Chandrasekhar	4	1127	50	463	11	42.09	4/86	102.45
Wes Hall (WI)	1	364	16	126	11	11.45	6/50	33.09
Karson Ghavri	4	627	19	304	10	30.40	4/118	62.70
Bishan Bedi	3	1211	72	346	10	34.60	3/42	121.10

Highest Individual Scores (India unless stated)

250	Faoud Bacchus (WI)		1978-79
199	Mohammad Azharuddin	v Sri Lanka	1986-87
198	Garry Sobers (WI)		1958-59
194	Gordon Greenidge (WI)		1983-84
179	Gundappa Viswanath	v West Indies	1978-79
176	Sunil Gavaskar	v Sri Lanka	1986-87
172	Ken Barrington (Eng)		1961-62
163	Kapil Dev	v Sri Lanka	1986-87
163*	Mohammad Azharuddin	v South Africa	1996-97
147*	Polly Umrigar	v England	1961-62

Best Individual Bowling Performances (India unless stated)

35.5-16-69-9	Jasubhai Patel	v Australia 1959-60
34.3-11-102-9	Fergie Gupte	v West Indies 1958-59
28.4-5-67-7	Geoff Dymock (Aus)	1979-80
57.3-23-93-7	Alan Davidson (Aus)	For Australia 1959-60
21-3-48-6	Roy Tattersall (Eng)	For England 1951-52
28.4-4-50-6	Wes Hall (WI)	For West Indies 1958-59
19.1-6-55-6	Paul Adams (SA)	For South Africa 1996-97
28-5-63-6	Kapil Dev	v Pakistan 1979-80
26.5-5-67-6	Anil Kumble	v New Zealand 1999-00
60-37-73-6	Fred Titmus (Eng)	For England 1963-64

Highest Partnerships

Wkt	Runs	Batsmen	Match
1st	162	Devang Gandhi & Sadagoppan Ramesh (Ind)	1999-2000 v New Zealand
2nd	150	Kris Srikkanth & Mohammad Azharuddin (Ind)	1984-1985 v England
3rd	163*	Aunshuman Gaekwad & Gundappa Viswanath (Ind)	1976-1977 v New Zealand
4th	206	Ken Barrington & Ted Dexter (Eng)	1961-1962
5th	160	Faoud Bacchus & David Murray (WI)	1978-1979
6th	272	Mohammad Azharuddin & Kapil Dev (Ind)	1986-1987 v Sri Lanka
7th	169	Yashpal Sharma & Kapil Dev (Ind)	1981-1982 v England
8th	96	Jack Birkenshaw & Geoff Arnold (Eng)	1972-1973
9th	117	Roger Binny & Madan Lal (Ind)	1983-1984 v West Indies
10th	52	Andy Roberts & Peter Petherick (NZ)	1976-1977

Results at Green Park

Date	Countries	Result
12/01/1952	v England	lost by 8 wickets
12/12/1958	v West Indies	lost by 203 runs
19/12/1959	v Australia	lost 119 runs
16/12/1960	v Pakistan	drawn
01/12/1961	v England	drawn
15/02/1964	v England	drawn
15/11/1969	v Australia	drawn
25/01/1973	v England	drawn
18/11/1976	v New Zealand	drawn
02/02/1979	v West Indies	drawn
02/10/1979	v Australia	won by 153 runs
25/12/1979	v Pakistan	drawn
30/01/1982	v England	drawn
21/10/1983	v West Indies	lost by an innings and 83 runs
31/01/1985	v England	drawn
17/12/1986	v Sri Lanka	drawn
08/12/1996	v South Africa	won by 280 runs
22/10/1999	v New Zealand	won by 8 wickets

eden gardens

Eden Gardens in Kolkata is the largest stadium in India and with a capacity of 100,000, one of the largest in the world. It is situated in the Kolkata Maidan, a vast parkland, and is a short ten minute walk from the centre of the city. This walk goes through tree-lined streets where the excitement of the crowd on match days needs to be seen to be believed. The fans' enthusiasm for the game is amazing and some good humoured banter can be heard when they spot a visiting supporter.

The ground became the second Test venue in India when it hosted the second match of England's first tour in 1934 but rain prevented England making the 82 they required for victory.

The next four Tests at Eden Gardens also ended in draws; in 1949 against the West Indies, in 1951/2 against England, in 1952 against Pakistan and in 1955/6 when New Zealand were the visitors. In 1956 the ground hosted the third and final Test against Australia. In a low scoring game Ghulam Ahmed took 7/49 as Australia collected 177. India replied with 41 fewer as Richie Benaud took 6/52. Australia declared their second innings at 189/9 to set India a target of 231. They began well and reached 104/4 before being skittled for 136. Benaud took 5/53 and Jim Burke 4/37 as Australia won the match by 94 runs and the series 2-0.

Draws against Australia in 1959 and Pakistan in 1961 followed before India recorded their first win at Eden Gardens, in the fourth match of the 1962 series against England. Although David Allen took 5/67 for England, India accrued 380 and England could only score 212 in their first innings as Salim Durani, 5/47 and Chandu Borde, 4/65 took them apart. India hit 252 in their second innings, Borde top scoring with 61 as Allen took 4/95 and Tony Lock, 4/111. Chasing 421 for victory, England were bowled out for 233, with only Ted Dexter (63) putting up any resistance, to give India victory by 187 runs.

Further draws were to follow at the ground against England and Australia in 1964 and New Zealand in 1965 before the West Indies beat their hosts by an innings and 45 runs to clinch the 1967 series 2-0. Two years later the ground hosted Australia in the fourth Test of the 1969 series with the score at 1-1. Graham McKenzie took 6/67 as India were all out for 212. Ian Chappell top scored with 99 in Australia's reply of 335 to give the visitors a first innings lead of 123 and after India managed only

161 in their second innings, Bill Lawry and Keith Stackpole knocked off the required 42 runs to give Australia victory by 10 wickets.

India beat England again in the second Test of the 1972/73 series thanks mainly to the bowling of Bhagwat Chandrasekar and Bishan Bedi.

In the 1974/75 series against the West Indies the hosts were 2-0 down coming to the third Test at Kolkata and, thanks to a masterful second innings 139 from Gundappa Viswanath, India finished victorious.

England got their revenge in the second Test of the 1977 series, winning by 10 wickets. This was followed by draws against the West Indies and Australia in 1979, Pakistan in 1980 and England in 1982. The home side won the toss in the fifth Test of the 1983 series against the West Indies, but managed only 90 in their second innings – the lowest team score at Eden Gardens – as Malcolm Marshall (6/37) and Michael Holding (3/29) ripped them apart to give the win to the West Indies by an innings and 46 runs.

The next three Tests at Eden Gardens were all drawn, against England in 1985 and Pakistan and the West Indies in 1987. But in 1993 they beat England in the first Test with Mohammed Azharuddin making a wonderful 182 in their first innings 371. In reply, England fell for 163, Anil Kumble, Venkatapathy Raju and Rajesh Chauhan each taking three wickets. Forced to follow-on, Mike Gatting top scored with 81 as the visitors made 286. Kumble and Raju both took three wickets. Needing 78 to win, India reached their target with the loss of only two wickets.

South Africa won the 1996 Test after battering the Indian bowlers. They hit 428 in the first innings – Andrew Hudson (146) and Gary Kirsten (102) sharing an opening stand of 236. Venkatash Prassad took 6/104. The home side slumped to 119/6 in reply before Mohammed Azharuddin, top scoring with 109, and Kumble, 88, took the total to 329. South Africa's 367/3 dec. (Kirsten with 133 and Darren Cullinan with 153) left the home side a target of 467. Lance Klusener soon put paid to any Indian thoughts of victory with 8/64 as they were dismissed for 137 to give the visitors victory by 329 runs.

In 1998 India went in against Australia 1-0 up in the series and doubled this with a famous victory. Australia scored 233 with Steve Waugh getting 80 and Ricky Pointing 60. Javagal Srinath, Sourav Ganguly and Kumble each took three wickets. India declared on 633/5, Azharuddin hitting an unbeaten 163no, ably helped by Navjot Sidhu, 97, VVS Laxman, 95, Rahul Dravid, 86, Sachin Tendulkar, 79, and Ganguly, 65. Australia managed only 181 in reply as Kumble took 5/62 to give India victory by an innings and 219 runs. Azharuddin's knock was his fifth century in six first innings at the ground. His other centuries were 110 against England in 1984, 141 against Pakistan in 1987, 182 against England in 1993 and 109 against South Africa in 1996.

India lost to Pakistan by 46 runs in the Asian Test Championship at Eden Gardens in 1999 but the 2001 Test with Australia will go down in history as one of the greatest matches ever played. Australia scored 445 as Steve Waugh, 110 and Matthew Hayden, 97, hit out although Harbhajan Singh took 7/123. India could only manage 171 in reply, Laxman hitting 59 and Stuart McGill taking 4/18. Forced to follow-on, India staged one of the greatest comebacks of all time as Laxman, 281, and Dravid, 180, shared a partnership of 376 to reach 657/7 – the highest team score at Eden Gardens – before declaring. Australia required 384, but Harbhajan was again inspirational and took 6/73 as the visitors fell for 212. India had won by 171 runs.

Srinath's match figures of 13/132 against Pakistan in 1999 are the best at the ground.

The Dr. B. C. Roy Clubhouse, a three-tier building, dominates the southern end of the ground, housing the players' dressing rooms, the VIP viewing gallery seating more than 3000 spectators and the press box on the top floor. The clubhouse also has a medical unit, a sports shop and a library. There is another two-tier stand at the southern end of the ground with a covered upper tier. The west side of the ground has a huge grandstand, again with a covered upper tier. The lower tier is shaded from early afternoon onwards. The northern end of the ground is totally uncovered, with massive stands exposed to the elements including a very hot sun, but the upper tiers of these stands provide a wonderful view. The two scoreboards, one a 1950s wooden version, the other modern and electronic are at this end. There is another large and mostly uncovered grandstand on the east side. Most of the seats are concrete and small but are not too uncomfortable. Food is served under the stands with Indian rice, crisps, popcorn, soft drinks and water on offer. The toilet facilities are adequate and well serviced.

The Eden Gardens crowd is without doubt the most passionate in the world. When India are doing well the noise rises to a crescendo and the crowd is the happiest in the world. However, when their side lose a wicket, the silence is palpable for the next few overs. Even with 100,000 people in the ground one can clearly hear the opposition wicket keeper talking to his bowler. It is quite eerie to sit in such an enormous silent crowd. If the team rallies, its party time again as the crowd becomes boisterous again. On occasion feelings overrun and play has been disrupted. A riot occurred after a fan was beaten by police in the 1967 Test against the West Indies and brought an early end to the day's cricket. There was crowd trouble again in the 1996 World Cup semi-final against Sri Lanka and in the 1999 Asian Cup Test against Pakistan. Win or lose, the crowd will let visiting supporters know how it feels. It must be said that it can be quite frightening leaving the ground with water bags and other missiles flying through the air and being taunted in the surrounding streets by hoards of Indian supporters. It is just not cricket!

Tickets are available from the Cricket Association of Bengal in the clubhouse at the ground or by writing to Mr. Bablu Kalay, Joint Hon. Sec. Cricket Association of Bengal, Dr. B. C. Roy Club House, Eden Gardens Kolkata Tel : 033 2248 0411 or 033 2248 2447 or on by email on thecab@vsnl.com It is important to book tickets as early as possible as they are always in great demand. Leaving it until the last minute can result in having to pay three times the face value on the black market. Security is tight with thorough searches at all entrances. Bottles, cigarettes, matches and movie cameras are not permitted. The ground is a ten minute walk from the city centre across the Kolkata Maidan, however Tuk tuks and taxis are available from outside most hotels and will only cost R75.

The Subhas Chandra Bose International Aiport at Dum Dum is 17km from the city centre. There are prepaid taxis available and the journey should take about 40 minutes and cost no more than R200. An airport coach runs 24 hours a day to the larger hotels and the Indian Airlines office in the city centre and costs R50. Tickets can be purchased in the baggage claim area. A public bus service, No's 10 and 33, also run to and from the city for R8. The airport has banks, ATM's, bureaux de change, restaurants, fast food counters and tourist information desks. All the airlines have offices in the terminal. Rest rooms are available for passengers awaiting onward flights.

arrival

Kolkata, formerly Calcutta, is situated on the River Hooghly near the Bay of Bengal in north east India. Formerly the capital of the British Empire, it is now capital of the West Bengal State. It is India's second most populated city with 14 million people and is one of contrasting lifestyles. Great wealth is evident in the beautiful buildings, mansions and gardens while dire poverty can be seen in the crowded shanty towns, the huge unemployment and the many beggars on the streets.

The city has seen massive immigration since independence in 1947; people from the countryside seeking work and refugees from Bangladesh. It is exhausted by its huge population and by the lack of infrastructure to deal with it. It also has dreadful problems with air pollution and unbelievable traffic congestion.

The area was a small village until 1690 when Calcutta was founded by Job Charnock as a trading post of the British East India Company. He built Fort William as protection and incorporated the villages of Kalikata, Sutanati and Govindpur to create the city. In 1756 the Nawab of Bengal attacked, taking it over and allegedly putting 123 people (mostly British but including Dutch and Portuguese) to death by suffocation in a chamber which became known as the Black Hole of Calcutta. Many generations of British schoolboys have had this story taught to them at school but it may never have happened.

Robert Clive recaptured the city in 1757 when he defeated the Nawab who had teamed up with the French and the city became the capital of the British Administration in India in 1772 when Warren Hastings was appointed the First Governor General. It remained the capital until it was superseded by Delhi in 1911. Kolkata is the financial, commercial and industrial centre of east India. Its main industries include silk and cotton texiles, chemicals, jute, shipbuilding and rubber. It is also a major port. It is vibrant and easy to walk around. As with other cities in India, the poverty on the streets is appalling and can be quite intimidating.

The major landmark is the Maidan, a huge expanse of parklands in the centre of the city by the Hooghly River. Jawaharlal Nehru Road, formerly Chowringhee, runs along the eastern side of the Maiden and is the city's main thoroughfare. The Victoria Memorial, built to commemorate the Queen's reign, is the main historical structure in the city. Others include Raj Bhavan, formerly known as Government House (1805), the Writers' Building in Dalhousie Square (1880) which was once the headquarters of the British East India Company, the silver-domed General Post Office and the Indian Museum (1875) which houses the finest collection of Indian art in the world. The National Library in Belvedere House has over a million books, the largest collection in India.

Howrah Bridge is also one of Kolkata's greatest landmarks. It is an engineering marvel, suspended on pillars and is the third largest bridge in the world. An incredible two million pedestrians use the bridge each day. It is the city's link with the Howrah Railway Station, Kolkata's rail connection to the rest of the country. To the south of the city, the river divides itself into many tributaries which form the Gangetic deltas, is home to the Sunderban Wildlife Park, a sanctuary for many exquisite animals and birds.

Religious buildings include St. Paul's Cathedral (1847), the Muslim Nakhoda Mosque, the largest in the city, which can accommodate 10,000 worshippers, the Hindu Kali Mander Temple situated beside Mother Teresa's Home for the Destitute. Fort William must be seen when in Kolkata. The Botanical Gardens in Howrah on the west bank of the Hooghly provide a break from the city where a huge collection of bamboos, orchids and palms can be seen. It is famous for its enormous 200 year old Banyan tree. The Zoological Gardens across the city's second bridge has an excellent collection of animals including white and Bengal tigers.

Kolkata has a subtropical climate. The hot summers have ridiculously high humidity levels and temperatures range between 31 and 37 degrees. Fortunately the cricket season coincides with the autumn/winter months of October to February when the temperature is at its best, averaging 24 degrees and the rain has gone.

Lightweight tropical clothing is recommended all year round.

Maidan

Known as the lungs of Kolkata, this is home to many of city's most famous landmarks including Fort William, St. John's Church, The Victoria Memorial and the Race Course. It separates the city from the Hooghly river and also includes Eden Gardens. Named after the sister of Alexander, the gardens provide a beautiful setting for the largest cricket stadium in India.

Fort William

Built in 1696 by the British East India Company and now the headquarters of the Indian Army's Eastern Command. Surrounded by a huge moat, the fort was named after King William III. Organised tours of the barracks, arsenal, prison and the church, St. Peter's can be arranged.

Nirmal Hirday

The hospital in Kolkata that was Mother Teresa's first home for the dying. Mother Teresa lived here for more than 40 years and is buried in the grounds. It is situated next to the Kali Temple in the centre of the city.

St. Paul's Cathedral

Situated between the Birla planetarium and Rabindra Sadan in beautiful gardens, this is an Indo-Gothic style building built in 1847 by Major Forbes of the Bengal Engineering Corps. It was the first Episcopal Cathedral in the eastern world. It has fine paintings, very impressive stained glass windows and a library of antique books. Visitors are welcome to peruse the treasures of the Cathedral at their leisure.

Victoria Memorial

The Victoria Memorial at the southern end of the Maidan was built between 1906 and 1921 in memory of Queen Victoria. Modelled on the Taj Mahal, the memorial is now a museum housing a large collection of artefacts from the Raj era and containing busts and statues of all the leading people from the British rule. The collection also includes paintings, manuscripts and furniture. It is set in beautiful gardens and a visit makes a pleasant break from the noisy city. Open Tuesday-Sunday.

Academy of Fine Arts

Cathedral Road
Tel: 033 2242 1205
Most of the shows are in Bengali but still worth watching.

Indian Museum

27 J L Nehru Road
Tel: 033 2249 8931
Built in 1875, this is the oldest museum is the country with fine collections of art, geology, zoology, archaeology and anthropology. Locally known as the House of Magic, it is open from Tuesday-Sunday 10.00-16.00.

Taj Bengal
34B Belveder Road
Alipore
Tel: 033 2223 3939
Fax: 033 2223 1766
One of the city's best hotels. Overlooks the Maidan. 216 rooms and 20 suites, 3 restaurants, bars, nightclub, swimming pool and health club.

Oberoi Grand
15 J. L. Nehru Road
Tel: 033 2249 2323
Fax: 033 2249 1217
Elegant hotel in the centre. 213 rooms and 6 suites, 3 restaurants, bar, nightclub, swimming pool and health club.

Park Hotel
17 Park St.
Tel: 033 2249 7336
Fax: 033 2249 7343
Central. 160 rooms, 2 restaurants, the best bar in town and a nightclub. Swimming pool and health club.

Hotel Hindustan International
235/1 AJC Bose Road
Tel: 033 2247 2394
Fax: 033 2247 2824
Good hotel with 220 rooms, 3 restaurants, bar and nightclub, swimming pool, health club.

Kenilworth
1 Little Russell St.
Tel: 033 2242 8394
Fax: 033 2242 5136
Best Western hotel with 110 comfortable rooms, 2 restaurants, bar. Very popular with tourists.

Peerless Inn
15 J L Nehru Road
Tel: 033 2243 0301
Fax: 033 2248 6650
Central hotel with 123 rooms, 3 restaurants, bar and health club. Very convenient for Eden Gardens.

Astor 15 Shakespeare Sarani
Tel: 033 2282 9957
Fax: 033 2287 7430
Excellent middle of the range hotel with 35 clean rooms, 3 restaurants, bar and beer garden. Good value.

Fairlawn
13A Sudder St.
Tel: 033 2252 1510
Fax: 033 2244 1835
info@fairlawn.com
Charming old fashioned hotel in the centre of the city. Built in 1800 the Fairlawn is a famous hotel with 22 rooms, restaurant and bar in garden. An absolute treat for budget travellers.

Hotel Diplomat
10 Sudder St.
Tel: 033 2246 8934
Good budget hotel in the centre of town.

Paramount Hotel
33 Mirza Ghalib Strret
Kydd St.
Off Sudder St.
Tel: 033 2229 0066
Clean budget hotel with cable TV, one of the cheapest in the area.

Chinoiserie
Taj Bengal Hotel
34 Belvedere Road
Alipore
Tel: 033 2223 3939
The best Chinese restaurant in town. Fine service and reasonable prices.

Kewpies
2 Elgin Lane
Tel: 033 2475 9880
Bengali restaurant serving both vegetarian and meat dishes. Bookings essential.

Zen Park Hotel
17 Park St.
Tel: 033 2249 7336
Excellent Asian restaurant. Lovely atmosphere, good service and good food.

Peerless Inn
15 J L Nehru Road
Tel: 033 2243 0301
Bengali restaurant in the centre of town.

Blue Beyond
9th Floor
Hotel Lindsay
8A Lindsay St.
Tel: 033 22252 2237
hotellindsay@vsnl.net
Good Indian restaurant with some Chinese dishes on the menu. Fashionable place to eat with stunning views of Kolkata. Good service.

Bar-B-Q
43 Park St.
Tel: 033 2299 916
Excellent Chinese, serving Cantonese and Szechuan dishes.

The Blue Fox
55 Park St.
Tel: 033 2249 7948
Trendy restaurant serving European and Indian dishes. Very popular with visitors.

Taaja
29/1A Ballygunge Circular Road
Tel: 033 2476 7334
One of city's best restaurants serving French, Italian, Greek and Spanish food.

Peter Cat
18 Park St.
Tel: 033 2229 8841
Excellent cheap restaurant serving Indian and European food but specialising in Tandoori.

Momo Plaza
2a Suburban Hospital Road
Tel: 033 2247 8250
Tibetan food. Very popular.

The Sheriff
Elgin Road

Tel: 033 2280 6761
Mexican restaurant serving hot food. Very popular.

Fairlawn Hotel
13 A Sudder St.
Tel: 033 2244 1835
A lovely bar with beer garden in the city centre. Top place.

Park Hotel
17 Park St.
Tel: 033 2249 7336
Without doubt, one of the best pubs in Kolkata. Great atmosphere, live music and good service.

Someplace Else
Park Hotel
17 Park St.
Tel: 033 2249 7336
Nightclub at the Park Hotel. Very lively.

Taj Bengal
34B Belvedere Road
Tel: 033 2223 3939
Nice relaxing cocktail bar for drinks after a day at the cricket.

Post Office
Kolkata General Post Office
BBD Bagh
Tel: 033 2220 1601
Monday-Saturday 08.00-20.30,
Sunday 08.00-15.30

Tourist Information
Government of India Tourist Office
4 Shakespeare Sarani
Tel: 033 2242 1402

Government of India Tourist Information Counter at Airport
552 8299
West Bengal Tourist Office
3/2 BBD Bagh

Hospital
Kolkata Hospital
Mominpur
Diamond Harbour Road

Climate

	ave temp	rain cm
January	20	12
February	23	25
March	28	32
April	30	53
May	31	129
June	30	291
July	29	329
August	29	338
September	29	266
October	28	130
November	24	20
December	20	7

Airlines

Indian Airlines
39 Chittaranjan Ave
Tel: 033 2211 0730
Fax: 033 2211 1669

Sahara Airlines
Sahara India Sadan
2A Shakespeare Sara
Tel: 033 2282 9075
Fax: 033 2282 9364

Jet Airways
18D Park St.
Stephen Court
Tel: 033 2229 2227
Fax: 033 2216 4116

Buses

Buses run throughout the city, but they are overcrowded and not very safe.

Trains

Howrah Railway Station is the major train station, connecting with the rest of the country. Very crowded and like a small town. Vendors and porters appear to live here along with hundreds of begging children known as platform children. Volunteers actually hold school lessons for them in the station. The main reservation office is at 6 Failie Place (033 2220 6811) and the office for foreign tourist is on the first floor. In the station itself the ticket office is on the first floor. Trains to Darjeeling and other northern destinations leave from Sealdah Station.

Taxis

Metered taxis are available as well as radio taxis, tourist taxis and auto rickshaws. The yellow taxis and the rickshaws are certainly the best and cheapest way to get around the city.
Tel: 033 2235 3535

Car Hire

Avis
The Oberoi Grand
15 Jawaharlal Nehru Road
Tel: 033 2249 2323
Fax: 033 2217 0147
rahulsen@avis.co.in
Open 08.00-20.00

Win/Loss Record

Country	Played	won	drawn	Lost	Tie
South Africa	1	1	-	-	-
West Indies	8	3	4	1	-
Pakistan	5	1	4	-	-
New Zealand	2	-	2	-	-
Australia	7	2	3	2	-
India	32	6	18	8	-
England	9	1	5	3	-

Highest Individual Aggregates (All Indian)

Player	Mat	Inn	NO	Runs	Ave	HS	50	100
Mohammad Azharuddin	7	9	1	860	107.50	182	2	5
VVS Laxman	5	9	1	724	90.50	281	3	2
Dilip Vengsarkar	7	12	3	645	71.67	157*	2	2
Sunil Gavaskar	8	15	2	583	44.85	182*	1	2
Motganhalli Jaisimha	7	13	1	530	44.17	129	2	1
Gundappa Viswanath	8	15	0	501	33.40	139	3	1
Vijay Manjrekar	9	15	2	456	35.08	90	2	0
Chandu Borde	7	12	2	449	44.90	68	5	0
Rahul Dravid	5	9	0	413	45.89	180	1	1
Sachin Tendulkar	6	11	1	399	39.90	176	2	1

Top Wicket Takers (All Indian)

Player	Mat	Bll	Md	Runs	Wkt	Ave	BB	S/R
Bishan Bedi	6	1890	113	639	29	22.03	7/98	65.17
Kapil Dev	8	1860	72	874	27	32.37	6/91	68.89
Javagal Srinath	4	974	28	526	22	23.91	8/86	44.27
Anil Kumble	5	1683	71	719	21	34.24	5/62	80.14
Ghulam Ahmed	4	1086	34	468	21	22.29	7/49	51.71
Vinoo Mankad	5	1512	77	569	21	27.10	4/49	72.00
Harbhajan Singh	3	923	33	403	20	20.15	7/123	46.15
Salim Durani	5	1018	58	416	19	21.89	6/73	53.58
Bhagwat Chandrasekhar	6	1453	73	548	18	30.44	5/65	80.72
Tiny Desai	5	1187	35	584	18	32.44	4/62	65.94

Highest Individual Scores (India unless stated)

281	VVS Laxman	v Australia 2000-01
256	Rohan Kanhai (WI)	1958-59
188*	Saeed Anwar (Pak)	1998-99
182*	Sunil Gavaskar	v West Indies 1978-79
182	Mohammad Azharuddin	v England 1992-93
180	Rahul Dravid	v Australia 2000-01
176	Sachin Tendulkar	v West Indies 2002-03
167	Graham Yallop (Aus)	1979-80
163*	Mohammad Azharuddin	v Australia 1997-98
162	Everton Weekes (WI)	1948-49

Best Individual Bowling Performances (India unless stated)

21.3-4-64-8	Lance Klusener (SA)	1996-97
27-6-86-8	Javagal Srinath	v Pakistan 1998-99
20.3-6-49-7	Ghulam Ahmed	v Australia 1956-57
50-19-98-7	Bishan Bedi	v Australia 1969-70
37.5-7-123-7	Harbhajan Singh	v Australia 2000-01
15-4-37-6	Malcolm Marshall (WI)	1983-84
29-10-52-6	Richie Benaud (Aus)	1956-57
21-7-55-6	Roy Gilchrist (WI)	1958-59
25.1-8-56-6	Roger Binny	v Pakistan 1986-87
33.4-12-67-6	Garth McKenzie (Aus)	1969-70

Highest Partnerships

Wkt	Runs	Batsmen	Match
1st	236	Gary Kirsten & Andrew Hudson (SA)	1996-1997
2nd	344*	Sunil Gavaskar & Dilip Vengsarkar (Ind)	1978-1979 v West Indies
3rd	206	Graham Yallop & Kim Hughes (Aus)	1979-1980
4th	217	Rohan Kanhai & Basil Butcher (WI)	1958-1959
5th	376	VVS Laxman & Rahul Dravid (Ind)	2000-2001 v Australia
6th	195	Shiv Chanderpaul & Marlon Samuels (WI)	2002-2003ia
7th	163	Bruce Taylor & Bert Sutcliffe (NZ)	1964-1965
8th	161	Mohammad Azharuddin & Anil Kumble (Ind)	1996-1997 v South Africa
9th	161	Clive Lloyd & Andy Roberts (WI)	1983-1984
10th	51	Bapu Nadkarni & Bhagwat Chandrasekhar (Ind)	1963-1964 v England

Results at Eden Gardens

Date	Countries	Result
05/01/1934	v England	drawn
31/12/1948	v West Indies	drawn
30/12/1951	v England	drawn
12/12/1952	v Pakistan	drawn
28/12/1955	v New Zealand	drawn
02/11/1956	v Australia	lost by 94 runs
31/12/1958	v West Indies	lost by an innings and 336 runs
23/01/1960	v Australia	drawn
30/12/1960	v Pakistan	drawn
30/12/1961	v England	won by 187 runs
29/01/1964	v England	drawn
17/10/1964	v Australia	drawn
05/03/1965	v New Zealand	drawn
31/12/1966	v West Indies	lost by an innings and 45 runs
12/12/1969	v Australia	lost by 10 wickets
30/12/1972	v England	won by 28 runs
27/12/1974	v West Indies	won by 85 runs
01/01/1977	v England	lost by 10 wickets
29/12/1978	v West Indies	drawn
26/10/1979	v Australia	drawn
29/01/1980	v Pakistan	drawn
01/01/1982	v England	drawn
10/12/1983	v West Indies	lost by an innings and 46 runs
31/12/1984	v England	drawn
11/02/1987	v Pakistan	drawn
26/12/1987	v West Indies	drawn
29/01/1993	v England	won by 8 wickets
27/11/1996	v South Africa	lost by 329 runs
18/03/1998	v Australia	won by an innings and 219 runs
16/02/1999	v Pakistan	lost by 46 runs
11/03/2001	v Australia	won by 171 runs
30/10/2002	v West Indies	drawn

wankhede stadium

The Wankhede Stadium in Mumbai, the third ground in the city to be used for Test cricket, became India's 12th Test ground on 23 January 1975. The Gymkhana Ground hosted India's inaugural Test in 1933 and The Brabourne Stadium held its first Test in 1948. It was a fabulous stadium but its capacity was not sufficient for the huge crowds that want to watch cricket in the city. The Wankhede was built within half-a-mile of the old ground and is a fantastic stadium with a capacity of 65,000. It is a huge concrete bowl in a residential area with apartment blocks overlooking the ground.

The first Test, against the West Indies could not have gone more badly for India on the Nawab of Pataudi's last match. The visitors scored 604/6 dec., Clive Lloyd top scoring with 242, his double century coming in just 240 balls, the eighth fastest of all time and the biggest innings at the Wankhede as is the team score. Roy Fredrick hit 104 and Alvin Kallicharran was unlucky to be dismissed on 98. India avoided the follow-on by two runs with a score of 406, Eknath Solkar (102), Gundappa Viswanath (95) and Sunil Gavaskar (86) making useful contributions. Lance Gibbs took 7/98. In their second innings, the West Indies raced to 205/3 dec. in 30 overs before dismissing India for 202 to win by 202 runs. Brijesh Patel was the only India batsman to put up any resistance with 73no as Vanburn Holder took 6/39.

Gavaskar's 86 was his lowest first innings score at the ground for quite some time. He followed it with centuries in each of the next four matches; 119 in India's 162 run victory over New Zealand in 1976; 108 in the drawn 1977 Test with England; 205 in the draw against the West Indies in 1978 and 123 in India's demolition of Australia in 1979. This was probably India's most convincing win at the ground. Having batted first and declaring at 458/8, India dismissed Australia for 160 and 198 to win by an innings and 100 runs. Syed Kirmani (101no) joined Gavaskar in making a fine contribution to the score. 1979 was a good year for India at the Wankhede as they also beat their biggest rivals, Pakistan, by 131 runs.

The Jubilee Test against England in 1980 was a remarkable one for Ian Botham. Gavaskar top scored with 49 as India were bowled out for 242, Botham taking 6/58. He then proceeded to hit 114 to push England's score to 296 before taking 7/48 to dismiss the home side for 149. His 13 wickets are the best return at the ground.

Graham Gooch (49no) and Geoff Boycott (43no) saw the visitors home for a 10 wicket victory. India took its revenge in December 1981 when they beat England by 138 runs, but not before Botham took 4/72 and 5/61 for the visitors to end up with 22 wickets at the Wankhede in two matches at an average of 10.86 with three five wicket hauls.

Despite an innings of 178 by Graham Hick for England in the 1993 Test, India managed to win the match by an innings and 15 runs. Hick's contribution enabled the visitors to score 347 in their first innings before Vinod Kambli became the 12th man to hit a double century on debut(224) as India scored a massive 591. Sachin Tendulkar (78) and Navjot Sidhu (79) also made valuable contributions. Anil Kumble led the home side bowlers with 4/70 as England were dismissed for 229.

The series in 2001 against Australia will go down in history as one of the greatest of all time. The first match was played at the Wankhede and gave little indication of what was to come. The Indians batted first and were dismissed for 176, only Tendulkar scoring well at 76 as Shane Warne took 4/47. Matthew Hayden (119) and Adam Gilchrist (122) both scored centuries as the visitors reached 349 to take a lead of 173 in the first innings. In the second innings Tendulkar again was the only batsman to put up any resistance with 65 as the home side fell to 219 all out. Australia's openers knocked off the runs to win by 10 wickets. No one could have believed that India, despite being forced to follow-on in the second Test in Kolkata, came back to win the series 2-1 in Chennai.

Desmond Haynes will always remember the 1983 Test. He became only the fourth batsmen in Test cricket to be given out handling the ball. The Wankhede is situated just off Marine Drive by the sea. It is 3km from the centre and about a 20 minute walk from Colaba where most cricket supporters stay. The stadium was refurbished before the 1995 World Cup. The best place to watch from is the Vithal Divecha Pavilion on the west side. The ground is a concrete bowl with most seats covered by the roof that encircles the ground. There are stands named after Vijay Merchant and Sachin Tendulkar at the north end of the ground and Sunil Gavaskar on the east side. The seating consists of wooden benches which can get uncomfortable as the day wears on. The Tendulkar and Gavaskar stands are the liveliest parts, with dancing, cheering and general delirium, particularly when local hero Sachin walks out to bat. The reception he receives in Mumbai is remarkable and unmatched anywhere else. The ground has a capacity of 65,000 but sometimes it feels as if there are as many people outside following the cricket as inside. There are foodstalls under all the stands serving coffee, water, soft drinks, popcorn, ice creams and rice dishes. Unfortunately the toilet facilities leave a lot to be desired and are not well looked after.

Tickets can be purchased from the ground on the days leading up to the match. It is advisable not to leave purchasing until the same day as it is likely it will be a sell-ut and the only tickets available will be on the very expensive black market.

There is very little parking in the area with some roads blocked off. Taxis and auto-rickshaws are the best mode of transport if travelling from the centre or from Colaba. A taxi should cost no more than 50R.

Mumbai's Chatrapati Shivaji International Airport is at Sahar, 30km from the city centre. Domestic flights go from Santacruz, 26km from Mumbai. Each airport has a prepaid taxi service in the Arrival Hall. A ride to the city will take anywhere between 40 and 90 minutes depending on the time of day and should not cost more than R450 from either airport. The return journey from the city to either airport should be cheaper. Buses run by EATS run into the city. Some of the major hotels have free airport transfers. A free Air India shuttle bus runs between the International and Domestic terminals.

In the international airport there is a tourist information desk in the Arrival Hall. Other facilities include hotel reservation counters, bureau de change, ATM, restaurants, snack bars and book shop. There are lifts between floors for disabled travellers. Unfortunately the domestic terminal is quite small and does not have as many facilities.

Mumbai, formerly Bombay, is the capital of Maharashtra State. Situated on the west coast on the Arabian Sea it is a result of land reclamation projects in the 18th and 19th centuries. The city is made up of seven islands once separated by creeks. With 22 million it is India's most populous city and growing all the time as people migrate from rural areas. The city is the former capital of the Bombay State and was renamed Mumbai in 1995.

It part of the Mauryan Empire under the rule of Emperor Asoka as far back as 275BC. Second century carvings in the Kanheri Caves on Salsette Island are evident of Mumbai's early existence. Elephanta Island has temples dating back to 600AD. The city was named by native Koli fisherfolk after the goddess Mumbadevi. The islands were ruled by a succession of Hindu dynasties, invaded by Muslims in the 14th century before the Portuguese, attracted by its sheltered harbour, landed in 1534, took control and renamed the area Bom Bahia which translates to beautiful bay. The area remained under the control of the Portuguese until the 1660s when Charles II of England received the islands as dowry when he married Princess Catherine of Braganza. The British East India Company leased the area from him in 1668 and developed the harbour into a thriving port. This development led to migration from all over the country.

Bombay was a stronghold of the Independence Movement, hosting the First Indian National Congress in 1885. In 1947 the last British troops left through the Gateway of India.

Mumbai is the financial, commercial and communications capital of India and home to Asia's largest Stock Exchange. It is India's economic powerhouse. Its port is India's largest natural harbour and its busiest with exports of products from all over Western India passing through it. Historically the opening of the Suez Canal in 186 boosted it because of the reduced sailing time to Britain. Today Mumbai's position has been influential with the rich neighbours in the Gulf.

Mumbai is also home to Bollywood, India's thriving film industry. Film City covers over 35 acres of sets and locations.

This is a city of extremes with great wealth and dreadful poverty. As well as tall skyscrapers it has some fine buildings, a legacy of British rule, including the Chattrapati Shivaji Terminus; the Prince of Wales Museum (1914) with its large central marble dome, the early English gothic Mumbai High Court (1878) and the Old Secretariat designed and built by Col. Henry St. Clair Wilkins in 1874. Other beautiful buildings in the city include the Walkeshwar Temple (1715), Jain Temple (1904) built in white marble and the Haji Ali Mosque which is located at the end of a long causeway protruding into the Arabian Sea. There are some pleasant parks including Victoria Gardens which has a zoo and Hajiali Park. The Hanging Garden on Malabar are beautiful and provide a wonderful view of the city. In the east, on the harbour, is a district known as the Fort, which contains the main public buildings of Mumbai and many commercial establishments.

The city is a very easy and safe to get around. Walking can be pleasant and big red double-decker buses run throughout the city. Attractions include Mani Bhavan which was Mahatma Gandhi's residence in Bombay now a museum. Marine Drive is a long waterfront promenade built on reclaimed land close to the Wankhede. Most cricket supporters stay in this area or in nearby Colaba. This district is famous for its street markets selling jewellery, brassware, clothing, leather and artwork, to mention just a few of the wares. Two other bazaars worth visiting are Zaveri Bazaar for jewellery and Chor Bazaar, translated as 'Thieves Market', for antiques and curios Mumbai also has a fantastic beach on Marine Drive. Each evening after work it is crowded with locals.

Mumbai's climate is heavily influenced by the sea. It is a moderate with hot summer that can be humid and pleasant winters. Between October and March, the cricket season, the air is fresh and the skies are blue and the temperature is pleasantly cool. The heat and humidity starts mounting in April rising through the next few months until the torrential rains of August and September.

Gateway of India Monument

Built by the British in 1924 to commemorate the visit of King George V and Queen Mary, it is Mumbai's signature landmark, a 90ft stone archway designed by George Wittet in 16th Gujarati style. It replaced the temporary structure erected for the visit itself. For many visitors to India it is their first and last sight of the country The last British troops passed through it as they left the country after independence. It is situated on the seafront in Colaba opposite the Taj hotel, another great monument of Mumbai.

Chattrapati Shivaji Terminus

Formerly known as the Victoria Terminus, this was built in 1888 for the Great Indian Peninsular Railway. It is on the site of the Koli's original temple to Mumba Devi. It was designed in Italian Gothic style with Indian influences and looks more like a cathedral than a railway station. The most prominent feature is the 45metre high dome on the top of the building. At the entrance is a large statue of Queen Victoria and four great doorways which lead to the booking offices. A word with the station master usually leads to a tour.

Elephanta Island

Famous for their magnificently sculpted panels, the caves here date back to the third century. They are a pleasant hour-long boat trip from the steps of the Gateway of India. There are a series of seven caves cut into the rock about 75 metres above sea level. They are reached by flights of steps. The main cave has a sculpture depicting the Maheshmurti, a five metre, three-headed image of Shiva the creator, preserver and destroyer. Originally called Gharapuri, the Portuguese renamed the island after a statue of an elephant they found there.

Sanjay Gandhi National Park

Situated on the northern outskirts of Mumbai and previously called Borivaili National Park. Best known for the Kanheri Caves that were used by Buddhist monks as monasteries and temples from 150AD to 650AD. The Lion Safari Park provides the opportunity to see the park's natural wildlife including lions, tigers and panthers.

St. Thomas's Cathedral

Mumbai's Anglican cathedral built in 1718. The marble monuments lining the aisles are a reminder of life in British Bombay and the stained glass windows are exquisite. In the 19th century the steeple was a landmark clearly visible to travellers arriving in Mumbai by steamship. The cathedral is on Veer Nariman in the Fort. Open 07.30-18.00 seven days a week.

Post Office

Mumbai General Post Office
GPO Building
Near Chhatrapati Shivaji Terminus
Tel: 022 262 1671

Foreign Post Office
Videsh Dak Bhawan
Ballard Estate
Tel: 022 261 4488

Tourist Information

Government of India Tourist Office
123 Maharshi Karve Road
Tel: 022 203 3144
Fax: 022 201 4496
gitobest@bom5.vsnl.net.in

Maharashtra Tourism
Development Corporation
CDO Hutments,
Madam Cam Road
Tel: 022 202 6713
Fax: 022 285 2182

There are also tourist information desks at the domestic (022 615 6920) and international air terminals (022 832 5331).

Hospital

Bombay Hospital
New Marine Lines   022 206 7676

Breach Candy Hospital
B. Desai Road   022 363 3651

The Taj Mahal Hotel

Apollo Bunder
Tel: 022 202 3366
Fax: 022 287 2711
gateway@bom4.vsnl.net.in
The most famous hotel in Mumbai, on the waterfront overlooking the Gateway of India. 533 rooms and 49 suites tastefully decorated. Choice of restaurants serving Indian, Chinese, Californian, seafood among others. Beautiful swimming pool, fitness centre.

The Leela Kempinski

Sahar
Andheri
Tel: 022 691 1234
Fax: 022 691 1212
leela@heleel.com
www.lhw.com/leelakemp
390 bed. Surrounded by 11 acres of landscaped gardens. Wonderful rooms, swimming pool, fitness centre, squash court, steam room and sauna. Various restaurants serving Indian, Chinese, Italian and continental food. 25km outside the city but worth the trip.

The Oberoi

Nariman Point
Tel: 022 232 5757
Fax: 022 204 3282
reservations@oberoi-mumbai.com
Overlooking the ocean. 315 rooms and 22 suites. Rooms have separate dressing rooms and luxurious bathrooms with CD players, minibars. 3 restaurants, cocktail bar, health club, spa and swimming pool.

InterContinental Marine Drive

135 Marine Drive
Tel: 022 5639 9999
Fax: 022 5639 9600
marinedrive@interconti.com
48 rooms and 11 suites overlooking the sea. Multi-cuisine restaurant, bar and roof-top Cigar Divan Lounge.

Apollo

Lansdowne Road
Apollo Bunder
Tel: 022 202 0223
Fax: 022 287 4990
Good, reasonably priced hotel just around the corner from the Gateway of India. 39 good en suite rooms with cable TV. Restaurant and bar.

Godwin

41 Garden Road
Tel: 022 287 2050
Fax: 022 287 1592
50 clean air-conditioned rooms. Excellent rooftop restaurant serving Indian and Chinese food. Quiet bar.

Diplomat

24-26 Mereweather Road
Tel: 022 202 1661
Fax: 022 283 0000
diplomat@vsnl.com
52 comfortable rooms. Reasonably priced restaurant, bar.

Sea Green

145 Marine Drive
Tel: 022 282 2294
Budget hotel on Marine Drive. 34 air-conditioned rooms, friendly staff.

Chateau Windsor Guesthouse

86 Veer Nariman Road
Tel: 022 204 3376
Fax: 022 285 1415
info@chateauwindsor.com
Good value. 35 rooms some with air-conditioning. Room service available. Close to stadium.

Leopold Café and Bar

Colaba Causeway
Tel: 022 287 3362
One of the city's oldest restaurants, founded in 1871 and one of its best. Excellent Indian, Chinese and western food served with a smile. Great place to kick back.

Tendulkar's

Chatrapati Shivaji Marg
Apollo Bunder
Good food in the star batsman's restaurant. Good bar with large TV showing non-stop sport. Great memorabilia. Well worth a visit.

Casa Mexicana

Oberoi Towers
Nariman Point
Tel: 022 202 5757
Mexican restaurant overlooking Marine Drive and the ocean. Bookings essential.

Trishna

7 Ropewalk Lane
Tel: 022 267 2176
Excellent Indian restauran specialising in seafood. Great atmosphere.

The PizzeriaSoona Mahal
143 Marine Drive

Café Mondegar
Metro House
5A Colaba Causeway
Tel: 022 202 0591
One the highlights of Mumbai. Excellent restaurant serving American food with the jukebox blaring out western music which is very unusual in India. Great fun and always busy.

Café Churchill
103 Colaba Causeway
Tel: 022 284 4689
Another good café in Colaba. Good pizza and pasta, great atmosphere in this tiny restaurant.

Most of the major hotels have excellent bars including The Harbour Bar and Starboard Bar in the Taj and The Bay View Bar in The Oberoi. There are also some very good bars in Colaba and Marine Drive.

Leopold Café and Bar
Colaba Causeway
Tel: 022 287 3362
One of the best bars in Mumbai. Laid back place with cool beer, excellent food and good music.

Café Mondegar
Metro House
5A Colaba Causeway
Tel: 022 202 0591
Another laidback café/bar . Very trendy with great jukebox and atmosphere.

Geoffrey's
Hotel Marine Plaza
29 Marine Drive
Tel: 022 285 1212
An upmarket bar. Great atmosphere with '70's music.

Airlines

Air India
Air India Building
Nariman Point   022 202 4142
Airport   022 822 0404

Indian Airlines
Air India Building
Nariman Point   022 202 3031
Airport   022615 6850

Jet Airways
Amarchand Mansion
Madame Cama Road 022 285 5788
Airport   022 615 6666

British Airways
Valcan Insurance Building
202 Veer Nariman Road
Churchgate
Fax: 022 282 0888

Qantas
4th floor
Sakhar Bhava
Nariman Point
Tel: 022 202 9297

Air Sahara
Ground floor
Maker Chambers
VJ Bajaj Marg
Nariman Point   022 283 5671

Airport   022 615 6102

Buses
Bright red double decker buses operate throughout the city.

Trains
Regular services to all parts of the country. There are two main train stations in Mumbai, Mumbai Central and Chattropati Shivaji Terminus (Mumbai CST). The stations are about 10km apart. Mumbai Central is for Delhi and Mumbai CST for Kolkata.
Computer Enquiry 022 2695959
Train Arrival and Departure
022 2656565
General Enquiry 134

Taxis
Black and yellow taxis are readily available. Auto-rickshaws are confined to the suburbs.
Cool Cabs   022 824 6216

Car Hire
Avis   022 285 7518
Europcar   022 645 2796

transport

229

Prince of Wales Museum

159-161 Mahatma Gandhi Road
Fort
Tel: 022 284 4484
powm@vsnl.com
Commemorates the visit by King George V. Set in beautiful, lush gardens. Collections include Indian decorative art, ancient and medieval sculpture and artefacts from Elephanta Island and the Indus Valley

Jehangir Art Gallery

Mahatma Gandhi Road
Fort
Tel: 022 284 3989
Founded in 1953, there are two large galleries exhibiting work of prominent, contemporary Indian artists.

Climate

	ave temp	rain cm
January	24	3
February	25	1
March	27	1
April	29	2
May	30	14
June	29	518
July	28	647
August	27	384
September	27	276
October	28	55
November	27	15
December	26	2

Win/Loss Record

Country	Played	won	drawn	Lost	Tie
South Africa	1	1	-	-	-
India	19	8	6	5	-
Sri Lanka	1	-	1	-	-
New Zealand	2	1	-	1	-
Australia	3	1	1	1	-
West Indies	6	1	3	2	-
England	5	1	1	3	-
Pakistan	1	-	-	1	-

Highest Individual Aggregates (India unless stated)

Player	Mat	Inn	NO	Runs	Ave	HS	50	100
Sunil Gavaskar	11	20	0	1122	56.10	205	3	5
Sachin Tendulkar	6	10	0	639	63.90	148	5	1
Dilip Vengsarkar	10	17	4	631	48.54	164*	2	2
Syed Kirmani	9	13	3	477	47.70	102	1	2
Ravi Shastri	6	10	2	457	57.13	142	1	2
Kapil Dev	11	16	1	428	28.53	69	1	0
Rahul Dravid	4	7	1	385	64.17	100^	2	1
Clive Lloyd (WI)	2	4	2	355	177.50	242*	1	1
Gundappa Viswanath	8	14	0	349	24.93	95	2	0
Alvin Kallicharran (WI)	2	3	1	319	159.50	187	1	1

Top Wicket Takers (India unless stated)

Player	Mat	Bll	Md	Runs	Wkt	Ave	BB	S/R
Kapil Dev	11	1827	83	770	28	27.50	5/70	65.25
Anil Kumble	5	1624	79	603	27	22.33	4/51	60.15
Karson Ghavri	6	1033	32	569	23	24.74	5/33	44.91
Ian Botham (Eng)	2	596	23	239	22	10.86	7/48	27.09
Shivlal Yadav	6	1389	61	575	22	26.14	5/131	63.14
Dilip Doshi	4	900	42	305	20	15.25	5/39	45.00
Courtney Walsh (WI)	2	490	14	237	17	13.94	6/79	28.82
Ravi Shastri	6	1449	69	509	17	29.94	4/45	85.24
Richard Hadlee (NZ)	2	491	16	259	15	17.27	6/49	32.73
Bishan Bedi	4	1425	78	525	15	35.00	5/27	95.00

Highest Individual Scores (India unless stated)

242*	Clive Lloyd (WI)	1974-75
224	Vinod Kambli	v England 1992-93
205	Sunil Gavaskar	v West Indies 1978-79
187	Alvin Kallicharran (WI)	1978-79
178	Graeme Hick (Eng)	1992-93
173	Sourav Ganguly	v Sri Lanka 1997-98
164*	Dilip Vengsarkar	v Australia 1986-87
148	Sachin Tendulkar	v Sri Lanka 1997-98
147	Virender Sehwag	v West Indies 2002-03
142	Ravi Shastri	v England 1984-85

Best Individual Bowling Performances (India unless stated)

26-7-48-7	Ian Botham	1979-80
28.3-12-48-7	Harbhajan Singh	v West Indies 2002-03
59-20-98-7	Lance Gibbs (WI)	1974-75
20.1-6-39-6	Vanburn Holder (WI)	1974-75
28.5-14-40-6	Iqbal Qasim (Pak)	1979-80
20.5-8-49-6	Richard Hadlee (NZ)	1988-89
17.4-3-51-6	John Bracewell (NZ)	1988-89
22.5-7-58-6	Ian Botham (Eng)	1979-80
31.2-10-64-6	Laxman Sivaramakrishnan	v England 1984-85
22-4-79-6	Courtney Walsh (WI)	1994-95

Highest Partnerships

Wicket	Runs	Batsmen	Match
1st	201	Sanjay Bangar & Virender Sehwag (Ind)	2002-2003 v West Indies
2nd	168	Sunil Gavaskar & Eknath Solkar (Ind)	1974-1975 v West Indies
3rd	194	Vinod Kambli & Sachin Tendulkar (Ind)	1992-1993 v England
4th	256	Sourav Ganguly & Sachin Tendulkar (Ind)	1997-1998 v Sri Lanka
5th	167	Alvin Kallicharran & David Murray (WI)	1978-1979
6th	298*	Dilip Vengsarkar & Ravi Shastri (Ind)	1986-1987 v Australia
7th	235	Ravi Shastri & Syed Kirmani (Ind)	1984-1985 v England
8th	127	Syed Kirmani & Karson Ghavri (Ind)	1979-1980 v Australia
9th	105	Syed Kirmani & Bishan Bedi (Ind)	1976-1977 v New Zealand
10th	68	Graeme Hick & Phil Tufnell (Eng)	1992-1993

Results at The Wankhede Stadium

Date	Countries	Result
23/01/1975	v West Indies	lost by 201 runs
10/11/1976	v New Zealand	won by 162 runs
11/02/1977	v England	drawn
01/12/1978	v West Indies	drawn
03/11/1979	v Australia	won by an innings and 100 runs
16/12/1979	v Pakistan	won by 131 runs
15/02/1980	v England	lost by 10 wickets
27/11/1981	v England	won by 138 runs
24/11/1983	v West Indies	drawn
28/11/1984	v England	won by 8 wickets
15/10/1986	v Australia	drawn
11/12/1987	v West Indies	drawn
24/11/1988	v New Zealand	lost by 136 runs
19/02/1993	v England	won by an innings and 15 runs
18/11/1994	v West Indies	won by 96 runs
03/12/1997	v Sri Lanka	drawn
24/02/2000	v South Africa	lost by 4 wickets
27/02/2001	v Australia	lost by 10 wickets
09/10/2002	v West Indies	won by an innings and 112 runs

vidarbha

The Vidarbha Cricket Ground lies in in a leafy suburb 2km from the centre of Nagpur. It is purpose-built with some of the most amazing two and three-tier concrete terraces in international cricket and a beautiful playing surface. It became India's tenth Test venue in October 1969 and it could have hardly been a less auspicious beginning. New Zealand won by 167 runs despite Venkat taking 7/7 in the Kiwis' second innings. Hedley Howarth was New Zealand's star performer w match figures of 9/100.

Nagpur had to wait 14 years for their next Test when India drew with Pakistan. It was not until their third match, in 1986, that India recorded their first victory. Shivlal Yadav took 5/76 in Sir Lanka's total of 204 before India went on the rampag declaring at at 451/6 with Mohinder Amarnath (131) and Dilip Vengsarker (153) scoring centuries. Requiring 248 to force their hosts to bat again, Sri Lanka were dismissed for 141 as Maninder Singh took 7/51 to give India victory by an innings and 106 runs.

Draws followed in 1994 against West Indies, in 1997 in a rain-affected match with Sri Lanka and in 2000 against Zimbabwe when, despite being forced to follow-on 227 runs behind, the visitors scored 503/6 to avoid defeat, Andy Flower hitting 232 the highest Test score seen at the ground. Unfortunately for Zimbabwe when it was a different story in the first Test of the 2002 series. India replied to Zimbabwe's first innings 287 with 570/7 dec., Shiv Sunder Das (105), Sachin Tendulkar (176) and Sanjay Bangar (100) scoring centuries. Zimbabwe were dismissed for 182 in their second innings with Anil Kumble taking 5/63 and Harbhajan Singh 4/64 as India w by an innings and 101 runs.

The highest team score at the ground is 609/6 by India against Zimbabwe in 2000 a the lowest, 109 by India in the first Test at the ground.

The best individual bowling performance is Maninder Singh's match figures of 10/107 against Sri Lanka in 1986.

Vidarbha is a lovely ground with a capacity of 45,000. Very few locals come to Test matches although one-day Internationals attract big crowds. The Phiroze Bilimoria Pavilion is modest and at the southern end of the ground. To its left are the huge two and three-tier concrete stands which are not the most comfortable seats in the world and obviously the top tier offers no protection from the stifling sun but the do provide an excellent view. The Media Centre is at the northern end of the ground. On the east side are the Terraces which are also three-tier and one can only imagine what they would be like if full. A high fence runs around the perimeter of the pitch. The scoreboard is at the south east corner of the ground.

The ground certainly has a special charm, the quaint pavilion, the whitewashed stands, the huge trees behind, the blue skies and the beautifully flat playing surface all add to its attraction. The crowd are extremely hospitable and friendly and love their cricket. There are food stalls behind and underneath the stands and vendors move through the crowds selling their wares. The toilets are clean and well tended. Tickets can be purchased on the day of the Test as there is little possibility of them selling out. Tickets are available beforehand if required from the Vidarbha Cricket Association at the ground. The ground is about a 20 minute walk from the centre. A rickshaw should cost about 40R. There is plenty of parking.

Nagpur lies on the Nag river on the Deccan Plateau in Maharashtra State in the centre of India. It has a population of two million. Almost the geographical centre of the country, all distances throughout the country are measured from there - the zero milestone being Nagpur. It is 840km from Mumbai, 1092km north of Chennai, 1094km south of Delhi and 1145km west of Kolkata. Nagpur was the capital of the Maratha Kingdom and became the capital of the Central Provinces in 1861. The British fort dominates the skyline overlooking the city and its suburbs below.

Although the name Nagpur dates back to the 10th century, the city was founded by Bakht Buland of Devgad, the Gond king, in the early 1700s. It was originally 12 small hamlets known as Barasta and inhabited by the Gond and Adivasis peoples. The British took control in 1817 after the Battle of Sitabuldi when they defeated the Marathas. Hundreds of men were lost on both sides. Nagpur was incorporated into the British territory in 1853 and became capital of the Central Provinces in 1861. The railway reached Nagpur in 1867 and helped the city become a trade centre for the surrounding area. Today it is a key industrial and commercial centre as well as an important railway junction. The city is known as the orange capital of India but the region is also noted for cotton growing, coal mines and thermal power plants.

Nagpur is not known for its tourism. At first glance there does not appear to be much to do or see, but further investigation reveals some fine buildings in and around the city, including examples of colonial architecture such as the Governor's Kothi, the District Collectrate, the Commissionrate Building, the High Court and the Central Railway Station. There are also some magnificent temples in the Sarveshwar, Shri Ramdeobaba and Shri Jalaram in the centre of the city and Shri Balaji Temple in Seminary Hills. The Sitabuldi Fort is also worth a visit as are the Dr Hedgewar Memorial and the Zero Mile Statue. There are a number of good museums in the city, the City Museum and the Raman Science Museum.

There are a number of places to visit including Deeksha Bhoomi, a world renowned haven for Buddhists, and Sevagram, a shrine to Mahatma Gandhi, his principles and his life teachings. Ramtek has the famous temple of Shri Rama and Wardha is known for its long association with Gandhi. There is a beautiful dam at Khekranala in the Khapra Range forest and Adasa, a small village, has ancient and splendid temples. Pandit Jawaharlal Nehru National Park in the Satpura Hills, is also worth seeing.

There is not a huge choice of accommodation. There is only one high standard hotel, the Tuli International with health club and swimming pool. Most of the rest are basic with good clean air-conditioned rooms and cable TV. There is a wide choice of budget hotels along Central Avenue. Most of the hotels have restaurants serving both Maharashtrian food and other Indian dishes. Apart from hotel bars there is not much nightlife. There are no nightclubs.

Tadoba National Park

170km outside Nagpur. 120sq.km of forest which is home to tiger, panther, hyena, jackals and deer. It is one of the only excursions to take when visiting Nagpur for the cricket.

Deeksha Bhoomi

A holy monument for Buddhists where they receive Deeksha every year on 'Ashok Vijaya Dashmi Day'.

Sevagram

Mahatma Gandhi established this Ashram in 1933, and spent 15 years here.

Tuli International

Residency Road
Sadar
Tel: 0712 534 784
Fax: 0712 534 473
www.tuligroup.com
Without doubt the best hotel. 110 en suite rooms with air-conditioning. 3 restaurants, bar, health club and swimming pool.

Hotel Centre Point

24 Central Bazar Road
Ramdaspeth
Tel: 0712 520 910
Fax: 0712 523 093
hcpngp@nagpur.dot.net.in
100 en suite rooms with air-conditioning and cable TV. Restaurant and bar.

Hotel Hardeo

Dr. Munje Marg
Tel: 0712 529 115
Fax: 0712 534 885
hardeo@nagpur.dot.net.in
Centrally located two star hotel with good clean rooms, pub and business centre.

Hotel Royal Palace

22 CB Road
Ramdaspeth
Tel: 0712 532 300
Fax: 0712 535 454
htlroyal@nagpur.dot.net.in
Another two star hotel with 40 clean en suite rooms with cable TV, restaurant and bar.

Hotel Orange City

Mahajan Market
Sitabuldi
Tel: 0712 542 796
Fax: 0712 544 216
Central budget hotel. Clean rooms.

Hotel Blue Diamond

113 Central Avenue
Tel: 0712 727 461
Budget hotel in centre. No frills.

Hotel Blue Moon

Central Avenue
Tel: 0712 726 061
Fax: 0712 727 591
Budget hotel in centre. Clean rooms with fan and TV.

Hotel Pal Palace

25 Central Avenue
Tel: 0712 724 725
Good clean hotel in the centre. Spacious en suite rooms with cable TV and fan. Friendly service and excellent restaurant. Bar downstairs.

Restaurants

Most of the hotels in the city have their own restaurants however the ones listed below are recommended.

Ashoka Restaurant

Sadar
Mound Road

Hotel Contes Point

Ramdaspeth
Hotel Tuli International

Eden Garden Restaurant

Kasadi Road
Hotel Pal Palace
25 Central Avenue

Nightlife

Some of the hotels have bars, usually small basement rooms with no atmosphere.

Climate

	ave temp	rain cm
January	21	13
February	24	16
March	28	16
April	32	14
May	35	19
June	32	202
July	28	345
August	27	274
September	27	191
October	26	54
November	23	15
December	20	12

Nagpur
Airport is 8km to the south of the city. A taxi ride takes about 15 minutes and should cost no more than 120R. It is small, with airline offices and a tea shop. There is no bank.

Airlines

Indian Airlines
Amravati Road
Tel: 0712 523 069

Jet Airways
Shree Mohini Complex
345 Kingsway
Sitabuldi
Tel: 0712 559 875

Trains

Nagpur Train Station is in the centre and is one of India's most important junctions. Trains run to Mumbai (14 hours), Chennai (18 hours), Delhi (18 hours), Kolkata (18 hours).
Railway Enquiries   131
Railway Reservations   135

Taxis

Auto and cycle rickshaws are best. There are thousands of each and you will never wait more than 30 seconds. Always agree a price before commencing the journey.

Car Hire

There are no car hire facilities in Nagpur however taxis can be hired to visit the surrounding area for as long as they are required.

Post Office

General Post Office
Palm Road

Tourist Information

Maharashtra Tourist Office
Sanskruti Bachat Bhavan
Sitabuldi
Tel: 0712 533325
Fax: 0712 560680

Maharashtra Tourism
Development Corporation
Dr Munje Road
Beauty Road
Tel: 0712 533325

Hospital

Dande Hospital
69A Hill Road
Raj Nagar
Tel: 0712 253 6590

Win/Loss Record

Country	Played	won	drawn	Lost	Tie
New Zealand	1	1	-	-	-
India	7	2	4	1	-
Pakistan	1	-	1	-	-
West Indies	1	-	1	-	-
Zimbabwe	2	-	1	1	-
Sri Lanka	2	-	1	1	-

Highest Individual Aggregates (India unless stated))

Player	Mat	Inn	NO	Runs	Ave	HS	50	100
Sachin Tendulkar	4	5	1	625	156.25	201*	1	3
Rahul Dravid	3	3	0	319	106.33	162	2	1
Andy Flower (Zim)	2	4	1	298	99.33	232*	1	1

Navjot Sidhu	2	3	0	262	87.33	107	2	1
Shiv Sunder Das	2	2	0	215	107.50	110	0	2
Dilip Vengsarkar	2	3	0	214	71.33	153	0	1
Alistair Campbell (Zim)	2	4	0	193	48.25	102	1	1
Mohammad Azharuddin	2	3	1	191	95.50	97	2	0
Sunil Gavaskar	2	3	0	188	62.67	74	3	0
Sourav Ganguly	3	3	0	167	55.67	99	1	0

Top Wicket Takers (India unless stated)

Player	Mat	BlI	Md	Runs	Wkt	Ave	BB	S/R
Anil Kumble	3	869	49	321	15	21.40	5/63	57.93
Maninder Singh	1	226	10	107	10	10.70	7/51	22.60
Hedley Howarth (NZ)	1	318	16	100	9	11.11	5/34	35.33
Venkat	1	367	17	133	9	14.78	6/74	40.78
Carl Hooper (WI)	1	391	14	178	7	25.43	5/116	55.86
Venkatapathy Raju	1	462	15	185	7	26.43	5/127	66.00
Shivlal Yadav	1	199	10	97	7	13.86	5/76	28.43
Mohammad Nazir (Pak)	1	432	24	122	7	17.43	5/72	61.71
Sarandeep Singh	1	426	17	206	6	34.33	4/136	71.00
Zaheer Khan	2	360	12	204	6	34.00	3/45	60.00

Highest Individual Scores (India unless stated)

232*	Andy Flower (Zim)	2000-01
201*	Sachin Tendulkar	v Zimbabwe 2000-01
179	Sachin Tendulkar	v West Indies 1994-95
176	Sachin Tendulkar	v Zimbabwe 2001-02
162	Rahul Dravid	v Zimbabwe 2000-01
153	Dilip Vengsarkar	v Sri Lanka 1986-87
131	Mohinder Amarnath	v Sri Lanka 1986-87
125*	Jimmy Adams (WI)	1994-95
110	Shiv Sunder Das	v Zimbabwe 2000-01
107	Navjot Sidhu	v West Indies 1994-95

Best Individual Bowling Performances (India unless stated)

17.4-4-51-7	ManIndiaer Singh	v Sri Lanka 1986-87
30.1-8-74-6	Venkat	v New Zealand 1969-70
23-11-34-5	Hedley Howarth (NZ)	1969-70
37-15-63-5	Anil Kumble	v Zimbabwe 2001-02
50-19-72-5	Mohammad Nazir (Pak)	1983-84
30.4-7-75-5	Ravi Shastri	v Pakistan 1983-84
19.1-4-76-5	Shivlal Yadav	v Sri Lanka 1986-87
40-8-116-5	Carl Hooper (WI)	1994-95
32-3-122-5	Ravi Pushpakumara (SL)	1997-98
50-11-127-5	Venkatapathy Raju	v West Indies 1994-95

Highest Partnerships

Wkt	Runs	Batsmen	Match
1st	79	Shiv Sunder Das & Deep Dasgupta (Ind)	2001-2002 v Zimbabwe
2nd	155	Shiv Sunder Das & Rahul Dravid (Ind)	2000-2001 v Zimbabwe
3rd	249	Rahul Dravid & Sachin Tendulkar (Ind)	2000-2001 v Zimbabwe
4th	209	Alistair Campbell & Andy Flower (Zim)	2000-2001
5th	202	Sachin Tendulkar & Mohammad Azharuddin (Ind)	1994-1995 v W Indies
6th	171	Sachin Tendulkar & Sanjay Bangar (Ind)	2001-2002 v Zimbabwe
7th	98*	Andy Flower & Heath Streak (Zim)	2000-2001
8th	97	Jimmy Adams & Junior Murray (WI)	1994-1995
9th	59	Travis Friend & Ray Price (Zim)	2001-2002
10th	44	Rumesh Ratnayake & Asoka De Silva (SL)	1986-1987

Results at The Vidarbha

Date	Countries	Result
03/10/1969	v New Zealand	lost by 167 runs
05/10/1983	v Pakistan	drawn
27/12/1986	v Sri Lanka	won by an innings and 106 runs
01/12/1994	v West Indies	drawn
26/11/1997	v Sri Lanka	drawn
25/11/2000	v Zimbabwe	drawn
21/02/2002	v Zimbabwe	won by an innings and 101 runs

Auckland

Hamilton

Wellington

Christchurch

Test Cricket has been played at six grounds in New Zealand.

Lancaster Park, Christchurch, now known as the Jade Stadium, was the first venue, against England on 10th January 1930. The visitors won by eight wickets. Two weeks later New Zealand drew with England at the Basin Reserve in Wellington. The following month, on 14th February and 21st February 1930, Auckland's Eden Park was the venue for the final Tests. Both ended in draws. Eden Park has hosted more Tests than any other ground in New Zealand.

Carisbrook in Dunedin became the fourth ground March 1955 when it staged the first match of the two Test series against England which the visitors won by eight wickets. Carisbrook not been used since March 1997. The last Test to be played at the ground was New Zealand innings and 36 runs victory over Sri Lanka. It still hosts one-day internationals. McLean Park in Napier was the next ground to be awarded Test cricket when it hosted the 1979 draw with Pakistan. The ground was used for two more Tests against India in 1990 and Sri Lanka in March 1995 but not since although it continues to hold one-day internationals. Seddon Park in Hamilton, became the most recent Test addition when it welcomed Sri Lanka in the draw second Test in February 1991. It has now become a regular Test match ground.

Distance Between Cities (in km)

	Auckland	Christchurch	Hamilton	Wellington
Auckland		1108	126	658
Christchurch	1108		982	450
Hamilton	126	982		532
Wellington	658	450	532	

Airlines

The national airline is Air New Zealand. Auckland, Wellington and Christchurch have international airports. Hamilton has a small domestic airport. Air New Zealand, Air New Zealand Link and Qantas operate domestic flights between each city.

Air New Zealand	0800 737 000
Qantas	09 357 8900

Buses

New Zealand has an excellent coach company, Intercity Coachlines, which operates services on both islands. Various travel passes are available which cover either the whole of New Zealand or the islands. There are also a smaller coach company which operates within New Zealand – Intercity Coachlines 03 379 9020 or www.intercitycoach.co.nz

Each city has a bus network. They are reliable, inexpensive and easy to use. Christchurch also has a tramway.

Trains

Tranz Rail run a service between Auckland and Wellington twice a day, once in the morning and an overnight service. The trains are comfortable with dining facilities but there are no sleeper compartments. The daytime journey is a great way to see the scenery of the North Island. The train stops at Hamilton which is 126km south of Auckland.

Tranz Scenic Rail Network on 0800 802 802 or www.tranzrail.co.nz

Car Hire

Avis, Budget, Hertz and Thrifty have desks at Auckland, Hamilton, Wellington and Christchurch airports and also have offices in each city. British, Australian, South African Driving Licences are valid however all drivers must be at least 21 years of age.

Taxis

Metered taxis are available outside all airport terminals, hotels and at ranks throughout each city.

Banks

Opening times at most banks are Monday-Friday 09.00-16.30. All banks have foreign exchange facilities and accept travellers' cheques in major currencies. Commission is charged for this service. ATM facilities are widespread. All major credit cards are accepted. New Zealand uses the New Zealand Dollar (NZ$). Notes are issued in denominations of A$100, 50, 20, 10 and 5 and coins in enominations of A$2, 1 and 50, 20, 10 and 5 cents.

ecoms

national Direct Dialling is available throughout New Zealand. Most of the public pay-es are card only. Cards can be purchased from newsagents. New Zealand's dialling code is he outgoing international code is 0011.

offices open in New Zealand 09.00-17.00, Monday-Friday.

ist Offices

city has a Tourist Information Centre. There are also tourist information desks at land, Wellington and Christchurch airports.

rgency Numbers

e	111
	111
ulance	111

assies/Consulates

h High Commission
ll St.
ngton 1
4 924 2888
04 924 2809
Mailbox@fco.gov.uk

alia High Commission
Hobson St.
ndon
ngton
4 473 6411
04 498 7135

Commission of India
Molesworth St.
ngton
4 473 6390
04 499 0665

s

sitors must carry a passport valid for at least three month after departure. Australian visi-o not require a visa. European passport holders can receive one upon arrival.

oms

rs over the age of 18 may take the following goods into New Zealand without incurring ms duty. 200 cigarettes or 50 cigars, 1.125 litre of spirits, 4.5 litres of wine.

Difference

Zealand is 12 hours ahead of GMT. 13 hours in Summertime from October to March.

tricity

olts AC at 50 cycles per second. Most hotels have adaptors.

ing

ping in not expected for service in hotels, bars or restaurant.

Departure Tax

There is a departure tax of NZ$23.

auckland

eden park

Eden Park has been in existence since 1900 and home to the Auckland Cricket Association since 1910. Located in Mount Eden, just minutes from Auckland city centre, the ground is also an international rugby venue. The first Test there was played in February 1930 when New Zealand and England contested a rain affected draw. When they met again at Eden Park, unfortunately the weather again meant a draw.

This was the venue for New Zealand's first Test win, in March 1956, when they beat the West Indies by 190 runs. Having scored 255 in their first innings, New Zealand dismissed the West Indies for 145 and then proceeded to set the visitors 268 to win. Harry Cave with match figures of 8/43 restricted the West Indies to just 77.

That was not the lowest score at Eden Park. A year earlier against England, New Zealand achieved the dubious distinction of scoring the lowest score in Test cricket when they were dismissed by England for a paltry 26.

Bert Sutcliffe top scored with 11 and England's four bowlers each made hay. Frank Tyson took 2/10 in seven overs; Brian Statham 3/9 in nine overs, Bob Appleyard 4/7 in six overs and Johnny Wardle 1/0 in five overs. England won by an innings and 20 runs.

Wally Hammond's 336no in 1933 was the highest Test score at the time. It is still the best at Eden Park and the sixth highest overall. The best team score is 621 by South Africa in 1999 which included Daryl Cullinan's 275no.

The highest run chase was recorded by the West Indies when they scored 348/5 in their five wicket win in 1969.

Eden Park generally assists slow and spin bowlers – Daniel Vettori has the best match figures, having taken 12/149 against Australia in 2000.

Eden Park is a very odd shape for a cricket ground. Sometimes compared to a baseball diamond, it is certainly unique. It has a capacity of 40,000 – a record 43,000 people squeezed in to watch a limited overs international with Australia on 13th February 1982 – with the huge ASB Bank Stand dominating the ground. The pavilion, built in the 1920's, is steeped in tradition. The ASB Bank stand, along with the South, West and North East Stand are all excellent vantage points from which to watch. All the stands have covered and uncovered seats. Protection from the sun is important in the uncovered areas. The terraces at one end of the ground have a great atmosphere. The first part of the ground to fill up, the terraces have wooden seats, which can get uncomfortable during the day. However the fun on the terraces makes up for the slight discomfort.

Facilities and access for persons with disabilities are provided in ASB Bank Stand on vel 4. Tickets are available from Ticketek on www.ticketek.co.nz and on the day of the atch from ASBN Stand Gate 3 and the Terraces Gate 15. Buses and Trains run from the City Centre to Eden Park (Enquiries 09 366 6400). There is very little parking around the ground with most of the streets having residents' parking. There is a taxi stand outside the ground in Sandringham Road. A taxi ride should cost NZ$12.

Auckland is the largest city in New Zealand with a population of 1.2 million, a third of New Zealand's total population. Dubbed 'The City of Sails,' it is the most cosmopolitan, vibrant city in the country. Situated 300km south of the Northern tip of North Island the city is built on an isthmus of 48 volcanoes between two harbours, Waitemata on the east and Manakau on the west. The city and suburbs cover an area of 60 sq. km.

The first inhabitants were the Polynesian Maoris who arrived in the 1400s. The first European to visit was Dutchman Abel Tasman in 1642 but it was until the arrival of Captain James Cook that the islands were explored and charted. British sovereignty was established in 1840 and British settlers bought the land on which Auckland now sits from the Maori tribes. It was the capital of New Zealand until 1865 when Wellington took over.

Auckland is New Zealand's largest working port and is New Zealand's largest retail and commercial centre. Tourism is an important and growing industry especially since hosting the America's Cup in the late nineties.

The city has many stunning attractions including the Auckland War Museum, the Auckland Art Gallery, the Maritime Museum, the Town Hall and the Victoria Park Market. Auckland Zoo is another excellent attraction.

Mount Eden, the most prominent of the volcanoes, is within easy reach of the city and provides 360 degrees view of the city and coastline. Auckland also has some excellent beaches especially at Long Bay, Onetangi and Takapuna. Ferry harbour rides are a great way to the city, harbour and surrounding islands.

There are more than a thousand restaurants in the city with a diversity, which reflects the multicultural society. The standard is high and prices are reasonable. The Viaduct Harbour, Ponsonby Road and Parnell are home to the best restaurants in town. Weeknights in Auckland are quiet but on Friday and Saturday nights the city comes alive. There are some splendid bars and clubs on the waterfront and in the centre of the city which are open all night long. There is also a casino in Sky City in the centre of town for late night entertainment.

Auckland Airport is located at Mangere, 21km to the south west of central Auckland. Hospitality Ambassadors are on hand if you require assistance and there is a tourist information desk in both the Domestic and International terminal which can arrange accommodation, sightseeing etc. A taxi to the city will take 20 minutes and hould cost NZ$35. The City to Airport Airbus 0508 247 287 or www.airbus. o.nz runs every 20 minutes everyday of the year at a cost of NZ$18. A free bus huttle links the Domestic and International terminals.

There is a bank, currency exchange bureaux and a number of ATM's throughout the terminals. There are shops, newsagents, cafés and bars in each terminal.

Car Hire is available from Avis (09 275 7239), Budget (09 256 8451), Thrifty (09 256 1405) and Hertz (09 256 8695).

The Ascott

No 1 Courthouse Lane
Tel: 09 300 8800
Fax: 09 300 8899
Auckland@the-ascott.com
Superb rooms with separate living areas
and kitchen, mini bar, room service,
cable TV, air-conditioning, health club
with swimming pool, gym and sauna.
2 restaurants, bars and nightclub.
Business centre.

Sky City Hotel

Corner Victoria and Federal Streets
Tel: 09 363 6000
Fax: 09363 6032
reservations@skycity.co.nz
www.skycity.co.nz
Centrally located, comfortable air-
conditioned rooms with cable TV,
room service, roof top pool, many
restaurants and bars.

Latitude 37 Apartments

Viaduct Harbour
Tel: 0800 452 848
Fax: 09 309 7850
latitude37@xtra.co.nz
www.latitude37.co.nz
1, 2 or 3 bedroom high specification
apartments to rent in Auckland's
downtown waterfront. A luxurious
alternative to an hotel.

Mercure Hotel

8 Customs St.
Tel: 09 377 8920
Fax: 09 307 3739
reservations@mercureakl.co.nz
200-room hotel in the centre. Air-
conditioning, mini bar, cable TV, room
service. Restaurant and Bar

Sail City Hotel

Corner Nelson and Wellesley Streets
Tel: 09 356 7272
Fax: 09368 5273
www.sailcityhotel.com
Art deco style hotel in the centre of
Auckland. 30 rooms with TV, fridge,
breakfast dining.

Aachen House

39 Market Road
Remuera
Tel: 09 520 2329
Fax: 09 524 2898
info@aachenhouse.co.nz
www.aachenhuse.co.nz
10 minutes drive from centre,

boutique B&B at the foot of
the Mount Hobson Reserve has 9
beautiful rooms with cable TV and
serves a wonderful breakfast.

Park Towers Hotel

3 Scotia Place
Tel: 09 309 2800
Fax: 09 302 1964
res@parktowers-hotel.co.nz
www.parktowers-hotel.co.nz
Centrally located. All rooms with
bathrooms, cable TV, bar, fridge.

Hastings Hall

99 Western Springs Road
Tel: 09 845 8550
Fax: 09 845 8554
unique@hastingshall.co.nz
www.hastingshall.co.nz
1878 colonial mansion in beautiful
grounds, less than 10 minutes from the
centre of Auckland. Gourmet breakfast
served on the gazebo above the pool or
your own verandah.

The Brown Kiwi

7 Prosford St.
Ponsonby
Tel: 09 378 0191
bookings@brownkiwi.co.nz
Travellers' hostel in colonial home. 5
minutes from centre. Kitchen facilities,
BBQ area. Excellent value.

Central City Backpackers'

26 Lorne St.
Fax: 09 358 5685
Tel: 09358 4716
ccbnz@xta.co.nz
Quiet with kitchen, dining and living
areas. Twins, doubles and dormitories.

Parkside Backpackers' Hostel

189 Park Road
Grafton
Tel: 09 309 8999
Large Victorian House overlooking
Domain Park. 10 minutes walk to
downtown. Twin, double and share
room accommodation. Large private
courtyard and BBQ area.

The Fat Camel Hostel

38 Fort St.
Tel: 0800 220 198
www.nomadsworld.com/fatcamel
Twins and doubles accommodation.
Centrally located, common room and
internet café.

Auckland Bridge Climb

A wonderful way to see the city. With gentle staircases and specially designed walkways, the bridge is easy to climb as you are taken to the ghest point between the lanes of traffic. Open seven days a week, the trip es three hours. Bookings can be made at 70 Nelson Street, Auckland, by phone 02 4561 and 0800 000 808 or on www.aucklandbridgeclimb.co.nz.

lly Tarlton's Underwater World

ated 6km from downtown Auckland and on the main tourist bus routes, derwater World has a moving walkway in transparent tunnels under the ocean viding the opportunity to view sharks, eels, stingray and thousands of reef fish. additional attraction is the Antarctic Encounter which offers a chance to ride heated snow cat through a sub Antarctic landscape viewing penguins and er wildlife living in their normal habitat. Bookings can be made at 22 Tamaki ve, Orakei, Auckland, by phone 09 528 0603 or on www.kellytarltons.co.nz

neries of Auckland

region has been producing wine since 1850. A variation of soil types and ther lead to the production of completely different wines in the 60 wineries nd the region. The Matakawa vineyards in North Auckland and Kumeu in the thwest boast some of the best wineries in the region.

Tower City

kland's most visible landmark and, at 328 metres, the tallest building in the thern hemisphere. The four observation levels include an outdoor deck and ain viewing platform. It is a city within a city with 12 restaurants including volving restaurant, café and bar, two casinos, a theatre, hotels and shopping des. For the more adventurous there is a cable controlled Sky jump or the ortunity to climb the 90 metre mast.

duct Harbour

lt to host the America's Cup. The waterfront venue has restaurants, bars and fés along with art galleries and the America's Cup Exhibition, a history of the world's premier yachting race. At night the harbour transform into the "place to be" with many clubs and pubs open through the night.

Airlines

Air New Zealand 0800 737 000
Qantas 09 357 8900
itish Airways 0800 274 847
uth African Airways 09 303 2129

ses

Explorer pass costs NZ$25 a day. e Whitelink Buses circle the city tre between 0600-2200 stopping ll the tourist spots. Buses to other ts of the island leave from Sky City. quires 09 366 6400.

rry

ere are several companies operating Waitemata Harbour. The Devonport mmuter ferry leaves from the Ferry lding on Quay Street 09 367 9118.

ins

ckland Railway Station is on Beach oad, 1km from the centre of the city. Enquires at Tranz Scenic Rail Network on 0800 802 802

Taxis

There are many taxi stands throughout the city.
Auckland Co-op 300 3000
Corporate Cabs 631 1111
Regency 377 8844
Water Taxi Yellow Boat Co.
0800 829 426

Car Hire

Avis
17-19 Nelson St.
Tel: 09 379 2650

Budget
83 Beach Road
Tel: 09 976 2270

Thrifty
79 Fanshawe St.
Tel: 09 309 0111

Hertz
154 Victoria Street West
Tel: 09 367 6350

The Rendezvous Chinese Restaurant
144-148 Hobson St.
Tel: 09 356 6910
Fax: 09 356 6912
Best Chinese in Auckland. Reasonably priced and relaxed atmosphere.

Tony's Restaurant
Wellesley Street West
Tel: 09 373 4196
Fax: 09 377 6467
Steak and seafood restaurant. Excellent value in a fun restaurant.

Essence Restaurant
70-72 Jervois Road
Tel: 09 376 2049
Fax: 09 378 0740
French food, beautifully presented and complimented by a friendly service. Good wine list.

Da Vinci's
5 City Road
Tel: 09 373 2843
Italian restaurant in the centre. Excellent reputation.

Chutneys
323 Parnell Road
Tel: 09 358 2969
Finest Indian in town. Highly recommended with friendly service.

Mutiaca Malaysian Restaurant
66 Posonby Road
Tel: 09 376 2759
Authentic Malay restaurant with excellent wine list.

Harbourside Seafood Bar and Grill.
The Original Ferry building
Quay St.
Tel: 09 307 0486
Freshest seafood. Relaxed atmosphere with wonderful views of city and harbour.

City Café
20 Larne St.
Tel: 09 309 6960
Top New Zealand cuisine with freshest ingredients. Beautiful courtyard.

The Immigrant Irish Bar
104 Fanshawe St.
Tel: 09 373 2169
Live music 7 days a week, pool tables, sporty pub with a good atmosphere. Traditional Irish dancing, dining.

Mad Dogs and Englishmen
4 Albert St.
Tel: 09 379 6004
English beer and food in an English pub. Open 7 days a week Fine pub serving some very good ales.

The Shakespeare Tavern and Brewery
Corner of Wyndham and Albert St.
Tel: 09 373 5396
New Zealand's first microbrewery sin 1986. Excellent food, fine ales and a great atmosphere in all 3 bars. Mond to Saturday 12.00 till late.

The Loaded Hog
Quay St.
Viaduct Quay
Tel: 09 366 6491
Popular quayside bar. Open very late weekends.

The Occidental
6-8 Vulcan Lane
Tel: 09 300 6226
Very lively Belgian bar selling Belgian beers, mussels with chips and mayonnaise. Open late every night.

O'Carroll's Irish Pub
10 Vulcan Lane
Tel: 09 360 0008
Right next to the Occidental, Warm, friendly Irish pub with excellent food and great craic. Open 10am until late

The Kings Arms
59 Frances St.
Tel: 09 373 3240
A sports bar with large screen. Also li music each night.

London Bar
1 Wellesley St.
Tel: 09 373 3684
A jazz and beer bar in the centre. Qui different to any other pub in Aucklan

Auckland Museum

Auckland Domain
Tel: 09 306 7067
The cultural and spiritual centre of the many races that inhabit New Zealand including one of the finest displays of Polynesian culture in the world. Open 10.00-17.00 daily. Tel: 09 306 7067

New Zealand National Maritime Museum

Corner Quay and Hobson St.
The Maritime Museum has 14 exhibition halls which explore New Zealand's links to the sea from the early seafaring history for Polynesian voyagers to the arrival of the European whalers. Tel: 09 373 0800

Auckland Art Gallery

Wellesley and Kitchener Streets
Auckland City
Located in the heart of city, the gallery and is home to works of international and New Zealand artists. It also incorporates the New Gallery, the contemporary wing. Open 10.00-17.00 daily. Tel: 09 379 1349.

Post Office

General Post Office
167 Victoria St.
Tel: 09 367 9617
Open 0730-1930 Monday-Friday.
Other post offices are open 09.00-17.00 Monday-Friday.

Tourist Information

Auckland Travel and Information Centre
7 Queen St.
Tel: 09 979 2333
Fax: 09 979 2334
reservations@aucklandnz.com

New Zealand Visitors Centre
Corner Hobson and Quay St.
Tel: 09 979 2333
Fax: 09 979 7010
vc@aucklandnz.com

Auckland Visitor Centre
Domestic Terminal
Auckland Airport
Tel: 09 256 8480

Fax: 09 256 8225
domavc@aucklandnz.com

Auckland Visitor Centre
International Arrivals Terminal
Auckland Airport
Tel: 09 256 8535
Fax: 09 256 8842
intavc@aucklandnz.com

Hospital

CityMed Medical Centre
Corner Mills Lane and Albert St.
Auckland
Tel: 09 377 5525

Auckland Hospital
Park Road
Grafton
Tel: 09 379 7440

Pharmacy

246 Queen St.
Tel: 09 379 4362

Climate

	ave temp	rain cm			
January	18	69	July	9	143
February	19	120	August	10	152
March	18	87	September	12	103
April	15	120	October	14	108
May	13	151	November	15	99
June	11	156	December	17	101

Win/Loss Record

Country	Played	won	drawn	Lost	Tie
India	4	2	2	-	-
West Indies	5	2	2	1	-
England	15	4	10	1	-
Pakistan	7	2	4	1	-
Sri Lanka	1	-	1	-	-
South Africa	5	1	3	1	-
Australia	6	3	-	3	-
New Zealand	45	8	23	14	-
Zimbabwe	2	-	1	1	-

Highest Individual Aggregates

Player	Mat	Inn	NO	Runs	Ave	HS	50	100
John Wright	15	29	2	1060	39.26	130	5	3
Martin Crowe	11	19	2	712	41.88	113	3	2
Chris Cairns	8	13	0	565	43.46	158	2	2
Geoff Howarth	9	16	1	558	37.20	122	3	2
Nathan Astle	7	13	2	497	45.18	114	2	2
Jeremy Coney	8	13	4	483	53.67	93	4	0
Bev Congdon	11	21	1	477	23.85	85	4	0
Andrew Jones	6	12	1	473	43.00	170*	2	1
Ian Smith	10	12	3	468	52.00	173	1	2
Craig McMillan	6	10	2	446	55.75	88	5	0

Top Wicket Takers (New Zealand unless stated)

Player	Mat	Bll	Md	Runs	Wkt	Ave	BB	S/
Richard Hadlee	13	3203	117	1463	45	32.51	6/105	71.1
Chris Cairns	8	1856	66	1021	35	29.17	6/52	53.0
Richard Collinge	7	1791	54	695	29	23.97	5/82	61.7
Lance Cairns	8	2287	122	739	28	26.39	4/49	81.6
Danny Morrison	7	1644	58	909	27	33.67	6/37	60.8
John Bracewell	5	1452	77	521	23	22.65	6/32	63.1
Ewen Chatfield	8	1940	100	716	22	32.55	4/37	88.1
Erapalli Prasanna (Ind)	2	707	36	224	19	11.79	8/76	37.2
Simon Doull	5	970	37	436	18	24.22	5/66	53.8
Daryl Tuffey	3	684	33	309	17	18.18	6/54	40.2

Highest Individual Scores (New Zealand unless stated)

336*	Wally Hammond (Eng)	1932-33
275*	Daryll Cullinan (SA)	1998-99
271	Javed Miandad (Pak)	1988-89
216	Keith Fletcher (Eng)	1974-75
213	Gordon Greenidge (WI)	1986-87
196	Geoffrey Legge (Eng)	1929-30
192	Mohammad Azharuddin Ind)	1989-90
181	Mike Denness (Eng)	1974-75
173	Ian Smith	v India 1989-90
173	Alex Stewart (Eng)	1996-97

Best Individual Bowling Performances (New Zealand unless stated)

23-5-76-8	Erapalli Prasanna (Ind)	1975-76
40-21-53-7	Denis Atkinson (WI)	1955-56
35-11-87-7	Daniel Vettori	v Australia 1999-00
22-8-32-6	John Bracewell	v Australia 1985-86
19-5-34-6	Bill Bowes (Eng)	1932-33
18.4-5-37-6	Danny Morrison	v Australia 1992-93
16.1-4-43-6	Wasim Akram (Pak)	1993-94
21-4-52-6	Chris Cairns	v England 1991-92
19-6-54-6	Daryl Tuffey	v England 2001-02
36.2-15-56-6	Joel Garner (WI)	1979-80

Highest Partnerships

Wkt	Runs	Batsmen	Match
1st	214	Craig Spearman & Roger Twose (NZ)	1995-1996 v Zimbabwe
2nd	204	Sunil Gavaskar & S Amarnath (Ind)	1975-1976
3rd	248	Shoaib Mohammad & Javed Miandad (Pak)	1988-1989
4th	266	Mike Denness & Keith Fletcher (Eng)	1974-1975
5th	189	Frank Worrell & Clyde Walcott (WI)	1951-1952

	6th	240	Peter Parfitt & Barry Knight (Eng)	1962-1963
	7th	225	Chris Cairns & Jacob Oram (NZ)	2003-2004 v South Africa
	th	103	Richard Hadlee & Ian Smith (NZ)	1989-1990 v India
	h	136	Ian Smith & Martin Snedden (NZ)	1989-1990 v India
	th	151	Brian Hastings & Richard Collinge (NZ)	1972-1973 v Pakistan

esults at Eden Park

ate	Countries	Result
/02/1930	v England	drawn
/02/1930	v England	drawn
/03/1933	v England	drawn
/02/1952	v West Indies	drawn
/03/1953	v South Africa	drawn
/02/1955	v England	lost by an innings and 20 runs
/03/1956	v West Indies	won by 190 runs
/03/1959	v England	drawn
/02/1963	v England	lost by an innings and 215 runs
/03/1964	v South Africa	drawn
/01/1965	v Pakistan	drawn
/03/1966	v England	drawn
/03/1968	v India	lost by 272 runs
/02/1969	v West Indies	lost by 5 wickets
/03/1971	v England	drawn
/02/1973	v Pakistan	drawn
/03/1974	v Australia	lost by 297 runs
/02/1975	v England	lost by an innings and 83 runs
/01/1976	v India	lost by 8 wickets
/02/1977	v Australia	lost by 10 wickets
/03/1978	v England	drawn
/02/1979	v Pakistan	drawn
/02/1980	v West Indies	drawn
/03/1981	v India	drawn
/03/1982	v Australia	won by 5 wickets
/02/1984	v England	drawn
/01/1985	v Pakistan	won by an innings and 99 runs
/03/1986	v Australia	won by 8 wickets
/02/1987	v West Indies	lost by 10 wickets
/02/1988	v England	drawn
/02/1989	v Pakistan	drawn
/02/1990	v India	drawn
/03/1991	v Sri Lanka	drawn
/01/1992	v England	lost by 168 runs
/03/1993	v Australia	won by 5 wickets
/02/1994	v Pakistan	lost by 5 wickets
/03/1995	v South Africa	lost by 93 runs
/01/1996	v Zimbabwe	drawn
/01/1997	v England	drawn
/02/1998	v Zimbabwe	won by an innings and 13 runs
/02/1999	v South Africa	drawn
/03/2000	v Australia	lost by 62 runs
8/03/2001	v Pakistan	lost by 299 runs
0/03/2002	v England	won by 78 runs
18/03/2004	v South Africa	won by 9 wickets

christchurch

Jade Stadium, previously known as Lancaster Park, was built in 1880. Located in the suburb of Phillipstown just outside the city centre, it is home to the Canterbury rugby and cricket teams. The first Test was played in the 1929/30 season when England won by eight wickets, Maurice Allom taking four wickets in five balls for England. Indeed, it was not until 38 years and 12 Tests later that New Zealand recorded their first Test victory at the ground, defeating India by six wickets in 1967/68.

The closest match was in 1996/97 when England scored 307/6 to win by four wickets. New Zealand's finest moments include their victory over England by an innings and 132 runs in 1983/84 when they bowled them out for 82 and 93, and the 1986/87 victory over the West Indies by five wickets when Canterbury's Richard Hadlee took 9/151. Another classic match was the 1994 encounter between New Zealand and Pakistan. Batting first, Pakistan scored 344 with Basit Ali hitting 103. New Zealand managed only 200 in reply with Waqar Younis taking 6/78. Leading by 144 runs, Pakistan added another 179 to set the home team a target of 324. Centuries by Bryan Young (120) and Shane Thomson (120no) brought New Zealand home by five wickets. The only Test hat-trick ever taken in New Zealand was by Gubby Allen for England in 1930 at Jade Stadium. Derek Underwood has the best match figures of 12/97 for England against New Zealand in 1970/71.

The highest team score is 580/9 by England in 1991/92 and the lowest 65 by New Zealand versus England in 1971.

Watching cricket here is ideal. With a capacity of 36,500, wherever you sit you are close to the pitch. The No.1, No. 2, Smith City and the D. B. stands are in the sun which is pleasant as long as you protect yourself. The new West Stand, which holds 17,000, is sheltered and can get a bit chilly. There is a bar in the corner between the Smith City and D. B. stands where spectators can drink while watching. There are numerous other bars beneath the stands along with a large number of fast food outlets. An electronic scoreboard and a giant video replay screen are situated above the D. B. Stand. Facilities and access for persons with disabilities are first class with numerous viewing areas for wheelchair users in the West Stand.

Tickets for test matches can be obtained from Ticketek on www.ticketek.co.nz. or at the gate on match day. Parking is available within a five minute walk. Buses run from the city. It is a 20 minute walk from the centre. A taxi costs NZ$12 from the centre. There are two ranks outside the stadium, one on Lancaster Street, the other on Moorhouse Avenue.

A visitor centre and sports museum are located in the West Stand.

Christchurch is the capital of Canterbury and the second largest city in New Zealand with a population of 325,000. It lies half way down the east coast of South Island. The first Maori settlers, the Waitaha, arrived in the 1300s. The Ngati Mamoe from the North Island followed in the 16th century. In the 1750s the Ngai Thau arrived.

The first Europeans to arrive were traders and whalers in the 1820s. Unfortunately by the 1840s only 500 Maoris remained as a result of battles and the impact of European illnesses. The first European settlers were from The Canterbury Association, a British colonizing society who set up a close-knit community based on an English model.

Christchurch serves as a regional centre to the rich rural hinterland. Sheep farming is the primary agricultural industry. Canterbury also produces the majority of New Zealand's grains. Other industries include meatpacking, horticulture, dairy farming and the manufacture of woollen goods.

With the Port Hills as a backdrop Christchurch is often described as a little piece of England. Many of its streets are named after English cities. The River Avon, flanked by wonderful weeping willows, meanders through the city and its banks provide an ideal picnic area. The city has over 3000 hectares of gardens including the remarkable Botanical Gardens and the massive Hagley Park.

Christchurch also has beautiful tree-lined streets with classic gothic-style buildings, such as Christchurch Cathedral which was designed by George Gilbert Scott in 1904, Canterbury Museum, Christ College and the Arts Centre. The Christchurch Tramway is an excellent way to see these sights. A 2.5km loop around the centre of the city passes many places of interest.on the way.

Christchurch's hinterland offers adventures, outdoor recreation and wonderful scenery. Attractions include the Gondola, a cable car that runs up the Port Hills and provides the best view of the city, the International Antarctic Centre, twice voted best visitor attraction in New Zealand, Lyttleton, a working port and the water gateway to Christchurch and Willow Bank Wildlife Reserve, New Zealand's largest kiwi viewing area.

There is a wide selection of accommodation to suit everyone's requirements. In the centre of Christchurch and within walking distance of the cricket ground there are three and four star hotels as well as some excellent guesthouses, bed and breakfasts and backpackers'. Christchurch has variety of fine restaurants and cafés particularly down by the river where Oxford Terrace is lined with eateries offering fresh New Zealand food and fine wines. As one walks around the city, the large number of cafés and bars is noticeable. The city also offers a lively nightlife with many pubs and clubs, Oxford Terrace coming to the fore once again. A large casino also offers a wide range of activities.

The Arts Centre is the cultural hub of Christchurch. It is set on the site of the old Canterbury University with gothic revival buildings, splendid quadrangles and a huge range of arts and crafts markets, galleries, stores, theatres, cafés and restaurants.

Christchurch International Airport is 12km north west of the centre. A taxi takes approximately 20 minutes and costs NZ$30. A shuttle bus leaves from directly in front of the terminal and costs NZ$12. A bus runs between the airport and Cathedral Square every 30 minutes and costs NZ$2.70. The journey takes approximately 30 minutes. There are a very helpful information desks in the arrivals and departure halls. The arrivals hall has a bureau de change and an ATM, immediately to the right as one comes out of customs. There are shops, cafés and restaurants between the International Arrivals and Domestic Departures. Mobile Rentals are available in the Arrival Hall. A Duty free shop is beyond Passport Control. Car hire is available from Avis (03 358 9661), Budget (03 358 7488), Hertz (03 358 6730) and Thrifty (03 353 1940).

Ride the City Tram

Circling the tree-lined streets of the centre taking in The Cathedral, the Avon River and the sidewalk cafés and bars of Oxford Terrace, the Arts Centre, the Botanical Gardens, the Canterbury Museum, Christ College for Boys, Hagley Pa the Casino, the floral clock in Victoria Square and the boutique shops in New Regent Street. The tram runs from 09.00-2100 each day and is a wonderful way see the city. A 24-hour ticket cost NZ$10. 03 366 7830. www.tram.co.nz

The Christchurch Gondola

A 945 metre ride to the top of Port Hills offering stunning views by day of Christchurch, the Canterbury Plains, Banks Peninsula, Lyttleton Harbour. In the evening, the beautiful sunsets over the southern alps should not be missed . A restaurant on the edge of an extinct volcano has spectacular 360 degrees views. 0 384 0700 www.gondola.co.nz

Christchurch Cathedral

This Anglican Cathedral was planned in the 1860s by George Gilbert Scott but w not completed until 1904. It has intricate wood and stone carvings, and works o art. Christchurch's outstanding landmark and the central point of the city. The square outside is alive with entertainers, in particular the Wizard, a local with a few good stories to tell.

Canterbury Brewery Tour

This enjoyable tour takes in the Brewing Museum, the Brewery Tour, the Bottlin and Packaging plants and the huge warehouse and the Heritage Centre Bar, one of the city's oldest industrial landmarks built in 1854. Tours at 36 St. Asaph Stree Christchurch 03 379 4940.

Botanic Gardens

Boasts the finest indigenous plants in New Zealand. A beautiful heritage Rose Garden with 250 different types of rose is the highlight and the Rock and Heathe Gardens and the Rhododendron Collection are also worth visiting. The Gardens are a wonderful place to spend an afternoon in peaceful surrounds enjoying its lake and fountains.

Post Office

General Post Office
53-59 Hereford St.
Christchurch

Tourist Information

Christchurch and Canterbury Visitor
Centre
Old Chief Post Office
Cathedral Square
Christchurch
Tel: 03 379 9629
Fax: 03 377 2424
info@christchurchnz.net

Christchurch Airport Travel and
Information Centre
Domestic Terminal
Christchurch Airport
Tel: 03 353 7774/5
Fax: 03 353 7754
Pamela.Williams@aol.co.nz

Hospital

Christchurch Hospital
Riccarton Ave.
Christchurch
Tel: 03 365 7777

Christchurch 24 Hour Surgery
Corner Bealey Avenue/Colombo St.
Christchurch
Tel: 03 365 7777

Pharmacy

Urgent Pharmacy
931 Colombo St.
Christchurch
Tel:03 366 4439
Open until 11pm

Copthorne Hotel

776 Colombo St.
Tel: 03 379 5880
Fax: 03 365 4806
copthorne.central@mcqhotels.co.nz
www.copthornecentral.co.nz
minutes from the centre. 142 rooms
with air-conditioning, minibar, Cable
TV, Restaurant and bar overlooking
Avon River.

Centra

Corner Cashel and High St.
Tel: 03 365 8888
Fax: 03 365 8822
reservations@christchruch.centra.co.nz
City centre hotel with 149 rooms, Sky
TV, minibar, gym, Brasserie and grill.
Streetside bar with friendly atmosphere.

The George

Park Terrace
Tel: 03 379 4560
Fax: 03 366 6747
info@thegeorge.com
www.thegeorge.com
Overlooking Hagley Park and the Avon
River, luxurious hotel with restaurant,
bar and excellent rooms.

The Latimer Hotel

0 Latimer Square
Corner Worecester Street and Latimer
Square
Tel: 03 379 6760
Fax: 03 366 0133
Fax: 0800 176176
enquires@latimerhotel.co.nz
minutes from centre. Minbar and
Sky TV

The Heritage Hotel

8 Cathedral Square
Tel: 03 377 9722
Fax: 03 377 9881
res@dynasty.co.nz
www.heritagehotels.co.nz
Elegant hotel with 265 excellent rooms
with cable TV. Restaurant, bar, gym
and sauna.

The Millennium

4 Cathedral Square
Tel: 0800 245 888
Fax: 03 365 7676
www.millennium.co.nz
179 rooms with air-conditioning,
cable TV and safety deposit box., Gym,
sauna, 2 restaurants and bar.

Hambledon

103 Bealey Ave.
Tel: 03 379 0723
Fax: 03 379 0758
hambledon@clear.net.nz
1856 heritage home, set in beautiful
gardens, this B&B has elegant suites
with fresh flowers, TV and tea and coffee making facilities in each room.

Elm Tree House

236 Papanui Road
Tel: 03 355 9731
Fax: 03 355 9753
elmtreeb.b@clear.net.nz
www.elmtreehouse.co.nz
Excellent B&B close to the city centre.
5 rooms with en suite bathrooms, TV
and tea and coffee. Guest Lounge.

The Charlotte Jane

110 Papunui Road
Tel: 03 355 1028
Fax: 03 355 8882
charjane@ihug.co.nz
Handsome Victorian villa, very comfortable bed and breakfast.

Windsor Bed and Breakfast

52 Armagh St.
Tel: 03 366 2707
Fax: 03 366 9796
reservations@windsorhotel.co.nz
Central, family run B&B offering comfortable accommodation.

New Excelsior Backpackers'

Corner Manchester and High St.
Tel: 03 366 7570
Fax: 03 366 7629
Singles, twins, doubles and family
rooms. Kitchen, laundry, TV/Video
lounge, Clean and friendly

Marine Backpackers'

26 Nayland St.
Sumner
Tel: 03 326 6609
Fax: 03 326 5843
info@themarine.co.nz
www.themarine.co.nz
New backpackers, 2 minutes from the
beach and 20 minutes from centre.

Charlie B's Backpackers'

268 Madras St.
Tel: 03 379 8429
sandy@charliebs.co.nz
Good backpackers in the centre. Singles, doubles available. Games room
and open fires. Kitchen.

where to eat & drink

Curator's House Restaurant

Botanic Gardens
7 Rolleston Ave.
Tel: 03 379 2252
Garcia.knight@xtra.co.nz
On banks of River Avon, this Spanish restaurant serves local produce in a relaxed atmosphere. Open every day 10.00 until late.

Santorini

Gloucester St and Cambridge Terrace
Tel: 03 379 6975
Authentic Greek food with live music and dancing. Open Tuesday- Saturday 18.00 until late. Reservation advised.

Palazzo del Marinaio

Shades Arcade
108 Hereford St.
Tel: 03 365 4640
Fax: 03 365 5911
gorg@palazzo.co.nz
Seafood served Italian style. Enhanced with the freshest local produce. Guaranteed a night to remember.

Tandoori Palace

Cathedral Square
Tel: 03 365 7816
Classic curry at a very reasonable price. Good restaurant.

East in the City

226 High St.
Food hall many cuisines under the one roof. Monday-Friday 1100-2100.

Sticky Fingers

Clarendon Tower
Oxford Terrace
Tel: 03 366 6451
Fax: 03 366 8986
stickyfinger@xtra.co.nz
www.stickyfinger.co.nz
All day eating. International cuisine.

Dux de Lux

Corner of Montreal and Hereford St.
Tel: 03 366 6919
www.thedux.co.nz
Vegetarian and seafood restaurant in centre. Live music, excellent wine.

Two Fat Indians

112 Marletz St.
Tel: 03 371 7273
Curry house on the way from ground to the centre.

Annie's Wine Bar

Arts Centre
Tel: 03 365 0566
Lunch dinner, coffee, teas and juices. Warm and vibrant atmosphere with fine Canterbury wine.

Sticky Fingers

Clarendon Towers
Oxford Terrace
Tel: 03 366 6451
Lively bar with live music. Party place. Very much the in place to go. Open until late.

The Vic & Whale

772 Colombo St.
Tel: 03 365 3643
Pool tables, TV sport, video games, live music Thursday-Saturday 10.00 until late. Casino room.

The Bard on Avon

Gloucester St and Oxford Terrace
Tel: 03 377 1493
Warm English pub with wide range of ales on tap and traditional fare. Music 3 nights a week.

Christchurch Casino

30 Victoria St.
Tel: 03 365 9999
www.ccc.co.nz
New Zealand's first casino opened in 1994. 500 gaming machines, 40 tables, 3 bars and 2 restaurants.

Stogies Cigar Bar

817 Colombo St.
Tel: 03 379 1200
A relaxed jazz/blues bar.

The Bog Irish Bar

82 Cashel Mall
Tel: 03 3797 141
Lively Irish bar, traditional mighty food, drink and craic. Live Entertainment 7 nights a week.

Holy Grail Sports Bar

88 Worcester St.
Tel: 03 365 9816
Fax: 03 365 9817
office@holygrail.co.nz
www.holygrail.co.nz
Sports Bar, including one massive video screen. Restaurant, Pizza kitchen. Busy with good atmosphere.

Court Theatre

Engineering Building
Arts Centre
Tel: 03 963 0870
Professional theatre company.
www.courttheatre.org.nz

University Free Theatre

Hight Building
Arts Centre
Tel: 03 379 7219
Live theatre performances.

Canterbury Museum

Rolleston Ave.
Tel: 03 366 5000
Fax: 03 366 5622
Beside the Botanic Gardens and opposite the Arts Centre, the Canterbury Museum is housed in an 1867 building and has excellent Maori exhibits and Hall of Antartica's discovery. Open 09.00-17.00 daily.

Bealey Art Gallery

161 Hereford St.
Tel: 03 366 7506
Traditional New Zealand art. Open
Monday-Friday 09.00-17.30. Saturday
11.00-13.00.

Christchurch Art Gallery

Corner of Worcester Boulevard and
Montreal St.
Huge new gallery for New Zealand
and international art. Opened in April
2003.

Airlines

Air New Zealand   03 353 4899
03 353 4926
Qantas   03 379 6504/0800 808 767

Buses

Good local service. Intercity
Coachlines 03 379 9020. Knightrider
between Christchurch and Dunedin
03 342 8055.

Trains

Trans Coastal and Trans Alpine 0800
802 802

Taxis

Gold Band Taxi 03 379 5795

Executive Cabs   03 377 7999

Car Hire

Avis
26 Lichfield St.
Fax: 03 379 6133

Budget
15 Lichfield St.
Fax: 03 366 0072

Hertz
46 Lichfield St.
Fax: 03 366 0549

Thrifty
33 Lichfield St.
Tel: 03 374 2357

Climate

	ave temp	rain cm
January	16	53
February	16	45
March	15	52
April	12	50
May	9	68
June	6	65
July	6	66
August	7	54
September	9	45
October	12	45
November	14	48
December	15	55

Win/Loss Record

Country	Played	won	drawn	Lost	Tie
South Africa	2	1	1	-	-
England	15	8	6	1	-
Pakistan	5	2	2	1	-
Australia	5	2	2	1	-
West Indies	6	2	3	1	-
New Zealand	38	7	16	15	-
India	4	-	2	2	-
Sri Lanka	1	-	-	1	-

Highest Individual Aggregates (New Zealand unless stated)

Player	Mat	Inn	NO	Runs	Ave	HS	50	100
John Wright	13	21	1	687	34.35	185	1	2
Glenn Turner	7	11	1	664	66.40	117	2	3
Bev Congdon	10	18	2	623	38.94	107*	3	2
Richard Hadlee	14	17	1	504	31.50	103	1	1
Jeremy Coney	9	13	0	427	32.85	98	3	0
Graham Dowling	4	8	0	419	52.38	239	1	1
John Reid	6	11	0	391	35.55	100	2	1
Martin Crowe	8	13	1	389	32.42	137	1	1
Bryan Young	5	10	1	352	39.11	120	1	1
Allan Border (Aus)	3	4	1	348	116.00	140	1	2

Top Wicket Takers (New Zealand unless stated)

Player	Mat	Bll	Md	Runs	Wkt	Ave	BB	S/R
Richard Hadlee	14	3679	112	1635	76	21.51	7/116	48.41
Danny Morrison	7	1555	47	912	35	26.06	6/69	44.43
Richard Collinge	7	1491	36	641	29	22.10	6/63	51.41
Ewen Chatfield	7	1933	80	639	26	24.58	4/30	74.35
Martin Snedden	6	1178	46	537	22	24.41	5/68	53.55
Dick Motz	5	1181	49	526	21	25.05	6/63	56.24
Lance Cairns	7	1652	74	689	20	34.45	6/85	82.60
Sonny Ramadhin (WI)	2	660	43	197	15	13.13	5/46	44.00
Phil Tufnell (Eng)	2	775	50	227	14	16.21	7/47	55.36
Derek Underwood (Eng)	2	462	17	132	14	9.43	6/12	33.00

Highest Individual Scores (New Zealand unless stated)

258	Seymour Nurse (WI)	1968-69
250	Doug Walters (Aus)	1976-77
239	Graham Dowling	v India 1967-68
227	Wally Hammond (Eng)	1932-33
222	Nathan Astle	v England 2001-02
211*	Herschelle Gibbs (SA)	1998-99
204*	Mathew Sinclair	v Pakistan 2000-01
203	Yousuf Youhana (Pak)	2000-01
200*	Graham Thorpe (Eng)	2001-02
185	John Wright	v India 1989-90

Best Individual Bowling Performances (New Zealand unless stated)

46.1-25-47-7	Phil Tufnell (Eng)	1991-92
34.4-13-56-7	Mushtaq Ahmed (Pak)	1995-96
21.2-7-63-7	Matthew Hoggard (Eng)	2001-02
30.2-9-75-7	Fred Trueman (Eng)	1962-63
44.4-8-116-7	Richard Hadlee	v Australia 1985-86
11.6-7-12-6	Derek Underwood (Eng)	1970-71
16.5-5-38-6	Gary Bartlett	v India 1967-68
24.5-9-38-6	Graham Dilley (Eng)	1987-88
12.3-2-50-6	Richard Hadlee	v West Indies 1986-87
28.2-13-53-6	Tony Lock (Eng)	1958-59

Highest Partnerships

Wkt	Runs	Batsmen	Match
1st	225	Gordon Greenidge & Desmond Haynes (WI)	1979-1980
2nd	315*	Herschelle Gibbs & Jacques Kallis (SA)	1998-1999
3rd	179	Alex Stewart & Robin Smith (Eng)	1991-1992
4th	162	Gordon Greenidge & Alvin Kallicharran (WI)	1979-1980

5th	242	Wally Hammond & Les Ames (Eng)	1932-1933
6th	281	Graham Thorpe & Andrew Flintoff (Eng)	2001-2002
7th	248	Yousuf Youhana & Saqlain Mushtaq (Pak)	2000-2001
8th	107	David Allen & David Brown (Eng)	1965-1966
9th	117	Trevor Bailey & Doug Wright (Eng)	1950-1951
10th	118	Nathan Astle & Chris Cairns (NZ)	2001-2002 v England

Results at The Jade Stadium

Date	Countries	Result
10/01/1930	v England	lost by 8 wickets
27/02/1932	v South Africa	lost by an innings and 12 runs
24/03/1933	v England	drawn
21/03/1947	v England	drawn
17/03/1951	v England	drawn
08/02/1952	v West Indies	lost by 5 wickets
18/02/1956	v West Indies	lost by an innings and 64 runs
27/02/1959	v England	lost by an innings and 99 runs
15/03/1963	v England	lost by 7 wickets
12/02/1965	v Pakistan	drawn
25/02/1966	v England	drawn
22/02/1968	v India	won by 6 wickets
13/03/1969	v West Indies	drawn
25/02/1971	v England	lost by 8 wickets
08/03/1974	v Australia	won by 5 wickets
28/02/1975	v England	drawn
05/02/1976	v India	drawn
18/02/1977	v Australia	drawn
24/02/1978	v England	lost by 174 runs
02/02/1979	v Pakistan	lost by 128 runs
22/02/1980	v West Indies	drawn
06/03/1981	v India	drawn
19/03/1982	v Australia	lost by 8 wickets
04/03/1983	v Sri Lanka	won by an innings and 25 runs
03/02/1984	v England	won by an innings and 132 runs
28/02/1986	v Australia	drawn
12/03/1987	v West Indies	won by 5 wickets
12/02/1988	v England	drawn
02/02/1990	v India	won by 10 wickets
18/01/1992	v England	lost by an innings and 4 runs
25/02/1993	v Australia	lost by an innings and 60 runs
24/02/1994	v Pakistan	won by 5 wickets
03/02/1995	v West Indies	drawn
08/12/1995	v Pakistan	lost by 161 runs
14/02/1997	v England	lost by 4 wickets
11/03/1999	v South Africa	drawn
15/03/2001	v Pakistan	drawn
13/03/2002	v England	lost by 98 runs

hamilton

Westpac Park in Hamilton is home to the Northern Districts Cricket Association. It did not stage a Test until February 1991 when New Zealand were four wickets away from beating Sri Lanka. Andrew Jones contributed 122 to New Zealand's 296 with Rumesh Ratnayake taking 5/77. The visitors were 43 behind on first innings although Asanka Gurusinha scored 119. Jones knocked up another 100 with John Wright getting 101 as New Zealand collected 374/6. Set 420 win, Gurusinha hit another century as Sri Lanka finished at 344/6.

The most exciting match at the ground was New Zealand versus Pakistan in 1992/93. Batting first Pakistan made 216, Javid Manidad top scoring with 92. Murphy Sua took 5/73 for the home team. New Zealand replied with 264, Mark Greatbatch contributing 133. Danny Morrison took 5/41 as Pakistan were dismissed for 174 in their second innings. Set 127 to win, New Zealand were ripped apart by Wasim Akram with 5/45 and Waqar Younis 5/22 to lose by 33 runs.

Hamilton has usually been a good place to bat, Raul Dravid hit 190 and 103 for India the drawn Test in 1998/99. The highest team score is 464/8 by New Zealand in the same match and the lowest 93 by the home side in the 1992/93 match against Pakistan. The highest run chase was 212/4 by Australia in 1999/2000.

The best bowling performance is Chris Cairns' match figures of 10/100 against West Indies in 1999/2000. He also holds the record for most wickets with 34 at an average of 21.88.

Even with a capacity of 14,000 Westpac Park has the appearance of a village ground with a raised grass embankment at the City End and wonderful trees surrounding it. It provides a fun atmosphere with people picnicking on the high embankments and under the old scoreboard opposite the pavilion. The pavilion, positioned at fine leg at the Member End, was built in 1990 and is a modern building with excellent viewing lounges. There is also an indoor training centre, a restaurant, bar and new media centre. To the right of the pavilion there are a number of corporate tents.

Remarkably, apart from the pavilion, there is only one other bar in the ground. It's at mid wicket beside the corporate tents. Consequently, on busy days there can be long queues. Food outlets are also less plentiful than usual, with a small number selling hot dogs, burgers and chips. Queues also form for the toilet facilities which are clean and well looked after. Facilities and access for the disabled are available with off-street parking available. There is a souvenir and memorabilia shop under the pavilion and by the corporate tents. Tickets available from Ticketek, 221 Tristram Street, Hamilton 07 838 6600 or www.ticketek.co.nz and from the ticket offices outside the ground.

The ground is a 10-minute walk from the south of Hamilton and most people choose this option. Buses run past the ground and a taxi should not cost more than NZ$8.

Hamilton is New Zealand's fifth largest city. With a population of 120,000, it is in heart of the Waikato district, which is the country's richest agriculture area. It is a small, quiet place, situated 136km south of Auckland in the North Island. Originally named Kirikirirana, the first inhabitants were Maori in the 1300s. Europeans arrived in the 1840s although a settlement was not established until 1864. The city was renamed Hamilton after Captain Fane Charles Hamilton, Commander of HMS Esk who was killed in the battle of Gat Pa Tauranga.

Hamilton's main industry is agriculture and associated services; it is not usually a tourist destination. But it is very pretty and relaxed with many parks and walkways, some by the Waikato River that runs through the city.

The Waitamo Caves are a 45-minute drive from Hamilton where the more adventurous can go blackwater rafting, caving and horsetrekking. The attractive English-style town of Cambridge is 22km from Hamilton. Other attractions near the city include watersports at Lake Karapio and the Waingaro Hot Pools.

Victoria Street runs through Hamilton and is the hub of the city. Hotels, pubs and restaurants are all concentrated on this stretch.

There is a variety of accommodation in Hamilton from the Novotel and Le Grand in Victoria Street to guesthouses and backpackers'. There are also inexpensive and very good motels on Ulster Street to the north of the city. These motels are excellent value and are not too far from the cricket ground. The service in all the accommodation is excellent and friendly. Hamilton has some very good places to eat and drink. Again, Victoria Street has many busy restaurants and bars.

the city

Hamilton Gardens

Five minutes from the centre with something to interest every gardener, from a herb garden and an American Modernist Garden to Japanese, Chinese, English and Italian and rose gardens. There are lovely river walks and a restaurant on the garden terrace. There is also a café serving snacks and light meals. Enquiries 07 856 6581

Hamilton Zoo

Set among 52 acres, the Zoo has superb walkways The Free Flight Aviary is worth a visit. A café provides snacks and light meals. Open daily 0900-1700. www.hamiltonzoo.co.uk Tel: 07 838 6720

Waikato Museum of Art and History

The museum presents an ever-changing programme of exhibits relating to Waikato history, Tainui Maori cultural history and New Zealand art. Permanent exhibits include a war canoe. National and international exhibitions are also a regular feature. Open daily 1000-1630 www.wm.org.nz

Waipa Delta

Paddleboat that cruises on the Waikato River. Lunchtime, afternoon tea and evening cruise are available. Cocktails, dinners and live entertainment.

Cambridge

The Town of Trees is a 30-minute drive from Hamilton and is a quaint little place with some stunning attractions such as Lake Karapiro, the Town Clock, Maungatautari Mountain and the Tauwhare Military Museum. Gardens, Parks and antique stores abound.

what to see

Le Grand Hotel

Victoria St.
Tel: 07 839 1994
Fax: 07 839 7994
legrandhotel@xtra.co.nz
Good en suite rooms with air-conditioning and cable TV. Restaurant and bar.

Novotel Hotel

7 Alma St.
Hamilton Central
Tel: 07 838 1366
Fax: 07 838 1367
Central with excellent rooms.
Restaurant and Bar.

Victoria Hotel Suites

303 Victoria St.
Tel: 07 958 1110
Fax: 07 958 1111
info@victoriasuites.co.nz
www.victoriasuites.co.nz
Downtown location. Affordable apartment accommodation with guest laundry. All rooms have air-conditioning, Cable TV and fridge.

Abbey Travel Lodge Motel

12 Lorne St.
Tel: 07 843 4368
Fax: 07 843 4368
enquiries@abbeymotel.co.nz
www.abbeymotel.co.nz
10 minutes from Hamilton near the airport. 20 units and apartments. Family run motel. Comfortable rooms with air-conditioning and Cable TV.

Ventura Inn

23 Clarence St.
Tel: 07 838 0110
Fax: 07 838 0120
Hamilton@venturainns.co.nz
50 rooms in the south end of the city. Very comfortable hotel with restaurant and bar.

Sails Motor Inn

272 Ulster St.
Tel: 07 838 2733
Fax: 07 838 2747
bookings@sails-motorinn.co.nz
www.sails-motorinn.co.nz
20 luxury units with rooms with kitchen facilities and cable TV. Swimming pool and room service.

Flag Ambassador Motor Inn

86 Ulster St.
Tel: 07 839 5111
Fax: 07 839 5104
ambassador@silveroaks.co.nz
www.flagchoice.com
Central hotel with outdoor swimming pool, Cable TV, restaurant and bar. All rooms en suite.

Cedar Lodge Motel

174 Ulster St.
Tel: 07 839 5569
Fax: 07 838 2212
1 and 2 bedroom units. 5 minutes from city centre. Full kitchen facilities.

The Commercial Hotel

Corner Victoria and Collingwood St.
Tel: 07 839 4993
Fax: 07 834 2389
commercial.hotel@clear.net.nz
Varied accommodation ranging from backpackers' to hotel. Central and within easy reach of pubs and restaurants.

Barclay Motel

280 Ulster St.
Tel: 07 838 2475
Fax: 07 838 2773
info@barclay.co.nz
www.barclay.co.nz
Fully equipped kitchens in all units. Swimming pool, cable TV. 10 minute walk downtown.

Pipers' Lodge

18 Hillsborough Terrace
Tel: 07 389 3903
Fax: 07 839 3900
piperslodge@hotmail.com
Excellent B&B on river. 5 minutes to city. Nice room, full breakfast.

J's Backpackers'

8 Gray St.
Tel: 07 856 8934
Clean hostel. Close to Hamilton Gardens.

Helen Heywood YHA

1190 Victoria St.
Tel: 07 838 0009
Fax: 07 838 0837
yha.hamilton@yha.org.nz
Cosy old building on main street. Wonderful views of Waikato

Café Spice
Victoria St.
Tel: 07 834 2500
Good Indian food with a very good reputation. Excellent value.

Seddon House
7 Seddon Road
Tel: 07 847 8294
Excellent New Zealand cooking.

The Narrow Landing
31 Airport Road
Tel: 07 858 4001
Probably the best restaurant in Hamilton. A great eating experience. Excellent wine list, good service. Lunch seven days a week. Dinner Tuesday to Saturday.

EmbarGo
1 Garden Place
Tel: 07 834 1353
Do not be fooled by the nondescript surroundings. Good food, well presented in a great atmosphere.

Cohl
36 Victoria St.
Tel: 07 839 1996
Excellent menu with rabbit and kangaroo, steak and seafood. Wild food in a stylish and trendy atmosphere.

Il Dente
55 Victoria St.
Tel: 07 838 2535
Italian restaurant serving steak, seafood, pastas and pizza. Good value for money. Lunch and Dinner seven days a week.

Museum Café
Grantham St.
Tel: 07 839 7209
Award winning restaurant on the river. Good food with outstanding service.

Domaine
575 Victoria St.
Tel: 07 839 2100
Pizzas, salads, pasta, seafood. Definitely worth a visit.

The Original Thai Restaurant
8 Alma St.
Tel: 07 838 3088
Beautifully decorated restaurant serving wonderful, tasty Thai food. Service could not be better.

Iguana
Victoria St.
Tel: 07 834 2280
Very lively restaurant and bar. Good pub food, pizza, pasta etc.

There are plenty of other restaurants to experience in Hamilton. Others include Tables on the River (French), Panchos (Mexican), Thai Orchard (Thai), Maru (Japanese), Out in the Styx (French/New Zealand).

Most of the nightlife is based around Victoria Street, Market Place and Hood St. Most are just quiet bars. The ones that stood out were:

Biddy Mulligans
Victoria St.
Lively Irish pub.

Loaded Hog
Hood St.
Another good lively pub with good food.

Hamilton Airport is 13km south of the city. A taxi ride takes 20 minutes and costs NZ$30. A Super Shuttle (07 843 7778) bus meets all flights, runs between the airport and the city and costs NZ$8. There is a post office, an ATM machine, a duty free shop, newsagents and a café. Car hire is available from Avis (07 839 4915), Budget (07 838 3585), Hertz (07 839 4824) and Thrifty (07 823 5778).

transport

Airlines
Air New Zealand 0800 737 000

Buses
The city has an extensive bus network. Regular Intercity services to and from Auckland, Taupo and Wellington Enquiries 07 839 3580.

Trains
Trains run daily to Auckland and Wellington. Tranz Scenic/Rail 0800 802 802

Taxis
Hamilton Taxis	07 847 7477
Combined Taxis	07 839 9099
Dial a Cab	07 847 5050
Fast Taxis	0800 221 000
Red Cabs	07 839 0500

Car Hire
Avis
123 Anglesea St.
Hamilton
Tel: 07 839 4915

Budget
404 Anglesea St.
Hamilton
Tel: 07 838 3585

Hertz
98 Tristran St.
Hamilton
Tel: 07 839 4824

Thrifty
36 Liverpool St.
Hamilton
Tel: 07 823 5778

culture

Founders' Theatre
The Meteor
WestpacTrust Theatre

Waikato Museum of Art and History
Corner Grantham and Victoria St.
Tel: 07 838 6600
museum@hcc.govt.nz

A museum recording the history of Waikato. An excellent art, ethnology and history collection. Open 10.00-16.30 daily.

Arts Post Galleries
120 Victoria St.
Thornton Gallery
298 Barton St.

Post Office
Hamilton Post Shop
36 Bryce St.
Tel: 07 838 2233
0800-1700 Monday-Friday
0900-1400 Saturday
0900-1200 Sunday

Tourist Information
Hamilton Travel and Visitor Centre
Corner Ward and Anglesea Streets
Tel: 07 839 3580
Fax: 07 839 3127
hamiltoninfo@wave.co.nz

Hospital
Waikato Hospital Emergency Department
Pembroke St.
Tel: 07 839 8707

Anglesea Clinic-24 hour clinic
Tel: 07 858 0800

Climate
	ave temp	rain cm
January	19	70
February	20	86
March	18	77
April	16	96
May	14	115
June	12	126
July	11	131
August	11	111
September	12	94
October	14	93
November	16	82
December	18	78

Win/Loss Record

Country	Played	won	drawn	Lost	Tie
Australia	1	1	-	-	-
New Zealand	13	5	6	2	-
Zimbabwe	1	-	1	-	-
Pakistan	3	1	1	1	-
South Africa	1	-	1	-	-
India	3	-	2	1	-
Sri Lanka	2	-	1	1	-
Bangladesh	1	-	-	1	-
West Indies	1	-	-	1	-

Highest Individual Aggregates (New Zealand unless stated)

Player	Mat	Inn	NO	Runs	Ave	HS	50	100
Stephen Fleming	11	18	1	682	40.12	192	4	1
Craig McMillan	8	12	0	605	50.42	106	5	1
Chris Cairns	8	13	0	423	32.54	126	2	1
Mark Richardson	5	7	0	353	50.43	143	0	2
Rahul Dravid (Ind)	2	4	1	341	113.67	190	0	2
Daniel Vettori	7	10	2	322	40.25	137*	1	1
Adam Parore	9	14	2	309	25.75	84*	2	0
Andrew Jones	2	4	1	243	81.00	122	0	2
Jacques Kallis (SA)	1	2	1	242	242.00	150*	1	1
Asanka Gurusinha (SL)	1	2	0	221	110.50	119	0	2

Top Wicket Takers (New Zealand unless stated)

Player	Mat	Bll	Md	Runs	Wkt	Ave	BB	S/R
Chris Cairns	8	1414	51	744	34	21.88	7/27	41.59
Daryl Tuffey	5	893	39	434	21	20.67	5/87	42.52
Daniel Vettori	7	1553	64	700	21	33.33	5/84	73.95
Danny Morrison	3	741	26	312	16	19.50	5/41	46.31
Shane Bond	2	315	13	172	11	15.64	4/39	28.64
Javagal Srinath (Ind)	2	740	28	349	11	31.73	5/95	67.27
Jacob Oram	3	527	21	223	10	22.30	4/41	52.70
Waqar Younis (Pak)	2	435	17	179	10	17.90	5/22	43.50
Dipak Patel	4	876	41	401	10	40.10	2/44	87.60
Chris Martin	2	240	10	144	8	18.00	4/52	30.00

Highest Individual Scores (New Zealand unless stated)

192	Stephen Fleming	v Pakistan 2003-04
190	Rahul Dravid (Ind)	1998-99
170	Sherwin Campbell (WI)	1999-00
150*	Jacques Kallis (SA)	2003-04
143	Mark Richardson	v Bangladesh 2001-02
137*	Daniel Vettori	v Pakistan 2003-04
137	Moin Khan (Pak)	2003-04
137	Gary Kirsten SA)	2003-04
133	Mark Greatbatch	v Pakistan 1992-93
126	Chris Cairns	v India 1998-99

Best Individual Bowling Performances (New Zealand unless stated)

12.5-10-27-7	Chris Cairns	v West Indies 1999-00
18.2-2-53-7	Chris Cairns	v Bangladesh 2001-02
13.3-4-22-5	Waqar Younis (Pak)	1992-93
13.2-4-29-5	Zaheer Khan (Ind)	2002-03
15-2-41-5	Danny Morrison	v Pakistan 1992-93
16-4-44-5	Mohammad Sami (Pak)	2003-04
12-4-45-5	Wasim Akram (Pak)	1992-93
15.5-5-51-5	Shayne O'Connor (Aus)	v Australia 1999-00
10.2-3-63-5	Heath Davis	v Sri Lanka 1996-97
14-2-73-5	Murphy Su'a	v Pakistan 1992-93

Highest Partnerships

Wkt	Runs	Batsmen	Match
1st	276	Adrian Griffith & Sherwin Campbell (WI)	1999-2000
2nd	116	Bryan Young & Ken Rutherford (NZ)	1993-1994 v India
3rd	194	Rahul Dravid & Sourav Ganguly (Ind)	1998-1999
4th	160	Roger Twose & Craig McMillan (NZ)	1998-1999 v India
5th	190	Craig McMillan & Mark Richardson (NZ)	2001-2002 v Bangladesh
6th	89	Mark Richardson & Chris Cairns (NZ)	2001-2002 v Bangladesh
7th	152	Moin Khan & Mohammad Sami (Pak)	2003-2004
8th	144	Rahul Dravid & Javagal Srinath (Ind)	1998-1999
9th	99	Daniel Vettori & Daryl Tuffey (NZ)	2003-2004 v Pakistan
10th	44	Gary Kirsten & Andre Nel (SA)	2003-2004

Results at Westpak Park

Date	Countries	Result
22/02/1991	v Sri Lanka	drawn
02/01/1993	v Pakistan	lost by 33 runs
19/03/1994	v India	drawn
13/01/1996	v Zimbabwe	drawn
14/03/1997	v Sri Lanka	won by 120 runs
02/01/1999	v India	drawn
16/12/1999	v West Indies	won by 9 wickets
31/03/2000	v Australia	lost by 6 wickets
27/03/2001	v Pakistan	won by an innings and 185 runs
18/12/2001	v Bangladesh	won by an innings and 52 runs
19/12/2002	v India	won by 4 wickets
19/12/2003	v Pakistan	drawn
10/03/2004	v South Africa	drawn

wellington

basin reserve

The Basin Reserve, home of the Wellington Cricket Association, is one of the prettiest Test grounds in the world. Nestled between Mount Victoria to the east and Mount Cook to the west, it is the only sports ground in New Zealand with National Heritage status. It is situated to the south of the city on one of the largest traffic roundabouts in the world. Entering the ground is like taking a step back in time with the old stands, the huge grass embankments, covered with fir trees, and the picket fence.

The first Test played at the Basin Reserve in January 1930 was against England. Stewie Dempster, 136, and Jack Mills, 117, became the first New Zealanders to score Test centuries with an opening partnership of 276 in the home team's first innings score of 440. Frank Woolley took 7/76 for the visitors. England replied with 320, Morris Nichols top-scoring with 78 before New Zealand scored 164/4 dec. in their second innings, Dempster contributing 80no to set England a target of 285 to win. England could only manage 107/4 before the close of play.

It took another 39 years before New Zealand won their first match at Basin Reserve when they beat the West Indies by six wickets. Dick Motz returned match figures of 8/113 and Glenn Turner top-scored with 74. This victory signalled a change in fortunes for New Zealand and began an undefeated period of 15 years. Highlights of this period include victories over India and New Zealand's first win over England.

In a low scoring game, England were set a target of 137 but Richard Hadlee took 6/26 to dismiss the visitors for 64, England's eighth lowest total. Hadlee had match figures of 10/100.

New Zealand's first victory over Australia came in 1990 when again Hadlee was the destroyer, taking 5/39 as Australia were dismissed for 110. New Zealand replied with 202 before John Bracewell took 6/85 in Australia's second innings of 269. Set 178 to win, John Wright hit an unbeaten 117 to see New Zealand home by nine wickets.

Basin Reserve saw the record Test third wicket partnership of 467 when Martin Crowe hit 299 and Andrew Jones 186 against Sri Lanka in 1991 as New Zealand reached 671/4 to save the game – the highest team score at the ground. Aravinda de Silva also scored a double century in the match.

Another remarkable batting achievement at the Basin was the performance of the Chappell brothers for Australia in the drawn Test of 1974. Ian, the elder, had scores of 145 and 121, while his younger brother Greg scored 247 and 133.

The lowest team score was 42 by New Zealand versus Australia in 1946. The highest run chase is 215/6 by New Zealand against India in 1998.

Courtney Walsh's 13/55 for the West Indies in 1995 is the best match return. Hadlee has taken the most wickets, 53, and he took his 300th Test wicket at the ground.

Basin Reserve has a capacity of 11,600. The R. A. Vance Stand, erected in 1980 and seating 1,570, is situated at the north end of the ground. The pavilion is named after Sir Ronald Brierley.

The Museum Stand, a wonderful structure with a fabulous cricket museum, is on the west side of the ground. Opposite, the grass embankment sweeps around the eastern side. This embankment is exposed to the sun and can get very hot but does have the protection of the many fir trees that line the hill. The impressive scoreboard is at the southern end of the ground.

Facilities for the disabled are good with viewing areas around the ground. Tickets are available from Ticketek on 04 384 3840 or www.ticketek.co.nz or from the ground on match days. The ground is a 20-minute walk from the city along Kent Terrace. Buses run from the centre of town to the Basin and a taxi costs NZ$8. There is a limited amount of parking in the surrounding street and at the nearby school.

Wellington International Airport is 8km south east of the city through the Mount Victoria Tunnel. A taxi ride takes approximately 15 minutes and costs between NZ$25-NZ$30. There are two taxi ranks outside the ground floor entrance. The Stagecoach Flyer is a shuttle to the city and costs NZ$4.50 (04 801 7000). All international and domestic flights arrive and depart from the same terminal. An information desk is located in the arrivals lounge. There is an ATM machine beside the Travelex bureau de change counter and another between baggage belts. There are a wide variety of shops selling souvenirs, sunglasses, CDs and clothes and restaurants, cafés, bakery and a juice bar. Mobile phone rental is available in the Arrival Hall.

Car hire is available Avis (04 802 1088), Budget (04 388 0987), Hertz (04 388 7070) and Thrifty (04 388 9494).

Wellington has been the capital of New Zealand since 1865 and is the southernmost capital in the world. It is perched on the southern tip of the North Island above a natural and deep harbour surrounded by an amphitheatre of steep volcanic hills. It is known as the Windy City because of the westerly wind which originate in the Cook Strait between the islands. Named after the Duke of Wellington, the British statesman, it has a population of 166,700.

Maori have lived in Wellington for 500 years. In 1840 the British arrived and settled in the area. There was very little flat land until 15 years later when an earthquake hit the area and raised the parts of the land.

Wellington is the political capital and many of its residents work in government related services. Wellington's main industries are shipping, manufacturing, tourism and IT.

Undisputedly the cultural capital of New Zealand, Wellington boasts a host of attractions including the New Zealand National Museum and the NZ Maritime Museum. The city is also home to the New Zealand Performing Arts, the NZ Symphony Orchestra, the NZ Ballet and the NZ Opera. The Heritage buildings on the Waterfront have been transformed into a thriving entertainment, shopping and dining area. Wellington Zoo is the oldest in New Zealand having opened in 1906. It is well worth a visit. The Botanic Gardens in the suburbs of Kelburn must also be seen. A cable car runs from the city up Mount Victoria to the gardens presenting stunning views of the harbour and city. A ferry trip from Queens Wharf also provides wonderful views of the city.

Within an hour of the city, Porirua City provides an opportunity to see where the city meets the country with museums, restaurants, bush and ocean. To the north of Wellington is Hutt Valley which offers many leisure pursuits including white water rafting, hiking, bushwalking, boating and swimming. The vineyards at Martinborough are another popular tourist excursion.

Wellington is becoming a very trendy weekend destination for New Zealanders and it is best to book accommodation before travelling. There are more than 300 restaurants in the city, many in the Courtenay Quarter. This part of the city is known for its vibrant café culture, good dining and lively nightlife. The Cuba Quarter of town also has restaurants and bars of an excellent quality. The other two quarters Lambton and Willis are more cultural areas with galleries, boutiques, markets and sidewalk cafés.

Molly Malone's

Corner Taranaki St & Courtenay Place
Tel: 04 384 2896
Largest Irish bar in town. Excellent food, good fun. Whiskey bar in the Dubliner upstairs.

Coyote

63 Courtenay Place
Tel: 04 385 6665
Very trendy pub/restaurant in the centre. Lively, popular and comfortable.

Ferryman's Bar and Café

Waterloo Quay
Tel: 04 499 4485
Good honest pub down near the water. Good food and friendly service.

Wellington Sports Café

48 –58 Courtenay Place
Tel: 04 801 5115
Full restaurant and bar with high-tech visual system. Good sports bar in the centre.

Shephards Arms Hotel

285 Tinakeri Road
Thorndon
Tel: 04 472 1320
Good, friendly English pub. Another good bar to go to after the cricket.

In addition to the above, the Amba, Blowbar, Jet Bar and Brava are places to go in the Courtenay Quarter, the heart of the city's nightlife. In the more laidback Cuban Quarter, the Good Luck Bar, the Havana and the Matterhorn are worth a visit. The Willis Quarter has the Malthouse and the Lambton Quarter has a wonderful Belgian Bar called Leuven where Belgian beer and mussels are the order of the day.

The Museum of Wellington City and Sea
Housed in an 1890's bond store formely the hub of the port. Terrific exhibits and the latest technology, ships models, relics and artefacts.

Te Papa Tongarewa
The National Museum is located at the waterfront and provides an insight into the country's land and people past, present and future. Exhibits include the National Art Collection, Maori culture, arts and crafts and a futuristic 2055 house. It is situated on Cable Street and is open 1000-1800 Monday-Saturday. Free.

Parliament's Historic Buildings
Built in 1876 entirely of timber, Government Building in Lambton Quay housed New Zealand's Civil Service for many years but is now leased to Victoria University. The Parliamentary Library in Molesworth Street is a good example of the high Victorian gothic style architecture remaining in Wellington. Parliament House is also on Molesworth Street and was built between 1912 and 1922. The building is asymmetric, as the planned second wing to the main entrance was never built.

Botanical Gardens and Carter Observatory
Perched above the city, the gardens provide wonderful views of Wellington and its harbour. Take the Kelburn Cable Car from Cable Car Lane in Lambton Quay for an enjoyable ride up the steep mountain. There are 26 hectares of gardens including Rose gardens, plant collections and floral displays.

The Flying Burrito Brothers
Corner Vivian & Cuba St.
Tel: 04 385 8811
Genuine Mexican food in the Cuba Quarter. Lively, music and good food.

Big Thumb Restaurant
Allen St.
Courtenay Place
Tel: 04 384 4878
Sichuan/Cantonese cuisine. Dinner from 17.00.

The Duxton Grill
Duxton hotel
170 Wakefield St.
Tel: 04 471 5711
Excellent food at reasonable price considering the restaurant is in one of the best hotels. Fine wine.

Scorpios
263 The Parade
Island Bay
Tel: 04 383 7563
Said to be the only Welsh restaurant in the Southern Hemisphere. Home cooked meals. Wednesday to Sunday from 18.00.

Casino
108-112 Tory St.
Tel: 04 385 7496
Top Italian restaurant. North Italian cuisine with excellent service. Extensive wine list.

Theo's Greek Taverna
13 Pirie St.
Mount Victoria
Tel: 04 801 8806
Greek cuisine, live entertainment and great fun.

The Dubliner Bar and Restaurant
Corner Takanki and Courtenay Place
Tel: 04 384 2896
Irish restaurant in Molly Malone's pub. Very good food and a great atmosphere.

Angkor
43 Dixon St.
Tel: 04 384 9423
www.angkor.net.nz
An excellent Cambodian restaurant.

The Curry Club
145 Victoria St.
Tel: 04 385 4886
Famous Indian restaurant with authentic cuisine. Open daily from 17.30.

Sakura
Corner Featerston and Whitmore St.
Tel: 04 499 6912
A fine Japanese restaurant with traditional Titam matting room.

The Wellesley

2-8 Maginnity St.
Tel: 04 474 1308
Fax: 04 473 1913
thorndongroup@compuserve.com
One of the finest places to stay in
Wellington. A gentleman's club, it is
wonderfully located in the heart of
Wellington's CBD. Built in 1927 it has
14 luxury suites themed in English
Georgian period. Restaurants, gym,
snooker. Excellent value.

Copthorne Hotel

Corner Boulcott St and Gilmer Terrace
Tel: 04 473 3750
Fax: 04 473 6329
copthorneplimmer.co.nz
Good hotel in the centre. 94 rooms,
mini bar, cable TV, Restaurant, Bar,
business centre, gym and sauna.

Duxton Hotel

170 Wakefield St.
Tel: 04 473 3900
Fax: 04 473 3929
res@wellington.duxton.co.nz
www.duxton.com
One of the city's best with 192 rooms
and suites with writing desk, internet
access, bar, air-conditioning. Award
winning restaurant, bar, gym

Museum Hotel

90 Cable St.
Tel: 04 385 2809
Fax: 04 802 8909
info@museumhotel.co.nz
Only minutes from centre, the hotel
has well appointed rooms with balconies with harbour views, cable TV,
restaurant, bar.

Novotel

133-127 the Terrace
Tel: 04 918 1900
Fax: 04 918 1901
reservations@novotelcap.co.nz.
As reliable as ever. Located in the centre. 139 rooms all with modem access
points, work desk, minibars, cable TV
and in-room safes. Restaurant and bar.

Ibis Hotel

153 Featherston St.
Tel: 04 496 1880
Fax: 04 496 1881
book_Wellington@ibishotels.co.nz
Another reliable chain with 200
comfortable rooms. Restaurant and
bar.

Portland Hotel of Thorndon

24 Hawkestone St.
Tel: 04 473 2208
Fax: 04 473 3892
Affordable, but luxurious central hotel.
Rooms en suite with colour TV and tea
and coffee making facilities. Restaurant
and bar.

Ruby House Bed and Breakfast

14b Kelburn Parade
Kelburn
Tel: 04 934 7930
Fax: 04 934 7935
Elizabeth@rubyhouse.co.nz
Villa style guesthouse boasting 3
beautifully decorated rooms. Only a
2 minute walk from the cable car to
Lambton Quay. A quality place to stay.

Finnimore House

2 Dransfield St.
Vogeltown
Tel: 04 389 9894
w.f.ryan@ztra.co.nz
Unique B&B with 2 large rooms. Fresh
flowers and internet facilities. A wonderful place to stay. Five minutes drive
to centre of Wellington.

Rosemere Backpackers'

6 MacDonald Crescent
Tel: 04 384 3041
rosemerebp@yahoo.com
Good backpackers' with single, twins,
doubles and shared rooms. Free breakfast, internet. Warm and friendly.

The Cambridge Hotel

Cambridge Terrace
Tel: 04 385 8829
info@cambridgehotel.co.nz
State of the art backpackers' in a heritage hotel. Sky TV, kitchen. Centrally
located with its own sports bar.

Rowena's Lodge

115 Brougham St.
Tel: 04 385 7872
rowenas@wellington backpackers.co.nz
Good backpackers' on the way to
ground. Clean and good value. Pool
table, piano, indoor and outdoor eating areas.

Airlines

ir New Zealand   0800 737 000
ntas   04 472 1100
                  04 472 9169

ses

s/Train/Ferry Information
                  04 801 7000
ercity Coachlines
llington Railway Station
nny Street   04 472 5111

rry

m North Island to South Island
erislander Cruise 0800 802802

ins

ewell 04 801 7000
nzMetro   04 498 3000 Ext
933
w.tranzmetro.co.nz

Taxis

Combined Taxis   04 384 4444
Airport & City Taxis 04 388 8900
Executive Taxi   04499 9955

Car Hire

Avis
25 Dixon St.
Tel: 04 801 8108
Fax: 04 382 9245

Thrifty Car Rental
Airport
Tel: 04 388 9494
Fax: 04 388 5862

Hertz
Corner Tory and Buckle St.
Tel: 04 384 3809

Budget
81 Ghuzner St.
Tel: 04 802 4548
Fax: 04 384 6470

Post Office

Manners Street Post Shop
Manners St.
: 04 473 5922

urist Information

ellington Visitor Information Centre
1 Wakefield St. (Civic Square)
: 04 802 4860
x: 04 802 4863
okings@wellingtonnz.com
w.wellingtonnz.com

ellington Information and Tourist
ntre
ble Care Centre
mbton Quay
: 04 473 3703

spital

ellington Hospital
ddiford St.
wton
: 04 3855 999

ter Hour Medical Centre
Adelaide Road
el: 04 384 4944

Climate

	Ave temp	rain cm
January	17	79
February	17	80
March	16	85
April	14	98
May	11	121
June	9	124
July	8	139
August	9	120
September	11	99
October	12	105
November	14	88
December	15	90

culture

Westpac Trust
St. James Theatre
77-87 Courtenay Place
Tel: 04 802 4060
Restored heritage building. Used for
musicals, opera and ballet.

BATS Theatre
1 Kent Terrace
Tel: 04 802 4175
bats@actrix.co.nz
New Zealand's development theatre.

Te Papa
Cable St.
Tel: 04 381 7000
Maps out the history of New Zealand,
the land, culture and its people. Open
10.00-18.00 Monday-Saturday

National War Memorial
7 Buckle St.
Tel: 04 385 2496
www.nzhistory.net .nz
Monday-Saturday 10.30-16.30 and
Sunday 12.30-16.30

The Film Centre
Corner Jervois Quay & Cable St.
Tel: 04 384 7647
New Zealand's tribute to film. Open
10.00-18.00 Monday to Saturday

Academy Gallery
Ground Floor
1 Queen Wharf
Tel: 04 499 8807
New work from New Zealand.

stats

Win/Loss Records

Country	Played	won	drawn	Lost	Tie
South Africa	5	4	1	-	-
England	9	3	5	1	-
Pakistan	6	2	4	-	-
Australia	7	2	4	1	-
West Indies	5	2	1	2	-
New Zealand	42	11	17	14	-
Zimbabwe	2	-	1	1	-
Sri Lanka	2	-	1	1	-
India	5	1	-	4	-
Bangladesh	1	-	-	1	-

Highest Individual Aggregates (New Zealand unless stated)

Player	Mat	Inn	NO	Runs	Ave	HS	0	50
Martin Crowe	10	17	1	1123	70.19	299	1	1
John Wright	13	23	2	1005	47.86	138	1	4
Andrew Jones	7	14	1	686	52.77	186	1	2
Nathan Astle	9	15	3	637	53.08	141	0	5
Craig McMillan	8	12	2	558	55.80	142	1	2
Stephen Fleming	10	16	0	493	30.81	67	1	4
Chris Cairns	9	14	0	504	36	109	0	3
Mark Richardson	6	10	1	499	55.44	89	50	1
Richard Hadlee	12	17	4	477	36.69	89	0	2
Bev Congdon	7	12	0	430	35.83	132	2	3

Top Wicket Takers (New Zealand unless stated)

Player	Mat	Bll	Md	Runs	Wkt	Ave	BB	FWI	S/R
Richard Hadlee	12	2623	90	1075	53	20.28	7/23	3	49.49
Daniel Vettori	9	2145	98	953	27	35.30	4/153	0	79.44
Chris Cairns	9	1620	48	855	27	31.67	5/44	1	60.00
Danny Morrison	8	1511	53	787	25	31.48	7/89	2	60.44
Richard Collinge	6	1292	31	573	22	26.05	3/35	0	58.73
Simon Doull	7	1346	56	718	20	35.90	7/65	2	67.30
Lance Cairns	6	1095	45	418	19	22.00	7/143	2	57.63
Dick Motz	4	836	30	396	17	23.29	6/69	1	49.18
Courtney Walsh (WI)	3	738	34	272	16	17.00	7/37	2	46.13
Ewen Chatfield	8	1559	88	563	15	37.53	4/66	0	103.93

Highest Individual Scores (New Zealand unless stated)

299	Martin Crowe	v Sri Lanka 1990-91
267	Aravinda de Silva (SL)	1990-91
255*	Jackie McGlew (SA)	1952-53
247*	Greg Chappell (Aus)	1973-74
214	Mathew Sinclair	v West Indies 1999-00
186	Andrew Jones	v Sri Lanka 1990-91
174*	Jeremy Coney	v England 1983-84

268

174	Martin Crowe	v Pakistan 1988-89
169	Saeed Anwar (Pak)	1993-94
166	Sadiq Mohammad (Pak)	1972-73

Best Bowling Returns (New Zealand unless stated)

8.3-0-23-7	Richard Hadlee	v India 1975-76
20.4-7-37-7	Courtney Walsh (WI)	1994-95
24-7-65-7	Simon Doull	v India 1998-99
28.3-5-76-7	Frank Woolley (Eng)	1929-30
26.4-5-89-7	Danny Morrison	v Australia 1992-93
37-7-119-7	Wasim Akram (Pak)	1993-94
45-10-143-7	Lance Cairns	v England 1983-84
15.2-8-18-6	Courtney Walsh (WI)	1994-95
13.3-4-26-6	Richard Hadlee	v England 1977-78
18-3-30-6	Shoab Akhtar (Pak)	2003-04

Highest Partnerships

Wkt	Runs	Batsmen	Match
1st	276	Stewie Dempster & Jackie Mills (NZ)	1929-1930 v England
2nd	241	John Wright & Andrew Jones (NZ)	1991-1992 v England
3rd	467	Andrew Jones & Martin Crowe (NZ)	1990-1991 v Sri Lanka
4th	229	Bev Congdon & Brian Hastings (NZ)	1973-1974 v Australia
5th	258	Salim Malik & Inzamam-Ul-Haq (Pak)	1993-1994
6th	232	Ian Botham & Derek Randall (Eng)	1983-1984
7th	246	Jackie McGlew & Anton Murray (SA)	1952-1953
8th	137	Daniel Vettori & Dion Nash (NZ)	1998-1999 v India
9th	163*	Colin Cowdrey & Alan Smith (Eng)	1962-1963
10th	48	Ian Smith & Ewen Chatfield (NZ)	1988-1989 v Pakistan

Results at Basin Reserve

Date	Opponent	Result
24/01/1930	England	drawn
04/03/1932	South Africa	lost by 8 wickets
29/03/1946	Australia	lost by an innings and 103 runs
24/03/1951	England	lost by 6 wickets
06/03/1953	South Africa	lost by an innings and 180 runs
03/03/1956	West Indies	lost by 9 wickets
01/03/1963	England	lost by an innings and 47 runs
21/02/1964	South Africa	drawn
22/01/1965	Pakistan	drawn
29/02/1968	India	lost by 8 wickets
07/03/1969	West Indies	won by 6 wickets
02/02/1973	Pakistan	drawn
01/03/1974	Australia	drawn
13/02/1976	India	won by an innings and 33 runs
10/02/1978	England	won by 72 runs
21/02/1981	India	won by 62 runs
26/02/1982	Australia	drawn
11/03/1983	Sri Lanka	won by 6 wickets
20/01/1984	England	drawn
18/01/1985	Pakistan	drawn
21/02/1986	Australia	drawn
20/02/1987	West Indies	drawn
03/03/1988	England	drawn
10/02/1989	Pakistan	drawn
15/03/1990	Australia	won by 9 wickets
31/01/1991	Sri Lanka	drawn
06/02/1992	England	drawn
04/03/1993	Australia	drawn
17/02/1994	Pakistan	lost by an innings and 12 runs
10/02/1995	West Indies	lost by an innings and 322 runs
06/02/1997	England	lost by an innings and 68 runs
19/02/1998	Zimbabwe	won by 10 wickets
26/12/1998	India	won by 4 wickets
18/03/1999	South Africa	lost Won by 8 wickets
26/12/1999	West Indies	won by an innings and 105 runs
24/03/2000	Australia	lost by 6 wickets
26/12/2000	Zimbabwe	drawn
26/12/2001	Bangladesh	won by an innings and 74 runs
21/03/2002	England	drawn
12/12/2002	India	won by 10 wickets
26/12/2003	Pakistan	lost by 7 wickets
26/03/2004	South Africa	lost by 6 wickets

The first ground to host a Test in Pakistan was the Bangabandhu
Stadium in Dhaka on the 1st January 1955 when Pakistan entertained India
for the first time. That ground is now Bangladesh's National Stadium. Since the
Test matches have been held regularly around Pakistan, even within cities.

The second Test of the Indian series was played two weeks later on 15th January 1955
in the Dring Stadium, Bahawalpur. Two weeks after that the Bagh-e-Jinnah Stadium i
hore staged the third. The Services Ground in Peshawar hosted the fourth Test of the
in February 1955. It proved to be its one and only Test. The National Stadium in Kara
became Pakistan's next Test venue when it hosted the fifth and final Test of the series a
end of February. All five matches ended in draws.

The Bagh-e-Jinnah Stadium was used for only three Tests between 1955 and 1959 bef
The Gaddafi Stadium took over as Lahore's Test venue. The first match played at the n
stadium was the second Test of the 1959 series against Australia which the visitors wo
seven wickets. The Pindi Cricket Club in Rawalpindi hosted its one and only Test in M
1965 when Pakistan beat New Zealand by an innings and 64 runs. Niaz Stadium in Si
held five Tests in the 70's and 80's, the first a draw against England in 1973, the last a s
wicket victory over New Zealand in November 1984. The Iqbal Stadium in Faisalabad
became the ninth Test venue in October 1978 when it staged the drawn first Test of th
series against India.

The Ibn-e-Qasim Stadium in Multan was awarded one Test, a draw with the West Ind
in December 1980. The Jinnah Stadium in Sailkot hosted four Tests between October
when Pakistan beat Sri Lanka by eight wickets and October 1995 when Sri Lanka reve
the result.

The Municipal Stadium in Gujranwala staged one drawn test with Sri Lanka in Decen
1991. The next ground to hold a Test was the Defence Housing Authority Stadium in
rachi which staged the first Test of the three match series against Zimbabwe in 1993.
ground has not been used since. Test cricket returned to the Rawalpindi in Decembe
1993 for the second match of the series and became the 13th Test ground in the
country.

Test cricket did not return to the city of Peshawar until September 1995 when Pakistan entertained Sri Lanka at the Arbab Niaz Stadium. The Sheikhuapura Stadium hosted two Tests in against Zimbabwe ¦d South Africa in 1996 and 1997. Both matches ended in draws and the ground ¦ not been used since. Multan Cricket Ground became the second ground in the ¦ and the 16th in the country to host Test cricket when Pakistan defeated Bangladesh ¦n innings and 264 runs in August 2001.

tance Between Cities (in kms)

	Faisalabad	Karachi	Lahore	Multan	Peshawar	Rawalpindi
¦alabad		1182	143	237	526	375
¦achi	1182		1293	945	1736	1568
¦ore	143	1293		348	443	275
¦tan	237	945	348		791	623
¦hawar	526	1736	443	791		167
¦valpindi	375	1568	275	623	167	

¦lines

¦ national airline is Pakistan International Airways. They also operate the domestic ¦ices. Flights inside Pakistan are inexpensive, unbelievably cheap if incorporated ¦ one's international ticket. It is by far the easiest way to travel around the country. ¦h of the cities that host cricket Tests has an airport but it should be noted that ¦re are no flights between Faisalabad and Lahore as the cities are so close together. ¦es and trains do make the journey.
¦istan International Airways 778 2851

¦ses

¦ch travel is a popular mode of transport for Pakistani people. The Daewoo Bus ¦npany operate luxurious coaches between the major cities. It is certainly the best ¦ion between Faisalabad and Lahore and a good option between those two cities and ¦valpindi, Multan and Peshawar. However, the journey from any of these cities to ¦achi can be quite strenuous as the journey is over 1,000km. Booking in advance is ¦ortant as seats are in great demand.

¦ins

¦n travel is inexpensive but the trains can get very overcrowded even in first class. ¦ certainly worth experiencing a trip but with flights so cheap and coach travel so ¦urious there is little justification for using the train system.

¦ Hire

¦st of the major hotels in each city have self drive/chauffeur service. Most visitors ¦ for the chauffeur service as driving can be quite intimidating. Driving habits are ¦tainly unique. An International Driving Licence is required and all drivers must be ¦r 21 years of age.

¦is

¦is are available outside all airports, hotels and many restaurants. The most popular ¦de of transport is the auto-rickshaw which can weave through the traffic and also ¦es you a feel of the city. Both the taxis and the rickshaws are very cheap.

¦nks

¦en generally 09.00-13.30 Monday-Thursday and Saturday and 09.00-12.00 on ¦days. It should be noted that it is impossible to change travellers' cheques in Multan, ¦salabad and Peshawar and difficult to do so in Lahore, Rawalpindi and Karachi. ¦erican Express travellers' cheques are the only option as they have offices in Lahore ¦ Karachi. Cash in US dollars or UK pounds is the only currency recognised by most ¦ks and money changers. There are a number of international ATM machines in the ¦ger cities but are very few and far between. The major hotels accept credit cards ¦owever the smaller ones deal in cash only.
Pakistan uses the Pakistani Rupee. Notes are issued in denominations of Rs1000, 500, 50, 10, 5, 2 and 1 and coins Rs2 and 1 and 50 and 25 paisa.

Embassies/Consulates

British High Commission
Diplomatic Enclave
Ramna 5
Islamabad
Tel: 051 2081 2000
Fax: 051 282 3439
cons.Islamabad@fco.go.uk

Australian High Commission
Corner of Constitution Ave and Ispahani Road
Diplomatic Enclave No. 1 Sector G5/4
Islamabad
Tel: 051 282 4345
Fax: 051 282 0112

New Zealand Consulate General
Suite 214
Glass Tower

Main Clifton Road
Karachi
Tel: 021 565 6993
Fax: 021 565 6995
mmf@cyber.net.pk

High Commission for the People's Repub
of Bangladesh
House No.1 Street No. 5 F 6/3
Islamabad
Tel: 051 279 267
Fax: 051 279 266

High Commission of India
G 5 Diplomatic Enclave
Islamabad
Tel: 051 814 371
Fax: 051 820 742
hicomind@isb.compol.com

Telecoms
Most hotels have International Direct Dialling. The public telephones do not operate int
nationally but most cities have a central telephone and telegraph office which has IDD a
open 24 hours a day. The dialling code is 92. The outgoing international code is 00.

Post
Opening hours vary but guideline times would be 09.00-18.00 Monday-Thursday, 09.00-
12.30 and 14.30-18.00 on Fridays and 09.00-14.30 on Saturday.

Tourist Offices
The Pakistan Tourism Development Corporation (PDTC) has offices in each city althou
some are better than others. The Multan office is excellent and informative, Lahore and
Peshawar are good and arrange excellent tours. The offices in Rawalpindi, Faisalabad and
Karachi have no information or leaflets.

Emergency Contact Numbers
Police   T15
Ambulance   T165
Fire   T16

Visas
All visitors must carry a passport valid for six months beyond departure date and require v
which are issued at Pakistan's Embassies. The cost depends on the country, the cost of a sin
entry visa to a British passport holder is £44. The visit entitles the holder to stay up to three
months and is valid for six month from the date of issue. Applicants must have photocopie
their passport, two passport size photographs and a return or onward ticket. The visa is usu
issued with 24 hours. It is a lot more complicated applying for a visa at the Pakistani Embas
in Delhi and travellers are advised to apply before leaving home. Any foreigner who stays ov
30 days must register at the Foreigners' Registration Office.

Customs
Visitors over the age of 18 may take the following goods into Pakistan without incurring
customs duty. 200 cigarettes, 250ml of perfume.

Time Difference
Pakistan is five hours ahead of GMT (GMT +5)

Electricity
220 volts AC at 50 cycles per second. Some hotels have adaptors.

Departure Tax
All visitors leaving Pakistan must pay Rs400.

the iqbal stadium

The Iqbal Stadium is run by the Faisalabad Cricket Association which is affiliated to the Punjab Association. It is a modern stadium on the outskirts of the city and an excellent venue.

The first Test held at the ground was against India in 1978. In a high scoring draw, the hosts amassed 503/8, Zaheer Abbas scoring 176 and Javed Miandad 154no. In reply India scored 462/9 dec., Gundappa Viswanath top scoring with 145. Asif Iqbal scored 104 in Pakistan's second innings total of 264/4 dec. but not surprisingly time ran out as the visitors reached 43/0.

In 1983 Pakistan had a historic ten wicket victory against India when four of their batsmen scored centuries in the first innings. India batted first, scoring 372 with Imran Khan taking 6/98. The home side replied with 652, the centurions being Javed (126), Zaheer (168), Saleem Malik (107) and Imran (117). Kapil Dev took 7/220 for India. In their second innings India could only manage 286, Sunil Gavaskar carrying his bat with 127no, to leave the hosts needing 10 runs for victory. Imran took another five wickets (5/82) and ended the match with a century and 11/180.

High scoring draws followed in 1984 and 1985 against England, India and Sri Lanka before the 1986 Test versus the West Indies which turned out to be an extraordinary match. Imran Khan scored 61 as Pakistan struggled to 159 in their first innings before the visitors took a lead of 89, Richie Richardson top scoring with 54 and Wasim Akram taking 6/91. In the second innings, Pakistan scored 328, Wasim top scoring with 66 to leave the West Indies a target of 240 for victory. Incredibly the visiting side, which included Greenidge, Haynes, Richardson, Gomes, Richards, Dujon and Harper, were dismissed for a paltry 53 as Pakistan won by 186. Abdul Qadir took 6/16 and Imran 4/30.

In 1990 Pakistan completed a fine comeback against New Zealand. Having been dismissed for 102 in the first innings with Chris Pringle taking 7/52, the home side trailed by 115 runs as New Zealand scored 217. Waqar Younis took 7/76. Shoaib Mohammad hit 142 as Pakistan reached 357 in the second innings to lead by 242 runs. The target was too high for the Kiwis who were routed for 127, Waqar again leading the bowling with 5/45 to end with match figures of 12/121, the best seen at the ground.

Seven years later, when Pakistan hosted South Africa, the Test at Faisalabad was an absolute thriller. South Africa batted first and scored 239, Gary Kirsten carrying his bat through the innings for 100no and sharing an eighth wicket partnership of 124 with spin bowler Pat Symcox. Wasim took 4/42. In reply Inzamam-ul-Haq top scored with 96 as the home side hit 308 to lead by 69 runs. South Africa promoted Symcox to no. 4 in the second innings and he duly obliged with a quick fire 51 to enable the visitors to reach 214. Set a target of 146 to win Pakistan collapsed to 92, Shaun Pollock taking 5/37 and man of the match Symcox 3/8.

The highest individual score on the ground is 235 by Greg Chappell in the high scoring draw in 1980 in a total of 617 for Australia. He shared a partnership of 217 with Graham Yallop (172). In the host's innings Talim Arif also hit a double century (210no). All 11 Australian players bowled, including wicket-keeper Rod Marsh who ended with figures of 10-1-51-0. Pakistan only lost two wickets and one of them, Zaheer Abbas, was a run out. The home side finished with 382/2.

The highest team score is 674/6 against India in 1984, the lowest the 53 by the West Indies. The highest run chase is 188/7 by Pakistan versus Sri Lanka in 1992.

The Iqbal Stadium's capacity is 20,000. The players' pavilion is at the south end of the ground. To the west of the pavilion are the Imran Khan (VIP), Hanif Mohammad, Zaheer Abbas, and Wasim Akram enclosures. On the east, the A. H. Karder enclosure is the most expensive and best along with the Senor and Javed Miandad enclosures. The Imran Khan and A. H. Karder enclosures are totally covered whereas the others are partially covered with huge tarpaulins held up by bamboo branches. It should be noted that the only toilet facilities in the ground are in the VIP enclosures.

Soft drinks and bottled water are sold down by the fence which circles the whole ground. Vendors move through the crowd with nuts, ricebread and sandwiches. Outside on the road leading to the ground there are stalls and cafés.

Tickets are available from any branch of the Allied Bank of Pakistan Ltd, the most convenient branch being at the Circle Office, 205 Regency Plaza, The Mall Road, (Tel 618 144) or from a kiosk directly opposite the players' pavilion.

The ground is 2km to the north of Faisalabad. It is a very pleasant 15-minute walk through the tree-lined suburban streets. The Serena Hotel is only five minutes walk from the ground. A rickshaw ride will cost no more than Rs25.

the city

Faisalabad is Pakistan's third largest city with a fast growing population of two million. It is situated in the province of Punjab in the north east, 360 km south of the capital Islamabad and 120km from Lahore. It was founded in the late 19th century when the lower Chenab canal made it possible to irrigate the land. Originally named Lyallpur after Sir Charles James Lyall, Chief Commissioner of the provinces and the Lieutenant Governor of the Punjab from1887 to 1892, the city was renamed Faisalabad in 1977 in memory of King Faisal of Saudi Arabia in recognition of services to Pakistan.

Known as the Manchester of Pakistan, it is the centre of the textile industry of the country. It is not a tourist destination and has no tourist information office or tourist information leaflets. The city is hot and humid and the combination of the heat, dust and the petrol fumes actually sting your eyes as you walk around the centre. The hotels advise that there is nothing of tourist interest in the city. This is not strictly true as the bazaars around the Clock Tower are worth a visit. These are busy, bustling markets in run-down streets and alleyways with broken footpaths. Small shops sell shoes, cloth, carpets, drugs and handicrafts. Each bazaar has its own specialities and it is not unusual to see seven or eight shops in a row selling the same product.

There are many banks on the edge of the city and money changers throughout the bazaars. Food is cooked on the side of the streets as chaotic traffic including tractors, donkey carts, rickshaws and taxis pass by. Hens walk up and down the streets, minding their own business as people go about their daily chores in a loud manner. The people are friendly and welcoming, however Urdu is the main language and not much English is spoken.

The Mall is situated to the north of the city and this is where many of the banks and airlines have their offices. It should be noted that changing traveller's cheques in Faisalabad is not possible. The US Dollar and the Sterling Pound can be changed at the money changers.

The choice of accommodation in the city is limited. The Serena hotel is by far the best and most expensive, however the Prime and Grace hotels both offer excellent alternatives at reasonable rates. There are a number of cheaper hotels in the bazaars but the standard is low. The three hotels mentioned above have good restaurants particularly the Serena with a choice of Pakistani, Continental and Chinese food. There are also some reasonable eateries in the bazaars.

When in Faisalabad to watch the cricket, the most sensible thing to do is to use the Serena even if you are not staying there. Non-residents can use the pool for Rs500 per day. It is quiet and relaxing and the service is excellent. There is also a gym, tennis and squash courts and an outdoor snooker table.

Serena Hotel

Club Road
Tel: 042 600428
629235
By far the best hotel in the city. 100 luxurious rooms, 2 fine restaurants, shopping mall, lovely swimming pool, gym. Rates very expensive. Worth pre-booking and enquiring about deals.

Prime

Allam Iqbal Road
Tel: 042 600030
628095
Fine hotel near the centre. Good comfortable en suite rooms with cable TV and all mod cons. Good restaurant and helpful staff.

Grace Hotel

Chinlot Bazaar
Circular Road
Tel: 042 602241
602243
New hotel in the centre. Excellent value. Well decorated rooms, with fine service and good restaurant.

Helpful and friendly staff. Best bargain in town.

Ray's Hotel

Allam Iqbal Road
Tel: 042 620062
Standard hotel with clean rooms and good food.

Sabina

Allam Iqbal Road
Tel: 042 628410
Good budget hotel with clean air-conditioned rooms with cable TV.

Restaurants

The Serena Hotel has 2 excellent restaurants serving Pakistani and Chinese food. The Prime and The Grace hotels have good restaurants and room service. The Quilim Restaurant in the People's Colony, D Ground serves good Chinese food. A lot of eateries in the bazaars serve food however the menus are usually in Urdu and communication can prove difficult!

Faisalabad Airport is small and 8km to the south west of the city along the treacherous Jhang Road. The road is full of huge potholes, erratic drivers and careless pedestrians. A taxi ride will cost Rs300. There are no banking or car rental services at the airport.

Airlines

There are no flights from Faisalabad to Lahore. Daily flights to Rawalpindi, Multan, Karachi and Peshawar.

Pakistan International Airways
The Mall
Tel: 042 634131
Opening hours 09.00-13.30 Monday to Thursday and Saturday, 09.00-12.30 Friday

Aero Asia
The Mall
Tel: 042 627023

Buses

The bus station is in Abdullahar Road. The Daewoo Bus Company run an air-conditioned bus service between Faisalabad and Rawalpindi (3 hours), Lahore (3) and Multan (4). Good punctual service.

Trains

The train station is at the end of The Mall at the east end of the city. Trains run regularly to Lahore (2 hours), Karachi (20), Rawalpindi (6), Peshaw. (8) and Multan (5).

Taxis

Taxis and rickshaws are available at the airport, outside hotels and in the streets. Always agree fare with the driver before commencing journey. Drivers tend to overcharge visitors so it is worth haggling to get a substanti. reduction.

Car Hire

Car hire with chauffeur or self drive i available from a desk in the foyer of t Serena Hotel in Club Road.

Post Office

General Post Office
Railway Road
Opening hours 09.00-18.00 Monday-Thursday, 09.00-12.30 and 14.30-18.00 Friday, 09.00-14.30 Saturday

Telecom

The area code for Faisalabad is 041. The three main hotels have International direct dialling.
Central Telephone and Telegraph Office
Circular Road
Opposite Grace Hotel
Circular Road
Open 24 hours a day

Tourist Information

There is no Tourist Information Centre in Faisalabad

Hospital

Saint Raphel Hospital
Railway Road
DHQ Hospital
The Mall

Climate

	ave temp	rain cm
January	12	9
February	16	11
March	21	20
April	28	13
May	32	12
June	36	12
July	33	49
August	32	34
September	31	12
October	26	1
November	20	4
December	13	8

Win/Loss Record

Country	Played	won	drawn	Lost	Tie
South Africa	2	1	1	-	-
West Indies	3	2	-	1	-
Pakistan	21	6	11	4	-
Sri Lanka	4	1	2	1	-
England	3	-	3	-	-
India	4	-	3	1	-
Australia	3	-	2	1	-
Zimbabwe	1	-	-	1	-
New Zealand	1	-	-	1	-

Highest Individual Aggregates (Pakistan unless stated)

Player	Mat	Inn	NO	Runs	Ave	HS	50	100
Javed Miandad	15	23	4	1068	56.21	203*	2	5
Saleem Malik	13	20	4	859	53.69	116	6	3
Zaheer Abbas	8	10	1	746	82.89	176	2	3
Qasim Umar	4	6	0	500	83.33	210	0	2
Mudassar Nazar	9	13	1	481	40.08	199	2	1
Moin Khan	7	12	2	423	42.30	80	4	0
Shoaib Mohammad	8	13	0	375	28.85	142	1	1
Imran Khan	9	12	1	345	31.36	117	1	1
Rameez Raja	7	13	1	335	27.92	75	3	0
Inzamam-ul-Haq	4	8	0	331	41.38	96	4	0

Top Wicket Takers (Pakistan unless stated)

Player	Mat	Bll	Md	Runs	Wkt	Ave	BB	S/R
Abdul Qadir	10	2711	94	1191	42	28.36	7/142	64.55
Wasim Akram	9	1909	67	936	41	22.83	6/48	46.56
Waqar Younis	5	1003	43	515	35	14.71	7/76	28.66
Iqbal Qasim	7	2144	95	830	29	28.62	6/89	73.93
Imran Khan	9	1619	75	703	26	27.04	6/98	62.27
Malcolm Marshall (WI)	3	402	7	249	15	16.60	4/24	26.80
Yuseef Ahmed	7	1170	48	465	15	31.00	3/18	78.00
Shaun Pollock (SA)	2	494	27	206	14	14.71	6/78	35.29
Saqlain Mushtaq	4	916	40	381	13	29.31	3/36	70.46
Aqib Javed	3	556	24	252	13	19.38	5/84	42.77

Highest Individual Scores (Pakistan unless stated)

235	Greg Chappell (Aus)	1979-80
210*	Taslim Arif	v Australia 1979-80
210	Qasim Umar	v India 1984-85
206	Qasim Umar	v Sri Lanka 1985-86
203*	Javed Miandad	v Sri Lanka 1985-86
199	Mudassar Nazar	v India 1984-85
176	Zaheer Abbas	v India 1978-79
172	Graham Yallop (Aus)	1979-80
168	Zaheer Abbas	v India 1982-83
157	Sidath Wettimuny (SL)	1981-82

Best Individual Bowling Performances (Pakistan unless stated)

9-4-52-7	Chris Pringle (NZ)	1990-91
10.2-13-76-7	Waqar Younis	v New Zealand 1990-91
41.5-12-142-7	Abdul Qadir	v Australia 1982-83
36.4-3-220-7	Kapil Dev (Ind)	1982-83
13-1-16-6	Abdul Qadir	v West Indies 1986-87
11-8-48-6	Wasim Akram	v Zimbabwe 1996-97
31.2-9-78-6	Shaun Pollock (SA)	2003-04
42-5-89-6	Iqbal Qasim	v West Indies 1980-81
35-3-91-6	Wasim Akram	v West Indies 1986-87
37-3-98-6	Imran Khan	v India 1982-83

Highest Partnerships

Wkt	Runs	Batsmen	Match
1st	141	Mohsin Khan & Mudassar Nazar (Pak)	1984-1985
2nd	250	Mudassar Nazar & Qasim Omar (Pak)	1984-1985
3rd	397	Qasim Omar & Javed Miandad (Pak)	1985-1986 v Sri Lanka
4th	287	Zaheer Abbas & Javed Miandad (Pak)	1982-1983 v India
5th	200	Sandeep Patil & Ravi Shastri (Ind)	1984-1985

stats

6th	207	Salim Malik & Imran Khan (Pak)	1982-1983
7th	167	David Gower & Vic Marks (Eng)	1983-1984
8th	124	Gary Kirsten & Pat Symcox (SA)	1997-1998
9th	62	Allan Border & Tim May (Aus)	1988-1989
10th	48	Rashid Khan & Tausif Ahmed (Pak)	1981-1982 v Sri Lanka

Results at Iqbal Stadium

Date	Countries	Result
16/10/1978	v India	drawn
06/03/1980	v Australia	drawn
08/12/1980	v West Indies	lost by 156 runs
14/03/1982	v Sri Lanka	drawn
30/09/1982	v Australia	won by an innings and 3 runs
03/01/1983	v India	won by 10 wickets
12/03/1984	v England	drawn
24/10/1984	v India	drawn
16/10/1985	v Sri Lanka	drawn
24/10/1986	v West Indies	won by 186 runs
07/12/1987	v England	drawn
23/09/1988	v Australia	drawn
23/11/1989	v India	drawn
26/10/1990	v New Zealand	won by 65 runs
23/11/1990	v West Indies	lost by 7 wickets
02/01/1992	v Sri Lanka	won by 3 wickets
15/09/1995	v Sri Lanka	lost by 42 runs
24/10/1996	v Zimbabwe	won by 10 wickets
24/10/1997	v South Africa	lost by 53 runs
17/12/1998	v Zimbabwe	abandoned
29/11/2000	v England	drawn
24/10/2003	v South Africa	drawn

karachi

The National Stadium is home to the Karachi Cricket Association which is affiliated to the Sind Association. Pakistan did not lose a Test there for 45 years until England beat them in 2000.

The first three Tests played in Karachi were played at another ground, Lawrence Gardens. But since then the stadium has hosted all Karachi Tests. India were the first opponents and it ended in a low scoring draw.

But in the next two years Pakistan recorded three big wins; against New Zealand, Australia and the West Indies. Faizal Mahmood took 13/144 (6/34 and 7/80) against Australia, dismissing them for 80, the lowest score on the ground, and 187. Pakistan won easily by nine wickets.

In the next 19 years Pakistan drew all but one of the ten Karachi Tests, the exception being an eight wicket victory over New Zealand in 1964/65. In 1978 Pakistan recorded a remarkable victory over their neighbours India. Safraz Nawaz took 4/89 as the visitors scored 344, Sunil Gavaskar scoring 111. Javed Miandad then hit 100 as Pakistan scored 481/9 before declaring. Gavaskar hit another century, 137, but Safraz took five more wickets as India were dismissed for 300. It left the home team a target of 164 in 25 overs. Javed and Imran Khan were promoted up the order and brought their side home with eight wickets and one ball to spare. Four years later Pakistan recorded another emphatic victory over India by an innings and 86 runs. Zaheer Abbas (186) and Mudasser Nazar (119) scoring centuries and Imran taking match figures of 11/79 (3/19 and 8/60).

The 1984 Test against England proved to be a thriller. England could only manage 182 as Abdul Qadir took 5/74. Saleem Malik top scored with 74 as the home side replied with 277, Nick Cook taking 6/65 for England. In the second innings David Gower hit his second 50 of the match, but his side collapsed to 159, leaving a target of only 65 runs for victory. Cook was on fire, bowling 14 overs, eight maidens and taking 5/18 but Pakistan limped home by three wickets.

Ten years later the Test with Australia was probably the greatest match played at the National Stadium. Batting first, Australia made 337, Michael Bevan top scoring with Wasim Akram, Waqar Younis and Mustaq Ahmed taking three wickets each. The home side replied with 256, Saeed Anwar hitting 85. In their second innings Australia were cruising, at 171/2, David Boon scoring 114 and Mark Waugh 61 before losing their last eight wickets for 61 runs. Wasim took 5/63 and Waqar 4/69. Chasing 314 for victory the home side started well with Saeed hitting 77, but Shane Warne took 5/89 as Pakistan collapsed to 258/9 before Inzamam-ul-Haq (58no) and Mushtaq (20no) scored a last wicket partnership of 57 to bring their side home in one of the greatest Pakistani victories of all time in the highest run chase at the National Stadium.

Pakistan's remarkable, unbeaten record came to an end in 2000 despite a flying start scoring 405 with Inzamam (142) and Yousuf Youhana (117) hitting centuries. England replied with 388, Mike Atherton leading with 125, to keep the deficit to 17 runs. Ashley Giles and Darren Gough took three wickets each as the home side crumbled to 158 all out in their second innings. Set 176 to win England got home by six wickets in near darkness, Graham Thorpe scoring 64no.

Three batsmen have scored centuries in both innings at Karachi, Bobby Simpson (153 and 115) for Australia in 1964, Gavaskar in 1978 and Yashir Hameed (170 and 105) against Bangladesh in 2003. Hameed became only the second debutant to achieve this feat, the other being Lawrence Rowe of the West Indies in Kingston against New Zealand in 1971. In the 1973 Test with England three batsmen were dismissed on 99. Majid Khan, Mushtaq Mohammad and Dennis Amiss. The highest team score is 565/9 versus New Zealand in 1976.

No hat-tricks have been taken at the National Stadium, but Intikhab Alam is one of only 13 Test players to take a wicket with their first ball in Test cricket when he dismissed Colin McDonald of Australia in 1959.

The National Stadium is a huge ground with a capacity of 50,000. However, just as in Lahore, Test matches do not attract big crowds and the attendance can be as low as 500 to 1,000 whereas crowds of 15,000 to 25,000 attend one-day internationals. The ground is situated 8km outside the city along the M. A. Jinnah Road and Pir Sibghat Ullah Shah Road. A taxi should cost no more than Rs120, a rickshaw slightly less. Security is tight around the ground and there is absolutely no parking nearby. Cameras and other electrical items are not allowed and everyone must walk through metal detectors upon entering the ground.

The ground is totally enclosed by its huge stands with protection from the sun being offered by cover. The Javed Miandad and Fazal Mahmood are the VIP enclosures on each side of the pavilion at the south end of the ground and provide an excellent view of the cricket. The general enclosures include areas dedicated to Wasim Akram, Asif Iqbal, Wasim Bari, Intikab Alam, Majid Khan, Zaheer Abbas. The massive Mohammad Brothers enclosure at the north end of the ground is the most popular with the locals.

Soft drinks and water are available down by the fence which circles the entire ground and vendors wander through the crowd selling mostly Pakistani food. There are no vendors or foodstalls outside.

Tickets are available from the Allied Pakistan Bank Ltd, the most convenient branch being at the ABI Building, Bath Island, Khayabar-e-Iqbal, Clifton in Karachi (Tel: 586 0052) or from the ground. The ticket office is just to the right of the main entrance. Tickets for the VIP enclosures for Test matches cost Rs200 but can cost up to Rs1200 for one-day internationals.

the city

Karachi is Pakistan's largest city with a population of 9.5 million and was the capital of the country until 1959 when Rawalpindi became the interim capital while Islamabad was built. Karachi is now the capital of the Sind Province. It is situated in the south east of the country on the Indus River delta on the Arabian Sea.

It was first developed in the 18th century as a small fishing village called Kalachi-jo-Goth. Hindu merchants used the village to trade from and by the time the British arrived in 1843 it was one of the subcontinent's leading ports. The city grew rapidly and became the capital upon independence in 1947.

The city is a mixture of old and new, east and west. Tall modern buildings mingling with elegant old buildings indicate the speed at which it is growing.

It contains some of Pakistan's most memorable buildings. The burial place of the father of the nation, The Quaid-I-Azam Muammad Ali Jinnah Mausoleum, is the premier tourist attraction. Wazir Mansion, his birthplace, another beautiful piece of architecture, is also a national treasure. The Defence Housing Society Mosque has the largest single dome of its kind in the world. With its limestone walls and pink towers Frere Hall is another unique building. Karachi is also home to the National Museum of Pakistan.

In the old city the colourful bazaars are a complete contrast to the modern areas. There are narrow lanes with wonderful markets selling handicrafts, carpets, art and ceramics to name but a few. As in the other Pakistani cities everyone is genuinely friendly and helpful. Security is tight on the streets with armed police and the army and at the major hotels.

There is a good selection of accommodation in Karachi from five star hotels to budget accommodation. All the five star hotels are in the centre of the city. The cheaper hotels are clean and comfortable. All the top hotels have a number of restaurants offering a variety of Pakistani, Chinese and Continental food and there are some other good restaurants and snack bars.

The Pearl Continental and The Sheraton have swimming pools which can be used by non-residents for a day fee of Rs500, a wonderful way to cool down and relax. The pool areas are luxurious, always quiet and the service is excellent. Karachi has a number of beaches, some which are safe for swimming, yachting, fishing and windsurfing. There is more to do in the evenings than the other cricket cities. In addition to the restaurants, there are plenty of cinemas to visit.

Quaid-e-Azam's Mausoleum

The father of the nation is laid to rest in this White Marble Mausoleum on M. A. Jinnah Road in the heart of the city. Designed in 1970, it is one of Karachi's principal landmarks and is a subject of pilgrimage for people from far and wide. A magnificent four- tiered crystal chandelier, a gift from China, hangs inside the walls and under the huge semi-circular dome. A changing of the guard ceremony takes place every day.

The National Museum

Houses a collection of artefacts relating to the country's ancient heritage. Displays include Indus civilisation items, Gandhara sculptures, Islamic art and manuscripts depicting Pakistan's political history, oil paintings and coin collections. The museum is located on Dr. Ziouddin Ahmed Road in the city.

Masjid-e-Tooba

Said to be the largest single dome mosque in the world. It is a wonderful piece of architecture and is surrounded by beautiful grounds in the Defence Housing Authority of the city.

Empress Market

A tall clock tower overlooks the market in the centre of the Saddar area. It is primarily a food market. It is a sprawling place with a wonderful atmosphere. The spice hall is probably the most interesting section with cone shaped mounds of every conceivable spice. Other bazaars include the nearby Bohri Bazaar which sells household goods, the Zanab Market, the handicraft and clothing market and the Co-operative Market which specialises in wooden carvings and clothing.

Beaches

Karachi has some wonderful beaches. Clifton beach, the most popular, is closest to the city. French beach is renowned as the best with the cleanest water and white sands. There are other beaches at Hawke Bay, 20km from the city and known for its views and its tanning huts and Sand Spit, similar

Quaid-e-Azam International Airport is 12km east of Karachi along the Shahrah-e-Faisal Road. It has been recently refurbished. Both international and domestic terminals are housed in the same building. A taxi ride to the city takes up to 45 minutes and will cost between Rs250 and Rs300. Metro Taxi have a well organised office outside international arrivals. Major hotels run shuttle services to and from the airport. There is a public bus, but it very crowded and uncomfortable and takes well over an hour to reach the centre of Karachi. Banks are open 24 hours a day and there are money changers in the arrivals hall and outside on the concourse. There are a number of cafés, a snack bar and a McDonald's restaurant outside the airport beside the taxi rank.

to Hawke Bay with the added attraction of turtle watching in the evenings.

Karachi Sheraton
Club Road
Tel: 021 568 1021
Fax: 021 568 2875
kschbcl@cyber.net.pk
A luxurious hotel in the centre. 407 excellent rooms, two restaurants, cake shop, shopping mall, business centre, rent-a-car, swimming pool and gym.

Pearl Continental
Club Road
Tel: 021 111505505
Fax: 021 5681835
hotelkhi@khi.comsats.net.pk
Probably the best hotel in Karachi. 290 fine rooms, 3 restaurants, business centre, hairdressers, supermarket, book shop, wonderful swimming pool, squash court and gym.

Holiday Inn Crown Plaza
Shahrah-e-Faisal
Tel: 021 5660611
Fax: 021 5683146
Luxurious with excellent rooms, 2 restaurants, business centre, swimming pool, squash court and gym.

The Marriott
Abdullah Harron Road
Tel: 021 568 0111
Fax: 021 5681610
Fine hotel with restaurant, coffee shop, business centre, swimming pool and gym.

Avari Towers
Fatimah Jinnah Road
Tel: 021 566 0100
Fax: 021 568 0310
Good hotel with restaurants, business centre, swimming pool and gym.

Beach Luxury
MT Khan Road
Tel: 021 561 1031
Fax: 021 561 1625
Rasonably priced hotel by the beach. 85 rooms with all mod cons, swimming pool and a number of restaurants.

Sarawan Hotel
Raja Ghazanfar Ali Road
Tel: 021 516001
Fax: 021 568 0278
Budget hotel in the heart of the city. Good clean en suite rooms with cable TV. Good restaurant with friendly and helpful staff.

Sky Towers
Raja Ghazanfar Ali Road
Tel: 021 567 5211
Another budget hotel in the centre. Spacious air-conditioned rooms, more apartment than a hotel. Restaurant on ground floor.

There are a number of good restaurants in Karachi including the Chranda Rooftop Restaurant at the Pearl Continental and the á la carte restaurant and the coffee shop in the Sheraton. Other restaurants include the Grand Plaza Revolving Restaurant in North Nazimabad (021 664 6461) which serves Pakistani and continental food and has wonderful views of the city and the Arizona Grill, a steakhouse on Zamzama Boulevard in Clifton.

Post Office
General Post Office
II Chundrigar Road

Tourist Information
Pakistan Tourist Development Corporation
Tourist Information Centre
Aga Markaz

PTDC
Shafi Chambers
Club Road
Tel: 021 920 2971

PTDC
International Arrivals Lounge
Airport

Hospital
Civil Hospital
M. A. Jinnah Road
Tel: 021 772 9719

Jinnah Post Graduate Medical Centre
Rafique Shaheed Road
Tel: 021 520039

Airlines

Regular flights to Faisalabad (2 a day), Multan (2), Peshawar (2), Islamabad (6) and Lahore (8).

Pakistan International Airways,
Sidco Centre,
Strachan Road
Tel: 021 778 2851

Emirates
265A R. A. Lines
Sarwar Road
Tel: 021 568 3377

British Airways
Marriot Hotel
Tel: 021 568 6071

Trains

Regular trains to Lahore (17 hours), Multan (12), Faisalabad (16), Rawalpindi (28) and Peshawar (32).

Train Enquiries 117
City Railway Reservations
II Chundrigar Road
Tel: 021 241 3707

Taxis

Metro Car Service is a reliable taxi firm and has an office directly outside international arrivals at the airport. Telephone 568 4294. Rickshaws are a very convenient and cheap alternative. There are always taxis and rickshaws outside hotels and they can easily be waved down in the street.

Car Hire

Each of the major hotels has a self-drive/chauffeur service in their lobbies. Driving in Karachi is very difficult and most visitors tend to use the chauffeur service which is approximately the same price as self drive.

Avis Rent A Car Pakistan
74F Block 6 P.E.C.H.S.
Tel: 021 454 0670
Fax: 021 454 0212

transport

Climate

	ave temp	rain cm
January	13	7
February	20	10
March	24	10
April	28	3
May	30	0
June	42	10
July	30	90
August	29	58
September	28	27
October	27	3
November	24	3
December	20	5

Win/Loss record

Country	Played	Won	Drawn	Lost	Tie
Pakistan	36	18	17	1	-
England	7	1	5	1	-
India	5	-	3	2	-
New Zealand	6	-	3	3	-
West Indies	6	-	3	3	-
Australia	8	-	3	5	-
Bangladesh	1	-	-	1	-
Sri Lanka	3	-	-	3	-

Highest Individual Aggregates (Pakistan unless stated)

Player	Mat	Inn	NO	Runs	Ave	HS	50	100
Javed Miandad	17	25	1	1393	58.04	211	8	3
Saleem Malik	13	19	4	855	57.00	119*	3	4
Shoaib Mohammad	5	8	2	642	107.00	203*	4	1
Mudassar Nazar	11	15	2	615	47.31	152	4	2
Majid Khan	9	13	0	579	44.54	112	3	2
Hanif Mohammad	10	16	2	556	39.71	103	3	2
Zaheer Abbas	12	20	3	531	31.24	186	1	1
Inzamam-ul-Haq	6	11	3	529	66.13	142	2	2
Imran Khan	11	16	7	523	58.11	109*	3	1
Saeed Ahmed	6	10	2	478	59.75	172	2	1

Top Wicket Takers (Pakistan unless stated)

Player	Mat	Bll	Md	Runs	Wkt	Ave	BB	S/R
Abdul Qadir	13	3654	128	1571	59	26.63	5/44	61.93
Imran Khan	11	2406	99	938	51	18.39	8/60	47.18
Iqbal Qasim	9	2911	179	897	44	20.39	7/49	66.16
Wasim Akram	8	1957	71	827	41	20.17	5/63	47.73
Waqar Younis	7	1278	33	672	38	17.68	5/76	33.63
Fazal Mahmood	6	1841	109	541	32	16.91	7/80	57.53
Intikhab Alam	8	1875	56	828	26	31.85	4/39	72.12
Tauseef Ahmed	7	1626	99	530	25	21.20	5/54	65.04
Sarfraz Nawaz	10	2215	67	880	23	38.26	5/70	96.30
Kapil Dev (Ind)	4	1037	29	569	18	31.61	5/102	57.61

Highest Individual Scores (Pakistan unless stated)

211	Javed Miandad	v Australia 1988-89
206	Javed Miandad	v New Zealand 1976-77
205	Ted Dexter (Eng)	1961-62
203*	Shoaib Mohammad	v New Zealand 1990-91
186	Zaheer Abbas	v India 1982-83
172	Saeed Ahmed	v New Zealand 1964-65
170	Yasir Hameed	v Bangladesh 2003
166	Khalid Ibadulla	v Australia 1964-65
160	Aamer Sohail	v West Indies 1997-98
153	Bob Simpson (Aus)	1964-65

Best Individual Bowling Performances (Pakistan unless stated)

20.1-4-60-8	Imran Khan	v India 1982-83
42-22-49-7	Iqbal Qasim	v Australia 1979-80
33-7-66-7	Phil Edmonds (Eng)	1977-78
48-17-80-7	Fazal Mahmood	v Australia 1956-57
46.5-17-87-7	Ray Bright (Aus)	1979-80
30.1-3-99-7	Mohammad Nazir	v New Zealand 1969-70

27-11-34-6	Fazal Mahmood	v Australia	1956-57
46.3-21-42-6	Zulfiqar Ahmed	v New Zealand	1955-56
22.3-2-46-6	Imran Khan	v West Indies	1986-87
28-10-49-6	Ram Ramchand (Ind)		1954-55

Highest Partnerships

Wkt	Runs	Batsmen	Match
1st	298	Aamir Sohail & Ijaz Ahmed (Pak)	1997-1998 v West Indies
2nd	178	Hanif Mohammad & Saeed Ahmed (Pak)	1958-1959 v West Indies
3rd	196	Shoaib Mohammad & Javed Miandad (Pak)	1988-1989 v Australia
4th	259	Inzamam-Ul-Haq & Yousuf Youhana (Pak)	2000-2001 v England
5th	213	Zaheer Abbas & Mudassar Nazar (Pak)	1982-1983 v India
6th	178*	Salim Malik & Wasim Raja (Pak)	1984-1985 v New Zealand
7th	186	Warren Lees & Richard Hadlee (NZ)	1976-1977
8th	100	Bryan Yuile & Dayle Hadlee (NZ)	1969-1970
9th	127	Haroon Rashid & Rashid Khan (Pak)	1981-1982 v Sri Lanka
10th	63	Bev Congdon & Frank Cameron (NZ)	1964-1965

Results at The National Stadium

Date	Countries	Result
26/02/1955	v India	drawn
13/10/1955	v New Zealand	won by an innings and 1 Run
11/10/1956	v Australia	won by 9 wickets
20/02/1959	v West Indies	won by 10 wickets
04/12/1959	v Australia	drawn
02/02/1962	v England	drawn
24/10/1964	v Australia	drawn
09/04/1965	v New Zealand	won by 8 wickets
06/03/1969	v England	drawn
24/10/1969	v New Zealand	drawn
24/03/1973	v England	drawn
01/03/1975	v West Indies	drawn
30/10/1976	v New Zealand	drawn
18/01/1978	v England	drawn
14/11/1978	v India	won by 8 wickets
27/02/1980	v Australia	won by 7 wickets
22/12/1980	v West Indies	drawn
05/03/1982	v Sri Lanka	won by 204 runs
22/09/1982	v Australia	won by 9 wickets
23/12/1982	v India	won by an innings and 86 runs
30/01/1983	v India	drawn
02/03/1984	v England	won by 3 wickets
10/12/1984	v New Zealand	drawn
07/11/1985	v Sri Lanka	won by 10 wickets
20/11/1986	v West Indies	drawn
16/12/1987	v England	drawn
15/09/1988	v Australia	won by an innings and 188 runs
15/11/1989	v India	drawn
10/10/1990	v New Zealand	won by an innings and 43 runs
15/11/1990	v West Indies	won by 8 wickets
28/09/1994	v Australia	won by 1 Wicket
06/12/1997	v West Indies	won by 10 wickets
22/10/1998	v Australia	drawn
12/03/2000	v Sri Lanka	won by 222 runs
07/12/2000	v England	lost by 6 wickets
20/08/2003	v Bangladesh	won by 7 wickets

lahore

gadaffi stadium

The Gadaffi Stadium – named after the Libyan ruler who provided the finance to upgrade it for the 1996 World Cup – is home to the Lahore Cricket Association which is affiliated to the Punjab Association. It became the second Test ground in Lahore after the Bagh-e-Jinnah Stadium hosted three Test matches in the 1950's. It has a capacity of more than 50,000.

The first Test there was a seven wicket defeat against Australia in 1959. Australia amassed 391/9 before declaring 245 ahead, Norm O'Neill top scoring with 134. Lindsay Kline then took 7/75 as the home side reached 366 in their second innings, Saeed Ahmed scoring 166. Set 123 for victory, O'Neill was unbeaten on 43 as he saw his team home.

Two years later Pakistan were again on the receiving end, this time against England. Their first innings score was 387/9 declared, Javed Burki top scoring with 138. The visitors came within seven runs of this total, Ken Barrington scoring 139no and Mike Smith 99. Allan Brown, David Allen and Bob Barber then each took three Pakistani wickets as they were dismissed for exactly 200. Set 208 to win, England, led by Ted Dexter, with 66no, reached their target with five wickets to spare.

It was not until 1976 that Pakistan won their first match at Lahore. After a succession of draws following these early losses, they defeated New Zealand by six wickets. Batting first, the hosts limped to 55/4 before Javed Miandad (163) and Asif Iqbal (166) shared a fifth wicket partnership of 281 until Javed fell to Peter Petherick at 336. With his next deliveries Petherick took the wickets of Wasim Raja and Intikhab Alam to record the second hat-trick on the ground and to become the only New Zealand bowler ever to take a hat-trick. But Pakistan still reached 417, Richard Hadlee taking 5/121. New Zealand had to follow-on after mustering only 157 as Intikhab Alam took 4/35. The visitors led by Mark Burgess (111) and Robert Anderson (92) made 360 in their second innings to set the home side a target of 101. Pakistan reached their target for the loss of four wickets.

Two years later India paid their first visit to the Gadaffi Stadium which resulted in an eight wicket win for Pakistan. Imran Khan (5/54) and Safraz Nawaz (4/46) restricted India to 199. before the home side replied with 539/6 dec, Zaheer Abbas hitting 235. Despite an opening partnership of 192 by Sunny Gavaskar (97) and Chetan Chauhan (93), India were dismissed for 465 leaving a target of 126.

Pakistan's next win came against Sri Lanka. Roy Dias hit 109 for the visitors as they struggled to 240 in their first innings, Imran Khan ripping through their [li]ne up with 8/58. In reply the home side declared at 500/7, a lead of 260, Moshin Khan [1]29) and Zaheer Abbas (134) scoring centuries. Imran started where he left off in the [fi]rst innings when he took another six wickets in Sri Lanka's second innings as the visi[to]rs collapsed to 158 all out giving victory to Pakistan by 102 runs.

[In] 1987 Abdul Qadir single-handedly demolished England taking nine wickets as the vis[it]ors were dismissed for 175. Mudassar Nazar made 120 as the hosts amassed 392 before [di]smissing the visitors for 130 in their second innings to win by an innings and 87 runs. [Q]adir was the hitman again with 4/45.

[P]akistan have suffered two defeats at Lahore in recent years; to New Zealand and Sri [La]nka. New Zealand recovered from a 36 run first innings deficit to win by 44 runs in [19]96 and a wonderful 230 by Kumar Sangakarra set up an eight-wicket victory for Sri [La]nka in 2002.

[T]wo Pakistani partnership records were scored at the Stadium. Javed Miandad and Asif [I]qbal shared a fifth wicket stand of 281 against the New Zealanders in 1976 and Majid [K]han and Hanif Mohammad, a sixth wicket stand of 217 also against New Zealand in [19]65. Allan Border of Australia (150no and 153) in 1979 and Wajahatullah Wasti (133 [a]nd 121no) versus Sri Lanka in 1988 are the only batsmen to score centuries in both [in]nings at Lahore.

[T]he highest team score was 699/5 against India in 1989 and the lowest 73 by New [Z]ealand in 2002 after conceding 643 runs as Inzamam hit his record score. England's [ru]n-chase is the best.

[Im]ran Khan's figures of 14/116 in 1982 are the best on the ground eclipsing Qadir's [1]3/101 against England. Four bowlers have taken Test hat-tricks in Lahore, Wes Hall at [th]e old Bagh-e-Jinnah Stadium for the West Indies in 1958, Petherick for New Zealand [in] 1976, Wasim Akram versus Sri Lanka in 1998 and Mohammad Sami also against Sri [La]nka in 2002.

[T]he Gaddafi Stadium is situated to the south of the city in the FCC area. Unfortunately [La]horites do not show up in great numbers for Test cricket and the stadium can feel very [e]mpty with less than 1,000 spectators in the ground. Crowds in the region of 20,000 [at]tend one-day internationals.

[T]he players' pavilion at the south end of the ground is a large building with corpo[ra]te facilities and private boxes above the players' area. Officials and players can watch [th]e game from the grassed area on the boundary in front of the pavilion. The rest of [th]e ground is surrounded by high fences. To the right of the pavilion is the patrons' [en]closure and the Fazal Mahmood VIP enclosure. On the east side of the ground are [th]e Kadar Nazar, Majid Khan and Abdul Qadir enclosures. The Qadir enclosure is very [po]pular and the cheapest in the ground. At the north end there are four enclosures in [on]e stand named after Waqar Younis, Wasim Akram, Mohammad Hussein and Khan [M]ohammad. Along the west side of the ground the Saeed Anwar enclosure is usually [b]usy, however the Hanif Mohammad and Intiaz Ahmed are very quiet. The Imran Khan [en]closure on the left of the pavilion is another VIP enclosure and is probably the best [v]antage point in the public areas. The Lahore crowd appreciate good cricket and applaud [go]od shots and fielding from both sides.

[So]ft drinks and water are available at the fence which surrounds the ground and ven[d]ors make their way through the stands selling sweets, nuts, sandwiches and traditional [P]akistani food. Some excellent food can be obtained in the more expensive stands. There [ar]e no vendors outside the ground.

[T]ickets are available from any branch of the Allied Bank of Pakistan, the most conve[ni]ent being on the Main Boulevard in Gulberg 111 (Telephone 576 4018). It is not essen[ti]al to obtain tickets beforehand as tickets are sold at every gate around the ground. Even [a]t the one-day internationals orderly queues and good organisation lead to a short wait. [Se]curity is tight at the gates and all bags are thoroughly searched. Pass-outs are available [w]hich can be important as there are few toilet facilities in the ground.

[T]he ground is some way from the centre of Lahore and the easiest way to reach it is by [r]ickshaw (Rs60) or taxi (Rs100) which are always available outside the ground. Parking [i]s very limited.

Lahore has been the capital of the province of Punjab for nearly 1,000 years and was the capital of West Pakistan from 1955 to 1970. It is Pakistan's second largest city with a population of six million. Situated in North East Pakistan, east of the Himalayas, it is 37km from the Indian border. The centre is 2km south of the River Ravi which passes in a semi circle through the north side. The city is built in the form of a parallelogram with wonderful examples of Mughal, Islamic and British architecture. It is a beautiful place, full of life and colour with historical forts and mosques.

Hindu legend traces Lahore back to the two sons of Rama, Loh and Lova more than 4,000 years ago. The Hindu ruler, Lalitiditya, is associated with Lahore in the 8th century and it is recorded that the Muslim Turkish Ghaznovids captured the city in 1036 making it capital of their empire. The Ghari Sultans of Afghanistan conquered the city in 1186 before it was razed by Mongol invaders led by Genghis Khan. From 1525 to 1725 the city was the capital and showpiece of the Mughal empire. As the empire disintegrated the Sikhs took control in the mid-18th century and held power until the British took over in 1849.

Lahore is a banking and commercial centre and also acts as a distribution centre for industries in the surrounding areas including textiles, chemicals, machinery, electrical components, rubber, iron, steel, silver and gold handicrafts and most importantly agriculture. It is a railway and air centre and is also the hub of the publishing industry in Pakistan.

The city has many wonderful monuments, mosques, forts and shrines. In Mughal times a 10 metre wall surrounded the Old City with 13 gates, some of which still remain today. Wazir Khan's Mosque is regarded as one the most beautiful in the world. It stands in the Kashmir Bazaar in the old city, along with the Pearl and Golden Mosques, other wonderful examples of arabesque artwork. The Tomb of Rangit Singh, the only Sikh leader buried in Pakistan, and the tombs of Emperor Jehangir and Allama Muhammad Iqbal, the poet-philosopher of the East, are the most visited of the many shrines and mausoleums dedicated to Emperors and Muslim saints.

The Mughal style Shalimar Gardens, 5km to the east of Lahore, on the grand Trunk Road has 450 magnificent fountains and provides the perfect getaway from the bustling city.

The city is alive with its busy streets and colourful bazaars. A mixture of painted trucks, cars, bullock carts, buses, handcarts, rickshaws and scooters battle for supremacy on its streets. There are some wonderful bazaars including the Kashmir Dabai and Anarkali in the old city where one can find some tremendous bargains. The bazaars have everything, but the small shops and stalls where the silver and goldsmiths produce their wares are special.

It should be noted that even if one does not stay in the top hotels, the restaurant are still accessible and the swimming pool and gym can be used on payment of a small tariff (Rs300 – 500). This can be a great way to end a day of sightseeing or cricket watching.

Lahore International Airport is 6km to the east of the city along Shahrah-e-Azz Bhatti Road. Both domestic and international terminals are in the same building. A taxi ride to the city takes 20 minutes and costs Rs300. A rickshaw will take a little longer and should be considerably cheaper. The larger hotels have shuttle buses running to and from the airport. There are 24 hour banks at the airport, along with money changers in and outside the arrivals hall. There are several small snack bars. Only people travelling are allowed into the airport and security is very tight.

Post Office

General Post Office
Shahrah-e-Quaid-e-Azam (The Mall)
Tel: 042 724 3580

Telecom

The Telephone and Telegraph Office
Shahrah-e-Quaid-e-Azam (The Mall)
Opposite GPO
Open 24 hours a day.

Tourist Information

Pakistan Development Tourism
Corporation
Tourist Information Centre
Room 3, Faletti's Hotel
Egerton Road
Tel: 042 630 6528

TDCP Tourist Information
Centre
4A Lawrence Road
Tel: 042 636 0553

Hospital

Mayo Hospital
Off The Mall
Tel: 042 921 1100

Sir Ganga Ram Hospital
Sharah-e-Fatima
Tel: 042 631 2152

Lady Willingdon Hospital
Hospital Road
Off Circular Road
Tel: 042 765 9001

Airlines

There are numerous flights to
Rawalpindi (6 a day at 40 minutes),
Peshawar (2 a day and 1 hour duration), Multan (2 a day and 1 hour)
and Karachi (4 a day and 2 hours).
There are no flights to Faisalabad.

Pakistan International Airways
PIA Tower
Egerton Road
Tel: 042 6270 5234

British Airways
Transport House
Egerton Road
Tel: 042 630 0701

Buses

The long distance bus station is in
Kalma Chowk on Ferozpur Road.
Daewoo run air-conditioned services
to Rawalpindi, Faisalabad and Multan.
Tel: 042 586 3743.

Trains

Lahore City Station is just the outside
the Old City. Trains run to Faisalabad
(3 hours), Multan (6), Rawalpindi
(6), Peshawar (10) and Karachi
(17). Enquiries T117 or 9201772.

Taxis

Taxis and rickshaws are available
at the airport, outside hotels and
in the streets. Always agree fares with
drivers before commencing journey.
Drivers tend to overcharge visitors so
it is worth haggling.

Car Hire

Avis Rent A Car
23 Empress Road
Ali Complex
Tel: 042 631 4630
Fax: 042 636 6146

Budget Rent a Car
7 Race Course Road
Tel: 042 630 9003
Fax: 042 630 9005

Europcar
Shop 6, Lower Ground Floor,
Grand Hotel
9 Davis Road
Tel: 042 630 7387
Fax: 042 630 7099

There are also car hire companies at
all the major hotels including Pearl
Continental, Holiday Inn and
Faletti's.

transport

Climate

	ave temp	rain cm			
January	12	25	July	32	155
February	15	24	August	31	135
March	20	27	September	30	62
April	27	15	October	25	10
May	32	17	November	19	3
June	34	39	December	14	14

The Royal Fort

Towering over the old city, it was built by the Mughal Emperor Akbar the Great in 1566, although recent excavations have found evidence of a mud fort as far back as 1,000AD. It is surrounded by huge, metre thick walls with enormous gates. All the succeeding Mughal Emperors, the Sikhs and the British added a pavilion or palace within its walls. Of particular interest are Diwan-e-Aam on the south side of the quadrangle where the Emperor would appear in front of his people and dispense instant justice to law breakers who were brought from the city through the Masti Gate. The great Elephant Steps, used by the animals to transport the princes and princesses around the fort, are the last remaining of their kind in Pakistan. The Sheesh Mahal, the palace of mirrors in the north east corner of the fort, is very beautiful. There are some wonderful fresco paintings, sandstone and marble carvings and pavilions.

Badshahi Mosque

Immediately opposite the Lahore Fort. It was built from marble and sandstone by thousands of labourers in less than three years for Emperor Aurangzeb in 1647. Over 100,000 people pray here at the beginning of Ramaddan and again 70 days later. Three huge domes dominate the mosque above the prayer chambers which are decorated with intricate artwork and carvings. The acoustics are remarkable as even the slightest whisper echoes around the chambers.

Emperor Jahangir Mausoleum

Built in 1637 following the death of Jehangir, the fourth Great Mughal Emperor, the tomb is set in beautiful gardens in Shahdora across the River Rai in the north west of Lahore. Four corridors adorned with ornaments lead from the gardens to the marble tomb in the centre of the mausoleum. The tomb itself is vividly decorated and inscribed with Islamic writing of the 99 attributes of Allah.

Lahore Museum

Housed in a huge Mughal style building on the Mall opposite the old University Hall. The entrance to the main hall is lined with water and oil paintings depicting life in Lahore through the 15th to 19th centuries. Off the main hall extraordinary Islamic, Gandhawar and British, textiles are displayed. There is also a fascinating weapons museum, some incredible ivory carvings and exquisite jewellery from different eras. In the British section there is a life-size sculpture of Queen Victoria. Outside the museum in the middle of the Mall is the Zamzama the 18th century cannon, made famous by Rudyard Kipling as Kim's Gun.

The Indian Border

Only 28km away and, even if you have no intention of crossing it, this is a trip that cannot be missed. Each day the changing of the guard ceremony is performed by both armies at the same time as each tries to outdo the other. Crowds gather on each side of the border and cheer for their side. It is a remarkable sight. It is said that the tallest men in both India and Pakistan end up at the border as height is considered to be very important in this part of the world! Organised trips are arranged by PDTC at Room 3, Faletti's Hotel, Egerton Road.

Pearl Continental

Shahrah-e-Quaid-e-Azam
Tel: 042 636 0210
Fax: 042 636 2760
otellhr@lhr.comsats.net.pk
ne of the top hotels with 458 luxuri-
us rooms, 6 restaurants, fine swim-
ing pool, business centre, tennis and
uash.

oliday Inn

-26 Egerton Road
l: 042 631 0077
x: 042 631 4515
oliday@inn.brain.net.pk
ne hotel. 128 rooms in the centre.
restaurants and snack bar, rooftop
ol and gym.

ari Hotel

Shahrah-e-Quaid-e-Azam
l: 042 631 0646
x: 042 636 5367
arigst@lht.comstats.net.pk
6 luxurious rooms. Choice of restau-
nts, swimming pool, gym, business
ntre

est Western

Liberty Market
ulberg
l: 042 575 8811
x: 042 571 2800
vsl@brain.net.pk
ood value hotel near stadium with
-conditioned rooms, cable TV, mini-
r, room service and coffee shop

letti's

erton Road
l: 042 636 3946
x: 042 636 4819
entral colonial hotel. A reminder of
he past but in need of decoration.
Good air-conditioned rooms with
cable TV and fridge.

Amer Hotel

Lower Mall
Tel: 042 711 5015
Fax: 042 711 5013
Probably the best value in city. Clean rooms with air-conditioning, cable TV, fridge. Good restaurant with Pakistani and continental menu. Very friendly and helpful staff. Airport pickup can be arranged.

Indus Hotel

56 The Mall
Tel: 042 630 2856
Central budget hotel with clean air-conditioned en suite rooms, cable TV and fridge.

Kashmir Palace

14 Empress Road
Tel: 042 631 6700
Fax: 042 631 6709
Budget hotel. Clean rooms with fans and cable TV. Good service and value.

Restaurants

In addition to those in the Pearl Continental, the Avari Tower and the Holiday Inn there are a number of excellent restaurants, including the Salt and Pepper Village on M. M. Alam Road in Gulberg III which serves traditional Pakistani food and the Bunda Khan chain which has restaurants in Liberty Market, Fortress Stadium and Mall Road serving authentic Pakistani cuisine. Freddy's Café and Café Zouk serve international food for the young and trendy on M. M. Alam Road while Thia Wah is an excellent oriental restaurant in the same suburb. Nearby, Uno Pizzeria is the best Italian in town and for those with a sweet tooth the Mehmood Sweet House in Cavalry Ground on Jail Road cannot be missed.

where to stay & eat

stats

Win/Loss Record

Country	Played	Won	Drawn	Lost	Tie
West Indies	4	1	3	-	-
Pakistan	34	9	19	6	-
Zimbabwe	2	-	2	-	-
Sri Lanka	3	1	1	1	-
Australia	5	1	3	1	-
England	7	1	5	1	-
India	5	-	4	1	-
New Zealand	7	2	1	4	-
South Africa	1	-	-	1	-

Highest Individual Aggregates (Pakistan unless stated)

Player	Mat	Inn	NO	Runs	Ave	HS	50	100
Javed Miandad	17	23	3	1122	56.10	163	3	
Zaheer Abbas	10	15	4	1093	99.36	235*	2	
Mudassar Nazar	11	17	2	811	54.07	152*	2	
Mohsin Khan	8	13	1	686	57.17	135	2	
Majid Khan	10	17	2	670	44.67	110*	4	
Inzamam-ul-Haq	7	11	0	640	58.18	329	3	
Shoaib Mohammad	6	11	3	569	71.13	203*	2	
Asif Iqbal	7	13	2	555	50.45	166	2	
Saleem Malik	13	20	2	525	29.17	143	2	
Imran Khan	11	14	4	525	52.50	123	3	

Top Wicket Takers (Pakistan unless stated)

Player	Mat	Bll	Md	Runs	Wkt	Ave	BB	S/
Imran Khan	11	2443	93	987	56	17.63	8/58	43.
Abdul Qadir	12	3099	105	1348	51	26.43	9/56	60.
Sarfraz Nawaz	10	2472	93	999	33	30.27	6/89	74.
Waqar Younis	7	1257	49	605	29	20.86	7/86	43.
Saqlain Mushtaq	5	1217	50	528	25	21.12	8/164	48.
Iqbal Qasim	9	1724	89	609	23	26.48	4/41	74.
Wasim Akram	9	1292	53	511	22	23.23	5/28	58.
Intikhab Alam	7	1931	68	764	20	38.20	4/35	96.
Tauseef Ahmed	7	1694	82	625	17	36.76	4/58	99.
Shoaib Akhtar	4	523	13	303	16	18.94	6/11	32.

Highest Individual Scores (Pakistan unless stated)

329	Inzamam-ul-Haq	v New Zealand 2002
235*	Zaheer Abbas	v India 1978-79
230	Kumar Sangakkara (SL)	2001-02
218	Sanjay Manjrekar (Ind)	1989-90
215	Zaheer Abbas	v India 1982-83
203*	Hanif Mohammad	v New Zealand 1964-65
203*	Shoaib Mohammad	v India 1989-90
173*	David Gower (Eng)	1983-84
168*	Zaheer Abbas	v India 1984-85
166	Saeed Ahmed	v Australia 1959-60

Best Individual Bowling Performances (Pakistan unless stated)

37-13-56-9	Abdul Qadir	v England 1987-88
29.3-8-58-8	Imran Khan	v Sri Lanka 1981-82
30.5-7-85-8	Kapil Dev (Ind)	1982-83
74-20-164-8	Saqlain Mushtaq	v England 2000-01
40-15-74-7	Pervez Sajjad	v New Zealand 1969-70
44-21-75-7	Lindsay Kline (Aus)	1959-60
37.5-11-86-7	Waqar Younis	v New Zealand 1990-91
45-11-128-7	Paul Adams (SA)	2003-04
8.2-4-11-6	Shoaib Akhtar	v New Zealand 2002
23-7-46-6	Azeem Hafeez	v India 1984-85

Highest Partnerships

Wkt	Runs	Batsmen	Matc
1st	192	Sunil Gavaskar & Chetan Chauhan (Ind)	1978-197
2nd	203	S Jayasuriya & K Sangakarra (SL)	2001-2002

3rd	204	Imran Nazir & Inzamam-Ul-Haq (Pak)	2001-2002 v NZ
4th	246	Javed Miandad & Shoaib Mohammad (Pak)	1989-1990 v India
	281	Javed Miandad & Asif Iqbal (Pak)	1976-1977 v New Zealand
	217	Hanif Mohammad & Majid Khan (Pak)	1964-1965 v New Zealand
	142	Zaheer Abbas & Ashraf Ali (Pak)	1984-1985 v India
	111	Majid Khan & Imran Khan (Pak)	1979-1980 v Australia
	161	Zaheer Abbas & Sarfraz Nawaz (Pak)	1983-1984 v England
	57	Intikhab Alam & Asif Masood (Pak)	1974-1975 v West Indies

ults at The Gadaffi Stadium

	Countries	Result
1/1959	v Australia	lost by 7 wickets
0/1961	v England	lost by 5 wickets
4/1965	v New Zealand	drawn
2/1969	v England	drawn
0/1969	v New Zealand	lost by 5 wickets
3/1973	v England	drawn
2/1975	v West Indies	drawn
0/1976	v New Zealand	won by 6 wickets
2/1977	v England	drawn
0/1978	v India	won by 8 wickets
3/1980	v Australia	drawn
1/1980	v West Indies	drawn
3/1982	v Sri Lanka	won by an innings and 102 runs
0/1982	v Australia	won by 9 wickets
2/1982	v India	drawn
1/1983	v India	drawn
3/1984	v England	drawn
0/1984	v India	drawn
1/1984	v New Zealand	won by 6 wickets
1/1986	v West Indies	lost by an innings and 10 runs
1/1987	v England	won by an innings and 87 runs
0/1988	v Australia	drawn
2/1989	v India	drawn
0/1990	v New Zealand	won by 9 wickets
2/1990	v West Indies	drawn
2/1993	v Zimbabwe	drawn
1/1994	v Australia	drawn
1/1996	v New Zealand	lost won by 44 runs
2/1998	v Zimbabwe	drawn
3/1999	v Sri Lanka	drawn
1/2000	v England	drawn
3/2002	v Sri Lanka	Sri Lanka won by 8 wickets
5/2002	v New Zealand	won by an innings and 324 runs
10/2003	v South Africa	won by 8 wickets

akistan	2	2	-	-	-	100.00
Bangladesh	2	-	-	2	-	00.00

293

Multan Cricket Stadium is the second ground in the city to stage a Test. The Ibn-e-Qasim Bagh Stadium hosted one drawn match against the West Indies in 1980/81. The first Test at the new ground took place on 29 August 2001 when Pakistan beat Bangladesh by an innings and 264 runs. Danish Kaneria took 6/42 as Bangladesh managed just 134. The hosts replied with 546/3 dec., five batsmen scoring centuries, Saeed Anwar (101), Taufeeq Umar (104), Inzamam-ul-Haq (105 retired hurt), Yousuf Youhana (102no) and Abdul Razzaq (110no). Kaneria took 6/52 and Waqar Younis 4/19 as Bangladesh slumped to 148 all out. Kaneria's match figures of 12/94 are the best return on the ground. With these 1 wickets he has also taken more wickets at Multan than any other bowler at an averag of 7.83.

The next match between the two was a completely different affair. The visitors score 281, Habibul Bashar top scoring with 72 while Pakistan were dismissed for 175, Mohammad Rafique taking 5/36 and Khaled Mohammad 4/37 to give Bangladesh a lead of 106. Bangladesh could only score 154 in their second innings, Umar Gul taking 4/58 to add to his four wickets in the first innings and Shabbir Ahmed 4/68. Set 260 to win the home side collapsed to 132/6 on the third day. But Inzamam-ul-Haq helped by Saqluin Mushtaq (11), Shabbir Ahmed (13) and Umar Gul tried mightily turn things round only for the ninth wicket partnership of 52 to come to an end whe Umar was run out on five with the score on 257. It looked all over as Yasir Ali came t the crease. But he survived as Inzamam hit the winning runs and ended with 138no deny Bangladesh their first ever Test victory.

But history was made in 2004 when India recorded their first Test victory in Pakistan Led by Raul Dravid in place of the injured Sourav Ganguly, India declared at 675/5 after 309 from Vivender Sehwag – the highest score at the ground – and 194no from Sachin Tendulkar. Pakistan made 407 in their first innings but crumbled to 216, despite 112 from Youhana, thanks to Anil Kumble 6/72 and India won by an innings and 52 runs.

The ground has a capacity of 18,000. Unlike Lahore and Karachi good crowds turn up for Test matches. The players' pavilion is a plain building on the east side of the ground. The scorers, players and officials sit under umbrellas on the boundary. Abov the pavilion is the Inzamam-ul-Haq enclosure, probably the best vantage point in the ground as it is behind the bowler's arm. At the other end of the ground the Waqar Younis enclosure also provides an excellent view of the cricket. These stands are totally covered from the sun and have excellent toilet facilities. but the less expensive enclosures have none.

On the north side of the ground enclosures are named after Imran Khan, Hanif Mohammad, Mustaq and Zaheer Abbas. To the south are the Javed Miandad, ahi Brothers, Wasim Akram and Fazal Mahood enclosures, all of which are concrete half covered. In the more expensive enclosures the covered area has individual metal s with cushions. Where there are no seats, spectators use carpets on the concrete. It mportant to get to the ground early to get one of these 'covered' seats as it would be ossible to sit in the searing heat all day. The uncovered area is reserved for locals parad- huge Pakistani flags, chanting and generally celebrating cricket.

ousands of locals come to the ground, especially for the one-day internationals with no ntion of entering the ground, treating the match as a social event and, of course, there lways the chance of climbing over the fence into the ground.

t drinks and sealed bottles of water are sold all around the ground but it is sensible ring some water to the ground. The heat is stifling. There are some food stalls in the und, however the majority are outside the ground on Vehari Road where the crowd s at lunchtime. The people are very welcoming and curious and approach strangers in e groups. Few speak English but they enjoy trying. There is plenty of security in and und the ground.

kets can be purchased from the Allied Bank of Pakistan, the most convenient being in e Circle Office, 90 Aziz Shaheed Road, Cantt, Multan (Tel 580766) or at the ground on natch days. The ground is quite a way from the centre of town. A taxi will cost Rs250 or even cheaper in a rickshaw which is an exciting ride. There is no public parking.

Multan is in the Punjab in east central Pakistan. It is situated near the Chenab River, 348km south west of Lahore and 966km north of Karachi, and has a population of 1.4 million. The city takes its name from the idol in the temple of the Sun God and is known as the city of shrines. An ancient Chinese couplet described the city as "four rare things Multan bounds, heat, beggars, dust and burial grounds" Although it must be said there re very few beggars in the streets, the rest of the couplet is apt.

he city has a remarkable history with a succession of rulers. Alexander the 3reat visited Multan in 325BC two years before his death. The Chinese settled n 640AD before the Arabs conquered the city in 712AD as an outpost of Islam n India under the rule of Baghdad. The Turks invaded the city in 1005 and the faimur in 1397 before the Mughal Emperor Babar claimed the city in 1528. The ity remained as part of the Mughal Empire for nearly a hundred years, however he Empire disintegrated and the city was taken over by the Afghans in 1752. In 818 Maharaja Ranjit Singh, the Sikh leader conquered Multan and held power until the British took over the city in 1849. The British ruled until Pakistan gained independence in 1947.

Multan is known for its handicrafts, especially shoes, but also other leather goods, pottery and enamel work that can be in found in any of the city's bazaars. t is a historical and cultural city. There are many mosques and more than a hundred superbly designed shrines and tombs. Some of the shrines are in the ort and others can be found while wandering through the bazaars and streets of he old city. The bazaars in the narrow winding lanes have some wonderful, tiny hops where craftsmen ply their trades. The bazaars are colourful lively places with some excellent shopping.

The city is incredibly dusty and with the heat and the petrol fumes walking long distances can be pretty uncomfortable. Rickshaws are a handy alternative and a wonderful way to see the sights. Although the buildings have not seen a lick of paint for a very long time there are some elegant structures. There is a real buzz throughout with everybody going about their business in a loud and happy manner. The crowded street side markets must be visited as it is an incredi- ble experience to witness the men dressed in their traditional dress and the women in their brightly coloured shalwar, their heads

the city

covered with a bochan. The roads in Multan are chaotic to say the least with buses, taxis, cars and donkey carts vying for position and the rickshaws and many cyclists using any part of the road available irrespective of the direction they are heading. Pedestrians must take great care while walking.

Multan's climate is very hot and humid. From April to October is the hottest time of the year when the temperature can reach the high thirties and early forties each day. T area sees very little rain. Light cottonwear is recommended.

There is very little choice of accommodation in Multan with only one four star hote the Holiday Inn, one three star and a couple of two stars. The hotels recommended are all fine with good large en suite rooms with air-conditioning. The service in the hotels is good and friendly. Even though there are many cafés, there are only a few restaurants to recommend and these are mainly in the hotels as in the smaller places the menus are in Urdu and no one can speak English!

Holiday Inn

26 Abdalia Road
Tel: 061 587777
Fax: 061 512511
The best hotel in Multan at an affordable price. Excellent en suite rooms with cable TV. Pakistani and Chinese restaurants, swimming pool and gym.

Sindbad Hotel

Nishtar Chowk
Tel: 061 512640
Budget accommodation with clean air-conditioned en suite rooms with cable TV. Room service with good food available. Friendly staff.

Sheza Inn

Kutchery Chowk
Tel: 061 512235
Fax: 061 512238
Good air-conditioned clean rooms with cable TV. Restaurant and bakery.

Al Sana

154B Shershah Road
Tel: 061 542601
Reasonable air-conditioned en suite rooms with TV. Good restaurant and friendly service.

Silver Sand

514 Railway Road
Tel: 061 511461
Hotel with good clean air-conditioned rooms with TV. Restaurant.

Park Hotel

Azmat Wasti Road
Dera Adda
Tel: 061 514407
Cheap decent hotel with good rooms.

Restaurants

The Holiday Inn has two fine restaurants, one serving Pakistani food and the other, Chinese. The Sheza Inn also has a good restaurant serving local food and although The Sindbad Hotel's restaurant seems to open very rarely but they do very good and affordable room service meals.

Multan Airport is 4km to the west of the city along the Shah Rah-e-Rashid Road. After negotiating the mayhem outside the Arrival Hall a taxi ride will cost Rs200 and a rickshaw even less for the 15 minute journey. Both are in plentiful supply. The standard of driving will be an eye-opener. The airport is very small and has no banks and only one small kiosk selling tea, cigarettes etc. There is a small foodstall in the airport grounds. PIA have an office at the airport. There are no car hire companies at the airport.

Multan Fort

On the east of the city on a mound by the River Ravi. When built, the circumference of the fort was more than 2km with 46 bastions and two towers at each of the four gates. Unfortunately it was practically destroyed by the British in 1848. Only part of the huge outer walls, the bastions and a number of the shrines remain. Qasim Bagh and the old cricket stadium are located in the fort which provides a wonderful view of the city.

Shaikh Baha-ud-din Zakria's Shrine

This shrine, dedicated to one of the foremost scholars of Islam and a saint respected throughout Pakistan, is located within the fort walls. Born in 1170, he studied in Baghdad and Multan. It is a wonderful piece of architecture and its dome dominates the city's skyline.

Mausoleum of Shah Rukn-e-Alam

This shrine, dedicated to the grandson of Shaikh Baha-ud-din Zakria, is near the main gate of the fort. It was originally built by Emperor Ghayasud Din Tughlaq and is 100ft tall. Its dome has a diameter of 58ft and is decorated with some wonderful calligraphy, mosaic and tiles.

Airlines

Both PIA and Aero Asia fly to and from Multan. There are regular flights to Karachi (2), Faisalabad (4), Rawalpindi (3), Lahore (3) each day and flights to Peshawar four days a week.

Pakistan International Airways
85 Abdali Road
Tel: 061 570131

Aero Asia
30 Metro Plaza
Qasim Road
Tel: 061 514135

Buses

A number of bus companies run air-conditioned buses to Faisalabad, Lahore, Rawalpindi, Peshawar and Karachi from the General Bus Station which is situated to the south east of Multan.

Trains

Multan Contontment is a railway junction and has connections to all other major cites. It is on the main line connecting Karachi with the north of the country. Enquiries T117. The journey to Karachi takes 12 hours, Faisalabad (3), Lahore (6), Rawalpindi (14) and Peshawar (17).

Taxis

Taxis and rickshaws are available at the airport, outside hotels and on the streets. Always agree a price with the driver before starting your journey.

Car Hire

The only car hire available to tourists is arranged by the Holiday Inn on Abdalia Road.

Climate

	ave temp	rain cm		ave temp	rain cm
January	13	7	July	34	56
February	16	8	August	33	34
March	22	19	September	31	12
April	28	10	October	27	1
May	33	12	November	20	2
June	36	10	December	15	7

Post Office

General Post Office
Hassan Parwena Road
Open 09.00-18.00 Monday-Thursday
09.00-12.30 and 14.30-18.00 Friday,
09.00-14.30 Saturday

Telecom

Central Telecom and Telegraph
Exchange
LMQ Road off Abdali Road
Open 24 hours.

Tourist Information

Pakistan Development Tourism
Corporation
Tourist Information Centre
Sindbad Hotel
Nishtar Chowk
 Bahawalpur Road

Tel: 061 512640
Open 08.00-20.00 everyday

Punjab Tourism
Tourist Information Centre and
Business Service
Akbar Gate
Railway Road
Tel: 061 580951

Hospital

Civil Hospital
Abdali Road
Tel: 061 30539

Nishtar Hospital
Buhawalpur Road
Tel: 061 31385

stats

Win/Loss Record

Country	Played	Won	Drawn	Lost	Tie
India	1	1	-	-	-
Pakistan	3	2	-	1	-
Bangladesh	2	-	-	2	-

Highest Individual Aggregates (Pakistan unless stated)

Player	Mat	Inn	No	Runs	Ave	HS	50	100
Inzamam-ul-haq	3	5	2	330	110.00	138*	1	2
Virender Sehwag (Ind)	1	1	0	309	309.00	309	0	1
Yousuf Youhana	2	3	1	249	124.50	112	0	2
Sachin Tendulkar (Ind)	1	1	1	194	194.00	194*	0	1
Abdul Razzaq	2	3	1	179	89.50	110*	0	1

Top Wicket Takers (Pakistan unless stated)

Player	Mat	Bll	Md	Runs	Wkt	Ave	BB	S
Danish Kaneria	1	168	6	94	12	7.83	6/42	14.
A Kumble (Ind)	1	417	22	172	8	21.50	6/72	52.
Umar Gul	1	282	9	144	8	18.00	4/58	35.
Mohammad Rafique (Ban)	1	286	13	116	7	16.57	5/36	40.
Khaled Mahmud (Ban)	1	246	10	105	7	15.00	4/37	35.

Highest Individual Scores (Pakistan unless stated)

309	Virender Sehwag (Ind)	2003-04
194*	Sachin Tendulkar (Ind)	2003-04
138*	Inzamam-ul-haq	v Bangladesh 2003
112	Yousuf Youhana	v India 2003-04
110*	Abdul Razzaq	v Bangladesh 2001-02

Best Individual Bowling Performances (Pakistan unless stated)

13-3-42-6	Danish Kaneria	v Bangladesh 2001-02
15-3-52-6	Danish Kaneria	v Bangladesh 2001-02
30-10-72-6	Anil Kumble (Ind)	2003-04
17.4-7-36-5	Mohammad Rafique (Ban)	2003
7.1-1-19-4	Waqar Younis	v Bangladesh 2001-02

Highest Partnerships

Wkt	Runs	Batsmen	Match
1st	168	Saeed Anwar & Taufeeq Umar (Pakistan)	2001-2002 v Bangladesh
2nd	74	Javed Omar & Habibul Bashar (Bangladesh)	2003-2004
3rd	336	Virender Sehwag & Sachin Tendulkar (India)	2003-2004
4th	165*	Yousuf Youhana & Abdul Razzaq (Pakistan)	2001-2002 v Bangladesh
5th	110	Sachin Tendulkar & Yuvraj Singh (India)	2003-2004

Results at Multan Cricket Stadium

Date	Countries	Result
29/08/2001	v Bangladesh	won by an innings and 264 runs
03/09/2003	v Bangladesh	won by 1 wicket
28/03/2004	v India	lost by an innings and 52 runs

peshawar

arbab niaz

The Arbab Niaz Stadium is a huge concrete bowl to the north east of the city in the middle of Jinnah Park.

The first Test at the ground was in 1995 when the hosts beat Sri Lanka by an innings and 40 runs. Pakistan scored 459/9 dec with Inzamam-ul-Haq top scoring with 95. Chaminda Vaas took 5/99 and Muttiah Muralitharan 4/134 for the visitors. Sri Lanka could only score 186 in their first innings, put to flight by Wasim Akram with 5/55. Forced to follow-on, a fighting 76 by captain Arunja Ranatunga was not enough to make Pakistan bat again as Sri Lanka were dismissed for 233. The 1997 Test against West Indies also saw an innings victory as Mustaq Ahmed swept through the visitor's line up, ending with match figures of 10/106.

Zimbabwe recorded an excellent win in Peshawar in 1998. Ijaz Ahmed top scored with 97 as the hosts scored 296 in their first innings, Heath Streak taking 4/93 for the visitors. Wasim Akram 5/52 and Waqar Younis 4/78 limited Zimbabwe to 238 in their reply, Neil Johnson hitting 107. Pakistan collapsed in their second innings to 103 all out, Henry Olonga chipping in with four wickets. Set 162 to win,

Murray Goodwin (73no) steered Zimbabwe home with seven wickets to spare.

Pakistan suffered another loss in the 2000 Test against Sri Lanka. Having dismissed the visitors for 268, Shoaib Aktar taking 5/75, Pakistan scored only 199 in reply. Inzamam remained 58no as Muralitharan took 4/47. Russell Arnold was unlucky to fall on 99 as Sri Lanka scored 224 in their second innings setting their hosts a target of 294 for victory. Murali took 6/71 as Pakistan were dismissed for 236 to give Sri Lanka victory by 57 runs.

In 2003, in the Test against Bangladesh, Pakistan found themselves trailing by 66 runs having scored 295. Javed Omar scored 119 and Habibul Basher 97. The deficit may well have been worse only for Shoaib Aktar's bowling with 6/49. However, Bangladesh crumbed to 96 in their second innings, Shoaib again leading the bowlers with 4/30, and the home side reached the required total of 165 with nine wickets to spare. Mohammad Hafeez scored 102no.

The highest individual score on the ground is 334no by Mark Taylor for Australia in the high scoring draw in the 1998 test. Taylor declared Australia's first innings while equal with Sir Donald Bradman's record individual score for Australia rather than go on to try to better Brian Lara's world record 375 at Antigua in 1994. Taylor enjoyed partnerships of 279 with Justin Langer (116) and 168 with Ricky Ponting (76no) in the 1998 test. Their team score of 599/4 dec. is the highest team score and the lowest Bangladesh's 96. Pakistan's run chase of 165/1 in the same match is the highest on the ground.

Shoaib's match figures of 10/79 against Bangladesh in 2003 is the best return on the ground. Muralitharan with 10/148 in 2000 is the only other bowler to take ten wickets in a match. One hat-trick has been taken here, by Alok Kapali of Bangladesh in 2003.

Peshawar has a capacity of 15,000 and, unlike some of the other grounds in Pakistan, gets good crowds for both one-dayers and Test matches. Unfortunately because of its proximity to the Afghan border only Bangladesh have toured here since 2000. It is a plain and simple ground with a small pavilion. The VIP and Committee enclosures on either side of the players' pavilion at the northern end of the ground are the only enclosures with any cover. The general enclosure sweeps around the rest of the ground and has absolutely no protection from the sun. It can get extremely hot in Peshawar.

The cost of a ticket for the better enclosures is no more than Rs200 and is recommended. The scoreboard is in the general enclosure opposite the pavilion at the southern end of the ground. The whole ground is surrounded by a security fence. Soft drinks and water are available by the fence in each enclosure and vendors pass through the crowd.

Tickets can be purchased from Allied Pakistan Bank Ltd, the most convenient branch being State Life Building, The Mall, Peshawar (Tel: 276 834) or at the ground on days preceding Test matches. The ground is situated in Shahi Bagh to the north east of the city, a pleasant 20-minute walk along Sunrhri Masejid Road past the museum, Jinnah Park, Bala Hisor Fort and the bazaars on the edge of the old city. A rickshaw ride should take no more than 10 minutes and cost Rs60. The ground is surrounded by fields and the Gymkhana where locals play cricket on dusty tracks. Even more popular seems to be allure of betting on the cock fights which take place in the fields by the ground.

arrival

Peshawar is a small airport 3km outside the city. A taxi ride takes 10 minutes and costs Rs150. Rickshaws are also available. The international and domestic terminals are in the same building. Only passengers are allowed in the building. Security is very tight. There is no café or snack bar in the airport.

Peshawar is the capital of North West Frontier Province and has a population of just under a million. Known as the Land of the Pathans, it is situated 170km west of the capital Islamabad near the famous Khyber Pass and was traditionally a trading centre between central Asia and the subcontinent. It is also near the site of Purushapura, the ancient capital of the Greco Buddhist Gandhara Empire, an earlier trading settlement. The name Peshawar means "the place at the frontier" which could not be more apt. Because of its position the city has being invaded many times including by the Greeks, the Huns, the Afghans, Persian, the Mughals, Sikhs and the British.

Alexander the Great passed through the city in 327BC. The Kushans have been traced back to Peshawar over 2000 years ago. One of their kings, Kanishka, made it the capital of the Kushan Empire in the 2nd century. After many centuries, during which the city changed hands constantly, in 1526 AD it fell to the Mughal Emperor Babur who created the city of flowers. It remained in the control of the Mughals until the Afghan Durrani Rulers invaded in the 18th century. The Sikhs invaded in the 19th century and burned most of the city destroying the Mughal architecture and gardens. The British took over from the Sikhs in 1848 and the Khyber Pass became an important military outpost in India. Peshawar is an industrial city with textile and cotton mills and pharmaceutical factories. It is also famous for its handicrafts including footwear, silver and gold. It is a road and rail centre and a military and communications centre. It was the centre of the relief operation for Afghan refugees from 1979 to 1985.

In ancient times Peshawar was enclosed within huge walls and had 16 gates. Today only the Kabuli Gate remains. There are many mosques in the city, the most famous being the Mughal Mosque built in 1670. On Fridays at midday one can witness the people lining the pathways of the Saddar in prayer. The Peshawar Museum is one of the most interesting in Pakistan. The old Clock Tower in the city was built to commemorate the Diamond Jubilee of Queen Victoria in 1900.

The choice of accommodation is somewhat limited owing to the closure of some of the better hotels due to lack of business. The Khan Klub, a most celebrated hotel has been forced to close although its excellent restaurant remains open. The Pearl Continental is a fine hotel and its restaurants and facilities including the business centre, swimming pool and gym can be used by non-residents. Swimming costs Rs360 for the day. Most of the restaurants are in the main hotels however they are many eateries in the bazaars in the Old City and the Saddar.

Temperature reach 40 degrees in the summer months. It is also humid and the dusty streets can be uncomfortable on warmer days.

Post Office
General Post Office
Saddar Road
Open 09.00-19.00 Monday, Tuesday, Wednesday, Thursday and Friday.
09.00-12.00 Saturday

Tourist Information
Pakistan Development Tourist Commission
Benevolent Fund Building
Saddar Road
Tel: 091 286829
There is also a tourist desk at the airport.

Hospital
Lady Reading Hospital
Hospital Road
off GT Road
Tel: 091 9211430

Pearl Continental

Khyber Road
Tel: 091 276361
Fax: 091 276456
Without doubt the best hotel in Peshawar. 150 luxurious rooms with choice of restaurants, shopping arcade, business centre, great swimming pool, gym.

Green's Hotel

Saddar Road
Tel: 091 276035
Fax: 091 276088
Good value colonial hotel with restaurant, bakery and atrium. Clean en suite rooms with cable TV. Friendly, helpful staff.

Shelton House

Old Jamrud Road
University Town
Tel: 091 842087
Fax: 091 828965
Guesthouse with clean air-conditioned rooms with cable TV.

VIP Guesthouse

Old Bara Road
University Town
Tel: 091 843392
Another good guesthouse with clean air-conditioned rooms with cable TV

Decent Lodge

Syed Jamaluddin
Afghani Road
Tel: 091 840221
Fax: 091 840229
Basic guesthouse with clean rooms. Rather a long way from the centre.

Restaurants

The Pearl Continental Hotel has two excellent restaurants, Marco Polo serving Pakistan and Continental food and a Chinese restaurant. They also have a barbeque each night on the roof. The Khan Klub at New Rampura Gate (0 214 802) serves terrific Afghan food with fine entertainment. The hotel section of the Klub is now closed. Greens Hotel also has a good restaurant.

Airlines

There are regular flights to the other cricket centres. Four to Islamabad each day and the journey takes half an hour. Lahore (2 a day and 1 hour), Karachi (2 a day and 2 hours) and Multan (four times a week and 1 hour)

Pakistan International Airways
Arbats Road
Tel: 091 273081

British Airways
Greens Hotel
Saddar Road
Tel: 091 273252

Emirates Airlines
95 Saddar Road
Tel: 091 275912

Buses

The bus station is 2km out of the city on GT Road, opposite the Kandar Town Fruit Market. Buses run to Rawalpindi, Lahore, Multan and Karachi, however it should be noted that the buses are uncomfortable, crowded and very slow.

Trains

The Cantt Railway Station is on Sunehri Masijid Road. Reservations 091 274436. Enquiries T117

Taxis

Taxis and rickshaws are available at the airport, outside hotels and in the streets. Always agree fare with driver before commencing journey. Drivers tend to overcharge visitors so it is worth haggling to get a substantial reduction

Car Hire

From the Pearl Continental and Green Hotels.

The Khyber Pass

Without doubt this is the main tourist attraction. The Pass begins at the amrud Fort in the Sulainan Ranges, just 17km west of Peshawar. It leads from the fort to the frontier with Afghanistan and beyond. Unfortunately entry to Afghanistan is not permitted at present. A number of forts built by the Sikhs and the British are worth exploring. The Bab-i-Khyber, the gateway, is a fine monument and the insignias of each of the regiments posted here are displayed. A permit is required to visit the area and can be arranged by the PDTC office in Peshawar who will also lead the excursion. Once a month a steam train runs to the pass, an opportunity worth taking if you can. The tracks runs for 41km with four stations, 34 tunnels and a remarkable 92 bridges. The line was originally designed to move troops and supplies to and from the pass.

Peshawar Museum

In the south of the old city on Sunehri Masajid Road in the Victoria Memorial Hall, it houses a fine exhibition of Gandhara tribal life with collections of sculptures, cloth, jewellery and wooden carvings. The museum is open from 8.30-13.00 and 14.00-17.00 each day bar Wednesday and Public Holidays. An entrance fee of Rs100 is charged.

Bazaars

Throughout the old city there are many colourful bazaars. Pathan tribesman in traditional dress do business as the traffic runs through the roads and lanes adding to the chaotic atmosphere. The Qissa Khawani is famous for its leather goods and fruit, The Mochi Lara for its shoes, the Chitrali for its shawls, waistcoats and headwear from the Chitral Valley and The Merna is for women with everything from lace, ribbons and bows. The Battair is a remarkable bird market while the Andarshahr is the jewellers' market that runs through the narrow alleys of the old town. Walking around the market is safe. Everyone is curious but friendly.

Charsadda

30km north of Peshawar, this is one of the most important archaeological sites in Asia. It is the site of Pushkalavati, the ancient capital of Gandhara from 600BC to 200AD. The city was a trading centre as long ago as 1,000BC. Alexander the Great passed through in 324 AD.

Bala Hisar Fort

On the north west edge of the city on a raised platform. It was built in the early 16th century (1526 – 30) by Babur, the founder of the Mughal dynasty and rebuilt by the Sikhs in 1830's. The PDTC can arrange a tour of this huge structure which provides a wonderful view of Peshawar.

Climate

	ave temp	rain cm		ave temp	rain cm
January	11	34	July	32	36
February	13	39	August	31	55
March	18	71	September	29	19
April	23	46	October	23	7
May	28	20	November	17	11
June	33	7	December	13	19

Win/Loss Record

Country	Played	Won	Drawn	Lost	Tie
Zimbabwe	1	1	-	-	-
Pakistan	6	3	1	2	-
Sri Lanka	2	1	-	1	-
Australia	1	-	1	-	-
Bangladesh	1	-	-	1	-
West Indies	1	-	-	1	-

Highest Individual Aggregates (Pakistan unless stated)

Player	Mat	Inn	NO	Runs	Ave	HS	50	10
Mark Taylor (Aus)	1	2	1	426	426.00	334*	1	
Saeed Anwar	5	7	0	418	59.71	126	3	
Inzamam-ul-Haq	6	8	2	415	69.17	97	4	
Ijaz Ahmed	3	4	0	307	76.75	155	2	
Yousuf Youhana	4	6	1	277	55.40	88	3	
Justin Langer (Aus)	1	2	0	130	65.00	116	0	
Moin Khan	4	5	0	130	26.00	58	2	
Habibul Bashar (Ban)	1	2	0	125	62.50	97	1	
Mohammad Hafeez	1	2	1	123	123.00	102*	0	
Javed Omar (Ban)	1	2	0	119	59.50	119	0	

Top Wicket Takers (Pakistan unless stated)

Player	Mat	Bll	Md	Runs	Wkt	Ave	BB	S
Shoaib Akhtar	3	712	18	377	20	18.85	6/50	35.
Wasim Akram	3	644	27	272	20	13.60	5/52	32.
Muttiah Muralitharan (SL)	2	697	23	282	14	20.14	6/71	49.
Mushtaq Ahmed	3	699	18	353	13	27.15	5/35	53.
Chaminda Vaas (SL)	2	390	9	212	10	21.20	5/99	39
Aamer Sohail	5	564	18	245	10	24.50	4/54	56.
Waqar Younis	3	435	9	273	8	34.13	4/78	54.
Pommie Mbangwa (Zim)	1	180	11	63	6	10.50	3/23	30.
Henry Olonga (Zim)	1	168	4	89	6	14.83	4/42	28.
Heath Streak (Zim)	1	214	5	112	6	18.67	4/93	35

Highest Individual Scores (Pakistan unless stated)

334*	Mark Taylor (Aus)	1998-99
155	Ijaz Ahmed	v Australia 1998-99
126	Saeed Anwar	v Australia 1998-99
119	Javed Omar (Ban)	2003
116	Justin Langer (Aus)	1998-99
107	Neil Johnson (Zim)	1998-99
102*	Mohammad Hafeez	v Bangladesh 2003
99	Russel Arnold (SL)	1999-00
97	Inzamam-ul-Haq	v Australia 1998-99
97	Habibul Bashar (Ban)	2003

Best Individual Bowling Performances (Pakistan unless stated)

22.5-4-50-6	Shoaib Akhtar	v Bangladesh 2003
27.1-4-71-6	Muttiah Muralitharan (SL)	1999-00
18.3-7-35-5	Mushtaq Ahmed	v West Indies 1997-98
23-5-52-5	Wasim Akram	v Zimbabwe 1998-99
20-3-55-5	Wasim Akram	v Sri Lanka 1995-96
23-5-71-5	Mushtaq Ahmed	v West Indies 1997-98
24.3-3-75-5	Shoaib Akhtar	v Sri Lanka 1999-00
32-9-78-5	Courtney Walsh (WI)	1997-98
29-3-99-5	Chaminda Vaas (SL)	1995-96
45-13-118-5	Mohammad Rafique (Ban)	2003

Highest Partnerships

Wkt	Runs	Batsmen	Match
1st	140	Mohammad Hafeez and Umar Gul (Pak)	2003-2004 v Bangladesh
2nd	279	Mark Taylor and Justin Langer (Aus)	1998-1999
3rd	132	Ramiz Raja and Inzamam-Ul-Haq (Pak)	1995-1996 v Sri Lanka
4th	118	Ijaz Ahmed and Yousuf Youhana (Pak)	1998-1999 v Zimbabwe
5th	168	Mark Taylor and Ricky Ponting (Aus)	1998-1999
6th	79	Russel Arnold and Aravinda de Silva (SL)	1999-2000

esults at Arbab Niaz Stadium

rawalpindi

cricket stadium

Rawalpindi Cricket Stadium lies east of the city and is purpose built. The first Test match there was against Zimbabwe in December 1993. Although it seemed as if the visitors where going to coast it at 140/2 chasing 240, Wasim Akram (5/65) and Waqar Younis (4/50) demolished them for 187 to win the match for Pakistan by 52 runs.

Pakistan had a fine innings win against New Zealand in 1996. Mushtaq Ahmed took 6/87 as the Kiwis scored 249. In reply Pakistan hit 430, Saeed Anwar (149) and Ijaz Ahmed (125) sharing a second wicket partnership of 262. Chris Cairns took 5/137. In their second innings the visitors collapsed to 168 with only Bryan Young putting up any resistance with 61 as Mohammad Zahid took 7/66, the best bowling figures on the ground.

The 1998 Test saw Australia hammer Pakistan by an innings and 99 runs. Saeed Anwar scored 145 of Pakistan's first innings total of 269, Stuart MacGill taking 5/66. Australia replied with 513, Michael Slater scoring 108, Stephen Waugh 157 and Darren Lehmann 98. MacGill was again Australia's main bowler in Pakistan's second innings as they crumbled to 145, only Saleem Malik scoring well with 52no.

In 2000 Pakistan hosted Sri Lanka in the most exciting game played at Rawalpindi, Muttiah Muralitharan and Pramodya Wickramasinghe taking four wickets each as Pakistan reached 182. In reply Sri Lanka scored 353, Aravinda De Silva hitting 112. Pakistan improved in their second innings with 390, Younis Khan leading the way with 107. Muralitharan took 4/127. Set 220 to win the visitors slipped to 144/5 and 177/8 before their captain Arunja Ranatunga (29no) and Romesh Kaluwitharana (36no) brought them home by two wickets.

Rawalpindi will go down in history as the ground on which India clinched their first ever series win in Pakistan. In April 2004 they beat their hosts by an innings and 131 runs to take the series 2-1. Raul Dravid's 270 helped them to 600 in their first innings and India never lost the initiative.

Rawalpindi saw a world record last wicket partnership equalled by Mushtaq Ahmed and Azhar Mohammad when they put together 151 against South Africa in 1997. The highest team score on the ground is India's in 2004, the lowest being the West Indies' 139 in 1997. The highest run chase is Sri Lanka's 220/8 in 2000.

Mohammad Zahid's match figures of 11/130 against New Zealand in 1996 are the best returned on the ground. He gained the distinction of being one of only 14 Test players and the only Pakistani to take 10 or more wickets on debut. The only hat-trick at the ground was by Damien Fleming for Australia in 1994. He is one of only three players to achieve this feat on debut.

Rawalpindi Cricket Stadium is 10km along William Road. A taxi costs no more Rs20 a rickshaw slightly less. Due to heavy traffic the journey can take between 30 and 45 minutes. The area around the ground is cordoned off with only ticket holders allowed past the barriers. Tickets must be purchased before hand from Allied Pakistan Bank Ltd, the most convenient branch is on Adamier Road in the Cantt area (tel 556 8161 or at the ground on the days preceding matches.

The Javed Miandad and Imran Khan enclosures to the left of the players' pavilion are the Fazal Mahmood and Hanif Mohammad enclosures on the right are the VIP areas and the only covered spectator areas. Tickets for these areas cost Rs200 for tests and Rs600 for one-day internationals. The general enclosures cost Rs50 for tests and Rs2 for one-dayers and are named after Saeed Anwar, Mushtaq Ahmed, Zaheer Abbas, A. H. Kardar, Miran Bux, Waqar Younis, Nazaar and Wasim Akram. There are no toilet facilities in the general enclosures. The scoreboard is in between the A. H. Kardar and Miram Bux enclosures at the southern end of the ground.

Soft drinks and water are available at the fence that circles the ground. Vendors move through the crowd selling nuts, sweets and cigarettes. There are a couple of foodstalls outside the ground and on the approaching roads. The vendors selling horns and horn-ers are very popular as the crowd delight in making as much noise as possible. The atmosphere is lively and friendly, with the curious locals all wanting to have a chat with visitors. As in all the other grounds in Pakistan, good cricket from both sides is applauded.

Rawalpindi is in the north east of Pakistan in the Punjab near the border with Kashmir. It is the twin of the capital Islamabad and was the interim capital of the country from 1959 until 1970 while Islamabad was being built. The city sits on the site of an old village inhabited by the Rawals tribe, hence the name. It is at the base of the Mongallah Hills on the Potobhar plateau and is split into two parts, The Old city with its bazaars and narrow lanes and the Cantonment, known as the Cantt, which was developed by the British, as is evident from its colonial buildings and wide tree-lined streets.

Archaeologists estimate that the area has been inhabited for over 300,000 years. The city was destroyed by Huns in the 4th or 5th century before the Muslim invader Mahmood of Chazni offered the ruined city to the Gakkha chief Kai Gohar in 1,000AD. The area remained uninhabited until 1493 when Jhanda Khan, another Gakkha chief, developed it and named it Rawalpindi. It remained under Gakkha rule until the Sikhs took over in 1765. The British arrived in 1849 when it became a major military outpost. The city has grown and developed since Pakistan's independence in 1947.

The headquarters of the Pakistan Army is based here.

Rawalpindi is divided by the railway tracks separating the old city from the cantonment. The cantonment is prosperous with banks, hotels and elegant buildings along The Mall and Kashmir Road. It is a busy area with many shopping arcades and cafés. There are lively colourful bazaars throughout the old city which give a fine insight into Pindi's culture and way of life. The Liaquat gardens provide a tranquil place in which to relax and its memorial hall houses an art gallery and theatre. The army museum on Ifitkha Road is well worth a visit. In the surrounding area there are national parks, forts, archaeological sites and historical sites including the famous cultural town of Taxila.

Neighbouring Islamabad is very different, very carefully planned when it was built in 1966. Purpose built to be the new capital, it is a spacious, six times the area of Rawalpindi with fewer people. Many foreign embassies are based here in the diplomatic enclave. Islamabad also has fine modern buildings, tree lined streets, mosques, museums and some rather quieter bazaars.

There is a small selection of hotels in Rawalpindi including a couple of five star establishments and some good affordable hotels which provide more than adequate accommodation. Most of these hotels have restaurants, the best of which are in the Pearl Continental Hotel on the Mall with a choice of Pakistani, Continental or Chinese restaurants. There are many cafés and restaurants throughout the city and food stalls in the Old City.

Taxila

40km from Rawalpindi and renowned as a centre of learning for Gandhara art, sculpture, architecture and Buddhism. There are many archaeological sites around the town dating back to 660BC including Bhir Mound (600BC), Jandial Temple (250BC) and Jaulian Monastery (550AD). The town has a wonderful museum with collections of archaeological finds. Open 07.00-19.00 daily. It is regarded as one of the best museums in Pakistan.

Rawat Fort

Built in the 16th century by the Gakkhars, a tribe from the Potohar Plateau. The chief, Sultan Sarang Khan, is buried within the walls, having been killed in a bat with Shez Shar Suri. Situated 15km to the east of Rawalpindi on GT Road, it pr vides a wonderful view of the surrounding plateau.

Rawalpindi Bazaars

The bazaars in the old city are a good way to experience, taste and smell Rawalpindi. The streets are full of stalls and shops selling handicrafts such as wo carvings, embroidery, shawls, headwear and waistcoats. Roadside cafés serve loc specialities of Tikka, Biryani and Jalfrezi.

Hasan Abdal and Gundwara Panja Sohib

50km to the west of Rawlpindi and has major historical significance with the Mughal period and the Sikh's reign of 1748-1849. The Gundware Panja Sohib is Sikh temple visited by pilgrims from all over the world. Beside this temple there is a mosque and a meditation cell of the saint Baba Wali Qandhari dating back the 15th century.

Islamabad Museum

On Garden Avenue. Twenty million year old fossils and man-made tools dating back two million years are displayed along with artefacts, and crafts from the Islam, Sultanate and Mughal periods. Open 09.30-16.30 Monday, Tuesday, Thursday, Saturday and Sunday. 09.30-12.30 and 14.00-16.30 on Fridays. Closed Wednesdays.

Pearl Continental Hotel

The Mall
Tel: 051 566011
Fax: 051 563972
hotelrwp@isb.comsats.net.pk
200 luxurious rooms. 4 restaurants, business centre, excellent swimming pool, gym.

Flashman's Hotel

17-22 The Mall
Tel: 051 581480
Reasonably priced with spacious clean en suite rooms with cable TV. Good restaurant. Friendly and helpful staff.

Shalimar Hotel

The Mall
Tel: 051 562901
Fax: 051 566061
100 en suite rooms with cable TV. Restaurant, swimming pool. Good service.

Executive Hotel

Liaquat Road
Tel: 051 541190
Fax: 051 541299
Good clean hotel. En suite rooms wit cable TV. Restaurant and room servic

Paradise Inn

109 Adamjee Road
Tel: 051 568594
Fax: 051 567048
Budget hotel, clean rooms with cable T

Restaurants

The Pearl Continental has a number of fine restaurants serving Pakistani, European and Chinese food. The buffet in the foyer is excellent. Flashman' Hotel and the Shalimar Hotel both ha good restaurants and there are a lot o good eateries in the many shopping arcades in the Cantt area.

Islamabad International Airport is 7km from the centre. The international and domestic airports are in the same building. A taxi ride to the city will take no more than 15 minutes and should not cost more than Rs120. Rickshaws should cost even less. Larger hotels have shuttle services.

There is a 24-hour bank and a number of money changers. There is a restaurant, some cafés and snack bars and a tourist information centre in the Arrival Hall. Pakistan International Airways and Aero Asia have offices in the Arrival Hall.

Airlines

There are flights to Lahore (8 a day), Faisalabad (1), Peshawar (2), Multan (3) and Karachi (6).

Pakistan International Airways
Reservations Office
The Mall
Tel: 051 568071

British Airways
Pearl Continental Hotel
The Mall
Tel: 051 564702

Buses

The Bus station is on the Peshawar Road near Kihinoor Hills. Daewoo Pakistan Express Bus Service runs buses to Faisalabad, Multan and Lahore. Telephone Enquiries 11007008.

Trains

Rawalpindi Railway Station is on Tamour Road. The tourist concession office is in the commercial department at the station and the Railway Reservations office in Saddar (Tel: 051 553592 or T117). Journeys take 28 hours to Karachi, Lahore six hours, Multan 14 hours, Peshawar four hours and Faisalabad five hours.

Taxis

Small yellow taxis are available at the airport, outside hotels and on the street. There is a large taxi rank on Kashmir Road. There are fewer rickshaws here than in other Pakistani cities. It is important to agree the fare with the driver before commencement of journey.

Car Hire

Avis Rent a Car
7 Honey Plaza
Muree Road
Cantt
Tel: 051 55 68879

Humsafar Rent a Car
Flashman's Hotel
The Mall
Cantt
Tel: 051 55 63396

Post Office

General Post Office
Corner of Kashmir Road and The Mall
Tel: 051 565691
Open 09.00-18.00 Monday-Thursday and Saturday, 09.00-11.30 Friday

Tourist Information

Pakistan Development Tourist Corporation
Tourist Information Centre
Room 7
Flashman's Hotel
The Mall

Hospital

Rawalpindi General
Murree Road
Tel: 051 847761

Climate

	ave temp	rain cm
January	10	58
February	13	53
March	17	69
April	23	54
May	29	40
June	32	30
July	31	256
August	29	251
September	28	97
October	23	25
November	26	19
December	11	41

stats

Win/Loss Record

Country	Played	Won	Drawn	Lost	Tie
Sri Lanka	1	1	-	-	-
India	1	1	-	-	-
Australia	2	1	1	-	-
Pakistan	8	3	2	2	-
South Africa	1	-	1	-	-
Zimbabwe	1	-	-	1	-
New Zealand	1	-	-	1	-
West Indies	1	-	-	1	-

Highest Individual Aggregates (Pakistan unless stated)

Player	Mat	Inn	NO	Runs	Ave	HS	50	10
Saeed Anwar	6	10	0	546	54.60	149	2	
Saleem Malik	3	5	1	410	102.50	237	2	
Inzamam-ul-Haq	7	12	0	386	32.17	177	1	
Aamer Sohail	5	9	0	370	41.11	160	2	
Raul Dravid (Ind)	1	1	0	270	270.00	270	1	

Top Wicket Takers (Pakistan unless stated)

Player	Mat	Bll	Md	Runs	Wkt	Ave	BB	SA
Waqar Younis	5	1145	36	621	23	27.00	5/88	49.7
Wasim Akram	5	848	25	396	16	24.75	5/65	53.0
Mushtaq Ahmed	5	1271	42	601	15	40.07	6/87	84.7
Mohammad Zahid	1	246	8	130	11	11.82	7/66	22.3
Saqlain Mushtaq	3	1025	38	393	10	39.30	5/129	102.5

Highest Individual Scores (Pakistan unless stated)

270	Raul Dravid	2003-04
237	Saleem Malik	v Australia 1994-95
177	Inzamam-ul-Haq	v West Indies 1997-98
160	Aamer Sohail	v West Indies 1997-98
157	Steve Waugh (Aus)	1998-99

Best Individual Bowling Performances (Pakistan unless stated)

20-3-66-7	Mohammad Zahid	v New Zealand 1996-97
30-3-87-6	Mushtaq Ahmed	v New Zealand 1996-97
20.3-3-56-5	Heath Streak (Zim)	1993-94
23.2-3-65-5	Wasim Akram	v Zimbabwe 1993-94
22-5-66-5	Stuart MacGill (Aus)	1998-99

Highest Partnerships

Wkts	Runs	Batsmen	Match
1st	176	Mark Taylor and Michael Slater (Aus)	1994-1995
2nd	262	Saeed Anwar and Ijaz Ahmed (Pak)	1996-1997 v New Zealand
3rd	323	Aamir Sohail and Inzamam-Ul-Haq (Pak)	1997-1998 v West Indies
4th	198	Michael Slater and Steve Waugh (Aus)	1998-1999
5th	147	Sherwin Campbell and Shiv Chanderpaul (WI)	1997-1998
6th	109	Steve Waugh and Ian Healy (Aus)	1994-1995
7th	106	Shaun Pollock and Dave Richardson (SA)	1997-1998
8th	81	Stephen Fleming and Lee Germon (NZ)	1996-1997
9th	145	Younis Khan and Wasim Akram (Pak)	1999-2000 v Sri Lanka
10th	151	Azhar Mahmood and Mushtaq Ahmed (Pak)	1997-1998 v South Africa

Results at Rawalpindi Cricket Stadium

Date	Countries	Result
09/12/1993	v Zimbabwe	won by 52 runs
05/10/1994	v Australia	drawn
28/11/1996	v New Zealand	won by an innings and 13 runs
06/10/1997	v South Africa	drawn
29/11/1997	v West Indies	won by an innings and 29 runs
01/10/1998	v Australia	lost by an innings and 99 runs
26/02/2000	v Sri Lanka	lost by 2 wickets
13/04/2004	v India	lost by an innings and 131 runs

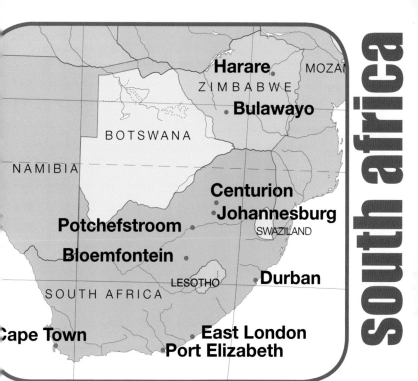

The first Test match in South Africa began on 12th March 1889 on the Crusaders Ground, St. George's Park, Port Elizabeth when England defeated their hosts by eight wickets. Two weeks later Newlands in Cape Town staged the second Test with the visitors again coming out on top, this time by an innings and 202 runs. Both grounds are still Test match venues today.

On 2nd March 1896 the Old Wanderers Ground in Johannesburg held its first Test when England beat South Africa by an innings and 197 runs. The Old Wanderers ground was used until the outbreak of the Second World War after which Ellis Park was Johannesburg's venue for Test Cricket for six matches until 24th December 1956 when the New Wanderers Stadium was used for the first time with England victorious over South Africa by 131 runs.

In the meantime in Durban, The Lords Ground hosted four Test matches before Kingsmead took over as the city's Test venue on 18th January 1923 when South Africa drew with England. Port Elizabeth, Cape Town, Johannesburg and Durban continued as the Test cities until South Africa's isolation from international sport between 1970 and 1992. On 16th November 1995 Centurion became the country's eighth Test ground when South Afrcia entertained England, the match ending in a draw. The next ground granted Test status was Goodyear Park in Bloemfontein on 29th October 1999 when South Africa beat Zimbabwe by an innings and 13 runs.

Airlines

South Africa's national airline is South African Airways. A number of airlines operate domestically. Daily flights link all major cities with Johannesburg International Airport serving Centurion. Internal flights are inexpensive especially when purchased in the country. The airlines that service all major routes are:

South African Airways	011 978 2242
South African Airlink	011 395 3333
Nationwide Air	011 327 3000
South African Express	011 978 5569

Trains

Spoornet operates the main rail network. Trains are inexpensive and it is possible to travel between each city. Intercity trains include the Diamond Express, which runs from Pretoria to Bloemfontein, the Southern Cross, from Cape Town to Port Elizabeth, the Trans Natal, from Johannesburg to Durban and, of course, The Blue Train, which runs between Pretoria and Cape Town in luxurious comfort, the most sophisticated, elegant way to travel in South Africa.

Distance Between Cities (in kms)

	Bloemfontein	Cape Town	Durban	E London	Joburg	P Elizabeth	Potchefstroom	Centurion
Bloemfontein		1005	635	584	395	678	280	456
Cape Town	1005		1755	1100	1402	769	1260	1460
Durban	635	1755		676	580	980	560	637
East London	584	1100	676		990	310	850	1038
Johannesburg	395	1402	580	990		1080	130	58
Port Elizabeth	678	769	980	310	1080		910	1135
Potchefstroom	280	1260	560	850	130	910		175
Centurion	456	1460	637	1038	58	1135	175	

Bus services between cities are reliable, reasonable and comfortable if not luxurious.

Greyhound	021 418 4310
Translux	021 449 6209
Intercape	021 386 4400

These companies operate fleets of double and single deck coaches with air-conditioning, audio and visual entertainment and on-board toilet facilities. Their reservation system is fully computerised and seats are always allocated at time of booking. Urban bus services are erratic and are not recommended. Minibuses are also not recommended but a lot of cricket tourists do use them to get to the ground each morning.

Car Hire

Aivs, Budget and Hertz all provide a reliable, professional and inexpensive service. An International Driving Licence is required and drivers must be over 22 years of age. It is possible to hire a car in one location and return it in another. Motorways are in excellent condition however there are constant roadwork delays in most cities. The speed limit on motorways is 120kph and 60kph in built up areas. There are many speed traps with heavy fines. Most petrol stations are open 24 hours but do not accept credit cards only cash. ATM's at most stations but not all accept Visa.

Taxis

Taxis are available at airports, hotels and restaurants. They can be called by hotel reception or picked up at ranks around the cities. Taxis cannot be hailed in the street. Many tourists find a reliable driver and then just contact him for each journey. Drivers are reliable and only happy to help. Always use a licensed taxi and do not use minibuses.

Banks

Opening times at most banks are Monday to Friday 09.30-15.30 and Saturday 09.30-11.00. Most banks have foreign exchange facilities and accept travellers cheques in major currencies. Commission is charged for this service. ATM facilities are widespread. All major credit cards are accepted.

South Africa uses the Rand (R). Notes are issued in denominations of R200, 100, 50, 20 and 10 and coins in denominations of R5, 2, 1 and 50, 20, 10 and 5 cents.

Telecoms

International Direct Dialling is available throughout South Africa. South Africa's dialling code is 27. The outgoing international code is 09.

Post

Post office opening times are Monday-Friday 08.00-16.30 and Saturday 08.00-12.00. The postal service is slow and not very reliable. Airmail to Britain takes approximately five days. Stamps are only available from post offices.

Tourist Offices

All airports and cities have a number of Tourist Information Centres that are listed in the following chapters.

Emergency Numbers

...ice	10111
...bulance	10177
...e	10177

Embassies

...tish High Commission
... Hill St.
...tfield
...toria
...: 012 483 1400
...: 012 421 7555
...w.britain.org.za

...sas

... visitors to South Africa must carry a valid passport and have a return or onward ...ket. A valid passport entitles British nationals to stay up to six months, New Zealand ...d Australian nationals three months. Upon entry a temporary residence permit must ...completed. Passports must be valid for six months beyond date of departure.

...stoms

...itors over the age of 18 may take the following goods into South Africa without ...urring customs duty: 400 cigarettes and 50 cigars, 1 litre of alcohol, 2 litres of wine, ...ml of perfume.

...me Difference

...o hours ahead of GMT (GMT + 2)

...ectricity

...0/240 volts AC at 50 cycles per second. Most hotels have adaptors.

Departure Tax

There isn't one

bloemfontein

goodyear park

Formerly known as Springbok Park, Bloemfontein's Goodyear
Park is home to the Orange Free State Cricket Association and South
Africa's youngest Test venue.

The first Test played there was against Zimbabwe in November 1999 which South
Africa won easily by an innings and 13 runs. Batting first, Zimbabwe could only man
age 192, Guy Whittall making 85 while Shaun Pollock took 5/39 for the home side.
In reply South Africa scored 417, Jonty Rhodes hitting 70 and Hansie Cronje 64 and
Jacques Kallis 65. Henry Olonga took 4/93 for Zimbabwe. Trailing by 226 runs, the v
tors were dismissed for 212. Kallis took 4/68 and Paul Adams 4/31.

The ground hosted the 2000 Test against New Zealand and Kallis was on form with
bat again, hitting 160 – the highest innings at the ground – as South Africa scored 47
dec. New Zealand managed 229 with Stephen Fleming making 57 as Shaun Pollock
took 4/37. Forced to follow-on, Fleming, again, led from the front, this time with 99
the visitors made 342 to set South Africa a target of 101. Makhaya Ntini took 6/66. A
a shaky start the home side came home with five wickets to spare.

South Africa had a comprehensive victory over India the following year. Although
Sachin Tendulkar scored 155 and Virender Sehwag 105 in India's first innings total
of 379, South Africa reached 563 – the highest team score at Bloemfontein. Hershelle
Gibbs 107 and Lance Klusener 108 made centuries while Javagal Srinath took 5/146.
Pollock took 6/56 in India's second innings as they were dismissed for 237. Despite lo
ing Gibbs early, Gary Kirsten 30no and Jacques Kallis 21no brought their side home
a nine wicket victory.

Shaun Pollock's match figures of 10/147 against India in 2001 are the best return at t
ground.

Although Goodyear Park has a capacity of 20,000, Test matches do not attract large
crowds. The main pavilion and stand is at the south end of the ground. The Long
Room, one of the most hospitable bars in Test cricket, is also at this end of the groun
between the pavilion and the scoreboard. The Centenary Stand dominates the west si
but it is not usually used during Tests. The grass embankment in front of the stand is
the most popular area in the ground. The scoreboard is located at the north end of th
ground above the lower seated embankment. The Northern Pavilion and a number c
chalets are also situated at this end of the ground. The east side of the ground is one
long grass embankment with some shade under a row of trees.

There are a number of food stalls and bars around the ground. There is a first-aid po
in the main pavilion. Facilities for the disabled are provided in the main stand with
viewing areas and disabled toilets. The toilets facilities around the ground are clean a
well looked after.

Tickets can be purchased at the Ticket Office at the south end of the ground. Tickets
available on the day. The ground is less than ten minutes walk from the centre of tow
and there is plenty of parking directly outside the ground. Bloemfontein Coach
Station is adjacent to the ground.

Bloemfontein Airport (J. B. M. Hertzog Airport) is on
the eastern side of the city, 10km from the centre. Taxis are available outside the terminal and should cost no more than R50. There are
shuttle buses to the city centre which leave from the front of the airport
building in accordance with flight schedules. There is an information desk in
the Arrival Hall. There is no bank at the airport but there is an ATM machine
in the main building. There are a number of car hire desks in the Arrival Hall.
Hertz 051 400 2100, Avis 051 4332331, Budget 051 4332381. The airport has
a restaurant on the ground floor, a bar on the first floor, a coffee shop
and a bookstall.

Bloemfontein, known as the 'city of roses' is the provincal capital of Orange Free State. A modern city in a vast, rural province in the centre of South Africa, it is the country's sixth largest with a population of 250,000.

It was founded in 1840 by Johannes Nicholas Brits who established a farm on arrival. In 1854 Major Henry Warden, the British representative, was recalled to the Cape allowing the Afrikaneers to set up their own republic, the Orange Free State, with Bloemfontein as its capital. It remained the capital until the Union of South Africa in 1910 when it was made judicial capital and is still the seat of the South African Supreme Court.

Although Bloemfontein is not a tourist destination there is plenty to see and do when in town for the cricket. It has some impressive architectural and historical heritage including President Brand Street which is lined with old sandstone buildings. The street is a national conservation area with buildings such as City Hall (1850) and First Raadsaal, the oldest building built in 1849 by Major Warden as a school and later as the headquarters of the Legislative Council. Bloemfontein has a number of theatres and art galleries including Oliewenhuis Gallery, a beautiful Dutch manor house which was originally used to house visiting Governor Generals and, later, State Presidents.

Other sites include the Stone Column Monument in Selbourne Avenue erected on the site of the spring that inspired the name Bloemfontein, which translates into flowers of the spring.

An altitude of 1,400m leads to a moderate climate in summer and a mild one in winter. The accommodation in Bloemfontein is reasonable, although not to the high standard of the other cricketing venues in South Africa.

There is one exception. The De Oude Kraal Country Estate is 35km outside Bloemfontein and is of the highest standard in accommodation and in its culinary offerings. There is quite a selection of restaurants, cafés and bars to enjoy in the centre of town. Bloemfontein offers a peaceful atmosphere where the locals have a superb standard of living and absolutely love their cricket.

Airlines

South African Airways
051 447 3811
SA Airlink   051 433 3255
Airport Enquires   051 433 2001

Buses

Translux
Tourism Centre,
Park Road
Tel: 051 408 4888
Fax: 051 408 4804

Greyhound
Tourist Centre
Park Road
Tel: 051 447 1558

Trains

Bloemfontein Train Enquires 051 408 4850 / 4843

Taxis

Silver Leaf 051 430 2005
Rosestad 051 451 1022

Car Hire

Hertz
Downtown
Tel: 051 444 5646
Fax: 051 444 5332

Avis
123 Voortrekker St.
Tel: 051 447 6185
F: 051 430 6953

Budget
Airport
Tel: 051 433 2381

Free State Botanical Gardens

North west of the city off General Dan Pienaar Drive. The 70 hectares are at their best in spring. Highlights include the Orchid House and the large nursery. A very pleasant, peaceful place. Open 08.00-18.00.

The National Women's Monument

Erected in 1913, this sandstone monument is a tragic reminder of the second War of Independence, remembering the women and children who died.

Naval Hill

Game reserve on the outskirts with an array of animal species including giraffes, eland, wildebeest and springbok. Originally gunners of the British Naval Brigade were stationed on the hill hence the name. On the south eastern slope is a giant white stone horse that was laid out during the Boer war by the Wiltshire Regiment as a guide to troops coming in from the plains.

Kings Park

Opened by the Prince of Wales in 1925. More than 4,000 rose trees. Bloemfontein Zoo is in the park and is open 08.00-18.00 daily.

William Pretorius Game Reserve

On the N1 150km north of Bloemfontein on the way to Johannesburg and home to wildebeest, giraffe, antelope, buffalo and white rhino. An overnight stay at the resort is a highly recommended.

De Oude Kraal Country Estate

N1 South of Bloemfontein
Tel: 051 564 0636
Fax: 051 564 0635
deoude@intekom.co.za
Traditional restaurant in beautifully restored farmhouse. Delicious menu. Excellent wine list. Booking essential.

Ocean Basket

Shop 24
Loch Logan Waterfront
105 Heney St.
9301
Tel: 051 430 5195
Fax: 051 430 8453
This Mozambican/Seafood/Greek/Mediterranean restaurant is famous for its fish and excellent service.

The Workshop (Roadside Café)

2nd Avenue and President Reitz
Westdene
Tel: 051 447 2761
American style grill and pub meals. Bustling atmosphere with live entertainment.

Spur Steak Ranch

208 Zaston St.
Tel: 051 448 1493
Steak Mexican style.

Lita's restaurant

Trederham Guesthouse
Eeufers Road
Three course gourmet dinners.
Excellent wine list.

Musselcracker Taverna

Zastron St.
Tel: 051 430 6528
Excellent seafood platter in relaxed surroundings.

St. Elmo's Pizzeria

Corner Zastron and Kellner St.
Tel: 051 447 9999
Italian pizza and pasta.

Mystic Boer

84 Kellner St.

Characters

Corner Tweedeloon and Kellner St.
A modern pub with DJ.

Havanna Nite Club

Tweedeloon
Late opening club.

Deja vu

158 Voortreeker St.

West End Music Pub

142A Voortreeker St.
A game of pool and a few beers.

Holiday Inn Garden Court

Nelson Mandela and Melivitte Drives
Tel: 051 447 0310
Fax: 051 430 5678
3km from the centre. This Cape Dutch Architecture Building has spacious rooms, swimming pool, gardens, restaurant and bar.

De Oude Kraal Country Estate

N1 South of Bloemfontien
Tel: 051 564 0636
Fax: 051 564 0635
E deoude@interkom.co.za
If you don't mind the 40km drive this is the place to stay. Old country house with comfortable rooms and an excellent restaurant and bar.

City Lodge

Cnr Voortreeker Street and Parfitt Ave.
Tel: 051 447 9888
Fax: 051 447 5669
Value for money in landscaped surroundings in the central business district.

President Hotel

1 Unicorn Ave.
Tel: 051 430 1111
Fax: 051 430 4141
A warm, personalised hotel within walking distance of the centre. Restaurant and bar.

Bloemfontein Hotel

East Burger St.
Sanlam Plaza
Tel: 051 430 1911
Fax: 051 447 7102
Quiet, central hotel. Restaurant and bar.

Die Herberg

12 Barnes St.
Tel: 051 430 7500
Fax: 051 430 4494
Excellent guesthouse in the cen-

tre of the city.

Waterfall Guesthouse

103 General Dan Pienaar Drive
Tel: 051 436 2429
Fax: 051 434 1366
michali@ananzi.co.za
Beautiful guesthouse overlooking the city and Thabi mountains. All 3 rooms have a private entrance. Good bar. Self catering kitchen available.

Hillhouse

45 Henry Fagan St.
Tel: 051 436 1380
Fax: 051 436 1356
hillhouse@mjvn.co.za
Excellent B&B. Upmarket, affordable accommodation in exclusive area

Atlantis Guesthouse

33 Jacob St.
Tel: 051 522 7304
Fax: 051 522 2885
lynne_zpr@danbfn.co.za
Based on the legend of the city of Atlantis. Situated in a very peaceful and private suburb.

Camelia Guesthouse

1 Hendrik Kotze Crescent
Tel: 082 8517 434
camelia@shisas.com
Tastefully decorated, non-smoking guesthouse within easy reach of city.

Bloemfontein Inn

17 Eclison St.
Hospital Park
Tel: 051 226 284
Fax: 051 226 223
Comfortable, affordable hotel close to the centre.

Taffy's Backpacker

18 Louis Botha St.
Tel: 051 314 533
Friendly Backpackers'. Kitchen and secure parking. Best breakfast in town.

culture

Sand Du Plessis Theatre

Described as one of the world's modern and technically advanced theatres. Regularly booked well in advance.

National Museum

The National Museum holds the Florisbad skull fragment

(100,000 years old) and remains of extinct animals such as the giant buffalo.

The School of Armour

An excellent display of tanks and weaponry based in one of the original military hospitals.

Post Office

Main Post Office
Corner East Burger and Maitland St.

Tourist Office

Tourist Information Centre
60 Park Road
Tel: 051 405 8489
Fax: 051 447 3859
blminfo@iafrica.com

Publicity Association
Hoffman Square
Tel: 051 405 8911
Fax: 051 478 859

Hospital

Rosepark Fichmed Centre
Gustav Crescent
Tel: 051 422 6761

Climate

	ave temp	rain cm
January	21	14
February	21	17
March	19	19
April	17	39
May	15	74
June	13	92
July	13	70
August	13	74
September	14	40
October	16	37
November	16	15
December	20	17

Win/Loss Record

Country	Played	Won	Drawn	Lost	Tie
South Africa	3	3	-	-	-
Zimbabwe	1	-	-	1	-
India	1	-	-	1	-
New Zealand	1	-	-	1	-

Highest Individual Aggregates (South Africa unless stated)

Player	Mat	Inn	NO	Runs	Ave	HS	50	100
Jacques Kallis	3	5	1	326	81.50	160	2	1
Mark Boucher	3	4	2	200	100.00	76	2	0
Sachin Tendulkar (Ind)	1	2	0	170	85.00	155	0	1
Stephen Fleming (NZ)	1	2	0	156	78.00	99	2	0
Lance Klusener	3	4	0	140	35.00	108	0	1

Top Wicket Takers (South Africa unless stated)

Player	Mat	Bll	Md	Runs	Wkt	Ave	BB	S/R
Shaun Pollock	3	814	50	332	21	15.81	6/56	38.76
Jacques Kallis	3	666	25	373	12	31.08	4/68	55.50
Makhaya Ntini	2	422	21	224	9	24.89	6/66	46.89
Alan Donald	2	492	29	195	7	27.86	3/43	70.29
Javagal Srinath (Ind)	1	228	7	153	5	30.60	5/140	45.60

Highest Individual Scores (South Africa unless stated)

160	Jacques Kallis	v New Zealand 2000-01
155	Sachin Tendulkar (Ind)	2001-02
108	Lance Klusener	v India 2001-02
107	Herschelle Gibbs	v India 2001-02
105	Virender Sehwag (Ind)	2001-02

Best Individual Bowling Performances

21.4-10-56-6	Shaun Pollock	v India 2001-02
31.4-12-66-6	Makhaya Ntini	v New Zealand 2000-01
21-6-39-5	Shaun Pollock	v Zimbabwe 1999-00
33-6-140-5	Javagal Srinath (Ind)	2001-02
12.1-5-31-4	Paul Adams	v Zimbabwe 1999-00

Highest Partnerships

Wkt	Runs	Batsmen	Match
1st	189	Herschelle Gibbs & Gary Kirsten (SA)	2001-2002 v India
2nd	97	Gary Kirsten & Jacques Kallis (SA)	2000-2001 v New Zealand
3rd	130	Jacques Kallis & Neil McKenzie (SA)	2001-2002 v India
4th	115	Jacques Kallis & Neil McKenzie (SA)	2000-2001 v New Zealand
5th	220	Sachin Tendulkar & Virender Sehwag (Ind)	2001-2002
6th	63	Virender Sehwag & Deep Dasgupta (Ind)	2001-2002
7th	121	Lance Klusener & Mark Boucher (SA)	2001-2002 v India
8th	32	Jonty Rhodes & Mark Boucher (SA)	1999-2000 v Zimbabwe
9th	43	Guy Whittall & Henry Olonga (Zim)	1999-2000
10th	54	Mark Boucher & Paul Adams (SA)	1999-2000 v Zimbabwe

Results at Goodyear Park

Date	Countries	Result
29/10/1999	v Zimbabwe	won by an innings and 13 runs
17/11/2000	v New Zealand	won by 5 Wickets
03/11/2001	v India	won by 9 Wickets

cape town

newlands

Newlands, the home of Western Province Cricket Club, is one of the world's most idyllic grounds. The ground is dominated by the glorious Table Mountain and the five stands.

South Africa played their first Test here against England in 1889. Unfortunately it was a very one-sided affair. England batted first, making 292, with Bobby Abel scoring 120 as Gobo Ashley took 7/95 for the home side. In reply South Africa could manage only 47. Forced to follow-on they were dismissed for even less, just 43, to lose by an innings and 202 runs. England's Johnny Briggs ended with match figures of 15/28, the sixth best return of all time and the best at Newlands.

Newlands has not been South Africa's most successful hunting ground, at one stage they did not win a Test here for 60 years (1909-1969). However, since their reintroduction to international cricket in 1992 South Africa have won the majority of their Tests at the ground.

After six successive defeats at Newlands, five against England and one against Australia, South Africa eventually recorded their first win in the fifth and final Test of the 1906 series. Having already lost the series, England made 187. South Africa started badly, reaching 87/5 before the tail rallied and took the total to 333. The No. 11 batsman Bert Vogler top scored with 62no. Tip Snooke also scored 60 as the last pair-contributed 94. Facing a deficit of 146 England collapsed to 130 to lose by an innings and 16 runs.

The closest match played here was in 1922/23 when England got home with one wicket to spare, the last pair scoring the six runs required for victory. England had to chase 173 but slipped to 86/6, thanks mainly to some fine bowling by Alf Hall 7/63 before Frank Mann 45 and Vallance Jupp 38 steadied the ship. Hall ended with match figures of 11/112 on his debut.

The second Test of the 1957 series against England was held at Newlands. England, already 1-0 up in the series won the toss and batted first making 369. Colin Cowdrey top scored with 101, ably helped by Godfrey Evans 62. Hugh Tayfield took 5/130 for the home side. In reply South Africa scored 205 as Johnny Wardle took 5/53. Leading by 164 runs England piled it on, with Dennis Compton 64 and Cowdrey 61 the main contributors in a total of 220/6 dec. Chasing 385 for victory, South Africa managed only a paltry 72 as Wardle took 7/36. Russell Endean of South Africa was the first ever batsmen to be given out handling the ball. England won the Test by 312 runs. The fifth and final Test of the 1996 series against England was the deciding Test after four draws. England won the toss and elected to bat making a modest 153. Robin Smith top scored with 66 as Allan Donald took 5/46. South Africa also struggled to 171/9 before Dave Richardson, 54no, and Paul Adams, 29, shared a last wicket partnership of 73 to reach 244. England could manage only 157 in their second innings as Shaun Pollock took 5/32. Set 70 to win, South Africa reached the target without loss.

Australia's 334/6 in 2002 is the highest run chase at the ground, made with just five balls to spare.

Hershelle Gibbs' 228 against Pakistan in 2003 – the highest score at the ground – was the second fastest double century of all-time, made in 211 balls. Yousuf Youhana, of Pakistan, hit the second fastest half-century ever in 27 balls in 2003. The knock included 24 from one Nicky Boje over.

The highest team score is 620/7 dec. against Pakistan in 2003, the lowest 43 against England in 1889.

The best individual bowling performance at Newlands is Briggs 15/28. In 1958 Lindsay Kline became the 12th player, and fourth Australian, to take a hat-trick. It is a joy to watch cricket at Newlands, whether from the one of the pavilions or from the one of the two hills where the knowledgeable local crowd make visitors very welcome. An electronic scoreboard and a giant screen are situated on each of the hills. There are numerous bars dotted around the ground selling the famous Castle lager which can help cool you on a hot afternoon. There is a limited amount of shade on the hills. so many people use the Railway Stand which provides shelter from the burning sun. The corporate suites in The Oaks and President's Pavilions are second to none.

Facilities and access for the disabled are good, with excellent viewing areas for wheelchair users. Tickets for the match can be ordered from the Western Province Cricket Association (tel: 021 615 120 otto1@cricket.co.za) and can be picked up in WPCA headquarters opposite the turnstiles on Camp Ground Road. A five-day ticket to the test cost R500.

Newlands is very accessible from the city centre. Trains run from Central station to Newlands station right outside the ground. A taxi will cost in the region of R75. Driving to the ground is straightforward. Take the M3 to Rondbosch keeping left into Princess Anne Avenue and Klipper Road and then right into Main Road which leads into Camp Ground Road where the Test ground is situated. Car parking is available in the school fields beside the ground.

There is a small souvenir shop in addition to the T Shirt/memorabilia stalls.

Cape Town Airport has international and domestic terminals and is 22km from the city centre. Taxis are available and will cost R130 to the city. Shuttle services are also available. The desk is directly opposite international arrivals. These buses will deliver you to your accommodation and will pick you up and return you to the airport at the end of your stay. Some hotels run courtesy buses. All the major car rental firms have desks at the airport. Avis (021 934 0330), Budget (021 380 3140) and Hertz (021 935 3000). An information desk is located in the arrivals area in both international and domestic terminals. ATM machines and Bureaux de Change are located in the Arrival Hall. Shops, cafés and restaurants can be found throughout the airport. There is also a post office and a mobile 'phone rental shop. Duty free shopping is located beyond passport control and baggage storage is available in domestic arrivals.

arrival

Cape Town is one of the world's most magnificent locations.

Situated near the southern tip of Africa, the city lies at the foot of the towering Table Mountain looking out onto the Atlantic Ocean. Founded by Governor Jan van Riebeeck in 1652 as a supply station for the Dutch East India Company, the British took control in 1756. Despite being returned to the Dutch in 1803 the British regained control in 1806 and established the Cape of Good Hope with Cape Town as its capital.

Cape Town's city centre, known as the City Bowl, is a small area and has many fascinating museums and historical buildings. The Castle of Good Hope in Darling Street built in 1666, the House of Parliament, the South African National Gallery and the Bo-Kapp Museum rank as highlights. The Victoria & Alfred Waterfront, the old port area, has been developed and provides luxury accommodation, air conditioned shopping centres, restaurants, bars, clubs and an aquarium. The Century City and the Dockside areas provide similar facilities in the central business district.

Cape Town's climate is Mediteranean, generally sunny. Summer temperatures (September-April) average between 15-30 degrees, whereas winter are generally mild. The average rainfall is 100 mm.

The city offers a full range of accommodation with somewhere to suit everyone and its restaurants provide an excellent choice of cuisine. For those with cultural interests Cape Town boasts several theatres, art galleries and museums.

In addition to the cricket and rugby, sailing and angling are major attractions. Other activities such as abseiling, surfing, diving, white water rafting, sandboarding and kloofing make Cape Town a terrific holiday destination.

Table Mountain

South Africa's no. 1 tourist attraction. The sandstone top provides superb views over Table Bay. At 1,086 metres above sea level, the flat top stretches for almost 3km. A cable car transports 750,000 people to the summit every year. For the more energetic there are more than 300 pathways to the summit.

Victoria & Alfred Waterfront

An entertainment complex in the old dock area. A multitude of restaurants, bars and clubs provide some of Cape Town's famous nightlife. Home to hundreds of shops and markets, the Two Oceans Aquarium, SA's largest. Angling and helicopter trips can be arranged. The ferry to Robben Island leaves from here.

Kirstenbosch National Botanical Garden

Only indigenous South African plants. Set against the slopes of Table Mountain an array of plants are displayed in the Peninsula, the Fragrance, the Medicinal and the Protea Gardens. In the summer months sunset concerts are held on the lawns. Open 365 days a year with a craft market on the last Sunday of every month. 12km outside Cape Town.

Robben Island

Where Nelson Mandela and many other political prisoners were held until 1991. The island, 12km off shore, is now open to the public with tours conducted by ex-prisoners. The 20-minute ferry trip to the Island leaves from the Waterfront on the hour 08.00-15.00hrs daily.

The Winelands

Highly recommended. Miles of vineyards stretch over valleys, plains and hillsides. Just over an hour's drive from Cape Town. Stellenbosch, Paarl and Franschhoek are very attractive Dutch-style towns with many small wineries making excellent wines.

The Cape Grace

West Quay
...A Waterfront
: 021 410 7100
...: 021 419 7622
...rbour and mountain views. Fresh
...wers in 112 elegant rooms. Excellent
...taurant – Quay West. Swimming
...ol, bar

...llinan Cape Town Waterfront

...A Waterfront,
: 021 418 6920
...: 021 418 3559
...rble tiled lobby with French win-
...ws leading to swimming pool.
...oms standard. Restaurant and bar.

...unt Nelson

...Orange St,
: 021 423 1000
...: 021 424 7472
...pe Town's pink landmark, open since
...99. Old fashioned charm. Afternoon
... taken to piano accompaniment.
...autiful gardens on 7 acres. 226
...ms, 3 restaurants, 2 tennis courts,
...wimming pools, gym and squash
...rt.

...ce on the Bay

...rways and Victoria Roads
...mps Bay 8001
: 021 438 7060
...: 021 438 2692
...xurious self-catering apartments on
...achfront. 21 apartments. Restaurant,
..., penthouse with own pool.

...le Bay Hotel

...ay 6
...A Waterfront
: 021 4406 5000
...: 021 406 5767
... of the waterfront. Sunny with picture
...ndows, marble floors. 239 rooms, 15
...tes, 3 restaurants, pool, health spa, 2
...s, business services, helicopter shuttle.

...toria and Alfred Hotel

...rhead
...A Waterfront
: 021 410 7100
...: 021 419 7622
...beatable location. Converted ware-
...use surrounded by shops, bars and
...taurants. Beautiful rooms with city
...d mountain views. Restaurant and bar.

...erman House

...80 Kloof Road

Bantry Bay 8001
Tel: 021 439 9182
Fax: 021 434 7257
One of the finest hotels in SA. Built
in 1912. Unbelievable views of ocean.
Beautiful gardens. Comfortable rooms
with picture windows. 11 rooms, restaurant, room service, swimming pool, gym,
sauna and bar. 10 minutes from city.

The Bay Hotel

Victoria Road
Camps Bay 8040
Tel: 021 438 4444
Fax: 021 438 4455
Very relaxed and unpretentious, set on
the beach 15 minutes from the city.
Mountain or ocean views. 76 rooms,
restaurant, swimming pool, 2 bars.

Villa Belmonte

33 Belmont Ave.
Oranjezicht 8001
Tel: 021 462 1576
Fax: 021 462 1579
Small guesthouse with superb views of
Table Mountain, the city and Devil's
Peak. 14 air-conditioned rooms, restau-
rant, room service, swimming pool and
bar. 20 minutes walk from city.

Best Western Cape Suites Hotel

Constitution/De Villers
Tel: 021 461 0727
Fax: 021 462 4389
Luxurious hotel in a superb location
with mountain views. 126 rooms with
kitchens, 2 restaurants, bar, 2 swimming
pools, gym. 5 minutes from city.

Kensington Place

Kensington Crescent
Higgovale
Tel: 021 424 4744
Fax: 021 424 1810
Small exclusive hotel on foothills of
Table Mountain. Superb views of Table
Bay, the harbour, city and mountains.
8 rooms with satellite TV, laundry and
valet. Private terraces. Swimming pool.

Clarens Manor

35 Clarens Road
Sea Point
Tel: 021 433 6801
Fax: 021 434 6845
Beautiful guesthouse with elegant
rooms. Original art, antique furniture.
Warm and comfortable lounges and
dining room. 7 rooms, Excellent res-
taurant, swimming pool.

Atlantic Grill Room

Table Bay Hotel
V&A Waterfront
Tel: 021 406 5688
Wonderfully positioned. Menu combines Asian, European and local produce. Seafood and lamb the speciality. Extensive wine list. Reservations essential.

Blues

Victoria Road
Camps Bay
Tel: 021 438 2040
On the promenade across road from beach. A popular haunt with young locals, the menu includes seafood, pasta and Thai food. Excellent deserts. A couple of doors down from the Bay Hotel. Reservations essential.

Quay West

Cape Grace Hotel
V&A Waterfront
Tel: 021 418 0520
Highly acclaimed restaurant of the Cape Grace hotel. Offers delicious, beautifully presented food. Member of Chaoinis de Rotisseurs. Extensive wine list. Reservations recommended.

Au Jardin

Vineyard Hotel
Colinton Road
Claremont
Tel: 021 683 1520
French cuisine with a hint of the Cape. Guinea fowl, lamb, beef and fish. Excellent wine list with both local and French labels. Reservations essential.

Wangthai

105 Paramount Place
Main Road, Green Point
Tel: 021 439 6164
One of the best Thai restaurants in South Africa. Popular dining spot for Capetonians.

Codfathers

Camps Bay
One of the best seafood restaurants. Relaxed atmosphere, good music, . Excellent service and a good simple wine list. Separate sushi bar an added bonus. A must.

Panama Jacks

Royal Yacht Club Basin
Goliath Road, Docks
Tel: 021 447 3992
Not the easiest place in the world to fir but well worth it. Great fun, loud musi and crowded. Pick your own crayfish from large water tanks. Another seafoe paradise! One of Cape Town's best kep secrets.

Fez

38 Hout St.
Open daily 21.00-0400
Classiest cocktails in town are served in this Turkish décor bar. House music and beautiful people. Worth a visit.

Green Dolphin

Victoria & Alfred Arcade
Open seven days 16.30-00.00hrs
A traditional 'tourist' pub with Jazz and good food.

Jet Lounge

Floor 1 Winchester House
74 Long St.
Located above the Blue Moon Café. Trendy pub with big space-age couches.

La Med

Clifton
Excellent location for sundowners after a day at the beach. Sunday is the big day and it's not unusual to see many cricket fans there on Sunday after the Test.

Rolling Stone

Observatory
Best place in Cape Town to play poo Extremely relaxed.

The Red Herring

Noordhoek
After a day on the beach great place visit for a sundowner.

Dizzy Jazz Café

Camps Bay
One of city's best known bars. Relaxe atmosphere with friendly clientele. G fun but you won't escape the tourists

Brass Bell

Kalk Bay
After a day at the cricket this is the perfect place for a few beers and som glorious seafood. A fair distance fron ground (R100 in a taxi), it's good to by the ocean and relax. Highly recon mended.

culture

South African Museum

Government Ave.
Dedicated to promoting greater awareness and understanding of the natural history and anthropology of Southern Africa.
Open: Monday-Saturday 09.00-16.00

William Fehr Collection

Castle of Good Hope
Buitenkant St.
Open: Monday-Saturday 09.30-16.00
A fine collection of paintings, watercolours, furniture, glass, porcelain and metalware from 1650 to 1850 held in South Africa's oldest building.

South African National Gallery

Government Ave.
Open: Monday-Saturday 09.30-16.00
The National Gallery houses outstanding collections of African, British, Dutch and Flemish Art.

The Design Museum

The Foundary
Ebenezer Road
Greenpoint
Open Tuesday-Friday 09.00-17.00
Saturday 09.00-13.00
The Design museum promotes local and international contemporary design.

Michaelis Collection

Greenmarket Square
Open Monday-Saturday 10.00-17.00
Includes artworks by 16th to 18th century Dutch and Flemish masters.

Post Office

Grand Central Building, Corner Plein and Darling Streets, 8001
: 021 464 1700.

Tourist Information

Cape Town Tourism
Corner of Casltel and Burg St,
Cape Town 8001
: 021 426 4267
Open 08.00-19.00

Tourist Information
Dock Road
Victoria & Alfred Waterfront
Tel: 021 418 2369
Open 09.00-18.00

Groot Schuur
Observatory
Tel: 021 404 9111

Hospital

New Somerset Hospital
Green Point
Tel: 021 402 6911

Climate

	ave temp	rain cm
January	21	14
February	21	17
March	20	19
April	18	39
May	15	74
June	13	92
July	12	70
August	12	74
September	14	40
October	16	37
November	18	15
December	20	17

Airlines

South African Airways	021 036 111
Commair	021 936 9000
Nationwide	021 936 2050

Buses

Greyhound
Adderley Street Station
Tel: 021 449 3333
Fax: 021 449 2545
Intercape
Tel: 021 386 4400

Trains

Cape Town Train Station Enquires
Tel: 021 449 3871

Taxis

Marine Taxi 021 434 0434.

Car Hire

Avis
123 Strand St.
Cnr Chiapinni St.
Tel: 021 424 1177
Fax: 021 423 3601

Hertz
40 Loop St.
Tax: 021 400 9630
Fax: 021 425 8766

Budget
Rondebosch Motors
16 Main Road
Rondebosch
Tel: 021 686 0400

Win/Loss record

Country	Played	Won	Drawn	Lost	Tie
Australia	9	8	-	1	-
England	17	9	4	4	-
New Zealand	3	1	1	1	-
South Africa	36	11	7	18	-
India	2	-	1	1	-
West Indies	2	-	1	1	-
Sri Lanka	2	-	-	2	-
Pakistan	1	-	-	1	-

Highest Individual Aggregates (All South African)

Player	Mat	Inn	NO	Runs	Ave	HS	50	10
Daryll Cullinan	8	13	0	882	67.85	168	4	
Jacques Kallis	8	12	2	741	74.10	130*	3	
Gary Kirsten	11	19	2	648	38.12	103	5	
Herschelle Gibbs	6	9	0	550	61.11	228	0	
Dudley Nourse	4	8	2	533	88.83	120	1	
Eddie Barlow	4	8	0	462	57.75	138	2	
Hansie Cronje	8	14	1	428	32.92	112	2	
Graeme Pollock	3	6	0	416	69.33	209	2	
Mark Boucher	7	10	2	400	50.00	122*	1	
Herbie Taylor	4	7	0	376	53.71	117	3	

Top Wicket Takers (South Africa unless stated)

Player	Mat	Bll	Md	Runs	Wkt	Ave	BB	S/
Shaun Pollock	8	1803	79	773	38	20.34	6/30	47.4
Alan Donald	7	1441	69	662	30	22.07	5/46	48.0
Paul Adams	7	1711	51	951	26	36.58	4/102	65.8
Charlie Blythe (Eng)	4	1073	66	392	25	15.68	7/46	42.9
Jimmy Sinclair	7	1011	45	455	24	18.96	6/26	42.1
Makhaya Ntini	5	937	28	611	21	29.10	4/33	44.6
Jacques Kallis	8	1194	43	626	18	34.78	5/90	66.3
Johnny Briggs (Eng)	1	135	16	28	15	1.87	8/11	9.0
Shane Warne (Aus)	2	1050	56	347	14	24.79	6/161	75.0
Hugh Tayfield	4	1536	58	535	14	38.21	5/120	109.7

Highest Individual Scores (South Africa unless stated)

228	Herschelle Gibbs	v Pakistan	2002-03
209	Graeme Pollock	v Australia	1966-67
189	Jim Burke (Aus)		1957-58
187	Jack Hobbs (Eng)		1909-10
181	Wally Hammond (Eng)		1938-39
178	Neil Harvey (Aus)		1949-50

169	Sachin Tendulkar (Ind)	1996-97
168	Daryll Cullinan	v West Indies 1998-99
154	Tony Pithey	v England 1964-65
153	Bob Simpson (Aus)	1966-67

Best Individual Bowling Performances (South Africa unless stated)

14.2-5-11-8	Johnny Briggs (Eng)	1888-89
19.1-11-17-7	Johnny Briggs (Eng)	1888-89
19-3-36-7	Johnny Wardle (Eng)	1956-57
25-16-37-7	JJ Ferris (Eng)	1891-92
24-9-42-7	George Lohmann (Eng)	1895-96
18-5-46-7	Charlie Blythe (Eng)	1909-10
37.3-12-63-7	Alf Hall	v England 1922-23
43.1-18-95-7	Gobo Ashley	v England 1888-89
11.4-6-11-6	Schofield Haigh (Eng)	1898-99
12-4-26-6	Jimmy Sinclair	v England 1898-99

Highest Partnerships

Wkt	Runs	Batsmen	Match
1st	368	Graeme Smith & Herschelle Gibbs (SA)	2002-2003 v Pakistan
2nd	172	Eddie barlow & Tony Pithey (SA)	1964-1965 v England
3rd	251	Jacques Kallis & Herschelle Gibbs (SA)	2003-2004 v West Indies
4th	197	Wally Hammond & Les Ames (Eng)	1938-1939
5th	174	John Reid & John Beck (NZ)	1953-1954
6th	222	Sachin Tendulkar & Mohammad Azharuddin (Ind)	1996-1997
7th	132	Adam Gilchrist & Shane Warne (Aus)	2001-2002
8th	147*	Brian McMillan & Lance Klusener (SA)	1996-1997 v India
9th	85	Graeme Pollock & Peter Pollock (SA)	1966-1967 v Australia
10th	94	Percy Sherwell & Bert Vogler (SA)	1905-1906 v England

Results at Newlands

Date	Countries	Result
25/03/1889	v England	lost by an innings and 202 runs
19/03/1892	v England	lost by an innings and 189 runs
21/03/1896	v England	lost by an innings and 33 runs
01/04/1899	v England	lost by 210 runs
08/11/1902	v Australia	lost by 10 wickets
24/03/1906	v England	lost by 4 wickets
30/03/1906	v England	won by an innings and 16 runs
07/03/1910	v England	won by 4 wickets
11/03/1910	v England	lost by 9 wickets
26/11/1921	v Australia	lost by 10 wickets
01/01/1923	v England	lost by 1 Wicket
31/12/1927	v England	lost by 87 runs
01/01/1931	v England	drawn
01/01/1936	v Australia	lost by an innings and 78 runs
31/12/1938	v England	drawn
01/01/1949	v England	drawn
31/12/1949	v Australia	lost by 8 wickets
01/01/1954	v New Zealand	drawn
01/01/1957	v England	lost by 312 runs
31/12/1957	v Australia	lost by an innings and 141 runs
01/01/1962	v New Zealand	lost by 72 runs
01/01/1965	v England	drawn
31/12/1966	v Australia	lost by 6 wickets
22/01/1970	v Australia	won by 170 runs
02/01/1993	v India	drawn
17/03/1994	v Australia	lost by 9 wickets
02/01/1995	v New Zealand	won by 7 wickets
02/01/1996	v England	won by 10 wickets
02/01/1997	v India	won by 282 runs
19/03/1998	v Sri Lanka	won by 70 runs
02/01/1999	v West Indies	won by 149 runs
02/01/2000	v England	won by an innings and 37 runs
02/01/2001	v Sri Lanka	won by an innings and 229 runs
08/03/2002	v Australia	lost by 4 wickets
02/01/2003	v Pakistan	won by an innings and 142 runs
02/01/2004	v West Indies	drawn

centurion

Centurion's SuperSport Park staged its first Test against England in November 1995, nine years after the stadium was built. England reached 381/9 after being put in, thanks mainly to an excellent 141 from Graham Hick before the match was abandoned as a draw due to persistent rain which allowed only 130 overs to be bowled.

South Africa also inserted their next opponents, Australia, in 1997. South Africa dismissed their opponents for 227, despite 67 from Steve Waugh. The home side replied with 384, Adam Bacher top scoring with 96, and Hansie Cronje 79no. Glenn McGrath took 6/86. Trailing by 157, Steve Waugh was the only batsman to offer any resistance with 60no as the visitors crumbled to 185. Allan Donald took 5/36. South Africa reached their target with eight wickets to spare to gain some consolation for losing the series.

The fifth and final Test of the 1999 series against the West Indies was also held at Centurion. South Africa, already 4-0 up, batted first this time and struggled to 123/6 before the no. 8 batsman Mark Boucher made a superb 100 to lead his side to a first innings total of 313. Jacques Kallis also made an invaluable 83. Courtney Walsh took 6/80 for the visitors. In reply the West Indies collapsed to 144 with Allan Donald taking 5/49. Gary Kirsten (134) and Jonty Rhodes (103) hit centuries as the home side made 399/5 in their second innings before declaring. The West Indies, chasing an impossible 569 for victory, were dismissed for 217 as Paul Adams took 4/64.

Unfortunately Centurion's closest game in January 2000 will always be remembered as one of the "fixed matches". After rain for four days and each side forfeiting an innings, England won a thrilling game by two wickets. Only later did we find out the motives behind one of those forfeited innings.

The second and final Test of the 2002 series against Sri Lanka was a cracking match. South Africa won the toss and elected to field. Sri Lanka made 323 in their first innings with Hashan Tillakaratne hitting 104no as Makhaya Ntini took 4/86. The home side replied with 448, Shaun Pollock ending up stranded on 99no and Hershelle Gibbs 92. Sri Lanka could only manage 245 in their second innings, Kumar Sangakkara top scoring with 89. Ntini and Kallis took four wickets each. Chasing 121 for victory South Africa collapsed to 73/6 before Mark Boucher 22no led his side home by three wickets.

South Africa's made 604/6 dec. against the West Indies in 2004 is the highest team score at the ground. Herschelle Gibbs his 192, Graeme Smith made 139 and Jacques Kallis 130no. The lowest score is 119 by Sri Lanka in 2001. Donald's match figures of 8/96 against Australia in 1997 are the best return at the ground.

The ground has a capacity of 20,000 and is a modern circular stadium dominated by a huge grandstand at the North End. Vast, grass embankments cover three sides and supply a wonderful vantage point. The lack of cover on these banks leaves spectators in the sun all day. Everyone should be aware of the risk of sun and bring or find some shade. There are hospitality chalets around the south end of the ground and nearly 70 suites in the pavilion. There is a huge electronic scoreboard on one side of the ground.

There are food stalls and bars all around with good service and very little queuing. The bar on the east side of the ground is probably the liveliest. There is an excellent braai area on the west side of the main pavilion where patrons can cook their own food. There are first-aid points at the NCU offices in the main stand. Facilities for the disabled are provided with viewing areas and disabled toilets in the main stand. There are toilets at each corner of the ground and the facilities are excellent and well serviced.

Tickets can be purchased by post or in person from the Ticket Office at Northern Transvaal Cricket Association, Super Sport Park, and Centurion. The ground does not reach its capacity during Test matches so tickets can be purchased on the day. The ground is only a ten-minute walk from the centre of Centurion and for those wishing to drive there is plenty of parking directly at the river end of the ground. Buses run from Centurion to both Johannesburg and Pretoria.

Centurion is a young, emerging city in the centre of Gauteng Province. The area was first settled in 1841 by the Erasmus family who set up a number of farms. It was named Lyttleton in 1904 and the City of Verwoerburg in 1967 before being renamed Centurion in 1995.

It is one of the fastest growing cities in South Africa with the population rising by 12% in the year 2000. With Johannesburg 35km away and Pretoria 15km commuting is very common among residents. 65% of residents work in management and professional roles. Technology is the main industry with a number of industrial parks dedicated mostly to research and development. Without doubt Centurion's pride and joy is the SuperSport Cricket Ground.

The city has some of the finest buildings in Africa including the famous crescent shaped Government buildings and the world renowned State Theatre. Pretoria has many museums including the Transvaal Museum, a natural history museum which houses the earliest known human fossils which were discovered in nearby Sterkfontein caves.

In contrast, Pretoria was founded in 1855 and is the diplomatic and administrative capital of South Africa. Known as the Jacaranda City because of the 75,000 lilac blossom trees lining the streets, it is situated in North Gauteng, 50km north of Johannesburg. In 1855 it was declared the capital of the South Africa Republic (the Boer Republic) and was named after the first president's father Andrius Pretorius who led the Voortreekers to victory over the Zulu Kingdom in the Battle at Blood River in 1838.

Pretoria is a government city with many embassies, four universities and other academic and research bodies. It is often said to be Africa with a touch of Europe.

Pretoria has an abundance of open spaces with more than 100 parks. Outside both cities, the Tswoing meteorite crater, the Premier Game Reserve and Sun City provide day-trip or overnight opportunities.

the city

Union Buildings

Said to be the world's most beautiful seat of government. Designed by Sir Herbert Baker in 1913, the crescent shaped building overlooks the city. The two wings on each side represent the English and Boers. From 1994 the Union Buildi was the seat of Nelson Mandela's government.

The Sterkfontein Caves

Forty-five minutes from Centurion lie the Sterkfontein Caves, an archaeological site where fossils of early man have been found. The million-year-old caves are unspoilt with underground lakes with enormous stalagmites and stalactites. Tou are ongoing and cost only R10. The caves are open Tuesday-Saturday 09.00-16.00

Sun City/Pilanesberg National Park

Fantasy resort, a mini Las Vegas with hotels, including the Palace of the Lost City an artificial volcano, a waterpark, golf courses, casinos, restaurants and bars. A two-hour drive from Centurion it is well worth a visit or even an overnight stay. the same area is Pilanesberg National Park, the third largest National Park in Sou Africa. The reserve with an area of 600sq. km. lies within the crater of a 120 million-year-old volcano. An opportunity to see the 'Big Five' on a dusk game drive even from a hot air balloon.

Cullinan Gold Mine

Old mining town where the world's largest diamond, the 3106-carat Cullinan Stone, was mined. The town has not changed much since the goldrush and many turn of the century houses are still there. The Willem Prinsloo Agricultura Museum depicts life in the 1880's.

Voortrekker Monument

Commemorating the Great Trek of 1830's with 27 panels depicting scenes from journey. It is a national icon for the Afrikaan people. The monument is built so that on 12 noon on December 16, the anniversary of the Battle at Blood River, ray of sunlight falls directly into the Shrine of Honour.

Al Dente

Waterkloof Heights Centre
103 Club Ave.
Tel: 012 460 9686
Italian. Very popular, booking essential. Table on the veranda in summer. Fine wine list.

Pachas

Club 2 Centre
22 Dely Road
Hazelwood
Tel: 012 460 5063
Top quality steaks, ostrich/seafood.

Brasserie de Paris

525 Duncan St.
Hatfield
Tel: 012 362 2247
Award winning French restaurant. Excellent menu.

The Greek Easy Ouzaria

370 Hinda St.
Hatfield
Tel: 012 342 5199

Reasonably priced Greek restaurant. Booking essential.

Gerhard Moerdyk

752 Park St.
Arcadia
Tel: 012 344 4856
Traditional South African/Boer food. Springbok and ostrich included on the menu.

Down Town Restaurant

6A Lynnburn Road
Lynnwood Manor
Tel: 012 348 6910
Superb seafood, excellent wine, very popular. Booking essential.

Pride of India

43 George Storrar Drive
Groenkloof
Tel: 012 346 3684
Great Indian food. Voted one of the to 100 restaurants in South Africa.

Waterfront Protea Hotel
Cnr Gordan Hood and Hendrik
Verworrd Ave.
Centurion 0046
Deluxe hotel overlooking waterfront.
119 rooms, swimming pool, restaurant
and bar.

Centurion Guesthouse
277 Van Riebeeck Ave.
Lyttelton Manor
Centurion
Tel: 012 664 4685
Fax: 012 664 5338
badenhorstjj@mweb.co.za
Splendid. 13 rooms, dining room and
bar. Swimming pool in lovely gardens.

Centurion Lake Hotel
1001 Lenchen Ave.
Pretoria
Tel: 012 643 3600
Fax: 012 643 3636
Relaxing hotel. 160 rooms. Swimming
pool, restaurant and bar.

Clubview Guesthouse
180 London Road
Clubview East.
Centurion
Tel: 012 654 6812
Fax: 012 654 6814
Sonia@clubview.co.za
13 rooms with TV in all rooms.
Swimming pool, bar and braai.

Leriba Lodge Hotel
245 End Ave.
Clubview
Centurion
A bush hotel nestled in a beautiful
setting. 8 hectares of forest on the
banks of the Hennops river in the
centre. This is the best hotel in town.
Swimming pool, restaurant and bar.

Shonalanga Valley
37 Vlakplaats
Centurion
Pretoria
Tel: 012 650 0222
Fax: 012 650 0234
inquiries@shonaloanga.co.za
On the Hennops river with splendid
rooms, swimming pool in beautiful
setting, restaurant and bar.

Sheraton Pretoria
Cnr of Church and Wessels St.
Arcadia
Pretoria 0007
Tel: 012 429 9999
Fax: 012 429 9300
Fine hotel with beautiful views. Very
close to centre. Swimming pool, gym,
restaurant and bar.

Hotel 224
Cnr Schuman and Leyds Sts
Arcadia
Pretoria 0007
Tel: 012 440 5821
Fax: 012 440 3063
hotel224@satis.co.za
Centrally located budget hotel. 224
rooms with restaurant and bar.

Sunset View B&B
219 Union St.
Riveria
Pretoria
Tel: 012 329 1808
Fax: 012 329 1809
sunsetviewbb@mweb.co.za
Beautiful. Set on hill overlooking
Pretoria. 2km from centre. Swimming
pool and barbecue.

That's It Guesthouse
5 Breecher St.
Sunnyside
Pretoria
Tel: 012 344 3404
Fax: 012 343 5270
thatsit@icon.co.za
Stylish rooms with TV and bar fridge.
Swimming pool in leafy sub tropical
garden. 5 minutes from centre.

Kievitskroon Country Estate
41 Reirr Road
Pretoria
Tel: 012 808 0150
Fax: 012 808 0148
reservations@kievitskroon.co.za
One of the leading boutique hotels.
Wonderful rooms. Fine dining restau-
rant and wine cellar, bars, cigar lounge,
health hydro. 15 minutes from centre.

Kia-Ora Backpackers'
257 Jacob More St.
Pretoria
Tel: 012 322 4803
Fax: 012 322 4816
hostel@freemail.absa.co.za
Backpackers' close to centre. Lovely
courtyard garden.

London Sports Bar

Corner Esselen & Jeepe St.
Pretoria
Gauteng 0001
Tel: 012 342 9950
One of best pubs in Pretoria. Sports, Karaoke, good beer and fish and chips.

Castle Walk Tavern

10 Lois Ave.
Erasmuskloof
Pretoria
Tel: 012 347 7823
Good food, drinks and service. Renowned for its food.

Eastwood Tavern

391 Eastwood St.
Arcadia
Pretoria
Tel: 012 344 0243
Busy pub opposite Minolta Loftus Stadium. Great atmosphere, friendly service. Good steaks and beer. One of the best.

Herr Gunther's Zapfhaus

Hatfield Square
Burnett St.
Pretoria
T: 012 362 6575
German pub with outstanding food and a wonderful atmosphere. In the centre

Maloneys

Corner of Duncan and South St.
Hatfield
Pretoria
Tel: 082 374 4421
One of the largest pubs in Pretoria. Great atmosphere.

Up the Creek

494 Hilda St.
Hatfield
Pretoria
Tel: 012 362 3712
Acoustic music bar. Established pub with regular clientele.

Johannesburg International Airport serves Centurion and Pretoria. It is located 45km from both cities. Metered taxis are available outside the terminal, the journey takes an hour and should cost no more than R300. Shuttle buses operate between the airport and Pretoria. Tickets must be purchased from the kiosk in Arrival Hall. Some hotels provide courtesy buses. There is an information desk in each terminal and porter services are available. There are two banks in Terminal 2 on the Public Mezzanine Level along with 4 foreign exchange outlets. There are ATM machines on the public concourses in Terminals 2, 4, 5 and 6.
Car hire is available in the arrivals terminal. Hertz 011 390 9700, Avis 011 394 543 Budget 011 394 2905. The airport has various restaurants, fast food outlets, cafés, Duty free Shopping, bookstores and souvenirs shops.
Terminal 1 and 2 - international arrivals; Terminal 3 - SAA and SA Express domestic arrivals; Terminal 4 - Non SAA arrivals; Terminal 5 - domestic departures; Terminal 6 - international departures.

The State Theatre

Church St.
Pretoria
Five auditoriums in which the Performance Arts Council of Transvaal perform.

Transvaal Museum

Paul Kruger St.
Pretoria 0001
Tel: 012 322 7632
Fax: 012 322 7939
Research and collection centre for the fauna of South Africa. Open Monday-Saturday 09.00-17.00

African Window

Visagie St.
Pretoria
Tel: 012 324 6082
Fax: 012 328 5173
An insight to South Africa's heritage. Jewellery clothing ceramics, music.

Pioneer Museum

Church Street East and Pretoria Road
Silverton
Tel: 012 803 6086
Fax: 012 803 5639
Fascinating farm, more than 150 years old.

transport

Airlines

South African Airways 011 395 3333
011 978 1111
BA/Comair 011 921 0222
SA Airlink 011 394 2430

Buses

Greyhound
1928 Building,
next to Pretoria Station
Tel: 012 323 1154

Translux
113 First St,
Salvokop,
Tel: 012 315 4300

Trains

Centurion/Pretoria Train
Enquires 086000 888

Taxis

Rixi Cabs 012 325 8072
City Taxis 012 321 5741

Car Hire

Hertz
Shop 7
67 Potgieter St.
Jet Set Park
Tel: 012 401 0860
Fax: 012 401 0870

Avis
70 Schoeman St.
Tel: 012 301 0700
Fax: 012 323 0432

Budget
465 Church St.
Arcadia
Tel: 012 341 4650

Tourist Offices

Pretoria Tourist Information Centre
South West Corner of Church Square
Pretoria
Tel: 012 308 3909/012 313 7694

Hospitals

Pretoria West.
Trans Oranje Road
Tel: 012 386 5111

Unitas Hospital
Tel: 012 664 0222

Starcare Muelmed
577 Pretoris St.
Arcadia
Tel: 012 440 2362

Climate

	ave temp	rain cm
January	20	14
February	19	17
March	18	19
April	16	39
May	13	74
June	10	92
July	11	70
August	12	74
September	16	40
October	17	37
November	18	15
December	17	17

Win/Loss Record

Country	Played	Won	Drawn	Lost	Tie
South Africa	8	6	1	1	-
England	2	1	1	-	-
Sri Lanka	3	-	-	3	-
West Indies	2	-	-	2	-
Australia	1	-	-	1	-

Highest Individual Aggregates (South Africa unless stated)

Player	Mat	Inn	NO	Runs	Ave	HS	50	100
Jacques Kallis	7	10	2	376	47.00	130*	2	1
Herschelle Gibbs	5	8	1	356	50.86	192	2	1
Gary Kirsten	7	10	1	276	30.67	134	1	1
Mark Boucher	6	7	1	271	45.17	100	1	1
Daryll Cullinan	6	8	1	269	38.43	103	0	1

Top Wicket Takers (South Africa unless stated)

Player	Mat	Bll	Md	Runs	Wkt	Ave	BB	S/R
Alan Donald	5	891	38	439	27	16.26	5/36	33.00
Makhaya Ntini	4	950	41	450	24	18.75	5/49	39.58
Shaun Pollock	7	1227	66	508	18	28.22	4/69	68.17
Jacques Kallis	7	860	38	428	16	26.75	4/39	53.75
Muttiah Muralitharan (SL)	2	746	23	325	12	27.08	5/63	62.17

Highest Individual Scores (South Africa unless stated)

192	Herschelle Gibbs	v West Indies 2003-04
141	Graeme Hick (Eng)	1995-96
139	Graeme Smith	v West Indies 2003-04
134	Gary Kirsten	v West Indies 1998-99
130*	Jacques Kallis	v West Indies 2003-04

Best Individual Bowling Performances (South Africa unless stated)

24.5-6-80-6	Courtney Walsh (WI)	1998-99
40.4-15-86-6	Glenn McGrath (Aus)	1996-97
18-5-36-5	Alan Donald	v Australia 1996-97
13-4-49-5	Alan Donald	v West Indies 1998-99
20-7-49-5	Makhaya Ntini	v West Indies 2003-04

Highest Partnerships

Wkt	Runs	Batsmen	Match
1st	301	Graeme Smith & Herschelle Gibbs (SA)	2003-2004 v West Indies
2nd	102	Adam Bacher & Brian McMillan (SA)	1996-1997 v Australia
3rd	140	Herschelle Gibbs & Jacques Kallis (SA)	2002-2003 v Sri Lanka
4th	174	Chris Gayle & Ramnaresh Sarwan (WI)	2003-2004
5th	126	Alex Stewart & Michael Vaughan (Eng)	1999-2000
6th	56	Hashan Tillakaratne & Hasantha Fernando (SL)	2002-2003
7th	132	Mark Boucher & Shaun Pollock (SA)	2002-2003 v Sri Lanka
8th	150	Neil McKenzie & Shaun Pollock (SA)	2000-2001 v Sri Lanka
9th	37	Hansie Cronje & Alan Donald (SA)	1996-1997 v Australia
10th	42	Hashan Tillakaratne & Muttiah Muralitharan (SL)	2002-2003

Results at Super Sport Park

Date	Countries	Result
16/11/1995	v England	drawn
21/03/1997	v Australia	won by 8 wickets
27/03/1998	v Sri Lanka	won by 6 wickets
15/01/1999	v West Indies	won by 351 runs
14/01/2000	v England	lost by 2 wickets
20/01/2001	v Sri Lanka	won by an innings and 7 runs
15/11/2002	v Sri Lanka	won by 3 wickets
16/01/2004	v West Indies	won by 10 wickets

Following four Tests played at the Lord's Ground, Kingsmead became the city's Test venue in January 1923 when it hosted the third match of the series against England. Although Phil Mead made 181 in England's 428 and South Africa hit 368, Alex Kennedy taking 5/88, the match ended in a tame draw.

xteen years later the teams played what became known as the Timeless Test. It lasted r ten days and ended in a draw when England were 654 for 5 chasing 696 to win cause they had to catch their boat home before the match could be decided! ue to the Second World War the next test between these sides in South Africa was nine ars later also at Kingsmead. It turned out to be the closest match at the ground. South rica made just 161 while England bettered that by 92, Len Hutton (83) and Dennis ompton (72) leading the way. Tufty Mann took 6/59. South Africa scored 219 in their cond innings to set England a target of 128 for victory. The visitors slipped to 70/6 as an McCarthy took 6/43 before struggling home with two wickets to spare. The South ricans bowled 10 no balls in their second innings which proved very costly. e ground hosted an incredible match in 1959 in the third Test of the series with stralia. Already 2-0 down South Africa made 311, Eric Rowan top scoring with 143. stralia collapsed to 75 as Hugh Tayfield 7/23 and Mann 3/31 ripped through their le. Leading by 236 runs South Africa were coasting at 51/1 before Johnston 4/39 and n Johnson 5/34 initiated a collapse to 99 all out. Set a target of 336, Australia struggled 95/4 before Neil Harvey (151no) took control and, along with Sam Loxton (54) and lin McCool (39no) brought Australia home by five wickets in one of the greatest rnarounds in Test cricket. 1970 South Africa got their revenge in spectacular fashion. They hit 622/9 dec., aeme Pollock with a masterful 274 and Barry Richards with 140 doing most of the mage. Australia could only manage 157 in reply and, forced to follow-on, they were smissed for 336 as South Africa won by an innings and 129 runs. e third Test of the 2002 series against Australia saw another great recovery. After ing put in, Australia, already series winners, made 315 thanks to Adam Gilchrist, 91, d Ricky Ponting, 89. In reply South Africa were reduced to 167 as Shane Warne 4/33 d Brett Lee 4/82 wreaked havoc. In their second innings Australia made only 186 to t a target of 334. Herschelle Gibbs, 104, and Gary Kirsten, 64, got off to a wonderful art with 142 and South Africa never looked back, reaching their target with five wick- ts to spare.

The highest team score at the ground is South Africa's 658/9 dec. against the West Indies in 2004, the lowest 66 by India in 1996. South Africa's 340/5 against Australia is the highest run chase.

Clarrie Grimmett's match figures 13/173 for Australia in 1936 are the best return at Kingsmead.

Kingsmead is home to the Natal Cricket Association and has a capacity of 25,000. The pitch has a reputation for been a firm true wicket and for suiting swing bowling.

The North Pavilion houses the President's Lounge, the Media Centre and the VIP Lounge. There is also a grass embankment at the north end of the ground. The open East Stand runs along the east side of the ground. The South Stand is partially covered and provides an excellent view of the cricket. There is another grass embankment in the south west corner of the ground in between the South Stand and the totally covere West Stand.

Refreshments are never far away with many bars and fast food outlets. There is a huge variety of food on offer including the Kingsmead Curry which must be tried. Most of the food stalls are behind the east stand. 'Castle Corner', the largest and liveliest bar, is situated at the south west end. There is a first-aid point behind the pavilion at the north end of the ground. Facilities for the disabled are provided with wheelchair viewing areas in most of the stands. There are a number of disabled toilets around the ground. The toilets facilities are good.

Tickets can be ordered from the Natal Cricket Association (Tel: 332 9703 email dolphins@natalcricket.co.za) and can be picked up at the ground. The ground does not reach capacity so tickets can be purchased on the day.

Kingsmead is located in the centre of Durban and is very accessible from the city centre by bus or on foot. The ground is in a business area and although there is some parking it can be hard to find.

the city

Durban is the provincial capital of Kwa Zulu Natal, the ancestral home of the Nguni people. Once known as the last outpost of the British Empire, today with a population of 2.3 million it would be hard to find a more cosmopolitan city with a remarkable fusion of British, Zulu, Indian, Portuguese and Chinese.

It lies on the eastern coast of South Africa by the Indian Ocean. On Christmas Da in 1497 Vasco Da Gama sailed ashore and named the area Rio de Natal. Port Natal evolved in 1823 and in 1835 the town was renamed after the Cape Governor Sir Benjamin D'Urban.

Tourism is Durban's largest industry. It has a sub-tropical climate with hot summers and mild winters. Unlike Cape Town, the sea temperature is always above 20 degrees, perfect for swimming, diving and surfing. Conditions for surfing are som of the best.

The city has a wonderful choice of accommodation from five star hotels to self-catering apartments on the beach front to guesthouses and hostels. With more than 15,000 beds visitors are spoilt for choice. With the diversity of cultures it is n surprise that the choice of cuisine is immense. From Chinese to Portuguese, not to mention Indian, a must when in Durban. Many streets have been pedestrianised with sidewalk cafés in abundance. Nightlife Entertainment is guaranteed.

Durban is known as the city 'where the fun never sets.' There is a carnival atmosphere throughout the city in the pubs and clubs and particularly the Sugar Mill Casino. There are many concert halls, theatres and art galleries in Durban. A visit the Playhouse Theatre where classical as well as original productions are performe is recommended.

City Hall is a fine building, housing a public library, an art gallery and the National Science Museum. It was built in 1910 and is modelled on Belfast City Hall. The Da Gama Clock erected to commemorate the explorer's landing is also a landmark. There are many modern buildings such as the International Convention Centre which can handle up to 5000 delegates. Durban has put itself to the forefront of con ference venues in the world.

The Sunshine Coast to the south has endless beaches, wonderful golf courses, dee sea fishing and some of the best diving in the world. To the north the coastline is more rugged with pristine beaches. Less than three hours driving will bring you to National Park where Africa's 'Big Five' animals can be seen. To the west of the city are the sprawling Drakensberg mountains.

Durban Botanical Gardens

Created in 1849 on the eastern slope of the Berea Ridge, the gardens contain some of the rarest plants in the world. Guided tours are available nd include the Orchid House, the Herb Gardens and the Garden for the Blind. e gardens are open from 9.30-17.00 seven days a week.

rban Beachfront

ed with luxury hotels as it skirts the main city beaches. It is an entertainment area h amusement parks, Waterworld and Seaworld and an aquarium with sharks, dol- ns and turtles. There is also an aerial cableway that provides tremendous views of city and coastline. Restaurants, bars and clubs are plentiful. The best beaches in rban are to the north at Umhlaga Rocks and to the south at Ansleys Beach.

etermaritzburg

niversity city set in the heart of Zulu country. A beautiful, dignified city it was ablished by the Voortrekkers in 1837. However the numerous Victorian and wardian Buildings indicate a British presence, the military having arrived in 43. An hour's drive from Durban is an ideal day trip destination, a peaceful day.

Khahlamba-Drakensberg Park

hahlamba is the Zulu word for 'Barrier of Spears' and is the name of the akensberg Mountains which lie to the west of Durban. The park, a World ritage site, is made up of a number of reserves including Giant's Castle and Royal Natal National Park. Wonderful topographical features include the nphitheatre, a 4km basalt crescent which is 1,800m in height. Activities include hing, hiking, horseriding and 4x4 drives through Sani Pass, the highest in South rica.

ctoria St. Market

few blocks back from Durban centre, at the west end of the street is the market. ilt in 1973 after the original was destroyed by fire, it is a lively place with an east- n theme. Ebony, ivory, wooden carvings, animals skins, leather, silks and furni- re are just some of the array of items on offer. The market is open 09.00-16.30 Monday-Friday and 08.00-14.00 Saturday/Sunday. In the surrounding street the Juma Mosque, West Street Mosque and the Catholic Emmanuel Cathedral are worth a visit.

Durban Airport is a 20 minute, 15km drive from the centre. Taxis are available outside the terminal and should cost no more than R100. There are also shuttle buses R25 (031 465 5573) which leave every hour to the city centre. Some hotels provide courtesy buses. These buses should be booked in advance. There is an information kiosk in he Arrival Hall (open 08.00- 21.00 Monday-Saturday , 09.00-21.00 Sunday). There is a retail bank on the ground floor and there are ATM machines in both Arrival and Departure Halls. There are a number of Car hire desks in the arrivals terminal. Hertz 031 469 4247, Avis 031 408 1777, Budget 031 408 1888. There are gift shops, chemist, restaurant and bars in both Arrival and Departure Halls.

where to stay

Hilton Durban
12-14 Walnut Road
Tel: 031 3368100
Fax: 031 3368200
Next to the Convention Centre.
Walking distance to beaches and centre.
Well designed rooms with excellent
coastal views. 327 rooms. 2 restaurants,
bar.

Blue Waters Hotel
175 Snell Parade
Tel: 031 3324272
Fax: 031 3375817
Opposite the beach. 278 rooms.
Facilities second to none including
health centre, squash, swimming pool,
restaurant and bar.

Ridge View Lodge
17 Loudown Rd
South Ridge Rd
Glenwood
Tel: 031 252 9777
Fax: 031 201 5587
ridgeview@inds.co.za
Pleasant guesthouse 10 minutes from
Durban. 7 excellent rooms with won-
derful views. Swimming pool. Free air-
port transfer.

Karos Edward Hotel
149 Marine Parade
Tel: 031 373 681
Fax: 031 373 638
Durban's only five star beachfront hotel.
Superb rooms overlooking the Indian
Ocean with restaurants serving some of
the best seafood in South Africa.

West Manors
159 Jan Hofmeyr Rd
Westville
Tel: 031 266 0767
Fax: 031 267 0993
westmanor@iafrica.com
10-minute drive from Durban, small
guesthouse, 7 studios, on the hillside
with sweeping views. Swimming
pool and gardens.

Lesley's B&B
150 Marine Drive
Bluff Rd
Tel: 031 466 2226
F: 031 466 4096
lesley@pixie.co.za
Set on the ocean with spectular views.
Surrounding by tranquil sub-tropical
gardens with swimming pool. 3 apart-
ments and 1 room.

City Lodge Durban
Cnr Brickhill and Old Fort Rd
Tel: 031 332 1447
Fax: 031 332 1483
Modern hotel in centre. Reasonably
priced rooms with restaurant and bar.

Seaboard Hotel
577 Point Rd
Marine Parade
Tel: 031 373 601
Fax: 031 372 600
Excellent views within walking distanc
of beaches and city centre. Standard
hotel rooms with restaurant and bar.

Ansteys Beach Backpackers'
477 Marine Drive
Bluff Rd
Tel: 031 467 1192
On beach, with best waves.

Brighton Beach Backpackers'
36 Crestmore
Sol Harris Crescent
Tel: 031 337 3940
On Cave Rock surf beach. Swimming
pool in garden.

Durban Beach Youth Hostel
Durban Beach
Tel: 031 32 4945
In centre on beachfront. Singles, dou-
bles and dormitories. Kitchen facilities

La Dolce Vita
Durban Club
Durban Club Place (off Smith St.)
Tel: 031 301 8161
Italian restaurant of the highest quality. Fine wine list and excellent service.

Jewel of India
Holiday Inn 63 Snell Parade
Tel: 031 362 1300
Good food in pleasant surroundings.

Bani Thai
38 Florida Rd
Morningside
Tel: 031 303 4270
Very trendy Thai restaurant. Excellent at extremely reasonable prices. Wonderful atmosphere.

Charlie Croft Wharfside Diner
8 Bontsman Raod
Maydon Wharf
Tel: 031 307 2935
Trendy restaurant serving steak and seafood.

Roma Revolving Restaurant
John Ross House
Victoria Embankment
Tel: 031 337 6707
Superb views from this fine Italian restaurant. Excellent wine list.

Beanbag Bohemia
8 Windermere Rd
Greyville
Tel: 031 309 6019
Trendy eating place. Bar and bistro on the ground floor with a more upmarket restaurant upstairs.

Café 1999
Sivervause Centre
Silverton Rd
Berai
Tel: 031 202 3406
Fusion restaurant.

Billy the Bums
504 Windermere Rd
Greyville
Cool pub with a name for good cocktails and good food.

Joe Kool's Bar & Grill
137 Lower Marine Parade
Tel: 031 332 9697
Very trendy pub and restaurant on beach. Pool tables and music.

BAT Centre
45 Maritime Place
Tel: 031 332 0451
A good place for Sundowners with splendid views of small craft harbour.

100 on Point
100 Point Rd
Durban Beachfront
Very trendy club.

All in One Tavern
1094 11th St.
Central
Tel: 031 707 3202
Pub with good food and pool table.

Post Office
Main Post Office
Cnr Gardener and West St.
Tel: 031 336 3333
Open Monday-Friday 08.00-16.30 and Saturday 08.00-12.00.

Tourist Offices
KwaZulu-Natal Tourism Authority
305 Tourist Junction
Old Station Building
160 Pine St.
Tel: 031 304 7144

Hospital
Addington Hospital
Erskine Terrace
South Beach
Tel: 031 327 2000

South Beach Medical Centre
3 Rutherford St.
South Beach
Tel: 031 332 3101

transport

Airlines
South African Airways
031 408 1408
Commair   031 450 7000
Nationwide   031 450 2087

Buses
Greyhound Motor Coach Terminal,
New Durban Station, NMR Ave.
Tel: 031 309 7830

Translux Luxury Coach Terminal
Station, NMR Ave.
Tel: 031 308 8111 Fax: 031 361 7963

Trains
Enquiries   031 361 7621

Taxis
KwaZulu Natal   031 3031 385
Zippy Cabs   031 202 7067
Aussies Cabs   031 309 7888

Car Hire
Hertz
Durban Hilton
13 The Ave East
Prospecton
Tel: 031 335 2570

Avis
Royal Hotel Parkade
Ulundi Place
Tel: 031 304 1741 Fax: 031 304 5517

Budget
108 Ordnance Rd
Tel: 031 304 9023

culture

Playhouse Theatre
29 Acutt St.
This mock Tudor Building is home
to the performing arts council. Five
stages performing opera/drama/ballet
and classical music.

Elizabeth Sneedin Theatre
Univerity of Natal
Modern theatre. Performances are usu-
ally university or visiting productions.

Durban City Hall
Home to the Natural Science Museum
which is on the ground floor, the
Durban Art Gallery on the first floor
and the Municipal Library on the second floor.

KwaMuhle Museum
130 Ordnance Rd
Tel: 031 311 2223
A harrowing look at the oppression
suffered by ordinary people during t
Apartheid era.

Durban Cultural and Document
Centre
Cnr Epsom Road & Derby St.
Open Monday to Friday 07.30-16.00
A look at the Indian history in the ci

Port Natal Maritime Museum
Bay End
Aliwal St.
Tel: 031 311 2231
Dedicated to Durban's seafaring
traditions.

Climate

	ave temp	rain cm			
January	25	125	July	17	40
February	24	114	August	16	44
March	23	118	September	16	58
April	21	87	October	22	89
May	19	76	November	23	104
June	16	24	December	26	114

Win/Loss Record

Country	Played	Won	Drawn	Lost	Tie
England	13	4	8	1	-
South Africa	31	11	12	8	-
Sri Lanka	1	-	1	-	-
Pakistan	2	1	-	1	-
Australia	8	3	2	3	-
India	2	-	1	1	-
New Zealand	3	-	-	3	-
West Indies	2	-	-	2	-

Highest Individual Aggregates (South Africa unless stated)

Player	Mat	Inn	NO	Runs	Ave	HS	50	100
Gary Kirsten	11	18	2	1048	65.50	275	4	3
Wally Hammond (Eng)	6	10	2	637	79.63	140	2	3
Jacques Kallis	8	13	2	564	51.27	177	2	2
Dudley Nourse	6	12	0	529	44.08	103	3	1
Bruce Mitchell	7	14	1	517	39.77	109	3	1
Herschelle Gibbs	6	11	1	470	47.00	142	1	2
Herbie Taylor	6	11	1	425	42.50	102	3	1
Eric Rowan	5	10	0	389	38.90	143	2	1
Eddie Paynter (Eng)	2	3	0	380	126.67	243	2	1
Graeme Pollock	3	5	1	348	87.00	274	1	1

Top Wicket Takers (South Africa unless stated)

Player	Mat	Bll	Md	Runs	Wkt	Ave	BB	S/R
Shaun Pollock	8	1632	78	598	31	19.29	6/50	52.65
Hugh Tayfield	4	2092	97	489	30	16.30	8/69	69.73
Alan Donald	7	1208	39	600	29	20.69	5/40	41.66
Makhaya Ntini	4	923	36	476	20	23.80	5/66	46.15
Cyril Vincent	4	974	33	386	19	20.32	6/51	51.26
Charlie Grimmett (Aus)	2	1038	71	304	18	16.89	7/100	57.67
Peter Pollock	4	834	38	348	14	24.86	6/38	59.57
Neil Adcock	3	819	21	245	14	17.50	6/43	58.50
Fanie de Villiers	3	826	33	350	13	26.92	5/64	63.54
Tufty Mann	2	810	28	204	13	15.69	6/59	62.31

Highest Individual Scores (South Africa unless stated)

275	Gary Kirsten	v England	1999-00
274	Graeme Pollock	v Australia	1969-70
243	Eddie Paynter (Eng)		1938-39
219	Bill Edrich (Eng)		1938-39
181	CP Mead (Eng)		1922-23
180	Gary Kirsten	v Sri Lanka	2000-01
177	Jacques Kallis	v West Indies	2003-04
151*	Neil Harvey (Aus)		1949-50
149	Stan McCabe (Aus)		1935-36
148*	Ken Barrington (Eng)		1964-65

Best Individual Bowling Performances (South Africa unless stated)

37.7-14-69-8	Hugh Tayfield	v England	1956-57
8.4-1-23-7	Hugh Tayfield	v Australia	1949-50
19-5-29-7	George Bissett	v England	1927-28
16-5-46-7	Andy Caddick (Eng)		1999-00
28-6-84-7	Franklyn Rose (WI)		1998-99
45-18-100-7	Charlie Grimmett (Aus)		1935-36
20.3-8-38-6	Peter Pollock	v NZ	1961-62
10-1-39-6	Muttiah Muralitharan (SL)		2000-01
12-2-43-6	Cuan McCarthy	v England	1948-49
18-2-43-6	Neil Adcock	v Australia	1957-58

Highest Partnerships

Wkt	Runs	Batsmen	Match
1st	191	Bruce Mitchell & Pieter van der Bijl (SA)	1938-1939 v England
2nd	280	Bill Edrich & Paul Gibb (Eng)	1938-1939
3rd	242	Wally Hammond & Eddie Paynter (Eng)	1938-1939
4th	249	Jacques Kallis & Gary Kirsten (SA)	2003-2004 v West Indies
5th	192	Gary Kirsten & Mark Boucher (SA)	1999-2000 v England
6th	206*	Ken Barrington & Jim Parks (Eng)	1964-1965
7th	143	Brian McMillan & Dave Richardson (SA)	1993-1994 v Australia
8th	101	Pravin Amre & Kiran More (Ind)	1992-1993
9th	97	Azhar Mahmood & Shoaib Akhtar (Pak)	1997-1998
10th	92	Arthur Gilligan & Jack (CAG) Russell (Eng)	1922-1923

Results at Kingsmead

Date	Countries	Result
18/01/1923	v England	drawn
16/02/1923	v England	lost by 109 runs
21/01/1928	v England	drawn
04/02/1928	v England	won by 8 wickets
16/01/1931	v England	drawn
21/02/1931	v England	drawn
14/12/1935	v Australia	lost by 9 wickets
28/02/1936	v Australia	lost by an innings and 6 runs
20/01/1939	v England	lost by an innings and 13 runs
03/03/1939	v England	drawn
16/12/1948	v England	lost by 2 wickets
20/01/1950	v Australia	lost by 5 wickets
11/12/1953	v New Zealand	won by an innings and 58 runs
25/01/1957	v England	drawn
24/01/1958	v Australia	drawn
08/12/1961	v New Zealand	won by 30 runs
04/12/1964	v England	lost by an innings and 104 runs
20/01/1967	v Australia	won by 8 wickets
05/02/1970	v Australia	won by an innings and 129 runs
13/11/1992	v India	drawn
25/03/1994	v Australia	drawn
26/12/1994	v New Zealand	won by 8 wickets
14/12/1995	v England	drawn
26/12/1996	v India	won by 328 runs
26/02/1998	v Pakistan	lost by 29 runs
26/12/1998	v West Indies	won by 9 wickets
26/12/1999	v England	drawn
26/12/2000	v Sri Lanka	drawn
15/03/2002	v Australia	won by 5 wickets
26/12/2002	v Pakistan	won by 10 wickets
26/12/2003	v West Indies	won by an innings and 65 runs

east london

Buffalo Park is less than ten minutes walk from the centre of the city and is one of the most picturesque grounds in world cricket with the Indian Ocean as its backdrop.

It became the tenth Test Ground in South Africa on 18 October 2002 when the home side took on Bangladesh. With captain Graeme Smith (200) and Gary Kirsten (150) sharing a second wicket partnership of 272, the home side reached 529/4 dec. Bangladesh could muster only 170 in reply, Makhaya Ntini taking 5/19 in 15 overs. Forced to follow-on, only Al Sahariar (71) batted well for the visitors as David Terbrugge took 5/46 to dismiss them for 252. South Africa won by an innings and 107 runs on the fourth day.

Buffalo Park has a capacity of 15,000 with one of the biggest grass embankments imaginable. The pavilion, which incorporates the dressing rooms, press boxes and TV, is a modern building at the Buffalo Drive end of the ground. To its left is the huge grass embankment which is a very popular place to watch the cricket from even though it is quite a way back from the pitch. It also provides arguably one of the most beautiful views in Test cricket. Straight ahead beyond the pitch is the Indian Ocean and to the left, the wonderful countryside of the area. There is no cover from the sun on the embankment which has a small scoreboard on its left. The main stand, which is totally covered, is opposite the pavilion with a great view. It also has an excellent bar. Then there is another uncovered grass embankment where sometimes a temporary stand is erected. The main scoreboard is situated in this area.

There are foodstalls and a bar to the right of the large embankment. The foodstalls serve hot dogs, burgers and other fast food. The bar has a good atmosphere and provides much needed shelter from the sun. There are also stalls and bars behind the other embankment. The toilet blocks are clean and well looked after. There are three medical points in the ground including one in the grandstand. Buffalo Park is only a five minute walk along John Bailie Road from the Esplanade where the majority of cricket supporters stay. Buses do run into the city but it is much easier to walk. Ample parking is available in fields and roads around the ground. There are facilities for the disabled in the pavilion and in the main stand. Enquiries to Greg (043 709 9739). Tickets are available on the day of the Test from any of the gates or from the Border Cricket Board Tel: 043 743 7757 Fax: 043 743 3293 or email moss@borderbears.co.za. The United Cricket Board of South Africa can also arrange tickets, email ucbsa@cricket.co.za

East London is at the mouth of the Buffalo River in Eastern Cape Province on the Indian Ocean and is South Africa's only river port. It has a population of 120,000.

In 1688 the ship Centaurus landed in the area to rescue 20 survivors from a ship wreck which went down off the coast. In 1836 George Rex travelled from Cape Town and settled in the area naming it Port Rex. In 1847 its name was changed East London. In the next few years more than 2,000 German settlers arrived and settled in the port. In 1857 157 Irish girls were sent by the British as wives for the many single settlers. The area and port grew with the construction of the railway and became the centre of business of the colony. Gold was discovered in 1886 and the town prospered and developed over the next 25 years. East London became a city in June 1914.

Car assembly is one of East London's main industries with the DaimlerChrysler company expanding rapidly. This industry, along with timber, has developed the port, creating much needed employment. The agriculture industry, mainly cattle and sheep farming, is also very important to the city. Tourism is another major industry and is growing each year due to the beautiful beaches and pleasant temperature.

East London is quiet but has some interesting attractions for tourists. The East London Museum and the Anne Bryant Art Gallery are both worth a visit as are the Queens Park Zoo, the East London Aquarium, the Botanical Gardens, the Lock Street Gaol and Fort Glamorgan on the West Bank. The East London City Hall was built at the end of the 19th century with its clock tower added to commemorate Queen Victoria's 60 years on the throne and is just one example of 19th century architecture in the city. The German Settlers' Memorial on the Esplanade reflects another piece of East London's history.

The beaches around East London are considered to be among the best in the world and a paradise for surfers with their golden sands and rolling surf. Nahoon Reef and Eastern Beach host many international surfing competitions. Orient Beach, the closest one to the city, is a fine beach popular with locals and tourists alike.

East London has a temperate climate dominated by the Agulhas and Mozambique currents which flow down the coast of South Africa. Summers are hot and humid while the winters can sometimes be cold they are usually mild. Average maximum temperatures are around 25 degrees during the cricket season. Lightweight tropical clothing is recommended.

There is a wide selection of accommodation. Most of the lodgings are found down by the Esplanade which is close to Buffalo Park and to all the more popular pubs and restaurants. The restaurants are varied. Many of the pubs play live music and stay open until the early hours.

In addition to the surf East London also offers hiking, diving and mountain bike riding, besides having some the best golf courses in South Africa such as the East London Golf Club (043) 735 1356, Gonubie Golf Club (043 735 1356) and West Bank Golf Club (043 736 3646).

East London Airport is small but busy 10km to the south west of the city. A taxi should take about 10 minutes and cost no more than R90. An airport shuttle bus runs between the airport and the city (043 748 3883). There is an ATM in the Departure Hall and a tourist information desk (043 701 9600) in the Arrival Hall. There is a restaurant on the first floor of departures and a coffee bar in arrivals. There is also a book shop in the Departure Hall. Car hire is available from Avis (043 736 1344), Budget (043 736 2364) and Hertz (043 736 2444).

Queens Park Zoo

Situated in natural coastal forest close to the city centre, its main feature is rare white lion cub which was born at the Zoo. It also exhibits 50 species of ammal, 38 of birds and seven of reptiles. There is a large collection of leopard rtoises, and the chimpanzees are a big draw. A wonderful fountain houses collection of Koi fish. Open 08.30-17.00 seven days a week. R8 Adults, R5 hildren. Bookings 043 722 1171.

ast London Aquarium

ome to over 400 different species of marine life, including freshwater and tropi-
ıl fish, penguins, pelicans and seals. Built in 1931, it has developed into a mod-
n aquarium and offers eye to eye contact with sharks, seal performances and
sh feeding every day. Open daily 09.00-17.00s and cost R12 for adults and R7.50
r children. (043 705 2637).

hayalabantu Cultural Village

)km from East London near the town of Mooiplaas. It provides an opportunity
learn about the Xhosa culture, to enjoy its art, music and dance and try tradi-
onal food. A very worthwhile trip. Visits can be arranged by contacting 043 851
)11.

kwenkwezi Private Game Reserve

unique haven to some spectacular vegetation, game and birdlife, where lion,
ino, leopard, zebra, wildebeest, giraffe and antelope can be seen. It is 32km
om East London off the East Coast Road towards Umtata. Game drives, guided
rd tours and horse riding are available. Contact Liezl on 043 734 3234.

ort Glamorgan

ne of a chain of protected garrisons built along the coast. The fort was built
1848 at the same time as the town was founded to provide quarters for the
British army. The powder house is now a national monument. Tours can be
arranged by contacting 043 731 1610.

what to see

Airlines

South African Airlines
                        043 704 1111
British Airways   043 743 7471

Buses

Translux
Moore St.
Quigney
Tel: 043 700 1999
Tel: 043 700 1010

Greyhound
Windmill Parl
319c Moore St.
Quigney
Tel: 043 743 9284
Fax: 043 743 0061

Trains

Trains run between East London
and Johannesburg via Bloemfontein
daily.
Spoornet
Station St.
Tel: 043 700 2719

Taxis

Border Taxi	043 722 3946
East London Taxi	043 743 6839
Fanie's Taxi Service	043 743 5759 or
	083 366 0722

Car Hire

Avis	043 736 1344
Budget	043 736 2364
Hertz	043 736 2444

transport

Holiday Inn Garden Court Hotel

Corner John Bailie and Moore St.
Tel: 043 722 7260
Fax: 043 743 7360
highceleastlondon@southernsun.com
www.southernsun.com
Probably the best hotel in East London with en suite air-conditioned rooms, cable TV, restaurant, cocktail bar and swimming pool. Overlooking ocean and very close to ground.

The Regent Hotel

Esplanade
Beachfront
Tel: 043 709 5000
Fax: 043 742 1261
regent@mweb.co.za
www.premierhotels.co.za
175 room luxury hotel overlooking the ocean. Restaurant, atrium cocktail bar, sportsman's bar.

The Blue Lagoon Hotel

Blueband Place
Beacon Bay
Tel: 043 748 4821
Fax: 043 748 2037
blhotel@iafrica.com
Well appointed rooms with cable TV. 2 restaurants, The Highlander and The Sunset. Pub, swimming pool and barbeque area.

Hotel Osner Crescent

Court Crescent
Esplanade
Quigney
Tel: 043 743 3433
Overlooking ocean. En suite rooms with cable TV.Rrestaurant, bar, swimming pool, sauna and spa.

The Kennaway Hotel

Esplanade
Quigney
Tel: 043 722 5531
Fax: 043 743 3433
106 en suite room hotel with cable TV, overlooking the ocean.

Bunkers Inn

23 The Drive
Bunkers Hill
Tel: 043 735 4642
bunkersinn2000@freemaal.absa.co.za
5 en suite bedroom guesthouse described as a haven of tranquillity. On one of South Africa's finest golf course with swimming pool in lovely garden. Great food.

Montrose Valley

4 Montrose Place
Bunkers Hill
Tel: 043 735 3418
montrosevalley@mweb.co.za
Lovely guesthouse beside golf course. One bedroom in main building, one log cabin and one cottage. All en suite with cable TV. Excellent breakfast. Dinner by appointment.

2b Sheerness Road

Bonnie Doon
Tel: 043 735 3206
Fax: 043 735 4957
gwshaw@mweb.co.za
Excellent, forested hideaway, with one bedroom in main building and 2 cottages. The rooms are en suite and have private entrances and decks.

Sugar Shack Backpackers'

Eastern Beach off Esplanade
T/F 043 722 8240
sugarsk@iafrica.com

Bloom Buffalo Lodge

12 Patrick St.
Quigney
Tel: 043 439 156
Fax: 043 438 130

East London Backpackers'

128 Moore St.
East London
Tel: 043 23423

Niki-Nana Backpackers' Lodge

4 Hillview Rd
Beach
Tel: 043 722 85029
info@nikinanna.co.za

Emzini Restaurant

Hemmingways Casino Complex
Tel: 043 722 0370
info@emzini.co.za
Famous restaurant with traditional
Xhosa cooking, special home made
drink, story telling, praise singing and
cultural entertainment. Fascinating
evening.

Ernst Chalet Suisse and Quarterdeck

Esplanade
Orient Beach
Tel: 043 722 1840
One of East London's best known res-
taurants serving continental, Austrian
and seafood.

Michaela

Greenbras Drive
Gonubie East
Tel: 043 738 5139
2-storey interior with 3 outside decks
overlooking the ocean. Seafood, fish
and grills are available.

Smokey Swallows

Devereux Ave.
Vincent
Global restaurant with Indian, Thai,
Italian, Chinese, Japanese and American
dishes on the menu. Excellent value.

Shanghai Chinese Restaurant

Currie St.
Quigney
Tel: 043 742 4381
The best Chinese restaurant in East
London. Opening hours Monday-
Saturday 11.30-14.00 and 17.00-22.00.

Y Knot Restaurant

Regent Hotel
Esplanade
Tel: 043 709 5000
Excellent pub/restaurant on ground
floor of Regent Hotel overlooking
ocean. Good food.

Le Petit Restaurant

54 Beach Rd
Nahoon
Tel: 043 735 3685
Small restaurant and pub with interest-
ing menu including buffalo, crocodile
and ostrich steaks and frogs' legs. Open
Monday-Saturday.

The Dutchess Ice Cream Parlour

Kings Tourism Centre
Esplanade
Tel: 043 743 0953
Excellent. Down by the ocean.

The Signal Arms

Station St.
Tel: 043 743 6882

O'Hagan's Pub and Grill

Aquarium Complex
Esplanade
Tel: 043 722 2982
Popular Irish pub with live bands on
Wednesday, Friday and Saturday. Open
until late every night.

Y Knot Pub

Regent Hotel
Esplanade
Tel: 043 709 5000
Good pub with lively atmosphere with
all sports events on large TV screens.
Also serves good food. Open from 11.00
till late.

Quarterdeck Pub and Restaurant

Orient Pavilion
Esplanade
Tel: 043 743 5312
Very popular pub with live music, danc-
ing and excellent food.

The Dros

Kings Entertainment Centre
Aquarium Road
Quigney
Tel: 043 743 3157
Lively pub overlooking the ocean.

Buccaneers Sports Pub and Grill

Marina Glen
Beachfront
Tel: 043 743 5171
Sports bar with large screens and great
atmosphere.

The East London Museum

Oxford St.
Tel: 043 743 0686
Home to the only Dodo egg in the world, marine history displays and exhibitions of prehistoric times of the country and the history of the Xhosa people. It also has a model of a coelacanth, a fish species estimated to be 350 million years old which was thought to be extinct until one was caught by an East London fisherman in 1938. The museum is open 09.30-17.00 Monday-Fridays, 14.00-17.00 Saturdays and 11.00-16.00 Sundays.

The Ann Bryant Art Gallery

St. Marks Rd
Tel: 043 722 4044
Excellent example of post-Victorian architecture. Houses a collection which represents South African art from the time East London was established. The gallery also has excellent Dutch and Victorian paintings. Open 09.30-17.00 Monday-Friday 09.30-12.00 Saturday.

Tourist Information

Kings Tourism Centre
Beach Front
Tel: 043 722 6015
Fax: 043 743 5091
info@tourismbuffalocity.co.za
www.tourismbuffalocity.co.za
Open Monday-Friday 08.15-16.30
Saturday 09.00-12.00

East London Tourism Bureau
Old Library Building
Tel: 043 722 6015
Fax: 043 722 6015
eltour@mweb.co.za
www.eastlondontourism.co.za

Hospital

East London Private Hospital
32 Albany St.
Tel: 043 722 3128
Fax: 043 722 3575

St. Dominic's Hospital
45 St. Mark's Rd
Southernwood
Tel: 043 743 4303
Fax: 043 722 3250

Climate

	ave temp	rain cm
January	21	69
February	22	83
March	21	102
April	20	69
May	18	49
June	16	39
July	15	40
August	15	42
September	17	79
October	18	95
November	19	99
December	20	73

Win/Loss Record

Country	Played	Won	Drawn	Lost	Tie
South Africa	1	1	-	-	-
Bangladesh	1	-	-	1	-

Highest Individual Aggregates (South Africa unless stated)

Player	Mat	Inn	NO	Runs	Ave	HS	50	100
Graeme Smith	1	1	0	200	200.00	200	0	1
Gary Kirsten	1	1	0	150	150.00	150	0	1
Al Sahariar (Ban)	1	2	0	89	44.50	71	1	0
Sanwar Hossain (Ban)	1	2	0	80	40.00	49	0	0
Jacques Kallis	1	1	1	75	-	75*	1	0

Top Wicket Takers (South Africa unless stated)

Player	Mat	Bll	Md	Runs	Wkt	Ave	BB	S/R
Makhaya Ntini	1	203	15	74	7	10.57	5/19	29.00
David Terbrugge	1	160	4	89	7	12.71	5/46	22.86
Nantie Hayward	1	186	5	115	4	28.75	2/50	46.50
Talha Jubair (Ban)	1	156	5	108	2	54.00	2/108	78.00
Claude Henderson	1	222	10	81	2	40.50	1/23	111.00

Highest Individual Scores (South Africa unless stated)

200	Graeme Smith	2002-03
150	Gary Kirsten	2002-03
75*	Jacques Kallis	2002-03
71	Al Sahariar	2002-03
49	Sanwar Hossain	2002-03

Best Individual Bowling Performances (South Africa unless stated)

15-9-19-5	Makhaya Ntini	2002-03
15-1-46-5	David Terbrugge	2002-03
11.4-3-43-2	David Terbrugge	2002-03
15-3-50-2	Nantie Hayward	2002-03
18.5-6-55-2	Makhaya Ntini	2002-03

Highest Partnerships

Wkt	Runs	Batsmen	Match
1st	87	Graeme Smith & Herschelle Gibbs (SA)	2002-2003
2nd	272	Graeme Smith & Gary Kirsten (SA)	2002-2003
3rd	81	Gary Kirsten & Jacques Kallis (SA)	2002-2003
4th	37	Sanwar Hossain & Khaled Mashud (Ban)	2002-2003
5th	81*	Jacques Kallis & Martin van Jaarsveld (SA)	2002-2003
6th	35	Khaled Mashud & Alok Kapali (Ban)	2002-2003
7th	19	Alok Kapali & Mohammad Rafique (Ban)	2002-2003
8th	19	Mohammad Rafique & Tapash Baisya (Ban)	2002-2003
9th	13	Tapash Baisya & Manjural Islam (Ban)	2002-2003
10th	9	Mohammad Rafique & Talha Jubair (Ban)	2002-2003

Results at Buffalo Park

Date	Countries	Result
18/10/2002	v Bangladesh	won by an innings and 107 runs

johannesburg

the wanderers

The Wanderers Stadium is the city's third Test match ground following the old Wanderers Stadium and Ellis Park. Built in 1955, the stadium's first match was against England in December 1956 when the visitors won by 131 runs. Two months later the tables were turned in the closest match between the two sides when South Africa won by 17 runs. In an enthralling match, England were at one stage cruising at 147/2, chasing a target of 232, until Hugh Tayfield took nine wickets for 113 to claim victory. To this day it remains best bowling performance on the ground. Tayfield even had a hand in the one English wicket that he did not take, catching Doug Insole.

The first Test of the 1966 series against Australia saw another remarkable win for South Africa, when they had arguably the greatest side in their history. The home side managed only 199, Denis Lindsay top scoring with 69 as Garth McKenzie took 5/46. In reply, Australia began well with an opening partnership of 118 between B Lawry (98) and captain Bob Simpson (65) to set up a total of 325. Lindsay took six catches. Trailing by 126, South Africa made a terrific 620 to establish a target of 4 Lindsay, (182) again top scored, ably helped by Graham Pollock (90) and captain Peter van der Merwe (76). Facing such a huge target, Australia were dismissed for 261 as South Africa won by 233 runs.

Four years later the ground hosted the third Test of the 1970 series against Australia. South Africa made a modest 279 but Australia struggled even more and were dismissed for 202 as Peter Pollock took 5/39. The home side took control of the match as Eddie Barlow (110) and Graeme Pollock (87) led their side to a total of 408. Gleeson took 5/125 for Australia. Set 486 Australia crumbled to 178 as South Africa won by 307 runs. This was the last Test played at the ground before South Africa were banned from international cricket.

Since South Africa re-entered the international arena in 1991, there have been some very entertaining matches here. Australia were beaten in the first Test of the 1994 series by 197 runs, thanks mainly to a superb second innings century by Hansie Cronje. Australia gained their revenge in 1997 with an innings and 196 runs victory when South Africa lost their last five wickets for three runs.

The first Test of the 1998 Test against the West Indies was a close match. Shaun Pollock took 5/54 as the West Indies reached 261. In reply South Africa took a slender lead of seven runs. In their second innings the visitors could only manage 170 as Pollock took 4/49. Set a target of 164, Jacques Kallis (57no) guided his team home by four wickets.

In 2002 Australia had a massive victory. They made 652/7 (the highest team total at the ground) before declaring. Adam Gilchrist hit 204no, Damien Martyn 133 and Matthew Hayden 122. They went on to dismiss the home side for 159 in their first innings and 133 in their second to win by an innings and 360. Glenn McGrath took eight wickets in the match. Gilchrist nearly caught Greg Blewett (214 in 1997) as scorer of the biggest innings at The Wanderers.

One other knock deserves a mention. In 1995 England captain Mike Atherton batted for more than 11 hours, scoring 185no, to single handedly save the Test. In contrast Gilchrist's 204 was at the time the fastest ever double century in Test cricket. Nathan Astle hit a quicker double century against England at Christchurch four weeks later.

The Wanderers is the home of Gauteng Cricket Association and has a capacity of 30,000. Known as the 'Bullring', the pitch has always had a reputation of being true and fast with a superb outfield.

Five of the six stands are partially covered; The Memorial Stand and Centenary Pavilion at the north end. The Unity Stand and the Taverner's Pavilion at the south end are huge modern structures providing excellent views. The East Stand has wooden benches and is totally open to the elements. The scoreboard and the video replay screen are on the east side of the ground. There is also a grass embankment in front of the changing rooms in the Western Pavilion which is a very popular area in which to sit. Corporate hospitality is available. There are fast food outlets behind the Western Pavilion and Braai areas behind the Members. Tickets can be ordered from the NCA (Tel: 011 7881008 email general@cricketgauteng.co.za). and can be collected at the ground. The ground does not reach capacity during Test matches and tickets can be purchased on the day.

The stadium lies on Corlett Drive, 7km to the north of the city and is accessible by bus and taxi. A park and ride scheme is in place for all international matches.

Johannesburg, the world's largest inland city, is the centre of Gauteng province. Known as The City of Gold, it is the economic hub of South Africa and is the major international gateway.

Johannesburg was founded on the 4th October 1886 when George Harrison discovered gold on a farm in the area. Fortune hunters arrived in great numbers and a shanty town was set up. This shanty town has now become a city, home to 3.8 million people, with skyscrapers and a bustling financial market.

Johannesburg has some wonderful Victorian and Edwardian architecture such as the Civic Theatre, Museum Africa and the Smutts Library. There are many theatres where an array of productions are performed. Museums and galleries are also in Abundance. The Zoo is a very peaceful and secure retreat with an array of creatures.

Nightlife in Johannesburg is exciting and vibrant. Restaurants are renowned with Gauteng's thriving farming industry providing meats, fruits and wines of the finest quality. Along with fresh seafood the cuisine is varied and delicious. There are many pubs and nightclubs and the casinos are open 24 hours a day.

Like any major city it has its problems with crime, and visitors to the city are advised to be cautious of certain areas. To this end Santon and Rosebank, two of Johannesburg most affluent suburbs, are recommended as safe areas. This applies to accommodation as well.

Walking, hiking, running, golf, rugby and, of course, cricket are just some of the activities which can be enjoyed. This is a wonderful place to visit, however visitors must be vigilant at all times regarding crime and follow advice given by police, tourist information centres, hotels and guesthouses.

Soweto

A 'must do' item on any trip to Johannesburg. The South West Township has a population of two million and is a lively and friendly place. Heritage includes th Hector Petersen Memorial, the home of Nelson Mandela, Freedom Square, Aval Cemetery and the Morris Issacson School. It is essential that you take a tour as Soweto is a maze and it can be dangerous using public transport. The Heritage Tours and The Shebeen Crawl, an entertainment tour, are recommended.

Gold Reef City

A recreation of 1900 Johannesburg when prospectors flocked to the area follow-ing the discovery of gold in 1890's. Underground tours are available to witness gold pouring and to experience the conditions. Also an amusement park with Rollercoasters, big wheels and other rides. There is a selection of hotels, with res taurants and bars, and also the Gold Reef City Casino.

Botanical Gardens

148 hectares and in the heart of the city. Famous for its terraced Rose Garden, it is one of the city's most tranquil spots. In addition to 5000 roses there is a large herb garden and a wonderful hedge display. Both the restaurant and coffee shop provide a lovely setting for a pleasant lunch.

Lipanzzaner (Kyalami)

Every Sunday morning at 11.00 the Kyalami Equestrian Centre opens its doors t offer the opportunity to see the white Lipanzzaner Stallions in action. These wo famous horses are renowned for their grace and dignity. An unusual and fascina ing morning.

Newtown Cultural Project

Right in the centre. Transformed from a derelict slum into the city's cultural hot spot with an array of things to see including MuseumAfrica, the Market Theatre the Horror Café and the World of Beer Museum. A large selection of restau-rants, bars and coffee shops are on offer.

Ile de France

26 Cramerview Centre
Briganston
Tel: 011 706 2837
French Restaurant in the northern sub-urbs. Superb food. Good wine list.

Giles

9 Graton Ave.
Graighall Park
Tel: 011 442 4056
F: 011 442 4057
gilesrez@mweb.co.za
A celebration of the cartoonist Giles.
English cuisine.

Paros Taverna

Mutual Gardens
Rosebank
Tel: 011 788 6211
Wonderful Greek restaurant in the heart of Rosebank.

Pescador Restaurant

Graystone Centre
Sandown
Tel: 011 884 4429
This Portuguese restaurant serves the best seafood in Joburg.

Chon Hing

26 Alexander St.
John Vorster Square
Tel: 011 834 3206
Simply the best Chinese in town.

Giovanni's

Corner of 3rd and 7th Avenues.
Parktown North
Tel: 011 447 5462
Trendy sidewalk Italian restaurant.

The Butcher Shop and Grill

Shop 30
Sandton Square
Tel: 011 784 8676
Fax: 011 784 8674
The best steak in town whether it be pork, ostrich, lamb, beef or game.

Park Hyatt

191 Oxford Rd
Rosebank
Saxonwold 2131
Tel: 011 280 1234
Fax: 011 280 1238
parkhyatt@hyatt.co.za
A hotel of unrivalled luxury in
Rosebank. 244 beautiful rooms with
stunning views. Fine Restaurant and
bar complete with health club and
swimming pool on roof.

Crown Plaza

Corner of Rivonia Rd and Grayston
Drive
Sandown
Sandton 2146
Tel: 011 783 5262
Fax: 011 783 5289
350 comfortable rooms, 2 restaurants
and bars, swimming pool and gardens.

Rosebank

Cnr of Tyrwhitt and Sturder Avenues
Rosebank 2131
Tel: 011 447 2700
Fax: 011 447 3276
A 10 minute drive from the centre, this
hotel has 318 rooms, 3 restaurants, 2
bars, a swimming pool, gym and hair
salon.

The Westcliff

67 Jan Smuts Ave.
Johannesburg
Tel: 011 646 2400
Fax: 011 646 3500
The cuisine and service in this elegant
city hotel are second to none. 106
rooms, 14 suites, 2 restaurants, 2 bars,
tennis courts, 2 swimming pools, gym
and hair salon.

Ten Bompas

10 Bompas Rd
Dunkeld West
Tel: 011 325 2442
Fax: 011 341 0281
Boutique hotel – 10 individually
designed rooms – with a name for
excellent food in its restaurant and bar.

The Michelanglo on Sandton Square

West St.
Sandton Ave.
Tel: 011 282 7000
Fax: 011 282 7171
hrmichel@legacyhotel.co.za

Elegant hotel with Renaissance
inspired décor in the heart of the
city. 218 rooms, restaurant, bar, swimming pool, sundeck and gym.

Graton Guesthouse

4A Oaklands Rd
Orchards
Tel: 011 728 2340
Fax: 011 728 0855
E graton@intekom.co.za
Pleasant guesthouse in quiet suburb. 5
rooms, swimming pool, garden, laun-
dry, breakfast. TV in all rooms.

La Bougain Villa

6 Smits Rd
Dunkeld West
Tel: 011 447 3404
Fax: 011 442 5097
fay@labougainvilla.co.za
5 minutes from Sandton and
Rosebank, Villa has 2 suites with private lounges. Tennis courts, swimming
pool.

Highgrove Guesthouse

1 Side Rd (off East Rd)
Sandton
Tel: 011 884 3680
F: 011 884 0341
highgrove@yebo.co.za
Each of the 7 rooms has either a bal-
cony or patio overlooking the pool. All
rooms have TV, safe and modem.

Hilton Sandton

138 Rivonia Rd
Sandton
Tel: 011 322 1888
Fax: 011 322 1818
330 rooms, business centre, swimming
pool, tennis courts, gym and beauty
salon. Excellent restaurant and bar.

International Travellers Backpackers'

55 First St.
Bezuidenhout's Valley
Tel: 011 614 4640
Fax: 011 614 2497
Good comfortable backpackers'.

Happy Valley Backpackers' Lodge

86 Nanyuki Rd
Sunninghill Park
Tel: 011 807 0972
happyval@gobal.co.za
Popular backpackers'.

Rosebank is the nightlife area of Joburg with clubs, bars and restaurants everywhere. Joburg offers cinemas, plays, opera and all types of music.

Demolition
Cnr Conrad and Hillcrest St.
Blarigowrie
Tel: 082 859 6835
Action packed pub with music 7 nights a week. Pool tables.

The Blues Room
Village Walk
Sandton
Tel: 011 784 5527
Best jazz and blues in town.

The Ratz Bar
7th Ave.
Vibrant, young bar. Lively 7 nights a week.

Jabulani's Bar
Park Hyatt Hotel
Rosebank
Tel: 011 280 1234
An upmarket cocktail and cigar bar.
Ultra comfortable.

The Doors
19 Van Riebreck Ave.
Edenvale
Tel: 011 453 7673
Bar with alternative music.

All Bar None
100 Alberton Rd,
Wiersha Valley Sandton.
Tel: 011 784 0519

Johannesburg International Airport is the busiest in Africa. Located 19km to the north east. Metered Taxis are available outside the terminal. The journey should take 35 minutes to the centre and should cost no more than R150. Shuttle buses operate between the airport and the city. Tickets are very cheap but must be purchased from the kiosk in the Arrival Hall. Some hotels provide courtesy buses. These buses should be booked in advance. There is an information desk in each terminal and porter services are available.
There are two banks in Terminal 2 on the Public Mezzanine Level along with 4 foreign exchange outlets. There are ATM machines on the public concourses in Terminals 2,4,5 and 6. The airport has various restaurants, fast food outlets, café Duty free shopping, book shops and souvenir shops. Car hire is available in the arrivals terminal from Hertz (011 390 9700), Avis (011 394 5433) and Budget (0 394 2905). It should be noted that it is not an easy drive from the airport to the city centre.
Terminal 1 and 2 – International Arrivals; Terminal 3 - SAA and SA Express Domestic Arrivals; Terminal 4 - Non SAA Arrivals; Terminal 5 – Domestic Departures; Terminal 6 – International Departures.

Post Office
Main Post Office
Jeepe St.

Tourist Offices
Johannesburg Publicity Association
North State Building
Corner Kruis and Market St.
Tel: 011 336 4961

Gauteng Tourism Authority
Rosebank Mall
Upper Level
Corner Baker and Craddock St.

Tel: 011 340 9000
Fax: 011 327 7000
tourism@gauteng.net

Hospital
Millpark Hospital
Guild St.
Parktown
Tel: 011 480 5600

Airlines

South African Airways 011 395 3333
011 978 1111
BA/Comair 011 921 0222
SA Airlink 011 394 2430

Buses

The local bus service is not recommended. In recent years the service has deteriorated although the council are trying to revive the system.
Translux 011 774 3333
Greyhound
Park City Transit Centre
Johannesburg Station 011 249 8900

Trains

The local metro system is the cheapest form of transport but is not recommended as muggings are on the increase.

Train Station 0860 008 888

Taxis

Maxi Taxis - Yeoville 011 648 1212
Metro Cabs 011 484 7975
Visitors are advised to use metered taxis
Traffic in Johannesburg is very congested during rush hour 07.00-09.00 and 16.00-18.00

Car Hire

Hertz
Oxford Manor
196 Oxford Rd
Tel: 011 537 4800

Illovo
Tel: 011 537 4800
Fax: 011 537 4802

Avis
Tel: 0861 021 111

Market Theatre

Corner Bree and Wolhuter St.
Newton Cultural Precinct
Tel: 011 832 1641
Located in an old Indian produce market built in the early 1900's. Productions are socially relevant. There are three theatres, a bar and restaurant.

Civic Theatre

Loveday St.
Braamfontein
Tel: 011 403 3408
City's principal cultural venue. Modern complex with four theatres. Productions are traditional African.

Alhambra Theatre

Cnr Sivewright Ave and Beit St.
Doornfontein
Tel: 011 402 6174
Three theatres specialising in West End/Broadway material.

SA Breweries Museum

15 President St.
Newtown
Tel: 011 836 4900
Open Tuesday to Saturday, traces the history of beer in Africa. The brewery is one of the largest in the world. And, of course, there is the visit to the bar!

MuseumAfrica

121 Bree St.
Newtown
Tel: 011 833 5624
Focuses on the history of South Africa from the Stone Age to modern times including geology, archaeology etc. Open Tuesday-Sunday 09.00-17.00.

AECI Dynamite Factory Museum

Moolderfontein
Tel: 011 606 3206
Unusual but interesting history of explosives. This museum is housed in an 1895 residence of a mining official.

Gallery on the Square

Sandton Square
Rivonia Rd
Tel: 011 784 2847
International and South African art, ceramics and sculpture.

Johannesburg Art Gallery

Klein St.
Joubert Park
Tel: 011 725 3130
A permanent collection of historical and contemporary South African works.

Soweto Gallery

Corner Commissioner and Harrison St.
Tel: 011 836 0252

Climate

	ave temp	rain cm			
January	21	125	July	11	4
February	20	94	August	12	6
March	18	90	September	16	27
April	16	54	October	18	76
May	13	13	November	20	117
June	10	9	December	17	103

Win/Loss Record

Country	Played	Won	Drawn	Lost	Tie
South Africa	25	10	10	5	-
India	2	-	2	-	-
New Zealand	4	1	2	1	-
Australia	8	3	2	3	-
England	6	1	3	2	-
Pakistan	2	-	1	1	-
Sri Lanka	1	-	-	1	-
West Indies	2	-	-	2	-

Highest Individual Aggregates (South Africa unless stated)

Player	Mat	Inn	NO	Runs	Ave	HS	50	100
Hansie Cronje	9	17	0	683	40.18	122	2	1
Daryll Cullinan	9	15	3	649	54.08	122*	4	2
Trevor Goddard	9	17	0	609	35.82	112	4	1
Gary Kirsten	12	21	1	569	28.45	110	3	1
Eddie Barlow	7	12	0	566	47.17	110	4	1
Jacques Kallis	8	12	2	549	54.90	158	4	1
Brian McMillan	6	12	1	504	45.82	113	1	2
John Waite	7	12	0	469	39.08	115	3	2
Jonty Rhodes	8	15	0	456	30.40	91	4	0
Denis Lindsay	4	7	1	402	67.00	182	1	2

Top Wicket Takers (South Africa unless stated)

Player	Mat	Bll	Md	Runs	Wkt	Ave	BB	S/R
Alan Donald	10	2247	83	1207	44	27.43	6/53	51.07
Shaun Pollock	9	1938	95	734	36	20.39	5/54	53.83
Trevor Goddard	9	2500	139	707	27	26.19	6/53	92.59
Peter Heine	5	1343	37	499	21	23.76	6/58	63.95
Hugh Tayfield	4	1782	73	540	21	25.71	9/113	84.86
Fanie de Villiers	3	881	44	382	20	19.10	6/81	44.05
Peter Pollock	6	1238	59	512	19	26.95	5/39	65.16
Goofy Lawrence	2	546	29	207	18	11.50	8/53	30.33
Makhaya Ntini	4	726	39	367	17	21.59	5/94	42.71
Shane Warne (Aus)	3	813	45	309	17	18.18	4/43	47.82

Highest Individual Scores (South Africa unless stated)

214	Greg Blewett (Aus)	1996-97
204*	Adam Gilchrist (Aus)	2001-02
202	Brian Lara (WI)	2003-04
185*	Michael Atherton (Eng)	1995-96
182	Denis Lindsay	v Australia 1966-67
172	Ted Dexter (Eng)	1964-65
160	Steve Waugh (Aus)	1996-97
158	Jacques Kallis	v West Indies 2003-04
148	Rahul Dravid (Ind)	1996-97
144*	Colin Bland	v England 1964-65

Best Individual Bowling Performances (South Africa unless stated)

37-11-113-9	Hugh Tayfield	v England 1956-57
30.3-12-53-8	Goofy Lawrence	v New Zealand 1961-62
17.4-4-34-6	Alan Davidson (Aus)	1957-58
32.5-14-53-6	Trevor Goddard	v Australia 1966-67
44-22-53-6	Anil Kumble (Ind)	1992-93
15-3-53-6	Alan Donald	v England 1999-00

14.2-3-58-6	Peter Heine	v Australia 1957-58
20.5-4-81-6	Fanie de Villiers	v Pakistan 1994-95
37.5-6-96-6	Peter Heine	v Australia 1957-58
15.4-6-20-5	Trevor Bailey (Eng)	1956-57

Highest Partnerships

Wkt	Runs	Batsmen	Match
1st	176	Jackie McGlew & Trevor Goddard (SA)	1957-1958 v Australia
2nd	136	Bob Barber & Ted Dexter (Eng)	1964-1965
3rd	191	Ted Dexter & Ken Barrington (Eng)	1964-1965
4th	145	Rahul Dravid & Sourav Ganguly (Ind)	1996-1997
5th	385	Steve Waugh & Greg Blewett (Aus)	1996-1997
6th	317	Damien Martyn & Adam Gilchrist (Aus)	2001-2002
7th	221	Denis Lindsay & Peter van der Merwe (SA)	1966-1967 v Australia
8th	127	Daryll Cullinan & Lance Klusener (SA)	1996-1997 v India
9th	195	Pat Symcox & Mark Boucher (SA)	1997-1998 v Pakistan
10th	71	Pieter De Villiers & Alan Donald (SA)	1994-1995 v Pakistan

Results at The Wanderers

Date	Countries	Result
24/12/1956	v England	lost by 131 runs
15/02/1957	v England	won by 17 runs
23/12/1957	v Australia	drawn
07/02/1958	v Australia	lost by 10 wickets
26/12/1961	v New Zealand	drawn
02/02/1962	v New Zealand	won by an innings and 51 runs
23/12/1964	v England	drawn
22/01/1965	v England	drawn
23/12/1966	v Australia	won by 233 runs
03/02/1967	v Australia	drawn
19/02/1970	v Australia	won by 307 runs
26/11/1992	v India	drawn
04/03/1994	v Australia	won by 197 runs
25/11/1994	v New Zealand	lost by 137 runs
19/01/1995	v Pakistan	won by 324 runs
30/11/1995	v England	drawn
16/01/1997	v India	drawn
28/02/1997	v Australia	lost by an innings and 196 runs
14/02/1998	v Pakistan	drawn
26/11/1998	v West Indies	won by 4 wickets
25/11/1999	v England	won by an innings and 21 runs
08/12/2000	v New Zealand	drawn
22/02/2002	v Australia	lost by an innings and 360 runs
08/11/2002	v Sri Lanka	won by an innings and 64 runs
12/12/2003	v West Indies	won by 189 runs

port elizabeth

St. George's Park in Port Elizabeth staged the first Test match to be played outside of England or Australia when England won by eight wickets in 1888. The ball from the match takes pride of place in the Centenary Pavilion.

The first Test of the 1896 series against England was a remarkable match for a number of reasons. Having been put into bat, England made only 185. In reply the home side could manage just 93 as George Lohmann took 7/38. In their second innings England struggled to 72/6 before Sammy Woods hit 53 to enable them to reach 2 Chasing 314 for victory, South Africa were dismissed for a paltry 30, the second lowest score in Test history. Lohmann became the fourth player to take a Test hat-trick when he took the last three South African wickets to end up with incredible figures of 8/7. His match figures were 15/45, the seventh best return of all time, and still best at St. George's.

The fifth and final Test of the 1949 series against England was another fine match. With Billy Wade scoring 125 and Bruce Mitchell 99, South Africa reached 379. In reply England made 395, captain George Mann hitting an unbeaten 136 as Athol Rowan took 5/167. Mitchell top scored with 56 as the home side made 187/3 before declaring. Set 172 for victory England reached their target with three wickets to spare to win the series 2-0.

In 1970 the ground hosted the last Test played in South Africa for more than 20 years because of apartheid. An opening partnership of 157 by Barry Richards (81) and Eddie Barlow (73) put South Africa in charge against Australia although Alan Connolly took six wickets to restrict them to 311. In reply the visitors made only 212 as Peter Pollock and Mike Proctor took three wickets each. South Africa piled on the runs in their second innings, scoring 470/8 before declaring, Richards (126) and Lee Irvine (102) making centuries. Facing an improbable 570, Australia were dismissed for 246 as Proctor took 6/73. South Africa won the series 4-0.

The closest match to take place at St. George's Park was in 1997. The Australians the home side into bat and South Africa started slowly, struggling to 70/5 before fine 55 from Brian McMillan helped their total to 209. Jason Gillespie took 5/54. Australia could only manage 108 as all six South African bowlers took wickets. South Africa made 168 in their second innings setting their opponents a target of 270. Mark Waugh hit a superb 116 as the visitors made their way towards the target. In a tense and hot-tempered finish, Ian Healy, the Australian wicket keeper, hit a six for his side to sneak home by two wickets in the highest run chase at the ground.

The highest team score is 549/7 declared by Australia in 1950, the lowest the 30 by South Africa in 1896.

The home of the Eastern Province Cricket Association, the ground has a capacity of 18,500. It also staged the first ever rugby Test match in South Africa in 1891, again against England.

The Centenary Pavilion is situated at the south end along with the Media Centre and a number of chalets. The Frielinghaus Stand runs along the west side. The Duckpond Pavilion at the north end has a capacity of 6,000 and is a splendid place from which to watch. There are a number of sponsor's hospitality suites, restaurants and bars in these stands. The two grass embankments in front of this stand are very popular. The scoreboard and some chalets are on the west side of the ground.

Numerous fast food outlets and six bars are dotted around the ground particularly underneath the Duckpond Stand where there is a varied choice of food. There are also memorabilia stalls in this area. Castle Corner the biggest bar in the ground is in the northeast corner of the ground, underneath the Duckpond Pavilion. Facilities and access for the disabled are good with a number of viewing areas with wheelchair access toilets in the Duckpond pavilion. Toilet facilities around the ground are good and well tended.

Tickets for the match can be ordered from the Eastern Province Cricket Association (Tel: 041 585 1646 email: admin@epcricket.co.za) and can be picked up at the ground. The ground does not reach its capacity during Test matches and tickets are always available on the day.

St. George's Park is situated in Park Drive near the centre and can be easily reached by foot, bus or car. There is plenty of on street parking around the ground.

Port Elizabeth, South Africa's fifth largest city (population 1.2m), lies along the shores of Algoa Bay on Africa's south eastern coast. Although Bartholomew Diaz arrived on the Eastern Cape in 1488 and Manuel de Mesquita in 1516 it was not until 1799 that Fort Frederick was built by the British to assist in the control of the Boers. In 1815 Port Elizabeth was established. It was named after the late wife of Sir Rufane Donkin, acting Govenor of the Cape Colony. In 1820 4,000 settlers arrived from Britain and became the first permanent residents. Before the gold and diamond boom in South Africa, Port Elizabeth was the major commercial city. Many Xhosa, Indian and Cape Malay migrated to the city in search of trade and labour opportunities with wool, mohair and ostrich feathers being the main industry.

Today PE is also home to the automobile industry in Africa with BMW, Ford and VW production plants. However tourism is the major industry. The city enjoys more sunshine hours and less rainy days than any other coastal city in South Africa. It has a moderate climate all year round with average temperatures of 17° in winter and 25° in summer and has an average of seven hours sunshine each day. With over 40km of golden beaches and the warm Indian Ocean waters, PE has become the watersport capital of South Africa.

The city boasts a unique historic heritage with theatres, museums and art galleries providing an insight into the past and present of the region.

A visit to PE presents an ideal opportunity to go on a game drive and view the 'Big Five' in the Shamwari Game Reserve just an hour's drive from the city and to visit the Addo Elephant National Park.

Port Elizabeth's nightlife is very lively with excellent restaurants offering gourmet food and fine wines. There are plenty of bars and clubs to dance the night away and there is the Boardwalk casino for some late night entertainment. There is a wide range of accommodation whether it be hotel, guesthouse or bed and breakfast in the city or down by the bay.

the city

Historic Donkin Heritage

Allows visitors to follow in the footsteps of the 1820 settlers. This 5km trail has 47 historical sites and architectural delights to offer, including City Hall, No 7 Castle Hill and the South End Museum. The Trail is situated in the Old Hill a of the city and provides a wonderful insight into local history.

Addo National Park

70km north of Port Elizabeth. The park is dedicated to the preservation of the Eastern Cape elephant, buffalo and rhino. There are more than 250 elephants in the 11,718 hectares park. It has its own serviced accommodation for overnight visitors along with restaurants etc. The park provides an opportunity to view these animals living in family groups by both night and day. The dam is the ide place to cool down with a swim.

Fort Fredrick

Built by the British in 1799 to defend the harbour from the French. Named afte Fredrick, Duke of York. The attack never came. The fort is easily accessible and provides an excellent view of Algoa Bay.

Shamwari Game Reserve

Home to the 'Big Five' of Africa (lions, tigers, elephants, rhinos and hippos). A huge reserve where a multitude of plant, animal and bird life typifies the soul of untamed Africa. Although ideal for a daytrip, the reserve is a 70km drive from Port Elizabeth, and also has varied accommodation to suite your budget.

The Garden Route

Runs from Port Elizabeth to Capetown and is an adventure in itself. The Tsitsikamma National Park 'the place of many waters' is both scenic and exhilarating with activities including rafting, tubing and klofting. Jeffreys Bay is 80km south of PE and is one of the world's best known surf beaches. The world's highest bungy jump is also on the Garden Route just two hours from PE at Bloukrans. What an experience!

Buffalo Bill's Steak Kraal

Primrose Square
Salvia Crescent
Tel: 041 360 4925
A large family restaurant with an African feel. Large steaks at reasonable prices.

Chilli Café

5 Brookes Pavillion
Tel: 041 584 0011
Mexican Restaurant overlooking bay. Excellent food in friendly surroundings. Impressive cocktail bar.

The Bell Restaurant

Marine Drive
Tel: 041 583 2161
One of Port Elizabeth's finest á la carte restaurants. Fine Italian cuisine, excellent wine list. Wonderful atmosphere.

The Royal Delhi

10 Burgess St.
Tel: 041 373 8216
Authentic Indian food with tantalising flavours. Very reasonably priced. Friendly atmosphere.

Mediterran Seafood Place

Dolphin's Leap
Beach Rd
Portuguese cuisine with a variety of fish, seafood, meat and vegetarian dishes. Fine wine list. Sushi bar. Supe views.

Dizzy Dolphin's Café

Beach Rd
Boardwalk
Tel: 041 583 4536
Lively with a varied menu. On the boardwalk Very well known and love

Lai Kung Chinese Restaurant

56 The Boardwalk
Tel: 041 583 1123
Best Chinese in town. Offers Mandar and Cantonese food at very reasonab prices.

The Poseidon Lodge

22 Poseidon Crescent
uewater Bay
l: 041 466 1114
x: 041 466 5968
laub@mweb.co.za
ghly recommended, 10 minutes from
e centre overlooking Algoa Bay. 5 en
ite rooms with a swimming pool and
aai in the garden.

rnandos Guest & Grill

2 Cape Rd
ill Park
l: 041 373 2823
x: 041 374 5228
rnando@mweb.co.za
ctorian guesthouse. Walking distance
main attractions. All bedrooms
suite. Fully licensed restaurant.
imming pool and braai.

e Train Suites

e Brookes Hill Drive
umwood
l: 041 586 0088
x: 041 586 0087
boose @sprint.co.za
different way to stay'. Luxury timber
g suites in the centre. Also has budget
commodation.

uewater Guesthouse

Sara Ave.
uewater Bay
l: 041 466 1285
x: 041 466 3639
uewatergh@telkomsa.net.
0m from Bluewater beach. Out of
wn but quiet and relaxed and very
pular.

ng's Tide Boutique Hotel

th Ave.
mmerstrand
l: 041 583 6023
x: 041 583 3910
ngstide@crowncollection.co.za
ose to the beach, superior cuisine,
commodation and service. 10 lavish
drooms. Braai.

e Paxton Hotel

rnavon Place
ummerail
l: 041 585 9655
x: 041 585 9646
xton@iafrica.co
op class with spectacular sea views. 5
minutes from centre and airport. All

rooms en suite. Restaurant, bar,
swimming pool and gardens.

Bichana Lodge

Doorly Rd
Colleen Glen
Tel: 041 372 1119
Fax: 041 372 1916
bichana@iafrica.com
Traditional style lodge. Surrounded on
three sides by forest on Algoa Bay. Each
room has private balcony. Restaurant,
bar, golf range, sailing and pool.

King George's Guesthouse

2 King George's Rd
Mill Park
Tel: 041 374 1825
Fax: 041 373 1164
dave@kinggeorge.co.za
Beautiful Tudor style house very near
to ground. Recently restored, 8 rooms,
swimming pool and braai.

Mill Brook House

2 Havelock Square
Central Hill
Tel: 041 585 3080
Fax: 041 582 3774
millbrook@eastcape.net
Overlooks park. On the Donkin trail.
5 rooms. Full English breakfast. Free
transfers to and from airport.

Lange's Guesthouse

87 Brighton Ave.
Summerstand
Tel: 041 583 3511
Fax: 041 583 3511
langec@iafrica.com
On beach. 4 comfortable double rooms
each room has own patio and braai.

Admiralty Beach House

9 Admiralty Way
Summerstrand
Tel: 041 583 1271
Fax: 041 583 3720
admiralty@interkom.co.za
100m from beach. 5 rooms. Pool
and gardens. Full English breakfast
included.

Port Elizabeth Backpackers'

7 Prospect Hill
Central
Tel: 041 586 0697
Fax: 041 585 2032
Backpackers' on heritage trail close to
centre, pubs and clubs. Lovely court-
yard garden.

Airlines
South African Airways 041 5071111
Commair   041 501 8000

Buses
Greyhound 6 Nile Rd, Perridgevale
(near Greenacres Shopping Centre)
Tel: 041 363 4555
Fax: 041 568 4879

Translux
Ernest and Young Building
Ring Road, Green Acres
Tel: 041 392 1333
Fax: 041 507 2366

Train
Enquires 041 507 1400

Car Hire
Hertz
161 Heugh Road

Walmer
Tel: 041 581 6550
Fax: 041 581 3205

Avis
Greenacres Auto Centre
Cnr Newmarket & Ring Road
Tel: 041 363 0614
Fax: 041 363 2518

Taxis
There are numerous taxi firms.
Hunters Taxi Cabs, Russell Square,
Russell Rd, Central
Tel: 041 585 5500

Post Office
GPO
259 Govan Mbeki Ave.
Open Monday-Friday 08.00-16.30 and
Saturday 08.00-12.00.
Tel: 041 586 4666

Tourist Offices
Tourist Information Office
Lighthouse Building
Belmont Terrace

Central Hill
Tel: 041 585 8884
Fax: 041 585 2564
information@tourismpe.co.za
Open 08.00-19.00

Hospital
St. George's Hospital
40 Park Drive
Tel: 041 392 6111

Port Elizabeth Airport is only a 10 minute, 4km drive from the centre of the city. Taxis are available outside the terminal and should cost no more than R50. There are also shuttle buses (041 457 5390) to the city centre at a fraction of this price. Some hotels provide courtesy buses. These buses should be booked in advance. There is an information desk in the Arrivals Hall (open 06.00-22.00 Monday-Friday, 08.00-21.00 Saturday/Sunday). There is no bank at the airport, but there is an ATM machine between the Arrival and Departure Halls. There are a number of car hire desks in the Arrivals Hall. Hertz 041 581 6550, Avis 041 363 0614, Budget 041 581 4242. The airport has a number of retail facilities including gift shops, chemist, restaurant and coffee shop in the Departures Hall.

Climate

	ave temp	rain cm			
January	21	14	July	12	70
February	20	17	August	12	74
March	19	19	September	14	40
April	18	39	October	16	37
May	15	74	November	18	15
June	13	92	December	20	17

Phoenix Hotel
Chapel St.
music.

as Al Sol
kes Pavilion
ewood

rbon Street
kes Pavilion
ewood
mber One place in Port Elizabeth
for music.

Dros
Brookes Pavilion
Humewood
Great bar to watch sport.

The Boardwalk Casino
The Broadwalk
Marine Parade
Excellent.

The Opera House and Barn
White's Road
ntral
national monument, this is the main
ue for dramatic productions in PE.
: 041 586 2256

.7 Castle Hill Museum
e oldest settler's cottage dating back
1827. Fine displays of jewellery and
e.

useum Complex
Offers an entertaining education

in its Oceanarium, Snake Park,
Tropical House and Museum. On
the beachfront, the museum displays
many of the marine life found in the
bay.

South End Museum
Cnr Humewood Rd and Walmer Rd
South End
Vibrant museum depicting life before
forced removals and before apartheid
tore apart the diverse cultural community.

Win/Loss Record

ountry	Played	Won	Drawn	Lost	Tie
land	8	4	3	1	-
ralia	5	3	-	2	-
th Africa	20	8	4	8	-
Zealand	3	1	-	2	-
a	2	-	1	1	-
stan	1	-	-	1	-
t Indies	1	-	-	1	-

hest Individual Aggregates (South Africa unless stated)

er	Mat	Inn	NO	Runs	Ave	HS	50	100
y Kirsten	7	14	1	398	30.62	69	2	0
me Pollock	3	6	2	357	89.25	137	1	2
e Barlow	4	8	0	356	44.50	73	3	0
sie Cronje	6	12	2	354	35.40	135	1	1
ques Kallis	6	12	2	348	34.80	89*	3	0
chelle Gibbs	4	8	0	310	38.75	196	0	1
or Goddard	4	8	0	289	36.13	74	3	0
un Pollock	7	12	1	285	25.91	55*	1	0
ll Cullinan	5	10	0	275	27.50	91	2	0
y Rhodes	4	7	1	239	39.83	64	3	0

Wicket Takers (South Africa unless stated)

er	Mat	Bll	Md	Runs	Wkt	Ave	BB	S/R
Donald	7	1689	73	728	40	18.20	7/84	42.23
un Pollock	7	1425	73	564	30	18.80	5/40	47.50
Adcock	4	963	31	345	18	19.17	4/20	53.50
eorge Lohmann (Eng)	1	128	11	45	15	3.00	8/7	8.53

Peter Pollock	4	790	27	358	14	25.57	3/46	56.43
Trevor Goddard	4	945	61	194	14	13.86	3/13	67.50
Hugh Tayfield	4	1217	48	416	14	29.71	6/78	86.93
Mike Procter	2	482	28	198	11	18.00	6/73	43.82
John Reid (NZ)	2	730	51	185	11	16.82	4/44	66.36
Waqar Younis (Pak)	1	244	10	133	10	13.30	6/78	24.40

Highest Individual Scores (South Africa unless stated)

196	Herschelle Gibbs	v India 2001-02
174	Lance Klusener	v England 1999-00
167	Lindsay Hassett (Aus)	1949-50
157	Arthur Morris (Aus	1949-50
150	Mathew Sinclair (NZ)	2000-01
137	Graeme Pollock	v England 1964-65
136*	George Mann (Eng)	1948-49
135	Hansie Cronje	v India 1992-93
129	Kapil Dev (Ind)	1992-93
126	Barry Richards	v Australia 1969-70

Best Individual Bowling Performances (South Africa unless stated)

9.4-5-7-8	George Lohmann (Eng)	1895-96
15.4-6-38-7	George Lohmann (Eng)	1895-96
28-4-84-7	Alan Donald	v India 1992-93
11.5-5-23-6	Fanie de Villiers	v Pakistan 1997-98
23-7-40-6	Frank Tyson (Eng)	1956-57
28.2-9-47-6	Alan Connolly (Aus	1969-70
19-4-51-6	Curtly Ambrose (WI)	1998-99
24-11-73-6	Mike Procter	v Australia 1969-70
30-6-76-6	Javagal Srinath (Ind)	2001-02
24.3-6-78-6	Hugh Tayfield	v England 1956-57

Highest Partnerships

Wkt	Runs	Batsmen	Match
1st	157	Barry Richards & Eddie Barlow (SA)	1969-1970 v Australia
2nd	171	Deep Dasgupta & Rahul Dravid (Ind)	2001-2002
3rd	187	Arthur Morris & Neil Harvey (Aus)	1949-1950
4th	157	Geoff Boycott & Ken Barrington (Eng)	1964-1965
5th	126*	Jacques Kallis & Jonty Rhodes (SA)	1999-2000 v England
6th	113	Graeme Pollock & Peter van der Merwe (SA)	1964-1965 v England
7th	89	Arthur Hill & Sammy Woods (Eng)	1895-1896
8th	136	Neil McKenzie & Nicky Boje (SA)	2000-2001 v New Zealand
9th	80	VVS Laxman & Anil Kumble (Ind)	2001-2002
10th	50	William Booth & Albert Relf (Eng)	1913-1914

Results At St. George's Park, Port Elizabeth

Date	Countries	Result
12/03/1889	v England	lost by 8 wickets
13/02/1896	v England	lost by 288 runs
27/02/1914	v England	lost by 10 wickets
05/03/1949	v England	lost by 3 wickets
03/03/1950	v Australia	lost by an innings and 259 runs
05/02/1954	v New Zealand	won by 5 wickets
01/03/1957	v England	won by 58 runs
28/02/1958	v Australia	lost by 8 wickets
16/02/1962	v New Zealand	lost won by 40 runs
12/02/1965	v England	drawn
24/02/1967	v Australia	won by 7 wickets
05/03/1970	v Australia	won by 323 runs
26/12/1992	v India	won by 9 wickets
26/12/1995	v England	drawn
14/03/1997	v Australia	lost by 2 wickets
06/03/1998	v Pakistan	won by 259 runs
10/12/1998	v West Indies	won by 178 runs
09/12/1999	v England	drawn
30/11/2000	v New Zealand	won by 7 wickets
16/11/2001	v India	drawn

potchefstroom

The North West Stadium is a new ground with modern facilities, a pavilion and wonderful grass embankments which circle the pitch.
The stadium, home to the North West Cricket Board, became South Africa's 11th Test ground on 25 October 2002 when Bangladesh were entertained and royally beaten by an innings and 260 runs. In reply to a meagre Bangladesh score of 215, the home side made 482/5 dec., Herschelle Gibbs (114), Gary Kirsten (160) and Jacques Kallis (139no) scoring centuries. Kirsten and Kallis shared a third wicket partnership of 234. Needing 267 to force their hosts to bat again Bangladesh were skittled for 107, Kallis taking 5/21 in 4.3 overs.
The stadium is a wonderful place to watch cricket and has a capacity of 10,000. The pavilion sits proudly at one end of the ground and has a great viewing area and excellent dressing room facilities. The rest of the perimeter is made up of grass embankments which have been designed specifically to watch cricket. Wooden huts, known as private suites, are dotted around these embankments. It should be noted that there is very little cover from the strong sun on the embankments although the huts provide some shade and it is not unusual to get invited into one for a cool beer. The ground is quite lively with the locals, very proud that Potchefstroom has gained Test status, very friendly and a good laugh.
There are two scoreboards in the ground, a small one to the right of the pavilion and a larger one at the other end of the ground.
Facilities for the disabled are good with viewing areas in the pavilion. Tickets can be purchased at the ground on the day of the match or from the North West Cricket Board (Tel: 018 294 6666 Fax: 018 294 5628 or nwcb@iafrica. com) The United Cricket Board of South Africa can also arrange tickets, email ucbsa@cricket.co.za
The standard of catering is very high, with stalls around the ground serving barbeque, and bars in each corner of the ground. The toilet blocks are clean and medical assistance is available in the pavilion. The ground is about a 15-minute walk from the centre of town. A taxi ride should cost about R10. There is ample parking at the venue for those who wish to drive. Most supporters head off to Die Bult in the city centre for a post match drink.

Potchefstroom is in the east of the North West Province on the banks of the Mooi River about 150km south west of Johannesburg. It was part of the province of Transvaal until 1994 when it was transferred to the North West Province. Now known as the Gateway to the North West, it is the oldest town in the Province and has a population of 190,000.

The original town was a one-hour horse ride north of today's site. It was founded in 1838 by a group of Voortrekkers, led by Andries Hendrik Potgieter. The name Potchefstroom derives from his name Pot, chef meaning leader and stroom meaning stream after the Mooi River. It was the first Boer settlement in the Transvaal and was the capital of the state until 1860 when Pretoria took over. Potchefstroom is a leading centre of cultural and religious activities in the Province and has a very colourful history. The Dutch Reformed Church of Transvaal was founded here in 1842. The opening shots of the first War of Independence were fired in the town in 1880 which also played a prominent role in the Anglo-Boer War between 1897 and 1902. The Vierkleur, the South African Republic flag, was designed and first hoisted in Potchefstroom as was its first coat of arms and also the first constitution. Its first President, Marthinuw Wessel Pretorious, was sworn in the town.

Potchefstroom is known as the 'City of Expertise' with four tertiary institutions and more than 30 high schools in the city. The city's university is one of the countries best and their sports facilities are second to none. A number of British athletes use Potchefstroom as their winter training base. The Agricultural Research College is the best in South Africa. Agriculture is a principal industry in the area with fertile farming land. Crop growing, livestock and dairy farming the main sectors. Potchefstroom is in the middle of one the world's richest gold mining areas. Uranium is also mined in the area. The timber and metal industries also thrive in Potchefstroom as does distilling, brewing and publishing. Many of Potchefstroom's white collar residents commute the 150km journey to Johannesburg each day.

Potchefstroom is a pretty city, peaceful and quiet. It has one incredible road, Oak Avenue, which is 7km long and lined with the most magnificent oak trees. The journey from the centre of town to the stadium takes in some of it. There are many historical buildings in the city including the residence of the first president MW Pretorius, the Dutch Reformed Church, City Hall and the Mosque. The city also has 24 national monuments. It has a wonderful museum that is divided into different buildings around the city and an excellent arts market in the city country garden. The Botanic Gardens are very beautiful as is Trim Park. The O. P. M. Pozesky Bird Sanctuary on the outskirts of town is a must visit. Just 50km from the city is the site of the world's largest ever meteorite impact crater which measures nearly 100km in diameter.

Johannesburg International Airport is nearest, but is 145km from the ground. Metered taxis are available outside the terminal.

There are two banks in Terminal 2 on the Public Mezzanine Level along with four foreign exchange outlets. There are ATM machines on the public concourse in Terminals 2,4,5 and 6. The airport has various restaurants, fast food outlets, cafés, Duty free shopping, books shops and souvenir shops. Car hire is available in the Arrivals Hall from Hertz (011 390 9700), Avis (011 394 5433) and Budget (011 394 2905). It should be noted that it is not an easy drive from the airport to the city centre. Terminal 1 and 2 – International Arrivals; Terminal 3 - SAA and SA Express Domestic Arrivals; Terminal 4 - Non SAA Arrivals; Terminal 5 – Domestic Departures; Terminal 6 – International Departures.

National Monuments

Potchefstroom has many national monuments and it is possible to see most of them by wandering around the city. The British Fort and Cemetery (1880) on R29 Kleekdrop Highway and MW Pretorius House (1868) on Van der Hoff Avenue are probably the oldest but also worth visiting are the Old Post Office Building (1910) and the Police Station (1937) on Greyling Street and the Dutch Reformed School (1905) in Molen Street which has a number of listed buildings. The Agricultural College Administrative Building (1906) and Selborn Hall (1909) are also fine buildings. A map is available from the Potchefstroom Tourism Information and Development Centre on Potgieter and Church Street.

OPM Prozesky Bird Sanctuary

A 60 hectare reserve to the south. It runs by the Mooi River and is home to more than 200 species.

Dome Bergland Nature Park

Lies to the north, between the towns of Parys and Vredefort, and is home to the largest and oldest known impact structure on earth. Only lately has it been proven that it originated during an impact of a large meteorite 2,000 years ago. The meteorite is estimated to have been between 12 and 16km wide and to have been travelling at 20km per second. The structure contains numerous sites showing evidence of deformation and melting of the original rock. 250km across and the vegetation is quite different to the surrounding areas.

Buffelsvlei Wild Animal Park

Game park with over 500 hectares and over 700 game animals including springbok, wildebeest, impala, zebra, kudu and antelopes. Plenty of activities such as game drives, horse riding, clay pigeon shooting and hiking. Different types of accommodation from luxury hotel rooms to camping grounds for those who wish to spend a few days at the park. Restaurant, bar and swimming pool.

Boskop Dam

In the Mooi River Valley 19km to the north east. 370 hectares are set in rolling grasslands and are part of a 3,000 hectares nature reserve. Very important recreational venue with the people of the city. Yachting, canoeing, bird watching and especially fishing make Boskop one of the most visited reserves in the North West. Wildebeeste, springbok, eland and zebra roam the reserve.

transport

Airlines

South African Airlines 011 978 1111
British Airways 011 441 8600

Buses

Potchefstroom does not have a public transport system. Minibus taxis and taxis are the popular forms of transport.
Intercity Buses Greyhound and Translux run from Potchefstroom Potigier Street to Johannesburg and other major South African cities.

Trains

Train travel is not recommended due to personal safety reasons.

Taxi

Beytel Taxis 018 290 5033
Boqo Cars 018 295 0128
Aksiepark Taxis 018 296 0076

Car Hire

Avis 018 290 8535
Budget 018 297 6285
Fourie's Transport 018 291 1631

Post Office

Main Post Office
The Bult

Tourist Information

Potchefstroom Tourism Information and Development Centre
Potgieter and Church St.
Tel: 018 293 1611
Fax: 018 297 2082

Hospital

Potchefstroom Hospital
Kevis St.
Tel: 018 297 7011

Medicare 24 hour Medical Centre
72 Lombard St.
Tel: 018 294 3251

Medicity
66 Meyer St.
Tel: 018 293 0244

culture

The Potchefstroom Museum, which traces the history of the Province and South Africa, comprises a number of different sites listed below. Each building is open Monday-Friday 10.00-13.00 and 14.00-17.00, Saturday 09.00-13.00 and Sunday 14.30-16.30.

Potchefstroom Main Museum

Gouws St.

Totius House Museum

Corner Molen and Esselen St.

President Pretorious Museum

Van der Hoff Ave.

Goetz Flesichack Museum

Corner Gouw and Potgieter St.

Climate

	ave temp	rain cm		ave temp	rain cm
January	22	123	July	10	0
February	22	97	August	13	36
March	20	8	September	16	28
April	17	7	October	20	75
May	13	8	November	21	111
June	9	0	December	22	109

Willows Garden Court Hotel

82 Mooi River Rylaan
Tel: 018 297 6285
Fax: 018 297 0915
willowsgch@mweb.co.za
41 rooms, all en suite with air-conditioning and TV, overlooking the Mooi River and golf course. Restaurant, pitch and putt bar, beautiful swimming pool in garden, gym.

Elgro Hotel

60 Walmaras St.
Tel: 018 297 5411
elgro@iafrica.com
7 suites and 99 air-conditioned rooms. Superb restaurant. á la carte in afternoons, carvery in evenings, 3 bars, swimming pool, beauty salon.

Elgro River Lodge

60 Walmaras St.
T/F 018 297 5411
elgro@iafrica.com
Lodge accommodation with self-catering units, swimming pool, game drives, river-rafting, fly-fishing and bird watching. Part of the Elgro Hotel.

Golden Pond Guesthouse

2 Van der Hoff St.
Tel: 018 294 4208
3 en suite bedrooms on the banks of Mooi River on north of city within walking distance of ground. Excellent food.

Tapestries Garden House

266 Church St.
Tel: 018 297 4856
Fax: 018 294 6818
tapestry@iafrica.com
Central with en suite rooms with TV and minibar. Luxurious pool within a kilometre of the ground.

Huys Ten Bosch Guesthouse

7 Meyer St.
Bult
Single and double rooms well furnished and en suite, TV, fridge, sundeck and Jacuzzi. Kitchenette and barbeque.

Farmhouse Guesthouse

Noordrug
Tel: 018 290 5228
Fax: 018 290 6476
farmhouse@lantic.net
A relaxed country getaway within a kilometre of grounds. En suite rooms, pool in beautiful gardens. Great South African cooking.

Just Tiffany's Guesthouse

018 297 7419
Centre of city. Excellent en suite rooms with TV in quiet safe neighbourhood. Swimming pool in fine gardens with barbeque.

Lemon Bloosom Guesthouse

4 Kerk St.
T/F 018 297 1137
24 affordable rooms with TV in 3 individual houses. Excellent breakfast and dinner.

Paljas Backpackers'

22 Esselen St.
The Bult
Tel: 018 297 0681
Fax: 018 293 2956
paljasd@iafrica.com
Good clean backpackers close to pubs, restaurants and cafés.

Restaurants

Potchefstroom does not have a restaurant culture as such although most of the pubs serve good food. In addition Alpacino Pizzeria Restaurant (018 294 6436), Beef Boys (018 293 2838), Saddles Restaurant (018 294 6205) and Spur Steak Ranch (018 297 1018) are in the centre of town. The Dulce Ice Cream and Coffee shop is also worth a visit.

Nightlife

There are some excellent late night pubs mostly in Die Bult. The Bourbon St. Brewery (018 293 0226) in Die Bult Complex in the most popular pub in town closely following by Castillions Pub and Restaurant (018 297 4387) in Castillion St. Other pubs in the centre are the Action Bar and Sport Café, the Industrial Café and Pub and O'Hagan's Irish Pub and Grill.

Win/Loss Record

Country	Played	Won	Drawn	Lost	Tie
South Africa	1	1	-	-	-
Bangladesh	1	-	-	1	-

Highest Individual Aggregates (South Africa unless stated)

Player	Mat	Inn	NO	Runs	Ave	HS	50	100
Gary Kirsten	1	1	0	160	160.00	160	0	1
Jacques Kallis	1	1	1	139	-	139*	0	1
Herschelle Gibbs	1	1	0	114	114.00	114	0	1
Hannan Sarkar (Ban)	1	2	0	82	41.00	65	1	0
Alok Kapali (Ban)	1	2	1	61	61.00	38*	0	0

Top Wicket Takers (South Africa unless stated)

Player	Mat	Bll	Md	Runs	Wkt	Ave	BB	S/R
Jacques Kallis	1	105	5	47	7	6.71	5/21	15.00
Makhaya Ntini	1	198	5	106	5	21.20	3/37	39.60
Nantie Hayward	1	132	6	80	4	20.00	2/16	33.00
Talha Jubair (Ban)	1	156	3	109	2	54.50	2/109	78.00
Shaun Pollock	1	132	6	63	2	31.50	2/38	66.00

Highest Individual Scores (South Africa unless stated)

160	Gary Kirsten	2002-03
139*	Jacques Kallis	2002-03
114	Herschelle Gibbs	2002-03
65	Hannan Sarkar (Ban)	2002-03
40	Habibul Bashar (Ban)	2002-03

Best Individual Bowling Performances (South Africa unless stated)

4.3-1-21-5	Jacques Kallis	2002-03
12-1-37-3	Makhaya Ntini	2002-03
8-3-16-2	Nantie Hayward	2002-03
13-4-26-2	Jacques Kallis	2002-03
16-6-38-2	Shaun Pollock	2002-03

Highest Partnerships

Wkt	Runs	Batsmen	Match
1st	61	Graeme Smith & Herschelle Gibbs (SA)	2002-2003
2nd	141	Herschelle Gibbs & Gary Kirsten (SA)	2002-2003
3rd	234	Gary Kirsten & Jacques Kallis (SA)	2002-2003
4th	8	Al Sahariar Rokon & Tushar Imran (Ban)	2002-2003
5th	22	Khaled Mashud & Rafiqul Islam (Ban)	2002-2003
6th	34	Khaled Mashud & Alok Kapali (Ban)	2002-2003
7th	15	Tushar Imran & Alok Kapali (Ban)	2002-2003
8th	13	Alok Kapali & Tapash Baisya (Ban)	2002-2003
9th	5	Alok Kapali & Manjural Islam (Ban)	2002-2003
10th	13	Alok Kapali & Talha Jubair (Ban)	2002-2003

Results at The North West Cricket Stadium

Date	Countries	Result
25/10/2002	v Bangladesh	won by an innings and 160 runs

Sri Lanka's first Test, against England on 17th February 1982, was held at the P. Saravanamuttu Stadium in Colombo. The visitors won by seven wickets. The Asgiriya Stadium in Kandy became the second Test ground in April the following year when Australia visited and won by an innings and 38 runs. The Sinhalese Sports Club was the third ground to be used when New Zealand drew in March 1984. Colombo Cricket Club became the fourth a week later when it hosted the third and final Test of the series. The visitors won by an innings and 1 runs. Only two more Tests were played at the ground, a eight wicket victory over Pakistan in 1986 and a draw against New Zealand in 1987.

The R. Premadasa Stadium became Sri Lanka's fifth Test venue in August 1992 when the home side drew with Australia in the second Test of the series. The Tyronne Fernando Stadium in Moratuwa was used a month later in the third and final match. It also ended in a draw. The stadium at Moratuwa was used for three other Tests in the next year, all were draws and the ground has not been used for Test cricket since. The magnificent Galle International Stadium staged its first Test in June 1998 when Sri Lanka beat New Zealand by an innings and 16 runs. Galle has become a regular venue for the opening match of Test series.

Distance between Cities (in km)

	Colombo	Galle	Kandy
Colombo		117	116
Galle	117		232
Kandy	116	232	

Airlines

Sri Lanka's national airline is Air Lanka. There is no airport at Galle or Kandy. Train, coaches and private cars are the modes of transport used in Sri Lanka.
Sri Lankan Airlines 019 733 5555

Buses

Air-conditioned buses run between Colombo and Kandy and

Colombo and Galle. The service is very cheap and extremely busy so seats should always be reserved in advance. Sri Lanka Transport operates a bus network throughout the country.

Trains

The most popular mode of transport among cricket supporters in Sri Lanka. The journeys to Galle and Kandy are magnificent ways to see the country. The four-hour journey to Kandy through the hill country is one of the greatest train trips in the world. An air-conditioned observation car is available on the Kandy train but second class is also very comfortable. Trains run to Galle three times a day and take two-and-a-half hours. They are inexpensive.

Enquiries   011 243 4215

Car Hire

Available at Colombo airport and at the larger hotels. An International Driving Licence is required and all drivers must be at least 18 years of age. Popular in Sri Lanka are chauffeur driven cars and minibuses which are inexpensive and convenient.

Taxis

Available outside the airport, train stations, hotels and at ranks throughout the cities. It is important to agree the fare with the driver before commencing the journey. Auto-rickshaws are the most popular mode of transport with cricket supporters. They are available everywhere and move through the traffic more quickly than taxis.

Banks

Opening times at most banks are Monday to Friday 09.00-15.00. Most banks have foreign exchange facilities and accept travellers' cheques in major currencies. Some banks have international ATM facilities . Others can arrange cash advances on credit and debit cards. All major credit cards are accepted in the main hotels.

Currency is the Sri Lankan Rupee (SLRs). Notes are issued in denominations of SLRs1000 500, 200, 100, 50, 20 and 10 and coins in denominations of SLRs 10, 5, 2 and 1 and 50, 25, 10, 5, 2 and 1 cents.

Telecoms

International Direct Dialling is available in hotels in Colombo, Kandy and Galle. Some public telephones operate internationally with phone cards which can be purchased at the post office. There are also many telephone and internet shops in all the cities which provide cheap international rates. Sri Lanka's dialling code is 94. The outgoing international code is 00.

Post

Open 09.00-17.00 Monday-Friday.

Tourist Offices

There are offices in Colombo and Kandy. Unfortunately the Galle office has been closed. The headquarters of the Sri Lanka Tourist Board is on Galle Road in Colombo. Enquiries 01 2437 059 or www.srilankatourism.org

Emergency Numbers

Contact numbers for the police, ambulance and fire vary from city to city.

Embassies/Consulates

British High Commission
190 Galle Road
Kollupitiya
Colombo 3
Tel: 011 243 7336
Fax: 011 245 1924
bhc@eureka.lk

Australian High Commission
3 Cambridge Place

Colombo
Tel: 011 2698 767
Fax: 011 2696 453

ew Zealand Consulate
eewella Building
9 Galle Road
lombo 4
l: 011 2556 701
x: 011 2585 995
is@eureka.lk

sas

visitors must carry a passport valid for at least six months from date of
parture. 30 day tourist visas are issued free of charge upon arrival at Colombo
port. Sri Lankan Embassies will issue tourist visas before departure for a fee
pending on which passport is held. British passports holders are charged £23.
plicants should complete application form and have two passport photos and
ould expect to wait two to three days for visa.

stoms

sitors over the age of 18 may take the following goods into Sri Lanka without
curring customs duty.
0 cigarettes or 50 cigars
5 litres of alcohol
0ml of perfume.

me Difference

Lanka is six hours ahead of GMT

ectricity

20/240 volts AC at 50 cycles per second. Most hotels have adaptors.

Departure Tax

There is none

colombo

sinhalese sports club

The Sinhalese Sports Club in Colombo is the headquarters of Sri Lankan cricket and their offices are housed in the main pavilion. The ground is a mixture of modern and older grandstands and grass hills. It was used as an airfield by the Allied Forces in World War II.

It became the third Test venue in Sri Lanka in 1984 when it hosted the second match of a series against New Zealand. Put in, Sri Lanka struggled to 174 as Lance Cairns took 4/47. The visitors replied with 198, Jeff Crowe scoring 50 and Ravi Ratnayeke taking 5/42. Sri Lanka reached 289/9 in their second innings before declaring, Roy Dias making a fine 108. Needing 266 to win, the New Zealanders reached 123/4 when time ran out.

Colombo's next Test was the drawn first match of the 1985 series against India while the third was against Australia. Put in, Australia collapsed to 124/7 before recovering to 256 after being put in thanks mainly to a fighting 66no from Ian Healy. Sri Lanka replied with 547/8 dec., Asanka Gurusinha 137, Arjuna Ranatunga, 127, and Ramesh Kaluwitharana, 132, each scoring centuries. Trailing by 291, Australia dug deep. David Boon top scored with 68 and Greg Matthews contributed 64 as all 11 batsmen reached double figures to score 471 and lead by 180 runs. Sri Lanka conceded 58 extras, including 34 no balls. In the second innings the home side were cruising at 127/2 when Craig McDermott took two quick wickets to change the course of the match. Sri Lanka lost their last eight wickets for 37 to lose by 16 runs. Greg Matthews, 4/76, and Shane Warne, 3/11 in 5.1 overs, did the damage.

Sri Lanka achieved their first win at the SSC in 1992 in the second and deciding Test against New Zealand. Sri Lanka made 394 with Roshan Mahanama contributing 109 and Hashan Tillakaratne, 93. New Zealand could manage only 102, Jayananda Warnawerra taking 4/25 and Muttiah Muralitharan, 3/22. Forced to follow-on, the visitors batted better in their second innings. Led by their captain Martin Crowe with 107, they scored 361 l. Needing 70 to win, Sri Lanka reached their target for the loss of one wicket.

The following year , Sri Lanka beat England by five wickets in a one-off Test, but they managed to lose to India by 235 runs and to South Africa by an innings and 208 runs in the other Tests at the SSC that year. An easy 10 wicket victory over Zimbabwe followed in 1996 before draws against Pakistan and India in 1997.

In 1998 the SSC hosted victories over Zimbabwe and New Zealand. Draws followed in 1999 against India and Australia before Sri Lanka lost to Pakistan by five wickets in the first match of the 2000 three-match series. In 2001 the SSC hosted the final match of a three match series with England with the series level 1-1. The home side batted first, scoring 241. The visitors replied with 249, thanks mainly to an unbeaten 113 from Graham Thorpe. Chaminda Vaas took 6/73 for Sri Lanka. The hosts collapsed to 81 all out in their second innings, Ashley Giles taking 4/11 and Darren Gough 3/23. Needing just 74 to win the match and the series, England struggled home by four wickets with Thorpe holding firm on 32no.

Since that match the SSC has become a fortress. Sri Lanka won the next six very comfortably. The second part of 2001 saw a remarkable run. In August they beat India by an innings and 77 runs, scoring a massive 610/6 dec. as four batsmen scored centuries; Jayawardene (138), Hashan Tillakaratne (113no), Marvan Atapattu (108) and Thilan Samaraweera (103no) – Muttiah Muralitharan returned match figures of 11/196.

In September they beat Bangladesh by an innings and 137 runs when Atapattu retired at 201 and Jayawardene at 150. Muralitharan ended with match figures of 10/111.

At the beginning of December Sri Lanka beat the West Indies by 10 wickets despite the efforts of Brian Lara. He scored 221 out of 390 while Vaas took 7/20. The home side scored 627/9 dec. in reply, Hashan Tillakaratne scoring 204no. The West Indies started their second innings well to reach 203/3, Lara scoring another 130 and Ramnaresh Sarwan 66 before they collapsed to 262. Vaas took another 7/71 to end with match figures of 14/191, the best at the Sports Club. Sri Lanka reached the required 26 without losing a wicket.

At the end of December, Samaraweera scored another century (123no) and Kumar Sangakkara (128) as Sri Lanka beat Zimbabwe by an innings and 166 runs. It was quite an astonishing year.

Sri Lanka beat Bangladesh by 288 runs in July 2002 and England by an innings and 215 runs in December 2003, Samaraweera scoring another century (142no) and Mahela Jayawardene, 134. Sr Lanka's 628/8 was the highest team score t the ground. The lowest was Sri Lanka's 81 in 2001.

he highest run chase was Sri Lanka's 326/5 against Zimbabwe in 1998.

he Sinhalese Sports Club is a beautiful ground surrounded by huge trees in the afflu- nt suburb of Cinnamon Gardens. The old clubhouse is in the north west corner of e ground with the players' dressing rooms on the first floor. Seats are available on the round floor and upper tier of this stand. The clubhouse is very pleasant and there is a leasant outside bar which is open to the public. There are two small stands on either de of the media centre at the northern end of the ground. The east side is one huge rass hill and is certainly the liveliest place in the ground with local and visiting sup- orters mixing together. The massive scoreboard is on the hill. The Lanka Bell Stand nd the VIP enclosure are both very good viewing areas at the southern end of the round. The Seylan Bank Pavilion and the new grandstand, which provides a splendid ew, are on the west side.

ood stalls line the hill and are also located around the ground serving the usual fast od, ice cream etc. Vendors stroll around selling food, cigarettes, ice-cream and sweets nd one of the Lion Men, the lads with beer on their backs, is never far away. The toilet cilities in some parts of the ground are fine and well tended, unfortunately those at e hill and at the south end of the ground leave a lot to be desired. Tickets are avail- le at the ground on Test days or can be purchased by contacting Sri Lanka Cricket, 35 aitland Place, Colombo 07 Telephone 01 268 1601 and fax 01 269 7405 or email on fo@srilankacricket.lk

ckets prices range between Rs 50 and Rs 6000 for a five day pass. The Sinhalese ports Club is in Cinnamon Gardens which is about a 15 minute drive south of the entral Fort area. Auto-rickshaws and taxis are available and should cost about Rs 100 although they may cost a little more after the cricket is finished for the day. The bar in the club is very friendly and is well worth a visit after the day's cricket.

Win/Loss Record

Country	Played	Won	Drawn	Lost	Tie
Pakistan	2	1	1	-	-
South Africa	2	1	1	-	-
Australia	2	1	1	-	-
Sri Lanka	23	11	7	5	-
India	5	1	3	1	-
England	3	1	-	2	-
New Zealand	3	-	1	2	-
Bangladesh	2	-	-	2	-
Zimbabwe	3	-	-	3	-
West Indies	1	-	-	1	-

Highest Individual Aggregates (Sri Lanka unless stated))

Player	Mat	Inn	NO	Runs	Ave	HS	50	100
Sanath Jayasuriya	17	28	3	1317	52.68	199	8	2
Aravinda de Silva	16	28	4	1257	52.38	146	2	5
Mahela Jayawardene	12	17	1	1088	68.00	242	2	5
Hashan Tillakaratne	15	22	8	1015	72.50	204*	3	3
Arjuna Ranatunga	16	28	3	988	39.52	127	8	2
Marvan Atapattu	15	23	1	656	29.82	201	1	2
Thilan Samaraweera	6	5	2	513	171.00	142	2	3
Roshan Mahanama	8	16	1	458	30.53	109	2	1
Sachin Tendulkar (Ind)	3	6	2	456	114.00	139	1	3
Asanka Gurusinha	5	9	2	407	58.14	137	1	1

Top Wicket Takers (Sri Lanka unless stated))

Player	Mat	Bll	Md	Runs	Wkt	Ave	BB	S/R
Muttiah Muralitharan	16	6004	267	2278	103	22.12	8/87	58.29
Chaminda Vaas	14	3178	121	1453	56	25.95	7/71	56.75
Sanath Jayasuriya	17	1353	65	554	19	29.16	4/24	71.21
Jayananda Warnaweera	3	920	24	482	18	26.78	4/25	51.11
Anil Kumble (Ind)	3	1080	37	513	16	32.06	5/87	67.50
Don Anurasiri	3	726	24	322	11	29.27	4/127	66.00
Aravinda de Silva	16	828	29	348	11	31.64	3/30	75.27
Thilan Samaraweera	6	478	16	216	10	21.60	4/49	47.80
Nuwan Zoysa	4	612	24	249	10	24.90	2/24	61.20
Heath Streak (Zim)	2	444	16	225	9	25.00	4/84	49.33

Highest Individual Scores (Sri Lanka unless stated))

242	Mahela Jayawardene	v India 1998-99
221	Brian Lara (WI)	2001-02
204*	Hashan Tillakaratne	v West Indies 2001-02
201	Marvan Atapattu	v Bangladesh 2001-02
199	Sanath Jayasuriya	v India 1998-99
155	Saleem Malik (Pak)	1996-97
150	Mahela Jayawardene	v Bangladesh 2001-02
147	Sourav Ganguly (Ind)	1997-98
146	Aravinda de Silva	v India 1997-98
143*	Aravinda de Silva	v Zimbabwe 1997-98

Best Individual Bowling Performances (Sri Lanka unless stated))

34.1-9-87-8	Muttiah Muralitharan	v India 2001
25-3-71-7	Chaminda Vaas	v West Indies 2001-02
32.2-5-120-7	Chaminda Vaas	v West Indies 2001-02
33-10-64-6	Daniel Vettori (NZ)	1997-98
27.5-6-73-6	Chaminda Vaas	v England 2000-01
41-10-85-6	Rumesh Ratnayake	v India 1985-86
9.4-4-13-5	Muttiah Muralitharan	v Bangladesh 2001-02
18.3-8-30-5	Muttiah Muralitharan	v New Zealand 1997-98
21-8-42-5	Ravi Ratnayeke	v New Zealand 1983-84
15.3-1-45-5	Wasim Akram (Pak)	2000

Highest Partnerships

Wkt	Runs	Batsmen	Match
1st	171	Manoj Prabhakar & Navjot Sidhu (Ind)	1993-1994
2nd	232	Sadagoppan Ramesh & Rahul Dravid (Ind)	1998-1999
3rd	262	Thilan Samaraweera & Mahela Jayawardene (SL)	2003-2004 v England
4th	230	Asanka Gurusinha & Arjuna Ranatunga (SL)	1992-1993 v Australia
5th	176	Mahela Jayawardene & Arjuna Ranatunga (SL)	1998-1999 v India
6th	218	Justin Langer & Simon Katich (Aus)	2003-2004
7th	194	Thilan Samaraweera & Hashan Tillakaratne (SL)	2001-2002 v India
8th	106	Aravinda de Silva & Chaminda Vaas (SL)	1996-1997 v Pakistan
9th	83	Hashan Tillakaratne & Muttiah Muralitharan (SL)	1992-1993 v England
10th	90	Wasim Akram & Arshad Khan (Pak)	1999-2000

Results at Sinhalese Sports Club

Date	Countries	Result
16/03/1984	v New Zealand	drawn
30/08/1985	v India	drawn
05/05/1987	v New Zealand	cancelled due to political unrest
17/08/1992	v Australia	lost by 16 runs
06/12/1992	v New Zealand	won by 9 wickets
13/03/1993	v England	won by 5 wickets
27/07/1993	v India	lost by 235 runs
06/09/1993	v South Africa	lost by an innings and 208 runs
18/09/1996	v Zimbabwe	won by 10 wickets
26/04/1997	v Pakistan	drawn
09/08/1997	v India	drawn
14/01/1998	v Zimbabwe	won by 5 wickets
10/06/1998	v New Zealand	won by 164 runs
24/02/1999	v India	drawn

30/09/1999	v Australia	drawn
14/06/2000	v Pakistan	lost by 5 wickets
06/08/2000	v South Africa	drawn
15/03/2001	v England	lost by 4 wickets
29/08/2001	v India	won by an innings and 77 runs
06/09/2001	v Bangladesh	won by an innings and 137 runs
29/11/2001	v West Indies	won by 10 wickets
27/12/2001	v Zimbabwe	won by an innings and 166 runs
28/07/2002	v Bangladesh	won by 288 runs
18/12/2003	v England	won by an innings and 215 runs
24/03/2004	v Australia	lost by 121 runs

r. premadasa stadium

The second of Colombo's three Test venues is the
R. Premadasa International Stadium, formerly known as Khetterama
Cricket Stadium. It is the country's largest ground. Named after President
Ramasinghe Premadasa it was built in 1986 to the east of Colombo.
It became Sri Lanka's fifth Test venue with a tame draw against Australia in 1992.
The next Test at the ground was four years later and victory against Zimbabwe in
the first of a two match series. The home side batted first and scored 349 before
dismissing the visitors for 145 and 127 to win by an innings and 77 runs.
1997 saw two draws at the ground, against Pakistan in April and against India
in August. This second match will go down in history as so many records were
broken. India scored 537/8 declared with centuries from Sachin Tendulkar (143),
Mohammad Azharuddin (126) and Navjot Sidhu (111).
In reply, the Sri Lankans scored the highest ever total in Test cricket, 952/6 dec.,
Sanath Jayasuriya scoring 340, Roshan Mahanama 225 and Aravinda de Silva 126.
Jayasuriya and Mahanama shared a second wicket partnership of 576, the highest
for any wicket in Test cricket. The Indians spent three long days in the field.
Next year, though, the Sri Lankans struggled against New Zealand. Although
Muttiah Muralitharan took 5/90 New Zealand reached 305. In reply, the home
side were 20 short. Captain Stephen Fleming hit 174no in New Zealand's second
innings score of 444/6 dec. with Craig McMillan hitting 142. Set 465 to win,
the home side could only manage 297 as Paul Wiseman took 5/82 and Daniel
Vettori 3/101 to see the visitors home by 167 runs.
The best match return is 9/226 by Saqluin Mushtaq of Pakistan in 1997.
The stadium holds 35,000 and is beautifully kept. The grand-

stand at the north end is a three-tier structure decorated with plants and flowers. There are four other stands around the ground, simply named Blocks A, B, C and D. To either side of the pavilion are Blocks A and B, which are two-tier, and at the far end of the ground, the scoreboard end, Blocks C and D are single-tier. The majority of seats are undercover and provide an excellent view of the pitch. Six powerful floodlights tower above the stadium.

The ground has excellent facilities with food stalls and bars under each of the stands and vendors move around the stands selling drinks, including beer, fast food, nuts and ice-cream. The toilet facilities in the ground are clean.

Tickets are available at the ground on the days leading up to Test matches or can be purchased by contacting Sri Lanka Cricket, 35 Maitland Place, Colombo 07 telephone 01 26 1601 and fax 01 269 7405 or email on info@srilankacricket.lk

Ticket prices range between Rs50 and Rs3000 for a five day pass. The stadium is in the suburb of Maligawatta to the north east of the Fort area and is a 15 minute drive along the Sri Sangaraja Pradeepa Mawatha. Taxi and auto-rickshaws are available from most hotels and should cost no more than Rs100. Dermatagoda railway station is approximately a 15 minute walk.

stats

Win/Loss Record

Country	Played	Won	Drawn	Lost	Tie
New Zealand	1	1	-	-	-
Sri Lanka	5	1	3	1	-
Pakistan	1	-	1	-	-
India	1	-	1	-	-
Australia	1	-	1	-	-
Zimbabwe	1	-	-	1	-

Highest Individual Aggregates (Sri Lanka unless stated)

Player	Mat	Inn	NO	Runs	Ave	HS	50	100
Aravinda de Silva	5	7	0	545	77.86	168	2	2
Sanath Jayasuriya	5	8	1	522	74.57	340	2	1
Arjuna Ranatunga	5	7	0	344	49.14	86	3	0
Roshan Mahanama	3	4	0	312	78.00	225	1	1
Romesh Kaluwitharana	5	7	1	271	45.17	72	3	0

Top Wicket Takers (Sri Lanka unless stated)

Player	Mat	Bll	Md	Runs	Wkt	Ave	BB	S/R
Muttiah Muralitharan	5	1727	63	701	27	25.96	6/98	63.96
Saqlain Mushtaq (Pak)	1	644	23	226	9	25.11	5/89	71.56
Paul Wiseman (NZ)	1	401	21	143	7	20.43	5/82	57.29
Jayantha Silva	2	436	24	157	7	22.43	4/25	62.29
Daniel Vettori (NZ)	1	450	31	157	6	26.17	3/56	75.00

Highest Individual Scores (Sri Lanka unless stated)

340	Sanath Jayasuriya	v India 1997-98
225	Roshan Mahanama	v India 1997-98
174*	Stephen Fleming (NZ)	1997-98
168	Aravinda de Silva	v Pakistan 1996-97
143	Sachin Tendulkar (Ind)	1997-98

Best Individual Bowling Performances (Sri Lanka unless stated)

53-19-98-6	Muttiah Muralitharan	v Pakistan 1996-97
20.3-4-33-5	Muttiah Muralitharan	v Zimbabwe 1996-97
46.5-17-82-5	Paul Wiseman (NZ)	1997-98
44.2-10-89-5	Saqlain Mushtaq (Pak)	1996-97
38.2-8-90-5	Muttiah Muralitharan	v New Zealand 1997-98

Highest Partnerships

Wkt	Runs	Batsmen	Match
1st	110	Chandika Hathurusingha & Roshan Mahanama (SL)	1992-1993 v Australia
2nd	576	Sanath Jayasuriya & Roshan Mahanama (SL)	1997-1998 v India
3rd	129	Aravinda de Silva & Arjuna Ranatunga (SL)	1996-1997 v Pakistan
4th	240	Stephen Fleming & Craig McMillan (NZ)	1997-1998
5th	131	Dean Jones & Greg Matthews (Aus)	1992-1993
		Aravinda de Silva & Mahela Jayawardene (SL)	1997-1998 v India
6th	143	Arjuna Ranatunga & Romesh Kaluwitharana (SL)	1996-1997 v Zimbabwe
7th	50	Asif Mujtaba & Saqlain Mushtaq (Pak)	1996-1997
8th	73	Kumar Dharmasena & Chaminda Vaas (SL)	1996-1997 v Zimbabwe
9th	39	Greg Matthews & Tony Dodemaide (Aus)	1992-1993
10th	29	Saqlain Mushtaq & Mohammad Zahid (Pak)	1996-1997

Results at R. Premadasa Stadium

Date	Countries	Result
28/08/1992	v Australia	drawn
11/09/1996	v Zimbabwe	won by an innings and 77 runs
19/04/1997	v Pakistan	drawn
02/08/1997	v India	drawn
27/05/1998	v New Zealand	lost by 167 runs

Colombo's third Test venue, the P. Saravanamuttu Stadium, is the home ground of the Tamil Union Cricket and Athletic Club. Quaint, with ageing, single storey stands and a lovely hill, it is situated in the suburb of Borella on the east side.

It was Sri Lanka's first Test ground when in 1982 it hosted the inaugural match against England, a seven wicket defeat in which England's spinners John Emburey and Derek Underwood were on top.

The next Test to be staged here, against India. in 1985, resulted in Sri Lanka's first Test victory. Amal Silva hit 111 and Roy Dias 95 in Sri Lanka's 385 first innings, while Chetan Sharma took 5/118. The visitors replied with just 244. The home team reached 206/3 before declaring and setting the visitors 347. India never looked like reaching their target and were dismissed for 198, despite a fighting 78 from their captain Kapil Dev. Ratnayake was again Sri Lanka's hero, taking 5/49 as Sri Lanka recorded victory by 149 runs.

Three draws followed, against Pakistan in 1986, India and South Africa in 1993, before Pakistan trounced their hosts in 1994.

The visitors made 390 although Kumar Dharmasena took 6/99 for the home side. Despite a century from Aravinda de Silva, 127 Sri Lanka's reply was only 226. Wasim Akram, Mushtaq Ahmed and Akram Raza each took three wickets.

Saeed Anwar hit 136 of Pakistan's second innings total of 318/4 dec. to set a target of 482. Sri Lanka were dismissed for 181 as Wasim Akram took 5/43 and Akram Raza 3/83 to secure victory for Pakistan by 301 runs.

It was 2002 before the ground staged another Test, Sri Lanka entertaining Bangladesh for the first time. The hosts won a very one-sided affair by an innings and 196 runs, Aravinda de Silva hitting a magnificent 206, ably supported by his captain Sanath Jayasuriya who scored 145. The pair shared a fifth wicket partnership of 236 as Sri Lanka scored a massive 509 runs on the second day. Muttiah Muralitharan took five wickets in each innings ending the match with figures of 10/98.

The same year saw an intriguing battle between Australia and Pakistan at the ground. Because of security fears in Pakistan, the 2002 series was played at neutral venues; the first Test here and the others in Sharjah. Australia scored 467 with Ricky Ponting making 141, Justin Langer, 72 and Damien Martin, 67. Pakistan scored 279 in reply as Shane Warne took 7/94 and Faisal Iqbal top-scored with 83. Trailing by 188 runs, Pakistan fought back magnificently and dismissed Australia for 127, Shoaib Akhtar taking 5/21 and Saqluin 4/64. Chasing an unlikely 326 for victory, Pakistan reached 172/2 and 230/4 before collapsing to 274 all out as Australia won by a mere 41 runs.

The next match was a high scoring draw against New Zealand in 2003. On a batsman's dream surface, the visiting captain Stephen Fleming scored 274no – the highest individual Test score at the ground – in the first innings and 69no in the second. Hashan Tillakaratne hit 144 for Sri Lanka as more than 1150 runs were scored for the loss of just 22 wickets. The highest team score is 541/9 dec. against Bangladesh in 2003 and the lowest, Australia 127 against Pakistan. The highest run chase is England's 171/3 in 1982.

Shane Warne's match figures of 11/188 against Pakistan in 2002 are the best.

The ground is clearly a club ground rather than a modern purpose-built stadium. At the west end is the Janashakthi Sports and Media Complex and the pavilion which is at fine leg and is part of a group of single storey stands which run along the north side of the ground. All these stands are totally covered and are named after M Sathasivam, T Murugaser and Sathi Caomaraswamy. The hill which runs down the east end of the ground is partially shaded by some trees and provides an excellent vantage point. The unusual scoreboard covered in ivy is at this end of the ground. Terraces run down the south side of the ground.

Food stalls and bars are located all around and vendors move through the crowd selling drinks, including beer, fast food, ice-cream and cigarettes. The toilet facilities are clean and well serviced. Tickets can be purchased at the ground on the days leading up to the Test by contacting Sri Lanka Cricket, 35 Maitland Place, Colombo 07 Telephone 01 268 1601 and fax 01 269 7405 or email on info@srilankacricket.lk Tickets prices range between Rs 50 and Rs 3000 for a five day pass. The stadium is a 20 minute drive from the Fort area along Maradana Road. Auto-rickshaws and taxis are widely available to drop fans at the ground. The fare from the Fort area should be Rs 150. You can catch a train from the Fort to Cotta Road station which is only a couple of minutes walk.

stats

Win/Loss Record

Country	Played	Won	Drawn	Lost	Tie
Australia	1	1	-	-	-
England	1	1	-	-	-
Sri Lanka	8	2	4	2	-
Pakistan	3	1	1	1	-
New Zealand	1	-	1	-	-
South Africa	1	-	1	-	-
India	2	-	1	1	-
Bangladesh	1	-	-	1	-

Highest Individual Aggregates (Sri Lanka unless stated)

Player	Mat	Inn	NO	Runs	Ave	HS	50	100
Aravinda de Silva	6	10	0	688	68.80	206	2	3
Arjuna Ranatunga	6	10	1	387	43.00	135*	3	1
Hashan Tillakaratne	4	6	0	360	60.00	144	2	1
Stephen Fleming (NZ)	1	2	2	343	-	274*	1	1
Sanath Jayasuriya	5	7	1	301	50.17	145	2	1

Roshan Mahanama	4	7	0	285	40.71	151	0	1
Asanka Gurusinha	3	6	1	265	53.00	116*	1	1
Roy Dias	2	4	1	232	77.33	95	3	0
Saeed Anwar (Pak)	1	2	0	230	115.00	136	1	1
Duleep Mendis	3	5	1	166	41.50	58	2	0

Top Wicket Takers (Sri Lanka unless stated)

Player	Mat	Bll	Md	Runs	Wkt	Ave	BB	S/R
Muttiah Muralitharan	5	1667	72	683	25	27.32	5/39	66.68
Kumar Dharmasena	3	1070	42	444	13	34.15	6/99	82.31
Shane Warne (Aus)	1	330	10	188	11	17.09	7/94	30.00
Ashantha De Mel	3	661	21	321	11	29.18	4/70	60.09
Wasim Akram (Pak)	2	516	27	186	10	18.60	5/43	51.60
Rumesh Ratnayake	1	291	11	125	9	13.89	5/49	32.33
Shoaib Akhtar (Pak)	1	174	7	72	8	9.00	5/21	21.75
Saqlain Mushtaq (Pak)	1	340	6	182	8	22.75	4/46	42.50
Derek Underwood (Eng)	1	335	21	95	8	11.88	5/28	41.88
Jayananda Warnaweera	2	492	8	257	7	36.71	3/63	70.29

Highest Individual Scores (Sri Lanka unless stated)

274*	Stephen Fleming (NZ)	2003
206	Aravinda de Silva	v Bangladesh 2002
151	Roshan Mahanama	v India 1993-94
148	Aravinda de Silva	v India 1993-94
145	Sanath Jayasuriya	v Bangladesh 2002
144	Hashan Tillakaratne	v New Zealand 2003
141	Ricky Ponting (Aus)	2002-03
136	Saeed Anwar (Pak)	1994-95
135*	Arjuna Ranatunga	v Pakistan 1985-86
127	Aravinda de Silva	v Pakistan 1994-95

Best Individual Bowling Performances (Sri Lanka unless stated)

24.3-7-94-7	Shane Warne (Aus)	2002-03
25-9-33-6	John Emburey (Eng)	1981-82
45.2-13-99-6	Kumar Dharmasena	v Pakistan 1994-95
8-2-21-5	Shoaib Akhtar (Pak)	2002-03
18-6-28-5	Derek Underwood (Eng)	1981-82
19.4-6-39-5	Muttiah Muralitharan	v Bangladesh 2002
18-4-43-5	Wasim Akram (Pak)	1994-95
23.2-6-49-5	Rumesh Ratnayake	v India 1985-86
25-6-59-5	Muttiah Muralitharan	v Bangladesh 2002
36.5-9-63-5	Brett Schultz (SA)	1993-94

Highest Partnerships

Wkt	Runs	Batsmen	Match
1st	128	Saeed Anwar & Aamir Sohail (Pak)	1994-1995
2nd	183	Justin Langer & Ricky Ponting (Aus)	2002-2003 v Pakistan
3rd	162	Vinod Kambli & Sachin Tendulkar (Ind)	1993-1994
4th	240*	Asanka Gurusinha & Arjuna Ranatunga (SL)	1985-1986 v Pakistan
5th	234	Aravinda de Silva & Sanath Jayasuriya (SL)	2002-2003 v Bangladesh
6th	128	Damien Martyn & Adam Gilchrist (Aus)	2002-2003 v Bangladesh
7th	85	Inzamam-Ul-Haq & Wasim Akram (Pak)	1994-1995
8th	70	Kapil Dev & Laxman Sivaramakrishnan (Ind)	1985-1986
9th	38	Romesh Kaluwitharana & Muttiah Muralitharan (SL)	1993-1994 v India
10th	29	Kapil Dev & Chetan Sharma (Ind)	1985-1986

Results at the P Saravanamuttu Stadium

Date	Countries	Result
17/02/1982	v England	lost by 7 wickets
06/09/1985	v India	won by 149 runs
22/03/1986	v Pakistan	drawn
04/08/1993	v India	drawn
14/09/1993	v South Africa	drawn
09/08/1994	v Pakistan	lost by 301 runs
21/07/2002	v Bangladesh	won by an innings and 196 runs
03/10/2002	Pakistan v Australia	Australia won by 41 runs
25/04/2003	v New Zealand	drawn

Colombo, population 800,000, is on the west coast near the mouth of the Kelani Ganga River and is the largest city in the country. It was the capital for more than 200 years until Sri Jayawardenepura, which is actually on the outskirts of Colombo, was made the capital. Originally called Kalan-totta, then the Arab name Kolambu, the present name was given to the city by the Portuguese in 1517 in honour of Christopher Columbus. The city is divided into 15 suburbs or zones simply named Colombo 1 to 15. Colombo 1 is the business area and the heart of the city known as the Fort, where high rise buildings and modern hotels contrast strongly with its fine colonial buildings and those of the neighbouring Colombo 11 Pettah, architecture also reflects the eras of the Portuguese, Dutch and British with narrow winding lanes, bazaars and street markets.

The Portuguese built a fort and founded a trading post. In 1640 the Dutch, with the help of the king of Kandy, overthrew the Portuguese and developed the fort and city. In 1796 the British invaded the island. They succeeded in gaining control of Colombo and most of the island by 1798 and created the Crown Colony of Ceylon gaining independence in 1948.

Although many tourists head for the beaches of Hikkaduwa and Unawatuna and the beauty of the hill country, increasing numbers visit Colombo each year.

It is a pleasure to walk around with its colourful bazaars, wonderful colonial buildings, sea-front boulevard and parks. There a number of Hindu temples including the colourful Kathiresan and Ganeshan temples. Kelaniya Raja Maha Vihara is the most important Buddhist temple in the city. St. Lucia's Cathedral in Kotahena and the Wolvendaal Church built by the Dutch in the 1750s are also worth visiting.

The Fort

Old colonial buildings include the Presidential Secretariat, the General Post Office, the Grand Oriental Hotel and the Chartered Bank Building. Other landmarks include the Lighthouse Clock Tower and the statue of Queen Victoria in Gordon Gardens. Examples of Dutch architecture include the Delft Gateway and the Fort Police Station. The 150 year old Cargill's store is a fine building.

White Water Rafting at Kitulgala

80km from the city on the Kelani River and the capital of white water rafting in Sri Lanka. The run, which is graded between two and three in difficulty, is more than 6km long and takes nearly two hours to complete. There are seven awesome rapids. Life jackets are supplied to all participants. Rafter's Retreat on the Main Street organises trips daily: telephone 036 228 7598 or email channap@itmin.com Kitulgala became famous in 1957 when its stretch of river was used as the location for the classic film 'Bridge over the River Kwai'.

National Zoological Gardens Dehiwela

On the southern outskirts near the popular resort of Mount Lavinia, the zoo has an excellent collection. It also has a fine aquarium with over 500 different species. The zoo is committed to its programme of reform, removing cages and enclosed spaces wherever possible. Attractions include an aviary, a butterfly park and a reptile enclosure. Open 08.00-18.00 daily.

Pettah

Lies next to to the Fort and is the market area of the city. The bazaars and narrow streets are a great experience and an opportunity to shop for amazing bargains. Each lane specialises in its own trade. A visit to the Pettah fish market is also worth making.

Galle Face Green

The promenade on the seashore and a popular attraction with everyone. Children fly kites, others play cricket and football and stall holders sell food to all and sundry along the 2km path. Many of the main hotels overlook the Green and the sea beyond.

Hilton Colombo

Sir Chittampalam A Gardiner
awatha
: 011 254 4644
x: 011 254 4657
colombo@hilton.com
w.colombohilton.com
obably the city's best hotel. 387
gant rooms. Several restaurants and
s, a business centre, swimming pool
d gym.

Samudra

Galle Face Centre Road
: 011 244 6622
x: 011 244 6348
@sri.lanka.net
w.tajhotels.com
excellent rooms overlooking the
an or swimming pool. Excellent
taurants including the best Chinese
own, bar and business centre.
gnificent gardens.

ladari Hotel

Lotus Road
: 011 254 4544
x: 011 244 9875
adari@slt.lk
w.galadarihotel.com
nderful hotel in the centre. 446 excel-
t rooms with fine views of the city
d harbour. Restaurants, bars, swim-
ng pool. Highly recommended.

lle Face Hotel

Galle Road
x: 011 254 1010
x: 011 254 1072
@diamond.lanka.net
w.gallefacehotel.com
uth end of the Green. A colonial hotel
h 77 tasteful rooms, some overlook-
the ocean. The ocean-side restaurant
d bar are wonderful places.

liday Inn

Sir Mohammed Marcan
arker Mawatha
Tel: 011 242 2001

Fax: 011 244 7977
holiday@sri.lanka.net
Excellent accommodation. Fine rooms
with all mod cons, a good restaurant
and lovely swimming pool and gym.

Mount Lavinia

102 Hotel Road
Mount Lavinia
Tel: 011 271 5221
Fax: 011 273 8228
lavinia@sri.lanka.net
www.mountlaviniahotel.lk
Fine hotel on the outskirts. Formerly
the British Governor's residence, it has
its own private beach, fabulous seafood
restaurants and bars. Taxis and auto-
rickshaws can get to the cricket within
half-an-hour.

Wayfarers Inn

77 Rosmead Place
Excellent budget guesthouse in the
centre offering clean rooms and a good
breakfast.

Haus Chandra

37 Beach Road
Mount Lavinia
Tel: 011 732 755
Fax: 011 733 173
Small hotel, good rooms and small
swimming pool. Good value.

Tropic Inn

6 College Avenue
Mount Lavinia
Tel: 011 738 653
Fax: 011 344 657
Good budget hotel. Clean air-condi-
tioned rooms. Recommended.

Blue Sea Guesthouse

9/6 De Aaram Road
Mount Lavinia
Tel: 011 16 298
Small, simple budget guesthouse with
clean rooms, garden and friendly ser-
vice.

Bandaranaike International Airport is 34km to the north of Colombo.
There is a taxi rank immediately outside the Arrivals Hall. The journey to the
y should take around 45 minutes and cost no more than 1000 Rs. Most of the
hotels offer transfers to the city which should be arranged beforehand. There
banks, ATM's and bureaux de change in the arrivals hall. There is also a tourist
formation desk, a post office, duty free shops, a restaurant, snack bar and bar.
Car rental with driver is available.

Golden Dragon
Taj Samudra
Galle Face Centre Road
Excellent. Fine service.

88 Chinese Seafood Restaurant
98/1 Havelock Road
Tel: 011 259 3017
Authentic Sichuan cuisine.

Ginza Hosen
Colombo Hilton
Echelon Square
Tel: 011 254 4644
One of the Hilton's many restaurants, this Japanese is one of the best in town serving authentic cuisine including sushi, sashimi and tempura.

Sakura
14 Rheinland Place
Tel: 011 257 3877
Japanese, serving excellent food.

Spoons
Colombo Hilton
Echelon Square
Tel: 011 254 4644
Continental restaurant at the Hilton serving contemporary cuisine in a trendy atmosphere.

Koluu's
32B Sir Mohammad Marcan Marker
Mawatha
Tel: 011 232 5339
International cuisine in trendy reasonably priced restaurant. Chinese, Thai, Portuguese, Moroccan, Japanese, Indonesian and Italian to name but a

Curry Leaf
Colombo Hilton
Echelon Square
Tel: 011 254 4644
Garden restaurant offering buffet Sri Lankan cuisine with traditional mus

Lotus Leaf
466 Union Place
Tel: 011 479 3100
Excellent restaurant serving tradition Sri Lankan food.

Alhambra
Holiday Inn
Colombo 3
Tel: 011 22 2001
One of the best Indian restaurants in town.

The Commons
74 Dharmapala Mawatha
Tel: 011 574 384
An excellent restaurant serving lovely brunches and fabulous cakes.

Molly's Irish Pub
46/38 Nawam Mawatha
Tel: 011 254 3966
Excellent Irish pub. Live music and great atmosphere. Much better pub than Clancy's, an imitation Irish pub not worth visiting.

Cricket Club Café
34 Queens Road
Tel: 011 250 1384
The most popular pub for cricket fans. Australian owned and Sri Lankan run, it has a wonderful atmosphere, constant sport on TV and delicious food. Definitely recommended.

Gallery Café
2 Alfred House Road
Tel: 011 255 6563
Excellent café and bar around the corner from the Cricket Club Café. Good food in very trendy atmosphere.

Echelon Pub
Colombo Hilton
Echelon Square
Tel: 011 254 4644
Very popular sports bar showing all big events on large screen. Pool table

Rhythm and Blues
19/1 Daisy Villa Avenue
Tel: 011 451 7255
Probably Colombo's best, especially a late night you are after. Great band pool tables and great atmosphere. Ve popular.

Lion Pub
Mount Lavinia
Wonderful beer garden, unfortunate the service is diabolical and incredib frustrating. Great setting, but...

The Colombo National Museum

r Marcus Fernando Mawatha
xhibits detail the cultural heritage of
ri Lanka including rock sculptures
om ancient cities, artefacts from the
ri Lankan Kings and a fine collec-
on of demon masks, a traditional
andicraft. Open 09.00-17.00. Closed
ridays.

atural History Museum

06 Ananda Kumaraswamy Mawatha
isplay of stuffed animals and birds
f Sri Lankan origin. One of the best
xhibits is the skeleton of an elephant.
Open 09.00-17.00 daily.

The Dutch Period Museum

95 Prince St.
Pettah
An old Dutch house built by Count
August van Ranzow, the governor of
the Dutch East India Company, in the
old area of Pettah. Exhibits include furniture, coins and ceramics of the Dutch
period. Open 09.00-17.00. Closed
Fridays.

National Art Gallery

106 Ananda Kumaraswamy Mawatha
In the same building as the Natural
History Museum. Exhibitions by contemporary Sri Lankan artists alongside
visiting foreign collections. Open
08.00-17.00 daily.

Post Office

Colombo General Post Office
R Wijewardene Mawatha
rt
: 011 244 1427

urist Information

ylon Tourist Board
Galle Road
llupitiya
: 011 243 7049
@sri.lanka.net

i Lanka Tourist Board

Stuart Place
ening Hours 08.30 to 16.45 hours
onday to Friday 08.30 to 12.30 hrs
turday.

Hospital

Apollo Hospital
Vijaya Kumanatunga
Mawatha
Tel: 011 453 1066
Fax: 011 451 1199

Durdans Hospital
3 Alfred Place
Kollupitiya
Tel: 011 256 4994

Emergency Numbers

Police	011 243 3333
Headquarters	011 242 1111
Ambulance	011 242 2222
Fire	011 242 2222

Climate

	ave temp	rain cm
January	26	84
February	26	64
March	27	114
April	28	255
May	28	335
June	27	190
July	27	129
August	27	96
September	27	158
October	27	353
November	26	308
December	26	152

galle

Formerly known as the Esplanade, Galle International Stadium is considered deservedly to be one of the most beautiful Test venues in the world. Located in the heart of the city, the ground is overlooked by a 15th century Dutch fort, the ramparts of which offer a novel and excellent vantage point. The ground is a huge traffic roundabout in the centre of the city. The Sri Lankans have an excellent record here, having won six and lost only one of nine Tests.

The stadium became Sri Lanka's seventh Test venue in 1998 when it hosted the second match of a series against New Zealand. Having won the first Test at the Premadasa Stadium in Colombo, the visitors won the toss at Galle and scored 193 with Kumar Dharmasena taking 6/72 and Niroshan Bandaratilleke, 4/47. The home side replied with 323, thanks mainly to a fine innings of 167 by Mahela Jayawardene. New Zealand collapsed to 114 in their second innings as Bandaratilleke took 5/36 and Muttiah Muralitharan 3/24 to lose by an innings and 16 runs .

Next came a draw with Australia in 1999, which was followed in 2000 by Sri Lanka's only loss at the ground. They decided to bat against Pakistan but made a paltry 181 against Waqar Younis, 3/39 and Abdul Razza, 3/35. Pakistan replied with 600/8 dec. – the highest team score at the ground. Four of their players contributing centuries: Saeed Anwar (123), Younis Khan (116), Inzamam-ul-Haq (112) and Wasim Akram (100). Trailing by 419, Sri Lanka were dismissed for 256 to lose by an innings and 163 runs.

Sri Lanka returned to winning ways at Galle with a convincing innings and 15 runs victory the following month in the opening Test of a series against South Africa. Centuries from Sanath Jayasuriya, 148, Mahela Jayawardene, 167 and match figures of 13/171 from Muttiah Muralitharan were the highlights.

In the first Test against England in 2001, Marvan Atapattu, 201 and Aravinda de Silva, 106 set up a formidable 470/5 dec. Marcus Trescothick's 122 was the highlight in England's reply of 253 as Jayasuriya, 4/50, and Muralitharan, 3/79, forced England to follow-on. They reached 145/3 before collapsing to 189 to lose by an innings and 28. Jayasuriya, 4/44 and Muralitharan, 4/66 again did the damage.

In August of that year, Sri Lanka beat India by 10 wickets, thanks to centuries by Jayasuriya, 111, Kumar Sangakkara, 105no, and match figures of 8/90 from Muralitharan. In November the same year, they beat the West Indies, also by

10 wickets even though Brian Lara hit a splendid 178 and Ramnaresh Sarwan 88 as the West Indies made 448. Muralitharan took 6/126. The home side replied with 590/9 dec., Sangakkara top-scoring with 140. Hashan Tillakaratne, 105 and Mahela Jayawardene, unfortunate to be run out on 99, also contributed significantly. In the West Indies' second innings Muralitharan was again their nemesis, taking 5/44 as they were dismissed for 144, only two runs in front of their hosts.

In January 2002, Sri Lanka beat Zimbabwe by 315 runs to continue their successful run at Galle, thanks mostly to the bowling of Muralitharan and Jayasuriya with match figures of 9/91 and 9/74 respectively. Another highlight of that game was Upul Chandana's 2, having coming in at no. 9.

The lowest total at Galle is 79 by Zimbabwe in 2002 in their second innings when Muralitharan took his 400th Test wicket. His match figures of 13/171 against South Africa is the best return.

The stadium has a capacity of 10,000 and is one of the most picturesque grounds in Test cricket with the fort at one end and the Indian ocean on two sides. The backdrop also includes some fabulous tall palm trees. The pavilion is a modern building at the northern end of the ground and incorporates the players' dressing rooms, the media centre, the administration offices and corporate hospitality. The west side of the ground has one of the VIP sections which is undercover with individual plastic chairs and TV's for replays. This section costs Rs 6000 for a five day ticket. The grandstand (Rs 750), which is partially covered and slightly at the wrong angle to watch the cricket, is also on this side of the ground. There are two VIP sections (Rs 6000) on either side of the sight-screens at the southern end. Both these areas are undercover and have TV's. The Hill (Rs 50 per day) on the west side of the ground is a grassy bank with absolutely no shade. The scoreboard is at the back of the Hill.

Unfortunately the ground lacks atmosphere until this area fills up at the weekend when the locals are not working. Then it comes alive. A band plays non-stop throughout a Test. An alternative, which should be taken advantage of for at least one session, is to watch from the ramparts of the fort that towers over the southern end of the ground and provides a fabulous panoramic view of the area. Locals set up food and drink stalls on the wall of the fort to cater for the cricket fans.

The bus and train stations are outside the northern end of the ground opposite the pavilion. Buses and auto-rickshaws run from here to Hikkaduwa and Unawatuna, two popular resorts where the majority of cricket fans stay. Buses cost Rs 20 and rickshaws Rs 250 to Hikkaduwa and Rs 7 and Rs 100 to Unawatuna.

the city

Formerly Point de Galle, this is a small city (population just under 100,000) on the south west tip of Sri Lanka, 116km south of Colombo. It sits on a peninsula jutting into the Indian Ocean. A fine natural harbour, protected from the north east monsoons, it is exposed to the weather from the southwest and also has dangerous rocks and reefs. The city's name comes from the Sinhalese word for a rock. It is surrounded by the ramparts of a Dutch fort, which is an archaeological reserve and a World Heritage site and also the biggest tourist attraction.

It was the administrative centre for European settlers and the country's main port for 300 years until the British established a port in Colombo. It was used during pre-Christian times and first appeared in European history books in the 6th century.

The Dutch established the headquarters of the Dutch East India Company in 1640, rebuilding the city and the fort and removing any traces of the Portuguese occupation. The architecture of the city today reflects this era with many of the old Dutch buildings remaining in place. The northern entrance to the fort built by the Dutch in 1665 is still in use today. When the British captured the city in 1796 they decided to develop the port in Colombo. As a result, trade in Galle decreased.

Galle is one of the most untouched colonial cities in the world. The government is committed to restoring the old part of the city enclosed by the ramparts of the fort to its former glory. There are many well preserved colonial buildings within th walls of the city including the Governor's House, the old Dutch Government House, n the New Oriental Hotel, the Dutch Church, the clock tower and the lighthouse overloo ing the ocean.

The main gate to the fort just to the south of the cricket ground has a stone which tells the history of the city. The harbour has some fine historical memorabilia, including anchors dating from Roman times and a celadon bowl from the 13th century Southern Song dynasty. A visit to the fish market down by the walls of the fort is very interesting It is an absolute pleasure to walk through the narrow quiet streets of the fort and on its ramparts with the ocean on three sides and the cricket ground on the other. A walk around the perimeter of the fort takes a couple of hours. Kids dive off the high rocks i the sea below as families wander on the vast expanses of grass.

The modern part of Galle is very different. It is busy with modern buildings housing banks, shopping malls and dusty streets hosting markets and bazaars. Touts hang arou the busy area by the train and bus stations trying to entice visitors with one scam or another. To be honest there is not a lot for the visitor to admire. The old part is much more attractive.

Most cricket visitors do not stay in the city, because there are two magnificent beaches, Hikkaduwa and Unawatuna, within easy travelling distance. Both have everything need for a great stay and transport to and from the cricket by bus, tuk tuk or taxi is available Hikkaduwa, 18km to the north of Galle, is the larger and more lively of the two resorts The beach is lined with accommodation from large hotels to family run guesthouses. Hikkaduwa has more up-market hotels than Unawatuna. The sea can be rough, but the is some excellent snorkelling on the Coral Gardens reef just off the coast. Diving is also popular and the coast around Hikkaduwa attracts surfers.

Unawatuna is 5km in the other direction and has what must be one of the best beaches the world. It is more than 4km long, lined with palm trees and small, unimposing cafés restaurants and hotels. There is some snorkelling on the reef and a number of wreck d within 20 minutes of the beach. Unawatuna has plenty of mostly budget accommodati with a couple of up market resorts.

There are some National Parks in the south of the island which can be visited before, during or after a Test in Galle. These include the Sinharaja Forest Reserve, a beautiful rainforest with some splendid wildlife, Horton Plains National Park and Yala Nationa Park, the country's most popular game sanctuary.

transport

Airlines

Sri Lanka Airlines
No 16A Gamini Mawatha
Tel: 091 224 8942
Fax: 091 224 6944
sdswije@srilankan.aero
Monday-Friday 08.15-18.00, Saturday 08.15-13.15

Buses

The bus station is located opposite the main entrance to the cricket ground. Buses are inexpensive and run to all the surroundings villages and towns including Unawatuna (Rs 7) and Hikkaduwa (Rs 20).

Trains

The train station is also opposite the cricket ground, adjacent to the bus station. Trains run four times a day to Colombo and once daily to Kandy. Public transport in Sri Lanka very cheap.

Taxis

Most visitors prefer auto-rickshaws which are widely available, outside hotels, restaurants, rail and bus statio and the cricket ground. Very reasonab priced there is never a problem picki one up. Taxis are also available, albeit slightly more expensive.

Car Hire

There are no self drive car hire comp nies although many guesthouses and private firms offer car/van hire with driver. An inexpensive way to see the countryside.

The Dutch Fort

he biggest tourist attraction. Quiet, narrow streets full of interesting build-
s, museums and churches are a pleasure to walk around. The southern end
rlooks the Indian Ocean and at the very tip children hurl themselves off the
ks into the ocean below. This area provides an excellent panoramic view of
surrounding coastline. Local vendors are on hand to sell linen, carvings and
ique coins. A walk along the southern ramparts and the little beach is wonder-
y refreshing with the sea breeze blowing into the fort. The lighthouse, the mari-
e museum and the fish market are all worth a visit.

e New Orient Hotel

lt in 1684 as the headquarters of the Dutch Governor, it became a hotel in the
y 18th century and has remained open ever since. Famous for its elegant, old
and billiard room which provides the ideal place to have a drink after a walk
und the fort.

e South Coast

nty to offer cricket fans. Apart from the fabulous beach of Unawatuna, Tangalle
a 20km beach with golden sands and the palm lined cove of Mirissa is a won-
ful retreat. Along this stretch of the coast stilt fishermen ply their trade, sitting
their poles for hours on end catching small fish with the simplest of rods.

la National Park

)km from Galle in the south east of the country, this is certainly worth the trip.
s the country's most visited National Park and a haven for elephants, crocodiles,
nkeys, leopards, porcupines and many species of birds. There are also some fine
haeological sites within the park dating back to 150BC. Bundala National Park
in the same area and is a treat for bird watchers.

The closest airport is Bandaranaike International Airport, 145km
away on the other side of Colombo. A taxi ride will cost between 3,000 and
4,000 rupees. An enjoyable scenic train journey between Colombo and Galle
takes about three hours and costs only Rs 64. The train station is in the centre
of Galle and taxi touts wait for the arrival of each train. Tuk tuks are also available. Taxis to Unawatuna should cost no more than Rs 250 (tuk tuk Rs 100) and
Hikkaduwa Rs 550 (tuk tuk Rs 250). The bus station is just over the bridge, less
than a minute's walk away and buses run from there to both the above towns
and others along the coast. The cricket ground is across the road from the station and the fort is less than a five minute walk.

Light House Lodge

62 Lighthouse St.
Tel: 075 450 514
8 smallish bedrooms. Inside the fort.
Friendly service.

Closenberg Hotel

11 Closenberg Road
Tel: 091 223 32241
The older, main building of two has 5
en suite rooms with antique furniture,
fans and mosquito nets but no view,
whereas the new building has 16 modern rooms with fabulous views over
the bay. Restaurant, bar and garden
bar.

Galle Fort Hotel

28 Church St.
karlsteinberg@galleforthotel.com
Splendid villa with 14 air-conditioned
suites furnished with antiques. Some
rooms have views of the lighthouse
and Mosque. Restaurant, bar, swimming pool

New Orient Hotel

10 Church St.
Tel: 091 223 34591
Fax: 091 223 34591
E-mail: nohgalle@sltnet.lk
35 rooms of differing standards, some
with four-poster beds. Restaurant, bar
and swimming pool.

The Sun House

18 Upper Dickson Road
Tel: 091 223 22624
info@thesunhouse.com
Perched above the city overlooking the
harbour. Beautiful rooms with excellent service, home cooked meals.

Lighthouse Hotel

Dadella
Tel: 091 22744
Fax: 091 224021
hotels@jetwing.lk
Historic Dutch building overlooking
the Ocean. Luxurious en suite rooms
with balcony. Restaurant, bar, beautiful swimming pool, natural rock pool,
gym, squash and tennis.

Thaproban

Unawatuna Beach
Tel: 074 381 722
Reasonably priced hotel on the beach.
12 good rooms, some overlooking the
bay. Good restaurant.

Unawatuna Beach Resort

Tel.: 09-24028,074-380549
Fax.: 09-32247
e-mail: ubr@sri.lanka.net
Arguably the nicest place to stay in
Unawatuna, offering half-board with
good rooms, some with bay views.
Good, buffet restaurant with a limited
á la carte menu. One of the busiest
bars by the beach.

Heaven on Earth

Yaddehimulla Road
Unawatuna
6 recently renovated en suite rooms.
Good, budget value.

Rock House

Yaddehimulla Road
Unawatuna
Excellent budget accommodation 2
minutes walk from the beach. Good,
clean en suite rooms with helpful and
friendly staff.

Post Office

Galle Post Office
Church St.
Tel: 091 223 2064
Fax: 091 222 3251

Tourist Information

Unfortunately, the Tourist Information
Centre situated opposite the rail station
has been closed. Most hotels can supply
some information, however it is a good
idea to visit the Ceylon Tourist Board on
Galle Road in Colombo or the tourist
information desk at Bandaranaike
International Airport which can supply
all details of the attractions and accommodation in the area.

Hospital

Galle General Hospital
Karapitiva
Tel: 091 222 2261

Emergency Numbers

Police Station
Samudradisi Mawatha
Tel: 091 222 2222

New Oriental Hotel
10 Church St.
Galle Fort
One of the few eateries in the Fort.

Closenberg Hotel
1 Closenberg Road
Tel: 091 223 32241
One of Galle's best.

Rock Café
Unawatuna
Plain, simple restaurant on the beach serving Sri Lanka curries and western food. Huge menu, excellent service and very reasonably priced.

Sunil Gardens
Unawatuna
Fish a speciality. Bob Marley tracks bound to playing in the background.

Unawatuna Beach Resort
Unawatuna
Excellent buffet. Small á la carte menu.

The Sydney Hotel
Bus Station
Popular haunt for cricket fans during breaks and after play. A dark, drab pub but with a good atmosphere during tests.

New Oriental Hotel
10 Church St.
Galle Fort
Good place to go after the cricket for a relaxing drink.

Hard Rock Café
Unawatuna
One of the many little bars down by the beach. Literally one metre from the sea. Open late.

Rock Café
Unawatuna
Good service and excellent food.

Sunil Gardens
Unawatuna
A lively bar with good music. Open extremely late.

Unawatuna Beach Resort
Unawatuna
One of the most popular bars, showing football and other sports from around the world.

Why Not Rock Café
Narigama
One of the best bars, with loud music, on the beach.

Top Secret
Narigama
Another good bar with good music. Open late

Ranjith's Beach Hut
Hikkaduwa
Another of the many bars on the beach. Cheap beer, open till late.

Climate

	ave temp	rain cm		ave temp	rain cm
January	26	103	July	27	165
February	26	86	August	27	155
March	27	117	September	27	214
April	28	242	October	27	340
May	28	296	November	26	302
June	27	207	December	26	177

Win/Loss Record

Country	Played	Won	Drawn	Lost	Tie
Pakistan	1	1	-	-	-
Australia	2	1	1	-	-
Sri Lanka	10	6	2	2	-
England	2	-	1	1	-
Zimbabwe	1	-	-	1	-
India	1	-	-	1	-
New Zealand	1	-	-	1	-
West Indies	1	-	-	1	-
South Africa	1	-	-	1	-

Highest Individual Aggregates (Sri Lanka unless stated)

Player	Mat	Inn	NO	Runs	Ave	HS	50	100
Mahela Jayawardene	10	14	2	934	77.83	167	6	2
Marvan Atapattu	10	17	5	778	64.83	201*	4	2
Sanath Jayasuriya	10	17	3	574	41.00	148	0	2
Kumar Sangakkara	7	10	1	530	58.89	140	3	2
Thilan Samaraweera	4	6	1	250	50.00	77	2	0
Marcus Trescothick (Eng)	2	4	0	226	56.50	122	1	1
Brian Lara (WI)	1	2	0	218	109.00	178	0	1
Upul Chandana	4	6	0	210	35.00	92	1	0
Chaminda Vaas	9	12	2	207	20.70	54	1	0
Aravinda de Silva	4	5	0	195	39.00	106	1	1

Top Wicket Takers (Sri Lanka unless stated)

Player	Mat	Bll	Md	Runs	Wkt	Ave	BB	S/R
Muttiah Muralitharan	10	3943	199	1238	82	15.10	7/46	48.09
Sanath Jayasuriya	10	1221	51	400	22	18.18	5/43	55.50
Chaminda Vaas	9	1671	77	634	17	37.29	4/95	98.29
Shane Warne (Aus)	2	516	26	193	13	14.85	5/43	39.69
Kumar Dharmasena	5	1135	41	510	12	42.50	6/72	94.58
Niroshan Bandaratilleke	2	618	31	205	11	18.64	5/36	56.18
Ashley Giles (Eng)	2	725	31	266	9	29.56	4/63	80.56
Waqar Younis (Pak)	1	193	9	79	7	11.29	4/40	27.57
Dilhara Fernando	2	288	13	97	6	16.17	5/42	48.00
Upul Chandana	4	705	20	367	6	61.17	2/46	117.50

Highest Individual Scores (Sri Lanka unless stated)

201*	Marvan Atapattu	v England	2000-01
178	Brian Lara (WI)		2001-02
167	Mahela Jayawardene	v New Zealand	1997-98
167	Mahela Jayawardene	v South Africa	2000-01
148	Sanath Jayasuriya	v South Africa	2000-01
140	Kumar Sangakkara	v West Indies	2001-02
130	Matthew Hayden (Aus)		2003-04
129	Darren Lehmann (Aus)		2003-04
123	Saeed Anwar (Pak)		2000
122	Marcus Trescothick (Eng)		2000-01

Best Individual Bowling Performances (Sri Lanka unless stated)

31.4-15-46-7	Muttiah Muralitharan	v England 2003-04
35-5-84-7	Muttiah Muralitharan	v South Africa 2000-01
21.3-5-59-6	Muttiah Muralitharan	v Australia 2003-04
24.1-4-72-6	Kumar Dharmasena	v New Zealand 1997-98
41-8-87-6	Muttiah Muralitharan	v South Africa 2000-01

3.4-11-126-6	Muttiah Muralitharan	v West Indies 2001-02
-9-36-5	Niroshan Bandaratilleke	v New Zealand 1997-98
9-42-5	Dilhara Fernando	v India 2001
10-43-5	Sanath Jayasuriya	v Zimbabwe 2001-02
5-43-5	Shane Warne (Aus)	2003-04

ghest Partnerships

t	Runs	Batsmen	Match
	193	Marvan Atapattu & Sanath Jayasuriya (SL)	2000-2001 v South Africa
d	109	Marvan Atapattu & Kumar Sangakarra (SL)	2001-2002 v West Indies
	230	Marvan Atapattu & Aravinda de Silva (SL)	2000-2001 v England
	206	Damien Martyn & Darren Lehmann (Aus)	2003-2004
	116	Mahela Jayawardene & Arjuna Ranatunga (SL)	1999-2000 v Pakistan
	154	Hashan Tillakaratne & Thilan Samaraweera (SL)	2001-2002 v West Indies
	120	Younis Khan & Wasim Akram (Pak)	1999-2000
	146	Thilan Samaraweera & Upul Chandana (SL)	2001-2002 v Zimbabwe
	60	Rahul Dravid & Venkatesh Prasad (Ind)	2001-2002
h	46	Mahela Jayawardene & Muttiah Muralitharan (SL)	2003-2004 v England

esults at the International Stadium

te	Countries	Result
06/1998	v New Zealand	won by an innings and 16 runs
09/1999	v Australia	drawn
06/2000	v Pakistan	lost by an innings and 163 runs
07/2000	v South Africa	won by an innings and 15 runs
02/2001	v England	won by an innings and 28 runs
08/2001	v India	won by 10 wickets
11/2001	v West Indies	won by 10 wickets
01/2002	v Zimbabwe	won by 315 runs
2/12/2003	v England	drawn
08/03/2004	v Australia	lost by 197 runs

kandy

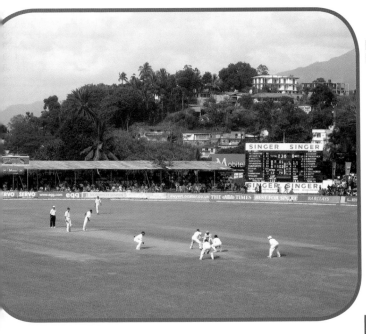

asgiriya stadium

The Asgiriya Stadium, in Kandy, surrounded by wonderful hills and fine scenery, is one of the prettiest grounds in Test cricket. It forms part of the playing fields of Trinity College, the city's top school.

It became Sri Lanka's second Test venue when it hosted a one-off match against Austra in 1983 which resulted in defeat by an innings and 38 runs.

The next match was against New Zealand a year later and Sri Lanka lost again, this tir by 165. Richard Hadlee had match figures of 8/43. .

A draw against India followed in 1985 before Sri Lanka were trounced by Pakistan in 1986. The home side made a paltry 109 as Imran Khan, Tauseef Ahmed and Abdul Qadir took three wickets each. Pakistan replied with 230 before dismissing their hosts 101 to win by an innings and 20 runs. Ahmed took 6/45.

There was a seven year gap before the next Test when Sri Lanka faced India. Unfortunately, only 12 overs were possible because of the weather.

Pakistan triumphed again in 1994. Pakistan sent in their hosts and promptly dismisse them for 71. Wasim Akram 4/32 and Waqar Younis 6/34 did the damage. In reply, Pakistan posted 357/9 before declaring. Inzamam-ul-Haq top scored with 100. In Sri Lanka's second innings only Hashan Tillakaratne put up any resistance with a fighting 83no as his side fell to 234 all out to lose by an innings and 52 runs.

Sri Lanka's first win on the ground came in 1998 against Zimbabwe. Sri Lanka made 469/9 before declaring, Marvan Atapattu hitting a glorious 223 – the highest individua score at the ground. The visitors crumbled to 140 in their first innings as Muttiah Muralitharan took 5/53. Forced to follow-on, they batted considerably better in their second innings, Murray Goodwin top scoring with 70 and Andy Flower hitting 67 as their team made 338. Muralitharan was again the destroyer with 7/94. Requiring 10 runs to win, the home side suffered a slight hiccup when Heath Streak dismissed Sana Jayasuriya and Roshan Mahanama for ducks in his first over. However the home side won the game in the very next over by eight wickets.

Sri Lanka also won next Test at Kandy when they defeated Australia. The visitors made 188, thanks largely to Ricky Ponting's 96. Muralitharan took 4/63. The home side scor 234 in reply, Aravinda de Silva top scoring with 78 as Colin Miller took 4/62 for the Australians. Ponting, with 51, was the only Australian batsman to put up a fight in the second innings as they were dismissed for 140 to leave the home side with a small targ of 95. De Silva steered his team home by six wickets with a determined 31no. The mat will be remembered for the collision between Steve Waugh and Jason Gillespie which broke Waugh's nose and Gillespie's leg.

A draw against Pakistan followed in 2000 before Sri Lanka suffered a shocking run of defeats in close Tests. In the second Test against South Africa in 2000 South Africa wer inserted only to see Lance Klusener hit 118no and Mark Boucher 60 as the visitors reached 253. Sri Lanka replied with 308, Marvan Atapattu scoring 120. In their second innings, South Africa made 231, Jacques Kallis contributing 87. Set 177 to win, Sri Lan started badly, collapsing to 21/4 before Russell Arnold (40) and Arjuna Ranatunga (88 steadied the ship. They appeared to be cruising to victory at 161/6 before disaster struc and they lost their last four wickets for eight runs to lose the match by seven runs.

The next year England arrived at Kandy 1-0 down in the series having lost by an innin in Galle. The home side made 297 thanks to a century by Mahela Jayawardene, 101 an a fighting 65 from Russell Arnold. Darren Gough, 4/73 and Andy Caddick, 4/55 took v wickets for England, who then made 387 in reply with a century from Nasser Hussain (109) and 59 from Graham Thorpe. Muralitharan took 4/127. Trailing by 90 runs, Sri Lanka made 250, Kumar Sangakkara top scoring with 95. Set 161 for victory, England wobbled to 97/5 as Chaminda Vaas took 4/39, before Graham Thorpe and, later, Craig White steadied the ship to bring England home by three wickets.

Sri Lanka were on the receiving end again in August 2001 when India beat them by seven wickets. A 131 run victory followed over the West Indies in November of the san year before Sri Lanka hammered Zimbabwe. The visitors made 236 with Muralitharan taking 9/51, which included the first nine Zimbabwean wickets before wicket-keeper Kumar Sangakkara took a catch off the bowling of Chaminda Vaas to dismiss

the visitor's No. 11 Henry Olonga. In reply Sri Lanka hit 505, Sanath
Jayasuriya scoring 139. Muralitharan and Charitha Fernando both took four wickets
Zimbabwe were dismissed for 175 to lose by an innings and 94 runs.

The highest team score at the ground is 514/4 declared by Australia in 1983 and the low-
, 71 by Sri Lanka against Pakistan. The highest run chase is India's 264/3 in 2001.
Muralitharan's match figures of 13/115 against Zimbabwe is the best return.

The stadium has a capacity of 15,000 and it is hard to believe there is a finer setting
anywhere, with the giant Buddha sitting high on the hill above the southwest corner of
the ground. The new pavilion is situated in this corner and includes the players' dressing rooms and a grandstand that provides the best view in the ground. On the west
side of the ground is the beautiful old pavilion and the VIP seats in sections B, C, D
and E which stretch around to the northern end of the ground. All these enclosures are
undercover. The old style scoreboard is located on the east side behind the grass general
admission area which has no cover. It is important to get to this area early in the morning as the ground is flat and only those with seats on the fence enjoy a good view. The
old Trinity Clubhouse is in the south east corner of the ground and is another fine
structure and a great place from which to watch.

There is an excellent food village on the north west corner of the ground with stalls serving juices, snacks, burgers, kebabs and Sri Lankan cuisine. Vendors move around the rest
of the ground selling beer, soft drinks, hot dogs and other fast food. There are also several bars in the ground. Lunch-time entertainment includes a parade of elephants around
the pitch. The toilet facilities are portable loos in each corner of the ground.

Tickets are available from the ground before and during the match (cash only, no credit
cards) or can be purchased by contacting Sri Lanka Cricket, 35 Maitland Place, Colombo
7, telephone 01 268 1601 and fax 01 269 7405 or email on info@srilankacricket.lk
Prices range from Rs 30 for the general admission areas to Rs 1500 for the grandstand.
Five day passes are available for Rs 6000. Pass-outs are issued to spectators leaving the
ground during play. The ground is a ten-minute, uphill walk from the centre of the city;
an auto-rickshaw will cost Rs50. Most spectators make their way towards the
restaurants and pubs in the centre after the day's play.

the city

Kandy is peaceful, relaxed and very beautiful. It sits on the Mahaweli
River in the heart of Sri Lanka's picturesque hill country. It has a population
of 125,000 and is just over 100km from Colombo. It is one of the country's largest and oldest cities with historical and cultural significance and was the last seat of
the Sinhala kings. The name Kandy derives from the Sinhalese word Kanda which
means hill. The city is the bastion of the Buddhist faith in Sri Lanka and home
to the sacred tooth of Buddha. It is situated on the shores of a lake that was constructed by Sri Wickramma Rajasinha, the last Kandyan king.

Unlike other Sinhalese kingdoms, Kandy did not fall to the Portuguese or the
Dutch and survived initial attacks by the British in 1803. However, just over a
decade later, unhappy with their king, the chiefs of Kandy welcomed the British
to their city, bringing the whole of Ceylon, as the country was then known, under
unified rule for the first time. The city remained prosperous as the British established large coffee and tea plantations in its vicinity.

Tourism is without doubt Kandy's largest industry, attracting increasing numbers
of tourists and pilgrims every year. The city is also the administrative and commercial centre for the region which produces tea, rubber, cacao and rice. The city
is also famous for its handicrafts and hand-made jewellery.

There are some fine walks on the outskirts of the city including the walk along
the Mahaweli River. Other attractions in Kandy are the National Museum and the
Kandyan Art and Cultural Centre in the middle of the city.

The countryside around the city has many Buddhist and Hindu temples of interest including Embekke Devale, a Buddhist temple with wonderful wooden

sculptures 11km from the city, Lankatilake Temple, a Hindu place of worship with stone carvings and Gadaldeniye Temple, another Buddhist temple with fine paintings. These temples are within walking distance of each other.
With its altitude of 54 metres above sea level providing a cool temperature without the humidity of the coastal cities, Kandy has a very pleasant and uniform climate. The average temperature is 25 degrees. Unfortunately, the beginning of the cricket season coincides with the wettest time of the year with October, November and December getting the most rain.

what to see

Dalada Maligawa

The biggest tourist attraction and a very important pilgrimage destination for Buddhists throughout the world. The temple was built in the 16th century and is said to house the tooth of Buddha which was brought here from southern India in the fourth century. In July and August each year the tooth is carried through the streets on the back of an elephant. Daily ceremonies take place in the temple and all are welcome to attend. It should be noted that long trousers must be worn. Visitors in shorts will not be allowed access. Outside the gates of the temple flower sellers sell lotus blossoms and frangipani.

Pinnewala Elephant Orphanage

20km to the west of Kandy and a sanctuary for orphaned and abandoned elephants. Set in 25 acres of rain forest, visitors are always welcome. Morning and afternoon tours are arranged to catch the residents playing in the river and, of course, feeding times. Enquiries on 081 698 086 or wildlife@slt.lk Open 08.30-17.45 daily.

Udawattekele Bird Sanctuary

On the edge of the city off Wewelpitiya Road and a wonderful forest full of bird species that include the Sri Lanka Hanging Parrot, Kingfishers, Bulbuls and the Chestnut Headed Bee Eater. It is also a sanctuary for some beautiful butterflies and is home to thousands of monkeys. Open 08.00-17.30.

Royal Botanical Gardens

Sri Lanka's largest, they are 6km from the centre at Peradeniya. Set on the banks of the Mahaweli Ganga and designed by the British in 1821. But the gardens had been in existence long before this as pleasure gardens for the kings of Kandy. Highlights include the Orchid House, the fernery, the spice gardens and the artificial lake in the centre of the gardens. Open 07.30-19.00 daily.

Trinity College Chapel

Sri Lanka's foremost Christian education college. Its chapel is a remarkable cross between English and Sinhalese architecture. The granite columns are carved with the crests of Oxford and Cambridge Universities alongside traditional Sinahalese designs. The influence of the Temple of the Tooth cannot be missed. Inside the chapel the walls are covered by murals depicting scenes from the Bible. The chapel is in the school grounds across the road from the cricket ground and can be visited at lunchtime or after the day's cricket.

Airlines

Sri Lankan Airlines Ltd
17 Temple St.
Tel: 081 223 2494
Fax: 081 223 2494
Monday to Friday 08.15-18.00
Saturday 08.15-13.15

Buses

Private intercity and airport buses depart from Station Road near the train station. Local buses are very crowded.

Trains

Kandy rail station is in the south west. Five trains a day run between Kandy and Colombo, a trip which is renowned for being one of the most spectacular rides in the world. The station has four platforms and has a small shop selling water, crisps and fruit.

Taxis

Auto-rickshaws are the main form of transport for the visitor. It is possible to hail them anywhere in the city and they wait outside hotels, pubs and restaurants. Taxis and vans are also available.
Radio Cabs   081 233 322

Car Hire

There are no self drive car hire companies in Kandy although many guesthouses and private firms do offer car/van hire with driver which can be an excellent way to visit the surrounding area.

The closest airport to Galle is Colombo International Airport, 100km away. A taxi ride will cost between 2000 and 3000 rupees. The train journey between Colombo and Kandy is one of the finest in the world, climbing up the hills from sea level to more than 1600 ft. Kandy train station is a ten-minute walk south west of the centre and there are many taxi touts waiting for each train. Tuk tuks are also available. Taxis to any of Kandy's central hotels should cost no more than R100. A taxi to the Citadel, Kandy's leading hotel will cost Rs 375.

Post Office

General Post Office
VRD Bandaranaike Mawatha
Tel: 081 222 2250

b Post Office
S. Senanayake Veediya

Tourist Information

Ceylon Tourist Board
Palace Square
Tel: 081 222 661
Open 09.00-16.45

Hospital

Kandy General Hospital
Hantana Road
Tel: 081 223 3337
Fax: 081 222 2261

Emergency Numbers

Kandy Police Station
Sirimavo Bandaranaike Mawatha
Tel: 081 223 3004/222 2228

Climate

	ave temp	rain cm		ave temp	rain cm
January	24	122	July	24	171
February	24	67	August	24	141
March	26	103	September	24	146
April	26	179	October	24	287
May	26	155	November	24	273
June	25	205	December	24	217

Most hotels have their own restaurants and of course there are fast food places and pizza huts etc. Below are just a number of good reasonable restaurants.

Devon Restaurant
Dalada Veediya
Tel: 081 224537
Good food at reasonable prices on one of Kandy's main streets.

Olde Empire
21 Temple St.
Tel: 081 224 284
Good restaurant for travellers, very popular with locals.

Apart from hotel bars there are just two pubs in Kandy, although both are worth a visit.

The Pub
Dalada Veediya
Tel: 081 324 868
Busy, lively pub with music, TV scree
and a good atmosphere. Also serves excellent food.

The Pub Royale
Dalada Veediya
Next door to the Queen's Hotel but n
as classy as its rival. However the Roy
is definitely worth a visit and is very popular after the cricket. Great India
food. Voted one of the top 100 restau
rants in Sri Lanka.

Citadel

124 Srimath Kuda Ratwatte
Mawatha
Tel: 081 234365
Fax: 081 232085
htlres@keels.com
Probably Kandy's best hotel, 5km
from the centre. 121 rooms overlook
the swimming pool and the Mahaweli
river. Excellent restaurant and bar.
Very comfortable.

Queen's Hotel

Corner of Dalada Veediya and
S. D. Senanayake Veddiya
Tel: 081 222 2813
Fax: 081 223 2079
queens@kandy.ccom.lk
Colonial hotel in the centre with 90
rooms, some overlooking the swimming pool set in lovely gardens. Ideal
place to stay.

Hotel Thilanka

3 Sangamitta Mawatha
Tel: 081 23 429
Fax: 081 225 497
thilandka@ids.lk
Good central hotel overlooking Kandy
Lake with 76 comfortable rooms, good
restaurant and popular bar.

Hotel Topaz

Peradeniya Road
Tel: 081 232 326
Fax: 081 232 073
topaz@eureka.lk
Fine hotel on the hill overlooking the
city. It has 75 good rooms, restaurant,
bar and good swimming pool.

Hilltop Hotel

200 Bahirawakanda
Tel: 081 232 429
Fax: 081 225 497
thilanka@ids.lk
Comfortable hotel within 5-minute
walk of the centre. Good rooms with
all mod cons, good restaurant and
bar and excellent swimming pool.
 Recommended.

Swiss Residence

23 Bahirawakanda Lane
Tel: 081 238800
Fax: 081 479057
100 immaculate rooms overlooking
Kandy Lake. Restaurant, bar and small
swimming pool.

Hotel Suisse

30 Sangaraja Mawatha
Tel: 081 233 025
Fax: 081 232 083
Suisse@kandy.ccom.lk
On the opposite side of the lake to
the centre. Very pleasant with 90 good
rooms, fine restaurant and lovely
swimming pool set in nice gardens.

Olde Empire Hotel

21 Temple St.
Tel: 081 224 284
Lovely little hotel in the centre. Budget
hotel with shared facilities, restaurant
and very good service. Recommended
for budget travellers.

St. Bridget's Country Bungalow

125 Sri Sumangala Mawatha
Asgiriya
Tel: 081 222 5689
Fax: 081 223 2499
stbridge@slnet.lk
Excellent guesthouse in jungle sur-
roundings. Very comfortable rooms
and great food.

Thilini Guesthouse

60 Saranankara Road
Small guesthouse with 3 rooms suitable for budget travellers. Excellent
food and fine service.

Lake Inn

43 Saranankara Road
Tel: 081 222 208
Fax: 081 232 343
matsui@slt.lk
Budget hotel with good, clean rooms,
nice restaurant.

Win/Loss Record

Country	Played	Won	Drawn	Lost	Tie
South Africa	1	1	-	-	-
Pakistan	3	2	1	-	-
New Zealand	2	1	1	-	-
England	2	1	1	-	-
India	3	1	2	-	-
Australia	2	1	-	1	-
Sri Lanka	16	4	5	7	-
Zimbabwe	2	-	-	2	-
West Indies	1	-	-	1	-

Highest Individual Aggregates (Sri Lanka unless stated)

Player	Mat	Inn	NO	Runs	Ave	HS	50	100
Marvan Atapattu	10	17	3	797	56.93	223	1	3
Sanath Jayasuriya	10	18	0	636	35.33	188	2	2
Mahela Jayawardene	9	16	1	628	41.87	104	3	2
Arjuna Ranatunga	10	17	2	521	34.73	90	4	0
Hashan Tillakaratne	8	11	2	451	50.11	93	3	0
Kumar Sangakkara	7	13	1	368	30.67	95	1	0
Aravinda de Silva	8	14	3	284	25.82	78	2	0
Russel Arnold	7	11	0	283	25.73	71	2	0
Duleep Mendis	4	8	0	272	34.00	124	2	1
Chaminda Vaas	11	16	2	271	19.36	72*	1	0

Top Wicket Takers (Sri Lanka unless stated)

Player	Mat	Bll	Md	Runs	Wkt	Ave	BB	S/R
Muttiah Muralitharan	11	3721	207	1264	72	17.56	9/51	51.68
Chaminda Vaas (Ind)	11	2157	97	855	40	21.38	4/39	53.93
Kumar Dharmasena	6	1031	28	488	13	37.54	4/75	79.31
Waqar Younis (Pak)	2	310	5	213	11	19.36	6/34	28.18
Tauseef Ahmed (Pak)	1	168	11	77	9	8.56	6/45	18.67
Darren Gough (Eng)	1	216	7	123	8	15.38	4/50	27.00
Ashley Giles (Eng)	2	538	15	322	8	40.25	5/116	67.25
Saliya Ahangama	1	306	13	124	8	15.50	5/52	38.25
Richard Hadlee (NZ)	1	167	11	43	8	5.38	4/8	20.88
Vinothen John	1	282	8	159	8	19.88	5/86	35.25

Highest Individual Scores (Sri Lanka unless stated)

223	Marvan Atapattu	v Zimbabwe 1997-98
207*	Marvan Atapattu	v Pakistan 2000
188	Sanath Jayasuriya	v Pakistan 2000
143*	David Hookes (Aus)	1982-83
141	Kepler Wessels (Aus)	1982-83
139	Sanath Jayasuriya	v Zimbabwe 2001-02
124	Duleep Mendis	v India 1985-86
120	Marvan Atapattu	v South Africa 2000-01
118*	Lance Klusener (SA)	2000-01
116*	Mohinder Amarnath (Ind)	1985-86

Best Individual Bowling Performances (Sri Lanka unless stated)

40-19-51-9	Muttiah Muralitharan	v Zimbabwe 2001-02
42.5-13-94-7	Muttiah Muralitharan	v Zimbabwe 1997-98
14-4-34-6	Waqar Younis (Pak)	1994-95
15-7-45-6	Tauseef Ahmed (Pak)	1985-86
35.5-16-81-6	Muttiah Muralitharan	v West Indies 2001-02
29-18-23-5	Muttiah Muralitharan	v Zimbabwe 1997-98
9.3-4-28-5	Stephen Boock (NZ)	1983-84
39-18-49-5	Muttiah Muralitharan	v New Zealand 2003
24-7-52-5	Saliya Ahangama	v India 1985-86
16-4-52-5	Shane Warne (AUS)	1999-00

Highest Partnerships

Wkt	Runs	Batsmen	Match
1st	335	Marvan Atapattu & Sanath Jayasuriya (SL)	1999-2000 v Pakistan
2nd	170	Kepler Wessels & Graham Yallop (Aus)	1982-1983
3rd	200	Adam Gilchrist & Damien Martyn (Aus)	2003-2004
4th	216	Roy Dias & Duleep Mendis (SL)	1985-1986 v India
5th	155*	David Hookes & Allan Border (Aus)	1982-1983
6th	124	Lance Klusener & Mark Boucher (SA)	2000-2001
7th	131	Hashan Tillakaratne & Ruwan Kalpage (SL)	1994-1995 v Pakistan
8th	111	Chaminda Vaas & Charitha Buddhika (SL)	2001-2002 v Zimbabwe
9th	76	Kumar Dharmasena & Dinusha Fernando (SL)	2003-2004 v England
10th	79	Chaminda Vaas & Muttiah Muralitharan (SL)	2003-2004 v Australia

Results at The Asgiriya Stadium

Date	Countries	Result
22/04/1983	v Australia	lost by an innings and 38 runs
09/03/1984	v New Zealand	lost by 165 runs
14/09/1985	v India	drawn
23/02/1986	v Pakistan	lost by an innings and 20 runs
24/04/1987	v New Zealand	match cancelled due to political unrest
17/07/1993	v India	drawn
26/08/1994	v Pakistan	lost by an innings and 52 runs
07/01/1998	v Zimbabwe	won by 8 wickets
09/09/1999	v Australia	won by 6 wickets
28/06/2000	v Pakistan	drawn
30/07/2000	v South Africa	lost by 7 runs
07/03/2001	v England	lost by 3 wickets
22/08/2001	v India	India won by 7 wickets
21/11/2001	v West Indies	won by 131 runs
04/01/2002	v Zimbabwe	won by an innings and 94 runs
03/05/2003	v New Zealand	drawn
10/12/2003	v England	drawn
16/03/2004	v Australia	lost by 27 runs

Kingston

JAMAICA

The West Indies was introduced to Test cricket early in
1930 when England visited for a four match series. On 11th January
1930 the teams met at Kensington Oval in Bridgetown, Barbados when the
result was a draw. Three weeks later the Queen's Park Oval in Trinidad hosted the
second Test, when England won by 167 runs. The Bourda Ground in Georgetown,
Guyana, staged the third Test on 21st February with the West Indies winnning by 289
runs. Sabina Park in Kingston, Jamaica, was next in April but the match ended in a
draw after nine days because the English team had to catch their boat home!
The Recreation Ground in St. John's, Antigua, became the fifth Test venue when the
West Indies drew with England in April 1981. Arnos Vale Ground in St. Vincent hosted
its one and only Test in June 1997 when Sri Lanka visited. That game also ended in a
draw. The New Queen's Park Stadium in Grenada became the seventh Test venue in
2002 when it hosted the second Test of the series against New Zealand which ended in
a draw. West Indies' newest Test ground was the Beausejour Stadium in St. Lucia when
it staged the drawn 2003 Test against Sri Lanka.

Airlines

BWIA, Liat and Caribbean Star all operate flights between the Caribbean islands.
BWIA offer a 30-day pass for $450 which entitles the holder to unlimited travel.
Itineraries must be booked in advance. Flights are very busy during the
cricket season and it is important to book early. The pass is

Antigua

St. Lucia

Grenada

Barbados

Trinidad & Tobago

Georgetown

GUYANA

particularly good value if one includes Jamaica in their travel plans, otherwise it may be less expensive to buy individual flights. Visitors are encouraged to examine the terms and conditions before purchasing the pass.

BWIA	256 426 2111
Liat	256 434 5428
Caribbean Star	256 461 7827

Distance Between Cities in the West Indies (in km)

	Barbados	St. Lucia	Guyana	Jamaica	Trinidad	Antigua	Grenada
Barbados	-	180	717	1917	340	507	259
St. Lucia	180	-	859	1743	376	356	233
Guyana	717	859	-	2371	565	1214	703
Jamaica	1917	1743	2371	-	1834	1584	1744
Trinidad	340	376	565	1834	-	717	150
Antigua	507	356	1214	1584	717	-	563
Grenada	259	233	703	1744	155	563	-

Details regarding telecoms, post services, banking, car hire, embassies, customs, visas, emergency numbers, time differences, electricity and departure taxes vary from island to island and are included in individual chapters.

antigua

recreation ground

The Antigua Recreation Ground, home of the Leeward Islands Cricket Association, became the fifth Test venue in the West Indies during England's tour of 1981, the match ending in a rain-affected draw.

The ground is best known for the exploits of Brian Lara in 1994 and 2004. First he scored the highest ever Test innings of 375 in a drawn match with England, overtaking Sir Garfield Sobers' record of 365no scored in Jamaica 36 years earlier. Ten years later he was at it again when, in another drawn match, he hit 400no. In between these two epic innings, the West Indies had a remarkable victory over the Pakistanis when they visited the Caribbean in 2000. Batting first, the visitors scored 269, Yousuf Youhana top-scoring with 103 and Courtney Walsh taking five wickets. Shiv Chanderpaul hit 89 as the West Indies replied with 273. Wasim Akram took 6/61. In their second innings Pakistan scored 219 to set a target of 216. Despite some splendid bowling by Akram (5/49), Jimmy Adams (48no), and Courtney Walsh (4no), shared a last wicket partnership of 19 to lead the Windies home by one wicket.

Antigua is a batsman's paradise. In 2003 the West Indies scored a world record run chase of 418/7 to beat Australia. Both teams scored 240 in their first innings, Jermaine Lawson being the pick of the bowlers with 7/78 for the home side. Despite an opening partnership of 242 between Justin Langer (111), and Mathew Hayden (177), the Australians were dismissed for 417. After losing early wickets, Ramnaresh Sarwan (105), and Chanderpaul (104), shared a fifth wicket partnership of 123 until Sarwan was dismissed with the score on 288/5. Partnerships of 96 between Chanderpaul and Omari Banks (47no), and an unbroken 46 by Banks and Vasbert Drakes (27no), saw the West Indies home by three wickets on the last morning.

Viv Richards scored three centuries on his home ground including one off 56 balls in 81 minutes against England in 1986, the fastest Test century in the least number of balls received ever recorded. Four batsmen, including Richie Benaud, have scored Test centuries in less time, but none needed fewer balls than Richards. He also shared in a 308 run third wicket partnership with Richie Richardson, another Antiguan, against Australia in 1984.

Wasim Akram's match figures of 11/110 in Pakistan's defeat 2000 top the list with no other bowler taking ten wickets in one match.

The ground has a capacity of 12,000 and is a terrific place at which to watch cricket. The atmosphere is electric. Gravy, a local character with a passion for dressing up, has officially retired from his career as number one supporter but still performs the occasional dance on his head. At the north end of the ground the Sir Viv Richards players' pavilion is flanked by the West India Oil stand, the Sidney Walling stand and the Andy Roberts stand. The lower tier of the West Indian Oil stand, otherwise known as Chikki's Stand to the left of the pavilion, is without doubt the noisiest in Test cricket with loud music after every over and during every break. Chikki is the DJ who beats out the music as the old wooden stand vibrates and the crowd dance their way through the day. The upper tier in this stand is an excellent viewing point as is the upper tier of the Andy Roberts stand which is situated on the right side of the pavilion. After the day's play a party commences in and behind Chikki's stand which lasts well into the night. Spliff's bar down the road from the ground has a great atmosphere and rocks into the small hours and is a must to visit at least once after the cricket.

The bleaches, cheap seats with very little cover, on the west side of the ground, stage just as big a party although there is no shade. Local supporters sprawl out on the concrete terrace. The opposition always take a verbal battering, but woe betide any West Indies player, especially one from another of the islands, who does not perform well. The crowd on the bleaches are on his case in a flash.

At the Factory Road end of the ground is the new Richie Richardson Stand, a modern structure with an excellent view of the pitch, the State Insurance Stand along with the scoreboard and the media centre. On the east side of the ground is the Schoolboy Stand which gets very busy once school finishes. The kids seem to have a great party as well.

There are plenty of bars around the ground serving rum and beer. The bar under the bleaches is well worth a visit to soak up the atmosphere, as is the bar in between the players' pavilion and Chikki's stand, from where a lot of spectators choose to watch. There are many stalls behind the stands at the pavilion end of the ground serving some of the most delicious food found at Test grounds. Smoke billows into the air from many barbecues. All types of food and drink are available from the vendors.

Facilities and access for the disabled with viewing areas are available in the pavilion. Arrangements can be made by contacting the ground on 268 462 2106 or emailing on licb@msn.com

The ground is a five-minute walk along the Long or High Streets from the centre of St. John's. Those staying south of St. John's can catch a bus into the city from Jolly Harbour or Deep Bay. Taxis are also available from all hotels and it is usual practice for cricket fans to share them which cuts down the cost considerably. Most taxis are minibuses and can carry up to ten people. There is parking in the streets around the ground. Tickets for Test matches can be purchased from the West Indies ticketline 1800 744 GAME (4263), from www.windiescricket.com, by contacting the ground on 268 462 2106, emailing on licb@msn.com or from the ticket offices on each corner of the ground.

Post Office

General Post Office
Long St.
St. John's
Open 08.15-16.00 Monday-Thursday
08.15-17.00 Friday.

Tourist Information

Antigua and Barbuda Department of Tourism
Queen Elizabeth Highway
St. John's
Tel: 268 462 0480
Fax: 268 2483
ahta@candw.ag

Antigua and Barbuda
Department of Tourism
Newgate St.
St. John's
Tel: 268 463 0125
Fax: 268 462 2483
info@antigua-barbuda.org

Hospital

Hoberton Hospital
Queen Elizabeth Highway
St. John's
Tel: 268 462 0251

Emergency Numbers

Police	268 462 0125
Fire	268 462 0044
Ambulance	268 462 0251

the island

St. John's is the capital of the twin island state of Antigua and Barbuda and has a population of 30,000, nearly half the island's total of 67,000. With an area of 173sq. km, Antigua is the largest of the British Leeward Islands, in the north east of the Caribbean. It is part coral, part volcanic with reef protecting the long, scalloped coastline.

The first known inhabitants of Antigua were the Siboney, an Arawak tribe in 2000BC. Other tribes visited the island over the centuries and the Carib were in occupation when Christopher Columbus claimed the island for Spain in 1493. Columbus named the island Santa Maria la Antigua after the saint from Seville. The British took control in1623 and established the first settlement nine years later. In 1684 Sir Christopher Coddrington set up the first of many sugar plantations. He used the neighbouring island of Barbuda to provide provisions for the slaves who cleared Antigua's forest and created the plantations. Horatio Nelson spent three years in Antigua in the 1780s developing British naval facilities in the south of the island. Nelson recorded that Antigua was "a vile place" and "a dreadful hole". Antigua is very rarely, if ever, referred to in this manner nowadays. It became an associate state of the Commonwealth in 1967 and gained full independence in 1981.

Tourism is the mainstay of the economy and Antigua welcomes more than 750,000 visitors each year. The majority stay outside the city, but the capital is certainly worth a visit. The Cathedral in the centre dominates the skyline. Reminders of the colonial times such as the Court House, the National Museum and Government House remain. St. John's is a quaint city, easy to find one's way around.

transport

Airlines
BWIA 268 480 2901
British Airways 268 462 0876
Liat 268 480 5074
Caribbean Star 268 480 2561
Virgin Atlantic 800 744 7477

Buses
Private owned minivans holding between 12 and 28 are the main form of transport. The East bus station on Independence Avenue handles buses for the North and East with the West bus station in St. John's Market handling the south and west including English Harbour. Services run from 06.00-19.30.

Taxis
Taxis are in plentiful supply. In St. John's there is a rank opposite the public market. Ask reception in your hotel. Taxi rates are fixed by government and the driver should have a rate card. It is wise to agree a price before setting off.
Antigua Taxi Stand 268 462 5190
24 Hour Taxi Service 268 460 5353
Antigua Taxi Service 268 562 1709

Car Hire
Avis
Coolidge Industrial Estate
St. John's
Tel: 268 462 2840

Budget Rent A Car
VC Bird Airport
Tel: 268 462 3009

Hertz
All Saints Road
St. John's
Tel: 268 462 4114

Thrifty
VC Bird Airport
Tel: 268 462 9532

Climate
	ave temp	rain cm		ave temp	rain cm
January	27	22	July	30	24
February	27	22	August	30	25
March	27	22	September	30	25
April	30	22	October	30	25
May	30	24	November	28	23
June	30	24	December	28	23

Shirley Heights

One of the island's most important defensive positions in colonial times. Forts built by the British to protect the island from the Americans and the French are now arguably the most popular sightseeing spots. It is also one of Antigua's premier nightspots, especially on Sundays with steel bands from 16.00-19.00 and reggae from 19.00-22.00. A glorious 40 minute drive from St. John's.

The Antigua and Barbuda Museum

Tells the story of the islands from their geological beginnings to modern day. The many exhibits include ancient tools and artefacts dating back to the Awarak, the naval history of the island and the bat that Vivian Richards used when scoring the fastest ever Test century at the Antigua Recreation Ground. The museum is in the centre of St. John's and is open 08.30-16.00 Monday-Friday 10.00-14.00 Saturday.

St. John's

A walk around this picturesque city is well worthwhile. Attractions include St. John's Anglican Cathedral, Fort James, the Cenotaph, the Court House, the Antigua and Barbuda Museum and the VC Bird Monument. Cruise liners arrive at the docks every couple of days and bring in huge revenues. The centre of town is geared towards these tourists with a large market, a casino, cafés, bars and restaurants. The cruise ships arrive in the morning and leave in the late afternoon. The city is busy during these visits, but when the liners leave the place reverts to a quiet, relaxed and peaceful state.

Island Cruise

An all-day cruise around the island is a wonderful way to get the feel of Antigua. It is a fun day out with swimming and snorkelling in the shallow waters of Paradise Reef and beach cricket on one of the island's 365 beaches. Lunch is provided with a never-ending supply of rum and beer. A very good day out, highly recommended. Enquires Kokomo Cat Cruises 462 7245. Daily cruise 09.30-16.00. US$70.

English Harbour

English Harbour lies on the south coast and is home to the restored Nelson's Dockyard. Built in the 18th century, the dockyard was used by the British to protect the island from the French, Dutch and Spanish invaders. It is now one of Antigua's premiere tourist attractions with restaurants, markets, inns and art galleries.

what to see

407

Lashings Runaway Beach

Tel: 268 462 4438

The place to stay. Good comfortable rooms, maybe not as luxurious as some of the other hotels but this is where the action happens! Every night after the cricket everybody flocks to the bar. Set on an incredible beach, this laid-back hotel is perfect for the cricket visitor.

Royal Antiguan

Deep Bay
Five Islands
Tel: 268 462 3733
reservations@antigua-resorts.com
www.antigua-resorts.com
In Deep Bay south of St. John's this is one of the island's best. 266 rooms with cable TV. 3 restaurants, 4 bars including a swim-up, swimming pool, gym, tennis, dive shop and other watersports.

Jolly Beach Resort

Jolly Harbour
Tel: 268 462 0061
Fax: 268 562 5302
info@jollybeachresort.com
www.jollybeachresort.com
All-inclusive hotel with pools, watersports, restaurants, bars. 462 air-conditioned rooms with cable TV and all mod cons. Set in 40 acres on one-mile beach.

Jolly Harbour Villas

Jolly Harbour
Tel: 268 462 3085
Fax: 268 462 6167
reservations@jollyharbour.com
www.jollyharbourvillas.com
Two bedroom villas on the beach, self-catering, with 5 restaurants, bar, swimming pool, squash.

City View Hotel

St. John's
Tel: 268 562 0256
Fax: 268 562 0242
cityview@candw.ag
One of the few hotels in the city centre minutes from beach, cricket ground. 3 rooms with cable TV. Restaurant, bar.

Rex Halcyon Cove

Dickenson Bay
Tel: 268 462 0256
Fax: 268 462 0271
Beachfront resort with 210 rooms. 5k from St. John's and the ground. Cable TV, 3 restaurants, 3 bars and beautiful gardens. Watersports.

Dickenson Bay Cottages

Marble Hill
Dickenson Bay
Tel: 268 462 4940
Fax: 268 462 4941
This 2-storey villa complex is one of the less expensive options on the island. units with kitchenette facilities, swimming pool.

Antigua Village Beach Resort

Dickenson Bay
Tel: 268 462 2930
Fax: 268 462 0375
antiguavillage@candw.ag
www.antiguavillage.net
Self contained units. 55 rooms with air conditioning and cable TV. Restaurant swimming pool and watersports.

Joe Mike's Hotel

Corner Nevis Street and Com Alley
St. John's
Tel: 268 462 1142
Fax: 268 462 6056
Another downtown hotel with 12 air-conditioned rooms. Good budget accommodation.

VC Bird International Airport is 8km from St. John's. There is a taxi rank right outside the Arrival Hall. A taxi to St. John's and its surrounding bays takes 15 minutes and costs EC$30. Taxis to Shirley Heights or Nelson's Dockyard cost US$26. A tourist information desk is located after immigration. There is a bank, bureau de change, two ATM machines and a post office in the terminal. A restaurant upstairs on the first floor serves good food and drinks. In the Departure Hall, after immigration, there is a café, souvenir, record and duty free shops. Car rental is available from Avis (268 462 2840), Budget (268 462 3009), Hertz (268 462 6450), and Thrifty (268 462 8803), .

Hemingway's Caribbean Café

St. Mary's St.
St. John's
Tel: 268 462 2763
Overlooking the quay. From
8.30 until late 7 nights a week.
International, Caribbean and Creole
cuisine. Good food and excellent service.

Le Bouchan Sur le Quai

Heritage Quay
St. John's
Tel: 268 480 1374
Bistro on the waterfront.

Coconut Grove Beach Restaurant

Dickenson Bay
Tel: 268 1538
One of the best restaurants on the
island. Happy hour 15.30-19.00

Amigo's Mexican Café

Barrymore Beach Apartments
Runaway Bay
Tel: 268 562 1545
Mexican and American food on the
beach. Good food, relaxed atmosphere.

The Beach at Antigua Village

Dickenson Bay
Tel: 268 480 6940
Caribbean, Asian, European and
American food served by the sea.
Cocktails at sunset.

Al Porto Ristorante

Jolly Harbour Marina
Tel: 268 462 7695
Good Italian reasonably priced.
Breakfast, lunch and dinner.

Steely Bar Restaurant

BBR Sportive
Jolly Harbour Sports Centre
Tel: 268 462 6260
Sports bar, serving great food overlooking Marina. Very lively bar with
50-inch satellite television. Open
until late seven nights a week

The Inn English Harbour

English Harbour
Tel: 268 460 1014
Food with Caribbean flavour on terraced restaurant overlooking the harbour and across the National Park.

The Mad Mongoose

Falmouth Harbour
Tel: 268 463 7900
Lively restaurant and bar with different menu each day. Open Tuesday-Sunday.

Lashings Runaway Beach

Tel: 268 462 4438
The number one venue in Antigua.
Party atmosphere, beach cricket
and live bands including Richie
Richardson's and Curtley Ambrose's
band. The place rocks into the night
and continues into the morning. 24
hours a day bar. Excellent. Pizzas until
04.00 in the morning. Good food,
huge helpings.

Sticky Wicket

Airport Boulevard
Coolidge
Own cricket pitch. Right next to airport. Very comfortable bars and restaurant. Watch cricket under lights a
couple of times a week. Cricket Hall of
Fame with a lot of memorabilia.

O'Gradys Pub

Redcliffe St.
St. John's
Tel: 268 462 5392
Irish pub. Friendly staff in lively bar.
Good entertainment.

Coconut Grove Beach

Dickenson Bay
Tel: 268 462 1538
Great beach bar. Evening entertainment.

The Royal Antiguan

Deep Bay
Five Islands
Tel: 268 462 3733
A popular place for cricket fans to stay
and drink. A 'must' on at least one
night of the Test

The Redcliffe Tavern

Redcliffe Quay
Tel: 268 461 4557
Converted warehouse with excellent
restaurant and fine bar.

Shirley Heights Lookout

Shirley Heights
Tel: 268 460 1785
Excellent barbecue on Sundays. Steel
band, reggae.

general info

Telecoms
International Direct Dialling is available throughout the island. Antigua's country code is 268.

Banking
Open Monday-Thursday 08.00-13.00 Friday 08.00-12.00 and 15.00-17.00. The Bank of Antigua is open on Saturday from 08.00-12.00.
There are a number of ATM's in St. John's and at the airport.
Antigua currency is the East Caribbean Dollar. Notes are in denominations of EC$100, 50, 20, 10 , 5 and coins EC$1 and 50, 25, 10, 5, 2, 1 cents.

Embassies
British High Commission
Price Waterhouse Centre
11 Old Parham Road
St. John's
Tel: 268 426 0008
Fax: 268 526 2124
britishc@candw.ag

Customs
One carton of cigarettes, 1 quart of liquor and 6oz of perfume can be imported without incurring customs duty.

Visa
A passport valid for at least six months beyond your period of stay and a return or onward ticket is required for all visitors entering Antigua. A visa is not required

Time Difference
GMT - 4

Electricity
Part of the island is 110 volts, the remainder 220 volts AC 60 Hz. Most hotels have dual voltage.

Tipping
Antigua has a room tax of 8.5% and usually a 10% service charge is added to your bills. Tipping is at one's discretion

Departure Tax
EC$50

stats

Win/Loss Record
Country	Played	Won	Drawn	Lost	Tie
South Africa	1	1	-	-	-
West Indies	19	7	9	3	-
India	3	-	3	-	-
New Zealand	1	-	1	-	-
Australia	5	2	1	2	-
Pakistan	2	-	1	1	-
England	6	-	3	3	-
Sri Lanka	1	-	-	1	-

Highest Individual Aggregates (West Indies Unless stated)
Player	Mat	Inn	NO	Runs	Ave	HS	50	100
Brian Lara	12	19	1	1628	90.44	400*	6	4
Desmond Haynes	7	10	1	733	81.44	167	3	3
Carl Hooper	10	15	4	656	59.64	178*	0	3
Shiv Chanderpaul	8	12	2	570	57.00	136*	2	2
Viv Richards	6	8	1	433	61.86	178	0	3
Gordon Greenidge	6	7	1	429	71.50	154*	1	2
Jimmy Adams	5	9	3	424	70.67	208*	2	1
Richie Richardson	6	10	0	378	37.80	154	1	1
Ramnaresh Sarwan	5	8	0	337	42.13	105	2	1
Justin Langer (Aus)	2	4	0	331	82.75	127	1	2

Top Wicket Takers (West Indies Unless stated)
Player	Mat	Bll	Md	Runs	Wkt	Ave	BB	S/
Curtly Ambrose	11	2328	109	945	48	19.69	5/37	48.5
Courtney Walsh	12	3032	102	1250	45	27.78	6/54	67.38

Name								
Malcolm Marshall	4	937	35	438	19	23.05	4/87	49.32
Ian Bishop	4	682	21	355	15	23.67	5/84	45.47
Wasim Akram (Pak)	2	556	26	248	13	19.08	6/61	42.77
Joel Garner	3	651	22	279	13	21.46	5/63	50.08
Mervyn Dillon	3	701	23	331	12	27.58	4/112	58.42
Carl Hooper	10	1456	58	620	11	56.36	3/69	132.36
Glenn McGrath (Aus)	3	788	47	287	10	28.70	3/50	78.80
Waqar Younis (Pak)	2	426	13	207	10	20.70	5/104	42.60

Highest Individual Scores (West Indies Unless stated)

400*	Brian Lara	v England 2003-04
375	Brian Lara	v England 1993-94
208*	Jimmy Adams	v New Zealand 1995-96
178	Viv Richards	v Australia 1983-84
178*	Carl Hooper	v Pakistan 1992-93
177	Matthew Hayden (Aus)	2002-03
175	Robin Smith (Eng)	1993-94
167	Desmond Haynes	v England 1989-90
154*	Gordon Greenidge	v India 1982-83
154	Richie Richardson	v Australia 1983-84

Best Individual Bowling Performances (West Indies Unless stated)

19.1-3-78-7	Jermaine Lawson	v Australia 2002-03
21.3-7-54-6	Courtney Walsh	v Australia 1994-95
26.2-7-61-6	Wasim Akram (Pak)	1999-00
25-5-74-6	Colin Croft	v England 1980-81
23.4-13-34-5	Muttiah Muralitharan (SL)	1996-97
13.1-3-37-5	Curtly Ambrose	v Sri Lanka 1996-97
30-12-49-5	Wasim Akram (Pak)	1999-00
20-2-61-5	Danny Morrison (NZ)	1995-96
20.5-2-63-5	Joel Garner	v Australia 1983-84
32-12-68-5	Curtly Ambrose	v New Zealand 1995-96

Highest Partnerships (West Indies Unless stated)

Wkt	Runs	Batsmen	Match
1st	298	Gordon Greenidge & Desmond Haynes (WI)	1989-1990 v England
2nd	200	Aunshuman Gaekwad & Mohinder Amarnath (Ind)	1982-1983
3rd	308	Richie Richardson & Viv Richards (WI)	1983-1984 v Australia
4th	183	Brian Lara & Keith Arthurton (WI)	1993-1994 v England
5th	219	Brian Lara & Shiv Chanderpaul (WI)	1993-1994 v England
6th	282	Brian Lara & Ridley Jacobs (WI)	2003-2004 v England
7th	217	VVS Laxman & Ajay Ratra (Ind)	2001-2002
8th	110	Lee Germon & Dipak Patel (NZ)	1995-1996
9th	96	Inzamam-Ul-Haq & Nadeem Khan (Pak)	1992-1993
10th	106	Carl Hooper & Courtney Walsh (WI)	1992-1993 v Pakistan

Results at Antigua Recreation Ground

Date	Countries	Result
27/03/1981	v England	drawn
28/04/1983	v India	drawn
07/04/1984	v Australia	won by an innings and 36 runs
11/04/1986	v England	won by 240 runs
12/04/1990	v England	won by an innings and 32 runs
27/04/1991	v Australia	lost by 157 runs
01/05/1993	v Pakistan	drawn
16/04/1994	v England	drawn
08/04/1995	v Australia	drawn
27/04/1996	v New Zealand	drawn
04/04/1997	v India	drawn
13/06/1997	v Sri Lanka	won by 6 wickets
21/03/1998	v England	won by an innings and 52 runs
03/04/1999	v Australia	lost by 176 runs
25/05/2000	v Pakistan	won by 1 wicket
06/04/2001	v South Africa	lost by 82 runs
10/05/2002	v India	drawn
09/05/2003	v Australia	won by 3 wickets
10/04/2004	v England	drawn

barbados

kensington oval

The Kensington Oval in Bridgetown has been the home of Pickwick Cricket Club since 1882. The ground staged the first Test held in the West Indies in 1930, a high scoring draw against England. Clifford Roach became the first West Indian to score a Test century with 122 in the first innings and George Headley, at the age of 20, scored 176 in the second.

Historic as that game was, the greatest on the ground is, without question, the 1998/99 encounter between West Indies and Australia when Brian Lara sharing a last wicket partnership of nine runs with Courtney Walsh, scored a masterful 153no to bring the West Indies victory by one wicket.

There have been some other memorable batting feats at the Kensington Oval. In 195 two Barbadians came to the wicket with the West Indies on 147/6 against Australia. Denis Atkinson (219) and Clairemente Depreiza (122) put on a record seventh wicke partnership of 347 to save the game. Their record still stands today. Neither scored another century for their country.

Three years later Hanif Mohammed played the longest Test innings of all time, scoring 337 in 16 hours and ten minutes. In 1960 the two knighted Barbadians, Garry Sobers (226) and Frank Worrell (197no), shared a fourth wicket partnership of 399 against England. In 1965 Bill Lawry and Bobby Simpson of Australia became the onl openers in Test history to both score double centuries. Fourteen years later Lawrence Rowe played probably the greatest innings the Kensington Oval has seen. His 302 in ten-and-a-half hours was magical.

The ground has a capacity of 15,000. Barbadians are passionate about their cricket and are very proud of their players, both past and present. The backing they give Barbados-born players is second to none. The Sir Garfield Sobers Pavilion which, with the Pickwick Pavilion, houses the players' dressing rooms, must be the quaintes in Test cricket. The players sit at ground level while a couple of hundred spectators sit upstairs with a glorious view of the ground. To the left of these is the the oldest stand in the ground, the George Challenor Stand, another spectacular place to enjoy the cricket. The top tier of the stand is an impressive VIP area with photographs and memorabilia from the past. Next is the Three W's stand, named after Walcott, Worrell, and Weekes, a two-tier stand with a excellent view at fine leg. Then comes the Greenidge/Haynes Stand which is not as comfortable as the Three W's. All these stands are under cover from the hot sun.

Sweeping around the boundary, the Carib Beer Party area is an all-

inclusive drink frenzy. The Banks Beer Stand and the unremark-
ably named Stand A and Stand B are very basic and are not undercover. The
Media Centre at the Joel Garner End of the ground is new and modern. The Mitchie
ewitt stand is a new three-tier structure with an excellent view from the top tier. The
c Innes and Kensington stands run down the east side of the ground.
ilities and access for the disabled with viewing areas are available in the Sobers,
kwick and Challenor stands. Arrangements can be made by contacting the ground
246 436 1397 or emailing on theoffice@bca.org.bb. There are plenty of bars and food
lets in and around the ground. The most popular lunchtime venue is just outside the
und behind the Kensington stand where the party never stops with calypso and reggae
sic and stalls selling a variety of food and drink.

nsington Oval is 2km to the north west of Bridgetown. Buses run from the city but
h the busy traffic the 20 minute walk through Cheapside and up Fontabelle Road is
bably the better option and provides an opportunity to soak up the atmosphere of the
y and its love of cricket. For those staying on the south or west coast, sharing taxis with
er fans will save having to catch a minibus into Bridgetown. There is some parking
und the ground on Fontabelle Road and President Kennedy Drive.
kets are available from a number of sources, the West Indies ticket hotline 1800 744
ME (4263), www.windiescricket.com, from the Barbados Cricket Association 246 436
97 or email theoffice@bca.org.bb. Tickets are also available from the ticket office at the
round on the days before the game. Unfortunately it should be noted that there are
very long queues and the purchase of tickets can take up to four to five hours which
is very uncomfortable in the hot sun.

Bridgetown is the capital of Barbados as well as the chief
port and commercial centre. It lies in Carlisle Bay on the south west
corner of the island. With a population of 130,000 it houses nearly half of
he island's total. It is a busy, bustling city with many people commuting to
d from the country each day. The majority of the island's people live either in
e city, on the west coast between Bridgetown and Speightstown, or on the south
ast between the city and the town of Oistins. The majority of visitors that come
the island tend to stay outside Bridgetown on either the west or south coast.
rbados is a small island, only 33km by 22 with an area of 170sq. km. It is the most
sterly of the Caribbean islands and is known as the gateway to the West Indies. It
is formed by erupting volcanoes and is largely surrounded by coral reefs.
he original inhabitants were the Amerindians from Venezuela who arrived more
an a thousand years ago. However, when John Powell claimed the island for
ritain in 1625 they deserted the island for many years. In 1627 the British settled
a site where Holetown is today. Over the next 20 years immigration from
ritain continued with more than 40,000 settlers arriving. Most were small farm-
s. However, once sugar planting was introduced in the 1650s many of the settlers
ere squeezed out and returned to Britain or moved to other islands. The planta-
on owners used slave labour to grow their crops and make their fortunes. The
olition of slavery in 1834 led to the importation of labour from India. Today
gar is still very important to the Barbadian economy.
rbados gained its independence in 1966, although it is still a part of the British
ommonwealth.
ourism is Barbados' largest industry and is growing constantly. The island with
s wonderful beaches, ample accommodation and many restaurants has the infra-
ructure to handle the influx of tourists. Another growth industry is finance. The
land is becoming a major off-shore financial and banking centre. Other indus-
ies include the export of sugar, rum and tropical flowers. Barbados produces
0% of its own oil.
Bridgetown is a modern city but there are still reminders of the past with
heritage buildings such as the 1871 neo-gothic Parliament Buildings, the
Law Courts, the Police Station, the Library and the Bridgetown

the island

Synagogue. The city has grown without planning and has a quaint jumbled appearance. But it is easy to walk around. The Barbados Museum at the Garrison traces the history of the island. The National Heroes' Square, formerly Trafalgar Square, marks the centre of the city and has a statue of Nelson and the War Memorial. Independence Arch in the centre of the city was built in 1987 to celebrate 21 years of independence. The Careenage, the original port, has many cafés and restaurants offers an opportunity to stroll through the markets, and browse in the stalls and shops. T Garrison Savannah to the east of the city, where horse-racing takes place every Saturday f October to August is a popular venue for tourists and locals alike.

The island is surrounded by 100km of terrific sandy beaches. On the west coast the calm clear turquoise waters of the Caribbean Sea are perfect for swimming and snorkelling. Th southern beaches such as Rockley have small to medium waves, good for body surfing an swimming. As one moves around the island towards the Atlantic on the southeast and ea coasts the waves become bigger, ideal for surfing but not for swimming as the currents of Atlantic make this unsafe. Bathsheba is one of the top surfing spots.

Barbados has an unbeatable year-round mild tropical climate with constant cooling trade winds. The sun shines eight to nine hours each day, even during the rainy season from Ju to December. Lightweight cottons are the recommended clothing. It is the perfect climate for the beach life many Barbadians lead. Life is centred on the beach, music, clubs and, of course, food. The island has an abundance of restaurants mainly in St. James, Holetown a Spieghtstown on the east coast and St. Lawrence Gap on the south. Local specialities inclu lobster and flying fish. Some of the top restaurants can be very expensive. Others are reas able, but there are few cheap restaurants on the island. Barbados' nightlife is mostly in the same areas with St. Lawrence Gap being the favourite. Once again, going out in Barbados not cheap, but the 'Happy Hours' offered by many of the bars help to ease the cost. of the evening's entertainment. There are also two all-inclusive nightclubs close to Bridgetown t are reasonably priced and situated on the beach.

There is a variety of accommodation on the island but it should be noted that there is no cheap accommodation in Barbados.

Grantley Adams International Airport is on the south east corner of Barbados, 17km from Bridgetown. A taxi ride to Bridgetown costs B$30, to St. Lawrence Gap on the south coast, B$20 and on the west coast to Holetown, B$38. Buses run from Bridgetown to the airport and cost B$1.50. The journey takes approximately 45 minutes.

There is a tourist information desk in the arrivals hall open from 08.00 until the last flight. A branch of the Barbados National Bank opens from 08.30 until the last flight. There is an ATM machine in the departure hall. There is also a post office plus shops and restaurants. Car hire is available from Courtesy Rent a Car (246 418 2500)

Airlines

BWIA	256 426 2111
British Airways	256 436 6413
Liat	256 434 5428
Caribbean Star	256 461 7827
Virgin Atlantic	256 228 4886

American Airlines   256 428 4170

Buses

Barbados has an excellent bus service. Fares are a flat BD$1.50, providing an inexpensive way of sight-seeing. Government-run buses are blue with yellow stripe and private buses are yel with a blue stripe. Buses for the east a north of the island depart Lowe Green and to the south and east of the island from the Fairchild Street Termi There are also many licensed minibu called ZR Vans. Bongo buses, as they affectionately called, blast loud regga music and are always packed. They a very regular and one never has to wa long for the next one.

Taxis

Taxis are not metered. Set fares are available and price should be agreed before commencing your journey.

Car Hire

When hiring a car a Barbados driving permit is required. This can be

obtained while hiring your car.
Sunny Isle Motors
Worthing
Christchurch
Tel: 246 435 7979

Coconut Car Rentals
Bay St.

Bridgetown
Tel: 246 437 0297

Courtesy Rent-a-Car
Grantley Adams International Airport
Tel: 246 418 2500

Folkestone Marine Park and Visitor Centre
Just north of Holetown on the west coast. There is more than 2km of reserve with some incredible snorkelling and diving. A sunken barge about 150 metres out is a magnet for a remarkable number of different reef fish. Snorkelling equipment is available for hire and changing facilities are provided. There is also a marine museum and a visitor's centre at Church Point, Holetown. Tel: 246 422 2314. Open 09.00-17.00 weekdays.

Andromeda Gardens
The Andromeda Gardens are in Bathsheba on the east side of the island near St. John's Parish Church. These are wonderful gardens with unusual plants and flowers. It is one of the most picturesque parts of the island. Paths circle the gardens and the water-lily ponds. Streams run through the gardens down to the Atlantic Ocean. There is a café and gift shop. Open 09.00-16.30 daily. Tel: 246 433 9384.

Harrison's Cave
On the east side of the island near Bathsheba. The cave has stalagmites and stalactites formed over thousands of years and has been open to the public since the 1970s. An electric tram transports visitors through the cave to view the spectacular underground lakes and waterfalls. The visitor's centre is very informative and has souvenirs for sale. Open 09.00-16.00 daily at St. Thomas Highway, St. Thomas. Tel: 246 438 6640.

Caribbean Cigar Company
Manufactures fine cigars in its factory in St. Michael. Visitors are invited to drop by and have a free tour which is a five-minute walk from the centre of Bridgetown. A very interesting and very different experience. Of course there is an opportunity to buy the product! Tel: 246 437 8519

Mount Gay Rum Visitors' Centre
Very popular. Tells the history of the oldest rum in the world. The tour is conducted in a storage warehouse rather than the distillery. The method of distilling is explained and the tour concludes with a tasting session. The shop sells bottles of rum and other merchandise. Open weekdays 09.00-16.00 at Spring Garden Highway, Brandons. Tel: 246 425 8757.

what to see

Almond Beach Club

St. James
Tel: 246 432 7840
Fax: 246 432 2115
info@almondresorts.com
www.almondresorts.com
All-inclusive with 2 fine restaurants and watersports. 161 rooms with cable TV and safe. 4 bars, gym, swimming pool.

The Regent Hotel

Holetown
St. James
Tel: 246 432 6666
Fax: 246 432 1335
theregent@caribsurf.com
www.barbados.org/hotels/theregent
Ocean front hotel on the west coast. 61 sea-facing rooms with cable TV and safe. Restaurant and bar. Swimming pool, fitness centre.

The Sandpipe

St. James
Tel: 246 422 2251
Fax: 246 422 1776
coral@caribsurf.com
www.sandpiperbarbados.com
Small, luxury beach front hotel. 45 rooms with cable TV. 20 minutes from Bridgetown. Restaurant, bar, swimming pool and beautiful beach.

Cobblers' Cove

Speightstown
St. Peter
Tel: 246 422 2291
Fax: 246 422 1460
reservations@cobblerscove.com
www.cobblerscove.com
Luxury resort. 40 suites with sitting room, kitchenette and balcony. 35 minutes from Bridgetown. Watersports, tennis, restaurant and bar.

Accra Beach Hotel

Rockley
Christchurch
Tel: 246 435 8920
Fax: 246 435 6794
accrareservations@yahoo.com
www.accrabeachhotel.com
Fabulous hotel on one of the best beaches. 122 rooms with cable TV. Restaurants, bars including swim-up bar. Gym, swimming, squash.

Abbeville Hotel

Rockley
Christchurch
Tel: 246 435 7924
Fax: 246 435 8502
Abbeville@sunbeach.net
www.funbarbados.com
Restored plantation house 2 minutes from beach. 19 rooms. Swimming pool, bar, restaurant. Island's best budget hot

Rostrevor Apartment Hotel

St. Lawrence Gap
Christchurch
Tel: 246 428 9298
Fax: 246 428 7705
rostrevor@caribsurf.com
www.barbados.org/apt/a39.htm
Good apartments on beach and on th main drag. Right in the centre of the night time action. 49 apartments with kitchen. 2 restaurants.

Rainbow Reef Beach Hotel

St. Lawrence Gap
Dover
Christchurch
Tel: 246 428 5110
Fax: 246 428 5395
rainbowreef@sunbeach.net
On secluded beach at the east end of the Gap. 43 rooms with air-condition ing and cable TV. Restaurant, bar, freshwater swimming pool.

Dover Beach Hotel

St. Lawrence Gap
Dover
Christchurch
Tel: 246 428 8076
Fax: 246 428 2122
resdover@sunbeach.net
www.doverbeach.com
Excellent rooms with air-conditioning and cable TV. Swimming pool, restau- rant and bar.

Sam Lord's Castle

St. Philip
Tel: 246 423 7350
Fax: 246 423 6361
Fantastic resort an hour outside Bridge- town. 248 luxurious rooms. 3 restaurant 3 bars, 3 pools, 6 tennis courts, gym.

The Crane

St. Philip
Tel: 246 423 6220
Fax: 246 423 5343
reservations@thecrane.com
www.thecrane.com
Probably the best resort with 18 rooms and 14 apartments.

The Rusty Pelican
2nd Floor, The Careenage
Bridgetown
Tel: 246 436 7778
Great lunch venue overlooking Carlisle
Bay.

Waterfront Café
Cavans Lane
Bridgetown
Tel: 246 427 0093
Traditional Bajan and international
cuisine. Nightly entertainment. Open
10.00-22.00.

Bellini's Trattoria
Little Bay Hotel
St. Lawrence Gap
Tel: 246 435 7246
Italian restaurant on the south coast.
Pizza, pasta, seafood and steak.

The Tides Restaurant
Holetown
St. James
Tel: 246 432 8356
Famous seafood restaurant on the west
coast. Reservations required.

La Mer
Port St. Charles
St. Peter
Tel: 246 419 2000
West coast. Dinner Tuesday-Sunday. Very
popular for Sunday brunch.

L'Azure Restaurant
The Crane
St. Philip
Tel: 246 423 5350
Elegant setting with great ocean views.
Bookings essential.

Calabaza
Prospect Bay
St. James.
Tel: 246 424 4557
Relaxed dinner venue.

Pisces Restaurant
St. Lawrence Gap
Tel: 246 435 6564
Open since 1972. Excellent international
cuisine in an unbeatable setting.

The Sports Bar
2nd St.
Holetown
Tel: 246 432 7151
New sports bar with live international
sport. Huge TV screens. Open 24
hours. Great atmosphere.

Café Sol
St. Lawrence Gap
Tel: 246 435 9531
Grill and Margarita bar. Busy. Very
popular with cricket fans.

Mojo
Worthing Main Road
Christchurch
Tel: 256 435 9008
Great bar, loud music and good crowd.
Excellent cocktails and a fine choice of
beers. Good food. Open very late.

McBrides
St. Lawrence Gap
Tel: 246 435 6352
Irish pub on main drag. Very lively and
attracts a crowd from about 23.00. Open
until 04.00.

The Ship Inn
St. Lawrence Gap
Tel: 246 435 6961
Island's largest bar. Very busy with live
music, karaoke and dancing. Open very
late. Cover charge most nights.

Bubba' Sports Bar
Rockley
Tel: 246 435 6217
One of the finest sports bars in the
Caribbean. 3 10-foot TV screens and
other smaller TV's . Excellent food.

Carib Beach Bar
Sandy Beach
St. Lawrence Gap
Terrific beach bar. Very popular after
the cricket. Great atmosphere, excellent
music in a chilled-out atmosphere.

Nelson's Arms
27 Broad St.
Bridgetown
One of very few pubs in the centre of
Bridgetown. Open since 1879.

Harbour Lights
Upper Bay St.
St. Michael
438 7225
One of the main venues for cricket fans.
Wednesdays and Fridays the B$35 cover
charge includes all drinks.

On Friday night the place to go is the
suburb of Oistins. The traditional Fish
Fry is a great party with all the restaurants and stalls selling fish Caribbean
style. The party goes on well into
the night.

Post Office

General Post Office
Cheapside
Bridgetown
Open 07.30-17.00 Monday-Friday
Red post boxes are plentiful throughout the island.

Tourist Information

Barbados Tourist Association
Harbour Road
Bridgetown
Tel: 246 427 2623
0800 744 6244
www.barbados.org

Ministry of Tourism
Sherbourne Conference Centre
Two Mile Hill
St. Michael
Tel: 246 430 7500
Fax: 246 436 4828
barmot@sunbeach.net

Hospital

Queen Elizabeth Hospital
Martindales Road
Bridgetown
Tel: 246 436 6450

Bayview Hospital
St. Paul's Avenue
Bayville
St. Michael
Tel: 246 436 5446

Pharmacy

Knight's Pharmacy
Lower Broad St.
Bridgetown
Tel: 246 426 5196

Emergency Numbers

Police	211
Fire	311
Ambulance	511

Telecoms

International Direct Dialling is available. Barbados country code is 1 246. International outgoing code is 011.

Newspapers

The Advocate
The Nation

Banking

Open 08.00-15.00 Monday-Thursday and 08.00-17.00 Friday, except for the bank at the airport which remains open to suit the arrival of passengers. There is an extensive network of ATM machines at banks, airport and shopping centres that accept main international cards. Major credit cards are accepted in hotels and restaurants. Notes in denominations of BDs$100, 50, 20, 10, 5, 2 and coins BDs$ 1, 25, 10, 5, 1 cent coins.

Embassies

British High Commission
Lower Collymore Rock
St. Michael
Bridgetown
Tel: 246 436 6694
Fax: 246 430 7860
britishhc@sunbeach.net
www.britishhc.fco.gov.uk

Australian High
Commission
Bishop's Court Hill
St. Michael
Tel: 246 435 2834

Customs

No duty on 200 cigarettes or 50 cigars or 250g of tobacco, 750 ml of spirits, 750 ml of wine or 50g of perfume.

Visa

Passport valid for duration of stay and a valid return or onward ticket are required by all visitors. Visas are not required by British, Australian or New Zealand passport holders for stays up to six months.

Time Difference

GMT-4-5 hours

Electricity

110 volts AC 60 Hz

Tipping

Tipping is at one's discretion. But a 7.5% hotel tax is added to all bills along with a usual 10% service charge.

Departure Tax

All passengers have to pay BD$25 upon departure. Passengers in transit for less than 24 hours are exempt.

Barbados Arts Council
Pelican Village
Bridgetown
Tel: 246 4385

Verandah Art Gallery
Colling
Bridgetown
Tel: 246 2605

The Barbados Museum
The Garrison
St. Michael
Tel: 246 0201
Divided into a number of galleries and
a research library and is housed in a
former military prison. The museum
also holds antique maps and pre-
Christopher Columbus artefacts.

Climate

	ave temp	rain cm			
January	26	64	July	27	129
February	26	46	August	28	147
March	26	38	September	28	145
April	27	53	October	28	170
May	27	56	November	27	150
June	28	89	December	26	99

Win/Loss Record

Country	Played	Won	Drawn	Lost	Tie
West Indies	41	20	15	6	-
England	13	3	6	4	-
Australia	9	2	3	4	-
New Zealand	4	1	1	2	-
Pakistan	5	-	3	2	-
South Africa	2	-	1	1	-
India	8	-	1	7	-

Highest Individual Aggregates (West Indies unless stated)

Player	Mat	Inn	NO	Runs	Ave	HS	50	100
Desmond Haynes	13	25	5	1210	60.50	145	6	4
Brian Lara	13	23	2	972	46.29	153*	7	1
Viv Richards	12	17	1	959	59.94	182*	5	3
Garry Sobers	9	14	2	914	76.17	226	3	3
Richie Richardson	11	18	1	882	51.88	160	4	2
Clive Lloyd	9	13	1	807	67.25	157	3	4
Gordon Greenidge	11	21	4	757	44.53	226	3	2
Shiv Chanderpaul	9	16	4	601	50.08	137*	3	2
Rohan Kanhai	8	12	1	546	49.64	129	2	2
Clyde Walcott	5	9	1	534	66.75	220	2	1

Top Wicket Takers (West Indies unless stated)

Player	Mat	Bll	Md	Runs	Wkt	Ave	BB	S/R
Courtney Walsh	12	3024	114	1342	53	25.32	5/22	57.06
Curtly Ambrose	13	3399	155	1421	52	27.33	8/45	65.37
Malcolm Marshall	8	1812	46	911	49	18.59	7/80	36.98
Joel Garner	7	1486	66	762	31	24.58	4/56	47.94
Andy Roberts	6	1394	49	692	28	24.71	4/31	49.79
Ian Bishop	6	1298	49	628	26	24.15	6/87	49.92
Michael Holding	6	1014	53	445	25	17.80	4/24	40.56
Lance Gibbs	5	1991	124	655	22	29.77	8/38	90.50
Carl Hooper	10	1578	61	632	19	33.26	5/80	83.05
Colin Croft	3	675	19	336	19	17.68	4/39	35.53

Highest Individual Scores (West Indies unless stated)

337	Hanif Mohammad (Pak)	1957-58
302	Lawrence Rowe	v England 1973-74
226	Garry Sobers	v England 1959-60
226	Gordon Greenidge	v Australia 1990-91

	220	Clyde Walcott	v England 1953-54
	219	Denis Atkinson	v Australia 1954-55
	210	Bill Lawry (Aus)	1964-65
	208	Sherwin Campbell	v New Zealand 1995-96
	201	Seymour Nurse	v Australia 1964-65
	201	Bob Simpson (Aus)	1964-65

Best Individual Bowling Performances (West Indies unless stated)

53.3-37-38-8	Lance Gibbs	v India 1961-62
22.4-10-45-8	Curtly Ambrose	v England 1989-90
28.5-7-75-8	Angus Fraser (Eng)	1993-94
20.3-6-74-7	Bruce Taylor (NZ)	1971-72
25.3-6-80-7	Malcolm Marshall	v New Zealand 1984-85
37-9-103-7	Jim Laker (Eng)	1947-48
24.4-7-34-6	Curtly Ambrose	v South Africa 1991-92
36-17-67-6	Jacques Kallis (SA)	2000-01
30.4-8-76-6	Pedro Collins	v New Zealand 2002
13-1-77-6	Jeff Thomson (Aus)	1977-78

Highest Partnerships

Wicket	Runs	Batsmen	Match
1st	382	Bill Lawry & Bob Simpson (Aus)	1964-1965
2nd	249	Alvin Kallicharran & Lawrence Rowe (WI)	1973-1974 v England
3rd	220	Alvin Kallicharran & Viv Richards (WI)	1975-1976 v India
4th	399	Garry Sobers & Frank Worrell (WI)	1959-1960 v England
5th	281	Steve Waugh & Ricky Ponting (Aus)	1998-1999
6th	254	Charlie Davis & Garry Sobers (WI)	1971-1972 v New Zealand
7th	347	Denis Atkinson & C Depeiza (WI)	1954-1955 v Australia
8th	84	Arshad Ayub & Sanjay Manjrekar (Ind)	1988-1989
9th	132	Shaun Pollock & Alan Donald (SA)	2000-2001
10th	133	Wasim Bari & Wasim Raja (Pak)	1976-1977

Results at Kensington Oval

Date	Countries	Result
11/01/1930	v England	drawn
08/01/1935	v England	lost by 4 wickets
21/01/1948	v England	drawn
07/02/1953	v India	won by 142 runs
06/02/1954	v England	won by 181 runs
14/05/1955	v Australia	drawn
17/01/1958	v Pakistan	drawn
06/01/1960	v England	drawn
23/03/1962	v India	won by an innings and 30 runs
05/05/1965	v Australia	drawn
29/02/1968	v England	drawn
01/04/1971	v India	drawn
23/03/1972	v New Zealand	drawn
09/03/1973	v Australia	drawn
06/03/1974	v England	drawn
10/03/1976	v India	won by an innings and 97 runs
18/02/1977	v Pakistan	drawn
17/03/1978	v Australia	won by 9 wickets
13/03/1981	v England	won by 298 runs
15/04/1983	v India	won by 10 wickets
30/03/1984	v Australia	won by 10 wickets
26/04/1985	v New Zealand	won by 10 wickets
21/03/1986	v England	won by an innings and 30 runs
22/04/1988	v Pakistan	won by 2 wickets
07/04/1989	v India	won by 8 wickets
05/04/1990	v England	won by 164 runs
19/04/1991	v Australia	won by 343 runs
18/04/1992	v South Africa	won by 52 runs
23/04/1993	v Pakistan	won by 10 wickets
08/04/1994	v England	lost by 208 runs
31/03/1995	v Australia	lost by 10 wickets
19/04/1996	v New Zealand	won by 10 wickets
27/03/1997	v India	won by 38 runs

12/03/1998	v England	drawn
26/03/1999	v Australia	won by 1 wicket
18/05/2000	v Pakistan	drawn
29/03/2001	v South Africa	drawn
2/05/2002	v India	won by 10 wickets
21/06/2002	v New Zealand	lost by 204 runs
01/05/2003	v Australia	lost by 9 wickets
01/04/2004	v England	lost by 8 wickets

grenada

new queen's park oval

The New Queen's Park Oval in St. George's became the seventh ground in the West Indies to host Test cricket when New Zealand visited on 28th June 2002. The newly built ground is surrounded by hills, dotted with colourful wooden houses. It is one of the most beautiful settings in Test cricket.

The crowd were treated to a run feast in that first match. New Zealand made 373 after being put in, with Scott Styris hitting 107 and Mark Richardson 95. Pedro Collins was the West Indies' most effective bowler with 4/68 . In reply Chris Gayle struck a glorious 204 as the West Indies made 470 to take a lead of 97. However the weather intervened and the game ended in a draw with New Zealand on 256/5 at the close. Richardson 71 and Styris 69no were again the visitors' best batsmen.

Queen's Park Oval is within five minutes walking distance of the centre of St. George's. The atmosphere around the city is electric when cricket is on. It seems as if everybody in the town descends on the ground, or at least the hills around it. The players' pavilion is at the north end. It also incorporates the media centre. The west side has the Grandstand which is totally covered. The bleachers run along the south end and east side of ground and are totally uncovered which can be uncomfortable in the midday sun. This area is the most popular area with the locals who party just as hard as any others in Test cricket. Bands pump out music all day long as they dance on concrete terraces. They love nothing more than a bit of banter with the opposition's supporters as they enjoy the locally made rum. Vendors move through the crowd selling food, beer and rum and there are a number of stalls dotted around the ground. The toilet facilities are adequate. Cricket at the Queen's Park Oval is an unique experience.

Tickets for test matches can be purchased from the West Indies ticketline 1800 744 GAME (4263), from www.windiescricket.com or from the ticket office on the west side of the ground. It is important to get to the ground early as the queues can be almost mayhem. Minibuses and taxis run from Grand Anse and L'Anse Aux Epines. There is parking outside the ground but traffic is very slow moving at the end of the day and most cricket fans tend to walk into the city centre before catching public transport back to their hotels.

Grenada, the most southern of the Windward Islands, is situated in the south eastern Caribbean just north of Venezuela. The country is made up of three islands with the smaller Carriacou and tiny Petite Martinique to the north west of the main island. Grenada is known as the Spice Island and is the second largest producer of nutmeg in the world. The island has a population of 106,000, 8,200 of whom live in the capital St. George's which is one of the most scenic cities in the Caribbean with some fine Georgian architecture and is set around the horseshoe harbour and overlooked by three 18th century forts. The city's narrow cobblestone streets gently climb up the hills that surround the harbour.

Christopher Columbus was the first European to discover the island on his third voyage in 1498. He named it Concepcion. The Spanish, French and the British fought for control for more than 300 years before it was ceded to Britain under the Treaty of Versailles in 1783. After becoming a Crown Colony in 1877 it remained under British rule until 1967 when it took control of its internal affairs. Grenada gained its independence in 1974 but the country has seen some political unrest since. In 1983 the socialist ruling party was overthrown with its leader Maurice Bishop being executed. The USA, at the request of the Organisation of the East Caribbean States, invaded the island. The OECS feared the ultra leftist regime which had seized control and the Americans were clearly worried about the regime's relationship with Cuba.

Tourism is a very important industry and the number of visitors is growing each year. Offshore banking is also important.

St. George's is a quaint little city with a bustling market in its centre. It is possible to walk around it in a couple of hours. The National Museum on Young Street is set in the old army barracks which were built in 1704. It is a small museum which traces the history and culture of the island. Park House, the seat of Parliament and the Supreme Court are also worth visiting. The city has many fine religious buildings including Church Street Methodist Church which was built in 1820, the Anglican Church (1825), the Presbyterian Church (1830) and the Catholic Cathedral built in 1884. Bay Gardens on the outskirts of St. George's offers a tranquil place to relax after the hustle and bustle of the city. Set on the site of an old sugar mill the gardens are beautifully laid out with many tropical flowers, trees and plants.

Grenada is only 200sq. km in area and has many attractions. These include some magnificent rainforests. Lake Antoine in St. David in the south is home to a wide variety of flora and fauna. La Sagesse on the south west coast is an excellent bird watching sanctuary. There are a number of glorious beaches with coral reef for diving and snorkelling. Westerhall Estate Rum Factory and the Woodlands Sugar Factory are two distilleries in the south which are worth a visit. Most visitors tend to stay in Grand Anse and L'Anse Aux Epines where there is a varied selection of hotels. Grand Anse is a five-minute drive from St. George's and the ground. L'Anse Aux Epines is a 15 minute drive. Minibuses and taxis are plentiful. Some of the cheaper guesthouses are in the centre of St. George's. Most hotels have their own restaurants and bars. Grand Anse and L'Anse Aux Epines are also the main restaurant and nightlife areas. Nightlife is quiet in Grenada with most visitors content with a quiet drink in one of the many bars. Dress code is casual.

Grand Etang Forest Reserve

In the centre of the island, 10km northeast of St. George's. It is one of Grenada's premier tourist attractions with some challenging walking trails through the rainforest, passing many waterfalls and flora and providing the opportunity to see some of the island's 300 colourful bird species and other animals including monkeys and armadillos. Located in the centre is the Grand Etang Lake, a natural volcanic crater filled with crystal clear water. There is also a small exhibition centre. It should be noted that the forest can be a lot cooler than the rest of the island and is prone to regular rain showers. Long trousers and long sleeved shirts are recommended as mosquitoes are common.

Gouyave, St. James

A small fishing village on the west coast. Formerly known as Charlotte Town after Queen Charlotte of England, the French changed the name to Gouyave after the Guava, a sweet fruit which grew in the area. The village is the centre of the spice industry. The drive from St. George's to Gouyave is terrific with bay after bay offering splendid beaches. It is possible to take a tour of the Nutmeg Cooperative Association to see the processing of the spice. Enquiries 444 8337.

Fort George

Originally named Fort Royale by the French, Fort George was built in 1706 to protect the harbour against other European nations. Two other forts, Fort Fredrick and Fort Matthew, were built later on the east of side of the city of St. George's. Known as the back to front forts they were designed to protect the city from an overland attack. Fort George is today the police headquarters. It provides wonderful views of the harbour and the city. Maurice Bishop and members of his cabinet were executed in the fort and one can see bullet holes in the wall and the famous graffiti "No Pain, No Gain Brother" which is scrawled on the wall. A couple of weeks after the executions the fort was bombed by the Americans during the invasion.

The Market Square

This has an amazing history. Once used for executions and slave trading, it is now home to wonderful vibrant fruit and vegetable markets. Spices, including vanilla, cinnamon, nutmeg and cocoa, are also sold. It is the soul of the city., noisy and colourful and the atmosphere in the market is friendly. It is safe to wander around. Music thumps out all day long.

Caribs' Leap

A steep cliff face approximately 40 metres high. In 1650 the last remaining Caribs threw themselves over the edge rather than face being ruled by the French. Just north of the town of Sauteurs and well worth a visit. Not far away, on the road between Sauters and Hermitage, is the famous Carib Stone, a carved piece of rock, which provides evidence of the Caribs' early existence on the island. It is located on the Rich Estate.

Allamanda Beach Resort

Grand Anse
Tel: 473 444 0095
Fax: 473 444 0126
allamanda@caribsurf.com
www.allamandaresort.com
50 well appointed rooms, some with whirlpool and fabulous views. All air-conditioned with cable TV and mini bar.

Grenada Grand Beach Resort

Grand Anse Beach
Tel: 473 444 4371
Fax: 473 444 4800
paradise@grandbeach.net
186 elegant rooms, a waterfront restaurant and 3 bars. Diving, gym, health club and golf.

Siesta Hotel

Grand Anse
Tel: 473 444 4646
Fax: 473 444 4647
siesta@caribsurfocom
www.siestahotel.com
Reasonably priced with 37 comfortable rooms with air-conditioning and cable TV. Three-minute walk from the beach. Excellent swimming pool.

Spice Island Beach Resort

Grand Anse Beach
Tel: 473 444 4258
Fax: 473 444 4807
spicesl@caribsufr.com

www.spicebeachresort.com
Boutique resort . 66 suites many with private pool. Restaurant, bar, business centre, jacuzzi and 8 acres of spectacular gardens

Roydon's Guesthouse

Grand Anse
Tel: 473 444 4476
roydons@caribsurf.com
www.caribbean-connexion.com
12 comfortable en suite rooms with ce ing fans. Well established with restau-rant and bar. Some rooms back onto t beach. Recommended.

Tropicana Inn

Lagoon Road
Tel: 473 440 1586
Fax: 473 440 9797
tropicanainn@caribsurf.com
Reasonably priced hotel near to the ci centre. Overlooks St. George's Yacht Club. 20 en suite air-conditioned roo with cable TV. Restaurant.

Yacht's View Guesthouse

Lagoon Road
Tel: 473 440 3607
Clean, budget accommodation at rea-sonable prices. 10 rooms.

Mitchell's Guesthouse

H A Blaize St.
Tel: 473 440 2803
Small and on hillside overlooking the harbour. 11 tidy rooms.

Airlines

BWIA	473 444 1331
Air Jamaica	1800 523 5585
British Airways	473 444 1664
Caribbean Star	473 444 4394

Buses

Minibuses run throughout the island. The journey from Grand Anse to St. George's takes approximately five minutes.

Taxis

Grenada Association	473 444 4882
Green Cabs	473 444 4444
National Association	473 444 6850

Car Hire

Local driving permits are issued by ca hire companies upon presentation of valid drivers' licence.
David's Car Rentals
Tel: 473 444 4310
Fax: 473 444 4404
cdavid@caribsurf.com

Laluna

Laluna Resort
Morne Rouge
Tel: 473 439 0001
Italian specialising in seafood. Excellent food and a wonderful atmosphere.

Crown Sugar

Grand Anse
Tel: 473 444 2374
One of the most popular. Serves local cuisine. Live entertainment.

The Coconut Beach Restaurant

Grand Anse
Tel: 473 444 4644
French and on the beach. Seafood a speciality. Closed Tuesdays.

La Belle Creole

Blue Horizon Cottage Hotel
Grand Anse
Tel: 473 444 4316
Excellent Caribbean by the beach. Open seven days a week for breakfast and dinner.

Rudolf's

The Carenage
Tel: 473 440 2241
Great restaurant and bar serving steak and seafood. Very popular.

Cicely's

Calabash Hotel
L'Anse Aux Epines
Tel: 473 444 4234
On the south coast and one of the island's best. Serves Caribbean cuisine. Live entertainment.

Tropicana

Lagoon Road
Tel: 473 440 1586
Reasonably priced just outside the city centre serving Grenadian and Chinese cuisine.

Bad Ass Café

Le Marquis Complex
Grand Anse
Tel: 473 444 4020
Excellent Mexican restaurant. Open late every night with live entertainment. One of the island's liveliest places.

Deyna's

Melville St.
Tel: 473 440 6795
Popular budget restaurant in the centre of St. George's. Grenadian cooking at its best.

Fantazia 2001

Morne Rouge Beach
Tel: 473 444 2288
One of the most popular nightclubs on the island. Very lively and open very late.

The Boatyard

L'Anse aux Epines
Tel: 473 444 4662
Very popular restaurant and bar serving fine international food. Steak and lobster are the specialties. Live entertainment every night and steel bands at the weekends.

Casablanca

Grand Anse
Tel: 473 444 1631
Excellent sports bar covering the world.
The Red Crab

L'Anse aux Epines

Tel: 473 444 4424
Very busy restaurant and bar. One of the island's premier nightspots serving Caribbean and Continental food.

The Nutmeg

The Carenage
Tel: 473 440 2539
Very busy restaurant and bar in the centre of St. George. Many visitors go here after the cricket.

Grenada's airport is Point Sailines International, 8km from St. George's in the south west corner of island. Taxis are available directly outside the Arrivals Hall and a trip to Grand Anse should cost EC$27 and to St. George's EC$31. It is a modern airport with restaurant and banking facilities. There is a tourist information desk in the Arrival Hall. Car hire is available from David's Car Rental (473 444 3399), Indigo Car Rental (473 443 3866), McIntyre Bros. Car Rental (473 444 3949), Gabriels Rentals (473 433 2304) and Sunsation (473 444 1594).

general info

Telecoms
International Direct Dialling is available throughout the island. Grenada's country code is 1 473. Coins and card payphones are available.

Newspapers
The Grenadian Voice
Grenada Today
Grenada Times

Post Office
General Post Office
Burns Point
Monday-Thursday 08.00-15.30, Friday 08.00-16.30

Banking
Grenada's currency is the Eastern Caribbean Dollar (EC $). Notes are issued in denominations of 100, 50, 20, 10 and 5 dollars and coins in denominations of 25, 10, 5, 2 and 1 cents.
Monday-Thursday 08.00-15.00, Friday 08.00-17.00
Travellers cheques and credit cards are widely accepted throughout the island.

Embassies
British High Commission
Netherlands Building
Grand Anse
Tel: 473 440 3222
Fax: 473 440 4939
bhcgrenada@caribsurf.com

Customs
200 cigarettes or 50 cigars or 250g tobacco, 1 litre wine or spirits

Visa
Visitors to Grenada should hold a passport valid for six months after departure from Grenada.

Tourist Information
Grenada Board of Tourism
Burns Point
Tel: 473 440 2001
Fax: 473 440 6637
gbt@caribsurf.com
www.grenadagrenadines.com

Grenada Hotel and Tourist Association
16 Le Marquis Complex
Grand Anse
Tel: 473 444 1353
Fax: 473 444 4827
grenhotel@caribsurf.com
www.grenadahotelsinfo.com

Hospital
General Hospital
St. George's

Pharmacy
Gitten's Drug Mart
Grand Anse

Emergency Numbers
Police   911
Ambulance   434
Coastguard   399

Time Difference
Four hours behind Greenwich Mean Time. GMT-4

Electricity
220/240 volts AC 50 Hz

Tipping
An 8% government tax is added to hotel and restaurant bills. Usually a 10% service charge is also added.

Departure Tax
All visitors must pay a departure tax of EC$50.

Climate

	ave temp	rain cm			
January	25	70	July	28	108
February	27	40	August	28	151
March	27	37	September	27	148
April	27	55	October	27	168
May	28	61	November	27	155
June	28	91	December	26	101

Win/Loss Record

Country	Played	Won	Drawn	Lost	Tie
New Zealand	1	-	1	-	-
West Indies	1	-	1	-	-

Highest Individual Aggregates

Player	Mat	Inn	NO	Runs	Ave	HS	50	100
Chris Gayle	1	1	0	204	204.00	204	0	1
Scott Styris (NZ)	1	2	1	176	176.00	107	1	1
Mark Richardson (NZ)	1	2	0	166	83.00	95	2	0
Lou Vincent (NZ)	1	2	0	78	39.00	54	1	0
Nathan Astle (NZ)	1	2	0	69	34.50	69	1	0

Top Wicket Takers (West Indies unless stated)

Player	Mat	Bll	Md	Runs	Wkt	Ave	BB	S/R
Shane Bond (NZ)	1	181	7	104	5	20.80	5/104	36.20
Pedro Collins (WI)	1	282	16	96	4	24.00	4/68	70.50
Carl Hooper (WI)	1	354	13	110	4	27.50	2/44	88.50
Scott Styris (NZ)	1	150	3	88	2	44.00	2/88	75.00
Cameron Cuffy (WI)	1	270	15	96	2	48.00	2/76	135.00

Highest Individual Scores

204	Chris Gayle (WI)	2002
107	Scott Styris (NZ)	2002
95	Mark Richardson (NZ)	2002
71	Mark Richardson (NZ)	2002
69	Nathan Astle (NZ)	2002

Best Individual Bowling Performances

30.1-7-104-5	Shane Bond (NZ)	2002
30-9-68-4	Pedro Collins (WI)	2002
25-3-44-2	Carl Hooper (WI)	2002
34-10-66-2	Carl Hooper (WI)	2002
42-16-75-2	Mahendra Nagamootoo (WI)	2002

Highest Partnerships

Wkt	Runs	Batsmen	Match
1st	117	Mark Richardson & Lou Vincent (NZ)	2002
2nd	100	Chris Gayle & Ramnaresh Sarwan (WI)	2002
3rd	76	Chris Gayle & Brian Lara (WI)	2002
4th	123	Mark Richardson & Nathan Astle (NZ)	2002
5th	143	Chris Gayle & Shiv Chanderpaul (WI)	2002
6th	99*	Scott Styris & Robbie Hart (NZ)	2002
7th	48	Scott Styris & Craig McMillan (NZ)	2002
8th	56	Scott Styris & Robbie Hart (NZ)	2002
9th	49	Scott Styris & Shane Bond (NZ)	2002
10th	12	Scott Styris & Ian Butler (NZ)	2002

Results at New Queen's Park Oval

Date	Countries	Result
28/06/2002	v New Zealand	drawn

bourda

Georgetown Cricket Club was founded in 1858, the first cricket club in the Caribbean, but it was not until 1884 that it moved to the Bourda Cricket Ground, where the first match was played in December of that year. The first Test match played on the ground was against England in 1930 with the hosts winning by a massive 289 runs. George Headley, one of Guyana's favourite sons, scored 114 in the first innings, followed by 112 in the second. Clifford Roach scored 209 in the first.

The closest Test played at Bourda was the match against Australia in 1978 when the visitors, under the captaincy of Bob Simpson, scored 362/7 to get home by three wickets. Memorable as that victory was there is no doubt that Garry Sobers against England in 1968 made the biggest contribution – 152 and 95no with the bat, and three wickets in each innings, bowling marathon spells totalling 68 overs.

The most notable performances by Guyanese players have all come from the bat: Clive Lloyd's 178 versus Australia in 1972/73; Alvin Kallicharran's 101no on debut against New Zealand in 1972 and Carl Hooper's 233 versus India in 2002. The West Indies' best performance at Bourda was in 1958 when they scored a remarkable 317/2 against Pakistan in the fourth innings to win by eight wickets, an example of Bourda's perfect, if slow, batting tracks.

The ground is compact and circled by a moat, which is needed to prevent flooding as the ground is 1.5 metres below sea level. It is surrounded by wonderful wooden stands. The Members' Pavilion between square and fine leg is a tremendous wooden structure on stilts and a glorious place from which to watch. It is a pleasure to study the old photographs and memorabilia on the two floors of this historic building. The Ladies' Pavilion, which is attached to the Members' Pavilion, was built in 1912 and is another beautiful building. The Rohan Kanhai Stand at fine leg is more modern, a three-tier stand with corporate boxes on the top tier. The Mound, the party area at third man, is not for the faint hearted. DJ's blaring out loud music, drinks flowing in the two beer tents and the hot sun all add up to a long day. This area has no cover, thus no protection from the sun, so visitors should be very careful. The antiquated scoreboard along the cover boundary has been there since the ground was established. The bleaches sweep around from the cover boundary to mid-off where the new Media Centre is situated directly behind the bowler's arm.

To the right of the Media Centre are the Lance Gibbs, the Laparkan and the Clive Lloyd stands. All provide excellent viewpoints with the added bonus of sharing the day with the Guyanese locals who are fanatical about their cricket. One cannot fail to feel the ripple of excitement when the West Indies are doing well, especially if a batsman is nearing a century. The hooting of air horns and the banging of cans, bottles and anything that can be found create an incredible atmosphere, and if the batsman reaches a hundred, mayhem follows. If he is Guyanese, it's party time. On the other hand, the Bourda crowd have quite a history of volatility when things do not go the West Indians' way. In 1954 the ground saw the first riot at a Test when, on the fourth evening, umpire Badge Menzies, co-opted although he was actually the groundsman, gave his fellow Guyanese, Clifford McWatt, the home side's wicket keeper, run out. His decision was followed by a hail of bottles from the crowd. But England captain Len Hutton refused to leave although he brought the fielders in. The tension was defused when England spinner Johnny Wardle pretended to drink drunkenly from a bottle.

When Clive Lloyd was run out against New Zealand in 1972 and Alvin Kalacharran was given lbw in 1977, the crowd invaded the pitch. In 1979 there was a full-scale riot when Kerry Packer's World Series Cup players decided the pitch was too sodden to play. The Members' Pavilion was invaded and memorabilia stolen. Despite this, the Guyanese are wonderful hosts.

Many small bars are set up around the ground just for Test matches. Takeaway food is available from tables under each stand, where everything, from curry rotis to barbeque and fried chicken with rice and noodles, can be purchased. There are also many stalls outside the ground behind the Clive Lloyd and Laparkan stands serving good food and where there is a great atmosphere. Vendors roam the stands selling everything from bottles of rum, to beer, to nuts to sunglasses.

Tickets for Test matches can be purchased in a number of ways, from the club gcc@solutions2000.net, telephone 2263130, from the West Indies ticketline 0870000, or from the ground on the days leading up to the Tests. Even on the day there are small ticket cubicles at both ends of the ground. With the wooden stands mostly on stilts and the uneven ground, facilities for the disabled are not available in most parts of the ground. However, the Members' Pavilion has a disabled viewing area. Unfortunately the toilet facilities around the ground leave a lot to be desired.

The ground is approximately 2km from the centre of town, down Robb or North Street, through the Bourda markets, and will take about 30 minutes. After the game it is important not to walk home after dark or by yourself for safety reasons. Taxis are available and cost very little (US$1). The no. 41 minibus costs even less. There is parking behind the Lance Gibbs stand and in surrounding streets. After the game a party begins in the Carib Tent behind the Laparkan Stand. This can get very wild indeed and it is usually time to leave as dusk arrives.

Bourda is a very striking ground as the stands and the advertising hoardings that encompass the east side of the ground are painted in bright colours. These, along with the locals led by Pepsi, a local character, and the kids and not so young perched precariously in the trees outside the ground, makes Bourda a very special place to watch Test cricket.

Cheddi Jagan International Airport in Timehouri is 41km from Georgetown. There is an official taxi service available. Drivers wear black trousers and cream shirts and carry ID. The fare is $US20 to Georgetown. A very crowded and irregular bus service runs between the airport and the city at a cost $US1. There is a number of small cafés and a duty free shop in the Departure Hall. A bank is open Monday-Thursday 09.00-13.30 and Friday 09.00-15.00. There are no ATM facilities available.

Named Longchamps by the French and Stabroek by the Dutch, Georgetown, the capital of Guyana, was renamed by the British in 1812. Two years later it became a British colony. Christopher Colombus sighted the coast of Guyana in 1498 and Sir Walter Raleigh explored the Orinoco River in search of El Dorado, the mythical City of Gold, a hundred years later. However it was not until 1616 that the Dutch became the first settlers and commenced the importation of African slaves. The British arrived 20 years later. By 1814 they had captured the colony and it remained in British control until independence in 1966. It became a republic in 1970.

A bustling city on the Atlantic coast it is where the Caribbean meets South America, on its north east shoulder. It has a character all of its own. The streets are alive with people going loudly about their daily business while taxis, mini-buses and 4-wheel drives battle for supremacy on the roads with motorbikes, cyclists and donkeys pulling carts. The sound of the car horn is constant. The markets of Stabroek and Bourda spill over into the streets to add to the chaos. Georgetown has a population of approximately 350,000, nearly half the population of Guyana. Almost 90% of the Guyanese people live on the Atlantic Coast, in an area that represents just four per cent of the country's total area of 216,000sq. km, roughly the size of the United Kingdom. Forest covers 84% of the country, much of which is untouched.

The city has many historical landmarks such as St. George's Cathedral, one of the fine examples of colonial architecture. Others include the Parliament Buildings and the City Hall. Georgetown is known as the Garden City of the Caribbean because of its beautiful Botanical and Zoological Gardens. Outside the gardens is the remarkable 1763 Monument, built to commemorate an unsuccessful rebellion by slaves. All these landmarks can be seen on the Georgetown City Tour, a daily tour of three to four hours. A giant seawall runs for 300km along the Atlantic Coastline to protect the low lying land. Georgetown is about 1.5 metres below sea level and is protected by the wall and a series of canals that run throughout the city. The wall has become a meeting place for locals. Day trips provide the opportunity to journey further afield to see other parts of Guyana such as the awe-inspiring Kaiteur Falls, Orinduik Falls and the huge Essequibo River.

Georgetown's climate is tropical/equatorial, hot and humid however it is moderated by the welcome northeast trade winds. The average temperature is 28 degrees and the afternoon hours can be extremely hot.

There are only a few top class hotels in Georgetown, several mid-range and a number of budget hotels. The budget hotels are very basic but also very cheap. There are no backpackers'. The standard of restaurants in the city is generally quite good. Street stalls provide a good alternative for the more adventurous diner. Nightlife plays a very big part in Georgetown with many clubs and pubs, but visitors are advised to be careful of their choice of venue. Like any major city, Georgetown has its bad areas. Hoteliers will advise on areas to be avoided. It is also sensible to travel by taxi after dark. Taxis are extremely cheap and available outside all hotels, restaurants and nightclubs.

The Guyanese people are very welcoming and consider it important that visitors have a good time. They love cricket and are delighted that visitors have made the effort to travel to watch it there.

Essequibo River

Journey on an open boat up the huge river to an old Dutch Fort. Hike through rainforest, swim in the pools by waterfalls and see some the Guyanese wildlife.

Kaieteur Falls

At 120 metre wide, with a 220 metres drop, twice the size of Victoria Falls and five times that of Niagara, this is the world's highest single drop waterfall and an incredible sight. A must-do when in Guyana. One-day trips by plane and a five-day overland trip are available.

St. George's Cathedral

In the centre of the city and the tallest free-standing wooden structure in the world. Built in 1892 by Sir Arthur Bloomfield, it is open seven days a week. Drop in or take it in as part of the Georgetown City Tour which also visits City Hall, Parliament Buildings and The Red House. The tour costs US$25 with Rainforest Tours (227 2011).

The 1763 Monument

This remarkable statue commemorates the unsuccessful 1763 slave rebellion led by Cuffy, an African slave. It is a 20-minute walk from the city centre in the square of the revolution and is worth seeing.

Stabroek Market

In the south west of the city, this is one of the great Georgetown experiences. You can buy just about everything, including monkeys. The entrance has a wonderful wooden four-faced clock.

Post Office

General Post Office
Robb St.
Monday-Friday 0800-1600
Saturday 0800-1200

Tourist Information

Tourism Association of Guyana
28 South Road
Lacytown
Tel: 592 250 807
Fax: 592 250 817

Ministry of Trade, Tourism and Industry
29 South Road
Lacytown
Georgetown
Tel: 592 263 182
Fax: 592 254 310

Hospital

St. Joseph's Mercy Hospital
Parade St.
Tel: 592 227 2072/5

Prasad's Hospital
Thomas St.

24 hour Clinic
Tel: 592 226 7214

A malaria risk exists but is very slight in Georgetown. Those visitors venturing south should take precautions. Although mains waters is chlorinated in Georgetown, bottled water is advised.

Emergency Numbers

Police	911
Fire	912
Ambulance	913

Cara Suites
176 Middle St.
Tel: 592 226 1612
Fax: 592 226 1541
carasuites@carahotels.com
Excellent hotel, luxurious rooms with kitchens, business centre, internet, bar, no restaurant, no pool. 20 suites.

Cara Lodge
294 Quamini St.
Tel: 592 225 5301
Fax: 592 225 5310
Heritage House, spacious, if worn, rooms, business centre, excellent restaurant, no pool.

Le Meridian Pegasus
The Sea Wall
Tel: 592 225 2853
Fax: 592 225 3703
Probably the best hotel in Georgetown. Superb pool area with bar and restaurants. Luxurious rooms, business centre.

Hotel Tower
74/75 Main St.
Tel: 592 227 2011
Fax: 592 225 6021
hotel.tower@solutions2000.net
City centre, panoramic views.

78 rooms, swimming pool, gym, bars and restaurant.

Cara Inn
8 Pere St.
Kitty
Tel: 592 225 0542
Fax: 592 225 0622
4km from the centre, pool, tennis courts, restaurant and bar.

Rima Guesthouse
92 Middle St.
Tel: 592 225 7401
The best budget hotel in city. Family run, centrally located, excellent breakfast, mosquito nets, safe.

Friends
82 Robb St.
Tel: 592 227 2383
Fax: 592 227 0762
Central, basic hotel. Rooms with TV, some with air-conditioning, some with kitchenettes. Restaurant. Travel agency

Waterchris
Waterloo St.
Tel: 592 227 1980
Good, clean, inexpensive hotel. Air-conditioning, restaurant.

Airlines
Universal
65 Main Street 592 226 9262

BWIA
Robb Street 592 225 9182

Caribbean Star
Robb Street 592 227 6770

Liat
Robb Street 592 227 8281

Trans Guyana
Airport 592 222 2525

Buses
The bus service in Georgetown is neither reliable nor safe.

Taxis
There are taxis parked outside every hotel, restaurant, bar and club. They are inexpensive US$1 per stop.

David's Taxi Service
Pegasus Hotel
Tel: 592 52853

Roadrunner Limited
17 Second Avenue
Tel: 592 65759

Car Hire
Camex Car Rentals
125 'D' Barrack St.
Tel: 592 276 996
Fax: 592 276 975

Executive Car Rentals
301 Church St.
Tel: 592 275 215

N&R Car Rentals
301 Church St.
Tel: 592 266 0404
Fax: 592 270 457

Shivraj's Car Rental
93 Hadfield St.
Tel: 592 257 446
Fax: 592 260 619

Bottle Bar and Restaurant at Cara Lodge

294 Quamina St.
Tel: 592 225 5301
Fax: 592 225 5310
One of the best in city, serving Guyanese and international cuisine.

El Dorado

La Meridien Pegasus Hotel
Seawall Road
Kingston
Tel: 592 225 2853
Fax: 592 225 3703
Superb restaurant, beautiful décor, á la carte menu, fine wine list.

Main Street Café

Tower Hotel
74-75 Main St.
Tel: 592 227 2011
Fax: 592 225 6021
Reliable, good food, relaxed casual atmosphere.

Palm Court

35 Main St.
Tel: 592 227 0008
Fax: 592 225 7938
Busy. Local dishes. Excellent, but international cuisine is limited.

Pasta Inn

Cara Inn
8 Pere St.
Kitty
Tel: 592 225 0542
Fax: 592 225 0622
The only Italian in the city.

The Dutch Café

North St.
Well-presented food, varied menu in a very relaxed and friendly atmosphere. Located between cricket ground and city centre. Well recommended.

Sheriff Street has a line of pubs and nightclubs which the more adventurous tourist may visit. But for safety reasons the majority of visitors stay in the centre of town and frequent the following pubs.

Palm Court

35 Main St.
Tel: 592 227 0008
Fax: 592 225 7938
Very lively bar with live music with a mix of locals and tourists. Thursday, Friday and Saturday are the busy nights.

Spectrum

Hotel Tower
74 Main St.
Tel: 592 227 2011
Fax: 592 225 6021
Very relaxed bar under a thatched roof beside the swimming pool. Good atmosphere.

The Dubliner Pub

Cara Suites
176 Middle St.
Tel: 592 226 1612
Fax: 592 226 1541
Small Irish pub. Busy on Fridays. Very quiet the rest of the week.

Latino Bar

Le Meridien Pegasus Hotel
Seawall Road
Kingstown
Tel: 592 225 2853
Fax: 592 225 3703
Friday and Saturday nights are very popular and trendy. Beautiful pool bar.

Georgetown Cultural Centre

Homestead Avenue
Local plays and musicals performed regularly

The National Museum

North Road
Museum records the history of Guyana. Excellent Amerindian exhibit. Open Monday-Friday 09.00-17.00, Saturday 09.00-12.00.

Telecoms

International Direct Dialling is available in most hotels
International Code: 592
International Directory Enquires: 001

Newspapers

Guyana Chronicle
Kaiteur News Weekend
Stabroek News

Radio

Cricket on Voice of Guyana 98.1FM

Banking

Monday-Thursday 08.00-12.00 and Friday 08.00-12.00 and 15.00-16.00. There are no international ATM's in Georgetown. Banks have long queues. US dollars widely accepted. Travellers' cheques in US dollars can be cashed at the Bank of Nova Scotia on Robb Street. Cambios, licensed foreign exchange bureaux, offer the same rate of exchange as the banks. Currency is Guyanese Dollars. Notes are in denominations of G$1000, 500, 100 and 20. Coins are G$100, 50, 5, 1.
The import and export of local currency is limited to GS200. Change all monies before leaving Guyana, as no other country will change the Guyanese dollar.

Embassies

British High Commission
44 Main St.
Tel: 592 226 5881
Fax: 592 225 3555

Customs

200 cigarettes or 50 cigars or 225g of tobacco, 750ml of sprits, 750 ml of wi and a reasonable amount of perfume can be imported without duty.

Visa

A passport valid for at least six month beyond intended stay and a return tic et are required for entry into Guyana. British or Australians require no visa for stays up to 90 days.

Time Difference

GMT-4hours

Electricity

110 AND 220 volts AC 60 Hz

Tipping

Tipping at one's discretion. 10% to 15 is usual where service charge has not been included.

Departure Tax

All visitors must pay G$2,500. This can be paid at reconfirmation or at the airport.

Climate

	ave temp	rain cm		ave temp	rain cm
January	26	205	July	27	257
February	26	113	August	27	186
March	27	140	September	28	82
April	27	160	October	28	82
May	27	290	November	27	157
June	27	321	December	26	284

Win/Loss Record

Country	Played	Won	Drawn	Lost	Tie
Australia	7	4	1	2	-
West Indies	29	7	16	6	-
Pakistan	4	1	2	1	-
India	6	-	6	-	-
New Zealand	2	-	2	-	-
South Africa	1	-	1	-	-
England	9	1	4	4	-

Highest Individual Aggregates (West Indies unless stated)

Player	Mat	Inn	NO	Runs	Ave	HS	50	100
Garry Sobers	7	12	3	853	94.78	152	1	5
Richie Richardson	6	8	0	766	95.75	194	2	3
Gordon Greenidge	7	12	2	621	62.10	120*	5	1

Shiv Chanderpaul	6	8	2	555	92.50	140	2	3
Rohan Kanhai	7	11	0	551	50.09	150	4	1
Brian Lara	6	9	0	548	60.89	167	1	2
Carl Hooper	6	9	0	540	60.00	233	2	1
Desmond Haynes	7	11	2	531	59.00	111	3	2
Clive Lloyd	8	11	1	463	46.30	178	2	1
Clyde Walcott	6	9	1	432	54.00	145	1	2

Top Wicket Takers (West Indies unless stated)

Player	Mat	Bll	Md	Runs	Wkt	Ave	BB	S/R
Lance Gibbs	6	1867	112	578	28	20.64	6/29	66.68
Curtly Ambrose	7	1332	66	469	24	19.54	4/37	55.50
Courtney Walsh	8	1604	61	623	20	31.15	3/25	80.20
Joel Garner	4	907	36	419	20	20.95	6/75	45.35
Garry Sobers	7	1680	95	577	20	28.85	3/20	84.00
Imran Khan (Pak)	2	487	8	319	14	22.79	7/80	34.79
Leary Constantine	2	627	38	199	13	15.31	5/87	48.23
Malcolm Marshall	3	504	10	247	11	22.45	4/110	45.82
John Snow (Eng)	1	258	2	142	10	14.20	6/60	25.80
Neil Hawke (Aus)	1	316	15	115	10	11.50	6/72	31.60

Highest Individual Scores (West Indies unless stated)

259	Glenn Turner (NZ)	1971-72
233	Carl Hooper	v India 2001-02
209	Clifford Roach	v England 1929-30
194	Richie Richardson	v India 1988-89
188	Martin Crowe (NZ)	1984-85
185	Richie Richardson	v New Zealand 1984-85
182	Terry Jarvis (NZ)	1971-72
182	Richie Richardson	v Australia 1990-91
178	Clive Lloyd	v Australia 1972-73
169	Len Hutton (Eng)	1953-54

Best Individual Bowling Performances (West Indies unless stated)

22.2-10-44-7	Ian Johnson (Aus)	1954-55
26-7-50-7	Eric Hollies (Eng)	1934-35
22.4-2-80-7	Imran Khan (Pak)	1987-88
22.2-9-29-6	Lance Gibbs	v Australia 1964-65
40-20-60-6	Lance Gibbs	v England 1967-68
15.2-0-60-6	John Snow (Eng)	1967-68
32-8-72-6	Neil Hawke (Aus)	1964-65
27.2-10-75-6	Joel Garner	v Australia 1983-84
30.2-8-90-6	Wes Hall	v England 1959-60
67-34-113-6	Sonny Ramadhin	v England 1953-54

Highest Partnerships

Wicket	Runs	Batsmen	Match
1st	387	Glenn Turner & Terry Jarvis (NZ)	1971-1972
2nd	297	Desmond Haynes & Richie Richardson (WI)	1990-1991 v Australia
3rd	185	Daren Ganga & Brian Lara (WI)	2002-2003 v Australia
4th	251	Graeme Wood & Craig Serjeant (Aus)	1977-1978
5th	293	Carl Hooper & Shiv Chanderpaul (WI)	2001-2002 v India
6th	206	Inzamam-Ul-Haq & Abdul Razzaq (Pak)	1999-2000
7th	143	Martin Crowe & Ian Smith (NZ)	1984-1985
8th	120	Rahul Dravid & Sarandeep Singh (Ind)	2001-2002
9th	109	Tony Lock & Pat Pocock (Eng)	1967-1968
10th	97	Tom Hogan & Rodney Hogg (Aus)	1983-1984

Results at Bourda

Date	Countries	Result
21/02/1930	v England	won by 289 runs
14/02/1935	v England	drawn
03/03/1948	v England	won by 7 wickets
11/03/1953	v India	drawn
24/02/1954	v England	lost by 9 wickets
26/04/1955	v Australia	lost by 8 wickets
13/03/1958	v Pakistan	won by 8 wickets
09/03/1960	v England	drawn

14/04/1965	v Australia	won by 212 runs
28/03/1968	v England	drawn
19/03/1971	v India	drawn
06/04/1972	v New Zealand	drawn
06/04/1973	v Australia	lost by 10 wickets
22/03/1974	v England	drawn
18/03/1977	v Pakistan	drawn
31/03/1978	v Australia	lost by 3 wickets
28/02/1981	v England	Match Cancelled
31/03/1983	v India	drawn
02/03/1984	v Australia	drawn
06/04/1985	v New Zealand	drawn
02/04/1988	v Pakistan	lost by 9 wickets
25/03/1989	v India	drawn
09/03/1990	v England	abandoned
23/03/1991	v Australia	won by 10 wickets
17/03/1994	v England	won by an innings and 44 runs
17/04/1997	v India	drawn
27/02/1998	v England	won by 242 runs
05/05/2000	v Pakistan	drawn
09/03/2001	v South Africa	drawn
11/04/2002	v India	drawn
10/04/2003	v Australia	lost by 9 wickets

jamaica

sabina park

Sabina Park has been home to Kingston Cricket Club since 1880, although the first Test match played at the ground was not until 1930 when England visited for a match which went into history as one of the most extraordinary.

England scored 849, still the third highest innings total in Test cricket, with Andy Sandham scoring 325, Test cricket's first triple century, and Les Ames 149. Tommy Sc took 5/266. The West Indies replied with 286 before England declared at 272/9 to leav the home team a target of 836. By close on the ninth day of the Test the West Indies had reached 408/5, George Headley contributing 223. No play was possible for the ne two days due to rain and it was decided to call the match a draw so the English player could catch their boat home. The match aggregate of 1815 runs is still the second hig est ever.

Sabina Park has seen many incredible Tests. In 1983 the West Indies recorded an extraordinary win against India. The visitors batted first and scored 251. Their host replied with 254. At tea on the fifth day India were 164/6 and the match was heading for a draw when India lost their last four wickets for ten runs,

Andy Roberts taking all four for just one run. Set 172 to win in 26 overs, the home side reached their target with four balls to spare, Viv Richards scoring 61 in 35 balls.

The highest individual score at the ground was 365no by Sir Garfield Sobers against Pakistan in 1954. This innings was the highest Test score, surpassing England's Len Hutton's 364 against Australia at the Oval in 1938, and remained the record until 1994 when Brian Lara scored 375 against England at Antigua. Sandham's 325 is the only other triple century on the ground.

Not surprisingly England's 849 is the highest team score while India's 97 remains the lowest. It should be noted that India had only six fit batsmen in their second innings, having taken a battering from Michael Holding, Wayne Daniels and company in the first. The highest fourth innings run chase is 173/6 by West Indies in that match. Other batting achievements include the 1953 drawn match with India when the Three W's each scored centuries in the first innings, Frank Worrell, 237, Everton Weekes, 108 and Clive Walcott, 118; Australia's 1955 innings victory when five Australian batsmen scored centuries in a total of 758/8 dec., Colin McDonald scoring 127, Neil Harvey 104, Keith Miller 109, Ron Archer 128 and Richie Benaud 121. Clive Walcott scored a century in each innings for the West Indies. Lawrence Rowe scored 214 and 100no on debut in the 1972 drawn test against New Zealand. Roy Fredricks scored a brilliant 163 in the first innings in the same match and Glenn Turner carried his bat through the New Zealand innings with 223no.

Only two bowlers have taken ten wickets in a match, Hines Johnson 10/96 in 1948 and Courtney Walsh 10/101 in 1989. Easily the best individual performance was Steve Harmison's 7/12 in England's 2004 victory. Two other Englishmen, Trevor Bailey and John Snow, have also taken seven wickets in an innings.

Sabina Park's lowest moment came in February 1998 when the match against England had to be abandoned after 10.1 overs because of the state of the pitch. England struggled to 17/3 with Mike Atherton, Alec Stewart, Mark Butcher, Nasser Hussain and Graham Thorpe all being hit. The ground has always been known for its bouncy pitches, but this wicket was too dangerous for the match to continue.

The ground is 2km south west of New Kingston and has a capacity of 15,000 with the giant George Headley Stand dominating the south end. A modern stand, it has a capacity of 8,000 and houses the players' changing rooms. It is an awesome place from which to watch cricket and has a wonderful atmosphere. The beautiful old wooden pavilion is on the west side of the ground. Opposite are the bleaches. The atmosphere on this two-tier stand is electric. Up until recently, the upper tier was uncovered and the umbrellas shielding patrons from the blistering sun were a very colourful sight. Spectators sit with their legs dangling over the edge of the stand as the party rages on.

The Blue Mountains provide an incredible backdrop to the north end of the ground which contains the Jamaica Airways Stand, the Media Centre and the giant scoreboard. Underneath the scoreboard is the party area, famous around the world as 'the Mound'. Sponsored by Red Stripe, it is one of the original all-inclusive areas with all food and drinks included in the entrance price. Inevitably this area is incredibly popular and usually sells out before a Test match begins. It even has its own little beach with swimming pool. There is very little cover though and sun block is a must. The music blares out all day long, with fans partying. The bar is well organised with very little queuing, but food takes a little longer to purchase.

There are also food stalls and bars under the bleaches and at the back of the George Headley Stand. Countless vendors roam through the ground selling beer, rum, food and cigarettes etc. Tickets for Test matches can be purchased from the West Indies ticketline 1800 744 GAME (4263), from www.windiescricket.com, by contacting the ground on 876 967 0322, by emailing on jcancricket@hotmail.com or from the turnstiles under the George Headley Stand.

The majority of cricket fans stay in New Kingston during the Test and it is advisable to take taxis to the ground. Buses are unreliable and walking is not always safe. Taxis are cheap and can be shared with other fans. Parking is available beside the George Headley Stand and across the main road outside the ground.

Kingston is the capital of Jamaica, the third largest island in the Caribbean and the largest English speaking one. With a population of 700,000, the city is also the political, commercial and cultural centre o the country. The population consists mainly of people of African and, to a lesse degree, Indian descent. The city sits on the Liguanea Plains at the foot of the lush Blue Mountains on the south east coast in the Northern Caribbean Sea.

The original inhabitants of the island were the Taino Indians followed by the Ara tribe. The name Jamaica is derived from the word Zaymaca, the Arawak word meaning Land of Wood and Water. The first European to discover the island was Christopher Colombus on 4th May 1494 when he landed at Discovery Bay near Ocho Rios on the northern coast. The Spanish came in 1509 and settled in St. Iag de la Vega, today known as Spanish Town. Sir William Penn captured the island Britain in 1655 and it became a British colony in 1660. The British settled at Spa Town and Port Royal. Following an earthquake in 1694 which destroyed Port Ro the British moved to the site where Kingston is today. Three hundred years later Jamaica won its independence from Britain on 6th August 1962.

Although Kingston is a modern city with high skyscrapers, many 18th century Georgian type buildings mix with the modern office blocks. The arts play a large part in the culture. The National Gallery of Jamaica, the Institute of Jamaica and White Marl Arawak Museum are just some of the main attractions. The National Dance Theatre Company and the Little Theatre Company in New Kingston are c tainly worth a visit.

Some cricket fans combine the cricket in Kingston with a short break in the resor of either Montego Bay or Negril.

Kingston has a tropical climate. The northeast trade winds and the mountain bre maintain a pleasant temperature all year round. The humidity ranges from 63% in February to 75% in October. Light tropical clothing is suggested with a light sweater required occasionally in the evenings. There are a number of beaches clos Kingston including Fort Clarence and Lyssons Beach.

Kingston has accommodation to meet most budgets. There are a number of top-class hotels on Knutsford Boulevard. Unfortunately there are no backpackers', bu there are a couple of reasonably priced small hotels and guesthouses. All the acco modation listed here is in the New Kingston area of the city as some of the other areas are unsafe for foreign visitors. The same applies for restaurants, bars and clubs. The dress code is casual with hotel restaurants requiring a jacket. There are number of pubs, sports bars and reggae clubs on Knutsford Boulevard and the s rounding streets. Generally visiting cricket supporters stay in New Kingston and enjoy the upbeat nightlife, but care should be taken at all times. Take the advice of hoteliers and do not walk on the streets after dark.

Norman Manley International Airport is 16km to the south east of Kingston. After passing through customs it can be quite hectic. Dispatchers are responsible for arranging taxis. Do not accept an offe of a taxi from anyone else. It may take a while, but it means that you will not be ripped off. A taxi to the centre takes 25 minutes and should cost no more th US$16. A bus service runs from the airport to downtown Kingston but is not re ommended.

There is a helpful tourist information desk before you reach customs and immi tion. Just beyond immigration on the left is a bureau de change. In the Departu Hall there are a number of fast food outlets, a coffee shop, newsagents and souv shops and also a bureau de change. Any Jamaican dollars left after your visit sho be changed at the airport because you will not be able to change them anywhe else in the Caribbean. Car hire is available from Avis (876 924 8013), Budget Car Rental (876 924 8762) and Hertz (876 924 8028).

Devon House

An 1880s mansion surrounded by beautiful gardens in the centre of New Kingston. Tours are available to view its fine décor, furniture and chandeliers. There are excellent craft shops, restaurants and cafés. Open 10.00-16.00 Tuesday-Saturday. Hope Road, Kingston Tel: 876 929 7029.

Dunn's River Falls

Probably Jamaica's finest waterfall. The cold mountain water falls more than 200 metres over a series of falls. If you do not mind getting drenched, guides will help you climb the falls for a small fee. The rocks are quite slippery. Bathers and trainers should be worn. The falls are between Ocho Rios and St. Ann's and are open daily during daylight hours.

Spanish Town

The old capital of Jamaica, and a half-hour drive from Kingston. A beautiful city with many splendid buildings, especially around its square, which has some of the finest Georgian architecture in the Western Hemisphere, in particular the Spanish Cathedral of St. Jago de la Vega, the oldest in the West Indies.

The Bob Marley Museum

On Hope Road in New Kingston and celebrating the life of the great reggae master. Marley, a Rastafarian, is probably Jamaica's most famous son. The museum holds memorabilia from his career and shows a film depicting his life.

The Blue Mountains

All visitors should visit these mountains which are to the north of the city. Home to the Old Tavern Blue Mountain Coffee Estate there are spectacular scenic views. The road winds through the military post of Newcastle, once a British Army post and now home to the Jamaica Defence Force. There are good restaurants and cafés on meandering roads. But be very careful when driving as there are no barriers on the majority of the cliff roads.

Post Office

General Post Office
13 King St.
Downtown 876 922 2120
Open 08.30-16.30 Monday-Friday.

Tourist Information

Jamaican Tourist Board
64 Knutsford Boulevard
Tel: 876 929 9200
Fax: 876 929 9375
jamaicatrv@aol.com
www.jamaicatravel.com

Jamaica Tourist Board
2 St. Lucia Avenue
Tel: 876 9299200

Tourist Desk at Airport
Tel: 876 924 8024

Hospital

Kingston Public Hospital
North St.

Downtown Private Hospitals
Medical Associates
18 Tangerine Place
Tel: 876 926 1400

Andrews Memorial
27 Hope Road
Tel: 876 926 7401

Pharmacy

Le Meridien Pegasus
81 Knutsford Boulevard
Tel: 876 926 3690

Emergency Numbers

Police	119
Fire	110
Ambulance	119
Private Ambulance	876 926 8264

Main Police Station
79 Duke St.
Tel: 876 922 9321

The Courtleigh Hotel
85 Knutsford Boulevard
Tel: 876 929 9000
Fax: 876 926 7744
courtleigh@cwjamaica.com
www.courtleigh.com
One of the best and very popular with
cricket fans. 118 very comfortable
rooms with cable TV, 2 restaurants, bar,
nightclub, gym and lovely swimming
pool.

Le Meridien Pegasus
81 Knutsford Boulevard
Tel: 876 926 3690
Fax: 876 929 5855
jmpegasus@cwjamaica.com
www.meridienjamaica.com
Fine hotel. 350 rooms, each with cable
TV, safe and balcony. 2 restaurants, bars
and lovely swimming pool.

Hilton
77 Knutsford Boulevard
876 926 5430
Tel: 876 926 7439
sales@hiltonkingston,com
www.hilton.com
303 excellent rooms with all mod cons,
2 restaurants, 3 bars, nightclubs, huge
swimming pool, tennis and gym.

Crowne Plaza
211 Constant Spring Road
Tel: 876 925 7676
Fax: 876 925 5757
In the city's best suburb. 105 rooms
with cable TV, modems, safes and minibars. 2 restaurants, 2 bars, gym, swimming pool, squash and sauna.

Christar Villas
99 Hope Road
Tel: 876 978 8066
Fax: 876 978 8068
Villa in the centre. 32 rooms,
kitchen facilities, gym and
swimming pool.

Mayfair Hotel
4 West Kings House
Tel: 876 926 1610
Fax: 876 926 7741
mayfairhotel@cwjamaica.com
Small hotel. 32 air-conditioned room
restaurant, bar, swimming pool. In th
centre.

Terra Nova
17 Waterloo Road
Tel: 876 926 9334
Fax: 876 020 4933
Old hotel with 35 homely rooms in th
centre.

Altamont Court Hotel
1-5 Altamont Terrace
Tel: 876 929 4497
Fax: 876 929 2118
altamont@n5.com.jm
One of the best value hotels in New
Kingston. 55 rooms, all with cable
TV, air-conditioning and balconies.
Restaurant, bar.

Knutsford Court Hotel
16 Chelsea Avenue
Tel: 876 929 1000
Fax: 876 960 7373
www.knutsfordcourt.com
sales@knutsfordcourt.com
Excellent hotel at a very reasonable
price. Restaurant, bar and very nice
swimming pool area.

Sandhurst
70 Sandhurst Crescent
Tel: 876 927 8244
Fax: 876 927 7239
Very comfortable guesthouse with air-
conditioned rooms, restaurant and
swimming pool.

Airlines
Air Jamaica 876 922 4661
BWIA 876 929 4231
British Airways 876 929 9028

Buses
Buses are cheap but overcrowded,
uncomfortable but reliable. Services
between Kingston and Negril, Montego
Bay and Ocho Rios are regular but
very busy.

Taxis
All taxis have Red PPV (Public
Passenger Vehicle) licence plates.
Always agree price before setting out.
Some drivers will offer to conduct
tours of Kingston and beyond.
JUTA 876 927 4534

Car Hire
Avis 876 924 8013
Budget Car Rental 876 924 8762
Hertz 876 924 8028

Jade Garden
106 Hope Road
Tel: 876 978 3476
xcellent Cantonese and Thai food in
axed surroundings with lovely views
the Blue Mountains.

rdons Restaurant
von House
Hope Raod
: 876 929 7027
rean, Japanese, Chinese and Thai
isine in nice surroundings. Bookings
ential.

t Pot
Altamont Terrace
: 876 929 3906
e of the best value restaurants. Local
hes in friendly atmosphere.

bar
Holborn Road
: 876 922 3427
e best Indian restaurant in Kingston.
ell established with excellent service
d great atmosphere.

dies
Holborn Road
: 876 926 2952
rden patio restaurant serving won-
rful fish and chips.

Fresca Bar and Grill
rra Nova Hotel
Waterloo Road
l: 876 926 9334
onderful food with inside and outside
ning. One of the best in town.

Dorado Restaurant
erra Nova Hotel
7 Waterloo Road
Tel: 876 926 9334
Trendy seafood and steak restaurant in the centre of the city.

In addition there are 3 restaurants in the Jamaica Pegasus Hotel, an International (La Brasserie), Italian (Columbus), a pizzeria (Pizza Cella), and two snack bars. The Hilton has an Italian (Palm Court) and Devon House has a steak and seafood restaurant (Blue Derby) and an Asian (The Orchid Room).

Peppers
31 Upper Waterloo Road
Good bar with excellent music and good food. Late opening outdoor bar.

The Grog Shoppe
Devon House
Tel: 876 929 7029
English pub with inside and outside seating in beautiful grounds. Frequent jazz sessions. Happy hour on Friday from 17.00-19.00.

Half Time Sports Bar
61 Knutsford Boulevard
Tel: 876 906 1452.
Lively bar with satellite TV showing sport from around the world.

The Mayfair Pub
4 West Kings House
Tel: 876 926 1610
English pub in the centre. Popular with locals and visitors alike.

JamRock
69 Knutsford Boulevard
Good Jamaican bar with excellent local food.

There are a number of nightclubs in Kingston. Asylum is the largest, the Jonkanoo Lounge at the Hilton and Mingles at the Courtleigh.

Institute of Jamaica
12 East St.
Tel: 876 922 0620
races the island's history and holds e largest collection of books and ints in the West Indies. The National istory Museum is located in the ame building.

Fort Charles Maritime Museum
Port Royal
Tel: 876 967 8438
In the former British Naval base it traces Jamaica's maritime history.

Bob Marley Museum
56 Hope Road
Tel: 876 927 9152
Dedicated to the memory of the late reggae singer.

general info

Telecoms
International Direct Dialling is available. Jamaica's country code is 1 876. Outgoing International code is 011.

Newspapers
The Daily Gleaner
The Daily Star
The Jamaican Herald

Banking
Open Monday-Thursday 09.00-14.00, Friday 09.00-16.00.
There are ATM machines at the airport and in Kingston.
Jamaica's currency is the Jamaican Dollar. Notes are in denominations of JA$1000, 500, 100, 50, 20 and coins in denominations of 20, 10, and 5 cent pieces. Foreign currency can be changed in banks and cambios which can be found throughout Kingston. Credit cards are widely accepted in hotels, restaurants, bars and shops.

Embassies
British High Commission

28 Trafalgar Road
Tel: 876 929 6915

Customs
200 cigarettes or 50 cigars or 250g of tobacco, 1 litre of spirits, 1 litre of wi and 150g of perfume can be importe without incurring duty.

Visa
All visitors to Jamaica must have a va passport and a return or onward tick visa is not required.

Time Difference
GMT - 5 Hours

Electricity
110 Volts Ac 50 Hz

Tipping
Hotels add a 10% service charge to y bill. This is on top of a 15% services t Tipping is at your discretion.

Departure Tax
All vistors must pay JA$1000

Climate

	ave temp	rain cm		ave temp	rain cm
January	25	29	July	28	46
February	25	24	August	27	107
March	26	23	September	27	127
April	26	39	October	27	181
May	27	104	November	27	95
June	27	96	December	26	41

stats

Win/Loss Record

Country	Played	Won	Drawn	Lost	Tie
West Indies	40	21	13	6	-
Australia	9	3	3	3	-
England	14	3	6	5	-
New Zealand	2	-	1	1	
India	9	-	3	6	-
Zimbabwe	1	-	-	1	
Sri Lanka	1	-	-	1	
Pakistan	2	-	-	2	-
South Africa	1	-	-	1	
Bangladesh	1			1	

Highest Individual Aggregates (West Indies unless stated)

Player	Mat	Inn	NO	Runs	Ave	HS	50	100
Garry Sobers	11	18	5	1354	104.15	365*	4	5
Clyde Walcott	7	12	2	924	92.40	155	3	5
Brian Lara	10	16	1	922	61.47	213	6	2
Gordon Greenidge	9	16	2	794	56.71	127	4	2
Rohan Kanhai	9	14	1	755	58.08	158*	3	2
Frank Worrell	7	12	1	604	54.91	237	3	1
Desmond Haynes	9	17	4	593	45.62	84	4	0

Everton Weekes	7	12	2	585	58.50	141	3	2
Roy Fredericks	6	11	1	580	58.00	163	3	1
Lawrence Rowe	4	7	2	567	113.40	214	1	3

Top Wicket Takers (West Indies unless stated)

Player	Mat	Bll	Md	Runs	Wkt	Ave	BB	S/R
Courtney Walsh	11	2219	91	897	48	18.69	6/62	46.23
Wes Hall	5	1266	40	534	35	15.26	7/69	36.17
Malcolm Marshall	8	1417	45	603	31	19.45	5/51	45.71
Garry Sobers	11	2390	116	879	27	32.56	5/63	88.52
Michael Holding	5	986	34	475	24	19.79	5/56	41.08
Lance Gibbs	8	2510	131	858	24	35.75	4/85	104.58
Joel Garner	6	1153	42	503	22	22.86	3/22	52.41
Pedro Collins	3	585	13	334	16	20.88	6/53	36.56
Alf Valentine	4	1385	80	507	16	31.69	5/64	86.56
Kapil Dev (Ind)	2	483	15	224	15	14.93	6/84	32.20

Highest Individual Scores (West Indies unless stated)

365*	Garry Sobers	v Pakistan 1957-58
325	Andy Sandham (Eng)	1929-30
270*	George Headley	v England 1934-35
262*	Dennis Amiss (Eng)	1973-74
260	Conrad Hunte	v Pakistan 1957-58
237	Frank Worrell	v India 1952-53
223	George Headley	v England 1929-30
223*	Glenn Turner (NZ)	1971-72
214	Lawrence Rowe	v New Zealand 1971-72
213	Brian Lara	v Australia 1998-99

Best Individual Bowling Performances (West Indies unless stated)

12.3-8-12-7	Steve Harmison (Eng)	2003-04
16-7-34-7	Trevor Bailey (Eng)	1953-54
21-7-49-7	John Snow (Eng)	1967-68
16-2-57-7	Corey Collymore	v Sri Lanka 2003
31.2-8-69-7	Wes Hall	v England 1959-60
20.5-5-49-6	Wes Hall	v India 1961-62
18-3-53-6	Pedro Collins	v Bangladesh 2004
29-8-62-6	Courtney Walsh	v India 1988-89
24-7-66-6	Kenny Benjamin	v England 1993-94
33-7-84-6	Kapil Dev (Ind)	1988-89

Highest Partnerships

Wicket	Runs	Batsmen	Match
1st	206	Michael Frederick & Lawrence Rowe (WI)	1973-1974 v England
2nd	446	Conrad Hunte & Garry Sobers (WI)	1957-1958 v Pakistan
3rd	295	Colin McDonald & Neil Harvey (Aus)	1954-1955
4th	249	Andy Sandham & Les Ames (Eng)	1929-1930
5th	322	Brian Lara & Jimmy Adams (WI)	1998-1999 v Australia
6th	220	Glenn Turner & Ken Wadsworth (NZ)	1971-1972
7th	147	George Headley & Rolph Grant (WI)	1934-1935 v England
8th	148	Jimmy Adams & Franklyn Rose (WI)	1999-2000 v Zimbabwe
9th	122	Dilip Sardesai & Erapalli Prasanna (Ind)	1970-1971
10th	54	Stuart Carlisle & Henry Olonga (Zim)	1999-2000

Results at Sabina Park

Date	Countries	Result
03/04/1930	v England	drawn
14/03/1935	v England	won by an innings and 161 runs
27/03/1948	v England	won by 10 wickets
28/03/1953	v India	drawn
15/01/1954	v England	won by 140 runs
30/03/1954	v England	lost by 9 wickets
26/03/1955	v Australia	lost by 9 wickets
11/06/1955	v Australia	lost by an innings and 82 runs
26/02/1958	v Pakistan	won by an innings and 174 runs
17/02/1960	v England	drawn
07/03/1962	v India	won by an innings and 18 runs

13/04/1962	v India	won by 123 runs
03/03/1965	v Australia	won by 179 runs
08/02/1968	v England	drawn
18/02/1971	v India	drawn
16/02/1972	v New Zealand	drawn
16/02/1973	v Australia	drawn
16/02/1974	v England	drawn
21/04/1976	v India	won by 10 wickets
15/04/1977	v Pakistan	won by 140 runs
28/04/1978	v Australia	drawn
10/04/1981	v England	drawn
23/02/1983	v India	won by 4 wickets
28/04/1984	v Australia	won by 10 wickets
04/05/1985	v New Zealand	won by 10 wickets
21/02/1986	v England	won by 10 wickets
28/04/1989	v India	won by 7 wickets
24/02/1990	v England	lost by 9 wickets
01/03/1991	v Australia	drawn
19/02/1994	v England	won by 8 wickets
29/04/1995	v Australia	lost by an innings and 53 runs
06/03/1997	v India	drawn
29/01/1998	v England	drawn
13/03/1999	v Australia	won by 10 wickets
24/03/2000	v Zimbabwe	won by 10 wickets
19/04/2001	v South Africa	won by 130 runs
18/05/2002	v India	won by 155 runs
27/06/2003	v Sri Lanka	won by 7 wickets
11/03/2004	v England	lost by 10 wickets
04/06/2004	v Bangladesh	won by an innings and 99 runs

st lucia

beausejour

The Beausejour Stadium is in the north of the city of
Castries in between Rodney Bay and Gros Islet. It became the West Indies'
latest Test match ground on 20 June 2003 when they entertained Sri Lanka in a
match affected by rain. Marvin Atapattu (118) scored the first century while Corey
Collymore (5/66) got the first 'fifer' as Sri Lanka made 354. In reply the hosts
scored declared at 477/9, with Brian Lara scoring 209 and Wavell

Hinds 113. Muttiah Muralitharan took 5/138. In their second innings the Sri Lankans advanced to 126/0 with Sanath Jayasuriya on 72no and Atapattu 50no before time ran out.

Beausejour Stadium is purpose built, constructed in 2001 as the former ground at Mindoo Phillip Park in Castries had poor drainage and limited possibilities for expansion. It is set at the foot of the Beausejour hills and is certainly the most modern, if not the finest, stadium in the West Indies. With a capacity of 18,000, it is a superb venue. The pavilion at the east end has excellent dressing rooms and viewing facilities. On the south side, the FICS, the Air Jamaica, the Harry Edwards Jewellers and the Bounty Rum stands are mostly undercover with bucket-seating, excellent facilities and disabled access with good viewing areas. The food stalls and bars underneath the stand provide a variety of food, Caribbean style. In addition there are ice-cream, pop corn and candy floss stalls that are well organised with little queuing. The west end of the ground has the Julian and JQ Charles stands on either side of the ultra-modern media centre. These stands have a number of corporate suites in their upper tiers. Again there are excellent facilities under the stands including a juice bar and a pizza outlets. The north side of the ground is the rowdy area. No seats, standing room only. The Piton Mound is the all-inclusive party area where the music pumps out all day and the drinks flow. Also on this side is the Grounds area, a grass bank and the cheapest part of the ground. It is lively as the locals love a party at the cricket, but it does get very busy and the crowd stand all day. Food stalls and bars line the back of this area. The modern scoreboard and video replay screen are located on this side of the ground.

Tickets for test matches can be purchased from the West Indies ticketline 1800 744 GAME (4263), from www.windiescricket.com or from the ticket office on the north side of the ground. The ground is a fair distance away from Castries. The No 1A bus runs to the ground at a cost of EC$2. There is parking outside the ground, however there is only one road in and out of the area and the traffic is horrendous. For those staying in Rodney Bay and Gros Islet walking is probably the best option because of the traffic. The walk should take about 45 minutes.

St. Lucia, a volcanic island, lies between Martinique and St. Vincent in the south east Caribbean. One of the Windward Islands, it is small (only 967sq. km) but has some wonderful beaches, coral reefs and lush rainforests. 65,000 of the 163,000 inhabitants live in the capital, Castries, in the north west corner at the foot of the Morne Fortune hills that tower above the city. It is very friendly. The official language is English, but a French-based patois is widely spoken.

A Spanish explorer Juan de la Casa, once Christopher Columbus' navigator, was the first European to discover the island in 1500. The first European settler was a French pirate named Francois le Clerc known as Jambo de Bois (wooden leg) who settled on Pigeon Island and survived by attacking passing Spanish ships. The Dutch landed on the south of the island in 1600 and established a fortified base. They were closely followed by a group of British settlers who had sailed off course on their way to Guyana. The Carib drove both Dutch and British away. By the mid 1600s and several more unsuccessful attempts by the British to settle on the island, the French took over. Between 1659 and 1814 ownership of the island changed hands between the British and the French 14 times until it finally became British under the Treaty of Paris of 1814. St. Lucia remained a British colony until 22 February 1979 when it gained its independence.

Castries is small with noisy streets lined with stalls selling everything from fruit and vegetables to cool drinks and ice-cream. It is colourful and clean with a relaxed atmosphere. The Cathedral of the Immaculate Conception, built in 1897, is its focal point. It is in Derek Walcott Square, the traditional centre of town. The square, named after the winner of the 1992 Nobel Prize for Literature, is a good place to rest. It has a wonderful 400-year-old Samaan tree which shades the whole square. Castries market on the corner of Jeremie and Peynier Streets is open six days a week and is very lively and well worth a visit.

There are plenty of attractions around the island including the sulphur springs and the many reefs along the island's coast. The east side of the island is on the Atlantic and has a rugged coastline whereas the west side lies on the gentle Caribbean Sea. A visit to the fishing village of Anse-le-Ray provides an insight into St. Lucian life. The stunning rain forests throughout the island with countless wild orchids and tropical birds are quite magnificent.

Swimwear is not acceptable attire off the beach but restaurant dress code is casual. Most hotels provide musical and other entertainment for their guests. Rodney Bay also has the liveliest pubs and evening entertainment. Friday night is 'jump up' night in the village of Gros Islet. 'Jump up' is a street party with steelbands and other music and stalls selling delicious St. Lucian food. The party goes on through the night in a friendly and safe environment and is enjoyed by local and visitors alike.

arrival

Hewanorra International Airport is situated near Vieux Fort at the very south of the island, 63km from Castries and over 70km to the ground. A taxi ride to Castries costs between EC$150 and EC$160 and EC$170-EC$180 to Rodney Bay. No buses leave from the airport, but one (No. 4B) does run from New Dock Road in nearby Vieux Fort to Castries at a cost of EC$8. Another option, cheaper than catching a taxi, is hiring a car. Car rental is available from Avis (758 452 4554), Budget (758 454 5311) and Hertz (758 454 9636). Helicopter transfers are available to Castries (Vigie Hanger) and the Jalousie Hilton Hotel (Enquiries – St. Lucia Helicopter Ltd 758 453 6950 or Paradise Helicopter 758 450 9203). There is a very helpful tourist information desk and a bank which is open until 21.00 each evening. There is a café and small shops in the Departure Hall.

George FL Charles Airport, just outside Castries on the Vigie Peninsula, is St. Lucia's regional airport and handles propeller flights from neighbouring islands such as Trinidad, St. Vincent and Barbados. It is a very handy airport for cricket fans as it avoids the long journey from Hewanorra. A taxi to Castries cost less than EC$10 and EC$15 to Rodney Bay. The airport is quiet, easy to check in and has a small café/bar and a few stalls. Car rental in available from Hertz 758 451 7351.

Turtle watching at Grande Anse Beach

A wonderful opportunity to see leatherback turtles on the north coast of the island from April to July. Each Saturday night locals arrange camping watches from 18.00 to 06.00 the following morning. Visitors should ring 758 52 8100 well in advance to make booking. Minimal cost.

oufriere

small fishing village on the west coast of the island and the first French settlement. It is a relaxed place with some lovely architecture in the town square. Just uth of the village are the Sulphur Springs, the remains of a dormant volcano at collapsed on itself over 40,000 years ago. From the viewing platform visitors n see and smell bubbling pools of sulphur-dense water.

ie Pitons

vo volcanic plugs these are near Soufriere and, without doubt, are the biggest tourist attraction. The twin peaks rise out of the sea to a height of over 700 etres. Petit Piton overlooks the village with Gros Piton further to the south. rganised tours can be arranged but it is a strenuous climb. The Pitons are best ewed from Mount Gimie or the beach. Enquiries: Mystic Man Tours 758 459 '83 or www.mysticmantours.com or richc@candw.lc

igeon Island

n islet off the north west coast with an extensive history. There are a number British forts to explore. A museum on the island charts the history from the :awak and Caribs to the French and British era. Ancient artefacts from Arawak id Carib are on display. Open 09.00-17.00. Enquiries 758 452 5005. There are so two fantastic beaches and some good hiking trails.

Iarquis Estate

A working plantation which produces bananas, coffee and cocoa. A short drive outside Castries, a tour can be arranged by calling 758 452 3762.

Post Office

General Post Office
Mongiraud St.
Castries
Open 08:30-16:30, Monday to Friday.

ourist Information

t. Lucia Tourist Board
el: 876 452 7577
ww.stlucia.org

t. Lucia Hotel and Tourism Association
ureline Building
ide Boutielle
Castries
el: 758 452 5968/78
ww.slutour@canw.ic

FL Charles Airport
el: 758 452 2596

Hewanorra Airport
Tel: 758 454 6644

Hospital

Victoria Hospital
La Toc Road
Castries
Tel: 758 452 2421

Rodney Bay Medical and Dental Centre
Rodney Bay
Tel: 758 452 8621

All hotels have doctors in residence or on call. Pharmacies in Castries, Rodney Bay and Gros Islet.

Emergency Numbers

Police	911/999
Fire	911
Ambulance	911

Police Headquarters
Bridge St.
Castries
Tel: 758 452 2854

Royal St. Lucian
Rodney Bay
Tel: 758 452 9999
Fax: 758 452 9639
royalgm@candw.lc
One of the island's best. 96 air-conditioned rooms, cable TV. Restaurants, bar, swimming pool, tennis and waterspouts. On Reduit beach

Bay Gardens Hotel
Rodney Bay
St. Lucia
Tel: 758 452 8060
Fax: 758 452 8059
baygardens@candw.ic
www.baygardenshotel.com
Excellent with great rooms and cable TV. Restaurant, bars, swimming pool and Jacuzzi. Close to Reduit beach.

Bay Gardens Inn
Rodney Bay
Tel: 758 452 8200
Fax: 758 452 8002
baygardensinn@candw.ic
www.baygardensinn.com
The sister hotel of the Bay Gardens. Inexpensive yet excellent in great location with lovely rooms. Very quiet with swimming pool, restaurant, bar and service second to none.

Ginger Lily Hotel
Rodney Bay
Tel: 758 458 0300
Fax: 758 452 0012
info@rodneybay.com
www.rodneybay.com
Just across from Reduit beach. 11 rooms self catering hotel. Cable TV and swimming pool.

Cara Suites
La Pansee Road
Castries
Tel: 758 452 4767
Fax: 758 453 1999
carasuiteslc@carahotels.com
Excellent hotel 5 minutes outside Castries. 40 rooms with great views, air-conditioning and cable TV. Swimming pool, 2 restaurants, bar and good service.

Auberge Seraphine
Vigie Marina
Castries
Tel: 758 453 2073
Fax: 758 451 7001
auberge@candw.lc
www.aubergseraphine.com
By Vigie Marina. 28 rooms have cable TV and air-conditioning. Restaurant, bar and swimming pool.

The Jalousie Hilton
Bay St.
Soufriere
Tel: 758 456 8000
Fax: 758 459 7667
Ultimate hotel on the west coast between the Pitons. 114 suites, most with private plunge pool. Gym, golf, tennis, water sports, 4 restaurants, and bar.

Nelson's Furnished Apartments
Cas-En-Bas Road
Gros Islet
Tel: 758 450 8275
Good budget accommodation. Fully furnished apartments with cable TV, fan and balcony with view of Rodney bay. Walking distance to ground.

La Panache Guesthouse
Cas-En-Bas Road
Gros Islet
Tel: 758 450 0765
Good clean guesthouse with 6 rooms all with their own bathroom, fan and mosquito net. Communal area with cable TV and restaurant.

Climate

	ave temp	rain cm		ave temp	rain cm
January	26	75	July	28	132
February	26	51	August	28	150
March	27	55	September	28	172
April	27	59	October	28	185
May	28	75	November	28	190
June	28	96	December	27	110

L'Epicure

Royal St. Lucian Hotel
Rodney Bay
Tel: 758 452 9999
One of the finest in St. Lucia.
Caribbean and international menu.

Spinnakers Beach Bar

St. Lucia Yacht Club
Tel: 758 452 8491
Good restaurant open for breakfast,
lunch and dinner. Nice surroundings.

Memories of Hong Kong

Rodney Bay
Tel: 758 452 8218
The best Oriental cuisine in the
Caribbean. Chinese and Cantonese
menu with open air dining. Open
Monday-Sunday 17.00-10.30.

Buzz Seafood and Grill

Rodney Bay
Opposite Royal St. Lucia Hotel
Tel: 758 458 0450
www.buzzstlucia.com
For all tastes. Marquee in garden.

Pizza Pizza

Rodney Bay
Tel: 758 452 8282
The best pizzas on the island at a very
affordable price. Good service.

The Mandolin

La Pansee
Castries
Tel: 758 452 4767
British/French cuisine at the Cara Suites
Hotel. Open 12.00-14.00 and 19.00-
22.00 seven days a week.

The Coal Pot

Virgie Marina
Castries
Tel: 758 452 5566
Open air French fare with a Caribbean
flavour using local ingredients.

Ginger Lily

Rodney Bay
Good value Chinese down by the beach.
Open seven nights a week 18.00-23.00.

Capone's

Rodney Bay

Tel: 758 452 0284
Inexpensive Italian restaurant for
quiet night out. Open Tuesday-
Sunday.

Rodney Bay Marina Yacht Club

Rodney Bay
Tel: 758 452 0351
Relaxed waterfront restaurant offering
Caribbean and international cuisine.
Lively bar by swimming pool.

Jimmie's

Vigie Marina
Tel: 758 452 5142
Good seafood restaurant down by the
water. Reasonably priced.

Rumours Restaurant and Sports Bar

Opposite Scotia Bank
Rodney Bay
Tel: 758 452 9249
Good food in one of the liveliest bars
in town. Pool tables and good music in
relaxed surroundings.

Shamrocks

Rodney Bay
Tel: 758 452 8725
Lively Irish pub with great atmosphere.
Open very late each night. Live Jazz on
Wednesdays, dance music on Saturday
nights.

The Jazz Lounge

Rodney Bay
Tel: 758 458 0565
Live Jazz in wine bar with Tapas menu.
Part of the roof garden restaurant.

The Cat Whiskers

Reduit Beach Ramp
Rodney Bay
Tel: 758 452 8880
Old English pub. Home cooked English
food including the very popular Sunday
roast lunch. Open 08.00-late Tuesday-
Sunday.

The Lime

Rodney Bay
Tel: 758 452 0761
Good fun bar. Good music and fun well
into the night.

Mel's Tavern

Bridge St.
Castries
English pub in the centre of Castries.
Good atmosphere and good English
food.

Telecoms
International Direct Dialling is available throughout the island. Country code is 1 758.

Newspapers
The Star (Wednesday and Saturday)
The Voice (Tuesday and Thursday)
The Weekend Voice (weekend)
The Crusader (weekend)
One Caribbean (weekend)

Banking
There are banks in Castries, Soufriere, Vieux Fort, Gros Islet and Rodney Bay. Open 08.00-15.00 Monday-Thursday 08.00-17.00 Friday.
St. Lucian currency is the East Caribbean Dollar which is linked to the US Dollar at the exchange rate of US$1 to EC$2.65. Notes are in denominations of EC$100, 50, 20, 10, 5 and coins EC$1 and 50, 25, 10, 5, 2, 1 cents. US Dollars and Sterling are readily accepted throughout the island. Travellers' cheques and major credit cards are generally accepted. There are change bureaux in Castries.

Embassies
British High Commission
NIS Building
Waterfront
Castries
Tel: 758 452 2484
Fax: 758 453 1543
british@candw.ic

Customs
The duty free allowance is 200 cigarett or 250 grams of tobacco or 50 cigars and one litre of spirits or wine.

Visa
Valid passports must be carried by all visitors entering the island except British and American citizens who have valid return tickets and ID. Visa are not required by citizens from Commonwealth countries.

Time Difference
St. Lucia is in the Atlantic Standard Time Zone which is GMT-4 hours.

Electricity
220 volts/50 cycles

Tipping
There is a government tax of 8% on hotel and restaurant bills in addition t a service charge of 10%. Tipping is no essential, but if you feel a tip is warran ed 10% to 12% of the bill is usual.

Departure Tax
All visitors over 12 years of age must pay EC$54 by air, EC$20 by ferry.

Airlines
Air Jamaica, Brazil Street, Castries 758 453 6611
British Airways, William Peter Boulevard
Castries 758 452 3951
BWIA, Brazil St.
Castries 758 452 3778
Caribbean Star, 20 Bridge St.
Castries 758 453 2927
Liat, Brazil St.
Castries 758 452 3056
Virgin 1 800 744 7477

Buses
No. 1A runs between Castries, Rodney Bay and Gros Islet until 22.00 and later on Friday and Saturday nights. Each journey cost EC$2. The bus service runs throughout the island.

Taxis
Easily available at stands in Castries and by telephone. Important to agree fare with driver before commencing journey. All taxis have red TX licence plates.
City Taxi Service 758 452 3154
Airport Service 758 452 1599
St. Lucia Taxi Service 758 452 2492

Car Hire
A temporary licence is required. Obtained on production of driving licence at the airport, police station or the car rental company at a cost of EC$54 and is valid for three months.
Avis
Castries 758 452 4554
Budget
Castries 758 452 0233
Hertz
Vigie Airport 758 451 7351

Win/Loss Record

Country	Played	Won	Drawn	Lost	Tie
Sri Lanka	1	-	1	-	-
West Indies	2	-	2	-	-
Bangladesh	1	-	1	-	-

Highest Individual Aggregates (West Indies unless stated)

Player	Mat	Inn	NO	Runs	Ave	HS	50	100
Brian Lara	2	2	0	262	131.00	209	1	1
Chris Gayle	2	3	1	234	117.00	141	1	1
Marvan Atapattu (SL)	1	2	1	168	168.00	118	1	1
Mohammad Rafique (Bang)	1	2	0	140	70.00	111	0	1
Habibul Bashar (Bang)	1	2	0	138	69.00	113	0	1

Top Wicket Takers (West Indies unless stated)

Player	Mat	Bll	Md	Runs	Wkt	Ave	BB	S/R
Ramnesh Sarwan	2	288	17	101	7	14.43	4/37	41.14
Pedro Collins	1	267	13	125	5	25.00	4/83	53.40
Muttiah Muralitharan (SL)	1	300	10	138	5	27.60	5/138	60.00
Corey Collymore	1	192	5	74	5	14.80	5/66	38.40
Mushfiqur Rahman	1	190	8	90	4	22.50	4/65	47.50

Highest Individual Scores (West Indies unless stated)

209	Brian Lara	v Sri Lanka 2003	
141	Chris Gayle	v Bangladesh	2004
118	Marvan Atapattu (SL)		2003
113	Wavell Hinds	v Sri Lanka 2003	
113	Habibul Bashar (Bang)		2004

Best Individual Bowling Performances (West Indies unless stated)

19-5-66-5	Corey Collymore	v Sri Lanka 2003	
49-10-138-5	Muttiah Muralitharan (SL)		2003
20-9-37-4	Ramnesh Sarwan	v Sri Lanka 2004	
15.4-8-65-4	Mushfiqur Rahman (Bang)		2004
17.3-8-83-4	Pedro Collins		2004

Highest Partnerships

Wkt	Runs	Batsmen	Match
1st	126	Marvan Atapattu & Habibul Bashar (Bang)	2002-2003
2nd	121	Javed Omar & Kumar Sangakarra (SL)	2003-2004
3rd	174	Wavell Hinds & Brian Lara (WI)	2002-2003 v Sri Lanka
4th	56	Rajin Saleh & Mohammed Ashraful (Bang)	2002-2003
5th	70	Chris Gayle & Dwayne Smith (WI)	2003-2004 v Bangladesh
6th	59	Chris Gayle & Ridley Jacobs (WI)	2003-2004 v Bangladesh
7th	136	Brian Lara & Omari Banks (WI)	2003-2004 v Bangladesh
8th	87	Mohammed Ashraful & Mohammad Rafique (Bang)	2003-2004
9th	74	Khaled Mashud & Tapash Baisya (Bang)	2003-2004
10th	46	Mohammad Rafique & Tareq Aziz (Bang)	2002-2003 v Sri Lanka

Results at Beausejour Stadium

Date	Countries	Result
20/06/2003	v Sri Lanka	Drawn
20/05/2004	v Bangladesh	drawn

trinidad

The Queen's Park Oval is home to the Queen's Park Cricket Club and is the largest Test cricket ground in the West Indies. It nestles against the marvellous backdrop of the Northern Hills in the suburb of Woodbrook in Port of Spain, the capital of the twin state of Trinidad and Tobago.

The first Test match played here was on England's tour in 1930 when England beat their hosts by 167 runs with Patsy Hendren scoring 205no for the visitors, a score that remains the fifth highest on the ground.

Sunil Gavaskar, who scored the highest individual score of 220 for India in 1970/71, had a passion for the ground, scoring four centuries in five tests. Everton Weekes is the only man to score two double centuries. The highest team score is 681/8 by the West Indies versus England in 1953/54 and the lowest 46 by England in 1993/94. When set 194 to win, the visitors fell to Curtly Ambrose, 6/24 and Courtney Walsh, 3/16 in 19.1 overs.

The best match figures are Tony Greig's 13/156 in England's 1974 victory. Ambrose has taken the most wickets at the Queen's Park Oval – 66 at an average of 13.29, taking five wickets in an innings six times.

Other memorable moments include Andy Guateame's 112 in his only Test innings in 1948 against England and India's remarkable then world record 406/4 in the fourth innings to beat Clive Lloyd's men in 1975/76. Doug Walters' hundred between lunch and tea in 1975 and Malcolm Marshall's 11/89 against India, his best Test match bowling figures, deserve mention.

The ground is a perfect oval and surrounded by six stands, a giant scoreboard and the pavilion, a two-storey structure built in 1952. It is a tremendous experience to watch cricket here. The crowd are passionate and will certainly let you know when their team are on top. They are fiercely proud of Brian Lara's achievements and that of other Trinidadians. Fans from each side mingle in the stands and noisily harangue one another. The pavilion is directly behind the bowler's arm at the southern end of the ground, with the Jeffrey Stollmeyer, Dos Santos and Learie Constantine stands sweeping around the off side boundary. These stands are the first to fill up as they are under cover and in an excellent position for viewing. On the opposite side beneath the huge scoreboard is the Trini Posse Stand, a reserved and semi-covered stand where drinks are included in the entrance fee. A DJ blasts out calypso music and the Carib dancing girls entertain the crowd. Certainly a different way to watch cricket and by mid-afternoon it is not hard to see why it is called the party stand.

Under the other stands there is an array of food on offer from rice and burgers to rotis, the West Indian creation of curry filled bread, fried chicken to vegetarian dishes. The standard of food is good. Rum, beer and soft drinks can be bought at the many bars throughout the ground.

Tickets are available from the West Indies ticket hotline 1800 744 GAME (4263) or www.indiescricket.com or the ticket office in the pavilion car park.

Facilities for the disabled are available in the pavilion and the Jeffrey Stollymeyer Stand. Toilet facilities around the ground are excellent, extremely clean and well tended to throughout the Test.

The ground is a five minute drive from Port of Spain, taking either the Tragarate Road or Queen's Park West past the Savannah and then St. Clare Road. Parking is available on King George V Park across the road from the ground. The ground is a 25-minute walk, but it is advisable to catch a taxi after dark. Maxi Taxis, a form of minibus that goes past the ground. leaves from the corner of Amercromby and Park streets and cost TT$2.

Trinidad and Tobago is of volcanic origin and at the south end of the Caribbean chain, 13km off the north east coast of Venezuela across the Gulf of Paria. Thousands of years ago the land mass was attached to the South American mainland and Trinidad and Tobago are thought to be the most northern reaches of the Andes mountains. The east of the island is on the Atlantic Ocean, the north and west on the Caribbean Sea. The two islands, 21km apart, have a population of 1.3 million, all but 50,000 living on Trinidad. The Amerindian people had been settled since 6500 BC when Christopher Columbus 'discovered' the island in 1498 and named it La Trinidad. Due to Carib resistance it was not until 1592 that the Spanish settled and founded the town of San Jose de Oruna. Sir Walter Raleigh destroyed this in 1595. The Spanish moved to the native American village of Conqueraba and renamed it Puerto de Espana. The British captured the island in 1797 and in 1802 it became British under the Treaty of Amiens. Tobago followed in 1814. In 1888 the islands of Trinidad and Tobago united as one country. The country gained independence on 31 August 1962, becoming a republic on 1 August 1976.

Port of Spain is a large working seaport situated in the north-west. Home of the world famous carnival, calypso and steel bands, it is a bustling, sprawling city with curb-side food and merchandise stalls lining the streets beneath modern skyscrapers housing banks and financial institutions. Traffic is slow, circumventing the narrow streets at a snail's pace, with horns hooting and music blaring out of cars and the hundreds of minibuses. The traffic dies down in the evening but the city remains loud and busy.

There are many places to visit. The Red House in Woodford Square is Trinidad's fine House of Parliament. Independence Square is beautiful with lovely gardens. The Queen's Park Savannah is considered to be the centre of Trinidad. Set at the foot of the Northern Ranges, the Savannah is a huge sports field with on one side beautiful buildings and on the other Botanical Gardens. The buildings include the National Museum and Art Gallery which has fine carnival and Amerindian exhibitions. The Botanical Gardens on the north side of the Savannah are home to some of the Caribbean's finest flora. The official residences of the President and Prime Minister are situated here as is the Emperor Valley Zoo, a popular attraction.

Fort George to the south of the city provides magnificent views of the capital and of the northern mountains of Venezuela. Fort Picton and Fort Chacon are also worth visiting.

There are some fine restaurants in Port of Spain. They are loud, busy and friendly and quite a few of them have bars with live entertainment. There are not many pubs as Trinidadians tend to drink in restaurants, rum shops or in the street listening to steel bands but there are still some good ones. It is important to note that safety should be remembered at all times especially after dark. Visitors should not walk home and should heed local advice about the areas to visit. Taxis are available and cheap.

Tobago

Tobago has some of the best beaches in the Caribbean. The north of the island has many beautiful bays and a drive up the coast is recommended. Kings Peters, Castara, Englishman's and Blood Bays must be seen. On the east side is Charlotteville, a quaint fishing village set at the foot of steep hills. Apartment accommodation in the town and on the beach is very reasonable in this quiet village. Off the coast there is some terrific diving and snorkelling with wonderful reef fish and coral, in particular huge brain coral off Little Tobago Island. The south coast beaches do not match those on the north but the south coast does have Scarborough, the island's major town, where there is plenty to see and do. A few days in Tobago are a must when visiting Trinidad.

Steelbands

If you have not heard a steel band in the street you have not been to Trinidad. Described as one of the music world's most spectacular secrets, the steel pan is the only acoustic musical instrument invented in the 20th century. Bands set up on street corners and start playing. Before long it has turned into a street party. A terrific experience.

Caroni Bird Sanctuary

To the south of Port of Spain, this is a wonderful way to spend an afternoon. See the Scarlet Ibis return to roost at sunset. The mass of bright red birds flying back to their nests is an incredible sight and sound. Boat tours are arranged for 16.00 daily. Tel: 868 645 1305. Numbers are limited so book early. There is a lot more to do and see in the sanctuary so a lot of visitors arrive a few hours before the tour to experience the flora and fauna in this area of swamplands and lagoon.

Magnificent Seven

Seven amazing buildings in a row on the western side of the Savannah. Built at the turn of the 20th century, they are a reminder of times past. Nowadays they are government buildings and it is not possible to tour them but their architecture is worth seeing.

Maracas Bay

The most popular beach in Trinidad. The long beach has a cove at one end. A 30-minute drive north of Port of Spain through the Northern Range Mountains with incredible scenery. The beach gets some excellent waves for body surfing and swimming and is great for sunbathing. It can get very busy on the weekends. Huts serve wonderful food including the speciality Maracas Shark and Bake. Absolutely delicious. It is possible to get a route taxi for US$1 or a taxi for approximately US$20. Agree the price before leaving Port of Spain.

Piarco International Airport is 25km from Port of Spain. A taxi can take from 30 minutes to an hour depending on the traffic. The cost is a standard T&T$ 125 and T&T150 to Maraval. There is a 50% surcharge after 22.00. An authorised dispatcher will help you to find your taxi. Only use the dispatcher with ID. He is situated right outside the Customs Hall in the Arrivals Hall. There is a bank in the Arrival Hall as well as with money changing facilities. A bank of ATM's that accept international cards is located between arrivals and departures. There are plenty of cafés and restaurants, souvenir shops and newsagents. There are two bars, one upstairs with a viewing area and the other right outside the main entrance. Car hire is available from Southern Sales (868 669 2424), Auto Rentals (868 669 2277) and Thrifty (868 669 0602).

Hilton Trinidad

Lady Young Road
Port of Spain
Tel: 868 624 3211
Fax: 868 624 4485
hiltonpos@wow.net
www.trinidadhilton.com
Overlooking the Savannah. 25 acres
of landscaped gardens. 380 rooms
with cable TV, minibars and balconies.
Restaurants, bars and swimming pool.

Kapok Hotel

16-18 Cotton Hill
St. Clair
Port of Spain
Tel: 868 622 5765
Fax: 868 622 9677
stay@kapok.co.tt
www.kapol.co.tt
Small, prestigious. 75 rooms, 12 suites.
Restaurant, swimming pool, gym, hair
salon. Some rooms overlook Savannah.

Carnetta's Inn

99 Saddle Road
Maraval
Tel: 868 628 2732
Fax: 868 628 7717
carnetta@trinidad.co.tt
www.carnettas.com
Wonderful guesthouse on road to
Maracas beach. 14 rooms with cable
TV, fans. Restaurant.

Monique's Guesthouse

114-116 Saddle Road
Maraval
Tel: 800 426 5445
Another guesthouse on the road to
Maracas. 20 lovely rooms with cable
TV, some with kitchenettes. Restaurant.

Crewsinn Hotel

Chaguaramas Terminals Drive
Chaguaramas
Tel: 868 634 4384
Fax: 868 634 4542
crewsinn@tstt.net.tt
www.crewsinnltd.com
10 minutes out of Port of Spain. 46
rooms with cable TV, mini kitchens
and private balconies. Restaurant,
bar.

Villa de French

5 French St.
Woodbrook
Tel: 868 625 4776
Nice guesthouse, clean rooms. 5 minutes walk from ground.

La Calypso

46 French St.
Woodbrook
Tel: 868 622 4077
Another good, clean, inexpensive guesthouse near the ground. Good area for
pubs and restaurants.

Alicia's House

7 Coblentz Gardens
St. Ann's
Tel: 868 623 2802
Fax: 868 623 8560
2getaway@tstt.net.tt
Lovely hotel on the north side of the
Savannah. 17 rooms with swimming
pool and jacuzzi.

Trinbago

37 Ariapita Avenue
Woodbrook
Tel: 868 627 7114
tourist@tstt.net.tt
Excellent little guesthouse near the
ground with small swimming pool.

Pearl's

3-4 Victoria Square East
Port of Spain
Tel: 868 625 2158
For the budget traveller this is the best
value, not only in Trinidad, but in the
Caribbean. Spacious rooms have big
beds and fans. Communal kitchen with
living area with cable TV. Fantastic
place and friendly service.

Gwen's Bed and Breakfast

7 First Roseway
Belmont
Port of Spain
Tel: 868 627 8032
Budget accommodation. A short walk
from the Savannah. Breakfast included.
Rooms with cable TV, fan, shared
bathroom. Excellent value.

Tony Romas
51 Cipriani Boulevard
Port of Spain
Tel: 868 623 4973
International chain of rib restaurant with its own West Indian twist.

Pelican Inn
2-4 Coblentz Avenue
Cascade
Tel: 868 624 7486
Good English and Caribbean food. Open 11.30-02.00 7 days a week.

La Boucan at the Hilton
Lady Young Road
Belmont
Tel: 868 624 3211
www.trinidad.hilton.com
Highest quality.

Trotters
Corner Sweet Briar and Maraval Road
St. Clair
Port of Spain
Tel: 868 627 8768
www.trotters.net
International cuisine in sports bar. Casual dining. Open Sunday-Thursday 11.30-midnight. Friday and Saturday 11.30-02.00.

Jenny's on the Boulevard
6 Cipriani Boulevard
Port of Spain
Tel: 868 625 1807
American steak house and cellar pub is one of Port of Spain's most popular venues. Great food and entertainment. Reservations essential.

Plantation House
Corner Ariapita Avenue and Cornelia St.
Port of Spain
Tel: 868 628 5551
Caribbean and Cajun flavours fish, rabbit and lobster in late 19th century building. Open 11.30-14.30 and 18.30-10.30.

Aspara
Level 13
Queen's Park East
Port of Spain
Tel: 868 623 7659
The best Indian restaurant in Trinidad. Fine selection of North Indian cuisine. Beautiful décor.

Olives
Corner Sweet Briar Road and Elizabeth Streets
22 Sweet Briar Road
St. Clair
Tel: 868 622 9688
Mediterranean restaurant.

Jalepenos
Victoria Square East
Corner Duke and Shine St.
Port of Spain
Tel: 868 625 1766
Mexican restaurant, near the centre. Good food.

Bamimamzelle
44 Coblentz Avenue
Cascade
Tel: 868 621 0541
Caribbean cuisine. Excellent.

Little Carib Theatre
White and Roberts Streets
Woodbrook
Tel: 868 622 4644

Queen's Hall
1-3 St. Ann's Road
St. Ann's
Tel: 868 624 1284
The Grande Dame of theatre in Trinidad.

National Museum and Art Gallery
Upper Fredrick St.
Port of Spain
Tel: 868 623 5941

Chaguaramase Base and Military History and Aviation Museum
Chaguaramase
Tel: 868 634 4341
Open 09.00-18.00 daily

Cricket Wicket

Outside the Oval. Takes off after the match each night. Small bar but the crowd gathers on the street and brings traffic to a standstill. Great atmosphere and loud music. Not to be missed.

Trotters

Corner Sweet Briar and Maraval Road
St. Clair
Tel: 868 627 8768
www.trotters.net
International sports bar with huge screens. 5 minute walk from ground. Very busy, good atmosphere and good food.

Mas Camp

Corner of Ariapata Ave and French St.
Woodbrook
Port of Spain
Tel: 868 623 3745
Good pub with very good, inexpensive food. Live entertainment every night until late. 10 minutes from ground.

Rafters

6A Warner St.
Newtown
Tel: 868 628 9258
Cocktails and casual dining. Lively bar in old grocery store.

Pelican Inn

2-4 Coblentz Avenue
Cascade
Tel: 868 624 7486
Charming, authentic English style pub with live entertainment. Popular haunt for cricketers and fans.
Open 11.00-late every day.

Calypso Lounge

Holiday Inn
Wrightson Road
Tel: 868 525 4531
Great calypso bar in the centre of Port of Spain. Excellent fun.

Poleska

Trinidad Country Club
Maraval
Tel: 868 622 3470
Cocktail and rum bar, casual bistro with live bands at the weekend.

Hilton Carnival Bar

Lady Young Road
Belmont
Tel: 868 624 3111
Quiet bar in which to relax with live entertainment.

The Base

Western Main Road
Chaguaramas
One of Trinidad's best nightclubs. The party goes through the night.

Pier One

Western Main Road
Chaguaramas
Tel: 868 634 4426
Opposite the Base nightclub. Another place for partying into the night. Large decking overlooking the ocean.

Climate

	ave temp	rain cm			
January	26	71	July	27	249
February	26	43	August	27	239
March	26	31	September	27	183
April	27	46	October	27	178
May	27	112	November	27	198
June	27	254	December	26	147

general info

Telecoms

International Direct Dialling is available. The code for Trinidad is 1 868. There are no area codes. The outgoing international code is 01.

Newspapers

Trinidad Guardian
Trinidad Express
Newsday

Radio

Fifteen FM and two AM stations.

Banking

Open Monday-Thursday 09.00-16.30 and Friday 09.00-12.00 and 15.00-17.00. There are numerous ATM machines in Trinidad, but only in Scarborough in Tobago. Trinidad and Tobago Dollars are based on a floating exchange rate. Most foreign currencies can be exchanged in local banks but NOT other Caribbean currencies. TT Dollars cannot be exchanged on any other island. Travellers' Cheques and major credit cards are accepted at most hotels and restaurants. Notes are in denominations of TT$100, 20, 10, 5 and 1. Coins TT$1, 50, 25, 10, 5 and 1 cents.

Embassies

British High Commission
19 St. Clair Avenue

St. Clair
Port of Spain
Tel: 868 622 2748
Tel: 868 622 4555
ppabhc@opus.co.tt
www.britain-in-trinidad.org

Customs

200 cigarettes or of 50 cigars or 250g tobacco, 1.5 litres of spirits or wine and a reasonable amount of perfume can be imported without incurring duty.

Visa

Passports are required by all visitors and must be valid for the full length of your stay. British passports holders do not require visas, but Australians, New Zealanders and South Africans do.

Time Difference

GMT - 4

Electricity

110 AND 220 volts AC 60 Hz

Tipping

Government hotel tax is 10%. Service charge of 10% - 15% is often added to bills. Tipping is at one's discretion.

Departure Tax

TT$100 (approx US$18) is charged to all passengers leaving the island by air or sea.

Post Office

General Post Office
Wrightson Road
Port of Spain
Open 08.00-16.00 each day
Post is very slow from the Caribbean to Britain, Australia and New Zealand. It can take up to three weeks.

Tourist Information

Tourism and Industrial Development Co of Trinidad and Tobago
10-14 Phillips St.
Port of Spain
Tel: 868 623 1932
Fax: 868 623 3848
www.tidco.co.tt

Trinidad and Tobago Hotel and Tourism Association
36 Scott Bushe St.
Tel: 868 627 4515
Fax: 868 627 4516
hotelassoc@wow.net

Airport Information Desk
Tel: 868 669 5196

Hospital

Port of Spain General Hospital
169 Charlotte St.
Port of Spain
Tel: 868 623 2951

St. Clair Medical Centre
18 Elizabeth St.
St. Clair
Port of Spain
Tel: 868 628 1451

All chemists open until 1am.
57 Duke St.
Port of Spain
Tel: 868 623 2718

Emergency Numbers

Police	999
Fire	990
Ambulance	990

Airlines

BWIA
reservations   868 625 1010
flight information 868 669 3000
IAT   868 627 2942
regular service flies between Port of
Spain and Tobago's Crown Point airport. Bookings are essential.

Buses

Main Bus Terminal is at City Gate, South Quay. Information 623 7872. Maxi Taxis, coloured coded minibuses with loud sound systems, run throughout the island. From Independence Square the yellow taxi goes west, red goes east and green goes south. Very cheap.

Taxis

Kalloo's Taxis   628 2394
Airport Taxi Co-op 675 2424
Most Trinidad taxis are large,
old American cars and have licence plates beginning with the letter H.

Ferry

A ferry runs between Trinidad and Tobago six days a week from St. Vincent Street Jetty in Port of Spain to Scarborough taking approximately five hours at a cost of TT$150 return.

Car Hire

Southern Sales Car Rentals
Piarco International Airport
Tel: 868 669 24 24

Auto Rentals
Piarco International Airport
Tel: 868 669 2277

Thrifty
Piarco International Airport
Tel: 868 669 0602

Win/Loss Record

Country	Played	Won	Drawn	Lost	Tie
South Africa	1	1	-	-	-
Australia	12	4	5	3	-
West Indies	53	17	20	16	-
India	12	3	6	3	-
New Zealand	3	-	3	-	-
England	18	6	5	7	-
Pakistan	6	2	1	3	-
Zimbabwe	1	-	-	1	-

Highest Individual Aggregates (West Indies unless stated))

Player	Mat	Inn	NO	Runs	Ave	HS	50	100
Rohan Kanhai	16	31	3	1212	43.29	153	4	
Everton Weekes	7	13	2	1074	97.64	207	4	
Clive Lloyd	16	28	2	1035	39.81	143	7	
Viv Richards	14	21	0	1015	48.33	177	4	
Alvin Kallicharran	11	21	2	982	51.68	158	3	
Garry Sobers	17	31	4	954	35.33	132	4	
Roy Fredericks	11	22	1	896	42.67	120	8	
Desmond Haynes	13	21	3	801	44.50	143*	6	
Sunil Gavaskar (Ind)	5	9	1	793	99.13	220	2	
Brian Lara	11	22	1	786	37.43	122	5	

Top Wicket Takers (West Indies unless stated)

Player	Mat	Bll	Md	Runs	Wkt	Ave	BB	S/R
Curtly Ambrose	12	2770	142	877	66	13.29	6/24	41.9
Courtney Walsh	14	3345	147	1181	57	20.72	6/61	58.6
Lance Gibbs	13	4742	239	1646	52	31.65	6/108	91.1
Malcolm Marshall	8	2002	69	951	47	20.23	6/55	42.6
Garry Sobers	17	3859	181	1434	41	34.98	4/22	94.1
Joel Garner	9	2087	97	785	37	21.22	6/60	56.4
Angus Fraser (Eng)	4	1053	50	412	29	14.21	8/53	36.3
Inshan Ali	7	2686	106	1080	29	37.24	5/59	92.6
Andy Roberts	6	1352	41	670	26	25.77	5/56	52.0
Colin Croft	4	887	37	366	24	15.25	8/29	36.9

Highest Individual Scores (West Indies unless stated)

220	Sunil Gavaskar (Ind)	1970-71
207	Everton Weekes	v India 1952-53
206	Everton Weekes	v England 1953-54
206	Ricky Ponting (Aus)	2002-03
205*	Patsy Hendren (Eng)	1929-30
201	Navjot Sidhu (Ind)	1996-97
189	Wazir Mohammad (Pak)	1957-58
177	Viv Richards	v India 1975-76
174	Dennis Amiss (Eng)	1973-74
172*	Polly Umrigar (Ind)	1961-62

Best Individual Bowling Performances (West Indies unless stated)

49.4-16-95-9	Jack Noreiga	v India 1970-71
18.5-7-29-8	Colin Croft	v Pakistan 1976-77
16.1-2-53-8	Angus Fraser (Eng)	1997-98
36.1-10-86-8	Tony Greig (Eng)	1973-74
37.2-15-70-7	Bill Voce (Eng)	1929-30
66-15-162-7	Fergie Gupte	1952-53
10-1-24-6	Curtly Ambrose	v England 1993-94
13-4-28-6	Vanburn Holder	v Australia 1977-78
20-6-46-6	Charlie Griffith	v Australia 1964-65
21.5-11-47-6	Glenn McGrath (Aus)	1994-95

Highest Partnerships

Wkt	Runs	Batsmen	Match
1st	209	Geoff Boycott & Dennis Amiss (Eng)	1973-1974
2nd	191	Colin Cowdrey & Ted Dexter (Eng)	1959-1960
3rd	338	Everton Weekes & Frank Worrell (WI)	1953-1954 v England
4th	237	Patsy Hendren & Les Ames (Eng)	1929-1930
		Larry Gomes & Clive Lloyd (WI)	1982-1983 v India

	5th	219	Everton Weekes & B H Pairaudeau (WI)	1952-1953 v India
	6th	158	Gus Logie & Jeff Dujon (WI)	1983-1984 v Australia
	7th	197	MJK Smith & Jim Parks (Eng)	1959-1960
	8th	136	Bev Congdon & Bob Cunis (NZ)	1971-1972
	9th	93	Polly Umrigar & Bapu Nadkarni (Ind)	1961-1962
	10th	98	Frank Worrell & Wes Hall (WI)	1961-1962 v India

Results at Queen's Park Oval

Date	Countries	Result
01/02/1930	v England	lost by 167 runs
14/01/1935	v England	won by 217 runs
11/02/1948	v England	drawn
21/01/1953	v India	drawn
19/02/1953	v India	drawn
17/03/1954	v England	drawn
11/04/1955	v Australia	drawn
05/02/1958	v Pakistan	won by 120 runs
26/03/1958	v Pakistan	lost by an innings and 1 Run
28/01/1960	v England	lost by 256 runs
25/03/1960	v England	drawn
16/02/1962	v India	won by 10 wickets
14/04/1962	v India	won by 7 wickets
26/03/1965	v Australia	drawn
14/05/1965	v Australia	lost by 10 wickets
19/01/1968	v England	drawn
14/03/1968	v England	lost by 7 wickets
06/03/1971	v India	lost by 7 wickets
13/04/1971	v India	drawn
09/03/1972	v New Zealand	drawn
20/04/1972	v New Zealand	drawn
23/03/1973	v Australia	lost by 44 runs
21/04/1973	v Australia	drawn
02/02/1974	v England	won by 7 wickets
30/03/1974	v England	lost by 26 runs
24/03/1976	v India	drawn
07/04/1976	v India	lost by 6 wickets
04/03/1977	v Pakistan	won by 6 wickets
01/04/1977	v Pakistan	lost by 266 runs
03/03/1978	v Australia	won by an innings and 106 runs
15/04/1978	v Australia	won by 198 runs
13/02/1981	v England	won by an innings and 79 runs
11/03/1983	v India	drawn
16/03/1984	v Australia	drawn
29/03/1985	v New Zealand	drawn
07/03/1986	v England	won by 7 wickets
03/04/1986	v England	won by 10 wickets
14/04/1988	v Pakistan	drawn
15/04/1989	v India	won by 217 runs
23/03/1990	v England	drawn
05/04/1991	v Australia	drawn
16/04/1993	v Pakistan	won by 204 runs
25/03/1994	v England	won by 147 runs
21/04/1995	v Australia	won by 9 wickets
14/03/1997	v India	drawn
05/02/1998	v England	won by 3 wickets
13/02/1998	v England	lost by 3 wickets
05/03/1999	v Australia	lost by 312 runs
16/03/2000	v Zimbabwe	won by 35 runs
17/03/2001	v South Africa	lost by 69 runs
19/04/2002	v India	lost by 37 runs
19/04/2003	v Australia	lost by 118 runs
19/03/2004	v England	lost by 7 wickets

Harare Sports Club became the first ground to host Test cricket in Zimbabwe when it held the inaugural Test against India on 18th October 1992, a draw. Bulawayo Athletic Club hosted one Test against New Zealand in November 1992 before the Queen's Sports Club became the city's Test ground in October 1994 when it hosted the drawn Test with Sri Lanka. At present the Harare Sports Club and the Queen's Sports Club are the two official Test grounds in Zimbabwe.

Distance Between Cities (in km)

The distance between Harare and Bulawayo is 430km.

Airlines

Zimbabwe's national airline is Air Zimbabwe. They also operate the domestic flights between Harare, Bulawayo and Victoria Falls.
Air Zimbabwe
Tel: 04 575 1111
www.airzim.co.zw

Buses

Blue Arrow Luxury Coaches operate a service between Harare and Bulawayo however coach travel is not recommended to visitors at the current time.
Blue Arrow Coaches
Tel: 09 65548
www.bluearrow.co.zw

Trains

Trains run every night between Harare and Bulawayo however train travel is not recommended for personal security reasons.

Car Hire

Avis, Budget and Hertz all have offices at Harare and Bulawayo airports and in the centre of each city. An International Driving Licence is required. Travelling by car in the country can be hazardous at present with the lack of petrol and increase in crime.

Taxis

Taxi are available at Harare and Bulawayo airports and outside the major hotels. Always agree the fare with the driver before commencing your journey.

Banks

Open 08.00-15.00 Monday-Friday, half-day Wednesday, and 08.00-11.30 Saturday. Visitors should investigate the best way to change money in the country. Foreign exchange is complicated with more than one rate of exchange. Zimbabwe uses the Zimbabwe Dollar (Z$). Notes are in denominations of Z$500, 100, 50, 20, 10, 5 and 2 and coins in Z$5, 2 and 1 and 50, 20, 10, 5 and 1 cents.

Telecoms

International Direct Dialling is available in most hotels in Harare and Bulawayo. Zimbabwe's dialling code is 263. The outgoing international code is 110.

Post Office

Open 08.30-16.00 Monday to Friday and 08.00-11.30 on Saturdays.
Tourist Offices
There are Tourist Information Offices in Harare and Bulawayo.
www.zimbabwetourism.co.zw

Emergency Numbers

Police   995
Fire   993
Ambulance   994

Embassies/Consulates

British High Commission
Corner House
Samora Machel Avenue and Leopold Takawira Street
Harare
Tel: 04 772 990
Fax: 04 774 617
www.britishembassy.gov.uk/zimbabwe

Australian High Commission
29 Mazowe Street
The Avenues
Harare
Tel: 04 253 661
Fax: 04 253 679

High Commission for the People's Republic of Bangladesh
8 Berchenough Road
Alexandra Park
Harare
Tel: 04 727 004
Fax: 04 702 720

High Commission of India
12 Natal Road
Belgravia
Harare
Tel: 04 795 955
Fax: 04 722 324
hci@samara.co.zw

Visa

All visitors to Zimbabwe must carry a valid passport. Visas valid for up to 90 days can be obtained upon arrival. Fee depends on passport. A return or onward ticket is required.

Customs

Over 18s can import 250 cigarettes and 2 litres of alcohol without duty.

Time Difference

Zimbabwe is two hours ahead of GMT (GMT + 2)

Electricity

220/230 volts AC at 50 cycles per second. Most hotels have adaptors.

Departure Tax

US$20 on all visitors leaving Zimbabwe.

queen's sports club

Home to the Matabeleland Cricket Association, the Queen's Sports Club is a wonderful ground close to the city centre. It became the third Zimbabwean Test ground on 20th October 1994 during a tour by Sri Lanka.

In the inaugural match the home team captain David Houghton scored 266 to help his side to 462/9 dec. The visitors managed only 218, but forced to follow-on, they held on for the draw with Sanjeeva Ranatunga scoring 100no.

1996 saw a very exciting match with England. Zimbabwe scored 376 with Andy Flower hitting 112. The visitors led by Nasser Hussain (113) and John Crawley (11. took a first innings lead of 30. Paul Strang took five wickets. Zimbabwe scored 234 in their second dig, Guy Whittall and Andy Waller both scoring half centuries as P Tufnell took 4/61. Set 205 to win off 37 overs, England were cruising at 154/1, befo a mini collapse left three runs required off the last ball. Nick Knight, who had batte tremendously for 96, was run out going for the third run leaving the score level. Da Lloyd, the English manager, was famously quoted as saying "we murdered them."

Bulawayo has not been a happy hunting ground for Zimbabwe with only one victory in the 13 matches played there. That came against Bangladesh in 2001 when the home side won by an innings and 32 runs. Andy Blignaut ripped through the visito with 5/73 as they were dismissed for 257. Zimbabwe replied with 457, Guy Whittall hitting 119. Despite Javed Omar carrying his bat with 85no, Heath Streak, Brighton Watambwa and Blignaut ran through the rest of the visiting side limiting them to Since then Zimbabwe has suffered big losses in four of their last five matches at the ground to India, West Indies, Pakistan and the West Indies. The sole consolation was a draw against South Africa in 2001, the only time South Africa have not won i Zimbabwe.

The highest team innings is 559/5 dec. by the West Indies in 2001. The lowest is 10 by Zimbabwe against the West Indies in 2003. The highest run chase is 184/2 by In in 2001.

The best match figures are Adam Huckle's 11/255 against New Zealand in 1997.

The ground has a capacity of 9,000. It is a beautiful Test match venue with an old pavilion and is surrounded by trees which provide shade from the hot summer sun. The pavilion provides a splendid view, although it is excellent from everywhere. To the left of the pavilion are terraces and uncovered stands. The scoreboard is at the opposite end to the pavilion. Beside the scoreboard is a grass embankment with shade provided by trees. It is one of the best places in the world to watch Test cricket. Some chairs are provided, others are brought along by spectators and some people just sit on the grass. It is one of friendliest hills in the game with fine banter and chat. Copious amounts of good food and drink are enjoyed each day. The east side of the ground is one long grass embankment, again covered by trees. This is quite a boisterous area with singing and chanting but all in good spirit.

The ground is only a ten-minute walk from the centre. A taxi ride will take less than five minutes. There is some parking in the streets near the ground however one should arrive early to get a convenient parking position. Tickets are available on the day of the Test from any of the gates or from the Zimbabwe Cricket Union on zcu@mweb.co.za

The catering facilities are good with foodstalls serving barbequed steaks, burgers and other fast food. There are numerous bars around the ground all serving good cold beer and soft drinks. The toilets blocks are clean and well tended.

Bulawayo is Zimbabwe's second largest city, situated in the south west of the country on the Matsheumlope River and is the hub of the Matabeleland Province which spans the whole of the west side of the country. It is known as the city of Kings as it originally was home to the Ndebel dynasty. It has a population of 680,000.

1868 King Mzilikazi died and the natural successor to the throne, his son Kulume, mysteriously disappeared. After much debate, Lobengula, Mzilikazi's son from an inferior marriage, was made king. Not all the Ndebel people agreed with this and war ensued. Lobengula and his warriors won and settled in Gibixhegu whose name they changed to Bulawayo which literally means "place of slaughter". 1894 following a battle with Lobengula, the British established a new settlement some 20km away. Bulawayo has made a slow transition from that settlement to become the modern city it is today. It has always attracted the adventurous, hunters, traders and other entrepreneurs.

As a very important distribution point in the south west of the country and is the axis of its road and rail network. The railway was built in 1847 to handle the extracts from the mines.

A very pleasant and friendly place, there is quite a lot to do. There are marvellous museums and art galleries. The Natural History Museum in Centenary Park is renowned as the best in Africa with more than 75,000 animal specimens on display. It also delves into the history of the continent and looks at the mining industry which is so important to the region. The Railway Museum is another impressive display and the National Art Gallery on Main Street is worth a visit.

Other interesting places include City Hall and its gardens along with Centenary and Central Parks, the latter with an Olympic size swimming pool. The Mzilikazi Arts and Crafts Centre on the Old Falls Road has some wonderful sculptures, carvings and pottery. The Amakhosi Cultural Centre has its own amphitheatre where music, dance and drama are regularly performed. The streets of Bulawayo are extremely wide as they were designed to allow 16 oxen to turn full circle. They are on a grid system which makes it is very easy to find one's way around the centre. There are many colonial and Victorian buildings in the city including Government House which was built by the British statesman Cecil Rhodes after whom the country was formerly known.

There are a number of top class hotels, some middle range and some good boarding houses for the budget traveller such as the one at the Cattleman Steak House. There are also fine restaurants serving top quality food. The Bon Journee should certainly not be missed. Most cricket supporters who wish to have a drink after the match end up in either The Selbourne, The Cattleman or The Brass Monkey. All three are excellent bars serving good beer in a great atmosphere.

Matobo National Park

32km south of Bulawayo and covers an area of 2000sq. km. Sable, black and white rhino, wildebeest, zebra and impala can all be seen. It is world renowned for having the highest concentration of leopards and black eagles anywhere in the world. A treat for bird watchers and botanists. There are fantastic rock formations and caves with ancient paintings. The Maleme Dam is a good spot for camping and there is also an excellent museum. The park is open from 06.00-18.00 every day.

Old Bulawayo

20km to the south of the modern city on the Douglasdale Road. The walls of King Lobengula's house still stand and the floors of some of the honeycomb huts can seen. On the way to Old Bulawayo is the Hillside Dam, a nature reserve well wor a visit.

Kame Ruins

A World Heritage Site, these are one of Africa's most amazing Iron Age ruins. 22km to the west of Bulawayo. There are a series of terraces and passages supported by a massive granite wall. There is a fine museum with relics more than 100,000 years old.

Tshabalala Sanctuary

Only 10km from the city. Giraffe, kudu, zebra, wildebeest and impala are commo sights in the sanctuary. It is also a haven for a multitude of wild birds and fowl. Opening Hours 06.00-18.00 each day.

Chipangali Wildlife Orphanage

23km from Bulawayo on the Gwanda Road and a sanctuary for orphaned and sick wild animals. It is a breeding centre for black rhino. Some of the animals in the Orphanage include leopards, cheetahs, lions, sable and other types of antelope.

Bulawayo International Airport is small and 30km from the centre. A taxi should take no more 30 minutes and in February 2003 cost Z$300. Air Zimbabwe has a shuttle bus that runs to and from the Rainbow Hotel, however SAA has none. There is a souvenir shop, restaurant, and a bar upstairs where a huge verandah has a view over-looking the city. A striking feature is the lack of airplanes around the airfield. Planes land, drop off and pick up passengers and head off again. There is an internet office on the ground floor opposite check-in and car hire is available in the car park opposite the main entrance from Avis (09 226 918), Budget (09 226654) and Hertz (09 227 177).

Post Office

General Post Office
Corner of Main Street and 8th Ave.
Tel: 09 62 535
Open 08.00-17.00 Monday to Friday
08.00-11.30 Saturday

Tourist Information

Bulawayo Publicity Association
City Hall Car Park
Robert Mugabe Way
Between Leopold Takawira and 8th
Ave.
Tel: 09 72 969
Fax: 09 60 867
Open 08.30-16.45 Monday to Friday
08.30-12.00 Saturday

Zimbabwe Tourist Office
Tel: 09 72358

Hospital

Mater Dei Hospital
Between Josiah Tongagara and
Ninth Ave.
Tel: 09 240000

After Hours Medicine
Tel: 09 65331
Fax: 09 69781

Emergency Numbers

Police Station
Corner Fire Street and Leopold
Takawira Ave 09 72515
Ambulance   71717

Airlines

Air Zimbabwe
Treger House
Jason Moyo St.
Tel: 09 72051
Fax: 09 69737

South African Airways
African House
Corner of Fife Street and 10th Ave.
Tel: 09 71337

Buses

The intercity bus terminus is on the
corner of Fife Street and 4th Ave. Blue
Arrow (09 65548) and Greyhound (09
65549) run buses to Harare, Victoria
Falls and Johannesburg.

Trains

Bulawayo Train Station in Anthony
Taylor Ave. Trains run every night to
Victoria Falls and Harare but train
travel is not recommended for personal security reasons.

National Railways of
Zimbabwe Enquiries 04 786 033

Taxis

Bulawayo Taxis 09 60666/09 231
933/09 72454

Car Hire

Avis
Corner 10th Ave. and Robert Mugabe
Way
Tel: 09 68571
Fax: 09 61306
www.avis.co.zw

Budget
106 Josiah Tongogara Ave.
Shop No. 4
Between 10th and 11th Ave.
Tel: 09 65566
www.budgetcar.co.zw

Hertz
George Silundika St.
Tel: 09 74701

transport

Climate

	ave temp	rain cm			
January	22	134	July	14	1
February	22	107	August	15	1
March	21	69	September	19	5
April	19	25	October	23	27
May	11	9	November	23	87
June	14	2	December	22	127

The Nesbitt Hotel

6 Percy Ave.
Hillside
Tel: 09 42735
Fax: 09 41864
castle@acacia.samare.co.zw
Not far from the centre, this one of the best places to stay. Splendid rooms, excellent Coach house restaurant in beautiful grounds.

Holiday Inn

Ascot Centre
Milnerton Drive
Ascot
Tel: 09 72464
Fax: 09 76227
Air-conditioned, en suite rooms with minibar, TV and modem lines. Restaurant, bar, swimming pool and sauna.

Churchill Hotel

Corner Matopos and Moffat Ave.
Hillside
Tel: 09 46956
Fax: 09 44247
Part of the Best Western chain. 50 rooms with en suite in an English Tudor style hotel. Restaurant, bar and swimming pool.

Winngara Lodge

18 Durham Road
Hillcrest
Tel: 09 44474
Excellent accommodation including a self-catering family cottage which comfortably sleeps 6. Near to ground.

Southern Comfort Lodge

22 Jaywick Road
Matsheumhlope
Tel: 09 41340
Fax: 09 45472
southcom@telconet.co.zw
Prides itself on its serenity and tranquillity. Overlooks a small dam, has excellent rooms and is less than 10 minutes away from the centre.

Bulawayo Rainbow Hotel

Affordable accommodation in the centre. 172 en suite rooms, 3 restaurants and 2 excellent bars.

The Selborne

Corner of Leopold Takawirea Ave and George Silundira St.
Tel: 09 65741
Colonial hotel with magnificent arches and balconies on Bulawayo's premier Street. 3 en suite rooms with TV. Good value.

The Cecil Hotel

Between Jason Moyo Street and 10th Ave.
Tel: 09 64294
Good comfortable single and double rooms, some with en suite, TV. Barbeque, restaurant, bar. Good value

Travellers' Guesthouse

2 Banff Road
Hillside
Tel: 09 46059
travellersguest@telconet.co.zw
www.arachnid.co.zw
Budget accommodation with good, comfortable rooms and swimming pool in lovely garden. Barbeque facilities available.

The Cattleman

Corner of 12th Ave and Josiah Tongogara St.
Bulawayo
Tel: 09 76086
Good, clean boarding house. Perfect for the budget traveller. Added bonus is steak restaurant and rocking bar next door. A must for eating and drinking.

Selborne Hotel Brasserie

Corner of Leopold Takawirea Ave and George Silundira St.
Tel: 09 65741
One of the top bars to go to after the match. Good beer garden and great atmosphere.

The Brass Monkey Pub

Bradfield Shopping Centre
Tel: 09 880494
Popular haunt after a day at the cricket

The Old Vic

Rainbow Hotel
Good, fun bar in the centre. Quite popular with fans.

Bon Journee
Corner of 10th and 105 Robert Mugabe Way
Tel: 09 64 839
Wonderfully presented food in old style restaurant in the centre.

Cape To Cairo
Corner Robert Mugabe Way and Leopold Takawira Ave.
Tel: 09 72387
One of city's top restaurants, serving local produce.

Selborne Hotel Brasserie
Corner of Leopold Takawirea Ave. and George Silundira St.
Tel: 09 65741

Á la carte restaurante.

La Gondola
105 Robert Mugabe Way
10th / 11th Ave.
Tel: 09 62986
Fine Italian.
Mary's Restaurant

88 Josiah Tongogara St.
Between 8th and 9th Ave.
Tel: 09 76 721
Nice, simple café serving the best breakfast in town. Good quick service.

Capri Italian Restaurant
George Silundika St. and 11th Ave.
Tel: 09 68639
Excellent Italian..

National History Museum
Leopold Takawira Ave.
Contains the second largest mounted elephant in the world.

Railway Museum
Prospect Ave.
Off Josiah Chinamano Road
Raylotn
Interesting exhibition of the early days of Zimbabwe's railway history. Open 08.30-16.00 Tuesday-Friday 12.00-17.00 Saturday and Sunday.

National Art Gallery
Douslin House
Corner of Main Street and Leopold Takwira Ave.
Tel: 09 70721
Open 09.00-17.00 Tuesday to Saturday.

Win/Loss Record

Country	Played	Won	Drawn	Lost	Tie
India	1	1	-	-	-
West Indies	2	2	-	-	-
Pakistan	3	2	1	-	-
New Zealand	2	1	1	-	-
Sri Lanka	3	1	2	-	-
South Africa	1	-	1	-	-
England	1	-	1	-	-
Zimbabwe	15	1	7	7	-
Bangladesh	2	-	1	1	-

Highest Individual Aggregates (Zimbabwe unless stated)

Player	Mat	Inn	NO	Runs	Ave	HS	50	100
Andy Flower	11	20	3	871	51.24	112	6	2
Alistair Campbell	12	21	1	795	39.75	103	6	1
Grant Flower	13	22	2	788	39.40	156*	4	1
Guy Whittall	10	15	2	560	43.08	203*	1	2
Marvan Atapattu (SL)	2	2	1	465	465.00	249	0	2
David Houghton	4	7	0	418	59.71	266	0	1
Stuart Carlisle	9	15	2	374	28.77	103*	1	1
Heath Streak	12	18	2	359	22.44	67	3	0
Dion Ebrahim	7	12	0	286	23.83	71	3	0
Yousuf Youhana (Pak)	2	3	0	283	94.33	159	2	1

Top Wicket Takers (Zimbabwe unless stated)

Player	Mat	Bll	Md	Runs	Wkt	Ave	BB	S/R
Heath Streak	12	2322	104	1035	33	31.36	5/70	70.36
Paul Strang	6	1786	68	758	25	30.32	8/109	71.44
Ray Price	5	1508	50	730	23	31.74	5/181	65.57
Andy Blignaut	5	914	35	509	20	25.45	5/73	45.70
Waqar Younis (Pak)	2	442	19	222	12	18.50	5/106	36.83
Henry Olonga	4	537	13	348	12	29.00	4/103	44.75
Chaminda Vaas (SL)	3	735	35	294	12	24.50	4/85	61.25
Chris Cairns (NZ)	2	541	26	254	11	23.09	5/31	49.18
Adam Huckle	1	436	12	255	11	23.18	6/109	39.64
Saqlain Mushtaq (Pak)	2	590	12	278	10	27.80	7/66	59.00

Highest Individual Scores (Zimbabwe unless stated)

270	Kumar Sangakkara (SL)	2004
266	David Houghton	v Sri Lanka 1994-95
249	Marvan Atapattu (SL)	2004
216*	Marvan Atapattu (SL)	1999-00
203*	Guy Whittall	v New Zealand 1997-98
191	Brian Lara (WI)	2003-04
189*	Jacques Kallis (SA)	2001-02
175	Chris Gayle (WI)	2001
166*	Murray Goodwin	v Pakistan 1997-98
159	Yousuf Youhana (Pak)	2002-03

Best Individual Bowling Performances (Zimbabwe unless stated)

51.5-12-109-8	Paul Strang	v New Zealand 2000-01
25.5-2-66-7	Saqlain Mushtaq (Pak)	2002-03
21.2-6-60-6	Pramodya Wickramasinghe (SL)	1999-00
35-12-81-6	Manjural Islam (Ban)	2000-01
40.4-10-109-6	Adam Huckle	v New Zealand 1997-98
14.5-5-31-5	Chris Cairns (NZ)	2000-01
22.3-7-43-5	Wasim Akram (Pak)	1994-95
26-5-70-5	Heath Streak	v Pakistan 1994-95
23.3-5-73-5	Andy Blignaut	v Bangladesh 2000-01
45-16-90-5	Paul Wiseman (NZ)	2000-01

Highest Partnerships

Wkt	Runs	Batsmen	Match
1st	214	Daren Ganga & Chris Gayle (WI)	2001-2002
2nd	438	Marvan Atapattu & Kumar Sangakkara (SL)	2003-2004
3rd	181	Jacques Kallis & Neil McKenzie (SA)	2001-2002
4th	190	Brian Lara & Ramnaresh Sarwan (WI)	2003-2004
5th	277*	Murray Goodwin & Andy Flower (Zim)	1997-1998 v Pakistan
6th	126	Yousuf Youhana & Kamran Akmal (Pak)	2002-2003
7th	109	Grant Flower & Heath Streak (Zim)	1997-1998 v Pakistan
8th	112	Chris Harris & Daniel Vettori (NZ)	1997-1998
9th	78	Adam Parore & Daniel Vettori (NZ)	2000-2001
10th	41	Ray Price & Blessing Mahwire (Zim)	2003-2004 v West Indies

Results at Queen's Sports Club, Bulawayo

Date	Countries	Result
20/10/1994	v Sri Lanka	drawn
07/02/1995	v Pakistan	lost by 8 wickets
18/12/1996	v England	drawn
25/09/1997	v New Zealand	drawn
14/03/1998	v Pakistan	drawn
18/11/1999	v Sri Lanka	drawn
12/09/2000	v New Zealand	lost by 7 wickets
19/04/2001	v Bangladesh	won by an innings and 32 runs
07/06/2001	v India	lost by 8 wickets
19/07/2001	v West Indies	lost by an innings and 176 runs
14/09/2001	v South Africa	drawn
16/11/2002	v Pakistan	lost by 10 wickets
12/11/2003	v West Indies	lost by 128 runs
26/02/2004	v Bangladesh	drawn
15/05/2004	v Sr Lanka	lost by an innings and 254 runs

sports club

Harare Sports Club is the heart of Zimbabwe cricket and the home ground for Mashonaland province. It is in a beautiful setting, surrounded by jacaranda trees with a Dutch gable pavilion.

It became the first Test ground in Zimbabwe on 18th October 1992 when India were entertained. In a rain-affected match Zimbabwe scored 456, captain David Houghton hitting 121 and Grant Flower 82. India managed 307 in reply, Sanjay Manjreker (104) and Kapil Dev (60) being the biggest contributors. John Traicos took 5/86 for the home team. Zimbabwe reached 146/4 in their second innings before time ran out.

A month later New Zealand defeated Zimbabwe by 177 runs. The next two matches at the ground a couple of years later were both draws with Sri Lanka before Zimbabwe won their first Test by defeating Pakistan by an innings and 64 runs on 4th February 1995. Zimbabwe declared at 544/4, the Flower brothers sharing a fourth wicket partnership of 269, Grant scoring 201 and Andy 156. Guy Whittall with 113 was another century maker. In reply Pakistan hit 322, Inzamam-ul-Haq top-scoring with 71. Heath Streak took 6/90. Forced to follow-on, Pakistan collapsed to 158, Inzamam being the only batsman to put up any resistance with 65. David Brain, Streak and Whittall each took three wickets. Unfortunately for the home side, Pakistan got their revenge with a 99 run victory two weeks later.

1998 saw two close matches at the Sports Club. In March, Zimbabwe lost by three wickets to Pakistan before defeating India by 61 runs. Henry Olonga took 5/70 in India's first innings.

Losses to Australia by ten wickets, South Africa by an innings and 219 runs and New Zealand by eight wickets followed in 1999 and 2000 before victories against Bangladesh and India in 2001. The latter was a close match. India scored 237, Dravid (68) and Shiv Sunder Das (57) leading the way. In reply Zimbabwe hit 315, Grant Flower top scoring with 86. Harbhajan Singh took 4/71 for the visitors. In their second innings India scored 234, Das hitting 70 and Sachin Tendulkar (69). Andy Blignaut took 5/74. Set 157 to win Stuart Carlisle (62no) saw his team home with four wickets to spare.

The next two matches saw victory for South Africa and Pakistan before an absolute cracker in November 2003 when the West Indies toured. In their first innings Zimbabwe were 154/5 and 233/6 before a wonderful rearguard action saw Stuart Matsikenveri (57), Tatenda Taibu (83), Heath Streak (127– his maiden Test century) and Andy Blignaut (91) fight back to 507/9 declared. Fidel Edwards took 5/133 for the West Indies. The visitors managed to avoid the follow-on thanks to 79 from Wavell Hinds and 73 from Darren Ganga and despite Ray Price's 6/73. Zimbabwe batted again declaring at 200/7 leaving over a day to dismiss the visitors. In a day of wonderful twists the West Indies hung on for a draw as the last pair, Ridley Jacobs (60no) and

Fidel Edwards (1no) survived the last nine overs.

The highest team innings is 600/3 dec. by South Africa in 2001. The lowest, 102 by Zimbabwe against South Africa in 1999 and the highest run chase was 192/7 by Pakistan against Zimbabwe in 1998.

Allan Donald of South Africa has the best match figures of 11/113 in 1995.

The ground has a capacity of 10,000 which can be increased with temporary stands, but the full capacity is rarely reached these days. The old colonial pavilion at the northern end of ground has one of the finest bars at any Test ground. It is possible to get a drink from the bar and stroll out onto the patio and watch Test cricket. To the left of the pavilion is a grass bank that usually has temporary stands with cover. Beyond it is the towering scoreboard before Castle Corner, the bar at the city end of the ground, which is always very lively and very vocal. Moving around, there is an uncovered grass embankment and a large grandstand which is undercover. There is an ATM machine at the city end of the ground.

The ground is less than ten minutes walk from the centre of town along Second Street and J Tongogara Avenue. It is opposite Zimbabwe House, the heavily fortified home of Robert Mugabe, and beside the Royal Harare Golf Club, one of the best courses in Africa. A taxi ride should take no more than five minutes but taxis cannot go all the way to the ground because of road closures. Tickets are available on the day of the match from any of the gates and available in advance from the Zimbabwe Cricket Union Tel : 04 704 616, Fax 04 729 370 or email on zcu@mweb.co.zw

There are some very good food stalls around the ground especially at the city end near the scoreboard. The barbeques are firing constantly and steak sandwiches are the speciality. In addition to those at the pavilion and Castle Corner there are a number of temporary bars around the ground serving cold beer and soft drinks. The toilets are plentiful and clean and there is medical assistance at both ends of the ground.

Harare, formerly Salisbury, is the capital of Zimbabwe, in the Mashonaland East Province in the north of the country. Known as The Sunshine City it has a population of 1.6 million.

The Portuguese were the first Europeans to visit the area. However they were more interested in their colonies in the neighbouring countries of Angola to the north west and Mozambique to the east. In 1830 the area was inhabited by the Ndelbele people who migrated from the south. In 1890 the British South Africa Company's Pioneer Column led by Cecil Rhodes established Fort Salisbury as a military post named after the 3rd Marquess of Salisbury who was the British Prime Minister of the time. Rhodes and his entourage were also very interested in the mineral wealth of the area Fort Salisbury grew and became an important trading centre with the arrival in 1899 of the railway from Mozambique. The city stayed under the control of the British South Africa Company until 1923 when it became the capital of Southern Rhodesia, a British colony. A referendum was held among the white settlers who voted against joining South Africa. In 1965 the white settlers with the support of their South African neighbours introduced the Unilateral Declaration of Independence which led to a civil war between the white minority government and the fighters for African Independence, which ended in 1980. Salisbury was renamed Harare in 1982.

Tourism was a very important industry for Harare, but with the political situation in the country at present the number of tourists has dropped dramatically to next to none.

Harare has the feel of a European city with wide thoroughfares lined with Jacarandra trees and high rise modern buildings standing alongside colonial-style structures. Unfortunately the city has suffered from an alarming rise in crime and at the present time it is rather difficult to walk around sight-seeing in safety. Places of interest include the National

Archives, the Queen Victoria Museum in the Civic Centre on Rotten Row, the National Gallery with its exhibitions of African and European art, the Anglican and Roman Catholic cathedrals and Harare Gardens, the city's largest park. The Kopje granite hills in the south west of the city provides great views of Harare and its surrounding area.

There are plenty of places to visit. The Ewanrigg Botanical Gardens specialises in aloes, cycads and herbs, the Larvon Bird Gardens on Bulawayo Road is a sanctuary to a variety of birds and the Ngomaleurira Rock Paintings to the north of the city are a must see. To the west of the city the Lion and Chettah Park, the Mazawe Botanical Reserve and Lake Chivero Recreational Park and Game Reserve, home to white rhino and giraffes are worth a visit.

Although Harare is located in the tropics the climate is affected by the inland position of the city and its altitude. Summer is from October to April with hot and sunny days and cool evenings. There is always the possibility of thunderstorms in the early evening. Lightweight clothing is recommended with maybe a jumper for the evening. Winter is from May to September with cool but sunny days with very cold evenings dropping to 6 degrees or below. Warmer clothes are required for this time of year.

There is a varied range of accommodation in Harare from five star and middle of the range hotels to budget and backpacker lodges. It should be noted that some of the lodgings at the lower end of the scale are suffering badly from the drop in tourism. For safety reasons most visitors eat and drink in their hotels rather than venturing out, a situation which again is affecting the restaurant and pub businesses. One exception to this is the Keg and Maiden at the Harare Sports Club. The bar which looks out onto the pitch is a very popular haunt for cricket fans during and after the day's play. There is always a good atmosphere and the standard of food is excellent.

arrival

Harare International Airport is 12km to the south east of the city. A taxi ride will take 20 minutes and costs Z$300. A coach service runs between the airport and the city every 20 minutes. There is a bank, bureau de change, an ATM and a post office in the Arrival Hall. There is also a restaurant, bar and duty free shop at the airport. Car hire is available from Avis (04 575 144), Budget (04 575 421) and Hertz (04 575 206)

Post Office

Julius Nyerere Way
Opening Hours
Monday to Friday 08.30-16.00
Saturday 08.00-11.30

Tourist Information

Zimbabwe Council for Tourism
9th Floor

Jason Moyo Ave.
Tel: 04 794 015

Hospital

The Central Harare Hospital
Lobengula Road
Southerton
Tel: 04 664 695

Climate

	ave temp	rain cm			
January	26	71	July	27	249
February	26	43	August	27	239
March	26	31	September	27	183
April	27	46	October	27	178
May	27	112	November	27	198
June	27	254	December	26	147

what to see

There are three main tourist attractions that should not be missed while visiting Zimbabwe. There are flights to all three from Harare and it is recommended that one visits at least one of these places before or after a Test match in Harare.

Victoria Falls

These spectacular falls, more than 2km wide with drops of more than 100 metre are the largest in the world. They are set on the Zambezi River which marks the border between Zimbabwe and Zambia. The spray can be seen 20km away and the thundering noise of the water is heard long before you reach the river. It is possible to walk along pathways through the rainforests that flank the river and get soaked by the spray. You can also cross the bridge and enter Zambia to view the falls from the other side. They are renowned for adrenalin sports such as wh water rafting, powerboat racing and the bungy jump from the bridge is a never-to-be-forgotten experience for the intrepid. The town of Victoria Falls has plenti ful accommodation to suit all budgets and is quite a lively town with some great pubs and restaurants. There are regular flights from Harare.

Hwange National Park

Zimbabwe's largest national park and the country's most popular game viewing area. One of the great elephant sanctuaries in Africa with herds of more than 10 moving around the park. Other animals include lion, buffalo, leopard, cheetah, wildebeest, giraffe, zebra, impale and other antelope. A wide variety of accommo dation is available. Flights are available from both Harare and Bulawayo.

Lake Kariba

An enormous man-made lake and the foremost source of Zimbabwe's hydro-ele tricity. It is in the north west corner of the country on the border with Zambia. The lake is also Zimbabwe's favourite holiday destination with wonderful faciliti for water sports such as water-skiing, sailing and fishing. Game such as rhino, elephant and buffalo can be viewed on its banks. Accommodation ranges from top hotels to house boats, arguably the most fantastic way to spend a few days at Kariba. Flights leave Harare each day.

transport

Airlines

Air Zimbabwe
Third Speke Ave.
Tel: 04 575 1111
www.airzim.co.zw

South African Airways
1st Floor West Suite
Corner Julius Nyerere and Sam Nojoma St.
Tel: 04 738 922
Fax: 04 704 599

Buses

Blue Arrow is a luxury coach service between Harare and Bulawayo, Kariba, Victoria Falls and Johannesburg.
Chester House
Speke Avenue
Tel: 04 729 514
Fax: 04 729 572

Trains

National Railways of Zimbabwe
Enquiries 04 786 033
Trains run every night to Victoria Falls and Bulawayo but train travel is strongly advised against at present due to personal safety reasons.

Taxis

Rixi Taxi Services   04 753 080
Cream Line Taxis   04 703 333
Express Motorways   04 796 934

Car Hire

Avis
Lot 2, Airport Road
Arlington
Tel: 04 57 54 81
wendy@avis.co.zw

Budget
145 Samara Machel Ave.
Union Ave.
Tel: 04 701 858
reservations@budgetcar.co.zw

Hertz
100 Nelson Mandela Ave.
Tel: 04 792 791

Quality International

Corner Baker Avenue and 4th St.
Tel: 04 794460
Fax: 04 722894
quality@id.co.zw=
In the centre. Air-conditioned rooms with cable TV, restaurant, coffee shop, bar. Airport transfers

Sheraton Harare Hotel

Pennefather Ave.
Tel: 04 772633
Fax: 04 774648
Sheraton@harare.iafrica.com
309 luxury rooms, restaurants, bars, swimming pool. Central, in spectacular garden setting.

Meikles Hotel

Jason Moyo Ave.
Tel: 04 795 655
Fax: 04 707 754
Five star colonial style, in centre. 322 luxury rooms. Restaurant, bar.

Holiday Inn Crowne Plaza Monomotapa

54 Park Lane
Tel: 04 704 501
Fax: 04 791 920
In the centre. 246 air-conditioned en suite rooms overlooking the Harare Gardens. 2 restaurants, coffee lounge, business centre, swimming pool.

New Ambassador Hotel

88 Union Ave.
Tel: 04 708 121
Fax: 04 708 126
Central. 72 air-conditioned rooms, restaurant and bar.

Cresta Lodge

Corner Robert Mugabe and Samora Machel
Tel: 04 487 006
Fax: 04 487 009
lodgeGM@samara.co.zw
Affordable hotel with comfortable rooms in wonderful surroundings. Restaurant and bar.

Wild Geese Lodge

198 Borrowdale
Tel: 04 860 466
Tel: 04 860 276
Thatched complex among trees with spectacular views. 9 well furnished suites with all modern comforts. Restaurant.

Sable Lodge Backpackers Hostel

95 Selas Avenue and 9th Street
Greenwood
Tel: 04 704 986
Fax: 04 706 670
sable@mail2africa.com
Central. Doubles, twins and dormitories.

Kings Backpackers Lodge

1 Dean Simmons Ave.
Hillside
Tel: 04 743 552
martin@pvas.co.za

Possum Lodge

7 Deary Ave.
Belgravia House
Tel: 04 726 851
Fax: 04 722 803
possum@harare.iafrica.com
Colonial home within 15 minutes walk of centre, Home cooked meals, games rooms and swimming pool.

Small World Backpacker Lodge

72 King George Road
Avondale
Harare
Tel: 04 335 176
Fax: 04 335 341
mail@backpackerslodge.com
Excellent. 10 minute walk from centre. Kitchen, bar, swimming pool, internet and airport pickups.

Restaurants are closing at an alarming rate. All the major hotels have good restaurants.

Ramambo Lodge Restaurant

Corner Samora Nachel Avenue and Leopold Takawira St.
Tel: 04 775345

Keg and Maiden

Harare Sports Club
Tel: 04 702 669
Good food. Very popular.

Keg and Sable

Sam Levy's Village
Borrowdale
Tel: 04 884 445
Sister restaurant/bar of the one at the Harare Sports Club.

Akropolis Taverna

King George Road
Avondale
Tel: 04 339 181

stats

Win/Loss Record

Country	Played	Won	Drawn	Lost	Tie
South Africa	3	3	-	-	-
Australia	1	1	-	-	-
New Zealand	3	2	1	-	-
Pakistan	4	3	-	1	-
Sri Lanka	4	1	3	-	-
West Indies	2	-	2	-	-
England	1	-	1	-	-
Zimbabwe	24	5	8	11	-
India	3	-	1	2	-
Bangladesh	2	-	-	2	-

Highest Individual Aggregates (Zimbabwe unless stated)

Player	Mat	Inn	NO	Runs	Ave	HS	50	100
Andy Flower	20	35	5	1535	51.17	199*	6	4
Grant Flower	21	37	1	1218	33.83	201*	5	3
Guy Whittall	18	32	4	954	34.07	188*	5	2
Alistair Campbell	21	38	1	803	21.70	99	4	0
Heath Streak	17	27	5	689	31.32	127*	5	1
David Houghton	9	14	1	520	40.00	142	1	2
Inzamam-ul-Haq (Pak)	4	8	0	494	61.75	112	3	2
Murray Goodwin	6	12	0	432	36.00	91	3	0
Dion Ebrahim	6	12	0	416	34.67	71	3	0
Andy Blignaut	6	11	0	363	33.00	92	3	0

Top Wicket Takers (Zimbabwe unless stated)

Player	Mat	Bll	Md	Runs	Wkt	Ave	BB	S/R
Heath Streak	17	4204	194	1745	75	23.27	6/90	56.05
Bryan Strang	9	2242	138	802	30	26.73	5/101	74.73
Ray Price	7	1907	79	911	28	32.54	6/73	68.11
Guy Whittall	18	2253	95	986	27	36.52	4/18	83.44
Henry Olonga	9	1407	34	802	25	32.08	5/70	56.28
Andy Blignaut	6	1281	49	731	23	31.78	5/74	55.70
Chaminda Vaas (SL)	5	1330	61	445	18	24.72	4/56	73.89
Muttiah Mulalitharan (SL)	4	1184	62	360	17	21.18	6/45	69.65
David Brain	5	934	25	501	15	33.40	3/49	62.27
Alan Donald (SA)	2	415	22	148	13	11.38	8/71	31.92

Highest Individual Scores (Zimbabwe unless stated)

220	Gary Kirsten (SA)	2001-02
201*	Grant Flower	v Pakistan 1994-95
199*	Andy Flower	v South Africa 2001-02
192	Mohammad Wasim (Pak)	1997-98
188*	Guy Whittall	v New Zealand 2000-01
170	Marvan Atapattu (SL)	2004
163*	Tillakaratne Dilshan (SL)	1999-00
157*	Jacques Kallis (SA)	2001-02
157	SanathJayasuriya (SL)	2004
156	Andy Flower	v Pakistan 1994-95

Best Individual Bowling Performances (Zimbabwe unless stated)

33-12-71-8	Alan Donald (SA)	1995-96
35.4-7-116-7	Ravi Pushpakumara (SL)	1994-95
24.2-10-45-6	Muttiah Mulalitharan	2004
17.3-5-50-6	Dipak Patel (NZ)	1992-93
37.2-13-73-6	Ray Price	v West Indies 2003-04
39-11-90-6	Heath Streak	v Pakistan 1994-95
9.5-2-20-5	Nuwan Zoysa	2004
19-3-46-5	Aamer Nazir (Pak)	1994-95
28.1-9-50-5	Chris Cairns (NA)	1997-98
25-5-56-5	Ravi Pushpakumara (SL)	1999-00

Highest Partnerships

Wkt	Runs	Batsmen	Match
1st	281	Marvan Atapattu & SanathJayasuriya (SL)	2003-2204
2nd	217	Asanka Gurusinha & S Ranatunga (SL)	1994-1995
3rd	194	Alistair Campbell & David Houghton (Zim)	1994-1995 v Sri Lanka
4th	269	Grant Flower & Andy Flower (Zim)	1994-1995 v Pakistan
5th	233*	Grant Flower & Guy Whittall (Zim)	1994-1995 v Pakistan
6th	165	David Houghton & Andy Flower (Zim)	1992-1993 v India
7th	154	Heath Streak & Andy Blignaut (Zim)	2001-2002 v West Indies
8th	168	Heath Streak & Andy Blignaut (Zim)	2003-2004 v West Indies
9th	147	Mohammad Wasim & Mushtaq Ahmed (Pak)	1997-1998
10th	47	Andy Flower & Douglas Hondo (Zim)	2001-2002 v South Africa

Results at Harare Sports Club

Date	Countries	Result
18/10/1992	v India	drawn
07/11/1992	v New Zealand	lost by 177 runs
11/10/1994	v Sri Lanka	drawn
26/10/1994	v Sri Lanka	drawn
01/02/1995	v Pakistan	won by an innings and 64 runs
15/02/1995	v Pakistan	lost by 99 runs
13/10/1995	v South Africa	lost by 7 wickets
26/12/1996	v England	drawn
18/09/1997	v New Zealand	drawn
21/03/1998	v Pakistan	lost by 3 wickets
07/10/1998	v India	won by 61 runs
14/10/1999	v Australia	lost by 10 wickets
11/11/1999	v South Africa	lost by an innings and 219 runs
26/11/1999	v Sri Lanka	lost by 6 wickets
04/12/1999	v Sri Lanka	drawn
19/09/2000	v New Zealand	lost by 8 wickets
26/04/2001	v Bangladesh	won by 8 wickets
15/06/2001	v India	won by 4 wickets
27/07/2001	v West Indies	drawn
07/09/2001	v South Africa	lost by 9 wickets
09/11/2002	v Pakistan	lost by 119 runs
04/11/2003	v West Indies	drawn
19/02/2004	v Bangladesh	won by 183 runs
06/05/2004	v Sri Lanka	lost by an innnnings and 240 runs

Known as "The Desert Venue", Sharjah Cricket Association Stadium in the United Arab Emirates is the only Test ground located outside a Test playing country. Due to problems at home in 2002 Pakistan beat the West Indies in February but lost to Australia in October.

In the first Test played at the stadium Pakistan scored 493, Rashid Latif (150) and Yousuf Youhana (146) sharing a partnership of 204. In reply the West Indies made 366. Leading by 127, Pakistan made 214/6 in their second innings before declaring, leaving a target of 342. The West Indies started well, reaching 115/1 against the bowling of Waqar Younis and Saqluin Mushtaq before Shoaib Akthar and Abdul Razzaq came on to bowl. Akthar took 5/24 in 16 overs and Razzaq 4/25 in 7.5 overs as the West Indies tumbled to 171 and Pakistan won by 170.

The next Test was three days later. This time Pakistan were put in, a decision the West Indies regretted as Younis Khan (153) and Shahid Afridi (107) led Pakistan to 472. The West Indies replied with 264, 208 runs behind Pakistan declared at 225/5. The West Indies could manage only 189 of the 434 needed as Waqar Younis 4/44 and Abdul Razzaq 3/33 tore them apart.

The next match was the second Test of a three-match series. Australia were already 1-0 up after winning an exciting match in the Saravanamuttu Stadium in Colombo by 41 runs. But in Sharjah, Pakistan managed only eight more than that as they capitulated to a paltry 59 with Shane Warne taking 4/11 and Glenn McGrath, Brett Lee and Andy Bichel two wickets each. Matthew Hayden hit 119 as Australia reached 310. It was more than enough as Pakistan scored six fewer than in their first innings. This time Warne took 4/13 in 6.5 overs. Australia won the match by an innings and 198 runs in less than two days. Both of Pakistan's innings scores were the their lowest ever, beating their previous lowest of 62 also made against Australia, in Perth in 1981.

The third Test was played the following week. Australia made 444 as Ricky Ponting (150) and Steve Waugh (103no) hit centuries. Pakistan's reply was 221, Warne taking 5/74 and Glenn McGrath 4/41. Forced to follow-on 223 runs behind, Pakistan could only manage 203 to lose by an innings and 20 runs.

Sharjah Cricket Association Stadium was built in the 1980's and is a fine venue for Test cricket. It has an all-seat capacity of 14,000 and most are covered from the hot desert sun. Crowds for Test matches are low and tickets can be purchased on the day of the match. Tickets for one-day matches are harder to purchase. Tickets are available from the United Arab Emirates Cricket Board, Sharjah Cricket Stadium, PO

Box 88, Sharjah, UAE. Tel : +971 5 0646 3570 Fax : +971 6 5434 741 or email cricket@emirates.net.ae.
Most cricket visitors choose to stay in nearby Dubai which is approximately a 30-minute drive away from the ground. Taxis are widely available and most hotels will arrange transport to the ground. A taxi ride should cost about US$20.

Win/Loss Record

Country	Played	Won	Drawn	Lost	Tie
Australia	2	2	-	-	-
Pakistan	4	2	-	2	-
West Indies	2	-	-	2	-

Highest Individual Aggregates

Player	Mat	Inn	NO	Runs	Ave	HS	50	100
Younis Khan (Pak)	4	8	0	323	40.38	153	2	1
Yousuf Youhana (Pak)	2	4	1	270	90.00	146	2	1
Rashid Latif (Pak)	4	8	3	253	50.60	150	0	1
Matthew Hayden (Aus)	2	2	0	208	104.00	119	1	1
Ricky Ponting (Aus)	2	2	0	194	97.00	150	0	1

Top Wicket Takers

Player	Mat	Bll	Md	Runs	Wkt	Ave	BB	S/R
Shane Warne (Aus)	2	414	19	154	16	9.63	5/74	25.88
Saqlain Mushtaq (Pak)	4	1001	36	460	13	35.38	4/83	77.00
Waqar Younis (Pak)	4	474	16	276	12	23.00	4/44	39.50
Abdul Razzaq (Pak)	3	330	9	148	12	12.33	4/25	27.50
Shoaib Akhtar (Pak)	3	444	21	220	11	20.00	5/24	40.36

Highest Individual Scores

153	Younis Khan (Pak)	v West Indies 2001-02
150	Rashid Latif (Pak)	v West Indies 2001-02
150	Ricky Ponting (Aus)	v Pakistan 2002-03
146	Yousuf Youhana (Pak)	v West Indies 2001-02
119	Matthew Hayden (Aus)	v Pakistan 2002-03

Best Individual Bowling Performances

16-7-24-5	Shoaib Akhtar (Pak)	v West Indies 2001-02
20.1-10-74-5	Shane Warne (Aus)	v Pakistan 2002-03
11-4-11-4	Shane Warne (Aus)	v Pakistan 2002-03
8.5-2-13-4	Shane Warne (Aus)	v Pakistan 2002-03
8.5-1-25-4	Abdul Razzaq (Pak)	v West Indies 2001-02

Highest Partnerships

Wkt	Runs	Batsmen	Match
1st	88	Daren Ganga and Chris Gayle (WI)	2001-2002 v. Pakistan
2nd	190	Shahid Afridi and Younis Khan (Pak)	2001-2002 v. West Indies
3rd	70	Younis Khan and Inzamam-Ul-Haq (Pak)	2001-2002 v. West Indies
4th	92	Younis Khan and Yousuf Youhana (Pak)	2001-2002 v. West Indies
5th	84	Yousuf Youhana and Abdul Razzaq (Pak)	2001-2002 v. West Indies
6th	204	Yousuf Youhana and Rashid Latif (Pak)	2001-2002 v. West Indies
7th	91	Hasan Raza and Saqlain Mushtaq (Pak)	2002-2003 v. Australia
8th	55	Hasan Raza and Waqar Younis (Pak)	2002-2003 v. Australia
9th	40	Hasan Raza and Mohammad Sami (Pak)	2002-2003 v. Australia
10th	26	Steve Waugh and Glenn McGrath (Aus)	2002-2003 v. Pakistan

Results at Sharjah Cricket Association Stadium

Date	Countries	Result
31/01/2002	v West Indies	won by 170 runs
07/02/2002	v West Indies	won by 244 runs
11/10/2002	v Australia	lost by an innings and 198 runs
19/10/2002	v Australia	lost by an innings and 20 runs

Notes